Chess Opening Essentials
Volume 1 – The Complete 1.e4

- ■ **Comprehensive:** covers all main variations likely to arise
- ■ **Easy-to-use:** important moves and key positions are highlighted in colour
- ■ **Long-lasting:** doesn't outdate because it is about the basics – not about the latest fashions
- ■ **Complete:** explains the plans and counterplans for *both* Black and White
- ■ **Down-to-earth:** simple, verbal introductions (not a database dump full of dead trees)
- ■ **Convenient:** every opening is illustrated with a number of instructive games
- ■ **Prize-winning:** received the Golden Award of the Italian Chess Federation

The series is now complete:

Stefan Djuric – Dimitri Komarov – Claudio Pantaleoni

Chess Opening Essentials

Volume 1 – The Complete 1.e4

THIRD EDITION

New In Chess 2010

2010 New In Chess
© Messaggerie Scacchistiche 2004
Revised and updated English edition published by New In Chess, Alkmaar, The
Netherlands
First English Edition May 2007
Second English Edition January 2008
Third English Edition June 2010
www.newinchess.com
This edition is published by arrangement with Le due Torri — Chess Department Store
— Italy — www.chess.it

Editor: Pierluigi Passerotti
Cover design: Steven Boland
Supervisor: Peter Boel
Translator: Richard Jones
Proofreading: René Olthof
Production: Anton Schermer

ISBN-13: 978-90-5691-203-1

Throughout our entire lives we all need a game
that lets us play like children;
something we can take seriously
and to which we apply ourselves in earnest,
knowing all along that it is of no real importance at all.

G. Rensi *Letters on the spiritual*

This opening book is chiefly intended for the average player. Yet at the same time, it should prove to be of use to both beginners and master-strength players. I know that I have certainly learnt a great deal while editing this book. Above all it has given me the opportunity to apply, re-examine, and deepen my knowledge of chess within the context of what we can learn from the historical development of chess theory. The book underlines the importance of understanding the subtle thread that runs through and unites the various phases of the game. I believe that opening books of this quality are rare indeed. I hope that by using this book readers will enjoy improved practical results, as well as the satisfaction that comes from having a deeper understanding of our 'royal game'.

To finish with, a quick look at some of the book's features.

Coloured text highlights moves which are of great importance; the names of the main variations, key initial positions and positions arising after important sequences which are all useful for evaluating the opening variation in question. Bold type, be it in black or in colour, indicates main lines, which are also classified and sub-classified (A1, B22, etc.). Lines in italics are unsound lines or errors to be avoided. But this is not all. Two-colour printing makes consulting the book easier, and there are numerous graphic features more often associated with sophisticated chess computer software than with chess books.

In short, no effort has been spared to create a truly exceptional book.

Pierluigi Passerotti
Editor

Glossary of chess symbols

!!	brilliant move	+−	White has a decisive advantage
!?	interesting move	±	White has a clear advantage
?!	dubious move	±	White has a slight advantage
?	mistake	=	equal
??	blunder	∓	Black has a slight advantage
N	novelty	−+	Black has a decisive advantage
↑	initiative	#	checkmate

Contents

Open Games   11

Semi-Open Games   117

Introduction

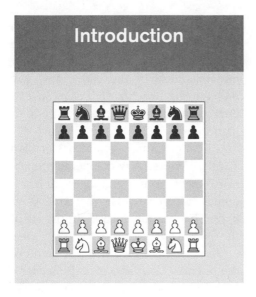

What is the best move in this position?

Our great-grandparents would not have hesitated for a second: the move 1.e4!. It occupies the centre and allows for the development of the king's bishop and the queen. This book is about this move, and all of Black's probable replies. We will discuss Closed Games in the later volumes of this series, thus completing this overview of the ideas and objectives of all the openings.

And what is Black's best response to 1.e4? Once again there used to be few doubts: 1...e5!. This fights against White's expansion in the most natural way, or so it was thought at the end of the 19th century. Indeed, until that time the vast majority of games had begun with these two moves. Why then is it that today only 10% of the games begin 1.e4 e5, which are the moves that define the branch of opening theory known as the Open Games? The answer is that over a hundred years of tournament experience has demonstrated that

there is no single opening or variation that is able to magically give a clear advantage to White, or easy equality to Black. Instead there are various systems that are more or less equal in terms of statistical success in tournaments, but that are very different indeed in terms of style and the type of positions they create.

Some could say that the Sicilian is the best defence against 1.e4, given that Black wins 47% of the games, compared to 44% for the Open Games, or 45% for the Caro-Kann. But this begs the question why a player such as Karpov, who was World Champion for 10 years, virtually never plays the Sicilian. Evidently, such an aggressive defence is not suited to his solid positional style.

For this reason it is important to know, at least in general terms, the characteristics of all the openings, so as to choose the one that is best suited to your own personal taste and style. And once we have decided on an opening, should we remain faithful to it for the rest of our lives, or should we frequently flirt with other systems? Here opinions differ.

Needless to say, if a player always uses the same opening they will end up knowing it very well (Grandmaster Wolfgang Uhlmann's dedication to the French Defence comes to mind). On the other hand, in the age of computers and the Internet, it only takes a few seconds to find the details of another player's repertoire. As a result, players with a predictable repertoire will find themselves sitting opposite adversaries who are very well prepared. The renowned English grandmaster and opening expert John Nunn wrote that until recently the advantages and disadvantages of a limited opening repertoire balanced themselves out, but with the advent of the computer age the balance was now clearly in favour of the player with a large repertoire. Indeed, today it is very easy to familiarize yourself with a new system with the help of a book or DVD that explains the opening's general concepts, a good database, and a variation table. This preparation allows you to surprise your opponent and to play the variation most suited to the occasion, and also perhaps to your mood at the time. It is no mere coincidence that a player like Karpov, with his highly limited opening repertoire, has difficulty in the opening phase when playing against the younger champions who were born in the computer age. Obviously, most of us are not champion players, and we have neither the time, nor the desire, to expand our opening repertoire. However, we would suggest

— if possible — that you use a minimum of two opening systems for both White and Black. This will also enlarge your understanding of the game, and you will see the benefits of this in an improved performance in the middlegame.

As the Dutch grandmaster Jan Timman wrote, 'A wide opening repertoire keeps your thinking flexible'. It comes as no surprise that this great player knows, and plays, almost all of the openings.

In these books we will discuss all of the openings, so as to give the reader a broad but not superficial overview. We will not only give you the specific moves played, but more importantly an understanding of the ideas behind each system. To help us with this goal we will observe the traditional division into Open, Semi-Open and Closed Games; not only for clear organization but also because it makes learning about them easier.

Open Games

Centre Game
Danish Gambit
Bishop's Opening
Vienna Game
King's Gambit
Latvian Counter-Gambit and other minor variations
Philidor Defence
Petroff Defence
Ponziani Opening
Göring Gambit and Scotch Gambit
Scotch Game
Four Knights Opening
Hungarian Defence
Evans Gambit
Giuoco Piano
Italian Opening
Two Knights Defence
Ruy Lopez

Centre Game

1.e2-e4 e7-e5 2.d2-d4 e5xd4 3.♕d1xd4

White is playing a type of Scandinavian with an extra tempo (the pawn is already well placed on e4, while in the Scandinavian it is rare that Black manages to get his pawn to e5). White prepares for a quick **0-0-0**. White will have active piece play and he will be able to exploit the space advantage which arises from the central pawn structure with a white pawn on e4 and a black pawn on d6.

Of course Black has his own trumps to play: after the natural

3. ...   ♘b8-c6

The white queen is forced to move and White loses a tempo. This in itself was sufficient reason for the Centre Game to quickly become a museum piece and to be scoffed at for decades. However, its recent adoption, even if occasional, by very strong players the likes of Morozevich, Adams and Judit Polgar has, in part, led to a re-evaluation of the opening.

4. ♕d4-e3!

With this move (suggested by the Syrian player Stamma in the 18th century!) White prevents the freeing move d5 by Black and prepares ♘c3, ♗d2 followed by 0-0-0 with good piece play.

4. ...   ♘g8-f6!

Black must play actively, so as not to be left with a structurally inferior position without compensation.

5. ♘b1-c3   ♗f8-b4

5...♗e7!? 6.♗c4! (after the uninspired 6.♗d2, Black obtains good play with 6...d5!) 6...0-0 7.♗d2!.

6. ♗c1-d2   0-0
7. 0-0-0   ♖f8-e8

Now the e4-pawn is under a great deal of pressure and White sacrifices it to maintain active play. This can be done in two different ways.

Method No 1:
8. ♗f1-c4

See the Romero Holmes-Karpov example game in the appendix.

Method No 2:
8. ♕e3-g3

The strongest response to this move is **8...♖xe4!**

The resulting positions are dynamically balanced, and even against correct play White cannot expect an objective advantage, it is clear that in practical play the opening is still an excellent surprise weapon. Most of the time black players will be unprepared for an opening that is so rarely played, and which is very much better than its reputation would suggest.

**Romero Holmes, Alfonso
Karpov, Anatoly**

Madrid 1992 (8)

1.e4 e5 2.d4 exd4 3.♕xd4 ♘c6 4.♕e3 ♘f6! [4...♗e7 5.♗d2 ♘f6 6.♘c3 0-0 7.0-0-0 d5 8.exd5 ♘xd5 9.♕g3 with chances for both sides, Mieses-Alekhine, Scheveningen 1913] **5.♘c3 ♗b4 6.♗d2 0-0 7.0-0-0 ♖e8 8.♗c4 d6** [8...♗xc3 9.♗xc3 ♘xe4 10.♕f4 ♘f6 11.♘f3 d6 12.♘g5 ♗e6 13.♗d3 h6 14.h4 Winawer-Steinitz 1896 (1-0 at move 26)] **9.f3 ♘a5 10.♗b3 ♘xb3+ 11.axb3 a5!** [11...d5? 12.♘xd5 ♘xd5 13.♕d4!] **12.♕f2 ♗d7 13.♘ge2 a4 14.bxa4 ♗xa4 15.♘b1 ♗c5 16.♗e3 b6 17.♗d4 ♗d7 18.g4 ♖a5 19.♘f4 ♗c6 20.♖hg1 ♘d7 21.♘h5!? g6 22.♕d2!? ♗xd4 23.♕xd4 gxh5 24.gxh5+ ♔f8 25.♕g7+ ♔e7 26.♖g5?** [26.f4! ♕a8 (26...♗xe4!? 27.♖ge1 d5 28.b4! ♖a2 29.♖xe4+ dxe4 30.♕g5+ ♔f8 31.♕h6+=) 27.e5! dxe5 28.♕g5+! (28.fxe5 ♖xe5−+ is Karpov's evaluation) 28...f6 (28...♔f8! 29.♕h6+ ♔e7 30.♕g5+=) 29.♕f5!! ♔d8 30.♖g7 ♔c8 31.♖dxd7 ♗xd7 32.♕xd7+ ♔b7 33.♕xc7+ ♔a6 34.b4! ♖c8! 35.♕f7! ♖a4 36.♕b3 b5 with an unclear position] **26...♕a8 27.b4 ♖xg5 28.♕xg5+ f6 29.♕g7+ ♔d8 30.♕xh7 ♕a2 31.♕h6 ♔c8 32.♕f4 ♖h8 33.h6 ♕g8 34.♖d3 ♕g5** **0-1**

Danish Gambit

1.e2-e4 e7-e5 2.d2-d4 e5xd4 3.c2-c3

Here we have a gambit where White sacrifices two pawns for a clear lead in development. If Black takes both pawns with

3. ...   **d4xc3**
4. ♗f1-c4   **c3xb2**
5. ♗c1xb2

he would be well advised to return at least one of the two pawns with

5. ...   **d7-d5!**

given the fact that hanging on to the material with 5...d6 appears to be dangerous (see the Mieses-Marshall game for an illustration of this).

White's best move is

6. ♗c4xd5!

and Black responds with

6. ...   **♘g8-f6!**

Black also returns the second pawn to achieve complete equality after

7. ♗d5xf7+   **♚e8xf7**
8. ♕d1xd8   **♗f8-b4+**
9. ♕d8-d2   **♗b4xd2+**
10. ♘b1xd2

This position, even if objectively equal, contains winning possibilities, as both sides have pawn majorities they can mobilize.

Black can also refuse to accept the pawn on offer and play 3...d5.

After 4.exd5 ♕xd5, the position involves the typical strategic considerations and potential long-term prob-

Alexeev,Evgeny
Shirov,Alexey

Germany Bundesliga 2006/07 (8)

1.e4 e5 2.♗c4 ♘f6 3.d3 c6 4.♘f3 d5 5.♗b3 ♗d6 6.exd5 ♘xd5!? [6...cxd5 7.♗g5 ♘c6 8.♘c3 d4 9.♘d5 ♗e6 10.0-0 ♗xd5 11.♗xd5 h6 12.♗xf6 ♕xf6 13.c3 dxc3 14.bxc3 0-0 15.♖b1 ♖ab8 16.♕a4 ♗c5 17.♕e4 ♗b6 18.♗xc6 bxc6 19.♕xe5± Ivanchuk-L.Dominguez, Havana 2005] **7.0-0 0-0 8.♖e1 ♗g4 9.h3 ♗h5 10.g4 ♗g6 11.♘xe5 ♗xe5 12.♖xe5 ♘d7 13.♖e1 ♕h4 14.♕f3 ♖ae8 15.♖f1 h5 16.♘c3 ♘xc3 17.bxc3 ♔h7 18.gxh5 ♕xh5 19.♕xh5+ ♗xh5 20.♗a3 ♖h8 21.♖fe1 ♘e5 22.♔g2 ♘f3 23.♖e3 ♘h4+ 24.♔f1 ♘f3 25.♗d6 g5 26.d4 ♔g6 27.c4 ♘xd4 28.c5 ♗f3 29.♔e1 ♘f5 30.♖xe8 ♖xe8+ 31.♔d2 ♖e2+ 32.♔d3 ♖xf2 33.♖e1 ♗g2 34.♖e8 ♗xh3 35.♖g8+ ♔f6 36.♗c7 ♖f3+ 37.♔d2 g4 38.♗d8+ ♔e5 39.♗c7+ ♔d4 40.♗d6 g3 41.♖d8** **0-1**

Adams,Michael
Kramnik,Vladimir

Tilburg 1998 (7)

1.e4 e5 2.♗c4 ♘f6 3.d3 c6 4.♘f3 d5 5.♗b3 ♗d6 6.♘c3 dxe4! [6...♗e6?! 7.♗g5!; 6...d4 not ideal for Black, nevertheless playable] **7.♘g5!** [7.dxe4 ♘a6 is satisfactory for Black] **7...0-0 8.♘cxe4 ♘xe4 9.♘xe4** [9.dxe4

♗b4+ 10.c3 ♕xd1+ 11.♔xd1 ♗c5=] **9...♗f5! 10.♕f3 ♗xe4 11.dxe4 ♘d7 12.c3** [12.0-0 ♘c5 13.♗c4 b5 14.♗d3 (14.♗e2 ♕h4) 14...♘e6 15.c3 ♗c5=] **12...a5 13.a4** [13.0-0 (allows) 13...a4 14.♗c2 ♘c5=] **13...♘c5 14.♗c2 b5!?** [14...♘e6 15.0-0 ♕e7=] **15.0-0 ♕c7 16.♖d1 ♖ab8 17.axb5 cxb5 18.g3 b4 19.cxb4 ♖xb4 20.♗d2 ♖xb2** ½-½

Fedorov,Alexey
Shirov,Alexey

Leon Ech-tt 2001 (8)

1.e4 e5 2.♗c4 ♘f6 3.d3 c6 4.♘f3 d5 5.♗b3 ♗d6 6.♘c3 dxe4 7.♘g5 0-0 8.♘cxe4 ♘xe4 9.♘xe4 a5 10.♕h5!♗b4+! [10...♗e7 11.a3 a4 12.♗a2 ♘d7 13.0-0 with a slight advantage for White] **11.♔f1!?** [11.c3 ♗e7=; 11...♕xd3? 12.♘g5! ♗xc3+ 13.bxc3 ♕xc3+ 14.♔e2 ♗g4+ (14...♗f5 15.♗xf7+ ♔h8 16.♖d1! ♕xa1 17.♗a3+—) 15.♕xg4 ♕xa1 16.♕f5 with a strong attack] **11...♗e7 12.a4 ♘d7 13.h4 ♘c5 14.♘xc5 ♗xc5 15.♕xe5 ♗d4 16.♕g5?! ♕b6! 17.♗e3 ♗e6 18.♖a3 ♖fe8 19.♔g1** [19.♗xe6 ♗xe3! 20.♕xe3 ♕xb2=] **19...h6 20.♕f4 ♖ad8 21.♖h3 ♕b4 22.♗xe6?** [22.c3!? dynamically maintains the balance] **22...♖xe6 23.♗xd4 ♖xd4 24.♕b8+ ♔h7 25.♖b3 ♕e1+ 26.♔h2 ♕xf2 27.♕g3 ♕xc2 28.♖c3 ♕xb2 29.♖c4 ♖g6 30.♕f3 ♖xd3** 0-1

Vienna Game

1.e2-e4 e7-e5 2.♘b1-c3

White controls the d5-square and plans the advance of the f-pawn. The **Vienna Game** was developed in Vienna around 1850 by Carl Hamppe, as an attempt to play an improved version of the **King's Gambit**.

However, in the modern approach the choice of 2.♘c3 is not always made with the intention of advancing the f2-pawn, but rather as part of a more solid deployment with the move ♗c4, or even g3, developing the f1-bishop by way of a fianchetto.

However, after 2...♘c6, White can in fact create some headaches for Black with 3.f4!.

More logical would be the move

2. ... ♘g8-f6

which, by counterbalancing the pressure on the centre squares, makes it possible to respond to the thematic 3.f4 with 3...d5! 4.fxe5 ♘xe4 with a complex but balanced position.

Black should not have many problems if White plays the solid 3.g3.

After

3. ♗f1-c4

Black has a more complicated task, and must choose between two very different continuations:

A) 3. ... ♘f6xe4

An apparent knight sacrifice: However, in reality after 4.♘xe4 d5, Black regains the piece, with a fluid game.

If White instead avoids the pawn fork by first sacrificing the bishop with 4.♗xf7+, then 4...♔xf7 5.♘xe4 d5!, and Black's dominant centre is more than sufficient compensation for the exposed king.

However, the best move for White is

4. ♕d1-h5!

This move leads to a long sequence of forced moves with the inventively picturesque name **Frankenstein-Dracula Variation**. It is very popular with correspondence players.

After

4.	...	**♘e4-d6**
5.	**♗c4-b3!**	**♘b8-c6**
6.	**♘c3-b5!**	**g7-g6**
7.	**♕h5-f3**	**f7-f5**
8.	**♕f3-d5**	

the threat to f7 forces Black to move his queen, losing control of the c7-square.

Now after

8. ...   ♛d8-e7
9. ♞b5xc7+   ♚e8-d8
10. ♞c7xa8

Black loses a rook. But with

10. ...   b7-b6

followed by ...♝b7, he wins the a8-knight, and it is not clear, notwithstanding the large number of examples from tournament play, if Black's initiative along the light-square diagonal a8-h1 compensates for the exchange.

What we can say is that with correct play White should maintain a certain advantage. However, in practice Black's position is not only easier to play, but also more fun.

B)   3. ...   ♞b8-c6

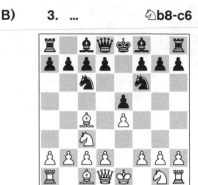

The most solid line: Black continues normally and after

4. d2-d3

he takes advantage of the fact that the knight is already on c3 by playing

4. ...   ♝f8-b4

which puts White's centre under pressure and prepares for ...d5.

A slightly more ambitious alternative exists for Black: 4...♞a5

The objective is to acquire the bishop pair. The downside is that the move neglects development and concedes White good control of the centre after 5.♘ge2 ♘xc4 6.dxc4 ♗c5.

If Black is playing to win, but does not feel up to dealing with the complications inherent in 3...♘xe4, this move would be a good choice.

After

5.	♗c1-g5	h7-h6!
6.	♗g5xf6	♗b4xc3+!
7.	b2xc3	♕d8xf6

we have a balanced position in which White's central predominance compensates for the doubled pawn on c3.

Gjedsted,Soren Havn
Thingstad,Tormod

Copenhagen 2006 (7)

1.e4 e5 2.♘c3 ♘c6 3.♗c4 ♗c5 4.♕g4 ♕f6 5.♘d5 ♗xf2+ 6.♔f1 ♕d6 7.♕xg7 ♗b6 8.♕xh8 ♕g6 9.♘f3 ♔f8 10.d3 d6 11.♘h4 ♕g4 12.♗h6+ ♔e8 13.♘f6+ 1-0

Mariotti,Sergio
Kortchnoi,Viktor

Rome 1982 (8)

1.e4 e5 2.♘c3 ♘f6 3.g3 ♗b4 4.♗g2 0-0 5.♘ge2 c6 6.0-0 d5 7.exd5 cxd5 8.d4 exd4 9.♘xd4 ♗xc3 10.bxc3 ♘bd7 11.♗f4 ♘b6 12.♘b5 ♗f5 13.♘d6 ♗e4 14.♗h3 ♘c4 15.♘xe4 ♘xe4 16.♕d4 ♕a5 17.♖fe1 ♖ae8 18.♗f1 ♘a3 19.♗d3 ♖e6 20.f3 ♘c5 21.♗f5 ♖f6 22.♕xd5 ♕xc3 23.♖ad1 ♖xf5 24.♕xf5 ♘xc2 25.♗e5 ♕c4 26.♗xg7 ♔xg7 27.♕g5+ ♔h8 28.♖d8 ♘d7 29.♖ee8 ♕d4+ 30.♔g2 ♕g7 31.♕e7 ♕g8 32.♕xd7 1-0

Ost Hansen,Jacob
Nunn,John

Teesside tt 1974

1.e4 e5 2.♘c3 ♘f6 3.♗c4 ♘xe4 4.♕h5 ♘d6 5.♗b3 ♘c6 6.♘b5 g6 7.♕f3 f5 8.♕d5 ♕e7 9.♘xc7+ ♔d8 10.♘xa8 b6 11.d3 ♗b7 12.h4 f4 13.♕f3 ♗h6 14.♕g4 e4 15.♗xf4 exd3+ 16.♔f1 ♗xf4 17.♕xf4 ♖f8 18.♕g3 ♘e4 19.♕c7+ ♔e8 20.♘h3 ♘xf2 21.♘xf2 ♕e2+ 22.♔g1 ♕xf2+ 23.♔h2 ♕xh4+ 24.♔g1 ♕d4+ 25.♔h2 ♘e5 26.♖hf1 ♘g4+ 27.♔h3 ♕e3+ 28.♔xg4 h5+ 29.♔h4 g5+ 30.♔xh5 ♖h8+ 31.♔g6 ♗e4+ 32.♖f5 ♗xf5+ 33.♔xf5 ♖f8+ 34.♔g6 ♕e4+ 35.♔g7 ♕e7+ 36.♔g6 ♕f6+ 37.♔h5 ♕h8+ 38.♔g4 ♕h4X 0-1

King's Gambit

1.e2-e4 e7-e5 2.f2-f4

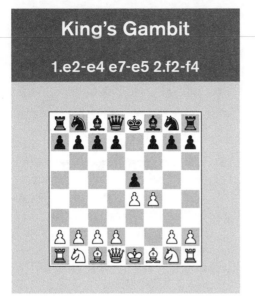

The **King's Gambit** is one of those openings which have made chess history. It was enormously popular in the 19th century at the height of the Romantic era. However, it all but disappeared with the advent of the positional school at the beginning of the 20th century. In the 1930s there was a partial re-evaluation thanks to the Swedish grandmaster Gösta Stoltz, who highlighted the positional merits of this gambit. The King's Gambit was now no longer seen simply as a means of violently attacking the f7-square via the f-file and the usual ♗c4, but as a way of conquering the centre, without ruling out the possibility of later simplification and an early endgame. Its occasional use by champion players such as Keres, Spassky, Bronstein, and even the great Bobby Fischer, and more recently Gallagher and Fedorov, has made the opening popular with lovers of sparkling and aggressive play. However, the King's Gambit is still viewed with a certain scepticism by top players; and indeed, if Black is well prepared, it is difficult for White to achieve an objective advantage. Black is naturally not obliged to accept the offered pawn, and for this reason – depending on Black's choice – the gambit is classified as either being declined or accepted.

King's Gambit Declined

Black usually either continues solidly with 2...♗c5, or he counterattacks with 2...d5; but there is also a novelty: 2...♘c6. *It should never be forgotten that White is not really threatening 3.fxe5??, because of 3...♕h4+ followed by 4...♕xe4+ and Black is winning.*

A)   2.   ...   ♗c5

This is highly logical, as it takes possession of the diagonal which has been weakened by advancing the pawn to f4. After the obvious

3. ♘g1-f3   d7-d6

White can play along the lines of the **Giuoco Pianissimo** with

4. ♘b1-c3   ♘g8-f6
5. ♗f1-c4   ♘b8-c6
6. d2-d3

and White has a minute advantage, but both players have chances.

Alternatively, he can more ambitiously prepare to take possession of the centre with 4.c3. After 4...♘f6 5.d4 exd4 6.cxd4 ♗b6, it is not clear if White's impressive-looking centre is in actual fact a strength or a weakness.

The Falkbeer Counter-Gambit

is without doubt the most active way to decline the King's Gambit.
After

B)   **2.**   **...**   **d7-d5**
       3. e4xd5
Black's original idea was to push the pawn to e4: 3...e4

with the ambitious goal of creating an obstacle to White's development and to highlight the unhappy placement of the f4-pawn, which in this position would be certainly better placed on f2. However, White will obviously play **4.d3!**, threatening the advanced black pawn, and after 4...♘f6! 5.dxe4! ♘xe4 6.♘f3 ♗c5 7.♕e2 ♗f5 (or 7...f5) 8.♘c3 ♕e7, a position is reached where Black, with active piece play, will try to compensate for his material deficit. Opinions differ as to how much compensation there really is, but there is no rea-

son to think that Black – having played all the logical moves – has not at least a playable position.
However, the most frequent move in modern times is

      3. ...   **c7-c6!?**

This is just another of Aaron Nimzowitsch's countless contributions. For White to now take on c6 appears to be dangerous. The following line has proved to be the best for both players:

      4.   ♘**b1-c3**   **e5xf4!**
      5.   ♘**g1-f3**   ♗**f8-d6**
      6.   **d2-d4**   ♘**g8-e7**
      7.   **d5xc6**   ♘**b8xc6**
      8.   ♗**f1-c4**   **0-0**
      9.   **0-0**   ♗**c8-g4**
   10.   ♘**c3-e4**   ♗**d6-c7**
   11.   **c2-c3**   ♘**e7-g6**

and we have a position in which White's strong centre is compensated for by the well-protected f4-pawn, which impedes White's development – e.g. of the c1-bishop – and those are the ingredients of good piece play for Black.
Remember that with 3...exf4!? 4.♘f3 Black transposes to the modern variation of the **King's Gambit Accepted**, having avoided the **Bishop's Gambit** 3.♗c4.

C)   **2. ...**   **♘b8-c6!?**
          3. ♘g1-f3   f7-f5!?

This is the latest fashion, but it is still not clear how good it is. There are some who have opined that it represents the refutation of the King's Gambit! But even if this line were as strong for Black as has been suggested, it is worth remembering that with 3.♘c3 instead of 3.♘f3, White can enter a favourable variation of the **Vienna Game.**

King's Gambit Accepted

          2. ...   e5xf4

Now the move ...♛h4+ is such a threat that White generally plays either 3.♗c4 (freeing the f1-square for the king) or 3.♘f3 (controlling h4). Eccentric moves such as 3.♘c3 or 3.d4 – with the idea of moving the king to e2 after the queen check on h4 – would have some appeal to a player from the Romantic period, but are fundamentally ill advised.

3.♗c4, sometimes called the **Bishop's Gambit**, is not to be underestimated. Evidence of this is its employment by Fischer on several occasions, admittedly against lesser players, but with a noteworthy performance of 100%.

To continue with 3...♛h4+ 4.♔f1 at this point would facilitate White's development, as he can play ♘f3 with tempo, followed by d2-d4.

Therefore Black should seek counterplay in the centre with **3...♘f6!** 4.♘c3 c6!

and after 5.♗b3 d5, you reach a dynamically balanced position.

          3. ♘g1-f3

After this knight move, which is by far the most popular, Black has eight perfectly playable replies:

A)   3. ...   h7-h6

In the Becker Defence Black prepares the pawn push ...g7-g5, ready to respond to h4 with ...♗g7. Now an interesting move is 4.b3!? to prepare the occupation of the long dark-squared diagonal.

B)   3. ...   ♘g8-e7

has been undervalued because of a beautiful victory by Fischer playing with the white pieces. In reality this knight move is much better than its reputation would suggest: it supports d5 and it prepares to defend the f4-pawn from g6 or d5.

Now the natural moves are 4.d4 d5 5.♘c3 dxe4 6.♘xe4.

The discovery of the move **6...♘d5!** has led to a re-evaluation of this continuation.

C)   3. ...   ♘g8-f6

is the **Schallopp Defence**, which counterattacks the e4-pawn and which also allows the knight to transfer to h5 supporting the f4-pawn. After 4.e5 (4.♘c3 is interesting) 4...♘h5 5.d4.

White's central domination seems more significant than Black's extra pawn.

D)   3. ...   ♗f8-e7

is the **Cunningham Defence**: after 4.♗c4 or 4.♘c3, Black can continue solidly with ...♘f6. Otherwise he could risk giving check with ...♗h4. This would prevent White from castling but leaves the bishop badly placed on h4. In both cases the resulting positions are complex and difficult to evaluate.

E)   3. ...   d7-d5

is the **Modern Variation**: it was inspired by the old saying that the antidote to all gambits is to push the pawn to d5 (!!).

    4. e4xd5   ♘g8-f6!

Black has denied White the pawn advance to e5, which is so dangerous in the King's Gambit. However, after

5. ♗f1-c4 ♘f6xd5

Black needs to be careful: a well-timed, even if unnatural exchange on d5 by the bishop could give White a slight positional advantage, and at times a dangerous initiative. Nevertheless, with correct play Black maintains equality. For example:

6. ♗c4xd5 ♕d8xd5
7. ♘b1-c3 ♕d5-d8

7...♕f5!?

8. d2-d4 ♗f8-e7
9. ♗c1xf4 0-0
10. 0-0 ♗c8-f5
11. ♕d1-d2

F) **3. ...** ♘b8-c6!?
  4. ♘b1-c3

We have transposed to the **Vienna Game**.

G) **3. ...** d7-d6

The **Fischer Defence**, which was so named following the publication of an article in which the American champion maintained that it refuted the King's Gambit! The goal is to play the ...g5 variations without having to deal with ♘e5. But after

4. d2-d4 g7-g5
5. h2-h4! g5-g4
6. ♘f3-g1!

you reach a strange position in which after six moves all of both player's pieces are still on their original squares! Strange in an opening where development is the most noteworthy characteristic! This is a clear example of the modern interpretation of this opening: White seeks to exploit the weakness of the pawns on f4 and g4 positionally, renouncing the classic attack against f7.

6. ... ♗f8-h6
7. ♘b1-c3 c7-c6
8. ♘g1-e2 ♕d8-f6
9. g2-g3!

Play is complex, with possibilities for both sides.

H) **3. ...** g7-g5

This is called the **Classical Variation**. It is now well accepted that aggressive variations such as the **Muzio Gambit**

and the like, which come from 4.♗c4 g4 (4...♗g7!) 5.0-0!? gxf3 6.♕xf3, do not promise White any advantage. The only serious attempt remains

4. h2-h4!

Undermining Black's pawn chain.

4. ... g5-g4

5. ♘f3-e5!

*The move 5.♘g5 introduces the **Allgaier Gambit**, which is considered unsound. After 5...h6! 6.♘xf7 ♔xf7, White does not have enough compensation for the piece.*

The next diagram (after 5.♘e5!) is the key position of the **Kieseritzky Gambit**.

White moves the knight several times, but gains the g4-pawn or the one on f4, at times losing the e4-pawn. The pawn push to h4 weakens White's kingside (in some variations a black knight lands on g3 via h5), but Black's king is also in a rather precarious position. As a result the continuations that arise are tactically complex and have strategic possibilities for both players.

Black can continue with 5...d6, sacrificing the g4-pawn in exchange for good piece play after 6.♘xg4 ♘f6 7.♘xf6 ♕xf6, or he can play the classical

5. ... ♘g8-f6

Now, modern theory suggests

6. d2-d4

Preparing for the knight's retreat to d3.

The old move 6.♗c4 has proved to be ineffective because of 6...d5 7.exd5 ♗d6.

6. ... d7-d6

7. ♘e5-d3 ♘f6xe4

8. ♗c1xf4

The key position of the Classical Variation of the King's Gambit Accepted.

It seems to go against common sense to concede the e4-pawn for the one on f4: in addition Black has an extra pawn and an active knight on e4. Nonetheless, White receives good compensation: Black's kingside has many weaknesses, the g4-pawn, even though a material advantage, has the negative quality of restricting black activity on that wing, and perhaps Black would be better off without it (as is the case in the 5...d6 variation). In addition, White's rooks on e1 and f1 will exert unpleasant and ongoing positional pressure. This is also the case in variations in which the queens are exchanged. Black almost always castles queenside. White sometimes castles queenside too, and on other occasions he moves the king to d2 or otherwise to f2. In conclusion, after 8...♕e7 or 8...♗g7, the position is dynamically balanced.

Spielmann,Rudolf
Tarrasch,Siegbert

Karlsbad 1923 (7)

1.e4 e5 2.f4 ♗c5 3.♘f3 d6 4.c3 ♗g4 5.fxe5 dxe5 6.♕a4+ ♗d7 7.♕c2 ♘c6 8.b4 ♗d6 9.♗c4 ♘f6 10.d3 ♘e7 11.0-0 ♘g6 12.♗e3 b5 13.♗b3 a5 14.a3 axb4 15.cxb4 0-0 16.♘c3 c6 17.h3 ♕e7 18.♘e2 ♗b8 19.♔h2 ♗a7 20.♗g5 h6 21.♗xf6 ♕xf6 22.♘fd4 ♕d6 23.♘f5 ♗xf5 24.♖xf5 ♘f4 25.♖f1 g6 26.♖1xf4 exf4 27.e5 ♕e7 28.♖f6 ♔g7 29.d4 ♗xd4 30.♗xf7 ♗xe5 31.♕xg6+   1-0

Schulten,John William
Morphy,Paul

New York blind m 1857

1.e4 e5 2.f4 d5 3.exd5 e4 4.♘c3 ♘f6 5.d3 ♗b4 6.♗d2 e3 7.♗xe3 0-0 8.♗d2 ♗xc3 9.bxc3 ♖e8+ 10.♗e2 ♗g4 11.c4 c6 12.dxc6 ♘xc6 13.♔f1 ♖xe2 14.♘xe2 ♘d4 15.♕b1 ♗xe2+ 16.♔f2 ♘g4+ 17.♔g1 ♘f3+ 18.gxf3 ♕d4+ 19.♔g2 ♕f2+ 20.♔h3 ♕xf3+ 21.♔h4 ♘h6 22.♕g1 ♘f5+   0-1

Spielmann,Rudolf
Tarrasch,Siegbert

Mährisch Ostrau 1923 (11)

1.e4 e5 2.f4 d5 [2...exf4 3.♕f3!?, Spielmann-Tarrasch, Gothenburg 1920] **3.exd5 e4 4.d3 ♘f6 5.dxe4 ♘xe4 6.♘f3 ♗c5 7.♕e2 ♗f5 8.g4 0-0 9.gxf5 ♖e8 10.♗g2 ♘f2 11.♘e5 ♘xh1 12.♗xh1 ♘d7** [12...f6 13.d6!] **13.♘c3 f6 14.♘e4 fxe5 15.♘xc5 ♘xc5 16.fxe5 ♕h4+ 17.♔f1 ♖f8 18.♔g1 ♕d4+ 19.♗e3 ♕xe5 20.♖e1 ♘d7 21.♕c4 ♘h8 22.♗e4 ♖ae8 23.♗d4 ♕f4 24.♖e2 ♘f6 25.♗xf6 gxf6 26.h3 ♖g8+**   0-1

Anderssen,Adolf
Kieseritzky,Lionel

London 1851

1.e4 e5 2.f4 exf4 3.♗c4 ♕h4+ 4.♔f1 b5 5.♗xb5 ♘f6 6.♘f3 ♕h6 7.d3 [7.♘c3!] **7...♘h5?! 8.♘h4?! ♕g5 9.♘f5 c6 10.g4?** [10.♗a4±] **10...♘f6** [10...g6!?] **11.♖g1! cxb5? 12.h4 ♕g6 13.h5 ♕g5 14.♕f3 ♘g8 15.♗xf4 ♕f6 16.♘c3 ♗c5 17.♘d5 ♕xb2 18.♗d6** [criticized by Euwe: 18. d4 was winning. But in spite of all the mistakes (it was a friendly game) this is known as the Immortal Game because of its brilliant finish] **18...♗xg1?** [18...♕xa1+ 19.♔e2 ♕b2!] **19.e5! ♕xa1+ 20.♔e2 ♘a6 21.♘xg7+ ♔d8 22.♕f6+!! ♘xf6 23.♗e7X**   1-0

Pasik,Ron
Fernandez,Jaime

Wichita 2006 (5)

1.e4 e5 2.f4 exf4 3.♘f3 h6 4.h4 ♘f6 5.♘c3 ♘h5 6.♗c4 ♘g3 7.♖h2 ♘xe4 8.♕e2   1-0

Réti,Richard
Flamberg,Alexander

Opatija 1912 (4)

1.e4 e5 2.f4 exf4 3.♘f3 g5 4.♗c4 g4 5.0-0 d5 6.exd5 gxf3 7.♕xf3 ♗d6 8.d4 ♕f6 9.♕e4+ ♕e7 10.♘c3 ♘d7 11.♗xf4 ♕xe4 12.♘xe4 ♗xf4 13.♖xf4 f5 [13...♘e7 14.d6] **14.♖xf5 ♘e7 15.♖e1!** ♘b6 [15...♘xf5 16.♘d6+ ♔f8 17.♖e8+ ♔g7 18.♘xf5+ ♔f6 19.♖xh8 ♔xf5 20.♖xh7±] **16.♗b5+ ♔d8** [16...c6 17.dxc6 bxc6 18.♖e5 cxb5 19.♘g5; 16...♗d7 17.♖e5 ♗xb5 18.d6±] **17.♖e5 ♘g6** [17...♘bxd5 18.♘g5 ♖f8

19.Rxd5+ Nxd5 20.Nf7+ Rxf7 21.Re8X] **18.Ng5 Nxe5 19.Rxe5 Bd7 20.Nf7+ Nc8 21.Nxh8 Bxb5 22.Rh5 Bc4 23.Rxh7 Bxd5 24.h4 Be4 25.Rg7 Bxc2 26.h5 a5 27.h6 a4 28.h7 Bxh7 29.Rxh7 Nc4 30.Nf7 Ra6 31.g4 Nxb2 32.Rh8+ Kd7 33.Ne5+ Ke6 34.g5 Nd1 35.Rf8 Ne3 36.Kf2 Nd5 37.g6** 1-0

Spielmann,Rudolf
Grünfeld,Ernst

Teplitz-Schönau 1922 (7)

1.e4 e5 2.f4 exf4 3.Bc4 Nc6 4.Nf3 g5 5.0-0 d6 6.d4 Bg7 7.c3 h6 8.g3 g4 9.Nh4 f3 10.Nd2 Bf6 11.Ndxf3 gxf3 12.Qxf3 Rh7 13.Ng6 Rg7 14.Nf4 Bg4 15.Qg2 Bg5 16.h3 Bd7 17.Nh5 Rh7 18.e5 dxe5 19.Qe4 f5 20.Rxf5 Bxf5 21.Qxf5 [Tartakower: 'A position in the best tradition of the King's Gambit: Black, even though he is a rook up, is in a completely hopeless position'] **21...Re7 22.Bxg5 hxg5 23.Rf1 Qd6 24.Bxg8 exd4 25.Qf8+ Kd7 26.Qxa8 Qc5 27.Nf6+ Kd6 28.Qf8 Qe5 29.Kg2 d3 30.Rf2 Qe1 31.Qh6** 1-0

Fedorov,Alexey
Shirov,Alexey

Polanica Zdroj 2000 (5)

1.e4 e5 2.f4 exf4 3.Nf3 g5 4.h4 g4 5.Ne5 d6 6.Nxg4 Nf6 7.Nf2 Rg8 8.d4 Bh6 9.Nc3 Nc6 10.Nd5 Nxd5 11.exd5 Qe7+ 12.Be2 Nb4 13.c4 Bf5 14.Qa4+ Kf8 15.Qxb4 Re8 16.Qd2 Rxg2 17.Kf1 Rg3 18.Qd1 Be4 19.Rh2 f5 20.Nxe4 fxe4 21.Bg4 e3 22.Bf3 Qg7 23.Rh1 Rg2 0-1

Spassky,Boris
Fischer,Robert

Mar del Plata 1960 (2)

1.e4 e5 2.f4 exf4 3.Nf3 g5 [afterwards Fischer suggested 3...d6!] **4.h4 g4 5.Ne5 Nf6 6.d4** [6.Nxg4] **6...d6 7.Nd3 Nxe4 8.Bxf4 Bg7 9.Nc3∓** [9.c3! Qe7! (Fischer) 10.Qe2 Bf5∓] **9...Nxc3 10.bxc3 c5! 11.Be2 cxd4 12.0-0 Nc6** [12...h5 13.Bg5 f6 14.Bc1 and Nf4; g6<, e6<, h5<] **13.Bxg4 0-0 14.Bxc8 Rxc8 15.Qg4 f5 16.Qg3 dxc3 17.Rae1** [17.Rxd6 Rf6 18.Bf4 Rg6↑ explains why Fischer, always seeking active play, had preferred 15... f5 to the quieter 15...Kh8] **17...Kh8** [17...Qd7 18.Bxd6 Rfe8 19.Nc5 Qf7∓ Fischer was better according to an analysis by Kmoch and Antoshin] **18.Kh1?** [≥ 18.Bxd6 Rf6 19.Be5 Nxe5 20.Nxe5 with some compensation for the pawn] **18...Rg8 19.Bxd6 Bf8!** [19...Bd4] **20.Be5+ Nxe5 21.Qxe5+ Rg7! 22.Rxf5** [22.Qxf5 Qxh4+ 23.Kg1 Qg4 24.Qxg4 (24.Qf2 Bd6→) 24...Rxg4∓; 22.Rf4? Bd6-+; 22.Qf4? Rg4-+] **22...Qxh4+ 23.Kg1 Qg4?** [Fischer's first mistake, but a rather serious one; 23...Qg3! was given by Spassky himself as very good for Black: 24.Qxg3 (24.Qe2 Bd6) 24...Rxg3∓ Δ 25...Rxc3] **24.Rf2 Be7 25.Re4 Qg5 26.Qd4! Rf8?** [Fischer admitted to having overlooked Spassky's intended reply; 26...Bf8! was enough for a dynamic balance: 27.Qxa7 (27.Ne5 Bc5 28.Nf7+ Kg8 29.Nxg5 Bxd4 30.Rxd4 Rxg5=) 27...Bd6=] **27.Re5!** [strangely Black now loses a piece] **27...Rd8** [27...Qg6 28.Rxe7+-; 27...Qh4 28.Rxf8++-; 27...Bf6 28.Qd6!+-] **28.Qe4 Qh4 29.Rf4** [29...Qg3 30.Rxe7+-] 1-0

Latvian Counter-Gambit

1.e2-e4 e7-e5 2.♘g1-f3 f7-f5

This is sometimes called the **Greco Counter-Gambit**, after the Calabrian Gioacchino Greco, who analysed a variety of lines in the early part of the 17th century. It was later revived by the Latvian Karl Behting, who studied it at the beginning of the 20th century.

To play a type of King's Gambit with a tempo less is certainly not a particularly appealing choice for Black: the only advantage is that there is not the possibility of a queen check on h5 and thus Black is genuinely threatening 3...fxe4, whereas fxe5 in the **King's Gambit** is only an illusory threat.

The best policy for White is to content himself with the good positional advantage that comes from

A)   **3. ♘f3xe5!**

threatening both 4.♗c4 and 4.♕h5+.

     3. ...   **♕d8-f6**

     4. ♘e5-c4!

Better than 4.d4: the d-pawn is better placed on d2, so that at the right mo-

ment White can attack Black's centre by pushing it to d3.

     4. ...   **f5xe4**

     5. ♘b1-c3!

The active knights, the weak e4-pawn and the exposed black queen are all favourable for White.

If White tries to aggressively punish the Latvian Counter-Gambit, Black's position will prove to have unexpected resources.

B)   **3. ♗f1-c4!?**   **f5xe4**

     4. ♘f3xe5

This position is so complex that it was not until the 1970s that the move

     4. ...   **d7-d5!?**

was considered playable.

The classical continuation 4...♕g5 would appear to give White an advantage after 5.d4! ♕xg2! 6.♕h5+ g6 7.♗f7+! ♔d8 8.♗xg6 ♕xh1+ 9.♔e2.

However, opinions still differ on this adventurous line and Black can still use it in practical games.

  5. ♕d1-h5+ g7-g6
  6. ♘e5xg6 h7xg6!

White should be able to maintain some advantage here by taking on either h8 or g6. Nonetheless, the introduction of 4...d5!? brought about a brief period of popularity for the Latvian Counter-Gambit. Today it is almost never played at a serious level, except by correspondence players, who in general like long forced lines of play. The Latvian fits the bill nicely in this respect and thus enjoys a certain popularity with this group of players.

Macieja,Bartlomiej
Vasquez,Rafael
Willemstad 2001 (3)

1.e4 e5 2.♘f3 f5 3.♘xe5 ♕f6 4.♘c4 fxe4 5.♘c3 ♕f7 6.♘e3 c6 7.♘xe4 d5 8.♘g3 h5 9.d4 h4 10.♘e2 ♗d6 11.♘g1 ♘f6 12.♘f3 ♘e4 13.♗e2 ♘d7 14.h3 ♘df6 15.0-0 ♕c7 16.c4 g5 17.♘e5 ♗xe5 18.dxe5 ♕xe5

19.cxd5 cxd5 20.♗f3 ♗e6 21.♖e1 ♔f7 22.♘g4 ♘xg4 23.♗xg4 ♗xg4 24.♕xg4 ♕d6 25.♗g5 ♖ag8 26.♕f5+ ♔e8 27.♖ac1 ♖xg5 28.♖c8+   **1-0**

Borozan,Nikola
Kovacevic,Slobodan
Igalo tt 1994 (2)

1.e4 e5 2.♘f3 f5 3.♗c4 fxe4 4.♘xe5 ♕g5 5.d4 ♕xg2 6.♕h5+ g6 7.♗f7+ ♔d8 8.♗xg6 ♕xh1+ 9.♔e2 c6 10.♘c3 ♘f6 11.♕h4 ♗e7 [11...d6 12.♗g5 (12.♕xf6+ ♔c7 13.♕xh8±) 12...♕xa1 13.♗xf6+ ♔c7 14.♗d8X] **12.♗g5 ♕xa1 13.♗xf6 ♗xf6 14.♕xf6+ ♔c7 15.♘c4 ♖g8 16.♕e5+ ♔d8 17.♘d6 ♖f8 18.♕g5+ ♔c7 19.♘db5+** **1-0**

Guido,Flavio
Hector,Jonny
Genova 1989 (10)

1.e4 e5 2.♘f3 f5 3.♗c4 fxe4 4.♘xe5 d5 5.♕h5+ g6 6.♘xg6 hxg6 7.♕xg6+ ♔d7 8.♗xd5 ♘f6 9.♘c3 ♕e7 10.d4 exd3+ 11.♗e3 dxc2 12.♕xc2 ♕h7 13.♕a4+ ♔d8 14.♗g5 ♗e7 15.♗f3 ♘fd7 16.♗f4 ♘c5 17.0-0-0 ♗d7 18.♕c4 ♖f8 19.♘d5 ♗d6 20.♗e3 ♘ba6 21.♖he1 b5 22.♕c3 b4 23.♕c4 b3 24.axb3 ♖b8 25.♗g5+ ♔c8 26.♖e3 ♕xh2 27.♘e7+ ♗xe7 28.♗xe7 ♕f4 29.♖d4 ♘xb3+ 30.♔d1 ♕xd4+ 31.♕xd4 ♘xd4 32.♗xf8 ♘xf3 33.gxf3 ♖xb2   **0-1**

Other Minor Lines after 2.♘f3

Among the alternative minor lines for Black after 2.♘f3, we can cite defences which are passive, such as 2...♕e7, or those which are quite clearly unsound, such as 2...f6.

This last move was the subject of **analysis by Damiano** in the 16th century. A brief examination of this move, apart from being of historical interest, is instructive for learning some typical tactical motifs in the opening: **3.♘xe5! ♕e7!** (3...fxe5? 4.♕h5+ g6 5.♕xe5+ followed by 6.♕xh8 wins a decisive material advantage. The attempt to not lose the h8-rook with 4...♔e7? is even worse: 5.♕xe5+ ♔f7 6.♗c4+ d5 7.♗xd5+ ♔g6 8.h4 – threatening to push this pawn further, with checkmate – 8...h5 9.♗xb7! gives White a decisive material advantage on account of the fact that 9...♗xb7 allows 10.♕f5+ ♔h6 11.d4+, which is winning) 4.♘f3 ♕xe4+ 5.♗e2 and after 6.0-0, White will gain several tempi for his development and for an attack along the e-file with ♖e1 and/or ♘c3.

Elephant Gambit

Of the minor variations, the so-called 'Elephant Gambit' is the most popular, and it has a significant number of enthusiastic adherents, especially at club level.

2. ...   d5

As a surprise weapon it may prove to be effective, but after the correct

3. e4xd5   e5-e4
4. ♕d1-e2!

it is extremely unlikely that Black will gain sufficient compensation for the pawn.

Landa,Konstantin
Vogiatzis,Dimitrios
Bad Wiessee 2006 (1)
1.e4 e5 2.♘f3 d5 3.exd5 ♗d6 4.d4 e4 5.♘e5 ♘e7 6.♘c3 ♗b4 7.♗b5+ c6 8.dxc6 bxc6 9.♗c4 0-0 10.0-0 ♗f5 11.♗g5 ♕d6 12.♗xe7 ♕xe7 13.f3 e3 14.♖e1 ♕g5 15.♕e2 c5 16.a3 cxd4 17.axb4 ♗e6 18.♗xe6 fxe6 19.♘c4 dxc3 20.bxc3   1-0

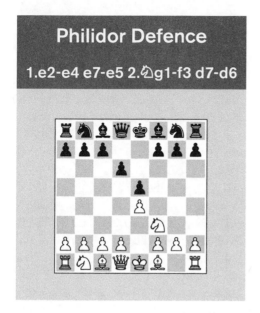

Philidor Defence

1.e2-e4 e7-e5 2.♘g1-f3 d7-d6

the following line is virtually forced:
5.0-0 ♗e7 6.dxe5! dxe5 7.♘g5! ♗xg5
8.♕h5 g6 9.♕xg5 ♕xg5 10.♗xg5
with a superior endgame for White.

However, the best response is without doubt

3.	...	♘g8-f6!
4.	♘b1-c3	♘b8-d7
5.	♗f1-c4	♗f8-e7
6.	0-0	0-0
7.	♖f1-e1	c7-c6
8.	a2-a4	

The **Philidor Defence** is named in honour of the famous 18th century chess theoretician-composer, who advocated this defence, albeit with the idea of pushing the pawn to f5 as early as the third move; a concept which today is viewed with great suspicion. Philidor's aggressive approach could have some validity after the moves 3.♘c3 or 3.♗c4, which is the very reason that Morphy's favourite move 3.d4! is so appropriate. The modern treatment of this defence tends towards a more solid approach, with Black developing his pieces on the back ranks, usually ...♘bd7, ...♘gf6, ...♗e7, ...c6, ...♕c7. 2...d6 has the obvious defect of blocking the f8-bishop. Nonetheless, such a natural move could not be considered bad... or, more precisely: not really bad!

3. d2-d4

Here it is worth mentioning the old Hanham Variation 3...♘d7, which is not often played nowadays. After 4.♗c4 c6!

Black's solid but passive position is reminiscent of several **Pirc** variations and the **Old Indian Defence**. White has to content himself with a small advantage that may arise from his possession of the d-file and the weakness of the d6-square. It is for this reason that White should strive to exchange on e5.

As this grants mobility to the e7-bishop, the exchange should take place at the most opportune moment. More rarely, White succeeds in the course of the game in preparing the pawn advance f2-f4, with the idea of undermining Black's centre.

Black, for his part, has to play a waiting game – putting his faith in the solidity of his position.

The following sequence has become an increasingly popular way of reaching this position: 1.e4 d6 2.d4 ♘f6 3.♘c3 e5!? (with 3...g6 we land in the **Pirc**) 4.♘f3 (exchanging queens does not give White any particular advantage) 4...♘bd7 5.♗c4 ♗e7, etc.

In conclusion, this is a defence that is in the process of being re-evaluated. It is certainly not as bad as has been thought in the past. It is suitable for solid, patient players, and it has the advantage of not requiring a lot of theoretical study.

Rodzinski
Alekhine,Alexander
Paris 1913

1.e2-e4 e7-e5 2.♘g1-f3 d7-d6 3.♗f1-c4 ♘b8-c6 4.c2-c3 ♗c8-g4 5.♕d1-b3 ♕d8-d7 6.♘f3-g5?! [6.♕xb7; 6.♗xf7+ ♔xf7 7.♕xb7 ♔d7 8.♕xa8 ♗xf3 9.gxf3 ♕xf3=] **6...♘g8-h6 7.♗c4xf7+?** [7.♕xb7] **7...♘h6xf7 8.♘g5xf7 ♕d7xf7?** [8...♗e6-+] **9.♕b3xb7 ♔e8-d7 10.♕b7xa8 ♕f7-c4 11.f2-f3 ♗g4xf3 12.g2xf3 ♘c6-d4 13.d2-d3?** [13.cxd4=] **13...♕c4xd3 14.c3xd4 ♗f8-e7 15.♕a8xh8 ♗e7-h4X** 0-1

Kaufmann,Arthur
Marco,Georg
Trebic 1915

1.e2-e4 e7-e5 2.♘g1-f3 d7-d6 3.d2-d4 ♘b8-d7 4.♗f1-c4 c7-c6 5.0-0 ♗e7 6.dxe5 dxe5 [6...♘xe5 7.♘xe5 dxe5 8.♕h5±] **7.♕e2** [7.♘g5! ♗xg5 8.♕h5 g6 9.♕xg5±] **7...♘gf6 8.♖d1 ♕c7?!** [8...♕a5 9.♘g5 0-0 △ 10.♗xf7+ ♖xf7 11.♕c4 ♘d5] **9.♘g5! ♖f8** [9...0-0 10.♗xf7+ ♖xf7 11.♕c4+-] **10.♗xf7+! ♖xf7 11.♕c4! ♖f8 12.♘e6 ♕b6 13.♘xg7+ ♔d8 14.♘e6+ ♔e8 15.♗e3 ♕b4 16.♘c7+ ♔d8 17.♕xb4 ♗xb4 18.♘xa8 b6 19.f3 ♗c5 20.♗xc5 bxc5 21.♖d3! ♗b7 22.♖a3 ♗c8** [22...♗xa8 23.♖xa7 ♔e7 24.♘a3+-] **23.♖xa7 ♔b8 24.♖a5 ♗xa8 25.♘d2 ♔c7 26.♘c4 ♗b7 27.♖d1 ♖a8 28.♖xa8 ♗xa8 29.♖d3 ♗b7 30.♖a3 ♘e8 31.♔f2 ♘d6 32.♘xd6 ♔xd6 33.♖d3+ ♔c7 34.g3 c4 35.♖c3 ♗a6 36.f4 ♔d6 37.♖a3 ♘c5** [37...♗b5 38.♖a8] **38.♔e3 h5 39.♖a5 ♗b5 40.b3 ♘d7 41.a4 cxb3 42.cxb3 ♗f1 43.♖a8 ♗g2 44.♖e8 ♗xe4 45.fxe5+ ♔d5 46.a5** 1-0

Peng Xiaomin
Du Shan
Xiapu 2005 (19)

1.e2-e4 e7-e5 2.♘g1-f3 d7-d6 3.d2-d4 ♘b8-d7?! 4.♗f1-c4 c7-c6 5.0-0 h6? 6.dxe5 dxe5 7.♗xf7+! ♔xf7 8.♘xe5+ ♔f6 9.♕d4 ♔e6 10.♘g6 b5 11.♘xh8 ♕f6 12.♕xf6+ ♔xf6 13.b3 ♗d6 14.♗b2+ ♗e5 15.♗xe5+ ♘xe5 16.f4 ♘g4 17.e5+ ♔e6 18.♘c3 ♘e3 19.♖f3 ♘xc2 20.♖d1 ♘e7 21.♖d6+ ♔f5 22.♘e2 c5 23.h3 1-0

Castaldi,Vincenzo
Tartakower,Savielly

Stockholm ol 1937 (2)

1.e4 e5 2.♘f3 d6 3.d4 ♘f6 4.♘c3 ♘bd7 5.♗e2 ♗e7 6.0-0 h6 7.b3 c6 8.♗b2 ♕c7 9.♕d2 g5!? 10.♖fd1 ♘f8? 11.dxe5 dxe5 12.♘xe5!! ♗e6 [12...♕xe5 13.♘d5!!] **13.♘b5!! ♕b8 14.♕a5! ♗d8 15.♖xd8+! ♕xd8 16.♘c7+ ♔e7 17.♗a3+** 1-0

Rabinovich,Ilya
Ilyin Zhenevsky,Alexander

Soviet Union 1922

1.e2-e4 e7-e5 2.♘g1-f3 d7-d6 3.d2-d4 ♘g8-f6 4.♘b1-c3 ♘b8-d7 5.♗f1-c4 ♗f8-e7 6.♗c4xf7+? ♔e8xf7 7.♘f3-g5+ ♔f7-g8! 8.♘g5-e6 ♕d8-e8 9.♘e6xc7 ♕e8-g6 10.♘c7xa8 ♕g6xg2 11.♖h1-f1 e5xd4! 12.♕d1-e2 [12.♕xd4 ♘e5 13.f4 ♘fg4→ threatening 14...♗h4+] **12...d4xc3!** [12...♘e5 13.f4!] **13.♕e2-c4+ d6-d5 14.♕c4xc8+ ♔g8-f7♚ 15.♕c8xb7** [15.♕xh8 ♕xe4+ 16.♔d1 ♕f3+ 17.♔e1 cxb2 18.♗xb2 ♗b4+ 19.c3

♗xc3+ 20.♗xc3 ♕xc3+ 21.♔e2 ♕c2+ 22.♔e1 (22.♔f3 ♕e4+ 23.♔g3 ♕g4X) **22...♘e4 23.♖d1 ♘c3—+**]

15...♕g2xe4+ 16.♗c1-e3 ♖h8-b8 17.♕b7xa7 c3xb2 18.♔e1-d2 [18.♖b1 ♕xc2—+] **18...♕e4-b4+ 19.c2-c3 ♘f6-e4+ 20.♔d2-e2 ♘e4xc3+ 21.♔e2-f3 ♕b4-e4+ 22.♔f3-g3 ♘c3-e2+ 23.♔g3-h3 ♕e4-f3X** 0-1

Yu Shaoteng
Bauer,Christian

Paris tt 2006 (3)

1.e2-e4 d7-d6 2.d2-d4 ♘g8-f6 3.♘b1-c3 e7-e5 4.♘g1-f3 ♘b8-d7 5.♗f1-c4 ♗f8-e7 6.0-0 0-0 7.a4 c6 8.♗a2 a5 9.♕e2 exd4 10.♘xd4 ♘c5 11.♖d1 ♕b6 12.h3 ♗e6 13.♘xe6 fxe6 14.e5 ♘d5 15.exd6 ♗xd6 16.♘xd5 exd5 17.c4 ♖ae8 18.♗e3 ♗f4 19.♗xc5 ♕xc5 20.♕d3 d4 21.g3 ♗e3 22.♖f1 ♖xf2 23.♖xf2 ♗xf2+ 24.♔xf2 ♖e3 25.♕f1 ♕e5 26.c5+ ♔h8 27.♔g1 ♖xg3+ 28.♔h1 ♕e4+ 29.♔h2 ♖f3 30.♕e1 ♖e3 31.♕f1 ♖e2+ 32.♔g3 ♕e3+ 0-1

Petroff Defence

1.e2-e4 e7-e5 2.♘g1-f3 ♘g8-f6

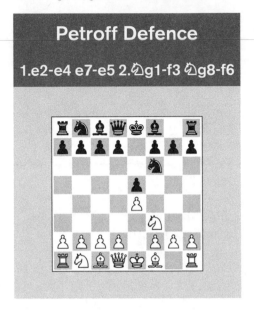

With 2...♘f6, Black does not defend the e5-pawn, but attacks the e4-pawn instead.

We are therefore talking about a defence which is conceptually ambitious and active. However, in practice, the resulting variations tend to lead to symmetrical and quiet positions, and the number of drawn games is unusually high.

If Black is looking for a win, other defences would be more suitable. On the other hand, it could be an excellent choice if you are Black against a stronger player, or one who plays ambitiously: indeed, if White plays too aggressively he may find that the more tactical variations will backfire on him.

The **Petroff Defence** is one of the most extraordinary examples of opening re-evaluation of all time: you only need to consult a 1970s opening book to realize how little it was appreciated then. The prospect of playing symmetrical positions with one or two tempi less was

sufficient for it to be considered unplayable. Only the Italo-Hungarian Bela Toth played it in those years, after which it began to appear in the repertoires of Yusupov, Karpov, Hort, Hübner and other champions.

From the beginning of the 1990s the Petroff Defence has been appreciated as one of the most effective means of drawing with the black pieces — especially by top-level players.

The Petroff is often called the **Russian Defence**. Alexander Petroff, who popularized it at the beginning of the 19th century, and Carl Jaenisch, who also contributed a great deal to its development, were both Russians. At the beginning of the 20th century the American Frank Marshall believed in the validity of several lines where Black plays very aggressively. Other very dynamic players, such as Harry Nelson Pillsbury, have also used the Petroff Defence with success. This makes you reflect on the common notion that certain openings are always solid and passive by nature, whereas others are always dynamic and aggressive. Fortunately, the possibility of personal interpretation in so many openings is so great that there is always room for creative play.

Now we will have a close look at some specific variations. After the defence of the e4-pawn with 3.♘c3, there is 3...♘c6, and you transpose to the innocuous **Four Knights Opening**.

For this reason, if White wishes to travel along more promising paths, there remain effectively two alternatives: either to take the pawn on e5 or to look for activity with 3.d4.

A)   3. ♘f3xe5

3. ...   d7-d6

Not 3...♘xe4? 4.♕e2 ♘f6 (4...d5 5.d3) 5.♘c6+.

4. ♘e5-f3

The move 4.♘xf7!? looks like the work of a drunken Irishman. Yet it is a part of chess theory and is even dignified with a name: the **Cochrane Gambit**. However, against correct play White will have his work set out for him trying to find sufficient compensation for the sacrificed piece.

4. ...   ♘f6xe4
5. d2-d4!

After 5.♕e2 ♕e7 6.d3 ♘f6 7.♗g5 ♕xe2+, even with the two extra tempi the position is too sterile to offer White a concrete advantage.

5.♘c3!? is interesting, as after 5...♘xc3 6.dxc3!, White's objective is quick development with 7.♗e3 or 7.♗f4, 8.♕d2 and 9.0-0-0.

5. ...   d6-d5
6. ♗f1-d3

In this almost symmetrical position White must exploit the presence of the black knight on e4, which appears to be actively placed, but which in reality renders Black's centre somewhat unstable. It is worth noting that if the knight

were on f6 we would be in the **Exchange Variation of the French**, which is notorious for leading to an easy draw. Black has three continuations:

A1)   6. ...   ♘b8-c6

7.	**0-0**	**♗c8-g4**
8.	**c2-c4!**	**♘e4-f6**
9.	**♘b1-c3!?**	**♗g4xf3**
10.	**♕d1xf3**	**♘c6xd4**
11.	**♕f3-h3**	

with good compensation for White.

A2)   6. ...   ♗f8-d6

7.	**0-0**	**0-0**
8.	**c2-c4**	**c7-c6**

is the most logical. Now the critical line appears to be 9.cxd5 cxd5 10.♘c3, and Black can no longer maintain the knight on e4.

After 10...♘xc3 11.bxc3 ♗g4 12.♖b1 White has an unpleasant initiative.

A3)   6. ...   ♗f8-e7

Here the bishop is more passively placed. However, the d5-pawn is defended by the queen, and Black does not have to move his pawn to c6 when White plays c4.

After 7.0-0 ♘c6 8.c4 – with 8.♖e1 ♗g4!?, the position becomes complex; especially after 9.c3 f5 – 8...♘f6, or 8...♘b4, you reach typical Petroff Defence positions, in which White's nice centre is compensated for by Black's active piece play.

B)   3. d2-d4

The most direct move. This was considered the best response in the 1970s, but now it is less common than the previously examined alternative.

**   3. ...   ♘f6xe4!**

Inadvisable is 3...exd4 4.e5 ♘e4 5.♕xd4!, which leads to a position that is considered to be difficult for Black.

**   4. ♗f1-d3   d7-d5**

The incredible 4...♘c6!? (invented by Yaacov Murey) is also playable. After 4.♗xe4 d5 and 5...e4 Black will regain the sacrificed piece.

**   5. ♘f3xe5**

you have a symmetrical position where White will have difficulty gaining any advantage from his extra tempo after either 5...♘d7, or the more complex

5.	...	♗f8-d6
6.	0-0	0-0
7.	c2-c4	♗d6xe5!
8.	d4xe5	♘b8-c6
9.	c4xd5	♕d8xd5
10.	♕d1-c2	♘c6-b4
11.	♗d3xe4	♘b4xc2
12.	♗e4xd5	♗c8-f5!
13.	g2-g4!	♗f5xg4
14.	♗d5-e4	

14.♗f4 ♘xa1 15.♗e4 f5!, and again the position is balanced.

14.	...	♘c2xa1
15.	♘b1-c3	♗g4-h3
16.	♖f1-e1	f7-f5!

White will receive two minor pieces for a rook and a pawn, and yet in the many games with this line, White has not been able to demonstrate any substantial advantage.

Karpov,Anatoly
Kortchnoi,Viktor

Moscow m 1974 (6)

1.e4 e5 2.♘f3 ♘f6 3.♘xe5 d6 4.♘f3 ♘xe4 5.d4 d5 6.♗d3 ♗e7 7.0-0 ♘c6 8.♖e1 ♗g4 9.c3 f5 10.♕b3 0-0 11.♘bd2 ♔h8 12.h3 ♗h5 13.♕xb7 ♖f6 14.♕b3 ♖g6 15.♗e2 ♗h4 16.♖f1 ♗xf3 17.♘xf3 ♗xf2+ 18.♖xf2 ♘xf2 19.♔xf2 ♕d6 20.♘g5 ♖f8 21.♕a3 ♕d8 22.♗f4 h6 23.♘f3 ♖e8 24.♗d3 ♖e4 25.g3 ♖f6 26.♕c5 g5 27.♘xg5 hxg5 28.♗xg5 ♖ee6 29.♖e1 ♕g8 30.h4 ♖g6 31.♖xe6 1-0

Anand,Viswanathan
Kramnik,Vladimir

Tilburg 1998 (2)

1.e4 e5 2.♘f3 ♘f6 3.♘xe5 d6 4.♘f3 ♘xe4 5.d4 d5 6.♗d3 ♘c6 7.0-0 ♗e7 8.♖e1 ♗g4 9.c3 f5 10.♕b3 0-0 11.♘bd2 ♘a5 12.♕a4 ♘c6 13.♗b5 ♘xd2 14.♘xd2 ♕d6 15.h3! [before this suggestion by Ubilava 15. ♘b3 was played immediately] 15...♗h5 16.♘b3 ♗h4 17.♘c5 ♗xf2+? [insufficient, but

the alternatives are no better; 17...♖ae8? 18.♗g5!!+−; 17...f4 18.♖e6! ♕d8 19.♘xb7 ♕g5 20.♗f1!] 18.♔xf2 ♕h2 19.♗xc6 bxc6 20.♕xc6 f4 21.♕xd5+ ♔h8 22.♕xh5 f3 23.♕xf3 ♖xf3+ 24.♔xf3 ♖f8+ 25.♔e2 ♕xg2+ 26.♔d3 ♕xh3+ 27.♔c2! [27.♗e3 ♖f2] 27...♕g2+ 28.♗d2 ♕g6+ 29.♖e4! h5 30.♖e1 ♖e8 31.♔c1 ♖xe4 32.♘xe4 h4 33.♘g5 ♕h5 34.♖e3 ♔g8 35.c4 1-0

Kavalek,Lubosh
Toth,Bela

Haifa ol 1976 (4)

1.e4 e5 2.♘f3 ♘f6 3.♘xe5 d6 4.♘f3 ♘xe4 5.d4 d5 6.♗d3 ♗e7 7.0-0 ♘c6 8.♖e1 ♗g4 9.c4 ♘f6 10.cxd5 ♕xd5 11.♘c3 ♗xf3 12.♘xd5 ♗xd1 13.♘xc7+ ♔d7 14.♗f4 ♗g4 15.d5 ♘d4 16.♘xa8 ♖xa8 17.♗e5 ♗f5 18.♗f1 ♘c2 19.♗b5+ ♔d8 20.d6 ♘xe1 21.♖xe1 ♗e6 22.dxe7+ ♔xe7 23.♗d4 b6 24.a4 g6 25.a5 bxa5 26.♖a1 a6 27.♗e2 ♖d8 28.♗c3 ♘d5 29.♗d4 ♘b4 30.♗c5+ ♔e8 31.♗d1 ♖d2 32.♗a4+ ♗d7 33.♖e1+ ♔d8 34.♗b6+ ♔c8 35.♖c1+ ♔b7 36.♗xd7 ♔xb6 37.♗e8 f6 38.b3 ♖c2 39.♖d1 ♘d3 40.f4 ♖c1 41.♖xc1 ♘xc1 42.♗f7 ♘e2+ 43.♔f2 ♘xf4 44.♗c4 ♔c5 45.♗g8 h6 46.♗f7 ♔d4 47.♔g3 ♘e2+ 48.♔g4 ♘c1 49.h4 f5+ 50.♔f3 g5 51.hxg5 hxg5 52.♗e6 ♔c3 0-1

Kasparov,Garry
Karpov,Anatoly

Moscow Wch m 1985 (48)

1.e4 e5 2.♘f3 ♘f6 3.♘xe5 d6 4.♘f3 ♘xe4 5.d4 d5 6.♗d3 ♘c6 7.0-0 ♗e7 8.c4 ♘f6 9.♘c3 0-0 10.h3 dxc4

11.♗xc4 ♘a5 12.♗d3 ♗e6 13.♖e1 ♘c6 14.a3 a6 15.♗f4 ♕d7 16.♘e5 ♘xe5 17.dxe5 ♘d5 18.♗xd5 ♗xd5 19.♕c2 g6 20.♖ad1 c6 21.♗h6 ♖fd8 22.e6 fxe6 23.♗xg6 ♗f8 24.♗xf8 ♖xf8 25.♗e4 ♖f7 26.♖e3 ♖g7 27.♖dd3 ♖f8 28.♖g3 ♔h8 29.♕c3 ♖f7 30.♖de3 ♔g8 31.♕e5 ♕c7 32.♖xg7+ ♖xg7 33.♗xd5 ♕xe5 34.♗xe6+ ♕xe6 35.♖xe6 ♖d7 36.b4 ♔f7 37.♖e3 ♖d1+ 38.♔h2 ♖c1 39.g4 b5 40.f4 c5 41.bxc5 ♖xc5 42.♖d3 ♔e7 43.♔g3 a5 44.♔f3 b4 45.axb4 axb4 46.♔e4 ♖b5 47.♖b3 ♖b8 48.♔d5 ♔f6 49.♔c5 ♖e8 50.♖xb4 ♖e3 51.h4 ♖h3 52.h5 ♖h4 53.f5 ♖h1 54.♔d5 ♖d1+ 55.♖d4 ♖e1 56.♔d6 ♖e8 57.♔d7 ♖g8 58.h6 ♔f7 59.♖c4 ♔f6 60.♖e4 ♔f7 61.♔d6 ♔f6 62.♖e6+ ♔f7 63.♖e7+ ♔f6 64.♖g7 ♖d8+ 65.♔c5 ♖d5+ 66.♔c4 ♖d4+ 67.♔c3 **1-0**

Anand,Viswanathan
Kramnik,Vladimir

Frankfurt rapid 1999 (7)

1.e4 e5 2.♘f3 ♘f6 3.♘xe5 d6 4.♘f3 ♘xe4 5.d4 d5 6.♗d3 ♘c6 7.0-0 ♗e7 8.c4 ♘b4 9.cxd5 ♘xd3 10.♕xd3 ♕xd5 11.♖e1 ♗f5 12.g4 ♗g6 13.♘c3 ♘xc3 14.♕xc3 ♔f8?! [after this game it became clear that the right move is 14...f6] **15.♗f4 c6 16.♖xe7!! ♔xe7 17.♕b4+ ♔d8?!** [17...c5 18.dxc5 ♔d8 (18...♕xf3 19.c6+ ♔d8 20.♕d4+ ♔e8 21.♖e1+ ♔f8 22.♗b8!!+–) 19.c6! with a winning attack] **18.♕xb7 ♖c8 19.♗g5+ f6 20.♕xg7+– fxg5 21.♕xh8+ ♔c7 22.♕e5+ ♕xe5 23.dxe5 h6 24.♖e1 ♖e8 25.h4 gxh4 26.♘xh4 ♗f7 27.♘f5** **1-0**

Leko,Peter
Kramnik,Vladimir

Brissago Wch m 2004 (1)

1.e4 e5 2.♘f3 ♘f6 3.♘xe5 d6 4.♘f3 ♘xe4 5.d4 d5 6.♗d3 ♘c6 7.0-0 ♗e7 8.c4 ♘b4 9.♗e2 0-0 10.♘c3 ♗f5 11.a3 ♘xc3 12.bxc3 ♘c6 13.♖e1 ♖e8 14.cxd5 ♕xd5 15.♗f4 ♖ac8 16.h3 ♗e4 17.♗e3 ♘a5 18.c4?! ♘xc4 19.♗xc4 ♕xc4 20.♘d2 ♕d5 21.♘xe4 ♕xe4 22.♗g5 ♕xe1+ 23.♕xe1 ♗xg5 24.♕a5 ♗f6 25.♕xa7 c5 26.♕xb7 ♗xd4 27.♖a2 c4 28.♖e2 ♖ed8 29.a4?! c3 30.♕e4 ♗b6! 31.♕c2 g6 32.♕b3 ♖d6! 33.♖c2 ♗a5 34.g4 ♖d2 35.♔g2 ♖cd8 36.♖xc3 ♗xc3 37.♕xc3 ♖2d5 38.♕c6 ♖a5 39.♔g3 ♖da8 40.h4 ♖5a6 41.♕c1 ♖a5 42.♕h6 ♖xa4 43.h5 ♖4a5 44.♕f4?? g5! 45.♕f6 h6!–+ 46.f3 ♖5a6 47.♕c3 ♖a4 48.♕c6 ♖8a6 49.♕e8+ ♔g7 50.♕b5 ♖4a5 51.♕b4 ♖d5 52.♕b3 ♖ad6 53.♕c4 ♖d3 54.♔f2 ♖a3 55.♕c5 ♖a2+ 56.♔g3 ♖f6 57.♕b4 ♖aa6 58.♔g2 ♖f4 59.♕b2+ ♖af6 60.♕e5 ♖xf3 61.♕a1 ♖f1 62.♕c3 ♖f2+ 63.♔g3? ♖f3+ 64.♕xf3 ♖xf3+ 65.♔xf3 ♔f6 **0-1**

Fischer,Robert
German,Eugenio

Stockholm izt 1962 (13)

1.e4 e5 2.♘f3 ♘f6 3.d4 exd4 4.e5 ♘e4 5.♕e2 ♘c5 6.♘xd4 ♘c6 7.♘xc6 bxc6 8.♘c3 ♖b8 9.f4 ♗e7 10.♕f2 d5 11.♗e3 ♘d7 12.0-0-0 0-0 13.g4 ♗b4 14.♗e2 ♘b6 15.♘d4 ♕e8 16.c3 ♗e7 17.f5 c5 18.♘b5 d4 19.♗f4 dxc3 20.♘xc3 ♘a4 21.♗b5 ♖xb5 22.♘xa4 ♖b4 23.♘c3 ♗b7

24.♖he1 ♔h8 25.f6 ♗d8 26.♗g5
♖d4 27.fxg7+ ♔xg7 28.♗f6+ ♔g8
29.♕h4 ♖xd1+ 30.♘xd1   1-0

Smyslov, Vasily
Lilienthal, Andor

Leningrad/Moscow ch-URS 1941 (2)

1.e4 e5 2.♘f3 ♘f6 3.d4 ♘xe4 4.♗d3
d5 5.♘xe5 ♗d6 6.♘c3 ♘xc3 7.bxc3
♕h4 8.0-0 0-0 9.♖e1 ♘d7 10.g3
♕h3 11.♗f1 ♕f5 12.♗d3 ♕h3
13.♗f1 ♕f5 14.♘g4 ♘b6 15.♘e3
♕f6 16.♗d3 ♗e6 17.♘g4 ♕d8
18.♘e5 c5 19.♕h5 f5 20.♘f3 ♕e8
21.♕h4 ♕g6 22.dxc5 ♗xc5 23.♗e3
♗xe3 24.♖xe3 ♘c4 25.♖e2 ♘d6
26.♕b4 ♘e4 27.♘d4 ♗d7 28.f3
♘d6 29.♕c5 ♔h8 30.♕xd5 ♖ad8
31.♘e6 ♗xe6 32.♖xe6 ♕f7 33.♕e5
♖fe8 34.♖xe8+ ♕xe8 35.♖e1 ♕c6
36.♔g2 ♖e8 37.♕xd6   1-0

Kasparov, Garry
Anand, Viswanathan

Linares 1991 (11)

1.e4 e5 2.♘f3 ♘f6 3.d4 ♘xe4 4.♗d3
d5 5.♘xe5 ♗d6 6.0-0 0-0 7.c4 ♗xe5
8.dxe5 ♘c6 9.cxd5 ♕xd5 10.♕c2
♘b4 11.♗xe4 ♘xc2 12.♗xd5 ♗f5
13.g4 ♗xg4 14.♗e4 ♘xa1 15.♗f4 f5
16.♗d5+ [16.♗xb7 ♘c2 17.f3 ♗h5
18.♗d5+ ♔h8 19.♗xa8 ♖xa8 20.♖d1
c5!∞] 16...♔h8 17.♖c1 c6 18.♗g2
♖fd8 19.♘d2 [19.f3 ♗h5 20.♘a3 ♖d4
21.♗e3 ♖b4 22.♘c4 ♖a4 23.♘a3 ½-½
Sax-Yusupov, Thessaloniki ol 1988]
19...♖xd2 20.♗xd2 ♖d8 21.♗c3
♖d1+ 22.♖xd1 ♗xd1 23.f4?
[23.♗f1! gives White a clear advantage
according to Rozentalis] 23...♘c2
24.♔f2 ♔g8 25.a4 a5!= 26.♗xa5
♘d4 27.♗f1 ♗b3 [draw in prevision of
28.♔e3 ♘e6 29.♗b6 ♗xa4 30.♗c4
♔f7 31.♗xe6+ ♔xe6 32.♔d4=] ½-½

Ponziani Opening
1.e2-e4 e7-e5 2.♘g1-f3
♘b8-c6 3.c2-c3

Domenico Lorenzo Ponziani, from the Italian town of Modena, analysed various important lines in the 18th century. He was also a member of the Pope's inner circle. The c2-c3 push is logical in that it supports d2-d4. But it has two drawbacks: it leaves the e4-pawn undefended and it prevents the development of the queen's knight to c3. Black's two best responses are 3...♘f6 and 3...d5, both of which highlight these drawbacks.

A)

3.	...	♘g8-f6
4.	d2-d4	♘f6xe4!

5. d4-d5   ♘c6-e7

42

5...♘b8 is also playable.

6. ♘f3xe5   ♘e7-g6

with equality.

B)   3. ...   d7-d5

The most active, and best if Black wants to win. However, Black will usually know relatively little about the theory of such a rare opening.

4. ♗f1-b5

4.♕a4 is also playable. *With the pawn on c3, opening the d-file with 4.exd5 does not make much sense because of the weaknesses that result on this file.*

4. ...   d5xe4

5. ♘f3xe5

Either 5...♕d5 or 5...♕g5 appears to give Black positions that are rich in potential. It will certainly not be to the taste of every player to deal with the position that arises after

5.	...	♕d8-g5
6.	♕d1-a4	♕g5xg2
7.	♖h1-f1	♗c8-h3
8.	♗b5xc6+	b7xc6
9.	♕a4xc6+	♔e8-d8!
10.	♕c6xa8+	♔d8-e7
11.	♔e1-d1	♕g2xf1+
12.	♔d1-c2	

Now we have a chaotic situation, but Black probably has a satisfactory position and he may even have the upper hand.

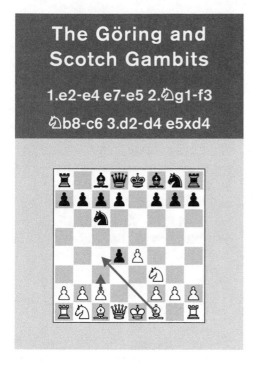

Black can prevent his adversary from castling with

8.	...	&g4xf3!
9.	&e2xf3	♛d5-c4

with a balanced game. World Champion José Raul Capablanca was the first to play this way with Black.

Alternatively, Black can be more ambitious and accept the sacrifice.

After 4...dxc3, White can continue with 5.&c4 along the lines of the **Danish Gambit** with the advantage that Black no longer has the simplifying ...d5. Black's best option is 5...d6 6.&xc3 &f6 7.♛b3 ♛d7 8.&g5 &e5 9.&b5 c6 10.f4

with a promising position after either 10...cxb5 or 10...&eg4.

If on the fifth move White plays 5.&xc3, Black can re-enter the variation we have just looked at by playing 5...d6, or he could try the more interesting 5...&b4!?.

In the standard **Scotch Game,** White takes on d4 with the f3-knight. If you wish to be more aggressive, you can sacrifice a pawn for quick development by playing 4.c3, or play another sacrifice option by developing the bishop with 4.&c4.

Göring Gambit

4. c3

With the c3-square unavailable for the queen's knight, it is logical for Black to reply with the thematic advance

4. ... d7-d5

declining the pawn on offer.
After

5.	e4xd5	♛d8xd5
6.	c3xd4	&c8-g4
7.	&f1-e2	&f8-b4+
8.	&b1-c3	

Scotch Gambit

4. ♗f1-c4

Black's safest option is probably to enter into a favourable variation of the **Two Knights Defence** with 4...♘f6.

4. ... ♗f8-c5

is playable, but riskier. It can be met by

5. c2-c3!? d4xc3

For 5...♘f6!, see the **Italian Game**.

6.	♗c4xf7+	♔e8xf7
7.	♕d1-d5+	♔f7-f8
8.	♕d5xc5+	♕d8-e7
9.	♕c5xc3!	♕e7xe4+
10.	♗c1-e3	

In this line, most players would prefer to be White.

In conclusion, these gambits are dangerous against an unprepared opponent. However, against correct play, not only does White not gain anything, he often has difficulty even to maintain equality.

Miles,Anthony
Nunn,John
Islington jr 1970 (5)

1.e4 e5 2.d4 exd4 3.c3 d5 4.exd5 ♕xd5 5.cxd4 ♘c6 6.♘f3 ♗g4 7.♗e2 ♗b4+ 8.♘c3 ♗xf3 9.♗xf3 ♕c4 10.♗xc6+ bxc6 11.♕e2+ ♕xe2+ 12.♔xe2 0-0-0 13.♗e3 ♘e7 14.♖hd1

♖he8 15.a3 ♗a5 16.♔f3 ♗b6 17.♘a4 ♘f5 18.♘c5 ♖d5 19.♖ac1 ♖ed8 20.b4 ♘xd4+ 21.♗xd4 ♖xd4 22.♖xd4 ♖xd4 23.♖c3 ♗xc5 24.bxc5 ♔d7 25.♔e3 ♖a4 26.♔d3 ♔e6 27.♔c2 ♔d5 28.♔b3 ♖d4 29.♖h3 ♖g4 30.♖h5+ ♔d4 31.g3 h6 32.♖f5 f6 33.♖f3 ♖e4 34.♖c3 ♖e2 35.♖c4+ ♔d5 36.♖f4 ♔xc5 37.h4 ♔d5 38.♔c3 c5 39.♖f3 a6 40.♖f5+ ♖e5 41.♖f4 ♖e4 42.♖f5+ ♔c6 43.♔b3 ♔b5 44.♖d5 ♖d4 45.♖f5 ♖d3+ 46.♔b2 ♔c4 47.♖f4+ ♖d4 48.♖f3 ♖d2+ 49.♔c1 ♖d3 **0-1**

Alekhine,Alexander
Verlinsky,Boris
Odessa m 1918

1.e4 e5 2.d4 exd4 3.c3 dxc3 4.♘xc3 ♘c6 [4...♗b4 5.♗c4 (5.♘f3 ♘c6) 5...d6? (5...♗xc3+ 6.bxc3 d6 7.♕b3 ♕e7 8.♘e2 ♘c6 9.0-0 ♘f6 10.♘d4 ♘xd4 11.cxd4 0-0 12.♖e1 h6 13.♗a3± Alekhine-Pomar Salamanca, Madrid 1943) 6.♗xf7+! ♔xf7 7.♕b3+ ♗e6 8.♕xb4 ♘c6 9.♕a4 ♘f6 10.♘f3 h6 11.0-0 ♖e8 12.♖d1 Alekhine-Stegerhoek, Malang simul 1933 1-0 (36)] **5.♗c4 d6** [5...♗b4!? 6.♘f3 d6 7.♕b3 ♗xc3+ 8.bxc3 ♕d7 9.♕c2 ♘f6 10.0-0 0-0 11.h3 ♖e8 12.♗d3 h6 13.♖b1 a6 14.♖e1 ♘e5 15.♘xe5 dxe5 16.f4 ♕d6 17.f5 White does not have enough compensation for the pawn, Ciocaltea-L.Kovacs, Baja 1971] **6.♘f3 ♘f6 7.♕b3 ♕d7 8.♘g5 ♘e5 9.♗b5 c6 10.f4 cxb5 11.fxe5 dxe5 12.♗e3 ♗d6 13.♘xb5 0-0 14.♖d1 ♘e8 15.0-0 ♕e7 16.♘xd6 ♘xd6 17.♕a3 ♖d8 18.♘xf7 ♗g4 19.♖xd6 ♖e8 20.♗g5 ♕c7 21.♕b3 ♗e2 22.♘xe5+ ♔h8 23.♖c1 ♖f8 24.♕d1 ♕a5 25.♕xe2 ♕xe5 26.♖d5** **1-0**

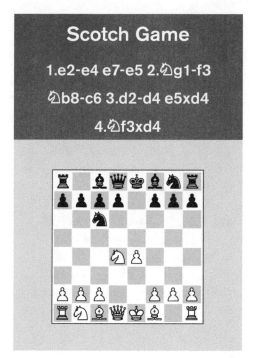

Scotch Game

1.e2-e4 e7-e5 2.♘g1-f3
♘b8-c6 3.d2-d4 e5xd4
4.♘f3xd4

The **Scotch Game** picked up its name after its use in a match between the Edinburgh and London Chess Clubs in 1824. This opening has had many highs and lows over the years. After its employment by Jacques Mieses and Savielly Tartakower at the beginning of the 20th century, the Scotch Game was a rarity until its successful adoption by Garry Kasparov from 1990 on. Another extraordinary example of a completely reassessed opening. Today the Scotch Game, along with the Ruy Lopez, is considered to be the only serious attempt for White to gain an advantage after 1.e4 e5.

In a certain sense 3.d4 is the most logical move: as in the **Open Sicilian** (i.e. the variations with 3.d4), White obtains the classic space advantage (4 ranks versus 3) and does not have to worry about an enemy central pawn majority such as is typical of the Sicilian Defence. However,

there is a drawback: with the pawn on c7 instead of on e7 the f8-bishop is ready to enter the fray on c5 or on b4, exerting a pressure on White's centre that is rare in the Sicilian. This is the reason why Scotch lines often have great positional tension: if White succeeds in neutralizing Black's active piece play, he can begin to exploit his space advantage and possession of the centre.

After 4.♘xd4, Black can choose from two main lines and three minor ones. We will begin with the three minor variations:

A)   4. ...   ♛d8-h4

Steinitz's move seeks to profit from the absence of the knight on f3 to attack the e4-pawn, which Black usually wins! Therefore, in a certain sense the Scotch Game is a gambit! However, the pawn comes at too high a price, and this variation remains a rarity. The best line for White is probably

5.	♘b1-c3	♝f8-b4
6.	♝f1-e2!	♛h4xe4
7.	♘d4-b5	♝b4xc3+
8.	b2xc3	♚e8-d8
9.	0-0	

and the lead in development, the bishop pair and the black king on d8 are more than enough compensation for the pawn.

B)   **4. ...**   ♗**f8-b4+**

A paradoxical move that is becoming increasingly popular. After 5.♘c3, 5...♘f6 transposes to the 4...♘f6 variation, reducing White's options. After 5.c3, Black's bishop retreats to e7 or to c5 hoping that the move c3, which prevents ♘c3, will prove to be to Black's advantage. It is not clear if this is the case, but at least in this way Black succeeds in avoiding many highly theoretical lines.

C)   **4. ...**   ♛**d8-f6**

This usually transposes to Variation D3 after 5.♘xc6 ♗c5.

D)   **4. ...**   ♗**f8-c5**

If we exclude the dubious 5.♘f5, White can now continue with:

D1)   **5. ♗c1-e3**   ♛**d8-f6!**

The pressure on d4 forces White to make the disagreeable move

       6. c3

and after 6...♘ge7 or 6...♛g6, Black has good piece play with equal possibilities for both sides.

D2)   **5. ♘d4-b3**   ♗**c5-b6**
       6. a2-a4   **a7-a6**
       7. ♘b1-c3   **d7-d6**
       8. ♘c3-d5   ♗**b6-a7**

White has a space advantage, but Black has no weaknesses and he can develop his forces smoothly.

D3)   **5. ♘d4xc6**

Another move that has been completely reassessed: the old line of thinking was that after

       5. ...   ♛**d8-f6!**

threatening mate on f2, Black had a good game. Then the move

       6. ♛d1-d2

was discovered. Ugly, as it blocks the bishop's view from c1, but quite effective.

       6. ...   **d7xc6**
       7. ♘b1-c3

There is a lot of play for both sides: Black has easy development, but the doubled pawn on the c-file will give White a favourable endgame. This is a recurrent theme in Open Games. Practice seems to slightly favour White.

E)   4.   ...   ♘g8-f6

This is the most ambitious move. Black encourages White to push the pawn to e5, hoping to then undermine the centre. If White decides not to rise to the bait, he can continue with 5.♘c3, or otherwise he can exchange on c6 to facilitate the pawn advance to e5:

E1)   5.   ♘b1-c3   ♗c5-b4
**   6.   ♘d4xc6**

In order to play ♗d3.

	6.	...	b7xc6
	7.	♗f1-d3	d7-d5
	8.	e4xd5	c6xd5
	9.	0-0	0-0
	10.	♗c1-g5	c7-c6

Black does not have any serious problems, but White has play against the weakened queenside with ♘a4 and c4.

E2)   5.   ♘d4xc6   b7xc6
**   6.   e4-e5**

The Mieses Variation. Black now plays

	6.	...	♕d8-e7

even if it locks in his own f8-bishop. However, White must imprison his own bishop, too.

**   7.   ♕d1-e2   ♘f6-d5**
**   8.   c2-c4**

and at this point Black can immediately retreat his knight with 8...♘b6, or he can pin the c4-pawn with 8...♗a6. In both cases there is complex play with chances for both sides. This becomes clear when you consider that both White and Black can castle either short or long, and that the pawns on e5 and c4 are weak but they also have the potential to suffocate the opponent, who is somewhat lacking for space. In short, a typical position where the stronger player should win. This also holds true because opening theory has not explored all the available possibilities yet and therefore there is still room for creative play.

Ponomariov,Ruslan
Godena,Michele
Plovdiv Ech-tt 2003 (4)
1.e4 e5 2.♘f3 ♘c6 3.d4 exd4 4.♘xd4 ♗c5 5.♗e3 ♕f6 6.♘b5 ♗xe3 7.fxe3 ♕h4+ 8.g3 ♕d8 9.♕g4 g5! [aesthetically ugly, but actually an important novelty] 10.♘1c3 d6 11.♕e2 a6 12.♘d4 ♘e5 13.♕g2 ♗e6 14.0-0-0 ♕d7 15.h4 gxh4

16.gxh4 ♗g4 17.♗e2 ♘e7 18.♗xg4
♕xg4 19.♕f2 0-0-0 20.♕f6 ♕d7
21.h5 ♖hg8 22.♖hg1 ♕h3 23.♖ge1
♖de8 24.♕h6 ♖g2 25.♖h1 ♕g3
26.♕xh7 ♕xe3+ 27.♔b1 ♖eg8
28.♘f5 ♖xf5 29.♕xf5+ ♔b8 30.h6
♖2g6 31.♘d5 ♕g5 32.♖df1 ♖h8
33.h7 c6 34.♘f6 ♕xf5 35.♖xf5 ♔c7
36.b3 ♔d8 37.♘g8 ♖g7 38.♖d1
♖gxh7 39.♖xd6+ ♔c7 40.♖d2 ♖xg8
41.♖xe5 f6 42.♖f5 ♖e8 43.♖f4 ♖he7
44.♖d4 ♖d7 45.c3 ♖e5 46.♔c2 c5
47.♖xd7+ ♔xd7 48.♔d3 ♖e6
49.♔e3 ♖d6 50.♖f5 b6 51.♖d5 ♔e6
52.c4 ♖d7 53.♔f4 ♖h7 54.♖d8
♖h4+ 55.♔f3 ♖h3+ 56.♔g4 ♖h2
57.♖e8+ ♔d6 58.♔f5 ♖f2+ 59.♔g6
♖xa2 60.♔f7 b5 61.♖e6+ ♔d7
62.♔xf6 ♖f2+ 63.♔e5 ♖b2
64.♖d6+ ♔c7 65.♖d3 ♔c6 66.♔e6
bxc4 67.bxc4 ♖c2 68.♖d6+ ♔c7
69.♖xa6 ♖xc4 70.e5 ♖h4 71.♔d5
♖d4+ 72.♔xc5 ♖d1 73.♖d6 ♖xd6
74.exd6+ ♔d7 75.♔d5 ♔d8 76.♔e6
♔e8 77.d7+ ♔d8 78.♔d6 [stalemate]

½-½

Ponomariov,Ruslan
Grischuk,Alexander

Lausanne 2000 (3)

1.e4 e5 2.♘f3 ♘c6 3.d4 exd4 4.♘xd4
♗c5 5.♗e3 ♕f6 6.c3 ♘ge7 7.♗c4 b6
8.0-0 ♗b7 9.♘b3 ♘e5 10.♘xc5 bxc5
11.♗e2 ♗xe4 12.f3 ♗b7 13.♗xc5 0-0
14.♘d2 d6 15.♗d4 ♘d5 16.g3 ♕g6
17.♔h1 ♘g4 18.♘c4 ♕h6 19.♗g1
♖ae8 20.♕c2 f5 21.♗d3 f4 22.♕d2
♘de3 23.gxf4 ♘xf1 24.♖xf1 ♖xf4
25.♕g2 ♖e1 26.♘d2 ♖xf1 27.♗xf1
♖f8 28.♕e2 ♘e5 29.♗g2 a6 30.♗d4
♕f4 31.♗xe5 ♕xe5 32.♕xe5 dxe5
33.♔g1 ♖d8 34.♘c4 ♖d1+ 35.♗f1

♗xf3 36.♔f2 ♗b7 37.a4 ♔f8 38.h4
♔e7 39.♗e2 ♖h1 40.h5 ♔f6 41.b4
♖c1 42.♘e3 ♖xc3 43.♗xa6 ♖xe3
44.♗xb7 ♖b3 45.a5 ♖xb4 46.a6 ♖a4

0-1

Zukertort,Johannes Hermann
Schallopp,Emil

Leipzig 1877 (10)

1.e4 e5 2.♘f3 ♘c6 3.d4 exd4
4.♘xd4 ♗c5 5.♘b3 ♗b6 6.♘c3
♘ge7 7.♗g5 f6 8.♗f4 ♘g6 9.♗g3 d6
10.f4 f5 11.♗c4 h5 12.♕d5 ♕f6
13.0-0-0 h4 14.e5 dxe5 15.fxe5
♕g5+ 16.♔b1 ♖f8 17.♗b5 ♘e7
18.♕d8+ ♔f7 19.♗c4+ ♗e6
20.♗xe6+ ♔xe6 21.♕d7+ ♔f7
22.e6+ ♔g6 23.♗xc7 ♖ad8
24.♗xd8 ♖xd8 25.♕xb7 ♕xg2
26.♖xd8 ♕xh1+ 27.♖d1 ♕xh2
28.♕d7 ♕b8 29.♘d5 ♘xd5
30.♖xd5 ♘e5 31.♕b5 a6 32.♕e2
♘g4 33.e7 ♘f6 34.♕e6

1-0

Monticelli,Mario
Vidmar,Milan Sr

San Remo 1930 (13)

1.e4 e5 2.♘f3 ♘c6 3.♘c3 ♘f6 4.d4
exd4 5.♘xd4 ♗b4 6.♘xc6 bxc6
7.♗d3 d5 8.exd5 ♕e7+ 9.♕e2
♕xe2+ 10.♗xe2 cxd5 11.♗d2 0-0
12.0-0-0 c6 13.f3 ♗e6 14.a3 ♗d6
15.♗a6 ♗c8 16.♗xc8 ♖fxc8
17.♖de1 ♘d7 18.♘e2 ♘b6 19.♘f4
♘c4 20.♘d3 ♖ab8 21.♗c3 c5
22.♘e5 ♗xe5 23.♗xe5 ♖b7 24.b3
♘xa3 25.♗b2 ♘b5 26.♖e5 d4
27.♖he1 f6 28.♖e8+ ♖xe8
29.♖xe8+ ♔f7 30.♖c8 ♖c7 31.♖b8
♘d6 32.b4 cxb4 33.♗xd4 a5
34.♗b6 ♖b7 35.♖xb7+ ♘xb7
36.♔b2 a4 37.c3 ♘d6

0-1

Four Knights Opening

1.e2-e4 e7-e5 2.♘g1-f3 ♘b8-c6 3.♘b1-c3 ♘g8-f6

The **Four Knights Opening** is one of White's most solid set-ups against 1...e5, and it was very widely played at the beginning of the 20th century. Then it all but disappeared until the 1980s and '90s, when it made a hesitant comeback, its chief use being to avoid highly theoretical lines. Black has few problems achieving equality if White plays 4.♗b5 (sometimes called the **Spanish Four Knights Game**) or 4.d4, which is in the spirit of the **Scotch Game**.

The fact that Black has few problems is not surprising, as practice has taught us that if White wishes to gain a significant advantage in the Open Games he must usually occupy the centre with pawns. However, this is rarely possible without the support of the c3-pawn: in this context the move ♘c3, made purely as a developing move, is too mechanical to offer concrete prospects.

If White decides on 4.d4, then after 4...exd4 you transpose to an innocuous variation of the **Scotch Game** that we have discussed in the previous chapter. If Black is not pleased by the prospect of playing the somewhat sterile positions that ensue, he can try 4...♗b4, but after 5.♘xe5, the resulting complications seem to favour White.

It is worth mentioning the minor variation 4.g3. However, by far the most frequent continuation is:

4. ♗f1-b5

Now, unlike in the **Ruy Lopez**, the e4-pawn is defended, and therefore the threat 5.♗xc6 and 6.♘xe5 is real. Black can respond in two completely different ways.

A) 4. ... ♗f8-b4
is a solid continuation that indirectly defends e5 by attacking e4.

5. 0-0 0-0
5...d6? allows 6.♘d5!.
6. d2-d3 d7-d6
7. ♗c1-g5
Now threatening ♘d5, and Black cannot go on copying White's moves. Therefore:

7. ... ♗b4xc3!
8. b2xc3 ♕d8-e7!

with the idea of ...♞d8-e6 to lift the pin by the g5-bishop.

9. ♖f1-e1   ♞c6-d8
10. d3-d4   ♞d8-e6
11. ♗g5-c1

With the possibility of repositioning the bishop on a3. Now we reach a strategically complex position in which White has good control of the centre and the bishop pair, while Black has a solid position with good endgame prospects.

B)   4. ...   ♞c6-d4

Rubinstein's move (who was usually a very solid player!) is appropriate if Black wants to unbalance the position.
It would appear that this move contravenes the general principles of opening theory, which always advise against moving the same piece twice in the

opening. However, in this case the attack is specifically aimed at b5 and, above all, the presence of the knight on c3 renders a capture on d4 unwise. Moreover, it prevents the pawn push c2-c3. This gives Black resources that are not present, for example, in the **Bird Defence of the Ruy Lopez** (3...♞d4), a borderline variation in terms of playability.

5. ♗b5-a4

Probably best. It maintains the pin on the d7-pawn and reduces the impact of Black's counterplay with ...c6 and ...d5. Now Black usually makes a positional sacrifice of a pawn in one of two ways:

B1)   5. ...   c7-c6

Enabling ...d6.

6. ♞f3xe5   d7-d6
7. ♞e5-f3   ♗c8-g4

with compensation, or, more violently:

B2)   5. ...   ♗f8-c5
6. ♞f3xe5   0-0
7. ♞e5-d3

Here one of the disadvantages of ...♗c5 is revealed; White now gains a tempo with this move.

7. ...   ♗c5-b6

At the moment Black threatens 8...d5.

8. e4-e5   ♞f6-e8

White's kingside is a little exposed and White now plans to protect it with

9. ♘c3-d5!

and then ♘e3, keeping the extra pawn.

9. ... d7-d6!

Opening the game and putting his trust in his superior development, his control of the e-file and White's weakly-defended king. The position after 10.♘e3 is difficult to evaluate, even if the results are slightly in White's favour.

As a testimony to the vitality of the game of chess, it is worth mentioning Black's final alternative. A move which began to become popular, even at higher levels, at the beginning of the new millennium: the 'beginner's move' 4...♗d6!?.

Dogmatism is truly a thing of the past! From the time of our first chess lessons, we have had it drummed into our heads that we mustn't place our bishop in front of a centre pawn, as only the advance of these pawns allows us to develop freely. We are not suggesting for a moment that such general strategic guidelines are no longer valid. It is just that they should never again be viewed as the Word of God.

Rublevsky,Sergey
Mamedyarov,Shakhriyar
Foros 2006 (1)

1.e4 e5 2.♘f3 ♘c6 3.♘c3 ♘f6 4.♗b5 ♘d4 5.♗a4 c6 6.♘xe5 d5 7.d3 ♗d6 8.f4 ♗c5 9.exd5 0-0 10.♘e4 ♘xe4 11.dxe4 ♕h4+ 12.g3 ♕h3 13.♗e3 ♕g2 14.♖g1 ♕xe4 15.♔f2 ♖e8 16.♕d3 ♖xe5 17.fxe5 ♕f3+ 18.♔e1 ♗f5 19.♖f1 ♗b4+ 20.c3 ♗xd3 21.♖xf3 ♘xf3+ 22.♔f2 ♘xh2 23.cxb4 ♘g4+ 24.♔f3 ♘xe5+ 25.♔f4 ♘g6+ 26.♔f3 cxd5 27.♖c1 ♘e5+ 28.♔f4 ♘g6+ 29.♔f3 b5 30.♗b3 ♗c4 31.♗c2 ♘e5+ 32.♔f4 f6 33.♖d1 ♗xa2 34.b3 ♖c8 35.♗c5 a5 36.♗f5 ♗xb3 37.♖b1 ♗c2 38.♗e6+ ♔h8 39.♖a1 ♖e8 40.bxa5 ♘d3+ 41.♔f3 ♘xc5 42.♗xd5 b4 43.a6 ♘xa6 **0-1**

Hungarian Defence

1.e2-e4 e7-e5 2.♘g1-f3 ♘b8-c6 3.♗f1-c4 ♗f8-e7

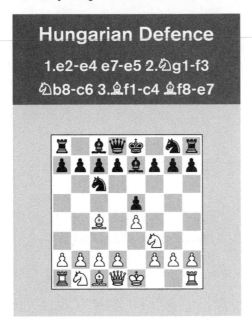

The move 3...♗e7 has never been popular since it first appeared in the middle of the 19th century in a postal game between the cities of Paris and Pest. It usually leads to strategic plans typically associated with the **Philidor Defence** or the **Steinitz Variation of the Ruy Lopez**: Black has a solid position but without any real prospects. After the natural

4.	d2-d4	d7-d6
5.	h2-h3!	

No pin!

5.	...	♘g8-f6
6.	♘b1-c3	0-0
7.	0-0	

White has a little more room to breathe, even if the solidity of Black's position must not be underestimated.

It is worth remembering that 3...d6 is playable on the 3rd move, with a likely return to the **Hungarian Defence** after 4.d4 ♗e7, given that 4...♗g4 is dubious because of 5.h3.

Let's go back a little, so as to explain the idea behind the Hungarian Defence. The development of the c4-bishop on the 3rd move, even if slightly inconsistent with the previous move, was one of the primary moves in the early development of opening theory. The vulnerability of the f7-square and related tactics have attracted and delighted players and chess scholars for centuries. Such is the brilliant quality of the playing style so closely associated with the Romantic era. But the advent of the Positional School and the realization that Black has nothing to fear from the most violent lines, directed White's attention towards the **Ruy Lopez** and also towards the **Scotch**; openings that are configured with a more correct strategic concern in mind: the control of the centre.

However, 3.♗c4 has not disappeared from practical play and it still has a charm, perhaps because of its associations with a golden past, even though by playing 3...♘f6 (**Two Knights**) or 3...♗c5, Black obtains completely playable positions with good prospects of equality.

OK then. Why play the Hungarian? The answer is simple: the variations to remember if you play 3...♘f6 or 3...♗c5 are so numerous, that there are many who prefer a quiet position which is slightly inferior to the risks associated with the more violent alternatives.

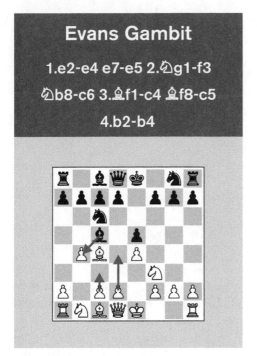

Evans Gambit

1.e2-e4 e7-e5 2.♘g1-f3
♘b8-c6 3.♗f1-c4 ♗f8-c5
4.b2-b4

Invented at the beginning of the 19th century, the **Evans Gambit** became so immensely popular that it threatened the supremacy of the **King's Gambit**. It was repeatedly played, even in World Championship matches, by players of the calibre of McDonnell, De la Bourdonnais, Morphy, Anderssen, Zukertort and Chigorin. However, with the development of more sophisticated defensive techniques at the beginning of the 20th century its popularity waned rapidly. To understand why, just look at the impact made by the **Lasker Defence**, where Black returns the pawn in exchange for a promising endgame. As a result of this defence many a white player has lost his taste for this romantic style of play.

Even if later on a method was devised to avoid the Lasker Defence, the Evans Gambit remains chiefly the property of correspondence players and is rarely seen in grandmaster tournament games. An exception was the Italian Sergio Mariotti's victory against the strong grandmaster Svetozar Gligoric (Venice 1971).

Later, in the 1990s, Kasparov, the great scholar of opening theory, won a couple of brilliant victories employing the Evans. This led to a partial rebound in the popularity of the Evans Gambit.

4. ...   ♗c5xb4

Black can also decline with 4...♗b6 and reach an acceptable position.

5. c2-c3

To occupy the centre with d2-d4. Now the idea behind the gambit becomes clear; White wants to play an Italian Game with an extra tempo. Avoiding 5...♗c5, which makes d2-d4 easier, the most solid retreat was always considered to be 5...♗e7, returning the pawn after 6.d4 ♘a5 7.♘xe5 ♘xc4 8.♘xc4 d5, with equality. However, Kasparov's introduction of **7.♗e2!? exd4 8.♕xd4!** has added new spice to this line.

The ugly 5...♗d6 also seems playable. But Black's principal alternative remains

5. ...   ♗b4-a5

which maintains the pin on the c3-pawn. White's best continuation is to immediately push the pawn to d4, given that 6.0-0 leads to the famous **Lasker Defence 6...d6 7.d4 ♗b6!**,

which is characterized by the return of the pawn with 8.dxe5 dxe5 9.♕xd8+ ♘xd8 10.♘xe5 ♗e6. In so doing, Black is left with a superior pawn structure.

6. d2-d4!

Now the main line is

6. ...	**d7-d6**
7. ♕d1-b3!	**♕d8-d7!**
8. d4xe5	**♗a5-b6!**

With the idea of ...♘a5.

9. ♘b1-d2!

In order to recapture with the knight.

9. ...	**♘c6-a5**
10. ♕b3-c2	**♘a5xc4**
11. ♘d2xc4	**d6-d5!**

Before this novelty, the perfectly reasonable 11...♗c5 was played.

12. e4xd5	**♕d7xd5**
13. ♕c2-a4+	**♗c8-d7**
14. ♘c4xb6!	**c7xb6**

A necessary evil: both pawn structures look ugly, but the opposite-coloured bishops give both players chances.

The following line has recently become popular:

6. ...	**e5xd4**
7. 0-0	**♘g8-e7**
8. c3xd4	**d7-d5**
9. e4xd5	**♘f6xd5**
10. ♕d1-b3	**♗c8-e6**

with a complex game.

Kasparov, Garry
Piket, Jeroen
Amsterdam Euwe mem 1995 (2)

1.e4 e5 2.♘f3 ♘c6 3.♗c4 ♗c5 4.b4 ♗b6 5.a4 a5 6.b5 ♘d4 7.♘xd4 ♗xd4 8.c3 ♗b6 9.d4 exd4?! [9...♕e7! 10.0-0 (10.♕g4 ♘f6 11.♕xg7 ♖g8 12.♕h6 ♖g6∞) 10...d6 (10...♘f6!? 11.♖e1 (11.♗a3 d6 12.♖e1 0-0 13.♕d3 ♖e8 14.♘d2) 11...d6 12.♘a3 0-0 13.♗b3 ♗g4 14.♕d3 ♗e6 15.♗xe6 fxe6 16.♘c4± Grosar-Barle, Geneva 1996) 11.♕d3! (11.f4 ♗e6!? (11...♘f6?! 12.fxe5 dxe5 13.♗a3±; 13.♗g5!?; 11...exd4 12.cxd4 ♘f6 (12...♗g4?! 13.♕d2 (13.♕d3!? ♗e2 14.♕xe2 ♗xd4+ 15.♗e3 ♗xa1 16.♗d5 ♖b8 17.♘d2⊠) 13...♘f6 14.♘c3 0-0 15.♖e1±) 13.♘c3 ♗e6=) 12.♘a3 exd4 13.cxd4 0-0-0 14.♗e2 ♘f6 15.♗f3 d5 16.e5 ♘e4 17.♘c2 h5!= Nunn-Hecht, Buenos Aires ol 1978) 11...♘f6 12.♘d2; 9...d6? 10.dxe5 dxe5 11.♗xf7++−] **10.0-0 ♘e7 11.♗g5!** [11.♗a3 d6, ⬀a3-f8] **11...h6 12.♗xe7** [12.♗h4 0-0 13.cxd4 g5 14.♗g3 d5 15.exd5 ♘xd5 Van der Sterren] **12...♕xe7 13.cxd4 ♕d6?** [13...0-0 14.♘c3; 13...d6 14.♘c3 ♗e6 15.♘d5; 13...♗b4!? 14.♘a3 0-0 15.♕d3 d5! 16.exd5

(16.Bxd5!? Qxd4 17.Qxd4 Bxd4
18.Rad1 Bc5 19.Nc4) 16...Bd7
17.Nc2 Qd6 18.Ne3± Kasparov]
14.Nc3! Bxd4 [14...Qxd4 15.Nd5!
Qe5!? (15...Qxd1 16.Rfxd1±;
15...Qxc4 16.Rc1 Qa2 17.Rxc7! Bxc7
18.Nxc7+ Ke7 (18...Kd8 19.Nxa8±)
19.Nxa8 d6 20.Qc1+− Kasparov)
16.Nxb6 (16.Kh1!? 0-0 17.Qc2 d6
18.f4♔) 16...cxb6 17.Bd5 0-0
18.Rc1±] **15.Nd5! Bxa1 16.Qxa1
0-0** [16...f6 17.b6! cxb6 18.e5
(18.Rb1→) 18...fxe5 19.Re1 Kd8
20.Rxe5±] **17.e5 Qc5 18.Rc1+−** [△
Nc7, Bf7] **18...c6 19.Ba2 Qa3
20.Nb6 d5 21.Nxa8+− Kh8
22.Nb6 Be6 23.h3 Rd8 24.bxc6
bxc6 25.Rc3 Qb4 26.Rxc6 Rb8
27.Nxd5 Qxa4 28.Rc1 Qa3 29.Bc4**
1-0

Chigorin,Mikhail
Lasker,Emanuel
St Petersburg 1895 (1)

**1.e4 e5 2.Nf3 Nc6 3.Bc4 Bc5 4.b4
Bxb4 5.c3 Bc5 6.0-0 d6 7.d4 Bb6
8.a4 Nf6 9.Bb5 a6 10.Bxc6+ bxc6
11.a5 Ba7 12.dxe5 Nxe4 13.Qe2
d5 14.Nd4 Nxc3 15.Nxc3 Bxd4
16.Qd3 c5 17.Qg3 Be6 18.Bg5
Qd7 19.Rac1 f6 20.exf6 gxf6 21.Bf4
Rg8 22.Qf3 0-0-0 23.Rfe1 c4
24.Qe2 Bf5 25.Qa2 Rxg2+ 26.Kh1
Rxf2** 0-1

Chigorin,Mikhail
Pillsbury,Harry Nelson
London 1899 (1)

**1.e4 e5 2.Nf3 Nc6 3.Bc4 Bc5 4.b4
Bxb4 5.c3 Bc5 6.0-0 d6 7.d4 Bb6
8.dxe5 dxe5 9.Qxd8+ Nxd8
10.Nxe5 Be6 11.Nd2 Ne7 12.Ba3**

f6 **13.Nd3 Ng6 14.Rab1 Kf7
15.Bd5 Re8 16.c4 c6 17.Bxe6+
Nxe6 18.Nb3 Rad8 19.Nbc1 Rd7
20.c5 Bc7 21.g3 Be5 22.Nxe5+
Bxe5 23.Nb3 g5 24.Rfd1 Red8
25.Rxd7+ Rxd7 26.h3 Bc7 27.Kf1
b5 28.Bb4 h5 29.Kg2 Rd3 30.Rc1
Nd4 31.Rc3 Rxc3 32.Bxc3 Nxb3
33.axb3 a5 34.Kf3 Be6 35.Ke3 g4
36.hxg4 hxg4 37.Kd3 a4 38.bxa4
bxa4 39.Bb4 Be5 40.Ba3 Ba1
41.Bc1 f5 42.Ba3 Ke5 43.exf5
Kxf5 44.Ke3 Ke5 45.f4+ Kd5
46.f5 Be5 47.Kf2 Ke4** 0-1

Kasparov,Garry
Anand,Viswanathan
Riga Tal mem 1995 (4)

**1.e4 e5 2.Nf3 Nc6 3.Bc4 Bc5 4.b4
Bxb4 5.c3 Be7 6.d4 Na5 7.Be2
exd4 8.Qxd4 Nf6 9.e5 Nc6 10.Qh4
Nd5 11.Qg3 g6 12.0-0 Nb6 13.c4
d6 14.Rd1 Nd7 15.Bh6 Ncxe5
16.Nxe5 Nxe5 17.Nc3 f6 18.c5 Nf7
19.cxd6 cxd6 20.Qe3 Nxh6
21.Qxh6 Bf8 22.Qe3+ Kf7 23.Nd5
Be6 24.Nf4 Qe7 25.Re1** 1-0

Short,Nigel
Gupta,Abhijeet
Mumbai 2006 (5)

**1.e4 e5 2.Nf3 Nc6 3.Bc4 Bc5 4.b4
Bxb4 5.c3 Ba5 6.d4 exd4 7.Qb3
Qf6 8.0-0 b5 9.Bxb5 Nge7 10.Bg5
Qg6 11.Bxe7 Nxe7 12.cxd4 0-0
13.Na3 Rb8 14.Qa4 Bc3 15.Rac1
Bb2 16.Rxc7 Qd6 17.Rxc8 Nxc8
18.Nc4 Qc7 19.Nxb2 Nd6 20.Bxd7
Rxb2 21.Bc6 Rfb8 22.a3 Rb1 23.g3
h6 24.e5 Nf5 25.Be4 Rxf1+
26.Kxf1 Ne7 27.d5 Qc5 28.d6 Nd5
29.Qd4 Qb5+ 30.Kg2 Nb6 31.Ne1**

♕a5 32.♘d3 ♕xa3 33.♘c5 ♖c8 34.d7 ♘xd7 35.♘xd7 ♕c3 36.♕xa7 ♕d2 37.♕b7 ♖d8 38.♗c6 ♕c3 39.h4 h5 40.♗e4 ♕d2 41.♗d5 1-0

Anderssen,Adolf
Dufresne,Jean
Berlin 1852

1.e4 e5 2.♘f3 ♘c6 3.♗c4 ♗c5 4.b4 ♗xb4 5.c3 ♗a5 6.d4 exd4 7.0-0 d3?! [avoids the creation of a central pawn duo on d4 and e4] **8.♕b3! ♕f6 9.e5 ♕g6 10.♖e1 ♘ge7 11.♗a3 b5?! 12.♕xb5 ♖b8 13.♕a4 ♗b6 14.♘bd2 ♗b7 15.♘e4 ♕f5 16.♗xd3 ♕h5 17.♘f6+!?** [17.♘g3! (this would have won more easily, but Anderssen plays in the romantic spirit of the time, and this encounter is rightly remembered as the Evergreen Game) 17...♕h6 18.♗c1+—] **17...gxf6 18.exf6 ♖g8! 19.♖ad1!** [this move is indeed the work of a genius] **19...♕xf3?** [losing: Lasker's 19...♖g4!! was better] **20.♖xe7+! ♘xe7!?** [20...♔d8 21.♖xd7+! ♔c8! (21...♔xd7 22.♗f5+ ♔e8 23.♗d7+ ♔d8 24.♗xc6+) 22.♖d8+! ♔xd8 (22...♘xd8 23.♕d7+!! ♔xd7 24.♗f5+ ♔c6 (24...♔e8 25.♗d7X) 25.♗d7X) 23.♗e2+ ♘d4 24.♗xf3 ♗xf3 25.g3 ♗xd1 26.♕xd1+—] **21.♕xd7+!! ♔xd7 22.♗f5+ ♔e8 23.♗d7+ ♔f8 24.♗xe7X** 1-0

Fischer,Robert
Fine,Reuben
New York 1963

1.e4 e5 2.♘f3 ♘c6 3.♗c4 ♗c5 4.b4 ♗xb4 5.c3 ♗a5 6.d4 exd4 7.0-0 dxc3 8.♕b3 ♕e7 9.♘xc3 ♘f6?

[9...♗xc3 10.♕xc3 f6 (10...♘f6 11.♗a3 d6 12.e5 ♘e4 13.♕b2 ♘xe5 14.♘xe5 ♕xe5 15.♖fe1!+—) 11.♗a3 d6 12.♗d5! ♗d7 13.♖ab1 0-0-0 14.♘d4+—; a little better is this suggestion of Fischer himself: 9...♕b4! 10.♗xf7+ ♔d8 11.♗g5+ (11.♗xg8? ♕xb3!) 11...♘ge7 12.♘d5 ♕xb3 13.axb3 with an attack] **10.♘d5! ♘xd5** [10...♕xe4□ 11.♗g5→ with the initiative] **11.exd5 ♘e5** [11...♘d8 12.♗a3 d6 13.♕b5+!+—] **12.♘xe5 ♕xe5 13.♗b2 ♕g5 14.h4! ♕xh4** [14...♕h6 15.♕a3+— △ 16.♖fe1+; 14...♕g4 15.♖fe1+ ♗xe1 (15...♔d8 16.♕e3 ♗b4 17.♕h6!! gxh6 18.♗f6+ ♗e7 19.♗xe7+ ♔e8 20.♗g5+! ♔f8 21.♗xh6+ ♕g7 22.♖e8+!! ♔xe8 23.♗xg7+—) 16.♖xe1+ ♔d8 17.♕e3 ♕xh4 18.g3!] **15.♗xg7 ♖g8 16.♖fe1+ ♔d8** [16...♗xe1 17.♖xe1+] **17.♕g3!** [17...♕xg3 18.♗f6X] 1-0

Mariotti,Sergio
Gligoric,Svetozar
Venice 1971 (8)

1.e4 e5 2.♘f3 ♘c6 3.♗c4 ♗c5 4.b4 ♗xb4 5.c3 ♗a5 6.d4 exd4 7.0-0 ♗b6 8.cxd4 d6 9.h3 ♘f6 10.♖e1 h6 11.♗a3 0-0 12.♘c3 ♖e8 13.♖c1 ♘h7 14.♖e3 ♘a5 15.♗d3 ♗e6 16.♕e2 ♘f8 17.♘a4 ♘g6 18.♘xb6 axb6 19.d5 ♗d7 20.♗b2 ♘f4 21.♕c2 c6 22.♕c3 f6 23.dxc6 bxc6 24.♗f1 c5 25.♘h4 d5 26.exd5 ♘xd5 27.♖xe8+ ♕xe8 28.♕g3 ♕e4 29.♖d1 ♖e8 30.♗d3 ♕a4 31.♗h7+ ♔xh7 32.♖xd5 ♖e7 33.♗xf6 ♕e4 34.♘g6 ♕xg6 35.♗xe7 ♗e6 36.♖d6 ♕f7 37.♖xb6 ♘c4 38.♖b7 ♗f5 39.♖c7 ♗g6 40.♗xc5 ♕f6 41.♗b4 1-0

Giuoco Piano

1.e2-e4 e7-e5 2.♘g1-f3

♞b8-c6 3.♗f1-c4 ♝f8-c5

4.d2-d3

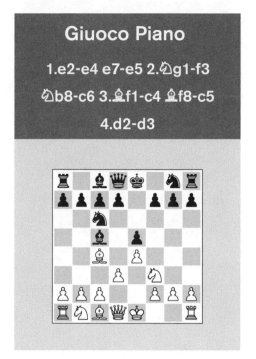

The name **Giuoco Piano** (in Italian: the quiet game) is often wrongly considered synonymous with the Italian Game, but in fact the two openings have game plans with very different strategic characteristics.

The reason why this opening is called the Giuoco Piano is clear: White does not seek to ambitiously conquer the centre with c2-c3 and d2-d4. Instead, he contents himself with slow, natural piece development: ♙d3, ♘c3, 0-0, ♗g5. In some lines White puts off ♘c3, reserving the option of c2-c3 in order to calmly prepare the d2-d4 pawn advance, with slow manoeuvring play.

Sometimes the name Giuoco Pianissimo (in Italian: the very quiet game) is used for the lines in which White does not try to push his pawn to d4, even when his development is completed,

preferring to just get his pieces out instead.

In the Giuoco Piano both players have equal opportunities. The main line is considered to be

4.	...	♞g8-f6
5.	♘b1-c3	d7-d6
6.	♗c1-g5	

6.♗e3 is interesting.

6.	...	h7-h6
7.	♗g5xf6	♛d8xf6
8.	♘c3-d5	♛f6-d8
9.	c2-c3	

Next, with the d3-d4 pawn advance White will conquer the centre, but Black's pair of bishops is adequate compensation.

In these variations, which frequently feature castling on opposite sides, beginners will be wise to remember the old maxim: 'Black should never castle before White does'. In other words, if Black wishes to avoid unpleasant assaults by White, it is advisable to wait and see where the latter castles, so as to castle on the same side!

Another common system also features White moving the pawn to c3. It is most often reached by transposition from the Two Knights or the Italian Game:

4.	**...**	♘g8-f6
5.	**c2-c3**	**d7-d6**
6.	**0-0**	**a7-a6**

With the idea of 7...♘a5.

7.	**♗c4-b3**	**♗c5-a7**

Prophylactically reducing the effectiveness of d2-d4.

8.	**♘b1-d2**	**0-0**
9.	**h2-h3**	

with slow manoeuvring play.

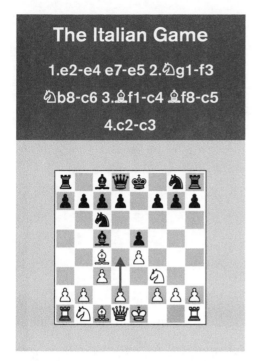

The Italian Game

1.e2-e4 e7-e5 2.♘g1-f3

♘b8-c6 3.♗f1-c4 ♗f8-c5

4.c2-c3

One of the oldest of all openings. Black's best continuation (4...♘f6) was suggested by the Portuguese author Pedro Damiano in 1512! In the **Italian Game** White plans to rapidly occupy the centre with c2-c3 and d2-d4, with the advantage, compared to the Ponziani Opening, of gaining a tempo by attacking the bishop on c5. Indeed, if Black responds with the passive 4...d6, after 5.d4 exd4 6.cxd4 ♗b6 7.h3!, White achieves his strategic objective of occupying the centre with his d-pawn and e-pawn without suffering any effective pressure on them. Black can fight against White's plan with two very different strategic set-ups:

A)   **4. ...**   **♕d8-e7**
Alekhine's move.
  5. d2-d4   **♗c5-b6**
  6. 0-0   **d7-d6**

which maintains the e5 outpost without conceding space to White.

B)   **4. ...**   **♘g8-f6**
Black attacks the weak point in White's position, namely the e4-pawn, which can no longer be defended by ♘c3, and concedes the centre in exchange for good piece play.
  5. d2-d4

The timid, but nonetheless commonly played 5.d3 transposes to the **Giuoco Piano**.

  5. ...   **e5xd4**
  6. c3xd4   **♗c5-b4+**
and you reach a crucial position where White has to make a fundamental strategic choice: sacrifice a pawn in exchange for the initiative with 7.♘c3, or steer the game towards a quiet positional struggle with 7.♗d2.

B1)   **7. ♘b1-c3**

This is more attractive looking, but probably less correct than 7.♗d2. It has a fascinating history: suggested by Greco as early as 1619 (!) it was revived by Steinitz in his match against Lasker in 1896.

7.   ...   ♘f6xe4
8.   0-0!

Here it was already understood how dangerous the double capture on c3 is: 8...♘xc3?! 9.bxc3 ♗xc3? (but 9...d5! still gives Black a playable position) 10.♗a3!! with a winning attack. Therefore, it was routine to play

8.   ...   ♗b4xc3!

with the idea, after 9.bxc3, to play 9...d5!, with a good game for Black. In the Lasker match mentioned before, Steinitz tried — with little success — to breathe new life into the **Greco Variation** by playing the dubious 10.♗a3. Fortunately, the renewed interest for this line led to Möller's extraordinary discovery of

9.   d4-d5!?

as an alternative to recapturing on c3. After years of intense theoretical study, the following came to be considered the main line:

9.   ...   ♗c3-f6

10. ♖f1-e1   ♘c6-e7
11. ♖e1xe4   d7-d6
12. ♗c1-g5   ♗f6xg5
13. ♘f3xg5   h7-h6
14. ♕d1-e2   h6xg5
15. ♖a1-e1

and now Black closes the e-file by means of 15...♗e6 16.dxe6 f6!, with a position that was for years thought to be advantageous for Black. However, in the in 1980s there was yet another development: the discovery of 17.♖e3!, with the idea of ♖h3 and a queen check on h5. The resulting position is not so clear. However, White's position continues to be viewed with some scepticism.

B2)   **7. ♗c1-d2**

This is the most played move: now Black can ambitiously continue with the rare but promising 7...♘xe4!? 8.♗xb4 ♘xb4 9.♗xf7+ ♔xf7 10.♕b3+ d5 11.♘e5+ ♔e6!. However, more often than not he opts for the solid

7.   ...   ♗b4xd2+
8.   ♘b1xd2   d7-d5

Necessary to free up play.

9.   e4xd5   ♘f6xd5
10. ♕d1-b3   ♘c6-e7
11. 0-0   0-0
12. ♖f1-e1

This position is reminiscent of several variations of the **Queen's Gambit Accepted**. White has more active pieces and a slight initiative. Still, the isolated d4-pawn and the excellent outpost on d5 for his knight give Black adequate resources.

22.♘a6 ♖a8 (22...bxa6 23.♕xd5+) 23.♕xd5+ ♔g6 24.♘c5 ♖d8 25.♕e4+ f5 26.♕h4→] **20.♕g4! g6 21.♘g5+ ♔e8** [21...fxg5?? 22.♕xd7+−] **22.♖xe7+ ♔f8** [22...♖xe7 23.♖xc8+; 22...♔xe7 23.♖e1+] **23.♖f7+! ♔g8! 24.♖g7+! ♔h8!** [24...♔f8 25.♘xh7+ ♔xg7 26.♕xd7++−] **25.♖xh7+!**
[Black, livid with rage after this show of artistry, left the playing hall without actually resigning! Mate would have followed in 10 moves: 25...♔g8 26.♖g7+ ♔h8 27.♕h4+ ♔xg7 28.♕h7+ ♔f8 29.♕h8+ ♔e7 30.♕g7+ ♔e8 31.♕g8+ ♔e7 32.♕f7+ ♔d8 33.♕f8+ ♕e8 34.♘f7+ ♔d7 35.♕d6X] **1-0**

Steinitz,Wilhelm
Von Bardeleben,Curt

Hastings 1895 (10)

1.e4 e5 2.♘f3 ♘c6 3.♗c4 ♗c5 4.c3 ♘f6 5.d4 exd4 6.cxd4 ♗b4+ 7.♘c3 d5? 8.exd5 ♘xd5 9.0-0 ♗e6 10.♗g5 ♗e7 11.♗xd5! ♗xd5 12.♘xd5 ♕xd5 13.♗xe7 ♘xe7 14.♖e1 f6 15.♕e2 ♕d7 [15...♕d6? 16.♕b5+ ♕c6 17.♕b4 ♕d6 18.♕xh7] **16.♖ac1?!** [16.♖ad1! was the right way to exploit White's better development: 16...♔f7 17.♕c4+ ♘d5 18.♘e5+ fxe5 19.dxe5+−] **16...c6?** [16...♔f7! was the correct defence, enough to maintain equality: 17.♕xe7+? (17.♕c4+ ♘d5) 17...♖xe7 18.♖xe7+ ♔xe7 19.♖xc7+ ♔d6 20.♖xb7 ♖hb8 21.♖xg7 (21.♖xb8 ♖xb8 22.b3 ♔d5∓) 21...♖xb2 22.h3 ♖xa2∞ with an unclear position; 16...♔f8; 16...♔d8] **17.d5!! cxd5** [17...♔f7 18.dxc6 ♘xc6 19.♖cd1→] **18.♘d4 ♔f7 19.♘e6 ♖hc8** [19...♘c6 20.♘c5 ♕c8 21.♕b5 ♖b8 (21...♘d8 22.♘d7 ♘c6 23.♕xd5+ ♔g6 24.g4→)

Van den Doel,Erik
Sokolov,Ivan

Leeuwarden ch-NED 2004 (8)

1.e4 e5 2.♘f3 ♘c6 3.♗c4 ♗c5 4.c3 ♘f6 5.d4 exd4 6.cxd4 ♗b4+ 7.♗d2 ♗xd2+ 8.♘bxd2 d5 9.exd5 ♘xd5 10.♕b3 ♘ce7 11.0-0 0-0 12.♖fe1 c6 13.♘e4 ♘b6 14.♗d3 ♘ed5 15.♘c5 ♖b8 16.♖ac1 ♘f4 17.♗b1 ♕f6 18.♘e5 ♕g5 19.♕f3 f6 20.♘ed3 ♘bd5 21.♘xf4 ♘xf4 22.h4 ♕h6 23.g3 ♘d5 24.♗e4 ♘b6 25.♕b3+ ♔h8 26.♕a3 ♖a8 27.♕e3 ♕xe3 28.♖xe3 ♖e8 29.♖ce1 ♘c4 30.♖3e2 ♘d6 31.♗d3 ♖xe2 32.♖xe2 ♔g8 33.♗c2 b6 34.♗b3+ ♔f8 35.♘e6+ ♗xe6 36.♖xe6 ♘f5 37.♖xc6 ♘xd4 38.♖c7 ♘xb3 39.axb3 ♖d8 40.♖xa7 ♖d3 41.♖a3 b5 42.b4 ♖d4 43.♖b3 h5 44.♔g2 ♔f7 45.♔f3 ♖c4 46.♔e3 g5 47.f4 gxh4 48.gxh4 ♔g6 49.♖c3 ♖xb4 50.♖c5 ♖b3+ 51.♔e4 ♖xb2 52.f5+ ♔h6 53.♖c6 ♖b4+ 54.♔f3 ♖xh4 55.♖xf6+ ♔g5 56.♖g6+ ♔xf5 57.♖b6 ♖b4 **0-1**

Two Knights Defence

**1.e2-e4 e7-e5 2.♘g1-f3
♘b8-c6 3.♗f1-c4 ♘g8-f6**

This defence was noted by the Abruzzian Giulio Cesare Polerio in the 16th century, and discussed again by Giambattista Lolli and Domenico Lorenzo Ponziani two centuries later. In the 19th century it was adopted chiefly as a means of avoiding the much-feared consequences of the then reigning **Evans Gambit**. Why was it used just as an expedience in the past, given its popularity today? It should be remembered that even though 3...♘f6 is the most natural move (it attacks the unprotected e4-pawn), it is in effect a pawn sacrifice... at least from the modern viewpoint!
4.♘g5 d5 5.exd5 used to be automatically followed by 5...♘xd5?!, *but at this point either 6.♘xf7!? (the celebrated* **Fried Liver Attack** – *also known by the original Italian name* **Fegatello Attack**), *or 6.d4!, produces positions which are undoubtedly advantageous to White.*

It was only at the beginning of the 20th century, when the playability of 5...♘a5! was discovered (as were 5...b5!? and 5...♘d4!?) that the popularity of this defence boomed, as it was now seen as an effective way for Black to fight for the initiative. Indeed, 3...♘f6 has currently overtaken 3...♗c5 in popularity.

Against the Two Knights White has fundamentally three lines to consider – *excluding 4.♘c3?!, which allows 4...♘xe4! with the idea of ...d7-d5.*

A)   4.   d2-d3
The most solid and currently the most popular move. It is in line with the modern tendency to play 3.♗c4 with a positional approach. After 4...♗c5, we are back in the **Giuoco Piano**. However, 4...♗e7 is the more popular choice. It is solid, even if slightly passive, and it generally leads to positions which are strategically similar to the **Closed Spanish**.

B)   4.   d2-d4
is a natural response in the centre, to which
4.   ...   e5xd4
is the best reply. You may be wondering why 3...♘xe4 is valid after 3.d4 in the **Petroff Defence**, whereas in the **Two Knights** 4...♘xe4? is considered to be so bad. The answer is that in the Two Knights after 5.dxe5, White already threatens 6.♕d5 with a clear advantage, whereas in the Petroff after 4.dxe5, Black gains easy equality with 4...d5 (there is no bishop on c4 to prevent this move).

B1) 5. e4-e5

In modern play this positional approach is the most usual continuation.

> 5. ... **d7-d5**
> 6. **♗c4-b5!**

With the g7-pawn defended, 6.exf6 does not make sense.

> 6. ... **♞f6-e4**
> 7. **♞f3xd4**

Arriving at a complex position. Black obtains satisfactory play after either the solid 7...♗d7 or the aggressive 7...♗c5.

B2) 5. 0-0

This classical move is currently less popular (5.c3 ♞xe4!). Black can respond 5...♞xe4 6.♖e1 d5 7.♗xd5! ♕xd5 8.♞c3 ♕a5 (or 8...♕h5) with a balanced position and results that tend to favour Black.

Another response is the more ambitious

> 5. ... **♗f8-c5**
> 6. **e4-e5**

We have arrived at the famous **Max Lange Attack**.

> 6. ... **d7-d5**
> 7. **e5xf6**

Now yes!

> 7. ... **d5xc4**
> 8. **♖f1-e1+** **♗c8-e6**
> 9. **♞f3-g5**

The threat is 10.♞xe6 followed by 11.♕h5+ and then 12.♕xc5. After the virtually forced

> 9. ... **♕d8-d5**

comes

> 10. **♞b1-c3**

This knight is immune because of the undefended ♕d5.

> 10. ... **♕d5-f5**
> 11. **♞c3-e4**

and the threat is 12.g4. It is surprising that with such active pieces White does not obtain anything after

> 11. ... **0-0-0!**
> 12. **g2-g4** **♕f5-e5**

Keeping the c5-bishop defended.

> 13. **♞g5xe6** **f7xe6**
> 14. **f6xg7** **♖h8-g8**
> 15. **♗c1-h6** **d4-d3**

Dozens of games have demonstrated that the position is dynamically balanced with possibilities for both players.

C) 4. ♞f3-g5

The critical move, at least in terms of the application of chess theory, is this now comparatively little-played and romantic move.

A 'beginner's move', huffed Tarrasch, who was famous for such dogmatic dismissals.

> 4. ... **d7-d5**

Before examining this line, let's look at another surprising move available to Black: **4...♗c5!?**

which delightfully ignores the attack on f7, so as to counterattack f2. This is the **Traxler Variation** (or **Wilkes-Barre** for the Americans), and it dates back to the end of the 19th century. After 5.♘xf7 ♗xf2+!, Black seems to have sufficient counterplay, even if a hundred years of analysis has not fully explored the resulting positions. Let's just say that in practice it is easier to play the black side. It is therefore not surprising that White prefers the safer 5.♗xf7+, even if after 5...♔e7 (threatening 6...h6) 6.♗b3 or 6.♗d5, Black receives a certain degree of compensation with ...♖hf8-♕d8-e8-g6 and ...d7-d6 followed by ...♗g4. It must be said that White, in addition to having an extra pawn, should be able to take advantage of the unhappy position of the black king on e7 if he can play a well-timed c3 and d4. In short, this counterattack is perhaps not 100% sound, but it is dangerous and greatly feared.

5. e4xd5

As we have already said, 5...♘xd5?! gives White the advantage after either 6.♘xf7!? (the Fegatello) or 6.d4!.

At this point the main move is

5. ... ♘c6-a5

Also interesting are the **Ulvestad Variation** 5...b5!? and the **Fritz Variation** 5...♘d4, which often merge at various stages: the following is a line that exemplifies the furious complications that can arise from 5...♘d4: 6.c3 b5 7.♗f1! ♘xd5 8.♘e4 ♕h4!? (8...♘e6 is more solid) 9.♘g3 ♗g4 10.f3 e4!

clearing the diagonal for the f8-bishop to exploit the uncomfortable position of the knight on g3: 11.cxd4 ♗d6 12.♗xb5+ ♔d8 (the king is safer here than on f8), and now either the classical 13.0-0 or the more recent 13.♕b3!? ♗xg3+ 14.♔d1 seems to give White the advantage.

6. ♗c4-b5+

In case of 6.d3 h6 7.♘f3 e4!, Black obtains good play.

6. ... c7-c6

6...♗d7!? is also becoming popular.

7. d5xc6 b6xc6
8. ♗b5-e2

8.♕f3!? was not considered to be dangerous until recently. However, today it must be treated with respect: it was successfully employed by Karjakin in 2005 and by Short in 2006!

8. ... h7-h6

For the pawn Black has a fairly significant lead in development and he is ready to grab centre space with his pawns. If White doesn't want to lose another tempo after 9.♘f3 e4, he can continue with the unnatural but interesting 9.♘h3, which was played by Steinitz, and later by Fischer. Remember that White is a pawn up and that 9...♗xh3 – to create bad doubled pawns for White – removes the dynamic quality from Black's position. With his bishop pair and the weak c6-pawn, White can look to the future with confidence. Black's best option is to ignore the ♘h3 and continue development with 9...♗c5 and ...0-0, with good compensation.

The most common 9th move, however, remains 9.♘f3 and now 9...e4 10.♘e5 ♗d6 (10...♛c7 is also playable)

either 11.d4 or 11.f4. Black has compensation which is difficult to evaluate.

Brandenburg,Daan
Postny,Evgeny
Hoogeveen 2006 (4)
1.e4 e5 2.♘f3 ♘c6 3.d4 exd4 4.♗c4 ♘f6 5.e5 ♘e4 6.♕e2 ♘c5 7.0-0 ♗e7 8.♖d1 d5 9.♗b5 0-0 10.♗xc6 bxc6 11.♘xd4 ♕e8 12.c4 f6 13.♘c3 fxe5 14.♕xe5 ♕f7 15.♕e2 ♗d6 16.cxd5 ♗g4 17.f3 ♖ae8 18.♕d2 ♕h5 19.h3 ♕h4 20.♕f2 ♗g3 21.♕d2 ♗d6 22.♕f2 ♗g3 23.♕d2 ♗xh3 24.♕g5 ♕xd4+ **0-1**

Nakamura,Hikaru
Ganguly,Surya Shekhar
Khanty Mansiysk 2005 (1)
1.e4 e5 2.♘f3 ♘c6 3.d4 exd4 4.♗c4 ♘f6 5.e5 d5 6.♗b5 ♘e4 7.♘xd4 ♗d7 8.♗xc6 bxc6 9.0-0 ♗c5 10.f3 ♘g5 11.f4 ♘e4 12.♗e3 ♕b8 13.♕c1 ♗xd4 14.♗xd4 c5 15.♗f2 ♗b5 16.♖d1 ♘xf2 17.♔xf2 ♗c6 18.♘d2 ♕b6 19.c4 d4 20.♕c2 0-0 21.f5 ♖ad8 22.♖f1 ♗a8 23.♔g1 d3 24.♕c3 ♖d4 25.♖f2 ♖e8 26.♖e1 ♕h6 27.♕a3 ♕g5 28.g3 h5 29.♕xc5 h4 30.♕xd4 hxg3 31.♔f1 gxf2 32.♕xf2 ♕g4 33.f6 gxf6 34.♖e3 ♕d1+ 35.♕e1 ♕xe1+ 36.♔xe1 fxe5 37.♖xd3 f5 38.♖d7 e4 39.♘b3 f4 40.♘d4 e3 41.♘f5 ♔h8 42.♘h4 ♔g8 43.♘g6 f3 44.♖e7 ♖xe7 45.♘xe7+ ♔f7 46.♘f5 e2 47.♘d4 ♔f6 48.♘b5 ♔e5 49.♘xc7 ♗e4 50.♘b5 ♗d3 51.b3 ♔e4 52.♘c7 ♗xc4 **0-1**

Canal,Esteban
Monticelli,Mario
Venice 1948
1.e4 e5 2.♘f3 ♘c6 3.d4 exd4 4.♗c4 ♘f6 5.0-0 [5.♘g5?! d5 6.exd5 ♘xd5?

7.0-0 ♗e7 8.♘xf7 ♔xf7 9.♕f3+ ♔e6
10.♘c3! dxc3 11.♖e1+ ♘e5 12.♗f4
♗d6 13.♗xe5 ♗xe5 14.♖xe5+ ♔xe5
15.♖e1+ ♔d4 16.♗xd5 ♖f8 17.♕d3+
♔c5 18.b4+ ♔xb4 19.♕d4+ 1-0
Morphy-Amateur, New Orleans 1858]
**5...♘xe4 6.♖e1 d5 7.♗xd5 ♕xd5
8.♘c3 ♕a5 9.♘xe4 ♗e6 10.♘eg5
0-0-0 11.♘xe6 fxe6 12.♖xe6 ♕d5
13.♕e2 ♗d6 14.♘g5 ♖df8 15.♗h4
d3 16.cxd3 g5 17.♗xg5 ♔d7 18.♖e4
♖xf3 19.♕xf3 ♕xg5 20.♕f7+ ♘e7
21.♖ae1 ♖e8 22.g3 ♕g6 23.♕b3
♔c8 24.♕a4 a6 25.♖g4 ♕f7 26.♖g7
♕f8 27.♖xh7 ♖d8 28.♕g4+ ♔b8
29.♖e4 ♘d5 30.♕e6 ♘b4 31.♖f7
♕h8 32.d4 ♕h5 33.a3 ♘d3 34.b4
♖h8 35.h4 ♖g8 36.♖e3 ♕d1+
37.♔g2 ♘xf2 38.♖xf2 ♖g7 39.♖ef3
♕xd4 40.♕e8+ ♔a7 41.♕e3** 1-0

Cueto Chajtur,Johny
Soppe,Guillermo

Buenos Aires 2000 (1)

**1.e4 e5 2.♘f3 ♘c6 3.d4 exd4 4.♗c4
♘f6 5.0-0 ♗c5 6.e5 d5 7.exf6 dxc4
8.♖e1+ ♗e6 9.♘g5 ♕d5 10.♘c3
♕f5 11.♘ce4 0-0-0 12.fxg7 ♖hg8
13.♘xc5 ♕xc5 14.♖xe6 fxe6
15.♘xe6 ♕d5 16.♘xd8 ♖xg7 17.♕f1
♘xd8 18.♗f4 ♘e6 19.♗d2 ♘c5**

20.♖d1 ♕f5 21.♗b4 ♘e6 22.♕xc4
♘f4 23.♖xd4 ♖xg2+ 24.♔f1 ♕g4
25.♔e1 ♖g1+ 26.♔d2 ♖d1+ 0-1

Polerio,Giulio Cesare
D'Arminio,Domenico

Rome 1610

**1.e4 e5 2.♘f3 ♘c6 3.♗c4 ♘f6
4.♘g5 d5 5.exd5 ♘xd5 6.♘xf7 ♔xf7
7.♕f3+ ♔e6 8.♘c3 ♘e7 9.d4 c6
10.♗g5 h6 11.♗xe7 ♗xe7 12.0-0-0
♖f8 13.♕e4 ♖xf2 14.dxe5 ♗g5+
15.♔b1 ♖d2 16.h4 ♖xd1+ 17.♖xd1
♗xh4 18.♘xd5 cxd5 19.♖xd5 ♕g5
20.♖d6+ ♔e7 21.♖g6 ♕d2
22.♖xg7+ ♔f8 23.♖g8+ ♔e7
24.♕h7X** 1-0

Radjabov,Teimour
Naiditsch,Arkadij

Warsaw Ech 2005 (8)

**1.e4 e5 2.♘f3 ♘c6 3.♗c4 ♘f6
4.♘g5 d5 5.exd5 ♘a5 6.♗b5+ c6
7.dxc6 bxc6 8.♗e2 h6 9.♘f3 e4
10.♘e5 ♗d6 11.d4 exd3 12.♘xd3
♕c7 13.b3 0-0 14.♗b2 ♘e4 15.♘c3
♗f5 16.h3 ♖ad8 17.0-0 c5 18.♗f3
♘g5 19.♘d5 ♕d7 20.h4 ♘e6
21.♘e5 ♕e8 22.♖e1 ♗b8 23.♕d2
♕b5 24.c4 ♕a6 25.♗c3 ♘b7
26.♘c6** 1-0

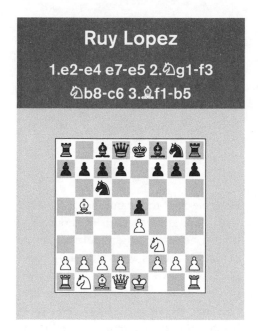

Ruy Lopez

1.e2-e4 e7-e5 2.♘g1-f3 ♞b8-c6 3.♗f1-b5

The **Ruy Lopez** (also called the Spanish Opening) is named after the Spanish clergyman who in 1561 declared 3.♗b5 to be White's best 3rd move. In his study he demonstrated that 3...♞ge7, which at that time was considered forced (!), is in fact unsatisfactory and he recommended that 2...d6 be played instead of 2...♞c6. A conclusion repeated by Philidor two centuries later! Naturally, it was quickly understood that the 'threat' ♗xc6 followed by ♘xe5 is not real because of ...♛d4, or better still ...♛g5, which regains the pawn with an advantage. With this information in mind, Black has a wide choice of playable lines.

In this light, it has been correctly noted that the Ruy Lopez is quite literally a 'threatening' opening: in the sense that White is continually threatening to exchange on c6 at the most opportune moment.

For this reason, at some point Black will have to defend the e5-pawn by moving his d-pawn to d6. However, this puts White in the most favourable position for expanding in the centre with d4. An alternative for Black in modern variations is to free himself of the annoying white bishop with ...a6 and ...b5, which is not without its negative consequences. It is important to understand what the negative positional aspects are of this preventive measure to defend the e5-pawn with a queenside expansion.

Let's compare the following two diagrams:

The first diagram shows the position in the Ruy Lopez after 3...a6 4.♗a4 b5 5.♗b3. The second shows the classical position after 3.♗c4.

If you were Black, which of the two positions would you choose? If you see the opening as a simple process of developing the pieces you will choose the first; Black has gained space on the queenside and is ready to continue developing with ...♗b7. However, this is not the best choice! Actually, chess opening theory assigns to White the advantage in the first position and equal possibilities for both players in the second. **Why?**

Because on b3 the bishop denies Black various tactical resources. One example is that in response to the natural 5...♗c5? there is the very strong 6.♘xe5! followed by a fork, a sequence that is obviously not available with the bishop on c4.

However, the real problem is the b5-pawn: its presence on that square favours a white queenside attack; a timely a2-a4 can be the basis for an enduring initiative. This consideration could seem esoteric, but for proof of its practical importance look at the following diagram:

Here we have the main line of the **Marshall Attack** (dealt with in more depth later), one of the most popular and feared of Black's options against the Ruy Lopez. Black is a pawn down, but he has a dangerous initiative on the kingside. White's only resource is the advance a2-a4; and he hopes that energetic counterplay on the queenside will make it impossible for Black to realize his aggressive plans on the other side of the board. If Black could play the pawn from b5 to b7 (!) his attack would probably be winning, but alas, this pawn move is against the rules.

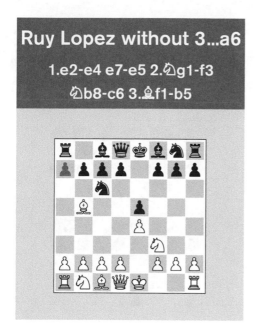

Ruy Lopez without 3...a6

1.e2-e4 e7-e5 2.♘g1-f3
♘b8-c6 3.♗f1-b5

We will now start to look at specific variations. After 3.♗b5, Black has many playable moves at his disposal of which 3...a6 is by far the most common. We will look at that move later. Let's begin with the **variations without 3...a6**, in ascending order of popularity.

A)　　3.　...　　　　**d7-d6**

The **Steinitz Defence**, similar to the **Steinitz Deferred**, which we will examine later, but with important differences. The Steinitz is solid, but a little passive.

4.	d2-d4	♗c8-d7
5.	♘b1-c3	♘g8-f6

The modern treatment: 5...exd4 6.♘xd4 g6!? is more dynamic.

| 6. | 0-0 | ♗f8-e7 |
| 7. | ♖f1-e1 | |

White threatens 8.♗xc6 and 9.dxe5, so Black must concede the centre with

| 7. | ... | **e5xd4** |
| 8. | ♘f3xd4 | |

With a position similar to the **Open Sicilian** with the difference that Black has a pawn on c7 instead of on e6. This reduces Black's possibilities of counterplay. White has a good space advantage, greater control of the centre and access to the f5-square, giving him good kingside prospects. This is not to say that Black's position is lost, only that it offers no exciting prospects.

B)　　3.　...　　　　**♘g8-e7**

The **Cozio Defence**, which was played when ♗xc6 was still considered a threat. In modern times it was reused by Bent Larsen, but it has never become popular.

4.	0-0	g7-g6
5.	c2-c3	♗f8-g7
6.	d2-d4	e5xd4
7.	c3xd4	d7-d5
8.	e4xd5	♘e7xd5
9.	♖f1-e1+	♗c8-e6
10.	♗c1-g5	♕d8-d6
11.	♘b1-d2	

White has good piece play and an unpleasant initiative.

C)   3. ...   ♘c6-d4

This is the **Bird Defence**, which every now and then pops up in tournament play. You reach a position not usually associated with the Ruy Lopez after

4.	♘f3xd4	e5xd4

It is unusual because there are not the customary opposing pawns on e4 and e5. Black has free play and the bishop on b5 seems to be a little out of play. The reality is that after

5.	0-0	♗f8-c5
6.	d2-d3	c7-c6
7.	♗b5-a4	♘g8-e7
8.	f2-f4	

White has a small but lasting advantage because of his better pawn structure and kingside initiative.

D)   3. ...   g7-g6

This is often called the **Smyslov Variation**. It remains a solid and reliable defence. Usually White gains central space with

4.	d2-d4	

4.c3!? a6! 5.♗a4 d6 transposes to a line of the Steinitz Deferred.

4. ... e5xd4

Practice has taught that recapturing on d4 gives Black a free game after ...♗g7 and ...♘f6, and for this reason White usually responds with

5. ♗c1-g5!?

speculating on the weakness of square f6.

5.	...	♗f8-e7
6.	♗g5xe7	♕d8xe7!
7.	♗b5xc6	d7xc6
8.	♕d1xd4	♘g8-f6
9.	♘b1-c3	♗c8-g4

White does not have an easy time exploiting his positional advantage.

E)   3. ...   ♗f8-c5

This is the **Classical Variation**, which is sometimes referred to as the **Cordel**

Variation. This is one of the oldest responses, which is hardly surprising given how natural it is for Black to play ...♗c5 in Open Games. However, a natural move is not necessarily also the best. Here the problem is evident. By placing the bishop on this square Black encourages White to occupy the centre with c3 followed by d4. An attentive reader may well ask: 'But doesn't the same thing happen in the **Italian Game**?'. The answer is that with the white bishop on c4 instead of b5 there are two differences: one strategic and the other tactical. Strategically, the bishop on b5 is applying pressure on the c6-knight; thematically, the idea is to apply pressure on the centre. Tactically, in some lines White has the extra resource of ♘xe5 followed by the fork on d4, a motif that is obviously not available with the bishop on c4.

4.	c2-c3	♘g8-f6
5.	0-0	0-0

5...♘xe4 is also playable.

| 6. | d2-d4 | ♗c5-b6! |

We have reached a position typical for Open Games, in which Black does not concede space and maintains his pawn on e5. However, there is an important difference with the Closed Spanish: instead of on e7 the dark-squared bishop is developed more actively. This is not to say that this placement of the dark-squared bishop is without negative aspects: it says enough that the results tend to favour White.

After 4.c3, a spectacular (even if not completely sound) gambit is 4...f5!? 5.d4 fxe4 6.♗xc6!? dxc6 7.♘fd2!.

The ensuing complications seem to favour White, considering that *7...exd4?? would lose a piece after 8.♕h5+.*

F)   3. ...   f7-f5

This is the popular and feared **Jaenisch Gambit** (also called the **Schliemann Defence** by some opening experts). It is perhaps not completely sound. However, its appeal continues to attract a host of amateur and correspondence players, while players on the professional tour-

nament circuit tend to regard it with a certain scepticism. It is true that if White knows all the complications of the main lines, he is sure to gain a concrete advantage. Otherwise he will be lucky to get out alive, as the unprepared player must work his way through the labyrinth of tactical and strategic complications presented by the gambit.

Black, in the spirit of the King's Gambit, immediately counterattacks the e4-pawn, relying on the fact that 4.exf5 will give him good counterplay after 4...e4. Radical attempts, such as 4.d4, have been used in an attempt to refute the Jaenisch Gambit: they have not borne fruit. In the end, people realized that White's best plan is simply to develop, relying on the fact that 3...f5 is not a developing move and that it also weakens the kingside. In this light

4.   ♘b1-c3!

which defends e4 and at the same time develops a piece, is the best move, even if after

4.   ...   f5xe4

4...♘f6 and 4...♘d4 are also played.

5.   ♘c3xe4

Black seems to be able to gain space in the centre and to gain tempi for his development with the pawn advance

5.   ...   d7-d5

But White, who enjoys a net advantage in terms of piece activity and development, does not pull back his knight, but instead aims for a tense position with

    6. ♘**f3xe5!**   **d5xe4**
    7. ♘**e5xc6**

The recapture of the knight on c6 gives White an advantage, and therefore Black moves the attacked queen to d5 or g5:

F1)   **7.** ...   ♛**d8-d5**

This has the advantage of immediately threatening 8...bxc6, but after the 'almost' forced sequence

    8. **c2-c4!**   ♛**d5-d6!**
    9. ♘**c6xa7+** ♝**c8-d7**
  10. ♛**d1-h5+** **g7-g6**
  11. ♝**b5xd7+** ♛**d6xd7**
  12. ♛**h5-e5+** ♚**e8-f7**
  13. ♘**a7-b5!** **c7-c6**
  14. ♛**e5-d4!**

White is better.

F2)   **7.** ...   ♛**d8-g5**

This counterattack on g2 is the most popular.

    8. ♛**d1-e2!**

Attacking e4 and defending b5 and – indirectly – g2 at the same time.

    8. ...   ♘**g8-f6**
    9. **f2-f4!**

This last move defends g2 with gain of a tempo.

    9. ...   ♛**g5xf4**

9...♛h4+ also gives White an advantage.

  10. ♘**c6-e5+** **c7-c6**
  11. **d2-d4**

Attacking the queen and gaining another tempo. This is the idea of 9.f4.

  11. ...   ♛**f4-h4+**
  12. **g2-g3**   ♛**h4-h3**
  13. ♝**b5-c4**   ♝**c8-e6**
  14. ♝**c1-g5**

and White has a clear advantage, even if the battle is not over yet.

G)   **3.** ...   ♘**g8-f6**

The **Berlin Defence**. It suddenly became fashionable at the end of the 20th century chiefly thanks to its adoption by Kramnik in his victorious match against Kasparov. Like the Petroff Defence, it is considered to be one of the best ways to draw as Black against very strong opponents, presuming of course that you have mastered the required technique.

The queens are exchanged very early on and often quickly an endgame is reached, where White's superior pawn structure is not at all easy to exploit. It is for this reason that some have christened it the **Berlin Wall**! It is a consoling thought that this symbol of the Cold War now only exists on the chessboard.

4. 0-0! ♘f6xe4

The capture that is the key move of the system. Instead, 4...d6 transposes to the Steinitz Defence, while with 4...♗c5 we reach the Classical Variation.

5. d2-d4!

White wants to open the e-file: practice has shown that 5.♖e1 ♘d6 does not cause Black problems.

5. ... ♘e4-d6!

This option is not available to Black in the Ruy Lopez with 3...a6, as there the white bishop is on a4. At this point, after 6.dxe5 ♘xb5, White will regain the piece with 7.a4, but it seems a little innocuous. If White wants to obtain anything he must give up his bishop pair and accept a queen trade-off.

6. ♗b5xc6 d7xc6
7. d4xe5 ♘d6-f5!

The most active square for the knight.

8. ♕d1xd8+ ♔e8xd8

We have a position that is strategically reminiscent of certain sub-variations of the **Exchange Variation of the Ruy Lopez** in which the queens leave the board very quickly. As in the Exchange Variation, here too the pawn ending is technically winning for White, given the doubled pawn on c6. However, Black's bishop pair and unhindered development make White's task of exchanging all the pieces very arduous. Here too, Black has the added advantage that the pawn on e5 supplies him with outposts on f4 and d4. This makes it easier to block White's kingside pawn majority. Statistically, the percentage of draws is very high (44%). At the same time the number of black victories is obviously well below average.

Nimzowitsch, Aaron
Capablanca, Jose Raul

St Petersburg 1914

1.e4 e5 2.♘f3 ♘c6 3.♘c3 ♘f6
4.♗b5 d6 5.d4 ♗d7 6.♗xc6 ♗xc6
7.♕d3 exd4 8.♘xd4 g6?! 9.♘xc6?!
[9.♗g5 ♗g7 10.0-0-0!?] 9...bxc6
10.♕a6 ♕d7 11.♕b7 ♖c8 12.♕xa7
♗g7 13.0-0 0-0 14.♕a6 ♖fe8
15.♕d3 [15.f3!?] 15...♕e6! 16.f3
♘d7 17.♗d2? [17.♗f4 ♘e5 18.♗xe5
♗xe5 19.♖ab1] 17...♘e5 18.♕e2 ♘c4
19.♖ab1 ♖a8 20.a4 ♘xd2 21.♕xd2
♕c4 22.♖fd1 ♖eb8 23.♕e3?
[23.♕d3 ♕c5+ 24.♔h1 ♖b4 25.♘e2
was the lesser evil] 23...♖b4 24.♕g5
♗d4+ 25.♔h1 ♖ab8 26.♖xd4 ♕xd4
27.♖d1 ♕c4 28.h4 ♖xb2 29.♕d2
♕c5 30.♖e1 ♕h5 31.♖a1 ♕xh4+
32.♔g1 ♕h5 33.a5 ♖a8 34.a6
♕c5+ 35.♔h1 ♕c4 36.a7 ♕c5
37.e5 ♕xe5 38.♖a4 ♕h5+ 39.♔g1
♕c5+ 40.♔h2 d5 41.♖h4 ♖xa7
42.♘d1   0-1

Murey, Yaacov
Dreev, Alexey

Moscow 1989 (2)

1.e4 e5 2.♘f3 ♘c6 3.♗b5 ♘ge7
4.♘c3 g6 5.d4 exd4 6.♘d5 ♗g7
7.♗g5 h6 8.♗f6 ♗xf6 9.♘xf6+ ♔f8
10.♘xd4 ♔g7? [10...♘f5] 11.♕d2!!
♘g8 [11...♗xf6 12.♕c3+−] 12.♘d5
[12.♘xg8 ♖xg8 13.0-0-0 ♕f6
14.♗xc6 bxc6 15.f4 Hübner] 12...♘f6
13.♘c3 ♘h5 [13...♖e8 14.0-0-0!
♘xe4 15.♘xe4 ♖xe4 16.♘xc6 bxc6
17.♗xc6+−] 14.g4 ♕g5? [14...♘f4]
15.♕xg5 hxg5 16.♗xc6+− dxc6
17.gxh5 ♖xh5 18.f3 g4 19.♔f2 ♖h3
20.fxg4 ♗xg4 21.♖ag1 ♖d8
22.♖xg4 ♖xd4 23.♔g2 ♖e3 24.♖f1

♖b4 25.♖f2 f5 26.♖gf4 fxe4 27.a3
♖d4 28.♘e2 ♖d7 29.♘g3 ♖e7
30.♖g4 ♔h7 31.♖ff4   1-0

Vul, Arkady
Arkhangelsky, Mikhail

Moscow 1999

1.e4 e5 2.♘f3 ♘c6 3.♗b5 g6 4.0-0
♗g7 5.c3 ♘ge7 6.d4 exd4 7.cxd4 d5
8.exd5 ♘xd5 9.♖e1+ ♗e6 10.♗g5!?
[10.♘g5 ♕d6; 10.♘e5 0-0! 11.♘xc6
bxc6 12.♗xc6 ♖b8] 10...♕d6 11.♘bd2
0-0 12.♘e4 ♕b4 13.♗xc6 bxc6
14.♕c1 ♗xd4? [14...♖fe8! 15.♗d2
♕b6; 15...♕b5] 15.♘xd4 ♕xd4
16.♕xc6 ♕xb2 17.♖ad1 ♕b6
18.♕c4! [18.♕c1 f6 19.♗h6 ♖fe8
20.h3 ♗f5? (20...♗f7 21.♕a1±)
21.♕c4 ♗xe4 22.♖xe4 c6 23.♖xd5! 1-0
Minic-Dely, Belgrade 1968] 18...♕b4
[18...f6 19.♘xf6+ ♖xf6 20.♗xf6 ♘e3
21.♕e4 ♘xd1 22.♕xa8+ ♔f7
23.♗h4+−; 18...c6 19.♖xd5!? (19.♖b1
♕a5 20.♗h6→) 19...f5 (19...cxd5
20.♘f6+ ♔h8 21.♕h4+−; 19...f6!
20.♘xf6+ ♖xf6 21.♗xf6 ♗xd5
22.♕c3→ Vul) 20.♘f6+! ♖xf6
21.♖xe6! ♕b1+ (21...♖xe6 22.♖d8+!
♖xd8 23.♕xe6+ ♔g7 24.♕e7++−)
22.♖d1! ♕xd1+ 23.♖e1+ ♕d5
24.♕xd5+ cxd5 25.♗xf6+−] 19.♘f6+
♔g7 [19...♘xf6 20.♕xb4+−; 19...♔h8
20.♘xd5! ♕xc4 21.♗f6+ ♔g8
22.♘e7X] 20.♕c1! ♘xf6 [20...c6
21.♖e4! ♕a5 22.♗h6+! ♔h8 23.♗xf8
♘xf6 24.♗b4 ♕a4 25.♗c3! ♕xe4
26.♗xf6+ ♔g8 27.♕h6+−] 21.♕a1!
♕e7 [21...h6 22.♗xf6+ ♔g8 23.♗h8
f6 24.♖xe6 ♔xh8 25.♖xf6+−;
21...♖fb8 22.♕xf6+ ♔g8 23.♗h6 ♕b2
24.♖d4+−] 22.♖d7!   1-0

Monticelli,Mario
Spielmann,Rudolf

Warsaw ol 1935 (16)

1.e4 e5 2.♘f3 ♘c6 3.♗b5 f5 4.♘c3 fxe4 5.♘xe4 ♘f6 6.♕e2 d5 7.♘xf6+ gxf6 8.d4 e4 9.♘h4 ♕e7 10.♗f4 ♗e6 11.g3 a6 12.♗xc6+ bxc6 13.♗h6 ♕b4+ 14.c3 ♕b5 15.♕xb5 cxb5 16.♗xf8 ♖xf8 17.♘g2 ♔d7 18.♘f4 b4 19.cxb4 ♖fb8 20.a3 a5 21.b3 axb4 22.a4 ♗f7 23.♖c1 ♖a5 24.♘e2 ♗h5 25.♔d2 ♖c8 26.♖c2 ♗xe2 27.♔xe2 c5 28.dxc5 ♖axc5 29.♖d2 ♖c2 30.♖a1 ♖xd2+ 31.♔xd2 ♖c3 32.a5 ♔c7 33.a6 ♔b8 34.♖a5 ♖d3+ 35.♔e2 ♔a7 36.♖b5 ♖xb3 37.♖xd5 ♔xa6 38.♖d6+ ♔b5 39.♖xf6 ♖d3 40.♖f7 h6 41.♖b7+ ♔c4 42.♖e7 b3 43.♖xe4+ ♔c3 44.♖e6 ♔c2 45.♖xh6 b2 46.♖c6+ ♖c3 47.♖b6 ♖b3 48.♖c6+ ♖c3 49.♖b6 b1♕ 50.♖xb1 ♔xb1 51.h4 ♔c2 52.h5 ♔b3 53.g4 ♔c4 54.h6 ♖h3 55.g5 ♔d4   0-1

Shtyrenkov,Veniamen
Annageldyev,Orazly

Alushta 2005 (6)

1.e4 e5 2.♘f3 ♘c6 3.♗b5 f5 4.♘c3 fxe4 5.♘xe4 ♘f6 6.♕e2 d5 7.♘xf6+ gxf6 8.d4 ♗g7 9.dxe5 fxe5 10.♘xe5 0-0 11.♘xc6 bxc6 12.♗xc6 ♖b8 13.c4 ♗a6 14.♗xd5+ ♔h8 15.♖b1 ♖e8 16.♗e3 c6 17.♗xc6 ♗c3+ 18.♔f1 ♖xb2 19.♕d1 ♗xc4+ 20.♔g1 ♖xb1 21.♕xb1 ♖xe3 22.fxe3 ♕d2 23.♕b8+ ♗g8 24.g4 ♕xe3+ 25.♔g2 ♕e2+ 26.♔h3 h5 27.♕f4 hxg4+ 28.♔h4 ♕e7+ 29.♔h5 ♕h7+ 30.♔g5 ♕g7+ 31.♔f5 ♕f6+ 32.♔xg4 ♕g6+   0-1

Kasparov,Garry
Kramnik,Vladimir

London Wch m 2000 (3)

1.e4 e5 2.♘f3 ♘c6 3.♗b5 ♘f6 4.0-0 ♘xe4 5.d4 ♘d6 6.♗xc6 dxc6 7.dxe5 ♘f5 8.♕xd8+ ♔xd8 9.♘c3 ♗d7 10.b3 h6 11.♗b2 ♔c8 12.♖ad1 b6 13.♘e2 c5 14.c4 ♗c6 15.♘f4!? ♗b7 16.♘d5 ♘e7 17.♖fe1 ♖g8!? 18.♘f4 g5! 19.♘h5 ♖g6 20.♘f6 ♗g7 21.♖d3 ♗xf3 22.♖xf3 ♗xf6 23.exf6 ♘c6 24.♖d3 ♖f8 25.♖e4 ♔c8 26.f4?! gxf4 27.♖xf4 ♖e8 28.♗c3 ♖e2 29.♖f2 ♖e4 30.♖h3 a5 31.♖h5 a4 32.bxa4!? ♖xc4 33.♗d2 ♖xa4 34.♖xh6 ♖g8 35.♖h7 ♖xa2 36.♖xf7 ♘e5 37.♖g7 ♖f8 38.h3 c4 39.♖e7 ♘d3 40.f7 ♘xf2 41.♖e8+ ♔d7 42.♖xf8 ♔e7 43.♖c8 ♔xf7 44.♖xc7+ ♔e6 45.♗e3 ♘d1 46.♗xb6 c3 47.h4!? ♖a6 48.♗d4 ♖a4= 49.♗xc3 ♘xc3 50.♖xc3 ♖xh4 51.♖f3 ♖h5 52.♔f2 ♖g5 53.♖f8 ♔e5   ½-½

Almasi,Zoltan
Alexandrov,Alexey

Moscow Aeroflot Open 2007 (3)

1.e4 e5 2.♘f3 ♘c6 3.♗b5 ♘f6 4.0-0 ♘xe4 5.d4 ♘d6 6.♗xc6 dxc6 7.dxe5 ♘f5 8.♕xd8+ ♔xd8 9.♘c3 ♗d7 10.b3 ♔c8 11.♗b2 ♗e7 12.♖ad1 a5 13.a4 ♖d8 14.h3 h5 15.♖d3 b6 16.♖fd1 ♗e8 17.♖xd8+ ♗xd8 18.♘e2 ♗e7 19.e6 fxe6 20.♘f4 b5 21.♘xe6 bxa4 22.bxa4 g6 23.g4 hxg4 24.hxg4 ♘h6 25.♘e5 c5 26.♗a3 ♖a6 27.♘xc5 ♗xc5 28.♗xc5 ♗xa4 29.♗e3 ♘g8 30.♗g5 ♖d6 31.♖a1 ♗xc2 32.♖xa5 ♘f6 33.♖c5 ♗e4 34.f3 ♗b7 35.♔f2 ♘d7 36.♖xd7 ♔xd7 37.♗f4   ½-½

Ruy Lopez with 3...a6

1.e2-e4 e7-e5 2.♘g1-f3
♘b8-c6 3.♗f1-b5 a7-a6

This move is the most popular response to the Ruy Lopez, even though there are other valid options, like the **Berlin Defence**. The philosophy behind the Berlin is very hazardous: I will accept doubled pawns, I will give my opponent space and a lead in development, but...!!! I have my bishop pair and my hope is that White's centre will be overextended.

The result is a draw rate which is much higher than average. Black players who want a more ambitious system turn to more active defences such as the **Sicilian**, the **Modern/Pirc**, the **Alekhine**, or in some cases the **French**. Some variations of the Ruy Lopez can also be recommended, such as the **Jaenisch Gambit**, which was examined in the previous section on the Ruy Lopez without 3...a6.

In the Ruy Lopez with 3...a6 the most aggressive option is the **Marshall Attack**, but the dynamic possibilities of the **Archangel** and **New Archangel** variations should not be forgotten. Neither should those of several variations of the **Open Spanish**.

So now we have the most common move, 3...a6. Before continuing with his development, Black prefers to reserve the option of pushing the pawn to b5, so as to rid himself of the irritating pressure being applied on the c6-knight by White's bishop.

The most popular of the various responses to 3...a6 is 4.♗a4. This does not mean that the exchange on c6, which we will discuss in the next section, is to be underestimated, even though it has been dismissed by many as toothless. Nonetheless, some of the most famous white victories in the Ruy Lopez have been scored with this very variation, such as those of Lasker against Tarrasch and Capablanca, and more recently some brilliant victories with it by the 11th World Champion, the American Bobby Fischer.

Ruy Lopez Exchange Variation

1.e4 e5 2.♘f3 ♘c6 3.♗b5 a6

4.♗xc6

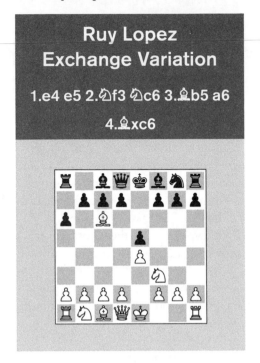

White usually retreats the bishop to a4, but 4.♗xc6, the **Exchange Variation**, is also a relatively frequent choice. After decades of stagnation, it became celebrated again through Fischer's successful employment of it during the 1960s. In the new millennium it still has its adherents. You may think that White's only winning strategy would be winning the pawn endings that the variation produces. However, variations characterized by opposite castling are not rare, and in these cases the predominate concern is the attack on the king.

4. ...　　d7xc6

Now taking on e5 is useless, as after 5...♕d4, Black will regain the pawn with an advantage. In the past, at this point either 5.d4 or 5.♘c3 was played, but Fischer's contribution was to demonstrate the power of

5. 0-0!

Before, castling had been mistakenly believed to be dubious because of **5...♗g4** (this move is still played, but has now been overshadowed by the classical 5...f6 and the modern 5...♕d6).

Now, castling is a move that leads to a flexible position. Depending on the circumstances, White keeps the possibility of the d2-d4 advance, with or without a preparatory c2-c3, or the option of simply plonking the pawn solidly on d3.

After 5.0-0, Black has many playable responses. If we can trust the statistics, the results with at least five alternative variations are more or less the same. We will ignore the minor lines that appear to be of doubtful merit. The following variations are in ascending order of popularity:

A)　　5. ...　　　　♘g8-e7

One of the most aggressive defences: it closes the e-file so that the queen can take on e4 after 6.♘xe5 ♕d4. In addition, the knight is ready to go to the excellent square g6, or at times to c6.

In the event of 6.♘xe5 ♕d4 White can try 7.♕h5!? g6 8.♕g5 (also of interest is 8.♘f3!? ♕xe4 9.♕a5) 8...♗g7 9.♘d3 f5! with complicated play.

B)   **5. ...   ♗f8-d6**

A little passive.

6. d2-d4   e5xd4
7. ♕d1xd4!   f7-f6
8. ♗c1-e3

White has the freer game.

C)   **5. ...   ♗c8-g4**

It seems logical to pin the f3-knight, but after

6. h2-h3!

Black would be in a crisis situation (6...♗h5 loses a pawn without compensation due to 7.g4, while 6...♗xf3 gives up the bishop pair too soon) if he did not have the continuation

6. ...   h7-h5!
7. d2-d3!

Not 7.hxg4? hxg4 and Black will deliver mate on the h-file.

7. ...   ♕d8-f6
8. ♘b1-d2   ♘g8-e7
9. ♖f1-e1   ♘e7-g6

and Black seems to have a dangerous initiative. But now it is time for White to play energetically *(avoid 10.hxg4? hxg4 11.♘h2 ♗c5 with the idea of 12...g3)*:

10. d3-d4!

With this move, White seeks to exploit his lead in development, effectively threatening to take the bishop on g4 (for example, 10...0-0-0? 11.hxg4 hxg4 12.♘h2 with the idea of 13.♕xg4+) or the pawn on e5 (10...exd4 11.e5!) with optimum results for White.

However, chess theory is constantly evolving: the move **10...♘f4!?** was considered to be lacking in the past, but according to the latest analysis it would appear to give Black sufficient re-

♗h6 16.♘e2 0-0-0 17.f4 g5 18.d3 gxf4 19.♘xf4 ♖hg8 20.g3 ♘g6 21.♘g2 f4 22.♘e1 fxg3 23.hxg3 ♗e3+ 24.♔h2 ♖df8 25.♖xf8+ ♖xf8 26.♘c3 ♗d4 27.♘a4 ♖f1 28.g4 ♖h1+ 29.♔g3 ♖g1+ 30.♔h2 ♗f2 0-1

Radjabov, Teimour
Harikrishna, Pentala
Cap d'Agde rapid 2006 (2)

1.e4 e5 2.♘f3 ♘c6 3.♗b5 a6 4.♗xc6 dxc6 5.0-0 ♗g4 6.h3 ♗xf3 7.♕xf3 ♕d7 8.d3 f6 9.♘d2 ♗d6 10.♘c4 ♘e7 11.♕h5+ ♘g6 12.♘xd6+ cxd6 13.f4 exf4 14.♗xf4 0-0 15.♗g3 d5 16.exd5 ♕xd5 17.♕xd5+ cxd5 18.c4 dxc4 19.dxc4 ♖fc8 20.♖ac1 ♖c6 21.b3 ♖ac8 22.♖cd1 b5 23.cxb5 axb5 24.♖d5 ♖c2 25.♖f2 ♖xf2 26.♔xf2 ♖c2+ 27.♔f3 ♖c3+ 28.♔f2 ♖c2+ 29.♔f3   ½-½

Mecking, Henrique
Kortchnoi, Viktor
Augusta m 1974 (12)

1.e4 e5 2.♘f3 ♘c6 3.♗b5 a6 4.♗xc6 dxc6 5.0-0 ♕d6!? 6.d3 [here the strategic goal is not the ending but to attack with opposite-side castling] 6...f6 7.♗e3 ♗g4 8.♘bd2 0-0-0 [8...♘e7] 9.♖b1 ♘e7 10.b4 g5 11.a4 ♘g6 12.b5 cxb5 13.axb5 axb5 14.♖xb5 ♕c6 15.♖b2 ♗c5 16.♘b3 ♗b4 17.♘fd4 exd4 18.♕xg4+ ♕d7 19.♕xd7+ ♖xd7 20.♘xd4 ♗c3 21.♖a2 ♖xd4 22.♖a3 ♖b4 23.♖xc3 ♖e8 24.f3 ♔d7 25.♖a1 ♖b5 26.♔f2 ♔d6 27.♖aa3 h5 28.♖a4 c6 29.♖ca3 g4 30.♖a5 ♖ee5 31.♖xb5 ♖xb5 32.fxg4 hxg4 33.♔g3 ♖b1 34.♗d4 ♖c1 35.♖c3 b5 36.♗xf6 b4 37.♖b3 ♖f1 38.♗g5 c5 39.c3 bxc3 40.♖xc3 ♖d1 41.♗e3 c4   1-0

Ruy Lopez
Minor Variations after

1.e4 e5 2.♘f3 ♘c6 3.♗b5 a6
4.♗a4

When White continues with the normal 4.♗a4, Black can hunt the bishop with 4...b5 5.♗b3 ♘a5, but after the simple 6.0-0 d6 7.d4, White's lead in development will make itself felt.

    4. ...   f7-f5!?

Against what is in effect a **Jaenisch Deferred**, we have the following very strong continuation:

    5. d2-d4!   e5xd4

After 5...fxe4?! 6.♘xe5 ♘xe5 7.dxe5, Black cannot play 7...c6, attacking the bishop on b5, as occurs in the normal **Jaenisch**, and follow up with a queen check on a5 after which the pawn on e5 falls.

    6. e4-e5!

Along the lines of the **Falkbeer** with reversed colours (see **King's Gambit**) in which Black has difficulty undermining the e5-pawn.

    6. ...   ♗f8-c5
    7. 0-0   ♘g8-e7
    8. ♗a4-b3

Now Black must play

    8. ...   d7-d5

so as to open up the position to facilitate development, but after

    9. e5xd6   ♕d8xd6
   10. ♖f1-e1

White is clearly better.

Karpov, Anatoly
Kortchnoi, Viktor
Moscow Candidates' final 1974 (20)

1.e4 e5 2.♘f3 ♘c6 3.♗b5 a6 4.♗a4 f5 5.d4 exd4 6.e5 ♗c5 7.0-0 ♘ge7 8.♗b3 d5 9.exd6 ♕xd6 10.♖e1 h6 11.♘bd2 b5 12.a4 ♗b7 13.axb5 axb5 14.♖xa8+ ♗xa8 15.♖e6 ♕d7 16.♕e2 d3 17.cxd3 ♔d8 18.♘f1 ♖e8 19.♘g3 ♘d4 20.♘xd4 ♗xd4 21.♗e3 ♗xe3 22.♕xe3 ♗d5 23.♗xd5 ♘xd5 24.♖xe8+ ♕xe8 25.♕d4 ♕d7 26.h4 ♔c8 27.♔h2 f4 28.♘e2 ♕f7 29.♕e4 c6 30.♘d4 ♕f6 31.♘xb5 ♕xh4+ 32.♔g1 ♕e7 33.♘d4 ♕f6 34.♕f5+ ♕xf5 35.♘xf5 ♘b4 36.d4 ♘d3 37.♘xg7 ♘xb2 38.♘f5 ♔d7 39.♘xh6 ♔e6 40.♔f1 ♔d5 41.♘f5 ♔e4 42.♘e7 ♔xd4 43.♘xc6+ ♔e4 44.♔e2 ♘c4 45.f3+ ♔d5 46.♘b4+ ♔e5 47.♘c2 ♔f5 48.♔d3 ♘e5+ 49.♔d4 ♘g6 50.♔d5 ♘h4 51.♘e1 ♘g6 ½-½

Ruy Lopez
Steinitz Defence
Deferred

1.e4 e5 2.♘f3 ♘c6 3.♗b5 a6
4.♗a4 d6

Unlike in the normal **Steinitz** with 3...d6, Black here has a sly tactical motif at his disposal that changes the strategic direction of the whole system. *If White continues with the normal 5.d4?!, after 5...b5 6.♗b3 ♘xd4 7.♘xd4 exd4*

he will be forced to sacrifice a pawn with 8.c3: taking back the d4-pawn unthinkingly with 8.♕xd4?? loses a piece after 8...c5 9.♕d5 ♗e6 10.♕c6+ ♗d7 11.♕d5 c4.

White can solve the problem of the exposed bishop with the radical 5.♗xc6+!? bxc6 6.d4, but after 6...f6!

Black's position is solid. He does not need to fear the weakening of the light squares, as he is the one with the light-squared bishop. This is why White usually proceeds with

5. c2-c3

which is not played — as is often believed — to support the d4 pawn advance, but to give the a4-bishop the escape square c2. Now Black has two continuations that are of a very different nature:

A)   5. ...   f7-f5

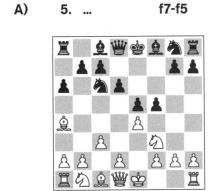

The aggressive **Siesta Variation**, which ambitiously aims to take advantage of the weakness of the d3-square.

6. e4xf5!   &c8xf5
7. 0-0

7.d4 gives Black a comfortable game because of 7...e4.

7. ...   &f5-d3
8. &f1-e1   &f8-e7
9. &a4-c2

By freeing himself of the annoying intruder, White gains a slight advantage.

B) 5. ...   &c8-d7
6. d2-d4

Now Black can prepare the fianchetto with 6...g6 and after 7.0-0 &g7 8.&e1 &ge7

he finds himself in a cramped but playable position.

Otherwise, he can continue with the classical

6. ...   &g8-e7

intending to trade off the bad bishop with the manoeuvre ...h6, ...&g6 and ...&e7-g5. White can frustrate Black's plan with the annoying h4-h5.

The other option is to change the nature of the position with 7.d5!? &b8 8.c4 with a type of Queen's Pawn Opening position in which White can free himself of his bad light-squared bishop.

Aronian,Levon
Yandemirov,Valery

Sochi tt 2005 (4)

1.e4 e5 2.&f3 &c6 3.&b5 a6 4.&a4 d6 5.0-0!? &g4!? 6.h3 h5 7.&xc6+ bxc6 8.d4 &xf3 9.&xf3 exd4 10.&d1 &f6 11.&b3 &e7 12.&b7 &c8 13.c3 &e5 14.&xa6 &xe4 15.cxd4 &f5 16.&c3 g6 17.&e1 &d7 18.&e3 &g7 19.&f3 &e6 20.&d2 f5 21.&e1 &f7 22.&g5 &he8 23.&fe3 &f6 24.&xf6 &xf6 25.&c4 d5 26.&e2 &a8 27.b3 f4 28.&e6 f3 29.&e3 &h4 30.g3 &xh3 31.&xe7+ &xe7 32.&xe7+ &c8 33.&f8+ &b7 34.&xf3 h4 35.&e7 &c8 36.&a4 hxg3 37.&c5+ &b6 38.&xg3 &h5 39.&c3   1-0

Steiner,Endre
Capablanca,Jose Raul

Budapest 1928 (6)

1.e4 e5 2.&f3 &c6 3.&b5 a6 4.&a4 d6 5.c3 f5 6.exf5 &xf5 7.d4 e4 8.&g5 &e7 9.&h4 &e6 10.&xe7 &xe7 11.&h5+ g6 12.&h6 &g8 13.&f4 &f6 14.&d2 0-0 15.0-0 d5 16.&g5 &h5 17.&xd8 &xd8 18.g3 &h3 19.&g2 &e6 20.&b3 c6 21.&d1 &ae8 22.&xh5 gxh5 23.f4 h4 24.&fe1 hxg3 25.hxg3 &xg2 26.&xg2 &e7 27.&f1 &g7 28.&h1

h5   29.c4   ♘xd4   30.♖ed1   ♘f3
31.cxd5 h4 32.d6 hxg3 33.♔g2
♘h4+ 34.♔g1 g2 35.♘h2 ♖xf4
36.♖d4 ♖d7 37.♖e1 ♘f5 38.♖dxe4
♖xe4 39.♖xe4 ♖xd6 40.♘f3 ♖g6
41.♖e5 ♘d6 42.♖e2 ♔f8 43.♖xg2
♖f6   44.♘e5   ♔e7   45.♖f2   ♖e6
46.♘d3 ♖e3 47.♘f4 ♘c4 48.b3 ♘e5
49.♘g2 ♖c3 50.♖e2 ♔d6 51.♔f1
♖c1+ 52.♔f2 ♘d3+ 53.♔e3 ♘b4
54.a3 ♖c3+ 55.♔d4 ♖c2 56.♖e1
c5+ 57.♔e4 ♖xg2 58.axb4 ♖g4+
59.♔d3 ♖xb4 60.♔c3 a5 61.♖a1 b6
62.♖a2 ♔c6 63.♖a1 ♔b5 64.♖a2 a4
65.bxa4+   ♖xa4   66.♖b2+   ♖b4
67.♖h2 ♖g4   0-1

Fischer,Robert
Ciocaltea,Victor
Varna ol 1962 (8)

1.e4 e5 2.♘f3 ♘c6 3.♗b5 a6 4.♗a4
d6 5.c3 ♗d7 6.d4 ♘ge7 7.♗b3 h6
8.♕e2 ♘g6 9.♕c4 ♕f6 [9...♕e7
10.d5 b5 11.♕e2 ♘a5=] 10.d5 b5
11.♕e2 ♘a5 12.♗d1 ♗e7 13.g3 0-0
[13...♗h3   14.a4] 14.h4   ♖fc8??
15.♗g5! hxg5 16.hxg5   ♕xg5
[16...♘f4 17.gxf6 ♘xe2 18.fxe7 and
the knight is lost] 17.♘xg5 ♗xg5
18.♘a3 c6 19.dxc6 ♗e6 20.♕h5
♗h6 21.♗g4 ♗xg4 22.♕xg4 ♘xc6
23.♖d1 b4 24.♘c4 bxc3 25.bxc3
♘d4 26.♘b6   1-0

Ruy Lopez Archangel and New Archangel Variation

1.e4 e5 2.♘f3 ♘c6 3.♗b5 a6 4.♗a4 ♘f6 5.0-0 b5 6.♗b3

Black's most popular fourth move remains 4...♘f6. After 5.0-0 (those of you who are not crazy about the idea of having to learn a lot of theory should consider 5.d3 or 5.♕e2), the normal response is 5...♗e7, or 5...♘xe4 (the **Open Spanish**), which we will look at soon. However, the immediate 5...b5 is being played more and more, and after 6.♗b3, 6...♗b7 (the **Classical Archangel**) or 6...♗c5 (the **New Archangel**). The two variations are similar, in that they both aim for more active play, even if by nature this involves taking more risks than with the **Closed Spanish**. Both bishop moves have good and bad points, and it is therefore difficult to decide which of the two is better, especially as the two variations often cross paths.

Classical Archangel

6. ...   ♗c8-b7

This variation has the plus of forcing White to play ♖e1 if he wishes to occupy the centre with d4. The move 7.c3

is in fact playable, but it amounts to a gambit. The bishop on b7 allows 7...♘xe4! 8.d4 ♘a5! 9.♗c2 exd4! and Black's position seems to be playable. Therefore, 7.d3 is often played. This robs the b7-bishop of much of its effectiveness and avoids a lot of theory. However, the critical line remains

7.   ♖f1-e1   ♗f8-c5
8.   c2-c3   d7-d6
9.   d2-d4   ♗c5-b6

with great strategic tension: White's centre is impressive, but it also runs the risk of collapsing. The ♗b6 increases Black's pressure on the centre, but at the same time his kingside is left weakened.

After the natural 10.♗g5, Black can respond with the effective 10...h6 11.♗h4 g5!?, or with 11...♕d7 followed by ...0-0-0. For this reason White usually reinforces the centre.

10. ♗c1-e3   0-0

10...♘xe4?? loses a piece after 11.d5.

11. ♘b1-d2   h7-h6

To play ...♘g4 hitting the bishop.

12. h2-h3

A strategically and tactically rich position for both sides: the kind that appeals to the contemporary player's taste.

New Archangel

The modern treatment involves a direct

6. ...   ♗f8-c5

This move became popular when it was realized that the presumed refutation 7.♘xe5 ♘xe5 8.d4 ♗xd4 9.♕xd4 d6 is in fact nothing special for White.

7. c2-c3   d7-d6

This line has an advantage over its sister variation: the c8-bishop can go to either b7 or g4, depending on the circumstances. The problem is that White, not having played ♖e1, can use the time saved to make more active moves, such as

8. a2-a4!

which puts pressure on the queenside. At this point the most popular move is

8. ...   ♖a8-b8

even if 8...♗b7 and 8...♗g4 are possible.

9. d2-d4   ♗c5-b6

10. ♘b1-a3!

Now Black sacrifices a pawn with

10. ...   0-0

11. a4xb5   a6xb5

12. ♘a3xb5   ♗c8-g4

(or 12...exd4 followed by 13...♗g4) with compensation which is difficult to evaluate.

Anderssen,Adolf
Paulsen,Louis

Leipzig m 1877 (4)

1.e4 e5 2.♘f3 ♘c6 3.♗b5 a6 4.♗a4 b5 5.♗b3 ♗b7 6.0-0 g6 7.c3 ♗g7 8.d4 d6 9.♗g5 ♘f6 10.♗d5 h6 11.♗xf6 ♕xf6 12.dxe5 dxe5 13.a4 0-0 14.♘a3 ♘d8 15.♗xb7 ♘xb7 16.axb5 axb5 17.♘xb5 ♕b6 18.♖xa8 ♖xa8 19.♘a3 ♕xb2 20.♘b1 ♘d6 21.h3 ♖a1 22.♘fd2 ♖a2 23.♕g4 ♕b5 24.c4 ♕b4 25.♕e2 ♖b2 26.♕d3 h5 27.g3 ♗h6 28.f4 ♕c5+ 29.♔h1 h4 30.♕c3 ♖a2 31.fxe5 ♗xd2 32.♘xd2 ♖a3 33.♕b2 ♘xc4 34.♕c2 ♖xg3 35.♘xc4 ♖xh3+ 36.♔g2 ♖g3+ 37.♔h2 ♔g7 38.e6 fxe6 39.♕b2+ ♔h6 40.♕h8+ ♔g5 41.♕f6+ ♔h5 42.♘e5 ♕e3 43.♕h8+ ♔g5 44.♕d8+ ♔h5 45.♕d1+ ♔h6 46.♘g4+ ♖xg4 47.♕xg4 ♕d2+ 48.♔h3 ♕e3+ 49.♖f3 ♕e2   1-0

Fischer,Robert
Bisguier,Arthur

Buenos Aires 1970 (12)

1.e4 e5 2.♘f3 ♘c6 3.♗b5 a6 4.♗a4 ♘f6 5.0-0 b5 6.♗b3 ♗b7 7.d4 ♘xd4 8.♘xd4 exd4 9.c3 ♘xe4 10.♖e1 ♗d6 11.♘d2 ♗xh2+ 12.♔f1 d5 13.♕h5 0-0 14.♕xh2 dxc3 15.♘xe4 dxe4 16.bxc3 c5 17.♖e3 c4 18.♗c2 ♕f6 19.♖f3 ♕e6 20.♖h3 ♕f5 21.♗e3 ♖ad8 22.♖e1 ♖d7 23.♗d4 ♖e8 24.♖h5 g5 25.g4   1-0

Vocaturo,Daniele
Godena,Michele

Cremona ch-ITA 2006 (7)

1.e4 e5 2.♘f3 ♘c6 3.♗b5 a6 4.♗a4 ♘f6 5.0-0 b5 6.♗b3 ♗c5 7.c3 d6

8.a4 [8.d4 exd4 9.cxd4 ♗b6 10.♗g5 ♗b7 11.♘c3 ♘e7 12.♖e1 h6 13.♗h4 g5 14.♗g3 ♔f8 15.♕d3 c5 16.e5 dxe5 17.♗xe5 ♗g7 18.♘e4 ♗xe4 19.♕xe4 ♘g6 20.♕b7 ♖a7 21.♕c6 c4 22.♗c2 ♗c7 23.♖ad1 ♕e7 24.♗xg6 ♗xg6 25.d5 ♗xe5 26.♘xe5+ ♔g7 27.♘g6+– Löwenthal-Morphy, London m-1 1859 (1-0, 38)] ♖b8 9.d4 ♗b6 10.axb5 axb5 11.♘a3 0-0 12.♘xb5 ♗g4 13.d5 ♘e7 14.♗c2 ♘g6 15.h3 ♗xh3 16.gxh3 ♕d7 17.c4 ♕xh3 18.♘g5 ♕g3+ 19.♔h1 ♕h4+ 20.♔g2 ♘f4+ 21.♗xf4 exf4 22.♘h3 g5 23.♖a3 ♘g4 24.♖h1 ♘xf2 25.♘xf2 ♕xf2+ 26.♔h3 f5 27.exf5 ♕h4+ 28.♔g2 ♕f2+ 29.♔h3 ♖be8 30.♖f3 ♖e3 31.♖xe3 ♕xe3+ 32.♔g4 h5+ 33.♔xh5 ♔f7 34.f6 ♖h8+ 35.♔g4 ♔xf6 36.♕e1 ♖h4+ 37.♖xh4 ♕xe1 38.♖h6+ ♔g7 39.♖h7+ ♔g8 40.♗g6 ♕g3+ 41.♔f5 f3   0-1

Schlechter,Carl
Chigorin,Mikhail

Berlin 1897 (15)

1.e4 e5 2.♘f3 ♘c6 3.♗b5 a6 4.♗a4 b5 5.♗b3 ♗b7 6.0-0 ♘f6 7.♘c3 ♗e7 8.d3 0-0 9.♗g5 d6 10.♘e2 ♘h5 11.♗d2 ♔h8 12.g4 ♘f6 13.h3 ♘d7 14.♘g3 ♘c5 15.♗d5 ♘e6 16.♔h2 ♖b8 17.c3 g6 18.d4 ♘g5 19.♘xg5 ♗xg5 20.f4 exf4 21.♗xf4 ♗xf4 22.♖xf4 ♕e7 23.♕f3 ♘d8 24.♖f1 ♔g7 25.g5 ♗xd5 26.exd5 h6 27.♖e4 ♕xg5 28.h4 ♕d2+ 29.♖e2 ♕xe2+ 30.♘xe2 f5 31.♘f4 g5 32.♘h5+ ♔g6 33.♘g3 f4 34.♕e4+ ♔f7 35.♕h7+   1-0

Ruy Lopez
Open Variation

1.e4 e5 2.♘f3 ♘c6 3.♗b5 a6
4.♗a4 ♘f6 5.0-0 ♘xe4

5...♘xe4 is the **Open Spanish**, which represents one of the most famous chapters in the history of the Ruy Lopez. Dr. Siegbert Tarrasch dogmatically declared it to be the only way for Black to obtain a good position. However, though it has always had many supporters, the Open Spanish has never been as popular as the **Closed**. Its most illustrious modern advocate is the Russo-Swiss champion Viktor Kortchnoi.

6. d2-d4!

Attempting to open the e-file is without doubt a good idea with an adversary's knight on e4.

The **Riga Variation**, though sometimes played, is undoubtedly favourable for White: 6...exd4 7.♖e1 d5 8.♘xd4 ♗d6!? 9.♘xc6 ♗xh2+! 10.♔h1! ♕h4 and now 11.♖xe4+! dxe4 12.♕d8+! ♕xd8 13.♘xd8+ ♔xd8 14.♔xh2

14...♗e6 (*14...f5 is rather inaccurate because of 15.♗g5 mate!*). White is better off. In view of the weak e4-pawn and his more active pieces it is safe to say that White's two minor pieces are stronger than Black's rook and two pawns.

So Black is virtually forced to weaken his queenside.

6. ... b7-b5!
7. ♗a4-b3

White threatens the paralyzing 8.dxe5 and, given that *7...exd4 8.♖e1 d5 9.♘c3!!* gives a clear advantage to White, Black has little choice but to play

7. ... d7-d5
8. d4xe5

Now Black has to defend d5.

8. ... ♗c8-e6

We have arrived at the initial position of the Open Spanish.

The black pawn on b5 facilitates White's opening of the queenside with a2-a4. The d4-square is often occupied by the f3-knight. Generally this is done after c3, ♗c2, which puts the adversary's e4-knight under pressure, and ♘bd2-b3 in order to be able to recapture on d4 with the knight or, alternatively, with the c3-pawn, which fixes the weakness on c7. In addition the move ♘f3-d4 clears the way for White's kingside pawn majority and the pawn advance f4-f5 can be devastating. Needless to say, Black has his resources. His pieces are active, the e5-pawn is weak, and his counterplay against f2 could become unpleasant, especially after ...f6, which opens the f-file for a rook. At this point White can choose between three main alternatives: 9.♕e2, 9.♘bd2, and 9.c3.

A)   9.   ♕d1-e2

The **Keres Variation**. White clears the d1-square for his rook in order to apply immediate pressure on the d5-pawn.

9. ...	♗f8-e7
10. ♖f1-d1	0-0
11. c2-c4!	b5xc4
12. ♗b3xc4	♗e7-c5
13. ♗c1-e3	♗c5xe3

14. ♕e2xe3   ♕d8-b8!
The pin is broken by the counterattack on b2.

15. ♗c4-b3   ♘c6-a5
Black has sufficient counterplay to maintain equality.

B)   9.   ♘b1-d2
This is increasingly popular: White does not vacate the c2-square for his bishop for now, but instead immediately attacks the outpost on e4.

9. ...	♘e4-c5
10. c2-c3	

If Black takes the bishop on b3, this would leave White with good control of the centre squares. As a result, the thematic move has always been considered to be

10. ...	d5-d4!?

even if in the light of recent developments, it may be preferable to play the more prudent 10...♗g4. After 10...d4, White has at his disposal one of the most important theoretical novelties of recent times:

11.   ♘f3-g5!!

Thought up by Igor Zaitsev and played for the first time by Anatoly Karpov against Kortchnoi in the 1978 World Championship match, this has been considered the best response from that moment on. It received its most famous seal of approval with Kasparov's famous victory over Anand in the 1995 World Championship.

The idea is to vacate the f3-square for the white queen, with the threat of ♘xf7. Taking the undefended knight with

11. ...   ♕d8xg5

is risky but still considered best: after

12. ♕d1-f3

the best thing for Black is to give back the piece with

12. ...   0-0-0

12...♔d7 13.♗d5 ♗xd5 14.♕xd5+ ♗d6 15.♘c4 gives White the advantage.

13.	♗b3xe6+	**f7xe6**
14.	♕f3xc6	**♕g5xe5**
15.	b2-b4	**♕e5-d5**
16.	♕c6xd5	**e6xd5**
17.	b4xc5	**d4xc3**
18.	♘d2-b3	**d5-d4**
19.	♗c1-a3!	

and although the earliest games from this position seemed to suggest that Black's mass of pawns is not sufficient compensation for the piece, more recent examples like Delchev-Gyimesi, Nova Gorica 2004, and

Morozevich-Ponomariov, Biel 2004, suggest that a draw is the most likely outcome.

The line previously thought to be safer, 11...dxc3, has been refuted by Kasparov: after 12.♘xe6 fxe6 13.bxc3 ♕d3, he found the brilliant 14.♗c2!! ♕xc3 15.♘b3!

and White's attack cannot be fought off.

C)   9. c2-c3

The standard move that clears the c2-square for the bishop and exerts influence on the d4-square.

Now Black, as is often the case in the Spanish, has to decide whether to place the bishop solidly on e7 or aggressively on c5.

C1) **9. ...** **♗f8-e7**

10. ♘b1-d2

First 10.♗e3, and then ♘bd2, is also interesting.

10. ... **0-0**

10...♘c5 11.♗c2 ♗g4!? is interesting.

11. ♗b3-c2

Ousting the black knight from e4.

11. ... **f7-f5**

12. ♘d2-b3 **♛d8-d7**

13. ♘f3-d4

A common move. Now 13...♘xe5 is too risky (14.f3!), and therefore:

13. ... **♘c6xd4**

14. ♘b3xd4 **c7-c5**

15. ♘d4xe6 **♛d7xe6**

16. f2-f3 **♘e4-g5**

17. a2-a4

and Black's impressive-looking centre is probably more of a weakness than a strength.

C2) **9. ...** **♗f8-c5**

This is the most played move, and probably the one which is most in the spirit of the Open Spanish, even if it is not necessarily the strongest reply. The price you pay to apply pressure on f2 and have an active position, is that it facilitates the common white manoeuvre ♘b1-d2-b3:

10. ♘b1-d2

10.♛d3, followed by 11.♗e3, is increasingly popular.

10. ... **0-0**

11. ♗b3-c2

Now Black has to decide what to do with the e4-knight: support it with 11...f5 or with 11...♗f5, or, alternatively, take the pawn on f2!!

C21) **11. ...** **♘e4xf2**

The controversial **Dilworth Variation**. Opening experts have always approached this line with suspicion, even though it is one of the few black systems with a performance superior to 50%! It seems strange that it could be a good idea to give up two more active minor pieces for a rook and a pawn.

12. ♖f1xf2 **f7-f6!**

Black can only obtain adequate counterplay by opening the f-file: 13.exf6 ♗xf2+! 14.♔xf2 ♛xf6 and now we see the point: Black's pressure is such that White usually concedes a pawn to open up the game with 15.♘f1 ♘e5 16.♗e3 ♖ae8 17.♔g1, and now the endgame that follows after 17...♘xf3+ 18.♛xf3 ♛xf3 19.gxf3 ♖xf3

is only favourable to White in theory: in practice Black's results are extremely good. This is presumably because it is easier to push a mass of passed pawns forward than for White to achieve a harmonious coordination of his minor pieces.

C22) 11. ...   ♗e6-f5

The most played of the three alternatives in modern times.

12. ♘d2-b3

White threatens to gain a piece.

12. ...   ♗f5-g6!

Black does not fear conceding the loss of his dark-squared bishop.

13. ♘f3-d4!

After 13.♘xc5 ♘xc5, the black knight heads for e6 with excellent control of the critical squares d4 and c5.

13. ...   ♗c5xd4!

It pays not to be too dogmatic. At times it is okay to give up the dark-squared bishop.

14. c3xd4

14.♘xd4 ♕d7! produces a balanced game. *Instead, 14...♘xd4?!, after which there is no further counterplay on a ♘b3, leaves White with the advantage after 15.cxd4, while 14...♘xe5? loses to 15.f4 with the idea of 16.f5.*

14. ...   a6-a5!

As in some variations of the **Closed Defence to the Spanish**, Black obtains counterplay with ...a5-a4, speculating on the presence of the white knight on b3:

15. ♗c1-e3   a5-a4
16. ♘b3-c1

If 16.♘d2 is played, then 16...f6!? is interesting; as is indeed 16...a3!? 17.b3 f6 with possibilities for both players.

C23) 11. ...   f7-f5

The classical continuation. Nowadays it is very rare, but this is a question of fashion, not objective inferiority, given that there are no known refutations. After 12.exf6 ♘xf6, Black has good piece play, and for this reason the following standard manoeuvre is preferred:

12. ♘d2-b3   ♗c5-b6
13. ♘f3-d4!   ♘c6xd4
14. ♘b3xd4

and once again Black concedes the bishop in exchange for the initiative .

14. ...   ♗b6xd4!

At this point, in the past the critical variation, which contains an incredible hidden Black sacrifice, was 15.cxd4 f4!.

Positionally forced: Black, who must play actively, threatens 16...f3. White occupies this square first with 16.f3 ♘g3! 17.hxg3 fxg3.

The question now is: how do you defend yourself against the threat of ...♕d8-h4-h2 mate? The answer is 18.♕d3! ♗f5 (*18...♕h4 19.♕xh7+ with an advantage for White*) 19.♕xf5 ♖xf5 20.♗xf5 ♕h4 21.♗h3 and mate has been prevented, but at the cost of two central pawns: 21...♕xd4+ 22.♔h1 ♕xe5.

The strange make-up of the opposing forces is something that you do not see every day: queen and three pawns against rook and two bishops. Who is better off? This line was first played in 1942, and no one is really any the wiser after more than 60 years!

There is an interesting story relating to this variation. The theory until the move 16...♘g3 was well-established as early as 1904 and many noted players (Cohn, Maroczy, Tarrasch, Vidmar) adopted it as Black. However, Isaac Boleslavsky was the first to appreciate the potential of 17.hxg3! (previously considered to be losing) followed by the queen sacrifice: he played this variation against Ragozin in1942 (1-0) as well as Botvinnik in 1943 (½-½). Two years later in 1945, a radio match was organized as part of the end-of-war celebrations: 10 Soviet players against 10 from the USA in a double-round match. The convincing win by the Soviets came as a great surprise: 15½-4½. On second board Vasily Smyslov found himself facing Samuel Reshevsky. In their first game Smyslov had the white pieces, and Reshevsky allowed him to employ this very variation, which was so well known to the Soviet players and completely unknown to the Americans. As a result Smyslov was able to beat his formidable opponent with unusual ease. This demonstrates how slowly news of chess developments spread in the days before the Internet.

It is understandable that White would want to seek an advantage without all these fireworks. With this in mind, it may be better to turn to

15. ♕d1xd4!

(instead of 15.cxd4)

15. ...   **c7-c5**

16. ♕d4-d1!

16. ...   **f5-f4**

17. f2-f3

Now the same manoeuvre *17...♘g3?* is no longer playable because at the end of the sequence there is no undefended pawn on d4, and therefore Black has to make do with

17. ...   **♘e4-g5**

18. a2-a4

White's position is more promising.

Smyslov, Vasily
Sokolsky, Alexey

Moscow Chigorin mem 1947 (14)

1.e4 e5 2.♘f3 ♘c6 3.♗b5 a6 4.♗a4 ♘f6 5.0-0 ♘xe4 6.d4 b5 7.♗b3 d5 8.dxe5 ♗e6 9.♕e2 ♘c5 10.♖d1 ♘xb3 11.axb3 ♗c5 12.♗e3 ♗xe3 13.♕xe3 ♕e7 14.♕c3 ♘d8 15.b4 0-0 16.♘bd2 ♗g4 17.h3 ♗xf3 18.♘xf3 c6 19.♖d2 h6 20.b3 ♖e8 21.♘d4 ♕g5 22.♖f1 ♘e6 23.f4 ♘xf4 24.♖df2 ♘e6 25.♘f5 ♖ec8 26.h4 ♕d8 27.♕g3 ♔h7 28.♘d6 ♖c7 29.♘xf7 ♕e7 30.♘d6 ♖g8 31.♕d3+

                                 1-0

Keres, Paul
Reshevsky, Samuel

The Hague/Moscow Wch 1948 (18)

1.e4 e5 2.♘f3 ♘c6 3.♗b5 a6 4.♗a4 ♘f6 5.0-0 ♘xe4 6.d4 b5 7.♗b3 d5 8.dxe5 ♗e6 9.♕e2 ♘c5 10.♖d1 ♘xb3 11.axb3 ♕c8 12.♗g5 h6 13.♗h4 ♗c5 14.♘c3 g5 15.♗g3 ♕b7 16.♘xd5 0-0-0 17.♘f6 g4 18.♘e1 ♘d4 19.♕f1 h5 20.♗f4 h4 21.♗e3 h3 22.♖d2 hxg2 23.♕xg2 ♘f3+ 24.♘xf3 ♗xe3 25.♖xd8+ ♖xd8 26.♘e1 ♗d4 27.♘d3 ♗f5 28.♖e1 a5 29.♘e4 ♔b8 30.b4 a4 31.c3 ♗xe4 32.♖xe4 ♗xc3 33.♖e3 ♕xg2+ 34.♔xg2 ♖xd3 35.♖xd3 ♗xb2 36.♖d5 c6 37.♖d8+ ♔c7 38.♖a8 ♔b7 39.♖f8 ♗e5 40.♖xf7+ ♔b6 41.f4

                                   0-1

Smyslov, Vasily
Euwe, Max

The Hague/Moscow Wch 1948 (19)

1.e4 e5 2.♘f3 ♘c6 3.♗b5 a6 4.♗a4 ♘f6 5.0-0 ♘xe4 6.d4 b5 7.♗b3 d5 8.dxe5 ♗e6 9.♕e2 ♘c5 10.♖d1 ♘xb3 11.axb3 ♕c8 12.c4 dxc4 13.bxc4 ♗xc4 14.♕e4 ♘e7 15.♘a3 c6 16.♘xc4 bxc4 17.♕xc4 ♕b7 18.e6 f6 19.♖d7 ♕b5 20.♕xb5 cxb5 21.♘d4 ♖c8 22.♗e3 ♘g6 23.♖xa6 ♘e5 24.♖b7 ♗c5 25.♘f5 0-0 26.h3

                                   1-0

Fischer, Robert
Ree, Hans

Netanya 1968 (7)

1.e4 e5 2.♘f3 ♘c6 3.♗b5 a6 4.♗a4 ♘f6 5.0-0 ♘xe4 6.d4 b5 7.♗b3 d5 8.dxe5 ♗e6 9.♕e2 ♗e7 10.♖d1 0-0 11.c4 bxc4 12.♗xc4 ♕d7 13.♘c3 ♘xc3 14.bxc3 f6 15.exf6 ♗xf6

16.♗g5 ♘a5 17.♕xe6+ ♕xe6
18.♗xd5 ♕xd5 19.♖xd5 ♗xc3
20.♖c1 ♗b4 21.♖xc7 ♖ac8 22.♖a7
♖c2 23.♖dd7 ♗c3 24.♖ac7 h6
25.♗e3   1-0

Kasparov,Garry
Anand,Viswanathan

New York Wch m 1995 (10)

1.e4 e5 2.♘f3 ♘c6 3.♗b5 a6 4.♗a4
♘f6 5.0-0 ♘xe4 6.d4 b5 7.♗b3 d5
8.dxe5 ♗e6 9.♘bd2 ♘c5 10.c3 d4
11.♘g5!? dxc3 12.♘xe6 fxe6
13.bxc3 ♕d3 14.♗c2!! ♕xc3
15.♘b3 ♘xb3 16.♗xb3 ♘d4 17.♕g4
♕xa1 18.♗xe6 ♖d8 19.♗h6! ♕c3!
20.♗xg7 ♕d3 21.♗xh8 ♕g6 22.♗f6
♗e7 23.♗xe7 ♕xg4 24.♗xg4 ♔xe7
25.♖c1! c6 26.f4 a5 27.♔f2 a4
28.♔e3 b4 29.♗d1! a3 30.g4+−
♖d5 31.♖c4 c5 32.♔e4 ♖d8
33.♖xc5 ♘e6 34.♖d5 ♖c8 35.f5
♖c4+ 36.♔e3 ♘c5 37.g5 ♖c1
38.♖d6   1-0

Morozevich,Alexander
Ponomariov,Ruslan

Biel 2004 (10)

1.e4 e5 2.♘f3 ♘c6 3.♗b5 a6 4.♗a4
♘f6 5.0-0 ♘xe4 6.d4 b5 7.♗b3 d5
8.dxe5 ♗e6 9.♘bd2 ♘c5 10.c3 d4
11.♘g5 ♕xg5 12.♕f3 0-0-0
13.♗xe6+ fxe6 14.♕xc6 ♕xe5
15.b4 ♕d5 16.♕xd5 exd5 17.bxc5
dxc3 18.♘b3 d4 19.♗a3 g6 20.♗b4
♗g7 21.a4 d3! 22.axb5 [½-½
Grischuk-Anand, Wijk aan Zee 2005]
22...d2 23.bxa6 [23.c6?! ♔b8
24.♖ad1 ♖d5 (24...axb5 25.♘c5 ♖d5
26.♘a6+ ♔c8 27.♘c5 △ 28.♖a1=)
25.bxa6 ♖hd8 26.♘a1 ♔a7 27.♘c2
♖b8 28.f4! (28.♖b1? (Shirov-Anand,

Mainz rapid 2004) 28...♗f8!−+)
28...♖db5 29.♗a3 ♔xa6 30.♔f2!∞]
23...c2 24.♘xd2 [24.♗xd2? ♗xa1
25.a7 ♔b7 26.♖xa1 ♖d3 27.♘a5+
♔a8 28.♘c4 ♖d4−+] 24...♗xa1
25.♖xa1 ♖he8 26.♖c1! [26.c6? ♔b8
27.♖c1 ♖e4! 28.♗c3 ♖c4 29.♖xc4
♖d3 30.♖b2+ ♔a8! 31.♗a5 ♖c1+
32.♘f1 ♖dd1∓ Gild.Garcia-V.Mikha-
levski, Montreal 2004; 26.a7!? ♔b7
27.a8♕+ ♖xa8 28.♖c1 ½-½ Delchev-
Gyimesi, Nova Gorica 2004] 26...♖e4
27.♗c3 ♖c4 28.♖xc2 ♖d3 29.♖b2
[29.♖a2?! ♔b8 30.♗a5 ♖c1+ 31.♘f1
♖dd1 32.g3 ♖xf1+ 33.♔g2 ♖g1+
34.♔f3 ♖xc5 35.♗d2] 29...♖cxc3
30.a7 ♖a3 31.♖b8+ ♔d7 32.a8♕
♖xa8 33.♖xa8 ♖xd2 [½-½ Külaots-
Rytshagov, Finland tt 2004/05] 34.g4
♔c6 35.♔g2 ♔xc5 36.♔g3 ♖d7
37.f4 ♔d4 38.♖a1 ♖f7 39.♖d1+ ♔e3
40.♖e1+ ♔d4 41.♖d1+   ½-½

Metger,Johannes
Tarrasch,Siegbert

Frankfurt ch-GER 1887 (13)

1.e4 e5 2.♘f3 ♘c6 3.♗b5 a6 4.♗a4
♘f6 5.0-0 ♘xe4 6.d4 b5 7.♗b3 d5
8.dxe5 ♗e6 9.c3 ♗c5 10.♗f4 g5
11.♗e3 ♗xe3 12.fxe3 g4 13.♘d4
♘xe5 14.♘d2 ♘c5 15.♕e1 0-0
16.♕g3 ♕g5 17.♖ae1 ♘cd3 18.♖e2
c5 19.♘4f3 ♕g7 20.♘xe5 ♕xe5
21.♕xe5 ♘xe5 22.e4 d4 23.cxd4
cxd4 24.♗xe6 fxe6 25.♘b3 ♖xf1+
26.♔xf1 ♖f8+ 27.♔e1 ♘d3+
28.♔d2 ♘f4 29.♖f2 e5 30.♘c5 ♖c8
31.♘d7 d3 32.♘f6+ ♔g7 33.♘xg4
♖c2+ 34.♔e1 ♘xg2+ 35.♔f1 d2
36.♔e2 h5 37.♔d1 ♖xb2 38.♖xg2
♖b1+ 39.♔xd2 ♖b2+   0-1

Boleslavsky,Isaak
Ragozin,Viacheslav
Moscow 1942

1.e4 e5 2.♘f3 ♘c6 3.♗b5 a6 4.♗a4 ♘f6 5.0-0 ♘xe4 6.d4 b5 7.♗b3 d5 8.dxe5 ♗e6 9.c3 ♗c5 10.♘bd2 0-0 11.♗c2 f5 12.♘b3 ♗a7 13.♘bd4 ♘xd4 14.♘xd4 ♗xd4 15.cxd4 f4 16.f3 ♘g3 17.hxg3 fxg3 18.♕d3 ♗f5 19.♕xf5 ♖xf5 20.♗xf5 ♕h4 21.♗h3 ♕xd4+ 22.♔h1 ♕xe5 23.♗d2 c5 24.♖ae1 ♕xb2 25.♗f4 ♕f6 26.♗xg3 d4 27.♖e6 ♕g5 28.♔h2 c4 29.f4 ♕h5 30.f5 d3 31.f6 gxf6 32.♖f5 ♕g6 33.♖exf6 ♕g7 34.♗f4 c3 35.♖g5 ♖d8 36.♗e6+ ♔h8 37.♗e5 1-0

Boleslavsky,Isaak
Botvinnik,Mikhail
Sverdlovsk 1943 (11)

1.e4 e5 2.♘f3 ♘c6 3.♗b5 a6 4.♗a4 ♘f6 5.0-0 ♘xe4 6.d4 b5 7.♗b3 d5 8.dxe5 ♗e6 9.c3 ♗c5 10.♘bd2 0-0 11.♗c2 f5 12.♘b3 ♗b6 13.♘bd4 ♘xd4 14.♘xd4 ♗xd4 15.cxd4 f4 16.f3 ♘g3 17.hxg3 fxg3 18.♕d3 ♗f5 19.♕xf5 ♖xf5 20.♗xf5 ♕h4 21.♗h3 ♕xd4+ 22.♔h1 ♕xe5 23.♗d2 c5 24.♖ae1 ♕xb2 25.♗f4 d4 26.♗xg3 d3 27.♗e5 ♕xa2 28.♗d6 ♕b2 29.♗e6+ ♔h8 30.♗e5 ♕d2 31.f4 c4 32.f5 ♖f8 33.♖e4 c3 34.♖ef4 ♖f6 35.♖4f2 ♕h6+ 36.♔g1 b4 37.♖f3 d2 38.♗b3 ♕h4 39.♖d3 ♖f8 40.♖g3 ♕e7 41.♗d4 ♖f6 42.♖e3 ♕d7 43.♖f4 a5 44.♖fe4 ♖f8 45.f6 gxf6

46.♖g3 h6 47.♖h4 ♔h7 48.♔h2 f5 49.♗e3 ♕c6 50.♗f4 ♖d8 51.♗e5 ♕b7 52.♗e6 ♖f8 53.♗f4 ♕g7 54.♖xg7+ ♔xg7 55.♗b3 ♖d8 56.♗e5+ ♔g6 57.♖d4 ♖e8 58.♗f4 ♖e1 59.♖d6+ ♔g7 60.♗xh6+ ♔h7 61.♗g5 ♖b1 62.♗c2 ♖c1 63.♗xf5+ ♔g7 64.♖d7+ ♔f8 65.♗xd2 cxd2 66.♖xd2 b3 67.♖d8+ ♔e7 68.♖a8 ♖a1 69.g4 ♔f6 70.♖b8 a4 71.♖b4 ♔g5 72.♔g2 ♔f6 73.♖b6+ ♔e5 74.♖b5+ ♔f6 75.♖b6+ ♔e5 76.♖b4 ♔f6 77.♔h2 ♔g5 78.♖b5 ♖c1 79.♗d7+ ♔f4 80.♗e6 ♖c2+ 81.♔h3 b2 82.♗a2 a3 83.♖f5+ ♔e3 84.♖a5 ♖c3 85.♔h4 ♔f4 86.♖a4+ ♔e5 87.g5 ♖c1 88.♖xa3 ♖a1 89.♖b3 ♖xa2 ½-½

Smyslov,Vasily
Reshevsky,Samuel
USA-URS radio m 1945 (1)

1.e4 e5 2.♘f3 ♘c6 3.♗b5 a6 4.♗a4 ♘f6 5.0-0 ♘xe4 6.d4 b5 7.♗b3 d5 8.dxe5 ♗e6 9.c3 ♗c5 10.♘bd2 0-0 11.♗c2 f5 12.♘b3 ♗b6 13.♘bd4 ♘xd4 14.♘xd4 ♗xd4 15.cxd4 f4 16.f3 ♘g3 17.hxg3 fxg3 18.♕d3 ♗f5 19.♕xf5 ♖xf5 20.♗xf5 ♕h4 21.♗h3 ♕xd4+ 22.♔h1 ♕xe5 23.♗d2 ♕xb2 24.♗f4 c5 25.♗e6+ ♔h8 26.♗xd5 ♖d8 27.♖ad1 c4 28.♗xg3 c3 29.♗e5 b4 30.♗b3 ♖d2 31.f4 h5 32.♖b1 ♖f2 33.♖fe1 ♕d2 34.♖bd1 ♕b2 35.♖d8+ ♔h7 36.♗g8+ ♔g6 37.♖d6+ ♔f5 38.♗e6+ ♔g6 39.♗d5+ ♔h7 40.♗e4+ ♔g8 41.♗g6 1-0

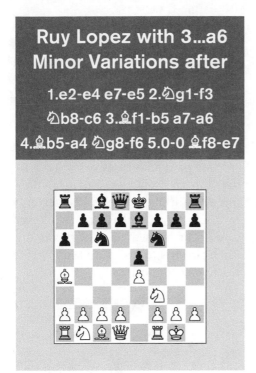

Ruy Lopez with 3...a6 Minor Variations after

1.e2-e4 e7-e5 2.♘g1-f3 ♘b8-c6 3.♗f1-b5 a7-a6 4.♗b5-a4 ♘g8-f6 5.0-0 ♗f8-e7

Black's most frequently played response on the fifth move in the above sequence is 5...♗e7, after which his threat to take on e4 becomes real. In addition to the main continuation 6.♖e1, which defends e4, White can also choose from several interesting alternatives:

A)   6. ♘b1-c3

Playable, but it lacks bite. It is more enterprising in the Ruy Lopez to occupy the centre with c3 and d4 and develop the knight with the moves ♘d2-f1-g3, with good prospects on the kingside.

	6. ...	**b7-b5**
	7. ♗a4-b3	**d7-d6**

The position is balanced.

B)   6. d2-d3

Less innocuous than it appears.

	6. ...	**b7-b5**

	7. ♗a4-b3	**d7-d6**

White has a flexible position: he can either play on the queenside with a4 or move the b1-knight to g3 by way of d2 and f1; or he can also slowly prepare the occupation of the centre with c3 and d4. The game is characterized by a slow positional struggle with opportunities for both sides; at times transposing to the **Anti-Archangel** or the **Anti-Marshall**, in which White plays the solid d3.

C)   6. d2-d4

opens the game, but Black has nothing to fear:

	6. ...	**e5xd4**
	7. ♖f1-e1	

Or 7.e5 ♘e4 8.♘xd4 ♘xd4 9.♕xd4 ♘c5 10.♘c3 0-0! with equality.

	7. ...	**b7-b5**
	8. e4-e5!?	

8.♗b3 d6 9.♗d5 *(9.♘xd4?? loses a piece after 9...♘xd4 10.♕xd4 c5 and 11...c4)* 9...♘xd5 10.exd5 ♘e5 11.♘xd4 with equality.

	8. ...	**♘c6xe5!**
	9. ♖e1xe5	**d7-d6!**

and Black does not have any problems; indeed he has the advantage of the two bishops.

D)   6. ♕d1-e2

The so-called **Worrall Attack**. White defends e4 with the queen so the rook can have the d1-square, thus making the pawn moves to c3 and d4 more effective. This plan is highly logical and dangerous, and Black's best way to counter would seem to be to play in the spirit of the Marshall:

6.   ...   b7-b5
7.   ♗a4-b3   0-0

8.   c2-c3   d7-d5!?

At this point, *9.exd5 seems to be dangerous because of 9...♗g4!, the idea being 10.dxc6 e4*. Therefore White falls back on 9.d3, and after 9...♖e8 10.♘bd2 ♗f8 11.♖e1 (to make the f1-square available for the knight) 11...♗b7, we have reached a middlegame position with equal possibilities for both players: White has some kingside prospects, while Black has good central control.

E)   6. ♗a4xc6

The most popular of the minor variations, and is called the **Exchange Varia-**

tion Deferred by some. It seems to go against common sense to take on c6 after having lost a tempo with the retreat to a4. However, in comparison with the exchange on the 4th move, the situation is different.

6.   ...   d7xc6

The knight on f6 and the bishop on e7 are not particularly active, whereas in the normal Exchange Variation these pieces are usually developed effectively by going respectively to g6 via e7, and to d6. The consequence of this is that Black also has to lose tempi in order to harmonize his position.

However, after

7.   d2-d3   ♘f6-d7
8.   ♘b1-d2   0-0
9.   ♘d2-c4   f7-f6
10. ♘f3-h4   ♘d7-c5

Black still maintains equality. It should be stressed that the percentage of draws with this variation is unusually high, and thus it could be an optimal choice for white players against stronger opponents.

Ruy Lopez Marshall Attack

1.e4 e5 2.♘f3 ♘c6 3.♗b5 a6
4.♗a4 ♘f6 5.0-0 ♗e7 6.♖e1
b5 7.♗b3 0-0 8.c3 d5

With 6.♖e1, White has defended the e4-pawn and made the threat of ♗xc6 and then ♘xe5 real. Apart from the rare 6...d6, which is along the lines of the **Steinitz Deferred**, Black almost always proceeds with 6...b5, and after 7.♗b3 he has two possibilities:

1) To head into the so-called **Closed Spanish** with ...d6 and ...0-0 (or first ...0-0 and then ...d6);

2) To continue ambitiously after 7...0-0 8.c2-c3, playing Frank Marshall's idea: the aggressive move 8...d7-d5!?. Black sacrifices the e5-pawn for a strong attack against the white king. The story goes that Marshall kept the idea of this pawn sacrifice secret for years, saving it up for a future encounter with Capablanca. He played it against him (New York 1918) in the hope of ruining the young Cuban's growing reputation. However, Capablanca met the prepared variation with sangfroid. He found the best moves over the board, 'refuting' the surprise weapon and winning.

The refutation was so convincing that the original move of the American player 11...♘f6 has now been replaced by 11...c6, as suggested by the very same Marshall 20 years after this losing encounter! Almost one hundred years of attempting to refute the Marshall has not borne fruit. Indeed, the results of hundreds of games demonstrate that the Marshall Attack is one of Black's best systems. Certainly the forcing nature of the line, in which a good memory is more important than creative play, is not always to many black players' taste. It also does not appeal to some because there are various lines in which White can force an early draw. As a consequence, this aggressive gambit is ironically seen by many professional players as a good way to get a draw against players of their own strength, while they prefer the Closed Spanish when looking for a win against weaker players.

However, we should take one step back:

There are many white players who do not enjoy playing against the Marshall. Among these is Garry Kasparov, who after 7...0-0 always chose one of the so-called **Anti-Marshall** lines: i.e. a variation in which White does not play 8.c3, and therefore the ...d5 advance is less appealing.

The most traditional Anti-Marshall line begins with **8.a4** (even if in the first years of the new millennium there has been a shift towards 8.h3 ♗b7 9.d3). During the 1990s, the most popular response to the a4 pawn advance was 8...♗b7 9.d3 d6, notwithstanding that after 10.♘bd2!

(Kasparov's move) White's win rate was good. However, also in this case opinions have changed, and the alternative move 8...b4!? is becoming more popular, even if in the past it was considered to be a move of dubious quality.

Another quick look at some of the subtle psychology that occurs in practical modern chess: as already stated, those intending to play the Closed Spanish can play 7...d6 and 8...0-0 in any order they like. However, if Black likes the positions that arise by employing Anti-Marshall lines, he can set off a smokescreen by beginning with

7...0-0, reserving the possibility of the Marshall, and if White plays unsuspectingly he can continue normally with 8...d6. If instead Black prefers the positions arising from the closed systems and does not like the Anti-Marshall systems, he will usually play 7...d6.

Let's see what happens after

9. e4xd5   ♘f6xd5

9...e4?! has not stood the test of time.

10. ♘f3xe5   ♘c6xe5
11. ♖e1xe5

Now we have the initial position of the **Marshall Attack**.

The d5-knight is *en prise* and needs to be either moved or defended, after which the white rook will be exposed, which facilitates Black's counterplay. When the variation was first introduced, 11...♘f6 was exclusively played. However, after 12.d4 ♗d6 13.♖e1 ♘g4 14.h3 ♕h4 15.♕f3! ♘xf2!? 16.♗d2!, or **16.♖e2!** (the move found by Capablanca over the board), experts agree that White has a clear advantage.

11...♗b7 is not often played, even if after 12.♕f3 ♗d6! 13.♗xd5! c6! 14.♖e2 cxd5 15.d4 ♕c7, Black has gained some positional compensation.

11. ...   c7-c6

By far the most popular move, and objectively the best. It has been used since the end of the 1930s – after Marshall first played his attack it took some twenty years to find the best move! In our age of the Internet and Fritz it could take as little as 20 minutes!

12. d2-d4

12.d3 prepares the lines in which White plays ♖e4. This is not often played, but the results with it are encouraging.

12. ...   ♗e7-d6
13. ♖e5-e1   ♕d8-h4
14. g2-g3

Black's attack is obviously too strong after 14.h3? ♗xh3.

14. ...   ♕h4-h3

Black has an obvious initiative against the weakened position of the castled white king. For years, at this point people have almost exclusively played 15.♗e3 ♗g4 16.♕d3 (the only option, to be able to return to f1 after ...♗f3) 16...♖ae8 17.♘d2 ♖e6 – in some lines this is a preparation for a transfer to h6 – 18.a4. White seeks counterplay on the queenside, and now, after 18...bxa4, 18...♕h5 or 18...f5, we reach highly theoretical po-

sitions on which we have yet to hear the last word. However, the general opinion is that the positions are dynamically balanced.

Recently, in the diagrammed position the move

15. ♖e1-e4!?

has become quite popular. The idea is to get rid of the intruder on h3 with the follow-up ♖h4. Black prevents this with

15. ...   g7-g5!

This pawn cannot be captured, because after 16.♗xg5 ♕f5 Black will win one of the two undefended white pieces.

16. ♕d1-f3   ♗c8-f5

The usual follow-up.

Here White makes an energetic exchange sacrifice with

17. ♗b3-c2!

Black can either accept this or refuse with 17...♗f4!?. After either of these options the position is difficult to assess.

Even after this short introduction you have probably already realized that the Marshall is alive and kicking. It is therefore fully understandable why many white players try to avoid it altogether.

Capablanca,Jose Raul
Marshall,Frank
New York 1918

1.e4 e5 2.♘f3 ♘c6 3.♗b5 a6 4.♗a4 ♘f6 5.0-0 ♗e7 6.♖e1 b5 7.♗b3 0-0 8.c3 d5 9.exd5 ♘xd5 10.♘xe5 ♘xe5 11.♖xe5 ♘f6 12.♖e1 ♗d6 13.h3 ♘g4 14.♕f3 ♕h4 15.d4 [15.hxg4 ♗h2+! 16.♔f1 ♗xg4 17.♕e4 ♗f4! 18.g3 ♕h2 19.♖e3 ♖ae8 20.♕d5 ♗xg3! 21.♖xg3 (21.♕xf7+ ♔h8!) 21...♗e2+ 22.♔e1 ♗f3+—+] **15...♘xf2 16.♖e2** [16.♗d2!] **16...♗g4 17.hxg4** [17.♕xf2 ♗g3 18.♕f1 ♗xe2 19.♕xe2 ♖ae8—+] **17...♗h2+ 18.♔f1 ♗g3 19.♖xf2 ♕h1+ 20.♔e2 ♗xf2 21.♗d2 ♗h4 22.♕h3 ♖ae8+ 23.♔d3 ♕f1+ 24.♔c2 ♗f2 25.♕f3 ♕g1 26.♗d5 c5 27.dxc5 ♗xc5 28.b4 ♗d6 29.a4 a5 30.axb5 axb4 31.♖a6 bxc3 32.♘xc3 ♗b4 33.b6 ♗xc3 34.♗xc3 h6 35.b7 ♖e3 36.♗xf7+** [36...♖xf7 (36...♔h7 37.♕f5+ ♔h8 38.♖xh6X) 37.b8♕+ ♔h7 38.♖xh6+ ♔xh6 (38...gxh6 39.♕xf7X) 39.♕h8+ ♔g6 40.♕h5X] **1-0**

Polgar,Judit
Adams,Michael
Dos Hermanas 1999 (6)

1.e4 e5 2.♘f3 ♘c6 3.♗b5 a6 4.♗a4 ♘f6 5.0-0 ♗e7 6.♖e1 b5 7.♗b3 0-0 8.c3 d5 9.exd5 ♘xd5 10.♘xe5 ♘xe5 11.♖xe5 c6 12.d3 ♗d6 13.♖e1 ♕h4 14.g3 ♕h3 15.♖e4 ♕f5 16.♘d2 ♕g6 17.♖e1 f5 18.♕f3 ♔h8 19.♗d1 f4 20.g4 h5 21.h3 ♘f6 22.♕g2 hxg4 23.hxg4 ♗xg4 24.♖e6 ♕h5 25.♗xg4 ♘xg4 26.♖xd6 ♖ae8 27.♘e4 ♘e5 28.f3 ♘xf3+ 29.♔f2 ♘h4 30.♕h1 g5 31.b4 g4 32.♗b2 g3+ 33.♔g1 ♘f3+

34.♔g2 ♘h2 35.c4+ ♔g8 36.♕d1 f3+ 37.♔xg3 ♕g4+ 38.♔f2 ♕h4+ 39.♔e3 ♕f4+ 40.♔d4 ♕e5+ 41.♔e3 ♘g4+ 42.♔d2 ♕xb2+ 43.♕c2 ♕xa1 44.♖g6+ ♔h7 45.♖xg4 f2 **0-1**

Kotronias,Vasilios
Beliavsky,Alexander
Istanbul Ech 2003 (3)

1.e4 e5 2.♘f3 ♘c6 3.♗b5 a6 4.♗a4 ♘f6 5.0-0 ♗e7 6.♖e1 b5 7.♗b3 0-0 8.c3 d5 9.exd5 ♘xd5 10.♘xe5 ♘xe5 11.♖xe5 c6 12.d3 ♗d6 13.♖e1 ♕h4 14.g3 ♕h3 15.♖e4 ♕f5 16.♘d2 ♕g6 17.♖e1 f5 18.f4 ♗xf4 19.♕f3 ♗b8 20.♗xd5+ cxd5 21.♘b3 ♗b7 22.♗f4 ♗xf4 23.♕xf4 d4 24.♘xd4 ♖ae8 25.♖xe8 ♕xe8 26.♔f2 ♕f7 27.♖e1 h6 28.♖e2 ♕d5 29.♔e1 ♕xa2 30.♘e6 ♖f7 31.♘d8 **1-0**

Leko,Peter
Anand,Viswanathan
Cap d'Agde rapid 2003 (3)

1.e4 e5 2.♘f3 ♘c6 3.♗b5 a6 4.♗a4 ♘f6 5.0-0 ♗e7 6.♖e1 b5 7.♗b3 0-0 8.c3 d5 9.exd5 ♘xd5 10.♘xe5 ♘xe5 11.♖xe5 c6 12.♖e1 ♗d6 13.g3 ♗f5 14.d4 ♕d7 15.♗e3 ♖ae8 16.♘d2 ♗g4 17.♕c2 ♗f5 18.♕c1 h5 19.♘f3 ♗g4 20.♘h4 ♖e6 21.♗d1 f5 22.♗xg4 hxg4 23.♗g5 f4 24.♕d2 ♖fe8 25.♖xe6 ♕xe6 26.gxf4 ♕e2 27.f5 ♕e4 28.♖f1 ♗f4 29.♗xf4 ♘xf4 30.f3 gxf3 31.♘xf3 ♖f8 32.♕e1 ♕xf5 33.♔h1 ♕h3 34.♕f2 ♘h5 35.♔g1 ♖f4 36.♕e3 ♕g4+ 37.♔h1 ♘g3+ 38.hxg3 ♕h3+ 39.♔g1 ♕xg3+ 40.♔h1 ♖h4+ 41.♘xh4 ♕xe3 42.♘g2 ♕e2 43.♖f5 ♕xb2 44.♖c5 ♕xa2 45.♖xc6 a5 **0-1**

Kuzmin,Gennady
Malinin,Vasily

Sudak 2002 (9)

1.e4 e5 2.♘f3 ♘c6 3.♗b5 a6 4.♗a4 ♘f6 5.0-0 ♗e7 6.♖e1 b5 7.♗b3 0-0 8.c3 d5 9.exd5 ♘xd5 10.♘xe5 ♘xe5 11.♖xe5 c6 12.d4 ♗d6 13.♖e1 ♛h4 14.g3 ♛h3 15.♗e3 ♗g4 16.♛d3 ♖ae8 17.♘d2 ♖e6 18.c4 ♗f4 19.cxd5 ♖h6 20.♛e4 ♛xh2+ 21.♔f1 ♗xe3 22.♖xe3 ♖f6　　0-1

Ponomariov,Ruslan
Anand,Viswanathan

Linares 2002 (14)

1.e4 e5 2.♘f3 ♘c6 3.♗b5 a6 4.♗a4 ♘f6 5.0-0 ♗e7 6.♖e1 b5 7.♗b3 0-0 8.c3 d5 9.exd5 ♘xd5 10.♘xe5 ♘xe5 11.♖xe5 c6 12.d4 ♗d6 13.♖e1 ♛h4 14.g3 ♛h3 15.♖e4 g5 16.♛e2 f5 17.♗xd5+ cxd5 18.♖e6 f4 19.♖xd6 ♗g4 20.♛f1 ♛xf1+ 21.♔xf1 ♖ae8 22.♗d2 ♗h3+ 23.♔g1 fxg3 24.hxg3 ♖e2 25.♗e3 ♖xe3 26.fxe3 ♖f1+ 27.♔h2 g4 28.♖xd5　　½-½

Kramnik,Vladimir
Leko,Peter

Brissago Wch m 2004 (8)

1.e4 e5 2.♘f3 ♘c6 3.♗b5 a6 4.♗a4 ♘f6 5.0-0 ♗e7 6.♖e1 b5 7.♗b3 0-0 8.c3 d5 9.exd5 ♘xd5 10.♘xe5 ♘xe5 11.♖xe5 c6 12.d4 ♗d6 13.♖e1 ♛h4 14.g3 ♛h3 15.♖e4 g5 16.♛f1 ♛h5 17.♘d2 ♗f5 18.f3 ♘f6 19.♖e1 ♖ae8 20.♖xe8 ♖xe8 21.a4 ♛g6 22.axb5 ♗d3 23.♛f2 ♖e2 24.♛xe2 ♗xe2 25.bxa6 ♛d3 26.♔f2 ♗xf3 27.♘xf3 ♘e4+ 28.♔e1 ♘xc3 29.bxc3 ♛xc3+ 30.♔f2 ♛xa1 31.a7 h6 32.h4 g4　　0-1

Shirov,Alexey
Aronian,Levon

Moscow Tal Memorial 2006 (4)

1.e4 e5 2.♘f3 ♘c6 3.♗b5 a6 4.♗a4 ♘f6 5.0-0 ♗e7 6.♖e1 b5 7.♗b3 0-0 8.c3 d5 9.exd5 ♘xd5 10.♘xe5 ♘xe5 11.♖xe5 c6 12.d4 ♗d6 13.♖e1 ♛h4 14.g3 ♛h3 15.♖e4 g5 16.♛f1 ♛h5 17.♘d2 ♗f5 18.f3 ♘f6 19.a4 ♘xe4 20.♘xe4 ♛g6 21.♘xd6 ♛xd6 22.♗xg5 ♛g6 23.♛c1 ♗d3 24.axb5 axb5 25.♖xa8 ♖xa8 26.♔f2 ♗c4 27.♗xc4 bxc4 28.g4 ♖e8 29.♗f4 ♛d3 30.♔g3 ♛e2 31.♛b1 ♛e1+ 32.♛xe1 ♖xe1 33.♗d6 ♖g1+ 34.♔f2 ♖b1 35.♗a3 ♔g7 36.♔g3 ♔g6 37.h3 h5 38.♔h4? ♖g1! 39.♗c5 ♖g2 40.♗a3 f6 41.gxh5+ ♔f5 42.f4 ♖g8 43.♗d6 ♔e6 44.h6?! ♔xd6 45.♔h5 f5 46.h7 ♖h8 47.♔g6 ♔e7 48.♔g7 ♔e8 49.♔g6 ♔f8 50.h4 ♔e7 51.♔g7 ♔e8 52.♔g6 ♔f8 53.h5 ♔e7 54.♔g7 ♔e8! 55.♔g6 ♔f8 56.h6 ♔e8–+ 57.♔f6 ♖xh7 58.♔g6 ♖f7 [59.h7 ♖f8 60.♔g7 ♖h8 61.♔xh8 ♔f8 62.b4 cxb3–+]　　0-1

Svidler,Peter
Leko,Peter

Morelia/Linares 2007 (5)

1.e4 e5 2.♘f3 ♘c6 3.♗b5 a6 4.♗a4 ♘f6 5.0-0 ♗e7 6.♖e1 b5 7.♗b3 0-0 8.c3 d5 9.exd5 ♘xd5 10.♘xe5 ♘xe5 11.♖xe5 c6 12.d4 ♗d6 13.♖e1 ♛h4 14.g3 ♛h3 15.♖e4 g5 16.♛f1 ♛h5 17.♘d2 f5 18.♗d1 ♛h6 19.♖e1 f4 20.♘e4 ♗c7 21.♗f3 ♗h3 22.♛d3 ♖f7 23.♗d2 ♖af8 24.♗h1 ♖g7 25.♗f3 ♖gf7 26.♗h1 ♖g7 27.♗f3 ♖gf7　　½-½

Ruy Lopez
Closed Variation

**1.e4 e5 2.♘f3 ♘c6 3.♗b5 a6
4.♗a4 ♘f6 5.0-0 ♗e7 6.♖e1 b5
7.♗b3 d6 8.c3**

Let's stop to look at the real reasons for White's last move, given the worrying fact that so many opening books do not explain the thinking behind it. 8.c2-c3 could seem to be preparation for d2-d4. However, the real reason is highly tactical. The most natural would appear to be the immediate 8.d2-d4, leaving the c3-square for the knight, but this allows an unpleasant tactical intermezzo: 8...♘xd4 9.♘xd4 exd4 10.♕xd4??

10...c5 followed by 11...c4, and the bishop on b3 is captured.

So as not to lose the bishop, the gambit continuation **10.c3!?** becomes necessary. It gives some compensation, but probably not enough. Now we can understand in what sense 8.c3 prepares for d4: it makes the c2-square available for the fleeing bishop.

8. ...   0-0

Here White usually plays the prophylactic move 9.h3 anticipating ...♗g4 which would indirectly put pressure on the centre.

It is worth mentioning the interesting possibility to get off the beaten path by proceeding to a direct occupation of the centre with

9. d2-d4   ♗c8-g4

Thematic. Black already threatens 10...♗xf3, requiring White to recapture with the g-pawn. However, White has resources with which he can liven up the game. This can be done in two ways:

A)   10. ♗c1-e3

defends d4 and keeps the position fluid. At this point Black concedes the centre, in order to attack it next with

10. ...   e5xd4
11. c3xd4   ♘c6-a5

12. ♗b3-c2   c7-c5

with active piece play.

The position is fluid and complex and provides both players with possibilities.

B)   10. d4-d5

A move typical of the Ruy Lopez. It gains space and closes the centre, giving Black a free hand on the flanks.

10. ...   ♘c6-a5
11. ♗b3-c2

11...c6! is a pawn move of fundamental theoretical importance. White cannot support the pawn chain with c3-c4, as he can in other variations, and must therefore take on c6. After 12.h3! ♗c8! 13.dxc6 ♕c7 14.♘bd2 ♕xc6, play is dynamic and the weakness of the e4-pawn is compensated for by the customary free play afforded to the white pieces.

Let's now go back to **9.h3**.

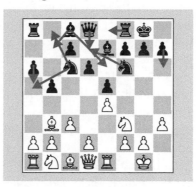

This is the most solid and the most popular move: White wishes to prevent ...♗g4 and postpones d2-d4 to the following move. This is the initial position of the **Closed Spanish**, the most popular system of all the Open Games and a chapter of fundamental importance in the history of chess openings. The number of arrows in the diagram shows the unusually high number of moves which can be played by Black, which is testimony to how flexible his position is. The subsequent game is usually characterized by heavy manoeuvring, with possible complications being played out at a later stage in the game. Now we will have a quick look at Black's options, in ascending order of popularity:

A)   9. ...   ♕d8-d7

One of Smyslov's many interesting ideas in the Closed Spanish: it frees the d8-square so Black can make the move ...♖e8 without having to worry about ♘g5, as f7 can be defended with ...♘d8.

10. d2-d4   ♖f8-e8
11. ♘b1-d2   ♗e7-f8

Black prevents the manoeuvre ♘f1-g3, as after ...exd4 the e4-pawn can be taken.

12. ♗b3-c2   ♗c8-b7

Now, 13.♘f1 does not work because of 13...exd4 followed by 14...♘b4.

13. a2-a3

and we have a customary Ruy Lopez position that is rich in opportunities for both sides.

B)   9. ...   a6-a5

Black's intention is to gain space on the queenside and also to exchange off White's light-squared bishop.

10. d2-d4   a5-a4
11. ♗b3-c2   e5xd4
12. c3xd4   ♘c6-b4

However, after

13. d4-d5!

with the idea of ♘d4, the weakness of the pawn on b5 and White's more harmonious development give White a clear advantage.

C)   9. ...   ♗c8-e6
10. d2-d4!

The threatened fork by the pawn obliges Black to exchange:

10. ...   ♗e6xb3
11. ♕d1xb3

The ambitious 11.axb3 is also playable because, after 11...exd4 12.cxd4, the badly placed pawn on b3 is compensated for by White's piece activity and occupation of the centre.

11. ...   ♕d8-d7
12. ♘b1-d2   ♖f8-e8
13. ♘d2-f1

White has an edge.

D)   9. ...   h7-h6

The **Smyslov Variation**. Here also, the idea is to play ...♖e8 and ...♗f8 without having to worry about ♘g5. However,

10. d2-d4   ♖f8-e8
11. ♘b1-d2   ♗e7-f8

12. ♘d2-f1!

Indeed, after 12...exd4?! 13.cxd4

13...♘xe4?? does not work because of 14.♗d5, which wins a piece: this is a tactical motif that does not exist in the 9...♕d7 variation.

12. ...   **♗c8-d7**

Also sometimes 12...♗b7 is seen.

13. ♘f1-g3   **♘c6-a5**

14. ♗b3-c2   **c7-c5**

We have a position reminiscent of the Chigorin Variation (9...♘a5 – see Variation I further on) with the usual slight advantage for White. Sometimes the knight goes to b6 with 14...♘c4 15.b3 ♘b6, which controls a4 and d5. The knight is certainly better placed on b6 than on a5. However, also in this case White has the freer position.

E)   **9. ...**   **♘f6-d7**

10. d2-d4   **♗e7-f6**

Keres's interesting idea: by putting d4 under pressure, you prevent the natural ♘bd2 because the d4-pawn would be left undefended. However, Black's two last moves were non-developing and White profits from this with the thematic

11. a2-a4   **♗c8-b7**

12. ♘b1-a3!

highlighting the Achilles' heel of many Ruy Lopez variations: the b5-pawn.

At this point Black usually responds with

12. ...   **e5xd4!?**

13. c3xd4   **♖f8-e8**

but if the truth be told, White's mobile centre seems to be more of a strength than a weakness.

F)   **9. ...**   **♖f8-e8**

transposes to the **Zaitsev Variation** after

10. d2-d4   **♗c8-b7**

G)   **9. ...**   **♗c8-b7**

The popular **Zaitsev Variation**.

Here we have a set-up which tries to prevent the manoeuvre ♘b1-d2-f1-g3 by exerting pressure on e4 at the opportune moment.

10. d2-d4   **♖f8-e8**

Preparing ...♗f8. It should now be noted that if White plays 11.♘g5, Black must return the rook to f8, with the tacit idea of a draw by repetition after 12.♘f3. If Black does not want the draw that would occur if he repeats the move 12...♖e8, he will need to fall back on minor lines that are not as effective.

After the usual

    11. ♘b1-d2

the reply

    11. ...   ♗e7-f8

prevents 12.♘f1 because after 12...exd4 13.cxd4 Black can win the pawn on e4; while 12.♘g5 is useless now because of 12...♖e7.

Here, White can choose between two very different plans:

G1)   12. ♗b3-c2

The positional approach. White defends the e4-pawn, but above all prepares d4-d5 followed by b2-b3 and c3-c4, to keep the pawn chain intact when Black attacks its head with ...c6.

    12. ...   g7-g6
    13. d4-d5   ♘c6-b8
    14. b2-b3   c7-c6
    15. c3-c4   ♘b8-d7

Black's position is solid, even if White can patiently try to exploit his space advantage.

G2)   12. a2-a4
More aggressive.

    12. ...   h7-h6
    13. ♗b3-c2

To transfer the bishop to d3 and attack b5. Black usually responds with the violent

    13. ...   e5xd4!?
    14. c3xd4   ♘c6-b4
    15. ♗c2-b1   c7-c5
    16. d4-d5   ♘f6-d7
    17. ♖a1-a3   f7-f5!?

This leads to strategically and tactically complex positions. White's centre will collapse, after which the b7-bishop becomes active and Black's mass of centre pawns can begin to march down.

Black's problem is the safety of his king: The manoeuvre ♘h2-g4, the ♖a3 ready to slide over to f3 or g3, and the two white bishops bearing down on the castled black king are ingredients for truly exciting play. Some of the best examples are to be found in the historic Kasparov-Karpov matches. We are yet to hear the last word on these variations, but on the whole the results favour White.

H)   9. ...   ♘c6-b8
The renowned **Breyer Variation**, which was advocated almost a hundred years ago by the strong Hungarian player of the same name.

With this paradoxical move Black intends to regroup his pieces more harmoniously. The knight is heading for d7 to give support to the e5-pawn and if the bishop is developed to b7, it will be immediately active. Furthermore, the way is cleared for the c-pawn.

Breyer's move is not as popular now as it was in the 1970s, when it was played at the highest level by the likes of Spassky and Karpov. However, it still has its supporters: Kramnik, Beliavsky and Mamedyarov, just to name some notable advocates.

 10. d2-d4   ♞b8-d7
 11. ♘b1-d2

Black's best response to 11.c4 is 11...c6!.

 11. ...   ♗c8-b7
 12. ♗b3-c2

Defending e4 in order to play 13.♘f1.

 12. ...   ♖f8-e8
 13. ♘d2-f1

It is worth noting that 13.b3!? is becoming increasingly popular, with the idea of playing d4-d5 and c3-c4.

 13. ...   ♗e7-f8
 14. ♘f1-g3 g7-g6
 15. a2-a4   c7-c5
 16. d4-d5   c5-c4
 17. ♗c1-g5 h7-h6
 18. ♗g5-e3 ♘d7-c5
 19. ♕d1-d2

White has some possibilities for taking the initiative on the kingside, and also at times on the queenside with ♖a3 and ♖ea1. That said, Black's position is both solid and flexible and tournament results have been satisfactory for the second player.

I) 9. ...   ♞c6-a5

The **Chigorin Variation**, which is the oldest, and over the years also the most popular line. However, it is not necessarily the best. Black immediately begins to become active on the queenside, which would appear to be the most natural plan. But on a5, the knight remains sidelined for a while and more often than not Black's pieces are less harmoniously coordinated in comparison to other variations of the Closed Spanish.

 10. ♗b3-c2 c7-c5

111

11. d2-d4 ♕**d8-c7**

Defending e5; another move which has its adherents is 11...♘d7, which was played many times by Keres.

12. ♘b1-d2

Now Black has two important strategic choices: to keep the position closed or to open up the c-file and start active piece play.

I1) **12. ...** ♘**a5-c6**

and now White can keep the game closed with 13.d5 ♘d8 14.a4, with a slightly better position thanks to his space advantage and the sad-looking knight on d8; otherwise he can open up the position with

13. d4xc5

hoping to take advantage of the outposts on d5 and f5. After

13. ... **d6xc5**

14. ♘d2-f1 ♗**c8-e6**
15. ♘f1-e3 ♖**a8-d8**
16. ♕d1-e2 **c5-c4**
17. ♘e3-f5

the position is difficult to evaluate.

I2) **12. ...** **c5xd4**

This is the most popular line.

13. c3xd4 ♘**a5-c6**

attacking the d4-pawn and preparing ...♘b4.

13...♗d7 is also played. Now, after 14.♘f1 ♖ac8 15.♘e3 ♘c6 16.d5 ♘b4 17.♗b1 a5 18.a3 ♘a6 19.b4!, White is a little better. Black cannot take twice on b4, because after 19...axb4 20.axb4 ♘xb4?? 21.♗d2

surprisingly, the knight on b4 cannot be defended (21...♕c5 22.♕b3) and it has no escape square.

14. ♘d2-b3

Why not the usual 14.♘f1? For the simple reason you would lose a pawn, as after the exchanges on d4 the bishop on c2 is unprotected.

14. ...   a6-a5

Threatening 15...a4.

15. ♗c1-e3

Defending d4.

15. ...   a5-a4
16. ♘b3-d2   ♘c6-b4
17. ♗c2-b1   ♗c8-d7
18. a2-a3   ♘b4-c6
19. ♗b1-d3   ♘c6-a5

Noteworthy is the 'knight's tour' made by this black knight: c6-a5-c6-b4-c6-a5.

20. ♕d1-e2   ♕c7-b8
21. ♖a1-c1

White will take advantage of the opening of the queenside.

Schlechter, Carl
Prokes, Ladislav
Prague 1908 (14)
1.e4 e5 2.♘f3 ♘c6 3.♗b5 a6 4.♗a4 ♘f6 5.0-0 ♗e7 6.♖e1 b5 7.♗b3 d6 8.c3 0-0 9.h3 h6 10.d4 exd4 11.cxd4 ♘a5 12.♗c2 ♗b7 13.♘bd2 ♖e8 14.♘f1 d5 15.e5 ♘e4 16.♘g3 ♘xg3 17.fxg3 c5 18.♕d3 g6 19.e6 f5 20.g4 ♗h4 21.♖e2 ♘c6 22.gxf5 ♘b4 23.♕d2 ♘xc2 24.♕xh6 ♕f6 25.♖xc2 ♕xf5 26.♖xc5 ♗f6 27.♖c7 ♖e7 28.♖xe7 ♗xe7 29.♘f4 ♕h5 30.♕xh5 gxh5 31.♗g5 ♗b4 32.a3 ♗a5 33.e7 ♗c7 34.♖e1 ♖e8 35.♖e6 ♔g7 36.♗h6+ ♔g8 37.♘g5   1-0

Adams, Michael
Beliavsky, Alexander
Leon Ech-tt 2001 (9)
1.e4 e5 2.♘f3 ♘c6 3.♗b5 a6 4.♗a4 ♘f6 5.0-0 ♗e7 6.♖e1 b5 7.♗b3 d6 8.c3 0-0 9.h3 ♖e8 10.d4 ♗b7 11.♘bd2 ♗f8 12.d5 ♘b8 13.♘f1 ♘bd7 14.♘3h2 ♘c5 15.♗c2 c6 16.b4 ♘cd7 17.dxc6 ♗xc6 18.♘g4 ♘xg4 19.hxg4 ♘b6 20.♕d3 g6 21.♖d1 ♕c7 22.♕f3 ♗d7 23.♗b3 ♗e6 24.♗g5 a5 25.♘e3 ♗xb3 26.axb3 axb4 27.cxb4 ♖xa1 28.♖xa1 d5!⇄ 29.♘xd5 ♘xd5 30.exd5 e4 31.♕e3 ♕d7 32.♕d2 ♕xg4 33.♖a6 ♗xb4 34.♕c1 ♗c5 35.♖c6 e3! 36.♗xe3 ♗xe3 37.fxe3 h5∓ 38.♖c7 ♖e5 39.♕f1 ♖f5 40.♕a1 ♔h7 41.d6 ♕g3 42.♖c8 ♕xe3+ 43.♔h1 f6 44.♖c3 ♕d2 45.♖c7+ ♔h6 46.d7 ♖e5 47.♕c3 ♕xc3 48.♖xc3 ♖d5-+ 49.♖c7 f5 50.b4 ♔g5 51.♖b7 ♔g4 52.♔h2 h4 53.♖xb5 ♖xd7 54.♖c5 ♖d2 55.♔g1 ♖b2

56.b5 h3 57.♖c4+ f4 58.gxh3+ ♔g3
59.♔f1 ♖xb5 60.♔e2 g5   0-1

Kasparov,Garry
Karpov,Anatoly

London/Leningrad Wch m 1986 (16)

1.e4 e5 2.♘f3 ♘c6 3.♗b5 a6 4.♗a4
♘f6 5.0-0 ♗e7 6.♖e1 b5 7.♗b3 d6
8.c3 0-0 9.h3 ♗b7 10.d4 ♖e8
11.♘bd2 ♗f8 12.a4 h6 13.♗c2 exd4
14.cxd4 ♘b4 15.♗b1 c5 16.d5 ♘d7
17.♖a3 c4 18.♘d4 ♕f6 19.♘2f3 ♘c5
20.axb5 axb5 21.♘xb5 ♖xa3
22.♘xa3 ♗a6 23.♖e3 ♖b8! 24.e5!
dxe5 25.♘xe5 ♘bd3? 26.♘g4?
♕b6! 27.♖g3 g6! 28.♗xh6 ♕xb2
29.♕f3! ♘d7?! 30.♗xf8 ♔xf8
31.♔h2! ♖b3! 32.♗xd3 cxd3?
[32...♖xa3!=]   33.♕f4   ♕xa3?
34.♘h6   ♕e7   35.♖xg6   ♕e5
36.♖g8+   ♔e7   37.d6++–   ♔e6
38.♖e8+   ♔d5   39.♖xe5+   ♘xe5
40.d7 ♖b8 41.♘xf7   1-0

Kasparov,Garry
Karpov,Anatoly

Lyon/New York Wch m 1990 (20)

1.e4 e5 2.♘f3 ♘c6 3.♗b5 a6 4.♗a4
♘f6 5.0-0 ♗e7 6.♖e1 b5 7.♗b3 d6
8.c3 0-0 9.h3 ♗b7 10.d4 ♖e8
11.♘bd2 ♗f8 12.a4 h6 13.♗c2 exd4
14.cxd4 ♘b4 15.♗b1 c5 16.d5 ♘d7
17.♖a3 f5 18.♖ae3 ♘f6 19.♘h2 ♔h8
20.b3 bxa4 21.bxa4 c4 22.♗b2 fxe4
23.♘xe4 ♘fxd5 24.♖g3 ♖e6 25.♘g4
♕e8 26.♘xh6 c3 27.♘f5 cxb2
28.♕g4 ♗c8 29.♕h4+ ♖h6 30.♘xh6
gxh6 31.♔h2 ♕e5 32.♘g5 ♕f6
33.♖e8 ♗f5 34.♕xh6+ ♕xh6
35.♘f7+ ♔h7 36.♗xf5+ ♕g6
37.♗xg6+ ♔g7 38.♖xa8 ♗e7 39.♖b8
a5 40.♗e4+ ♔xf7 41.♗xd5+   1-0

Anand,Viswanathan
Adams,Michael

San Luis Wch-FIDE 2005 (3)

1.e4 e5 2.♘f3 ♘c6 3.♗b5 a6 4.♗a4
♘f6 5.0-0 ♗e7 6.♖e1 b5 7.♗b3 d6
8.c3 0-0 9.h3 ♗b7 10.d4 ♖e8
11.♘bd2 ♗f8 12.a4 h6 13.♗c2 exd4
14.cxd4 ♘b4 15.♗b1 c5 16.d5 ♘d7
17.♖a3 c4 18.axb5 axb5 19.♘d4
♕b6 20.♘f5 ♘e5 21.♖g3 g6 22.♘f3
♘ed3 23.♕d2 ♗xd5 24.♘xh6+
♗xh6 25.♕xh6 ♕xf2+ 26.♔h2
♘xe1 27.♘h4 ♘ed3 28.♘xg6
♕xg3+ 29.♔xg3 fxg6 30.♕xg6+
♔f8 31.♕f6+ ♔g8 32.♗h6   1-0

Anand,Viswanathan
Kasimdzhanov,Rustam

Bastia rapid 2006 (4)

1.e4 e5 2.♘f3 ♘c6 3.♗b5 a6 4.♗a4
♘f6 5.0-0 ♗e7 6.♖e1 b5 7.♗b3 d6
8.c3 0-0 9.h3 ♖e8 10.d4 ♗b7 11.♘bd2
♗f8 12.a4 h6 13.♗c2 exd4 14.cxd4
♘b4 15.♗b1 c5 16.d5 ♘d7 17.♖a3 c4
18.♘d4 ♕f6 19.♘2f3 ♘c5 20.♖ee3
♘bd3 21.axb5 axb5 22.♘xb5 ♖xa3
23.♘xa3 ♖xe4 24.♘xc4 ♘xf2 25.♕e2
♘xh3+ 26.gxh3 ♕g6+ 27.♔f2 ♖xe3
28.♗xe3 ♕xb1 29.♘xc5 dxc5 30.♕e5
♕c2+ 31.♘fd2 ♕d3 32.d6 ♕xh3
33.♕e8 ♗c8 34.♘e5 ♕e6 35.♕xe6
♗xe6 36.♘e4 f5 37.d7 ♗xd7 38.♘f6+
gxf6 39.♘xd7 ♔f7 40.♔f3 ♗d6
41.♘b6 ♔e6 42.b3 h5 43.♘c4 h4   0-1

Kotronias,Vasilios
Bologan,Viktor

Moscow Aeroflot Open 2007 (6)

1.e4 e5 2.♘f3 ♘c6 3.♗b5 a6 4.♗a4
♘f6 5.0-0 ♗e7 6.♖e1 b5 7.♗b3 d6
8.c3 0-0 9.h3 ♗b7 10.d4 ♖e8
11.♘bd2 ♗f8 12.a4 h6 13.♗c2 exd4

14.cxd4 ♘b4 15.♗b1 c5 16.d5 ♘d7
17.♖a3 c4 18.axb5 axb5 19.♘d4
♛b6 20.♘f5 ♘e5 21.♖g3 g6 22.♘f3
♘ed3 23.♗e3 ♛d8 24.♗xh6 ♛f6
25.♛d2 ♘xe1 26.♘h2 ♖xc4
27.♗xe4 ♖a1 28.♘f1 ♗xd5 29.♗xd5
♛xf5 30.♗xf7+ ♔xf7 31.♗xf8 ♘bd3
32.♛h6 ♛xf2+ 33.♔h2 ♛f6
34.♘e3 ♘f2 35.♘c2 ♘xc2 36.♖f3
♖h1+ 37.♔g3 ♘e4+ 38.♔g4 ♖f1
39.♖xf6+ ♖xf6 40.♛g7+ ♔e6
41.♛e7+ ♔d5 42.♗h6 ♖f2 43.♛b7+
♔d4 44.g3 ♘e3+ 45.♗xe3+ ♔xe3
46.♛a7+ ♔d3 47.♛a3+ ♔e2
48.♛a8 d5 49.♛e8 ♖f3 50.h4 b4
51.♔h3 ♖xg3+ 52.♔h2 c3 53.bxc3
bxc3 54.h5 c2 55.♛b5+ ♖d3   0-1

Fischer,Robert
Spassky,Boris

Reykjavik Wch m 1972 (10)

1.e4 e5 2.♘f3 ♘c6 3.♗b5 a6 4.♗a4
♘f6 5.0-0 ♗e7 6.♖e1 b5 7.♗b3 d6
8.c3 0-0 9.h3 ♘b8 10.d4 ♘bd7
11.♘bd2 ♗b7 12.♗c2 ♖e8 13.b4 ♗f8
14.a4 ♘b6 15.a5 ♘bd7 16.♗b2 ♛b8
17.♖b1 c5 18.bxc5 dxc5 19.dxe5
♘xe5 20.♘xe5 ♛xe5 21.c4 ♛f4=
22.♗xf6 ♛xf6 23.cxb5 ♖ed8 24.♛c1
♛c3 25.♘f3 ♛xa5 26.♗b3! axb5
27.♛f4 ♖d7 28.♘e5 ♛c7 29.♖bd1!
♖e7 30.♗xf7+ ♖xf7 31.♛xf7+ ♛xf7
32.♘xf7 ♗xe4 33.♖xe4 ♔xf7 34.♖d7+
♔f6 35.♖b7 ♖a1+ [≥ 35...b4] 36.♔h2
♗d6+ 37.g3 b4 38.♔g2 h5 39.♖b6
♖d1 40.♔f3! ♔f7?! [40...g5!] 41.♔e2
♖d5 42.f4! g6 43.g4! hxg4 44.hxg4 g5
45.f5 ♗e5 46.♖b5 ♔f6 47.♖exb4 ♗d4
48.♖b6+ ♔e5 49.♔f3! ♖d8 50.♖b8
♖d7 51.♖4b7 ♖d6 52.♖b6 ♖d7 53.♖g6
♔d5 54.♖xg5 ♗e5 55.f6 ♔d4 56.♖b1!
                                1-0

Topalov,Veselin
Adams,Michael

Cap d'Agde rapid 2003 (2)

1.e4 e5 2.♘f3 ♘c6 3.♗b5 a6 4.♗a4
♘f6 5.0-0 ♗e7 6.♖e1 b5 7.♗b3 d6
8.c3 0-0 9.h3 ♘a5 10.♗c2 c5 11.d4
♘d7 12.♘bd2 exd4 13.cxd4 ♘c6
14.d5 ♘ce5 15.a4 ♗b7 16.♘xe5
♘xe5 17.f4 ♘d7 18.♘f3 ♖e8 19.♗d2
♗f6 20.♖a2 g6 21.♔h2 ♗g7 22.b3
♛c7 23.♗d3 c4 24.bxc4 ♘c5
25.♗c2 bxc4 26.♖a3 a5 27.♗c3
♗a6 28.♗xg7 ♔xg7 29.♘d4 ♘d3
30.♗xd3 cxd3 31.♘c6 ♔g8 32.♛d2
♖ac8 33.♖b3 f5 34.exf5 ♛f7
35.♖e6 ♗c4 36.♖xd3 ♗xd3
37.♛xd3 gxf5 38.♘d4 ♖f8 39.♘b5
♖cd8 40.♘xd6 ♛c7 41.♛g3+ ♛g7
42.♛e3 ♔h8 43.♘e8 ♛b2 44.d6
♖g8 45.♛e5+ ♛xe5 46.fxe5 ♖gxe8
47.♖xe8+ ♖xe8 48.d7   1-0

Karpov,Anatoly
Unzicker,Wolfgang

Nice ol 1974 (3)

1.e4 e5 2.♘f3 ♘c6 3.♗b5 a6 4.♗a4
♘f6 5.0-0 ♗e7 6.♖e1 b5 7.♗b3 d6
8.c3 0-0 9.h3 ♘a5 10.♗c2 c5 11.d4
♛c7 12.♘bd2 ♘c6 13.d5 ♘d8 14.a4
♖b8 15.axb5 axb5 16.b4 ♘b7 17.♘f1
♗d7 18.♗e3 ♖a8 19.♛d2 ♖fc8
20.♗d3 g6 21.♘g3 ♗f8 22.♖a2 c4
23.♗b1 ♛d8 24.♗a7!! [the idea is to
double the rooks on the a-file] 24...♘e8
25.♗c2 ♘c7 26.♖ea1 ♛e7 27.♗b1
♗e8 28.♘e2 ♘d8 29.♘h2 ♗g7 30.f4
f6 31.f5 g5 32.♗c2 ♗f7 33.♘g3 ♘b7
34.♗d1 h6 35.♗h5 ♛e8 36.♛d1
♘d8 37.♖a3 ♔f8 38.♖1a2 ♔g8
39.♘g4 ♔f8 40.♘e3 ♔g8 41.♗xf7+
♘xf7 42.♛h5 ♘d8 43.♛g6 ♔h8
44.♘h5   1-0

Semi-Open Games

Minor Defences after 1.e4
Owen Defence
Nimzowitsch Defence
Scandinavian Defence
Alekhine Defence
Modern Defence
Pirc Defence
Caro-Kann Defence
French Defence
Sicilian Defence

Minor Defences after

1.e2-e4

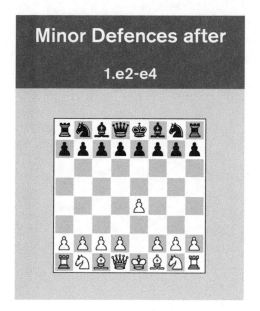

Now we enter the blood-stained battle-ground of the sceptics who have dared to challenge the sanctity of established theory. A word of warning: these minor defences should not be taken lightly. This is a lesson learnt the hard way by a World Champion, Anatoly Karpov, in a game against the late Tony Miles in 1980. The English grandmaster was an aficionado of minor systems, and to the dismay of Karpov as well as purists the world over, he won their encounter using the following minor defence:

| 1. | ... | a7-a6! |

| 2. | d2-d4 | b7-b5 |
| 3. | ♘g1-f3 | |

In some lines of the **Kan Variation of the Sicilian**, it's better to refrain from ♘c3, so as not to be bothered by ...b5-b4.

3.	...	♗c8-b7
4.	♗f1-d3	♘g8-f6
5.	♕d1-e2	e7-e6
6.	0-0	c7-c5
7.	c2-c3	

White has good prospects in the centre. In addition, with the pawn advance a2-a4, there are also attacking possibilities on the queenside. However, the solidity of Black's position should not be underestimated.

Even more provocative is **Basman's idea**

| 1. | ... | g7-g5?! |

Black can find himself in a type of Modern Defence after 2.d4 h6, with what is called an 'extended fianchetto'. In general it pays not to be dogmatic. However, the lost tempo and, more importantly, the weakening of the kingside seems to be a bit beyond the pale. Therefore, with correct play, these defects should guarantee White a clear advantage.

Owen Defence

1.e2-e4 b7-b6

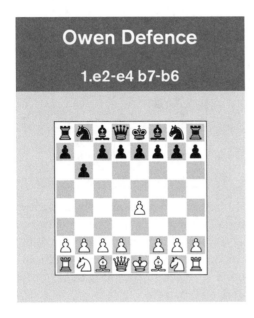

1...b6 is the **Owen Defence**. Following 2.c4 e6 3.d4, the position quickly transposes to the **English Defence**.

| | 2. | d2-d4 | ♗c8-b7 |
| 3. | ♗f1-d3! | e7-e6 |

3...f5?! 4.exf5! ♗xg2 5.♕h5+ g6 6.fxg6 ♗g7 seems to be too risky on account of 7.♕f5! (7.gxh7+ is also promising) 7...♘f6 8.♗h6! ♗xh6 9.gxh7 with 10.♕g6+ and 11.♕xh6 to come.

4.	♘g1-f3	c7-c5
5.	c2-c3	♘g8-f6
6.	♕d1-e2!	

with a small but meaningful advantage.

Nimzowitsch Defence

1.e2-e4 ♘b8-c6

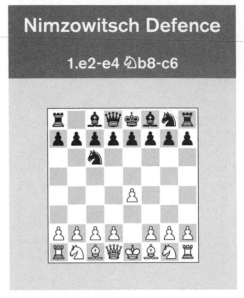

The most respectable of the minor systems is 1...♘c6. This defence was championed by the great Aaron Nimzowitsch, and thus carries his name. Its ambitious objective is to apply pressure to White's d4-pawn, but in practice this doesn't usually happen. Placing the two centre pawns side by side is the most natural and ambitious response for White.

2. d2-d4

You can also come across 2.♘f3, which gives Black the opportunity to 'repent' and to transpose to a more common member of the Open Games with 2...e5. However, the type of player who opts for 1...♘c6 is not likely to enjoy a mainstream opening, and will therefore probably go for 2...d6 or 2...d5.

The orthodox continuation is

2. ... d7-d5

You should note that 2...e5!? is increasingly being played nowadays, but after 3.dxe5! ♘xe5 4.♘f3!, White has a small but clear plus.

3. ♘b1-c3

It is better to maintain the tension. The alternatives 3.e5 ♗f5 or 3.exd5 ♕xd5, even though both plausible, would give Black the active game that he seeks.

3. ... d5xe4

After 3...e6 we have an inferior version of the **French**.

3...♘f6!? is interesting: after 4.e5 ♘d7, *the move 5.♘xd5?! would be weak because of 5...♘db8!.* However, a good move would be 5.♘ce2, which is inspired by the **Steinitz Variation of the French**.

4. d4-d5 ♘c6-e5

4...♘b8 looks too passive.

5. ♕d1-d4!? ♘e5-g6

6. ♕d4xe4!

6.♘xe4 e5!.

6. ... ♘g8-f6

7. ♕e4-a4+ ♗c8-d7

8. ♗f1-b5

White enjoys the advantage, since his d5-pawn renders ...e6, and thereby Black's development, more difficult.

Scandinavian Defence

1.e2-e4 d7-d5

As with the **Petroff Defence**, here is another case of recent re-evaluation. The move ...d7-d5 is the typical freeing move in many defences; just think of some of the examples from the **Sicilian** or the **Ruy Lopez**. Here, however, things are not so simple: after 2.exd5, if Black takes back with the queen he remains behind in development. If, on the other hand, he plays 2...♘f6 so as to take on d5 with the knight; after 3.d4, White gets a nice centre with prospects of further expansion with c2-c4. At least, that is what opening manuals have blindly repeated for years and years.

However, recent practice has demonstrated that this assessment is a little superficial and that there are structural elements present which are favourable for Black: to start with, Black frees himself of the irritating presence of the e4-pawn, which in King's Pawn openings lays the foundation for kingside attacks. In addition, we have a 4:3

kingside pawn majority, which tends to make kingside castling a safer proposition for Black.

It is still true that advancing his pawn to d4 gives White a certain central predominance, at least in terms of space, with greater piece activity as a consequence. It is no surprise that you have the same pawn structure as in the **Caro-Kann** and the **Rubinstein Variation of the French** – which are both solid positions *par excellence*.

2. e4xd5

Now Black can continue in two ways:

A)　2. ...　♕d8xd5

The queen now loses a tempo after

3. ♘b1-c3　♕d5-a5

3...♕d6 is a now relatively fashionable alternative, but it seems less natural.

4. d2-d4

This is thematic as it occupies the centre.

4. ...　♘g8-f6

5. ♘g1-f3

Now Black can play 5...♘c6 to apply pressure on d4 with ...♗g4 and ...0-0-0. However, this plan seems too ambitious to be realistic. Another choice is 5...♗g4 or 5...♗f5.

5. ...　c7-c6

This waiting move is generally preferred. It reserves the options of moving the queen's bishop to f5 or g4 and opens an escape route for the queen. The position is now practically that of a **Caro-Kann** where Black has lost some tempi, and he will lose another with a further queen move. On the other hand, White's knight is more passive on c3 than on e4. Moreover, by following this virtually forced sequence Black has avoided the dangerous **Advance Variation of the Caro-Kann**.

> **6. &f1-c4   &c8-f5**

6...&g4 is also playable.

> **7. &c1-d2   e7-e6**
> **8. ♛d1-e2!**

With the idea of d4-d5.

> **8. ...   &f8-b4!**
> **9. 0-0-0   ♞b8-d7**
> **10. a2-a3   &b4xc3**
> **11. &d2xc3   ♛a5-c7**

Despite White's possession of the bishop pair and a space advantage, Black's position is solid and well defended, and it is therefore not surprising that this line is becoming more and more popular among players who don't want to be overwhelmed by the avalanche of theoretical possibilities that awaits them in more mainstream openings in this computer age.

If Black does not wish to expose the queen, he may prefer:

> **B)   2. ...   ♞g8-f6**
> **3. d2-d4**

For the alternative 3.c4 c6! 4.d4! cxd5, see the **Panov-Botvinnik Attack in the Caro-Kann**. *Instead, after 4.dxc6?! ♞xc6 5.d3 e5, Black has optimum compensation for the pawn.*

> **3. ...   ♞f6xd5**

The sharp 3...&g4!? had a moment of popularity, but Black's compensation for the pawn seems doubtful after 4.f3, followed by 5.&b5+.

> **4. c2-c4**

Or first 4.♞f3.

> **4. ...   ♞d5-b6**
> **5. ♞g1-f3**

Here Black has two plans:

B1) **5. ...** **♝c8-g4**

This looks logical, but White's centre remains strong after

6. ♝f1-e2 **e7-e6**
7. 0-0 **♞b8-c6**
8. ♞b1-c3! **♝f8-e7**

After 8...♝xf3?! 9.♝xf3 ♞xc4 10.d5! White has the advantage.

9. d4-d5! **e6xd5**
10. c4xd5 **♞c6-b4**

11. ♛d1-d4!

Not only hitting the bishop on g4, but also the pawn on g7.

11. ... **♝g4xf3**
12. ♝e2xf3

And White is slightly better. Indeed, if *12...♛c2? 13.♛xg7 ♝f6 14.♛h6 ♞xa1? 15.♖e1+ ♚d7 16.♝g4+, checkmate follows.*

B2) **5. ...** **g7-g6**
6. h2-h3!

A useful prophylactic move.

6. ... **♝f8-g7**
7. ♞b1-c3 **0-0**
8. ♝c1-e3 **♞b8-c6**
9. ♛d1-d2

Preparing to castle queenside.

9. ... **e7-e5**

The only useful move for Black.

10. d4-d5

And now after either 10...♞a5 11.b3, or 10...♞e7 11.g4!, White's prospects seem to be better, even if the tactically and strategically complex game that follows offers Black good chances as well.

Spassky,Boris
Larsen,Bent
Montreal 1979 (17)

1.e4 d5 2.exd5 ♛xd5 3.♞c3 ♛a5 4.d4 ♞f6 5.♞f3 ♝f5 6.♝d2 ♞bd7 7.♝c4 c6 8.♛e2 e6 9.d5 cxd5 10.♞xd5 ♛c5 11.b4 ♛c8 12.♞xf6+ gxf6 13.♞d4 ♝g6 14.h4 h5 15.f4 ♝e7 16.♖h3 ♛c7 17.0-0-0 ♛b6 18.♝e1 0-0-0 19.♞b5 ♞b8 20.♖xd8+ ♚xd8 21.♝f2 ♛c6 22.♝xa7 ♞d7 23.a3 ♛e4 24.♝e3 ♝f5 25.♖g3 ♛c6 26.♞d4 ♛a4 27.♞xf5 ♛xa3+ 28.♚d1 ♛a1+ 29.♝c1 ♝xb4 30.♝b5 ♞b6 31.♛e4 ♛a5 32.♛xb7 1-0

Svidler,Peter
Tiviakov,Sergey
Wijk aan Zee 2007 (2)

1.e4 d5 2.exd5 ♛xd5 3.♞c3 ♛d6 4.d4 ♞f6 5.♞f3 a6 6.g3 ♝g4 7.h3 ♝h5 8.♝g2 ♞c6 9.0-0 0-0-0 10.♝f4 ♛b4 11.g4 ♝g6 12.a3 ♛c4 13.g5 ♞d5 14.♞xd5 ♖xd5 15.c3 ♖d8 16.b3

♕d3 17.♕c1 ♕c2 18.♕e3 e6 19.b4 ♕e4 20.♘d2 ♕xe3 21.fxe3 e5 22.♗g3 exd4 23.cxd4 ♗d6 24.♗xd6 cxd6 25.♖ac1 ♔d7 26.♘c4 h6 27.♘b6+ ♔e8 28.gxh6 ♖xh6 29.♘d5 f6 30.a4 ♗f7 31.b5 axb5 32.axb5 ♘a5 33.♖a1 ♘c4 34.♖a7 ♖h5 35.♘c7+ ♔f8 36.♗xb7 ♖xh3 37.♖f3 ♖h5 38.♗c6 ♖b8 39.♖g3 ♘b6 40.e4 ♘c8 41.♖a1 ♖h4 42.♘a6 ♖b6 43.♘b4 ♖b8 44.♖ga3 ♘b6 45.♖a7 d5 46.♘a6 ♖d8 47.♖b7 ♘c4 48.♘c5 dxe4 49.♖aa7 ♖g4+ 50.♔h2 ♘d6 51.♖xf7+ ♔xf7 52.♘e6+ ♔g8 53.♘xd8 ♘g5 54.♗d5+ ♔h7 55.♘e6 ♘f3+ 56.♔h3 f5 57.♖xg7+ ♖xg7

58.♘xg7 ♘xd4 59.b6 e3 60.♔g2 ♘c2 61.♔f1 ♘b4 62.b7 ♘a6 63.♘xf5 ♔g6 64.♘e7+ ♔f6 65.♘c6   1-0

Topalov, Veselin
Kamsky, Gata
Wijk aan Zee 2006 (1)

1.e4 d5 2.exd5 ♘f6 3.♘f3 ♘xd5 4.d4 ♗f5 5.♗d3 ♗xd3 6.♕xd3 e6 7.0-0 ♘c6 8.c4 ♘b6 9.♘c3 ♗e7 10.♗f4 g5 11.♗g3 g4 12.♘e5 ♘xd4 13.c5 ♗xc5 14.♖ad1 0-0 15.♘e4 ♗e7 16.♘xg4 c5 17.b4 ♘d5 18.bxc5 ♘f5 19.♕f3 ♖c8 20.♗d6 ♘xd6 21.cxd6 ♗h4 22.d7 ♖c6 23.♘e5 ♖c7 24.♕g4+ ♔h8 25.♘d6   1-0

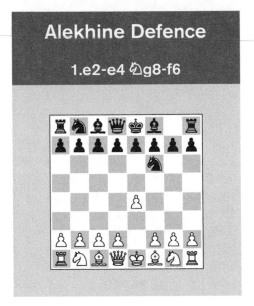

Alekhine Defence

1.e2-e4 ♞g8-f6

A)

4.	c2-c4	♞d5-b6
5.	f2-f4	

This is the **Four Pawns Attack**, unquestionably the critical line of the Alekhine, at least in terms of the philosophy behind strategic theory. It should be noted that instead of supporting the centre with the f-pawn, it has recently become very popular for White to adopt the quiet alternative 5.exd6!?, contenting himself with greater piece mobility and a slight space advantage.

But let's return to 5.f4. How do we evaluate such a position? Is White, with his imposing centre, ready to start a mating attack? Or is his centre a house of cards that is about to collapse? In practice, both of these events occur, and this is why we are looking at some of the most complex and exciting variations in opening literature.

Usually Black aims to put d4 under immediate pressure with

This is one of the most theoretically revolutionary openings in the history of the game. First made famous by the later World Champion Alexander Alekhine in 1921, it is based on a startling concept, which at the time bordered on heresy: to provoke White to advance his pawns in an attempt to prove that these advanced centre pawns are in fact a weakness rather than a strength.

2.	e4-e5	♞f6-d5
3.	d2-d4	

3.c4 ♞b6 4.c5 ♞d5 has its supporters, but it is not at all clear if White's pawn is better on c5 than on c2.

3.♞c3!? is interesting, with the idea of 3...♞xc3 4.dxc3! with active play to compensate for the doubled pawns.

3.	...	d7-d6

The attack on White's pawn centre begins. After ...dxe5 and ...♞c6, the d4-pawn becomes the target. Now White must decide whether to gain further space in the centre or content himself with a quieter approach.

5.	...	d6xe5

However, 5...g6!? or 5...♝f5 are both also possible.

6.	f4xe5	♞b8-c6

The hyper-aggressive 6...c5!? 7.d5 e6 is playable as well.

7.	♝c1-e3!	

If 7.♞f3? ♝g4, White's centre is in crisis.

7.	...	♝c8-f5
8.	♞b1-c3	e7-e6
9.	♞g1-f3	

Now Black generally continues with either the solid 9...♝g4, the ambitious 9...♛d7, or the normal developing move

9.	...	♝f8-e7

This is considered to be the main line, at least in terms of statistical frequency.

10. d4-d5	

Or 10.♝e2.

10.	...	e6xd5
11.	c4xd5	♞c6-b4
12.	♞f3-d4	♝f5-d7
13.	e5-e6	f7xe6
14.	d5xe6	♝d7-c6
15.	♛d1-g4	♝e7-h4+!
16.	g2-g3	♝c6xh1
17.	0-0-0	

This line is not forced, but it gives an idea of the complexity of these variations.

This being the case, it is not a surprise that the percentage of draws in these lines is very low. Nonetheless, years of practical experience, as well as statistics produced by hundreds of games, show that White wins more or less the same percentage of games as he would by employing any other opening. Therefore, the Four Pawns Attack does not refute the Alekhine, as

some believe; nor does it give Black an advantage, as others maintain.

B) 4. ♞g1-f3

Observing the Latin maxim 'in medio stat virtus', White does occupy the centre, but he doesn't overdo it! Play in this line is quiet and the variations are characterized by slow manoeuvring.

Now Black can choose from the following alternatives: 4...♞c6, 4...g6, 4...dxe5 or 4...♝g4.

B1) 4. ... ♞b8-c6

This is ambitious but premature. After

5.	c2-c4	♞d5-b6
6.	e5-e6!	f7xe6

White is on top after either 7.♞g5 or 7.♞c3.

B2) 4. ... g7-g6

This is known as the **Alburt Variation**. This line was very fashionable in the 1980s following its adoption by Fischer in his 1972 World Championship match against Spassky. Today, however, it is seldom used.

5. ♙f1-c4   ♞d5-b6
6. ♙c4-b3   ♙f8-g7

And now, White gains a promising position with either the aggressive 7.♞g5 e6 8.♕f3 or the solid 7.♕e2 ♞c6 8.0-0 0-0 9.h3.

B3)   4. ...   d6xe5

This move was underappreciated in the past, but it is now very popular.

5. ♞f3xe5!

In case of 5.dxe5?! ♗g4, the e5-pawn seems to be more of a weakness than a strength.

At this point 5...♞d7 is playable, but then Black exposes himself to 6.♞xf7!? ♚xf7 7.♕h5+ ♚e6

after which 8.c4 (or also 8.g3!?) 8...♞5f6 9.d5+ ♚d6 10.♕f7! is psychologically demanding for Black, even if it isn't necessarily winning for White. Therefore recently, Black has shown a preference to prepare ...♞d7 with 5...c6, or to fianchetto the ♗f8 with 5...g6, after which the game usually continues as follows: 6.♗c4 c6 7.0-0 ♗g7 8.♜e1 0-0

9.♗b3 ♞d7 10.♞f3! ♞7f6 11.h3, and White has a slight plus.

B4)   4. ...   ♗c8-g4

The **Classical Variation**.

5. ♗f1-e2

White gains nothing with the hyperactive 5.♗c4 c6.

5. ...   e7-e6

Flohr's move 5...c6!? is interesting. But it leaves the door open to the complications that ensue after 6.♞g5!?.

6. 0-0   ♗f8-e7
7. c2-c4   ♞d5-b6
8. ♞b1-c3   0-0
9. h2-h3

The c4-pawn is indirectly defended, as after ...♗xf3 the b7-pawn is hanging. White can also choose not to play h3, but it is generally a useful move.

9. ...   ♗g4-h5
10. ♗c1-e3   d6-d5

The moves 10...a6 and 10...a5 are both interesting, since 11...♗xf3 is a threat, as the a7-square is now free for the rook.

11. c4-c5

11.b3!? and 11.cxd5 are both rare, but playable.

11. ...   ♗h5xf3

In order to take the knight to c4 after 12.♗xf3. But, aware of this, White replies

12. g2xf3!   ♘b6-c8
13. f3-f4

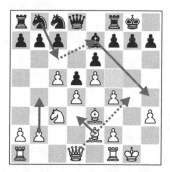

White has a good space advantage and seems to have easy attacking possibilities on the kingside. However, the doubling of the f-pawns makes it difficult to break with f4-f5, and Black's position usually proves surprisingly robust.

Steiner, Endre
Alekhine, Alexander
Budapest 1921 (9)

1.e4 ♘f6 2.e5 ♘d5 3.d4 d6 4.♗g5 dxe5 5.dxe5 ♘c6 6.♗b5 ♗f5 7.♘f3 ♘b4 8.♘a3 ♕xd1+ 9.♖xd1 ♘xc2+ 10.♘xc2 ♗xc2 11.♖c1 ♗e4 12.♘d4 ♗xg2 13.♖g1 0-0-0 14.♘xc6 ♗xc6 15.♗xc6 bxc6 16.♖xc6 ♖d5 17.♗f4 e6 18.♔e2 ♗c5 19.b4 ♗xb4 20.♖xg7 ♖d7 21.♗e3 a5 22.♖c4 h5 23.♖h4 ♗c3 24.♖g5 ♖d5 25.f4 f6 26.♖gxh5 ♖xh5 27.♖xh5 fxe5 28.fxe5 ♗xe5 29.♖h7 ♖b5 30.♔f3 ♖b2 31.♖h5 ♗xh2 32.♖xa5 ♗d6 33.♔e4 ♔d7 34.♗d4 ♖d2 35.♗e3 ♖e2 36.♔d3 ♖e1 37.♗d4 ♖c1 38.♗e3 ♖d1+ 39.♔e4 ♖e1 40.♔d3 e5 41.♗f2 ♖f1 42.♗e3 ♔e6 43.♔e4 ♖h1 44.♗f2 ♖h2 45.♗e3 ♖h4+ 46.♔d3 ♗b4 47.♖a7 c5 48.a3 c4+ 49.♔e2 ♗d6 50.♖a8 ♖h2+ 51.♔d1 ♖h3 52.♔d2 ♔d5 53.♖d8 c3+

54.♔e2 ♔e4 55.♖xd6 ♖xe3+ 56.♔f2 ♖d3 57.♖c6 ♖d2+ 58.♔e1 ♔d3 59.♖d6+ ♔c2 60.♖e6 ♖d5 61.♔e2 ♔b2 62.♖c6 c2   0-1

Leko, Peter
Ivanchuk, Vasily
Odessa rapid 2007 (4)

1.e4 ♘f6 2.e5 ♘d5 3.d4 d6 4.c4 ♘b6 5.exd6 exd6 6.♘c3 ♗e7 7.♗d3 ♘c6 8.♘ge2 ♗g4 9.f3 ♗h5 10.0-0 ♗g6 11.b3 0-0 12.♗e3 ♖e8 13.♗xg6 hxg6 14.♕d2 ♘f6 15.d5 ♘e5 16.♗f2 ♘bd7 17.♘e4 ♗h4 18.♗d4 ♘f6 19.♘4c3 ♘h7 20.♖ad1 a6 21.♔h1 ♕e7 22.♗g1 ♖ad8 23.♘d4 ♘d7 24.♕c2 ♗f6 25.♖d2 ♗e5 26.f4 ♗xd4 27.♗xd4 ♕h4 28.♖e2 ♘hf6 29.♕d3 ♖xe2 30.♕xe2 ♖e8 31.♕f3 ♘c5 32.♗f2 ♕h5 33.♕xh5 gxh5 34.♖e1 ♖xe1+ 35.♗xe1 ♔h7 36.g3 ♔g6 37.♔g2 ♘fe4 38.♘xe4 ♘xe4 39.♔f3 f5 40.h3 ♔f7 41.g4 g6 42.gxh5 gxh5 43.♔e3 ♔e8 44.♔d4 ♔d7 45.♗h4 c6 46.♗e1 c5+   ½-½

Nakamura, Hikaru
Benjamin, Joel
Philadelphia 2006 (4)

1.e4 ♘f6 2.e5 ♘d5 3.c4 ♘b6 4.d4 d6 5.f4 dxe5 6.fxe5 ♘c6 7.♗e3 ♗f5 8.♘c3 e6 9.♘f3 ♗g4 10.♕d2 ♗xf3 11.gxf3 ♕h4+ 12.♗f2 ♕h5 13.c5 ♕xf3 14.♖g1 ♘d5 15.♗g2 ♕f4 16.♘xd5 ♕xd2+ 17.♔xd2 exd5 18.♗xd5 ♖d8 19.♗xc6+ bxc6 20.♔c3 f5 21.b4 ♔d7 22.a4 ♖b8 23.♔c4 a6 24.♖ge1 ♔e6 25.♖ab1 ♗e7 26.b5 axb5+ 27.axb5 cxb5+ 28.♖xb5 c6 29.♖b6 ♖xb6 30.cxb6 ♖b8 31.♖b1 g5 32.b7 ♔d7 33.d5

cxd5+   34.♔xd5   ♔c7   35.♗b6+
♔xb7 36.♗c5+ ♔c7   1-0

Kotronias,Vasilios
Short,Nigel

Gibraltar 2003 (5)

1.e4 ♘f6 2.e5 ♘d5 3.d4 d6 4.c4
♘b6 5.f4 dxe5 6.fxe5 ♘c6 7.♗e3
♗f5 8.♘c3 e6 9.♘f3 ♕d7 10.♗e2
0-0-0 11.0-0 f6 12.d5 ♘xe5
13.♘xe5 fxe5 14.a4 a5 15.♘b5 ♗b4
16.d6 ♘a8 17.c5 ♔b8 18.♗f3 c6
19.♘a3 e4 20.♗e2 b6 21.cxb6
♕xd6 22.♕xd6+ ♖xd6 23.♖ad1
♖hd8 24.♖xd6 ♖xd6 25.g4 ♗d2
26.♗f2 ♔b7 27.♘c4 ♖d5 28.gxf5
exf5 29.♖d1 ♗b4 30.♗e3 g6 31.♔f2
♖xd1 32.♗xd1 c5 33.♗b3 ♘xb6
34.♘xb6 ♔xb6 35.♗g8   1-0

Velimirovic,Dragoljub
Martz,William

Vrnjacka Banja 1973

1.e4 ♘f6 2.e5 ♘d5 3.c4 ♘b6 4.d4
d6 5.f4 ♗f5 6.♘c3 dxe5 7.fxe5 e6
8.♘f3 ♗b4 9.♗d3 ♗g4 10.0-0 ♘c6
11.c5 ♗xc3 12.bxc3 ♘d5 13.♕e1
♘de7 14.♖b1 ♖b8 15.♘g5 ♗f5
16.♗xf5 ♘xf5 17.♕e4 ♕d7 18.d5
♘ce7 19.c4 c6 20.d6 ♘g6 21.g4
♘h6 22.♖b3 0-0 23.♖bf3 b6 24.h4
♖fe8 25.♘xh7 ♘xh4 26.♖h3   1-0

Short,Nigel
Timman,Jan

Tilburg 1991 (4)

1.e4 ♘f6 2.e5 ♘d5 3.d4 d6 4.♘f3 g6
5.♗c4 ♘b6 6.♗b3 ♗g7 7.♕e2 ♘c6
8.0-0 0-0 9.h3! a5 10.a4 dxe5 11.dxe5
♘d4 12.♘xd4 ♕xd4 13.♖e1 e6
14.♘d2! ♘d5 15.♘f3 ♕c5 16.♕e4
♕b4 17.♗c4! ♘b6 18.b3! ♘xc4

19.bxc4 ♖e8 20.♖d1 ♕c5 21.♕h4 b6
22.♗e3 ♕c6?! 23.♗h6 ♗h8 24.♖d8!
♗b7 25.♖ad1 ♗g7 26.♖8d7! ♖f8
27.♗xg7 ♔xg7 28.♖1d4 ♖ae8
29.♕f6+ ♔g8 30.h4 h5 31.♔h2 ♖c8
32.♔g3! ♖ce8 33.♔f4! ♗c8 34.♔g5!!
[34...♗xd7 35.♔h6! with mate on g7] 1-0

Spassky,Boris
Fischer,Robert

Reykjavik Wch m 1972 (19)

1.e4 ♘f6 2.e5 ♘d5 3.d4 d6 4.♘f3
♗g4 5.♗e2 e6 6.0-0 ♗e7 7.h3 ♗h5
8.c4 ♘b6 9.♘c3 0-0 10.♗e3 d5 11.c5
♗xf3 12.♗xf3 ♘c4 13.b3! ♘xe3
14.fxe3 b6 15.e4! c6 16.b4 bxc5
17.bxc5 ♕a5 18.♘xd5 ♗g5 19.♗h5!
cxd5 20.♗xf7+ [≥ 20.exd5] 20...♖xf7
21.♖xf7 ♕d2! 22.♕xd2 ♗xd2
23.♖af1 ♘c6 24.exd5= exd5 25.♖d7
♗e3+ 26.♔h1 ♗xd4 27.e6 ♗e5!
28.♖xd5 ♖e8 29.♖e1 ♖xe6 30.♖d6!
♔f7 31.♖xc6 ♖xc6 32.♖xe5 ♔f6
33.♖d5 ♔e6 34.♖h5 h6 35.♔h2 ♖a6
36.c6 ♖xc6 37.♖a5 a6 38.♔g3 ♔f6
39.♔f3 ♖c3+ 40.♔f2 ♖c2+   ½-½

Almasi,Zoltan
Varga,Zoltan

Budapest zt-playoff 1995 (1)

1.e4 ♘f6 2.e5 ♘d5 3.d4 d6 4.♘f3
♗g4 5.♗e2 e6 6.0-0 ♗e7 7.c4 ♘b6
8.h3 ♗h5 9.♘c3 0-0 10.♗e3 ♘8d7
11.exd6 cxd6 12.b3 d5 13.c5 ♘c8
14.b4 a6 15.♘d2 ♗xe2 16.♕xe2
♗f6 17.♘b3 ♘e7 18.♖fd1 ♘c6 19.a3
b6 20.♘a4 bxc5 21.♘axc5 ♘xc5
22.♘xc5 ♖a7 23.♘xa6 ♕a8 24.b5
♘b8 25.♘c5 ♖xa3 26.♕b2 ♖a5
27.♗d2 ♖a7 28.♗f4 ♖c8 29.b6 ♖xa1
30.♖xa1 ♕c6 31.b7 ♖e8 32.♗xb8
♖xb8 33.♖a8   1-0

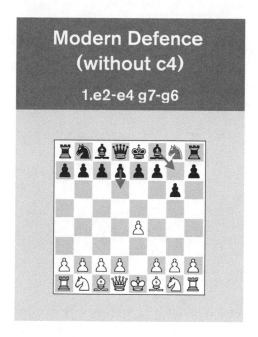

Modern Defence (without c4)

1.e2-e4 g7-g6

The development of the bishop on g7 and the pawn move to d6 signify that this is a close relative of the Pirc. However, the difference is that in the Modern the knight is absent from f6, or it develops to this square later on. When White pushes his pawn to c4, the game resembles the **Queen's Pawn Opening**: in other cases it remains more in the realm of the Semi-Open Games.

Here we have a very elastic defence. Black almost ignores what White does and develops on his own account with a wide number of plans to choose from. This makes the Modern an ideal defence for those among you that don't want a system for which you need to learn a lot of established theory. Black sometimes chooses not to make the classical pawn move ...d6, preferring instead to set up a **Modern/Caro-Kann hybrid** with pawns on c6 and d5.

However, usually Black does proceed with ...d6 (which can also be played on

the first move) and ...♗g7. He can push his pawns to e5 or to c5, or otherwise to c6-b5 or a6-b5. Black may decide to develop the b8-knight to d7 or to c6, and the g8-knight to f6 or e7. White is not urgently required to defend e4 as in the **Pirc**, and therefore he, too, has a wide variety of approaches available to him.

As a result of all this, it is very difficult to systematically examine this chameleonic defence.

2. d2-d4   ♗f8-g7

Now White can play 3.c4, which we will discuss in the second volume of this series. However, it is more common to play 3.♘f3 or 3.♘c3.

A)   3. ♘g1-f3   d7-d6
**   4. c2-c3!?**

The advance of the c-pawn, often already played on the 3rd move, is an option not available in the Pirc: White supports the centre and takes the bite out of a possible ...b7-b5. However, this is not a developing move and White must content himself with a minuscule advantage in the centre. However, for players who enjoy a slow manoeuvring struggle it could be the right choice.

4.♗e2 usually transposes to the **Classical Pirc** if Black plays ...♘f6.

4.	...	♘g8-f6
5.	♗f1-d3	0-0
6.	0-0	

The results are slightly in White's favour, but Black's position offers many resources.

B)   3. ♘b1-c3

White proceeds naturally, reserving the option to aggressively push the f-pawn. Or otherwise to continue in a less directly challenging way. The only drawback of the natural development of the knight to c3 is that it facilitates a counterattack by Black with ...b5-b4.

3.	...	d7-d6

B1)   4. f2-f4

Black can now play 4...♘f6 if he wishes to enter the Pirc. However, he usually opts for the interesting plan

4.	...	c7-c6!?
5.	♘g1-f3	♗c8-g4
6.	♗c1-e3	♕d8-b6

establishing an adventurous, but promising attack on the queenside. The following line is not forced, but reveals a lot about the position:

7.	♕d1-d2	♗g4xf3

8.	g2xf3	♘b8-d7
9.	0-0-0	♕b6-a5

Clearing the way for the b-pawn.

10.	♔c1-b1	b7-b5
11.	h2-h4	♘d7-b6

And it is not clear who will be the first to have a real threat against the opponent's king.

B2)   4. ♗c1-e3

This is a very fashionable move in the **Pirc**, and hence also in the **Modern Defence**. In the spirit of the **English Attack in the Sicilian**, White prepares for ♕d2 and 0-0-0. Usually Black postpones castling short, which could lead to a re-entry in the Pirc. This would not be a bad thing, if it did not give White the chance to use a simple plan of attack: to weaken the black kingside by removing the fianchettoed g7-bishop by means of ♗h6, with interesting chances of an attack against the black king.

For this reason, Black prefers to respond with

4.	...	c7-c6

so as to harass the c3-knight with ...b5-b4.

5.	♕d1-d2	b7-b5

And now it is natural for White to continue with

6. &f1-d3 &b8-d7

The position is strategically complex and offers both players chances, even if results tend to favour White.

B3) 4. &g1-f3

A positional choice.
Now Black can play

4. ... a7-a6

or

4. ... c7-c6

or otherwise transpose to the Pirc with

4. ... &g8-f6

White preserves the small advantage that is his birthright, but Black does not have to deal with any immediate threats. In these variations, more so than in the others, the player with the better strategic skill will win. Ignoring any tactical mishap along the way, of course.

Spassky,Boris
Olafsson,Fridrik
Moscow Alekhine mem 1971 (17)
1.e4 g6 2.d4 &g7 3.c3 &f6 4.&d3 d6 5.f4 e5 6.&f3 &g4 7.fxe5 dxe5 8.&g5 h6 9.&h4 g5 10.&f2 exd4 11.cxd4 &c6 12.&bd2 &h5 13.&b5 &f4 14.0-0 0-0 15.&a4 &e7 16.&fe1 &eg6 17.&f1 &d7 18.&c2 g4 19.&e5 &xe5 20.dxe5 &g6 21.&c4 &g5 22.&e3 &xe5 23.&xc7 &ac8 24.&d6 &c6 25.&a3 h5 26.&ad1 &e6 27.&d5 &xd5 28.exd5 &c2 29.&xa7 g3 30.hxg3 &g4 31.&e2 &xe2 32.&xe2 &xf2 33.&xf2 &e5 34.&d3 &c8 35.d6 &c1+ 36.&d1 &g6 37.&d2 &c8 38.d7 &d8 39.&b3 &g7 40.&f3 f5 41.&e6 f4 42.gxf4 &f6 43.&h2 h4 44.g4 &e4 45.&e3 &b4 46.b3 &d4 47.&e2 &c5 48.&f5 &f6 49.&e8 1-0

Tatai,Stefano
Timman,Jan
Amsterdam B 1970 (2)
1.e4 g6 2.d4 &g7 3.c3 d6 4.&f3 &f6 5.&bd2 0-0 6.&e2 &c6 7.0-0 e5 8.dxe5 &xe5 9.&xe5 dxe5 10.&c2 b6 11.&e1 &b7 12.&f1 &d7 13.&c4 &fe8 14.f3 a5 15.&e3 &c6 16.&a3 &ed8 17.&ad1 &f8 18.&b5 &e6 19.&b3 &xb3 20.axb3 c6 21.&xd8 &xd8 22.&xb6 &d2 23.&c4 &c2 24.&a4 &d7 25.&e3 &c5 26.&c1 &xc1+ 27.&xc1 &d3 28.&e3 &a6 29.&xa5 &xb2 30.&xc6 &d1 31.&b6 &xc3 32.&xe5 &d6 33.&g4 &d3 34.e5 &e7 35.&e3 &g5 36.&c6 &f4 37.&d5 &e2+ 38.&f2 &xh2 39.f4 &xf4 40.&f6+ &g7 41.&g4 1-0

Anand,Viswanathan
Svidler,Peter
Linares 1998 (2)

1.e4 g6 2.d4 ♗g7 3.♘c3 d6 4.♗e3
a6 5.♘f3 b5 6.♗d3 ♘d7 7.e5 ♗b7
8.e6 fxe6 9.♘g5 ♘f8 10.0-0♕ ♘f6
11.♖e1 ♕d7 12.♗d2 h6 13.♘f3 ♖b8
14.a4 b4 15.♘e4 ♘xe4 16.♗xe4
♗xe4 17.♖xe4 ♕c6!? 18.♖e3 ♕c4
19.c3 b3 20.♖e1 g5 21.♗e3 ♕d5
22.♕d3! a5 23.♖a3 ♔f7 24.♘d2
♘g6 25.♕e2! ♘h4 26.f3 ♘g6 27.c4
♕f5 28.♘e4! ♔g8 29.♕d1 ♖b4? [≥
29...g4] 30.♖xb3 ♖xc4?± 31.♖b5
♕f7 32.♖xa5 ♔h7 33.♖b5 d5?
34.♘c5 ♕f5 35.b3 ♖c3 36.♕d2 ♖c2
37.g4! ♘h4 38.gxf5 ♘xf3+ 39.♔h1
♘xd2 40.♖e2 ♘c4 41.♖xc2 ♘xe3
42.♖e2 [42...♘xf5 43.♘xe6 c6
44.♖b6 ♖c8 45.♖c2+−]   1-0

Dominguez,Lenier
Ivanchuk,Vasily
Barcelona 2006 (9)

1.e4 g6 2.d4 d6 3.♘c3 ♗g7 4.♗e3
a6 5.f4 b5 6.♗d3 ♗b7 7.♘f3 ♘d7
8.e5 ♘h6 9.♕e2 ♘b6 10.0-0-0 ♕d7
11.♖hg1 0-0 12.g4 ♘xg4 13.♘g5
♘xe3 14.♕xe3 e6 15.♕h3 h6
16.♘xf7 ♕xf7 17.♖xg6 ♕xf4+
18.♔b1 ♖f7 19.♖dg1 ♘h8 20.♖6g4
♕d2 21.♕h5 ♖af8 22.a3 ♖e7
23.♖xg7 ♖xg7 24.♖xg7 ♖f1+
25.♗xf1 ♔xg7 26.♗d3 ♕g5 27.♕e8
dxe5 28.dxe5 ♕xe5 29.♕e7+ ♔g8
30.♕e8+   ♔g7   31.♕e7+   ♔g8
32.♗h7+   ♔h8   33.♗g6   ♕g7
34.♕d8+   ♕g8   35.♕f6+   ♕g7
36.♕d8+   ♕g8   37.♕xc7   ♘d5
38.♕e5+   ♕g7   39.♕b8+   ♕g8
40.♕e5+   ♕g7   41.♕xe6   ♕f6
42.♕xf6+ ♘xf6 43.♗f5 ♔g7 44.♔c1

♘e8 45.♘e4 ♗xe4 46.♗xe4 ♘d6
47.♗d3 a5 48.♔d2 ♔f6 49.♔e3
♔e5 50.♔f3 b4 51.axb4 axb4
52.♔g4 ♔f6 53.♔f4 ♔e6 54.b3 ♔f6
55.♗c4 ♘f5 56.♔e4 h5 57.♗e2 h4
58.♗g4 ♘d6+ 59.♔f4 ♘b7 60.♗f5
♘c5 61.♔g4 h3 62.♗h7 ♘e6
63.♗d3 ♔e5 64.♔xh3 ♘f4+
65.♔g4 ♘xd3 66.cxd3 ♔d4 67.h4
♔c3 68.h5 ♔xb3 69.h6   1-0

Polgar,Judit
Shirov,Alexey
Linares 1994 (7)

1.e4 g6 2.d4 ♗g7 3.♘c3 c6 4.♘f3
d6 5.♗g5 ♕b6 6.♖b1 ♗g4 7.♗e3
♗xf3 8.gxf3 ♕c7 9.h4 e6 10.h5 d5
11.♕d2 ♘d7 12.b4 ♘gf6 13.h6 ♗f8
14.♗f4 ♕d8 15.♗d3 ♗e7 16.♘e2
0-0 17.c3 b5 18.♔f1 a5 19.a3 ♘b6
20.♖e1 ♘e8 21.♗e5 ♘d6 22.♗g7
♘dc4 23.♕c1 ♖e8 24.e5 axb4
25.axb4 ♖a2 26.♕f4 ♖d2 27.♗b1
♘a4 28.♔g2 ♘ab2 29.♕g4 ♘a3
30.♘f4 ♘xb1 31.♖xb1 ♘d3
32.♘xd3 ♖xd3 33.♖a1 ♖xc3 34.♖a7
♖c4 35.♖ha1 ♖xb4 36.♕f4 c5
37.♖xe7 ♕xe7 38.♗f6 ♕c7 39.♖a6
♖xd4 40.♕g5 ♖a4 41.♖d6 ♖aa8
42.♖c6 ♕a7 43.♗d8 f6 44.♗xf6 c4
45.♕g4 ♕f7 46.♕d4 ♖ec8 47.♕b6
♖xc6 48.♕xc6 ♖b8   0-1

Okhotnik,Vladimir
Beliavsky,Alexander
Hungary tt 2002/03 (9)

1.e4 d6 2.d4 g6 3.♘c3 ♗g7 4.♗g5
c5 5.dxc5 ♕a5 6.♕d2 ♕xc5 7.♘d5
♗e6 8.0-0-0 ♘d7 9.♗e3 ♕c8
10.♗b5 ♘f6 11.♘xf6+ ♗xf6 12.♗d4
♗xd4 13.♕xd4 0-0 14.♗xd7 ♕xd7
15.♔b1 ♖fc8 16.♘e2 a5 17.♘f4 ♖c4

18.♕d3 ♖ac8 19.♖d2 b5 20.♘d5
♕b7 21.♖e1 b4 22.b3 ♖4c5 23.♕d4
a4 24.f3 ♗xd5 25.exd5 ♕c7
26.♖ee2 axb3 27.axb3 ♕b7 28.♖d3
♖a8 29.♖de3 ♖xd5 30.♖xe7 ♕xe7
31.♕xd5 ♕a7   0-1

Lasker,Emanuel
Von Bardeleben,Curt
Berlin m 1889/90 (1)

1.e4 g6 2.d4 ♗g7 3.f4 c5 4.dxc5
♕a5+ 5.♗d2 ♕xc5 6.♗c3 ♘f6
7.♕d4 ♕c7 8.e5 ♘c6 9.♕d3 ♘h5
10.♘e2 f5 11.♘d2 0-0 12.g3 b6

13.♗g2 ♗b7 14.0-0 ♘d8 15.♖ad1
♗xg2 16.♔xg2 ♘e6 17.♘b3 ♖fd8
18.♕d5 ♔h8 19.♖d2 ♗f8 20.♖fd1
♘hg7 21.a4 a6 22.h4 ♕c6 23.a5 b5
24.♗b4 ♕c4 25.c3 ♖ac8 26.♘a1
♕c6 27.♘c2 ♘e8 28.♘e3 ♘8c7
29.♕f3 ♕xf3+ 30.♔xf3 ♔g7
31.♖xd7 ♔f7 32.♖xd8 ♖xd8
33.♖xd8 ♘xd8 34.♗c5 ♘b7 35.♗b6
♘a8 36.♘d5 ♔e6 37.♘b4 ♘xb6
38.axb6 ♔d7 39.♘xa6 e6 40.♘d4
b4 41.cxb4 ♘d8 42.♘c5+ ♔c8
43.♔e3 ♗e7 44.♔d3 h6 45.♔c4 g5
46.hxg5 hxg5 47.♘dxe6   1-0

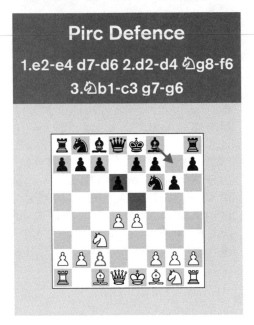

Pirc Defence

**1.e2-e4 d7-d6 2.d2-d4 ♞g8-f6
3.♞b1-c3 g7-g6**

The **Pirc Defence** is named after the strong Yugoslav player Vasja Pirc, who was born in the early part of the 20th century, and it is characterized by the kingside fianchetto. However, first Black plays 1...d6 to prevent e4-e5, and then 2...♞f6 provoking 3.♞c3, in doing so preventing White from playing c2-c4, entering into the **King's Indian**. This is not to suggest that the Pirc has proved itself to be superior to the King's Indian: as always, it is simply a matter of taste.

It should be said that White can also choose not to play 3.♞c3, and instead go for 3.f3 or 3.♗d3. In both these cases Black can decide not to fianchetto his f8-bishop and instead respond in the centre with 3...e5, creating a different type of game. As in the **Modern Defence**, Black concedes the centre in hopes of undermining it at a later stage. Therefore this is an ambitious defence and, as a result, rather demanding to play. For his part, White can react ag-gressively, or he can instead opt to begin with slow manoeuvring.

In ascending order of popularity, the most common options are:

A)   4. g2-g3

An underestimated variation.
   4. ...   ♗f8-g7
Now White solidly develops:
   5. ♗f1-g2   0-0
   6. ♞g1-e2   e7-e5
With another type of game in mind, people are increasingly beginning to play 6...♞bd7, which prepares ...c7-c5.
   7. h2-h3!   ♞b8-c6
   8. ♗c1-e3

If Black now takes on d4, he allows his opponent active piece play. If Black plays mechanically, White obtains an unpleasant initiative with moves such as 0-0 and f2-f4. Therefore this is a position which inspires differing assessments, depending on the taste of the commentator and ranging from equality to a small advantage for White.

B)   4. ♗c1-g5

An insidious move, even if comparatively uncommon. If Black allows, White will try ♕d2-♗h6 along the lines of the 4.♗e3 variation. Otherwise, he can continue with f2-f4, aiming to play an Austrian Attack, but with the bishop on g5, given the pressure it applies on e7, the e4-e5 advance is more effective. On the other hand, this takes a tempo, and it is not clear if all this is worth it.

Black, who may not appreciate the presence of the bishop on g5, can give it a kick with ...h6, and if he chooses, eliminate it with the common manoeuvre ...g5 and ...♘f6-h5xg3. However, here it is not clear either if this is positive or negative, given the lost tempi and the weaknesses on the kingside.

    4. **...**   **♗f8-g7**

White can now continue with:

B1)   **5.** **♕d1-d2**

At this point, kingside castling seems dangerous because of White's intention to exchange off the g7-bishop. Therefore:

B11)   **5.** **...**   **h7-h6**
       6. **♗g5-h4**   **g6-g5**
       7. **♗h4-g3**   **♘f6-h5**

By chasing the bishop we are heading for a complex middlegame, e.g. after 8.0-0-0.

B12)   **5.** **...**   **c7-c6**
       6. **♗g5-h6**   **♗g7xh6**
       7. **♕d2xh6**   **♕d8-a5**

Black immediately begins a counterattack on the queenside. It is difficult to judge which is more dangerous: White's kingside attack, or Black's on the queenside.

B2)   **5.** **f2-f4**

       5. **...**   **c7-c6**

Here also, it is better to postpone castling.

       6. **♘g1-f3**   **b7-b5**
       7. **♗f1-d3**   **b5-b4**
       8. **♘c3-e2**   **♗c8-g4**
       9. **0-0**   **♕d8-b6**
     10. **♔g1-h1**

White has a good centre, but Black has sufficient counterplay.

C)   **4. ♗c1-e3**

Preparing for ♕d2 and 0-0-0.

4. ...   **c7-c6!**

Black is correct to immediately seek counterplay on the queenside. After the natural 4...♗g7 5.♕d2 c6 *(here also, as after 4.♗g5, castling kingside would be dangerous because of ♗h6 followed by h4-h5 in the style of the Dragon Variation of the Sicilian)* 6.♘f3 (after 6.♗h6 ♗xh6! 7.♕xh6 ♕a5, you reach the position already seen in B12) 6...b5 7.♗d3 ♘bd7 8.♗h6 or 8.h3 the results tend to favour White.

    5. ♕d1-d2   **b7-b5**
    6. ♗f1-d3   **♘b8-d7**

The idea is that if White opts for ♗h6, Black will not waste a tempo, as he has not played ...♗g7. The resulting positions are complicated and they offer both sides chances.

The move 4.f4 — the Austrian Attack — has seen a decline in popularity, and as a result the 4.♗e3 variation is the most fashionable line at the moment.

The Austrian Attack

D)   **4. f2-f4**

The famous **Austrian Attack**'s great popularity began in the 1950s and gradually became the most frequently played variation against the Pirc until the 1990s. White develops his pieces (♘f3 and ♗d3) behind a central expansion, preparing for a future assault on the black king, which is generally initiated by pushing the pawn to e5 at an opportune moment. This plan is very dangerous and Black must respond by advancing a pawn to e5 or c5: either immediately, or after suitable preparation.

    4. ...   **♗f8-g7**
    5. ♘g1-f3

Now Black can counterattack the centre (with ...c5), or otherwise make non-committal moves.

D1)   **5. ...**   **c7-c5**

This pawn advance is inspired by tactical considerations: 6.dxc5 ♕a5! which attacks e4, winning back the pawn. After 7.♗d3 ♕xc5 a balanced position is reached that is structurally reminiscent of the more solid Dragon positions.

If White wants to play more aggressively, he chooses

6. &f1-b5+!?

Weakening Black's control of the e6-square.

6. ...   &c8-d7

7. e4-e5   &f6-g4
8. e5-e6

8.&xd7+ is more solid, but after 8...&xd7 9.d5 dxe5 10.h3 e4!, Black maintains equality. At this point there are two variations to consider:

D11) 8. ...   f7xe6!?

For years this was thought to be a simple error because of

9. &f3-g5   &d7xb5

and now after 10.&xe6

both Black's queen on d8 and the g7-bishop are under attack.

However, in the 1980s **10...&xd4!** was discovered. If White takes the queen, Black gives perpetual check on f2 and e3. Therefore White usually relies on

10. &c3xb5

but after

10. ...   &d8-a5+
11. c2-c3   &a5xb5
12. &g5xe6   &b8-a6!
13. &e6xg7+   &e8-f7

Black maintains equality notwithstanding his exposed king.

D12) 8. ...   &d7xb5

This old line is sound and still being played.

9. e6xf7+   &e8-d7!

The king is safer here than on f8!

10. &c3xb5   &d8-a5+
11. &b5-c3   c5xd4
12. &f3xd4

Now we have an intricate situation: even though hundreds of games have been played with this position it is still not clear who is attacking and who is defending.

D2)   **5. ...**   **0-0**
      6. ♗f1-d3

The most common move: it defends e4 and in the event of e4-e5, it enables the d-pawn to recapture without allowing the exchange of queens. 6.e5 seems to be premature. 6.♗e3 – which prepares for ♕d2 and 0-0-0 – has its admirers, but practice has shown that 6...b6!, preparing for both the ...c7-c5 advance and ...♗b7, gives Black sufficient counterplay.

Instead, 6.♗e2, which used to be played in the early days of the Austrian Attack, lacks bite because of 6...c5! 7.dxc5 ♕a5.

Let's return to 6.♗d3. Now the ...e7-e5 advance is no longer playable, and the other advance ...c7-c5 is weak because of 7.dxc5. As a result, Black usually prepares for the first with 6...♘c6, or for the second with 6...♘a6.

D21)   **6. ...**   **♘b8-c6**
       7. 0-0

The impetuous 7.e5 is risky but playable.

7. ...   **e7-e5!?**

Now White can either take with the d-pawn and then push f4-f5, or he can take with the f-pawn and then advance his d-pawn to d5. For his part, Black can move his c6-knight to b4 or to d4; in both cases with satisfactory results.

D22)   **6. ...**   **♘b8-a6**
       7. 0-0   **c7-c5**
       8. d4-d5   **♖a8-b8**

In response to 8...♗g4!?, the latest craze is **9.♗c4!**.

9. ♔g1-h1

The hyper-aggressive 9.e5!? or 9.f5!? is also possible.

In Benoni fashion, Black now seeks counterplay on the queenside, which is facilitated by the absence of the white pawn on c4 and because the knight on b4 harasses the bishop on d3. Yet at the same time, the manoeuvre ♕e1-h4 with the idea of f5, ♗h6 and ♘g5 can be very dangerous and practical results would appear to favour White.

Classical Variation

E)   4. ♘g1-f3

White continues in simple fashion, giving priority to development.

** 4. ...   ♗f8-g7**
** 5. ♗f1-e2**

5.♗e3 is also popular. The latter tends to lead to the 4.♗e3 variation if White continues with ♕d2. However, a specific line exists in which White chooses a solid plan that starts with h2-h3. An example is the variation 5...c6 6.h3 0-0 7.a4 ♘bd7 (7...d5!? loses a tempo, but it is interesting as it aims to take advantage of White's non-developing moves) 8.a5, with a small but unpleasant queenside initiative.

** 5. ...   0-0**
** 6. 0-0**

We have reached the key position of the **Classical Pirc**.

White doesn't have any immediate threats, so Black can choose between

various strategic plans. These generally involve putting White's centre under pressure either with ...♗g4 and ...♘c6, or more directly with the pawn advance ...c7-c5. Alternatively, Black can search for play on the queenside with ...c6. The variations below are indicative for each of the three different approaches.

E1)   6. ...   c7-c5
**   7. d4-d5!**

Thus we arrive at positions which are typical of the Franco-Benoni.

** 7. ...   ♘b8-a6**
** 8. h2-h3   ♘a6-c7**
** 9. a2-a4   b7-b6**
** 10. ♗c1-f4**

White is slightly better off.

E2)   6. ...   ♗c8-g4
**   7. ♗c1-e3   ♘b8-c6**
**   8. d4-d5!?**

The old main line 8.♕d2 is a little out of fashion: after 8...e5, neither 9.d5 nor the simplifying 9.dxe5 appears to give White anything special.

** 8. ...   ♗g4xf3**

8...♘b8!? seems provocative, but it makes sense now that White's centre has been compromised.

9.   ♗e2xf3   ♘c6-e5
10.   ♗f3-e2   c7-c6

Attacking the head of the pawn chain seems best here.

11.   a2-a4!   ♕d8-a5
12.   ♖a1-a3!

With the idea of ♖b3, leaving White with a small but insidious initiative.

E3)   6.   ...   c7-c6

is the most popular. White can prepare the pawn push e4-e5 with 7.h3 or 7.♖e1, but he usually proceeds with

7.   a2-a4

which prevents b5, and White also has a4-a5 in mind. The aim is to take away all of Black's manoeuvring space on the queenside.
In view of this, Black plays

7.   ...   a7-a5
8.   h2-h3   ♘b8-a6
9.   ♗c1-e3   ♘a6-b4

Now White can either prepare the f2-f4 advance with 10.♘d2, or develop normally with 10.♕d2 and 11.♖ad1 with that small advantage which is always nice to have, but against correct play does not guarantee anything substantial. Black could react with ...d7-d5, to exchange off the e4-pawn and make the f5-square available for the bishop on c8.

Lasker,Emanuel
Marshall,Frank
New York m 1940 (2)

1.e4 d6 2.d4 ♘f6 3.♘c3 g6 4.f3 ♗g7 5.♗e3 ♘bd7 6.♘ge2 a6 7.♕d2 c6 8.♗h6 ♗xh6 9.♕xh6 ♕a5 10.♕d2 b5 11.♘c1 ♗b7 12.♘b3 ♕c7 13.a4 b4 14.♘d1 a5 15.♘e3 d5 16.e5 ♘h5 17.g3 0-0 18.♗h3 e6 19.0-0 c5 20.f4 ♘g7 21.♖fd1 ♖fc8 22.♘xc5 ♘xc5 23.dxc5 ♕xc5 24.♕d4 ♕xd4 25.♖xd4 ♘f5 26.♗xf5 gxf5 27.♔f2 f6 28.♖g1 h5 29.h3 ♔f7 30.g4 hxg4 31.hxg4 fxg4 32.exf6 ♔xf6 33.♖xg4 ♖g8 34.c3 bxc3 35.bxc3 ♖xg4 36.♘xg4+ ♔f5 37.♘e3+ ♔f6 38.c4 ♖c8 39.cxd5 ♗xd5   ½-½

Stulik,Vlastimil
Pirc,Vasja
Karlovy Vary 1948 (11)

1.e4 d6 2.d4 ♘f6 3.♘c3 g6 4.♘f3 ♗g7 5.♗g5 0-0 6.♕d2 ♗g4 7.h3 ♗xf3 8.gxf3 e5 9.d5 c5 10.h4 h5 11.0-0-0 ♘bd7 12.♗h3 a6 13.♘e2 ♕c7 14.♖hg1 c4 15.♘g3 c3 16.bxc3 ♕a5 17.♔b1 ♘b6 18.c4 ♕xd2 19.♖xd2 ♘xc4 20.♖d3 ♘h7 21.♘xh5 ♘xg5 22.hxg5 gxh5 23.g6 fxg6 24.♖xg6 ♖f6 25.♖g5 ♖h6 26.♖d1 ♔h8 27.♖dg1 ♗f6 28.♖5g2 ♘d2+   0-1

Kasparov,Garry
Topalov,Veselin
Wijk aan Zee 1999 (4)

1.e4 d6 2.d4 ♘f6 3.♘c3 g6 4.♗e3 ♗g7?! 5.♕d2 c6 6.f3 b5 7.♘ge2 ♘bd7 8.♗h6 ♗xh6 9.♕xh6 ♗b7 [≥ 9...e5!?] 10.a3! e5 11.0-0-0 ♕e7 12.♔b1 a6 13.♘c1! 0-0-0 14.♘b3 exd4!? 15.♖xd4 c5 16.♖d1 ♘b6

17.g3 ♔b8 18.♘a5?! [≥ 18.♗h3!?]
18...♗a8 19.♗h3 d5 20.♕f4+ ♔a7
21.♖he1 d4 22.♘d5 ♘bxd5 23.exd5
♕d6 24.♖xd4! cxd4? [≥ 24...♔b6!=]
25.♖e7+!! ♔b6 26.♕xd4+ ♔xa5
27.b4+ ♔a4 28.♕c3!? [28.♖a7!]
28...♕xd5 29.♗a7 ♗b7□ 30.♖xb7
♕c4?! [30...♖he8!] 31.♕xf6 ♔xa3
[≥ 31...♖d1+] 32.♕xa6+ ♔xb4
33.c3+! ♔xc3 34.♕a1+ ♔d2□
35.♕b2+ ♔d1 36.♗f1! ♖d2□
37.♖d7! ♖xd7 38.♗xc4 bxc4□
39.♕xh8 ♖d3 40.♕a8 c3 41.♕a4+
♔e1 42.f4 f5 43.♔c1 ♖d2 44.♕a7
1-0

Svidler, Peter
Ivanchuk, Vasily

Spain tt 2006 (1)

1.e4 d6 2.d4 ♘f6 3.♘c3 g6 4.♗e3
c6 5.h3 ♗g7 6.g4 b5 7.e5 ♘fd7 8.f4
♘b6 9.♘f3 ♘8d7 10.♗d3 b4 11.♘e4
♘d5 12.♗d2 c5 13.♘fg5 ♕b6 14.c4
bxc3 15.bxc3 ♗a6 16.♖b1 ♗xd3
17.♖xb6 ♘5xb6 18.exd6 h6
19.♘xc5 ♘xc5 20.dxc5 0-0 21.♕f3
♗c4 22.cxb6 hxg5 23.b7 ♖ab8
24.♕c6 ♗xa2 25.0-0 exd6 26.♖a1
♗e6 27.♖xa7 gxf4 28.♖a8 ♗e5
29.♖xb8 ♖xb8 30.♕c7   **1-0**

Spassky, Boris
Fischer, Robert

Reykjavik Wch m 1972 (17)

1.e4 d6 2.d4 g6 3.♘c3 ♘f6 4.f4 ♗g7
5.♘f3 c5 6.dxc5 [6.e5 ♘fd7 7.exd6
cxd4 8.♘b5 0-0 9.♘c7 ♘c5 10.♘xa8
♕xd6 11.♗d3 ♘c6 12.0-0 ♗e6
13.♘g5 ♗d5 14.f5 ♖xa8 15.fxg6 hxg6
16.♕g4 ♘xd3 17.cxd3 f6 18.♘f3 ♗f7

19.♘h4 ♘e5 20.♕g3 ♕d7 21.♗f4 g5
22.♗xg5 fxg5 23.♘f5 ♗g6 24.♘xg7
♗f7 25.♖xf7 ♔xf7 26.♕e5 ♗xd3
27.♖d1 ♖g8 28.♖xd3 ♖xg7 29.♖xd4
♕e6 30.♕xe6+ ♔xe6 Kramnik-
Grischuk, Wijk aan Zee 2005 (½-½,
67)] 6...♕a5 7.♗d3 ♕xc5 8.♕e2 0-0
9.♗e3 ♕a5 10.0-0 ♗g4 11.♖ad1
♘c6 12.♗c4 ♘h5 13.♗b3 ♗xc3
14.bxc3 ♕xc3 15.f5 ♘f6 16.h3 ♗xf3
17.♕xf3 ♘a5 18.♖d3 ♕c7 19.♗h6
♘xb3 20.cxb3 ♕c5+ 21.♔h1 ♕e5
22.♗xf8 ♖xf8 23.♖e3 ♖c8 24.fxg6
hxg6 25.♕f4 ♕xf4 26.♖xf4 ♘d7
27.♖f2 ♘e5 28.♔h2 ♖c1 29.♖ee2
♘c6 30.♖c2 ♖e1 31.♖fe2 ♖a1
32.♔g3 ♔g7 33.♖cd2 ♖f1 34.♖f2
♖e1 35.♖fe2 ♖f1 36.♖e3 a6 37.♖c3
♖e1 38.♖c4 ♖f1 39.♖dc2 ♖a1
40.♖f2 ♖e1 41.♖fc2 g5 42.♖c1 ♖e2
43.♖1c2 ♖e1 44.♖c1 ♖e2 45.♖1c2
½-½

Karpov, Anatoly
Kortchnoi, Viktor

Baguio City Wch m 1978 (32)

1.e4 d6 2.d4 ♘f6 3.♘c3 g6 4.♘f3
♗g7 5.♗e2 0-0 6.0-0 c5 7.d5 ♘a6
8.♗f4 ♘c7 9.a4 b6 10.♖e1 ♗b7
11.♗c4 ♘h5 12.♗g5 ♘f6 13.♕d3 a6
14.♖ad1 ♖b8 15.h3 ♘d7 16.♕e3
♗a8 17.♗h6 b5 18.♗xg7 ♔xg7
19.♗f1 ♘f6 20.axb5 axb5 21.♘e2
♗b7 22.♘g3 ♖a8 23.c3 ♖a4 24.♗d3
♕a8 25.e5 dxe5 26.♕xe5 ♘xd5
27.♗xb5 ♖a7 28.♘h4 ♗c8 29.♗e2
♗e6 30.c4 ♘b4 31.♕xc5 ♕b8
32.♗f1 ♖c8 33.♕g5 ♔h8 34.♖d2
♘c6 35.♕h6 ♖g8 36.♘f3 ♕f8
37.♕e3 ♔g7 38.♘g5 ♗d7 39.b4
♕a8 40.b5 ♘a5 41.b6 ♖b7   **1-0**

Caro-Kann Defence

1.e2-e4 c7-c6

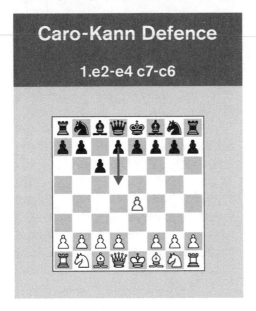

When Nimzowitsch wrote during the 1920s that the **Caro-Kann Defence** is the refutation of 1.e4, he was either kidding or he just wanted to stir the stagnant waters of a theoretical approach that resisted all attempts at innovation under the banner of Tarrasch's rigid and dogmatic principles. Nimzowitsch knew that if you want to rock the boat you need to exaggerate somewhat.

The proof that Nimzowitsch did not fully believe his pronouncement is demonstrated by the fact that he continued playing 1.e4 on a fairly regular basis after making this remark! What he really meant was that it isn't compulsory to answer 1.e4 with 1...e5 and that there are many potential strategies available besides pure frontal opposition based on simple space control.

In this sense 1...c6 is conceptually very ambitious. The e4-pawn, unlike its colleague to the immediate left, is unpro-

tected. And if we look a little closer, we notice that the e4-pawn is the strategic linchpin around which all Semi-Open Games are based. Let's have a look at the various starting positions.

- in the **Alekhine**:

with 1...♘f6, the e4-pawn is attacked immediately, but this leaves White with a sound space advantage;

- in the **Scandinavian**:

with 1...d5, Black immediately wants to exchange his d-pawn and create a pawn majority on the kingside, but in doing so he will either lag behind in development (2.exd5 ♕xd5 3.♘c3) or, in the line 2.exd5 ♘f6 3.d4 ♘xd5 4.c4 ♘b6, his knight on b6 is far removed from the action;

● in the **French Defence**:

after 1...e6, the e4-pawn is threatened on the second move when Black continues with 2...d5. However, now White often advances the pawn to e5, keeping the centre closed. In the Closed French, it is a good thing that the c8-bishop cannot speak, as it has plenty to grumble about;

● in the **Pirc Defence**:

with the move 1...d6, Black prevents the advance of the e-pawn's to e5 in order to attack it on his second move. But the drawback of this system is that White can successfully maintain his two central pawns side by side on e4 and d4;

● in the **Sicilian Defence**:

after 1...c5, Black prevents the two central pawns from standing side by side, usually attacking the e4-pawn on his fourth move (3.d4 cxd4 4.♘xd4 ♘f6), but often at the expense of his own king's safety.

Presented in this light, the **Caro-Kann** appears to be a perfect defence.

2. d2-d4   d7-d5

Here White's options are limited by the fact that the e4-pawn is threatened. The exchange 3.exd5 is excellent for White in the Scandinavian. In the Caro-Kann, after 3...cxd5 Black achieves a central pawn majority.

As for 3.e5, it gains space, but unlike in the Advance Variation of the French the c8-bishop has nothing to complain about here and it can go straight to f5. The remaining option is to defend the pawn with 3.♘c3 or with 3.♘d2 and after 3...dxe4 4.♘xe4, Black can safely continue his development, attacking the unprotected knight on e4 with 4...♗f5, or with 4...♘d7 followed by 5...♘gf6.

In real life, things are not so simple: in the first place 3.e5 and 3.exd5, even considering the previously discussed limitations, do not allow Black to take equality for granted. Furthermore, in the main line, even though the absence of the e-pawn takes some of the sting out of White's play, it is also true that in the ensuing long positional battle White obtains a spatial advantage anyhow, and a comfortable position. This might not be so easy to convert into a win, but it is also true that the risks of losing are minimal.

As a result, the Caro-Kann has gained a reputation as a very solid defence suitable for positional players. All this is true, but beware if your opponent chooses 3.e5, the Advance Variation — in particular if he replies to 3...♗f5 with the aggressive **4.♘c3**.

You will be dealing with one of the sharpest and most complex lines found in all opening theory!

1. e2-e4   c7-c6

Besides occupying the centre with 2.d4, White has other interesting options.

A)   2. c2-c4!?

Here White intends, after the thematic

2. ...   d7-d5

to continue with

3. e4xd5   c6xd5
4. c4xd5

and if Black captures with his queen, to transpose to a favourable line of the **Sicilian with 2.c3** (!).

If Black plays the more accurate

4. ...   ♘g8-f6

White can attempt to keep the d5-pawn with 5.♗b5+ ♗d7 6.♗c4, or try with

5. ♘b1-c3

to transpose to favourable lines of the **Panov-Botvinnik Attack** (see below), advancing his pawn to d4 at the most opportune moment. This is not as academic as it may seem:

A1)   5. ...   g7-g6

Compared to the similar line in the **Panov-Botvinnik Attack**, White, instead of advancing d2-d4, could decide to defend the d5-pawn with either ♕b3 and ♗e2-f3 or ♗c4, and it is difficult for Black to regain the pawn.

A2)   5.   ...   ♘f6xd5

In order to avoid the risk of not being able to recoup the pawn, Black usually captures on d5 right away.

6.   ♘g1-f3   ♘b8-c6
7.   d2-d4

Now 7...♗g4 transposes to a line of the **Panov-Botvinnik Attack**, which we will look at later. However, Black could also play the solid

7.   ...   e7-e6

and, incredibly, we end up on **Semi-Tarrasch** territory with possible transpositions to the **Queen's Gambit Accepted**! In addition, from the Panov-Botvinnik Attack we may transpose to the **Nimzo-Indian**.

All of this should suffice to convince us that opening theory is a coherent whole and not a group of segmented compartments, as is commonly believed. It is for this reason that, in order to have a full grasp of what you are doing, you should have a general understanding of ope-

nings, even if they are not part of your repertoire. For as much as we study or prepare for a particular type of game, sooner or later we will be confronted with unpredictable and ever-changing situations which require us to think for ourselves. Specialized preparation is all very fine, but by cultivating a more general awareness we develop mental 'elasticity', which is a fundamental requirement for a good chess player.

Once we admit that it is impossible to know everything about everything, we can reach a suitable compromise by learning a little about everything, and everything about a little.

B)   2.   d2-d3

This is a typical move in the **King's Indian Attack**, and it is playable against the **French Defence** and some lines of the **Sicilian**. But more frequently it features in 1.♘f3 followed by a kingside fianchetto and e4: therefore we're talking about a **King's Indian** with an extra tempo, and hence the name.

2.   ...   d7-d5
3.   ♘b1-d2

Now Black may occupy the centre with 3....e5, or he can continue with 3....g6. The game assumes the character of a

Caro-Kann
Advance Variation

1.e4 c6 2.d4 d5 3.e5

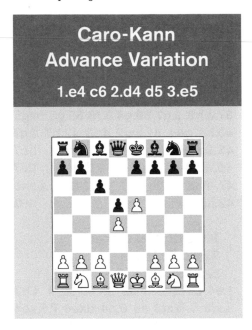

After 3.e5, the immediate

3. ...   ♗c8-f5

is the most natural, but 3...c5!?, a useful move for players who wish to avoid a lot of theory, could also be a good idea: compared to the **French**, Black has lost a tempo, but his potentially bad bishop can still be developed to f5 or g4. However, after 4.dxc5! – an ugly but effective move – Black has difficulty winning back the pawn and the results are sufficiently in White's favour.

Let's return to 3...♗f5. Now White can play several moves.

A)   4. ♘g1-f3
A solid choice, championed by Nigel Short.

4.	**...**	**e7-e6**
5.	**♗f1-e2**	**c6-c5**
6.	**c2-c3**	**♘b8-c6**
7.	**0-0**	

For decades, opening manuals have pronounced that Black is in effect playing an improved version of the French, with the bishop on f5 instead of c8. However, this has been revealed to be a somewhat blinkered analysis. Recently we have come to realize that the loss of two tempi (...c6-c5 and indeed ...♗f5) make it possible for White to develop a small but unpleasant initiative which has produced encouraging results.

B)   4. h2-h4!?

With this poisonous move, White gains space on the kingside and threatens to seriously harass the f5-bishop. Indeed, the natural 4...e6?? loses the bishop after g2-g4, f2-f3 and h4-h5. After 4...h6 5.g4, if Black continues with the normal-looking 5...♗h7?! (5...♗d7! is the right move), *White obtains optimal play on the light squares with 6.e6! fxe6 7.♗d3.*

Black's most common move is

4. ... h7-h5

and now it is not clear which of the two h-pawns is the weaker. At this point White responds with the committal

5. c2-c4!?

which is considered to be much better if played at this point than on the move before, because White has more comfortable access to the g5-square.

If Black now takes on c4, he gains control of the key d5-square, but at the same time he gives White the important e4-square. If Black dithers, White will have the usual initiative on the queenside. White's results are fairly good and it is strange that this variation is not played more often, especially considering that there is not too much theory to study.

C) 4. ♘b1-c3

This aggressive move allows White to control e4, reserving g2-g4 for a better moment later on.

At this stage, all sorts of moves have been tried, among which 4...♕d7, 4...h5, 4...♕b6, and recently also the interesting 4...a6. However, the most popular move by far is still

4. ... e7-e6
5. g2-g4

Now yes!

5. ... ♗f5-g6
6. ♘g1-e2!

White seeks to harass the g6-bishop with ♘f4 and/or h2-h4. However, this takes several tempi and Black responds thematically in the centre:

6. ... c6-c5

In order to dissuade White from the idea of ♘f4. 6...♘e7 and 6...f6 are also playable.

7. h2-h4

7.♗e3!? with the idea of 8.dxc5 contains a drop of poison too, but the text move is more common. Now Black gives the bishop some breathing space by advancing his h-pawn, or by capturing on d4. To give you an idea of the complexity of the variations that ensue, you only need to look at this line:

7.	...	c5xd4
8.	♘e2xd4	h7-h5
9.	f2-f4!	h5xg4
10.	♗f1-b5+	♘b8-d7
11.	f4-f5!	♖h8xh4
12.	♖h1-f1!	♖h4-h5!?

with unclear play.

D)   **4. ♗c1-e3**

Speaking of uncharted waters, this was played in 2002 by Garry Kasparov. His distinguished patronage is reason in itself to take this strange move seriously. Predictably, in the following years this variation became very fashionable and many of the top players in the world are now exploring its deeper mysteries. The idea of 4.♗e3 is to defend b2 with 5.♕c1 if Black plays 4...♕b6; the second idea is to make the freeing pawn advance ...c6-c5 more difficult if Black prepares for this with 4...e6.

Even if the 4.♗e3 variation is still in its infancy, the following move sequence is usually seen as the main line.

4.	...	e7-e6
5.	♘b1-d2	♘b8-d7
6.	♗f1-e2	♘g8-e7

The results for White after 7.f4 or 7.♘gf3 are encouraging, even if it is too early to speak of an indisputable advantage for White.

Morozevich,Alexander
Asrian,Karen
Fügen tt 2006 (5)
1.e4 c6 2.d4 d5 3.e5 ♗f5 4.♘f3 e6
5.♗e2 ♘e7 6.c3 ♘d7 7.♘h4 ♗g6
8.♘xg6 hxg6 9.♘d2 ♘f5 10.♘f3
♘h4 11.♘xh4 ♖xh4 12.g3 ♖h8
13.0-0 ♗e7 14.♗d3 ♕c7 15.♕e2 c5
16.♗e3 0-0-0 17.a4 ♔b8 18.a5 ♖c8
19.♖fc1 g5 20.♕g4 ♕c6 21.b4 c4
22.b5 ♕xb5 23.♗c2 ♕c6 24.♗xg5
f5 25.exf6 gxf6 26.♗f4+ ♗d6
27.♗a4 ♕c7 28.♗xd6 ♕xd6 29.♖e1
♖he8 30.♗xd7 ♕xd7 31.♕f4+ ♔a8
32.♕xf6 ♖e7 33.♖e5 ♖ce8 34.♖ae1
a6 35.h4 ♖f7 36.♕g6 ♖ef8 37.♕xe6
♕a4 38.♕xd5 ♖xf2 39.♖b1 ♖b2
40.♖be1 ♖c8 41.♕f3 ♖g8 42.g4
♕c6 43.♕g3 ♔a7 44.g5 ♖h8
45.♖5e2 ♖b5 46.♖e6 ♕c8 47.g6

♖xa5 48.g7 ♖g8 49.♖g6 ♕f5 50.♖f1
♕e4 51.♖g4 ♕e6 52.♖e1 ♕f5
53.♖f1 ♕e6 54.♖b1 ♕f5 55.♖b2
♖a1+ 56.♔h2 ♕d5 57.♖g2 ♕f7
58.♖f4 ♕c7 59.d5 ♖d1 60.♔f2+ b6
61.♖g3 ♖xd5 62.♖f7 ♖d7 63.♖xd7
♕xd7 64.♕f6 a5 65.h5 ♕e8
66.♕g5 a4 67.h6 ♕e2+ 68.♖g2
♕e4 69.♕g4 ♕e5+ 70.♖g3 ♕f6
71.♕g5 ♕d6 72.h7   1-0

Kramnik,Vladimir
Leko,Peter
Brissago Wch m 2004 (14)
1.e4 c6 2.d4 d5 3.e5 ♗f5 4.h4 h6
5.g4 ♗d7 6.♘d2 c5 7.dxc5 e6
8.♘b3 ♗xc5 9.♘xc5 ♕a5+ 10.c3
♕xc5 11.♘f3 ♘e7 12.♗d3 ♘bc6
13.♗e3 ♕a5 14.♕d2 ♘g6 15.♗d4
♘xd4 16.cxd4 ♕xd2+ 17.♔xd2 ♘f4
18.♖ac1 h5 19.♖hg1 ♗c6 20.gxh5
♘xh5 21.b4 a6 22.a4 ♔d8 23.♘g5
♗e8 24.b5 ♘f4 25.b6 ♘xd3
26.♔xd3 ♖c8 27.♖xc8+ ♔xc8
28.♖c1+ ♗c6 29.♘xf7 ♖xh4
30.♘d6+ ♔d8 31.♖g1 ♖h3+
32.♔e2 ♖a3 33.♖xg7 ♖xa4 34.f4
♖a2+ 35.♔f3 ♖a3+ 36.♔g4 ♖d3
37.f5 ♖xd4+ 38.♔g5 exf5 39.♔f6
♖g4 40.♖c7 ♖h4 41.♘f7+   1-0

Gelashvili,Tamaz
Nauryzgaliev,Amangeldy
Turin ol 2006 (1)
1.e4 c6 2.d4 d5 3.e5 ♗f5 4.h4 h6
5.g4 ♗e4 6.f3 ♗g6 7.h5 ♗h7 8.e6

fxe6 9.♗d3 ♗xd3 10.♕xd3 ♕d6
11.f4 ♘f6 12.♘f3 ♘bd7 13.♕g6+
♔d8 14.♘e5   1-0

Kasparov,Garry
Karpov,Anatoly
Linares 2001 (5)
1.e4 c6 2.d4 d5 3.e5 ♗f5 4.♘c3 e6
5.g4 ♗g6 6.♘ge2 ♘e7 7.♘f4 c5
8.dxc5 ♘d7 9.h4 ♘xe5 10.♗g2 h5
11.♕e2 ♘7c6 12.♘xg6 ♘xg6
13.♗g5 ♗e7 14.gxh5 ♘f8 15.♘b5
♘d7 16.h6 ♘xc5 17.♗f4 ♔f8
18.hxg7+ ♔xg7 19.0-0-0 ♔f8
20.♔b1 a6 21.♘c7 ♖c8 22.♗xd5
exd5 23.♖xd5 ♕xc7 24.♗xc7 ♖xc7
25.♖f5 ♖d7 26.c3 f6 27.♖g1 ♘d8
28.♕g4 ♔e8 29.♖h5 ♖f8 30.♖xc5
♗xc5 31.♕h5+   1-0

Morozevich,Alexander
Ivanchuk,Vasily
Calvia ol 2004 (4)
1.e4 c6 2.d4 d5 3.e5 ♗f5 4.f4 e6
5.♘f3 c5 6.♗e3 cxd4 7.♘xd4 ♘e7
8.♗b5+ ♘d7 9.0-0 a6 10.♗e2 g5
11.g4 gxf4 12.gxf5 ♘xf5 13.♘xf5
fxe3 14.♘c3 ♖g8+ 15.♔h1 ♕g5
16.♗f3 ♘xe5 17.♕e2 ♕xf5 18.♗xd5
♕h3 19.♗xb7 ♖a7 20.♗f3 ♗h6
21.♘e4 ♔e7 22.♕e1 f5 23.♕b4+
♔f7 24.♕d4 ♘xf3 25.♕f6+ ♔e8
26.♕xe6+ ♔f8 27.♕f6+ ♖f7
28.♕d6+ ♔g7 29.♖g1+ ♔h8
30.♘f6   0-1

Black can respond to this direct approach with the classical

6. ...   e7-e6

but there is also the paradoxical 6...♗e6 or the aggressive 6...♕a5. Each option results in a complicated game for both players.

C2)   6. ♘g1-f3

After this solid move, if Black doesn't want to head into variations of the **Queen's Gambit** or the **Nimzo-Indian** with 6...e6, he can maintain the tension by playing

6. ...   ♗c8-g4

This move has the virtue of putting pressure on the centre, and the defect of weakening the light squares on the queenside. Paradoxically for such an aggressive line, after the almost forced sequence

7. c4xd5   ♘f6xd5
8. ♕d1-b3!   ♗g4xf3
9. g2xf3   e7-e6!

9...♘b6 10.♗e3 e6 11.0-0-0 gives White the advantage.

10. ♕b3xb7   ♘c6xd4
11. ♗f1-b5+   ♘d4xb5
12. ♕b7-c6+!   ♔e8-e7
13. ♕c6xb5   ♕d8-d7
14. ♘c3xd5+   ♕d7xd5
15. ♕b5xd5   e6xd5

We have entered an endgame which the old opening manuals declared to be advantageous for White. This opinion held sway in spite of the doubled pawn on f3, because of White's queenside majority and Black's badly coordinated pieces (not to mention the isolated pawns on d5 and a7). In reality, hundreds of games have demonstrated that Black equalizes easily. The percentage of draws is unusually high: 65% against 35% for the entire Caro-Kann Defence.

Fischer, Robert
Petrosian, Tigran
Belgrade URS-World 1970 (1)
1.e4 c6 2.d4 d5 3.exd5 cxd5 4.♗d3 ♘c6 5.c3 ♘f6 6.♗f4 ♗g4 7.♕b3 ♘a5 8.♕a4+ ♗d7 9.♕c2 e6 10.♘f3 ♕b6 11.a4! [Fischer's novelty, in order to prevent the exchange of the bishops] 11...♖c8 12.♘bd2 ♘c6 13.♕b1 ♘h5 14.♗e3 h6 15.♘e5 ♘f6 16.h3 ♗d6 17.0-0 ♔f8 18.f4 ♗e8 19.♗f2! ♕c7 [19...g6 20.f5 gxf5 21.♗xf5 exf5 22.♕xf5 ♕d8 23.♗h4+– Fischer] 20.♗h4 ♘g8 21.f5 ♘xe5 22.dxe5 ♗xe5 23.fxe6 ♗f6 24.exf7 ♗xf7 25.♘f3! ♗xh4 26.♘xh4 ♘f6 27.♘g6+ ♗xg6 28.♗xg6 ♔e7 29.♕f5 ♔d8 30.♖ae1 ♕c5+ 31.♔h1

♖f8 32.♕e5! ♖c7 [32...♕c7
33.♕xd5+!] 33.b4! ♕c6 34.c4 dxc4
35.♗f5 ♖ff7 36.♖d1+ ♖fd7 37.♗xd7
♖xd7 38.♕b8+ ♔e7 39.♖de1+
[39...♔f7 40.♕e8X] 1-0

Ivanchuk, Vasily
Ehlvest, Jaan
New Delhi/Teheran FIDE-Wch 2000 (2)

1.c4 c6 2.e4 d5 3.exd5 ♘f6 4.♘c3
cxd5 5.d4 e6 6.♘f3 ♗b4 7.cxd5
♘xd5 8.♕c2 ♕c7 9.♗d2 ♘d7
10.♗d3 ♗xc3 11.bxc3 ♘5f6 12.a4
b6 13.0-0 ♗b7 14.♘h4 0-0 15.f4
♗d5 16.♘f3 ♗c4 17.♘e5 ♗xd3
18.♕xd3 ♖ac8 19.♖f3 ♘d5 20.♕b5
♖fd8 21.♖af1 f5 22.♗e1 ♘xe5
23.fxe5 ♕c4 24.♗h4 ♕xb5 25.axb5
♖d7 26.♖c1 ♖c4 27.♗e1 ♘c7 28.h3
♖dxd4 0-1

Sveshnikov, Evgeny
Malakhov, Vladimir
Moscow 2003 (9)

1.e4 c6 2.d4 d5 3.exd5 cxd5 4.c4
♘f6 5.♘c3 e6 6.♘f3 ♗b4 7.cxd5
♘xd5 8.♕c2 ♘c6 9.♗e2 0-0 10.0-0
♗e7 11.♖d1 ♗f6 12.♕e4 ♘ce7
13.h4 ♗d7 14.♗d3 g6 15.h5 ♖c8
16.hxg6 hxg6 17.♗h6 ♘xc3 18.bxc3
♗c6 19.♕f4 ♘d5 20.♕g4 ♗g7
21.♗xg7 ♔xg7 22.♘e5 ♕f6 23.c4
♘f4 24.♗f1 ♖h8 25.♘xc6 ♖h4
26.♕g3 ♖ch8 27.f3 bxc6 28.♖d2 c5
29.♖e1 cxd4 30.♖e4 e5 31.c5 ♕e7
32.♖c2 d3 33.♖cc4 d2 0-1

Gelfand, Boris
Morozevich, Alexander
Wijk aan Zee 2002 (11)

1.c4 c6 2.e4 d5 3.exd5 cxd5 4.d4
♘f6 5.♘c3 g6 6.♕b3 ♗g7 7.cxd5

0-0 8.♗e2 ♘a6 9.♘f3 ♕b6 10.♘ge2
♕xb3 11.axb3 ♘b4 12.0-0 ♖d8
13.♖a5 h6 14.h4 ♘d3 15.♖d1 ♘xc1
16.♖xc1 b6 17.♖a4 ♗b7 18.d6 ♗xf3
19.dxe7 ♖d7 20.gxf3 ♖e8 21.♖d1
♖exe7 22.♔f1 h5 23.♖da1 ♘d5
24.♘xd5 ♖xd5 25.♖xa7 ♖xa7
26.♖xa7 ♗xd4 27.♘c3 ♖a5 28.♖d7
♗xc3 29.bxc3 ♖a3 30.♔g2 ♖xb3
31.♖b7 ♔g7 32.c4 ♖b4 33.♔g3 ♘f6
34.f4 ♔e6 35.♖c7 ♖b3+ 36.f3 ♖b4
37.♖c6+ ♔d7 38.♖f6 ♔e7 39.♖c6
♔e8 40.♖f6 ♖xc4 41.♖xb6 ½-½

Kasparov, Garry
Anand, Viswanathan
Amsterdam 1996 (3)

1.e4 c6 2.d4 d5 3.exd5 cxd5 4.c4
♘f6 5.♘c3 ♘c6 6.♗g5 e6 7.♘f3
♗e7 8.c5 h6 9.♗f4 ♘e4 10.♗b5
♘xc3 11.bxc3 ♗d7 12.0-0 0-0
13.♖c1 ♖e8 14.♖e1 ♗f6 15.♖b1 b6
16.♗a6 ♗c8 17.♗b5 ♗d7 18.♗a6
♗c8 19.♗d3 bxc5 20.♘e5 ♗d7
21.♖b7 ♗xe5 22.dxe5 ♖b8 23.♖xb8
♕xb8 24.♕g4 ♘f8 25.♖e3 ♕d8
26.h4 ♕a5 27.♖g3 ♔e7 28.♕xg7
♔d8 29.♕xf7 ♕xc3 30.♗b5 ♕a5
31.♖g7 ♘e7 32.♗xd7 ♔xd7 33.♕f6
d4 34.♗xh6 c4 35.♗g5 ♕c5
36.♖xe7+ 1-0

Mamedyarov, Shakhriyar
Smeets, Jan
Wijk aan Zee B 2005 (13)

1.c4 c6 2.e4 d5 3.exd5 cxd5 4.d4
♘f6 5.♘c3 ♘c6 6.♗g5 dxc4 7.♗xc4
♕xd4 8.♕xd4 ♘xd4 9.0-0-0 e5
10.f4 ♗g4 11.♘f3 ♘xf3 12.gxf3
♗xf3 13.fxe5 ♗xh1 14.exf6 h6
15.♖e1+ ♔d7 16.♖d1+ ♔e8 17.♗h4
♖c8 18.♗e2 g5 19.♗g3 ♗e4

20.♗g4 ♖xc3+ 21.bxc3 ♗a3+
22.♔d2 h5 23.♔e3 ♗c2 24.♗d7+
♔f8 25.♖d5 ♗c1+ 26.♔d4 ♔g8
27.♗e8 h4 28.♗e5 ♗g6 29.♖d7 h3
30.♗g3 ♗f4 31.♖xb7 ♗xg3 32.hxg3
h2 33.♗c6 ♖h3 34.♗h1 ♖xg3
35.♖b8+ ♔h7 36.♖b2 ♖h3 37.c4
♗f5 38.c5 ♔g6 39.c6 ♔xf6 40.♖f2
♔g6 41.c7 ♖h8 42.♗e5 f6+ 43.♔d6
g4 44.♔c6 ♔g5 45.♖d2 g3 46.♖d8
♖h4 47.♔c5 ♖h7 48.♔c6 ♔f4
49.♖e8 ♗h3 50.♖e4+ ♔g5 51.♖e2
♖h8 52.♔b7 ♔f4 53.♖e4+ ♔f5
54.♖e2 g2 55.♖f2+ ♔e5 56.♖xg2
♗xg2+ 57.♗xg2 ♔f4   0-1

Tal,Mikhail
Bronstein,David

Leningrad ch-URS 1971 (4)

1.e4 c6 2.c4 d5 3.exd5 cxd5 4.d4
♘f6 5.♘c3 ♘c6 6.♗g5 ♗g4 7.♗e2
♗xe2 8.♘gxe2 dxc4 9.d5 ♘e5
10.0-0 h6 11.♗f4 ♘g6 12.♕a4+
♕d7 13.♕xc4 ♖c8 14.♕b3 e5
15.dxe6 ♕xe6 16.♕xb7 ♗c5

17.♘d4 ♗xd4 18.♖ae1 0-0 19.♖xe6
fxe6 20.♗d6 ♖fd8 21.♗c7 ♖f8
22.♘b5 ♗e5 23.♗xe5 ♘xe5
24.♕xa7 ♘d5 25.♕d4 ♘g6 26.h4
♘gf4 27.♕e4   1-0

Fischer,Robert
Euwe,Max

Leipzig ol 1960 (7)

1.e4 c6 2.d4 d5 3.exd5 cxd5 4.c4
♘f6 5.♘c3 ♘c6 6.♘f3 ♗g4 7.cxd5
♘xd5 8.♕b3 ♗xf3 9.gxf3 e6
10.♕xb7 ♘xd4 11.♗b5+ ♘xb5
12.♕c6+ ♔e7 13.♕xb5 ♘xc3?!
14.bxc3 ♕d7 15.♖b1 ♖d8 16.♗e3
♕xb5 17.♖xb5 ♖d7 18.♔e2 f6
19.♖d1! ♖xd1 20.♔xd1 ♔d7 21.♖b8
♔c6 22.♗xa7 g5 23.a4 ♗g7
24.♖b6+ ♔d5 25.♖b7 ♗f8 26.♖b8
♗g7 27.♖b5+ ♔c6 28.♖b6+ ♔d5
29.a5 f5 30.♗b8 ♖c8 [30...♗xc3?
31.a6] 31.a6 ♖xc3 32.♖b5+! [32.a7
♖a3 33.♖d6+ ♔c4 34.♖xe6 ♗d4]
32...♔c4 33.♖b7 ♗d4 34.♖c7+ ♔d3
35.♖xc3+ ♔xc3 36.♗e5!   1-0

Caro-Kann Main Line

1.e4 c6 2.d4 d5 3.♘c3

favour in the positional variations. The aggressive continuation 5...♘f6 6.e5 ♘e4 7.♘xe4 dxe4 8.♘g5 c5 9.♗c4 also seems to be doubtful for Black.

Returning to 3.♘c3 (3.♘d2), and now:

3.	...	**d5xe4**
4.	**♘c3xe4**	

We have reached the key position of the **Classical Variation of the Caro-Kann**. Black has three continuations:

A) 4...♘f6, which is provocative and controversial. Its reputation oscillates from 'dubious' to 'interesting';

B) 4...♘d7, the popular Smyslov Variation;

C) 4...♗f5, the old main line.

After 1.e4 c6 2.d4 d5, White's most usual choice continues to be defending e4 with the knight, usually with 3.♘c3. Over the last 20 years the pseudo-refinement 3.♘d2 is a frequent alternative. Given that nine times out of ten Black continues by taking on e4, this move does not make a big difference. Unless, of course, Black intends to play one of the **3...g6** systems. In that case ♘d2 proves to be more precise than ♘c3 given that, as in some lines of the **Modern Defence**, White keeps the option of supporting the centre with c3.

However, you need to contemplate the wisdom of discouraging a variation (3...g6) that has a worse performance statistically than other normal variations! Indeed, after 3.♘c3 g6, the position has the characteristics of many dubious variations of the **Pirc-Modern Defence**. For White 4.h3!, so as to prevent ...♗g4, seems best. After 4...♗g7 5.♘f3 the results tend to be in White's

A)   4.   ...   ♘g8-f6
Black allows the creation of an ugly doubled pawn, which has the virtue of controlling e5, the usual outpost for White's pieces in the Caro-Kann.

5. ♘e4xf6+
Now Black can recapture with either of the pawns.

A1)   5.   ...   e7xf6
This appears to be anti-positional, as it gives White a queenside pawn majority. Yet, it does have the advantage of being solid: the mass of pawns will protect

159

the king after subsequent kingside castling and, in addition, Black's two pawn islands are easier to defend than the three pawn islands created by taking with the other pawn. There is a very high percentage of draws with this line and for Black, it is difficult to win.

White can continue quietly, aiming for a slightly favourable endgame. Or he can play the more aggressive

6. c2-c3

Defending d4.

6.	**...**	**♗f8-d6**
7.	**♗f1-d3**	**0-0**
8.	**♕d1-c2**	**♖f8-e8+**
9.	**♘g1-e2**	**g7-g6**

9...h6 is safer.

10. h2-h4

with a dangerous attack.

A2)   5. ...   g7xf6

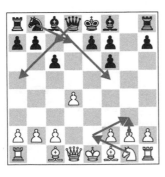

This recapture is enterprising and more popular. It is often called the **Bronstein/Larsen Variation**, after two of its most illustrious exponents – it is no coincidence that both players are associated with daring and creative chess.

Black enjoys better control of the centre, he has his eye on the g-file, and in some variations he succeeds in advancing his e-pawn to e5. Black will usually develop the c8-bishop to f5 or, less often, to g4; the knight goes to d7 and the queen is moved to c7 or a5.

However, Black's real problem is not his pawn structure – the active placement of his pieces makes this academic – but the much more urgent dilemma of his king's future. Kingside castling without the g7-pawn seems unsafe; and after Black castles queenside, White's pawn advance there should be quicker than Black's pawn march on the kingside.

White has several different plans. However, the most common, and probably also the strongest, has proved to be the waiting move

6. c2-c3!

White delays ♘f3, as he does not wish to encourage ...♗g4. He waits for

6. ...   ♗c8-f5

to harass the bishop with 7.♘e2 ♘d7 8.♘g3 ♗g6 9.h4. It is true that after 9...h5 10.♗e2 ♕a5, White can win a pawn with 11.b4 followed by ♘xh5, but Black's counterplay, based on the ...e7-e5 advance or, alternatively, ...a7-a5, has revealed itself to be insidious.

As a result, the plan of preparing for the kingside fianchetto

7.	**♘g1-f3**	**e7-e6**
8.	**g2-g3!**	

has recently caught on.

By doing this White aims to consolidate his king after castling, and in the case of opposite-side castling the g2-bishop becomes a dangerous weapon. If instead Black castles kingside, White's advantage is small but concrete, as his excellent percentage of more than 60% would appear to confirm.

B)   4. ...   ♘b8-d7

This has recently been called the **Smyslov Variation**, while in some of the older manuals it is referred to as the **Nimzowitsch Variation**.

Besides Smyslov, another famous and devoted practitioner was, and still is, Anatoly Karpov. For many, his continued support is the reason why this variation enjoys its current popularity. Black does not directly attack the knight on e4, but it 'threatens to threaten' on

the next move with ...♘gf6: perfectly in keeping with Nimzowitsch's style of play.

Now White has to decide what to do with his knight on e4 in the next two moves. Practice has shown that neither to defend it, nor to exchange it with the one on f6, nor to move it to g3, gives White any serious opportunities to gain an advantage.

Strangely, the best square has proven to be g5! and the knight can be moved there either immediately or after the preliminary 5.♗c4. Black cannot try to rid himself of the knight's ominous presence here right away because of various tactical resources centred around e6 or f7. First he must continue to develop, and after the knight — depending on the variation — returns from g5 to f3 or to e4, White maintains an unpleasant initiative.

However, the system is a hard nut to crack and it is well suited to black players who are not worried about the prospect of defending cramped but solid positions.

B1)   5. ♗f1-c4

The most natural continuation, and it was the most popular move until the 1980s.

> **5. ...   ♘g8-f6**
> **6. ♘e4-g5!   e7-e6**

6...♘d5 is playable, but it has never been popular.

> **7. ♕d1-e2!   ♘d7-b6!**

Black first defends the e6-pawn. Instead, the move *7...♗d6?? (or 7...h6??) would be followed by the brutal 8.♘xf7! ♔xf7 9.♕xe6+ ♔g6 10.♗d3+ ♔h5 11.♕h3*

Mate!

After 7...♘b6 White's bishop usually retreats to d3, having played out its role on the a2-g8 diagonal; namely, to force Black to block the way out of the c8-bishop with ...e6. However, 8.♗b3 also has its admirers and it is not necessarily inferior.

8. ♗c4-d3   h7-h6

It is inadvisable to take the d4-pawn: indeed, at first glance 8...♕xd4?! 9.♘1f3 ♕d5! 10.♘e5 ♕xg2 11.♖f1 ♗e7

seems very dubious. However, things are not as terrible as was thought before the advent of chess computer programs. For example, after 12.♘e5/♘g5xf7 0-0, it is even possible that Black is better; but after 12.♘ef3!, it is probable that White is in fact the one with the advantage: 12...♕g4 13.♘xf7! and now after 13...0-0?, we have 14.♘h6+!.

Computer programs are capable of finding hitherto unthought-of tactical resources in what appear to be desperately bad positions. As a result, many variations that had been uncritically accepted for decades have had to be subsequently re-evaluated.

Back to 8...h6.

9. ♘g5-f3

Now the d4-pawn was really undefended. Here Black's c8-bishop looks ugly. However, the g1-knight is hardly happy to find his fellow knight sitting on f3.

9. ...   c6-c5

Black attempts to free his game. With time, the main line has become

10. d4xc5   ♗f8xc5

The move 10...♘bd7 is playable, but this usually does not appeal to a Caro-Kann player's taste, given that after 11.b4 adequate compensation for the pawn is yet to be proved.

11. ♘f3-e5

Vacating f3 for the other knight.

11. ...   ♘b6-d7

12. ♘g1-f3   ♕d8-c7

13. 0-0

Keep in mind the following tactics: 13.♗d2? ♘xe5 14.♘xe5 ♗xf2+!! 15.♔xf2 ♕xe5 and after 16.♕xe5 Black regains the queen with

an advantage on account of the knight fork on g4.

13. ...   0-0

14. ♗c1-f4   ♗c5-d6

and White will have difficulty maintaining the outpost on e5. After 15.♖fe1 ♘c5 16.♖ad1 b6, Black concludes his development and the game is balanced.

B2)   5. ♘e4-g5

A paradoxical move that creates no immediate threat.

5. ...   ♘g8-f6

Or 5...h6?! 6.♘e6! ♕a5+ (the knight is immune from capture because of mate in two) 7.♗d2 ♕b6 8.♗d3 ♘gf6 (once again taking the knight on e6 doesn't work, this time because of 9.♕h5+ followed by 10.♗a5 and Black loses the queen) 9.♘xf8 ♘xf8 with a big, even though not decisive advantage for White.

6. ♗f1-d3

With 6.♗c4 we would be back in Variation B1.

6. ...   e7-e6

7. ♘g1-f3   ♗f8-d6!

7...h6?! is premature because of 8.♘xe6! fxe6 9.♗g6+ ♔e7 10.0-0 and only a computer would know how to defend this position with Black. In prac-

tice White's attack proves to be winning.

8. ♕d1-e2!

To take on e4 with the queen.

8. ...   h7-h6

Finally Black can force the troublesome knight to go elsewhere.

9. ♘g5-e4

With the f8-square free for the black king, the sacrifice on e6 does not lead to anything good.

9. ...   ♘f6xe4

10. ♕e2xe4

Black's problem is the c8-bishop, which is usually developed to b7. To make this possible, Black must defend c6 or force the white queen to leave e4. After 10...♕c7 11.♕g4! the black king's position is problematic, in that he must continue with 11...♔f8!, with a small plus for White.

For this reason, Black usually prefers the alternative

10. ...   ♘d7-f6

In the past the natural 11.♕h4 was played, putting the kingside under pressure and rendering kingside castling too risky for Black. However, in 1993 Karpov stunned the chess world with the sensational novelty 11...♔e7!!.

An incredible move which, by defending the rook on h8, puts the white queen in peril with the simple threat of 12...g5 13.♕h3 g4. In order to give the queen some space there remains only 12.♘e5, which, however, loses a pawn after 12...♗xe5 13.dxe5 ♕a5+.

Enthusiasm for Karpov's idea waned a little when it was discovered that after 14.c3 ♕xe5+ 15.♗e3, White has greater compensation than was originally thought and probably enough to continue, with an unclear game.

Obviously, however, most white players are looking for an objective advantage, and thus prefer the more solid

11. ♕e4-e2	b7-b6
12. ♗c1-d2	♗c8-b7
13. 0-0-0	♕d8-c7

Now Black will be wise to castle queenside – the h6-pawn makes it eas-

ier for White to open the g-file after short castling – after which the game turns into a slow positional struggle, typical of many variations of the Caro-Kann. White has slightly more possibilities thanks to his space advantage, but Black's position is solid and without weaknesses.

Classical Variation

C)   4. ...   ♗c8-f5

This is the **old main line**. It suffered a slump in popularity at the end of the 20th century because of the success of the **Smyslov Variation**. However, in the first years of the new millennium it has become more and more fashionable again. In the age of the computer and the Internet, in which new moves are available within seconds of being made, the following phenomenon turns up: during an important game a strong player employs a new variation, or dusts off a forgotten one; the game is subsequently discussed and analysed around the world; other new moves are proposed and discovered; lower-rated players imitate the stronger players by using the variation in question; and in no time at all there is such a big database of games available that it is very difficult to surprise your opponent – that is, until another creative player uses something else that's new and off we go again. An example of this is a move that we will look at soon: 7...♘f6. This move was even classified as a blunder in the old opening manuals.

It would appear that as a result of these developments there will soon be nothing left to discover in opening theory: a conviction that Capablanca already ventilated in the 1930s (!!). However, fortunately for us, history has demonstrated that this is far from being the case, and that there still exist large areas that have yet to be explored, and much from the past that needs to be reassessed in the light of what we know now. Even if one day we do manage to sift through everything there is to be known about chess, human memory is such that the old saying 'Everything new is something forgotten' will prove itself to be as true as ever.

Returning to where we left off, White almost always proceeds with

5. ♘e4-g3

By the way, even 5.♘c5 is playable and better than it would appear to be: as is so often the case with David Bronstein's ideas!

5. ... ♗f5-g6

Now we have reached **one of the most important positions of the Caro-Kann.**

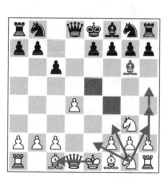

White can choose from many plans, whereas Black's scope for development is restricted. Usually White continues with 6.h4, but once in a while he also has plans that include ♘e2-f4 – with or without ♗c4. The advantage of the two

bishops after the possible exchange of the f4-knight for the g6-bishop is only academic. This is because in the closed positions that are typical of these variations it is not rare that a knight is more effective than a bishop. The sacrifice of a knight or bishop on e6 in these variations is interesting but not really sound. On the other hand, the idea of advancing the f-pawn is a double-edged sword, because if the subsequent advance to f5 becomes impossible, the pawn on f4 will become a pronounced positional weakness; for starters, just have a look at the poor bishop on c1.

White normally seeks to profit from the position of the g6-bishop to gain space on the kingside with

6. h2-h4

It is true that sometimes pawns that advance too far up the board can become weak, but in this specific case, experience has demonstrated that this is the only option that allows White to hope for a concrete advantage.

6. ... h7-h6

7. ♘g1-f3

White threatens 8.♘e5 before advancing the h-pawn again. Here we come to another point relevant to our previous discussions about the development of opening theory. For decades in this position Black automatically played

7. ... ♘b8-d7

to prevent the very move ♘e5.

Recently, it has become fashionable to ignore this threat and play 7...♘f6!?. After 8.♘e5 ♗h7, the most solid move is **9.♗d3!** (the old opening books believed the following line to be excellent for White: 9.♗c4 e6 10.♕e2, with the idea of 11.♘xf7. But in reality after

10...♘d5, White does not gain anything – indeed, the results favour Black)
9...♗xd3   (9...♕xd4?   10.♘xf7!)
10.♕xd3 e6.

White seems to have gained a tempo
compared to variations of the old main
line: the pawn on the h4-square has no
influence on the game compared to h5,
but the knight's placement on e5 rather
than f3 seems to be an advantage. However, the latter may in fact not be the
case. In certain variations of the **Petroff
Defence** also, the black knight is better
on f6 than on e4, where it facilitates
White's development).

The resulting positions are typical of
the Caro-Kann: solid but cramped, and
are variously described as equal or
slightly to White's advantage, depending on the taste of the commentator.
Let's return to 7...♘d7.

8. h4-h5

As the pawn has already been played to
h4, you may as well advance it one
more square before exchanging the
bishops.

8. ...	♗g6-h7
9. ♗f1-d3	♗h7xd3
10. ♕d1xd3	

Now, to stop ♗f4, Black usually proceeds with

10. ...	♕d8-c7
11. ♗c1-d2	e7-e6
12. 0-0-0	♘g8-f6

We have reached another key position
of the Caro-Kann (a so-called *tabiya*,
an Arabic term for 'key position'
which is derived from the medieval
predecessor of the game). Experience
gained from thousands of games
demonstrates that the best move for
White is either of the following two:
13.♕e2 or 13.♘e4.

C1)   13. ♕d3-e2

Spassky's aggressive idea: the queen defends e5, enabling ♘e5, to attack f7.

| 13. ... | 0-0-0 |

The recent idea 13...c5!? is intriguing,
as it undermines the control of e5 before White can occupy it.

| 14. ♘f3-e5 | |

And here Black generally plays

| 14. ... | ♘d7-b6 |

to defend f7 indirectly, given that
14...♘xe5 has not produced encouraging results. Indeed, a white pawn on e5
limits Black's mobility, also in a possible
endgame, and the g3-knight can immediately become very active on e4.
Back to 14...♘b6. White now mostly
continues with

15. &d2-a5

This defends d4 and threatens the annoying c4-c5. Black responds energetically.

15. ...   &d8-d5!

Liberating himself from the pin with every means available.

Now White can play the solid

16. &a5xb6

contenting himself with a slight positional advantage.

16. ...   a7xb6

The defence of f7 must be maintained.

17. c2-c4

Followed by 18.&e4, and if needs be f2-f4.

Alternatively, White can accept the challenge and defend the a5-bishop with 16.b4. Black must then continue energetically with 16...&xa5! 17.bxa5 &a3+ 18.&b1 &a4, but it is not clear if Black has achieved sufficient compensation for the exchange.

C2)   13. &g3-e4

is the most frequent and probably best move. This is despite the fact that it seems to contravene the principle that in a cramped position, every exchange favours the defender. However, as you know, the complexity of chess arises

from the fact that there are as many exceptions as there are rules: in this specific case the knight on g3 is White's most passive piece and it seems to be a good idea to exchange it for the knight on f6, which is playing an important defensive role. In addition, the move makes g2-g3 possible, with control of f4.

At this stage, Black almost always plays

13. ...   0-0-0

against which the best response is

14. g2-g3!

Preparing for 15.&f4. Black now usually simplifies with

14. ...   &f6xe4

14...&c5!? is playable, even if 15.&xc5 &xc5 16.c4!, with the idea of &c3, seems to give White a small plus.

15. &d3xe4   &f8-d6

15...&f6?! attacks the queen but gives up control of the e5- and c5-squares.

16. c2-c4!   c6-c5

And after 17.&c3 or 17.d5!? the results appear to be slightly in White's favour, with a decidedly high draw rate of around 50%.

This type of variation is typical of the Caro-Kann: suitable for patient players who have no problem with the prospect of a probable draw.

Réti,Richard
Tartakower,Savielly

Vienna 1910

1.e4 c6 2.d4 d5 3.♘c3 dxe4 4.♘xe4 ♘f6 5.♕d3 e5?! 6.dxe5 ♕a5+ 7.♗d2 ♕xe5 8.0-0-0 ♘xe4?? [Black was worse anyway: this game aptly illustrates the dangers of having your king in the centre when there are open lines and the development is lagging; 8...♕xe4 9.♖e1+−; 8...♘bd7 9.♘f3±; 8...♗e7 9.♘xf6+ ♕xf6 10.♘f3±] 9.♕d8+! ♔xd8 10.♗g5+ ♔c7 [10...♔e8 11.♖d8X] 11.♗d8X 1-0

Karpov,Anatoly
Miles,Anthony

Bath 1983

1.e4 c6 2.d4 d5 3.♘d2 dxe4 4.♘xe4 ♘f6 5.♘xf6+ gxf6 6.♘f3 ♗f5 7.♗f4 ♘d7 8.c3 ♕b6 9.b4 e5 10.♗g3 0-0-0 11.♗e2 h5 12.0-0 ♗e4 13.♘d2 ♗d5 14.♗xh5 exd4 15.c4 ♗e6 16.a3 ♘e5 17.♖e1 d3 18.c5 ♕b5 19.♖b1 ♗h6 20.a4 ♕a6 21.f4 ♘c4 22.b5 cxb5 23.♖xb5 ♘a3 24.♖b2 ♘c2 25.♗f3 ♗d5 26.♖e7 ♗f8 27.♗xd5 ♖xd5 28.♖bxb7 ♗xe7 29.♖xe7 ♕c6 30.♖xf7 ♖xc5 31.♕g4+ f5 32.♕g7 ♖e8 33.h4 ♘e3 34.♗f2 ♖c1+ 35.♔h2 ♘g4+ 36.♔g3 ♘xf2 37.♘f3 ♘e4+ 38.♔h2 d2 39.♘xd2 ♘xd2 0-1

Tal,Mikhail
Benko,Paul

Amsterdam izt 1964 (11)

1.e4 c6 2.d4 d5 3.♘c3 dxe4 4.♘xe4 ♘d7 5.♗c4 [5.♕e2?! (a clever trap) 5...♘gf6?? (5...♘df6! and the queen on e2 hinders White's development) 6.♘d6X] 5...♘gf6 6.♘g5 e6 7.♕e2 ♘b6 8.♗b3 h6 9.♘5f3 ♗e7 10.♘h3 c5 11.♗e3 ♘bd5 12.0-0-0 ♘xe3 13.fxe3 ♕c7 14.♘e5 a6 15.g4 ♗d6 16.g5 hxg5 17.♘xg5 ♗xe5 18.dxe5 ♕xe5 19.♖d8+ ♔e7 20.♖xh8 ♕xg5 21.♕d2 1-0

Anand,Viswanathan
Bologan,Viktor

Dortmund 2003 (7)

1.e4 c6 2.d4 d5 3.♘c3 dxe4 4.♘xe4 ♘d7 5.♘g5 ♘gf6 6.♗d3 e6 7.♘1f3 ♗d6 8.♕e2 h6 9.♘e4 ♘xe4 10.♕xe4 ♕c7 11.0-0 b6 12.♕g4 g5 13.♕h3 ♖g8 14.♖e1!! ♗f8 15.♕f5 ♗g7 16.h4 ♔f8 17.♕h3 ♖h8 18.hxg5 hxg5 19.♕g4 c5 20.♗xg5 cxd4 21.♖ad1 ♗b7 22.♖xe6 fxe6 23.♗e7+ ♔xe7 24.♕xg7+ ♔d6 25.♘xd4 ♕c5 26.♗f5 ♕e5 27.♘f3+ ♕d5 28.♕g3+ ♔e7 29.♖xd5 ♗xd5 30.♕g5+ ♔d6 31.♕f4+ ♔e7 32.♗e4 ♖h5 33.♘h4 ♖g8 34.♘g6+ ♔d8 35.♕f7 ♖e8 36.♗d3 1-0

Kramnik,Vladimir
Bareev,Evgeny

Wijk aan Zee 2003 (3)

1.e4 c6 2.d4 d5 3.♘c3 dxe4 4.♘xe4 ♗f5 5.♘g3 ♗g6 6.h4 h6 7.♘f3 ♘d7 8.h5 ♗h7 9.♗d3 ♗xd3 10.♕xd3 ♘gf6 11.♗f4 e6 12.0-0-0 ♗e7 13.♘e4 ♘xe4 14.♕xe4 ♘f6 15.♕d3 ♕d5 16.c4 ♕e4 17.♕xe4 ♘xe4 18.♗e3 ♘d6 19.b3 ♗f6 20.g4 b5 21.♘d2 ♔d7 22.♔c2 ♗d8 23.♘f3 ♗f6 24.♘e5+ ♔c7 25.c5 ♗xe5 26.dxe5 ♘c8 27.♖h3 ♘e7 28.♖f3 ♖hf8 29.♖d6 a5 30.g5 hxg5 31.♗xg5 ♘f5 32.♖d1 a4 33.b4 ♔c8 34.♖fd3 ♖a7 35.♖d8+ ♖xd8 36.♖xd8+ ♔b7 37.♔c3 ♔a6

38.♔d3 ♖c7 39.♔e4 ♔b7 40.♖d1
♔c8 41.♖d8+ ♔b7 42.♔f4 ♖c8
43.♖d7+ ♖c7 44.♖d3 ♔c8
45.♖d8+ ♔b7 46.♗f6 g6 47.hxg6
fxg6 48.♔g5   1-0

Kramnik,Vladimir
Leko,Peter
Brissago Wch m 2004 (12)

1.e4 c6 2.d4 d5 3.♘d2 dxe4 4.♘xe4
♗f5 5.♘g3 ♗g6 6.h4 h6 7.♘f3 ♘d7
8.h5 ♗h7 9.♗d3 ♗xd3 10.♕xd3 e6
11.♗f4 ♕a5+ 12.♗d2 ♕c7 13.0-0-0
♘gf6 14.♘e4 0-0-0 15.g3 ♘xe4
16.♕xe4 ♗d6 17.♔b1 ♖he8 18.♕h7
♖g8 19.c4 c5 20.d5 ♘f6 21.♕c2
exd5 22.cxd5 ♕d7 23.♗c3 ♖de8
24.♗xf6 gxf6 25.♕d3 f5 26.♘d2 b5
27.♖he1 ♔b8 28.♕c3 ♖xe1 29.♖xe1
c4 30.♘f3 f4 31.g4 ♗c7 32.♕d4
♕xg4 33.♕e4 ♕xh5 34.♘d4 ♕g6
                                    ½-½

Topalov,Veselin
Vallejo Pons,Francisco
Leon rapid 2006 (1)

1.e4 c6 2.d4 d5 3.♘d2 dxe4 4.♘xe4
♗f5 5.♘g3 ♗g6 6.h4 h6 7.♘f3 ♘d7
8.h5 ♗h7 9.♗d3 ♗xd3 10.♕xd3 e6
11.♗f4 ♗b4+ 12.c3 ♗e7 13.♘e4
♘gf6 14.♘xf6+ ♘xf6 15.♘e5 ♕a5
16.♕g3 ♖g8 17.♕h3 ♕a6 18.♕f3
♖d8 19.b4 ♘d7 20.♘d3 ♕c4
21.♗d2 ♕d5 22.♔e2 ♘f6 23.♕xd5
cxd5 24.f3 ♗d6 25.a4 ♔e7 26.♗d2
b6 27.g4 a5 28.♖hb1 ♖d7 29.bxa5
bxa5 30.♖b5 ♖a8 31.♘c1 ♖da7
32.♖ab1 ♘e8 33.♘d3 ♔d7 34.♗e3
♔c8 35.♖1b3 ♖b8 36.♖xb8+ ♗xb8
37.♘e5 ♗xe5 38.dxe5 ♖b7 39.♖xb7
♔xb7 40.♗c5 f6 41.f4 ♔c6 42.♗f8
fxe5 43.fxe5 ♔d7 44.♔d3 ♔c7
45.♔e3 ♔c6 46.♔f4 ♔d7 47.g5
♔d8 48.♗xg7 hxg5+ 49.♔xg5
♘xg7 50.h6 ♔e7 51.h7   1-0

French Defence

1.e2-e4 e7-e6

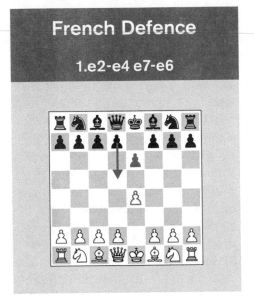

This defence had its successful debut in a London/Paris correspondence team match (hence the name) in 1834, and in the following years it was to become the 2nd most popular defence after the reigning 1...e5.

More than anything, 1...e6 is a radical way of avoiding all those f7-square based tactics that give Black headaches in the Open Games. It was only with the boom in the **Sicilian**'s popularity, which started in the middle of the 20th century, that the **French** became the third most popular choice against 1.e4.

Many champions have employed the French as one of the main weapons in their repertoire: Botvinnik is an illustrious exponent from the past, while Bareev, Yusupov, Dolmatov and Kortchnoi are noteworthy contemporary users.

For many, the French is a defence you either love or hate: in some it inspires an enthusiasm that borders on the fanatical – again, just think of Uhlmann,

who has never played anything else in his whole life. Others maintain that it is virtually losing from the start. White players also seem to be polarized by it: there are some that love to play against it, and others who feel so uncomfortable with it that it is not a rarity to see them switch to 1.d4, so as to be forever free of the French!

As is the case with the **Caro-Kann**, Black attacks the undefended e4-pawn on the second move, with the difference that the d5 advance is supported by the e-pawn instead of the c-pawn. This has the advantage that when White advances the pawn to e5

– as often happens – Black is ready to undermine the pawn chain d4-e5 with the ...c7-c5 advance in one go, or, more rarely, with the advance ...f7-f6.

The price to be paid for this is the passive bishop on c8, which in the Caro-Kann develops without problems. Conceptually speaking, the **French is an active defence** – contrary to what you would imagine, the percentage of draws in the French is lower than in the Open Games – even if many quiet lines can ensue. The Exchange Variation is a good example. Generally Black concedes space on the kingside in exchange for counterplay against White's centre and good prospects on the queenside. We could simplify things by saying that if Black gets through the middlegame alive, his possession of the c-file and the weakness of the white d4-pawn give him excellent endgame prospects. This is a very general assessment. Clearly there are some specific variations that have different characteristics. Just think of the Tarrasch Variation with 3...c5. Here Black's isolated d5-pawn favours White's endgame chances and Black must play all his cards in the middlegame!

Now we will have look at the specifics of the variations. After 1.e4 e6, nine times out of ten White responds with 2.d4. However, various other replies are possible:

2. ♘g1-f3   d7-d5
3. e4-e5   c7-c5
4. b2-b4!?

An interesting continuation along the lines of the Wing Gambit against the Sicilian. Here Black has already advanced his pawn to e6, and therefore this represents a better version. However, after 4...cxb4 5.a3 ♘c6 6.axb4 ♗xb4 7.c3

♗e7, the compensation is rather dubious, although, at lower levels, where players are usually less skilled in defence than in attack, it can be a highly dangerous weapon.

The move 2.d3 introduces the **King's Indian Attack**, as we have mentioned earlier in the section on the Caro-Kann. The King's Indian Attack is a **King's Indian Defence** played with the white pieces. Given that the best plan for White in the King's Indian is to advance his e-pawn to e4, here White profits from the fact that Black has already advanced his e-pawn to e6 to establish the same position with an extra tempo.

2. d2-d3   d7-d5
3. ♘b1-d2   c7-c5
4. ♘g1-f3

The position is strategically complex, and offers both players possibilities. Play is very similar to the **Sicilian**: 1.e4 c5 2.♘f3 e6 3.d3 with the usual continuation 3...d5 4.♘bd2, which we will look at in more detail later.

2.♕e2 is possible and runs along the lines of the preceding variation, but prevents the immediate 2...d5 if Black wants to recapture with the pawn. Black prepares to play ...d5 with 2...♗e7, or otherwise he plays 2...c5 and the game assumes the distinctive features of the King's Indian Attack. Alternatively, Black could reply with the paradoxical 2...e5!?

considering that in the Open Games you are worse off with your queen on e2 than on d1. For example, White now has a problem if he wants to play the **Ruy Lopez**!

However, as already mentioned, the most popular move is 2.d4 and after 2...d5

we arrive at the initial position of the French Defence. The e4-pawn is being attacked and White must decide what to do: advance it, exchange it or defend it.

Cosulich,Roberto
Pokojowczyk,Jerzy
Nice ol 1974 (2)

1.e4 e6 2.d3 d5 3.♘d2 ♘f6 4.♘gf3 b6 5.g3 ♗b7 6.e5 ♘fd7 7.♗g2 ♘c6 8.♕e2 ♘b4 9.♘b3 c5 10.0-0 ♗e7 11.h4 ♕c7 12.♖e1 a5 13.a3 ♘c6 14.♗f4 b5 15.♘bd2 0-0 16.♘f1 ♖fc8 17.c3 b4 18.♘e3 ♘f8 19.♘g4 ♗a6 20.♘f6+ gxf6 21.exf6 ♕d8 22.fxe7 ♕xe7 23.c4 ♕f6 24.♘e5 ♘d4 25.♕d1 ♗b7 26.♘g4 ♕e7 27.♗g5 ♕d6 28.♗f6 ♘d7 29.♘h6+ ♔f8 30.♕h5 1-0

Fischer,Robert
Miagmarsuren,Lhamsuren
Sousse izt 1967 (3)

1.e4 e6 2.d3 d5 3.♘d2 ♘f6 4.g3 c5 [4...dxe4!? 5.dxe4 e5 6.♘gf3 ♗c5] **5.♗g2 ♘c6 6.♘gf3 ♗e7 7.0-0 0-0 8.e5 ♘d7 9.♖e1 b5 10.♘f1 b4 11.h4 a5 12.♗f4 a4 13.a3!** [this idea of Fischer is still considered the best] **13...bxa3** [13...♗a6 14.♘1h2 c4 15.d4 c3 16.bxc3 bxc3 17.♘g5 ♘b6 18.♕h5 ♗xg5 19.♗xg5 ♕e8 20.♗f6 ♘xd4 21.♘g4 ♘f5 22.♕g5 ♔h8 23.♗xg7+ ♔xg7 24.♘f6 ♕d8 25.♕h6 Kaidanov-Nijboer, Elista ol 1998 (1-0, 31)] **14.bxa3 ♘a5 15.♘e3 ♗a6 16.♗h3** [16.h5!? with the idea of h6 and ♘g4] **16...d4 17.♘f1 ♘b6 18.♘g5 ♘d5 19.♗d2 ♗xg5 20.♗xg5 ♕d7 21.♕h5 ♖fc8 22.♘d2 ♘c3 23.♗f6 ♕e8 24.♘e4 g6 25.♕g5 ♘xe4 26.♖xe4 c4 27.h5 cxd3 28.♖h4 ♖a7** [28...dxc2 29.hxg6 fxg6 30.♖xh7+−] **29.♗g2 dxc2** [29...♕f8 30.♗e4 dxc2 31.hxg6 fxg6 32.♗xg6+−] **30.♕h6 ♕f8 31.♕xh7+** [31...♔xh7 32.hxg6+ ♔xg6 33.♗e4X] 1-0

French Defence Exchange Variation

1.e4 e6 2.d4 d5 3.exd5 exd5

The **Exchange Variation** is correctly considered to be unambitious and toothless. After 3...exd5, the resulting position is similar to the **Petroff Defence**. However, in the Petroff the placement of the black knight on e4 with the accompanying weakening of d5 gives White some chances. In the present case, Black achieves complete and immediate equality. However, equality does not mean a drawn game. In fact, Black has a better win rate than White in this variation!

The explanation for this lies in competitive psychology: sometimes, when facing a stronger opponent, a white player will choose this system, which is famous for it drawish nature, to score a precious half-point. Only later does he realize that thirty pieces still remain on the board and that their presence generally gives more than sufficient opportunity for the stronger player to win any-

way. This is why the percentage of draws is also much lower than you would expect.

White usually continues with 4.♗d3, reserving the e2-square for his king's knight. Draws are common with 4...♗d6 5.♘e2 ♘e7 6.0-0 0-0 7.♗f4 ♗f5.

Another development is

4.	**♘g1-f3**	**♘g8-f6**
5.	**♗f1-d3**	

Curiously, 5.♘e5?! produces a position from the Petroff Defence, but with reversed colours!

5.	...	**♗f8-d6**

An ambitious black player could break the symmetry with 5...c5!?, which gives his pieces activity at the cost of a weak pawn on d5.

6.	**0-0**	**0-0**
7.	**♗c1-g5**	**♗c8-g4**
8.	**♘b1-d2**	**♘b8-d7**
9.	**c2-c3**	**c7-c6**

with a symmetrical position. White's extra tempo does not give him any advantage in such a quiet position. After several exchanges of the major pieces on the e-file the game should head for a draw.

City London
City Paris
cr 1834

1.e4 e6 2.d4 d5 3.exd5 exd5 4.♘f3
♞f6 5.♗d3 c5 6.♕e2+ ♝e7 7.dxc5
0-0 8.♗e3 ♜e8 9.♗b5 ♞c6 10.♘d4
♝xc5 11.♗xc6 bxc6 12.c3 ♝xd4
13.cxd4 c5 14.♕d3 ♛b6 15.0-0
♗a6 16.♕b3 ♛xb3 17.axb3 ♝xf1
18.♔xf1 ♞g4 19.dxc5 ♞xe3+
20.fxe3 ♜xe3 21.♘d2 ♜ae8 22.b4
♜d3 23.♜xa7 ♜xd2 24.b5 ♜xb2

25.b6 d4 26.b7 d3 27.♜a8 ♚f8
28.c6 d2 29.♜xe8+ ♚xe8 30.♔e2
♚d8   0-1

Tatai,Stefano
Kortchnoi,Viktor
Beer-Sheva 1978 (6)

1.e4 e6 2.d4 d5 3.exd5 exd5 4.♗d3
c5 5.♘f3 ♞c6 6.♕e2+ ♝e7 7.dxc5
♞f6 8.h3 0-0 9.0-0 ♝xc5 10.c3 ♜e8
11.♕c2 ♛d6 12.♘bd2 ♛g3 13.♗f5
♜e2 14.♘d4 ♞xd4   0-1

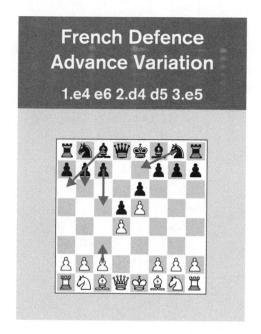

French Defence Advance Variation

1.e4 e6 2.d4 d5 3.e5

This is sometimes called the **Nimzowitsch Variation** – as if there weren't already enough variations with that man's name – and it represents one of White's most ambitious options.

White gains space on the kingside and he is not afraid to concede Black the initiative. Black will apply pressure to the d4-pawn for several moves, and White will be forced to defend it. This is the heart of the matter. Will this attack bring some concrete advantage, or will it come to nothing and will White then be able to exploit his structural advantage?

This subject has been a topic of debate since the time when Nimzowitsch disputed Dr. Siegbert Tarrasch's claims (i.e. that 3.e5 is strategically wrong) in the pages of his famous book My System. Nowadays, we do not have to rely on the inevitably subjective opinions of commentators on any given variation. Modern players have a resource that was

unavailable in the greater part of the last century: statistics.

With all its defects, statistical analysis can be very revealing and supply a lot of useful information. If, as in this case, statistics are available for thousands and thousands of games, and White's performance is within the standard result range (let's say 52-55%), then the results are normal and harsh judgements are unwarranted.

Perhaps the truth lies somewhere between the two conflicting viewpoints: 3.e5 does not give White the net advantage that Nimzowitsch claimed, nor does it give Black as easy a game as Tarrasch would have us believe.

Black almost always responds with the natural

3. ... c7-c5

But sometimes he will vary with 3...b6 or 3...♞e7, which are both playable moves that leave Black with a cramped position. At this point, White keeps the pawn chain intact by playing

4. c2-c3

The move 4.♕g4 seems too optimistic; while 4.♞f3 is interesting, as it is based on the idea of leaving the d4-pawn to its fate: 4...cxd4 5.♗d3 ♞c6 6.0-0 and if Black does not wish to be overwhelmed by White's kingside initiative, he must react energetically there with ...♞ge7-g6 or ...f7-f6.

4. ... ♞b8-c6

There are some who prefer 4...♕b6 5.♞f3 ♗d7, to exchange the bad bishop. However, with 6.♗e2 ♗b5 7.c4! White can open up the game to his advantage.

5. ♞g1-f3 ♕d8-b6

The most thematic, even though 5...♗d7 with the idea of ...♘ge7-f5 is becoming more and more popular. Black increases the pressure on the d4-pawn. Now White has three alternatives.

A)   6.   ♗f1-d3

Preparing an interesting but dubious pawn sacrifice.

6. ...	**c5xd4**
7. c3xd4	**♗c8-d7**

Obviously the double capture on d4 doesn't work because of 9.♗b5+, which wins the queen.

8.   0-0

To have second thoughts and defend d4 with 8.♗e2 does not make sense, as White would transpose to the next variation with loss of a tempo.

8. ...	**♘c6xd4**
9. ♘f3xd4	**♕b6xd4**
10. ♘b1-c3!?	

Giving up another pawn to increase his initiative. 10.♕e2 ♘e7! 11.♘c3 a6! is a simple transposition.

10. ...	**a7-a6!**

10...♕xe5 is playable but results in an unclear position. After 11.♖e1, White has the sort of game he has been looking for.

11. ♕d1-e2	**♘g8-e7**
12. ♔g1-h1	

Preparing f2-f4.

12. ...	**♘e7-c6**
13. f2-f4	**♗f8-c5!**
14. ♖f1-d1	**♘c6-b4!**

And after ♗xa6 or ♗xh7, the queen goes to f2, giving Black the advantage.

B)   6.   ♗f1-e2

The most natural move, quietly developing.

6. ...	**c5xd4!**

Black wants to relocate his knight to f5, but after 6...♘ge7 *a strong response is 7.dxc5, and after 6...♘h6 7.♗xh6!, Black cannot take on b2 because of the reply 8.♗e3!, and if 8...♕xa1 9.♕c2!, and the black queen will be captured.*

7. c3xd4	**♘g8-h6!**

The knight goes to f5 via h6 to allow the f8-bishop to maintain control of the a3 square. After 7...♘ge7 8.♘a3 ♘f5 9.♘c2 ♗b4+ 10.♔f1!, White castles by hand and will be a little better thanks to his space advantage.

8.   ♘b1-c3

After 8.♘a3, there follows 8...♗xa3; and after 8.♗xh6, without the c3-pawn, the move 8...♕xb2! is now good.

8. ...	**♘h6-f5**
9. ♘c3-a4!	**♕b6-a5+**
10. ♗c1-d2	**♗f8-b4**
11. ♗d2-c3!	**b7-b5**

12. a2-a3!   **♗b4xc3+**
13. ♘a4xc3   **b5-b4**
14. a3xb4   **♕a5xb4**

And it is not clear which is weaker: White's pawns on d4 and b2 or Black's pawn on a7: both sides have approximately equal chances.

C)   6. a2-a3

This is the most popular move. Before proceeding with his development, White prevents future checks from b4 or a5 – a common tactical resource for Black – and prepares for the b2-b4 advance, which gains space on the queenside.

However, every move has its negative consequences, and in this case the weakness created on b3 allows the ambitious

6. ...   **c5-c4!?**

Black can also permit White to advance the b-pawn with 6...♗d7 7.b4 cxd4 8.cxd4 ♖c8, waiting for 9.♗b2

in order to respond with 9...♘a5! 10.♘bd2 ♘c4 with a complicated game.

Let's go back to 6...c4.

This seems like a beginner's move, one of those moves computers used to play in their early days.

That would be the case if the white pawn were still on a2: but now, as soon as White wants to open up the queenside he has to recapture on b3 with a piece, and the outpost on c4 will give Black excellent chances. 6...c4 is therefore a prophylactic move that intends to completely restrict White's activity on the queenside, after which the strategic centre of gravity will shift to the centre and the kingside.

7. g2-g3!?

In anticipation of the ...f7-f6 break, White does well to move his bishop to g2 or h3. It is wise for Black to continue with the solid

7. ...   **♗c8-d7**

followed by ...♘a5 and ...0-0-0, with slow manoeuvring play and chances for both sides.

Bondarevsky,Igor
Botvinnik,Mikhail
Leningrad/Moscow ch-URS 1941 (2)
1.e4 e6 2.d4 d5 3.e5 c5 4.♘f3 ♘c6 5.♗d3 cxd4 6.0-0 ♗c5 7.a3 ♘ge7 8.♘bd2 ♘g6 9.♘b3 ♗b6 10.♖e1 ♗d7 11.g3 f6 12.♗xg6+ hxg6 13.♕d3 ♔f7 14.h4 ♕g8 15.♗d2 ♕h7 16.♗b4 g5 17.♕xh7 ♖xh7 18.exf6 gxf6 19.hxg5 e5 20.gxf6 ♔xf6 21.♗d6 ♖e8 22.♘h4 ♖g8

23.♔h2 ♗f5 24.♖e2 d3 25.♖d2 dxc2 26.f4 ♗e3 27.♗xe5+ ♞xe5 28.fxe5+ ♔e7 29.♖f1 c1♛ 0-1

Sveshnikov,Evgeny
Bischoff,Klaus
Calvia ol 2004 (2)

1.e4 e6 2.d4 d5 3.e5 c5 4.c3 ♞c6 5.♞f3 ♗d7 6.♗e3 cxd4 7.cxd4 ♞ge7 8.♗d3 h6 9.♞c3 ♞c8 10.0-0 a6 11.♞d2 ♞b6 12.♖c1 ♖c8 13.f4 g6 14.g4 ♞e7 15.♛e2 h5 16.h3 hxg4 17.hxg4 ♞c6 18.♞f3 ♞b4 19.♗b1 ♞c4 20.♔g2 ♗e7 21.♖h1 ♖g8 22.♗f2 ♞c6 23.♖h7 ♛b6 24.♞a4 ♛b5 25.♞c5 ♗xc5 26.dxc5 ♛xb2 27.♛xb2 ♞xb2 28.♖ch1 ♞e7 29.♞g5 ♖f8 30.♖g7 ♗c6 31.♗d4 ♞c4 32.♖hh7 ♔d7 33.♗xg6 ♞xg6 34.♖xg6 ♖cd8 35.♖gg7 ♔c8 36.♖xf7 ♖xf7 37.♖xf7 ♞a3 38.♞f3 ♞c2 39.♔g3 ♗b5 40.♗f2 ♗e2 41.♖g7 ♗d3 42.♞d4 1-0

Nimzowitsch,Aaron
Salwe,Georg
Karlsbad 1911

1.e4 e6 2.d4 d5 3.e5 c5 4.c3 ♞c6 5.♞f3 ♛b6 6.♗d3 ♗d7?! 7.dxc5!? ♗xc5 8.0-0 f6? [≥ 8...a5] 9.b4! ♗e7

10.♗f4 fxe5 11.♞xe5 ♞xe5 12.♗xe5 ♗f6 13.♞d2 0-0 14.♞f3 ♗d6 15.♛e2 ♖ac8 16.♗d4 ♛c7 17.♞e5 ♗e8 18.♖ae1 ♗xe5 19.♗xe5 ♛c6 20.♗d4 ♗d7 21.♛c2 ♖f7 22.♖e3! b6 23.♖g3 ♔h8 24.♗xh7!± e5!? [24...♞xh7 25.♛g6!+−] 25.♗g6 ♖e7 26.♖e1 ♛d6 27.♗e3 d4 28.♗g5 ♖xc3 29.♖xc3 dxc3 30.♛xc3 ♔g8 31.a3 ♔f8 32.♗h4 ♗e8 33.♗f5 ♛d4 34.♛xd4 exd4 35.♖xe7 ♔xe7 36.♗d3 ♔d6 37.♗xf6 gxf6 38.♔f1 ♗c6 39.h4 1-0

Maslak,Konstantin
Asrian,Karen
Moscow 2007 (5)

1.e4 e6 2.d4 d5 3.e5 c5 4.c3 ♞c6 5.♞f3 ♛b6 6.a3 c4 7.g3 ♗d7 8.♞bd2 ♞a5 9.h4 0-0-0 10.h5 ♞h6 11.♗h3 f6 12.♛e2 ♞f7 13.0-0 f5 14.♞h2 g6 15.f4 ♗e7 16.g4 g5 17.♗g2 gxf4 18.gxf5 exf5 19.♗xd5 ♖hg8+ 20.♔h1 ♗e6 21.♗xe6+ ♛xe6 22.♞df3 ♞b3 23.♖b1 ♞xc1 24.♖bxc1 ♛c6 25.♖g1 ♞g5 26.♖g2 ♞e4 27.♔g1 ♛d5 28.♞f1 ♖xg2+ 29.♔xg2 ♖g8+ 30.♔h1 ♗h4 31.♔h2 ♗f2 32.♖c2 ♛f7 33.♞3d2 ♗g1+ 0-1

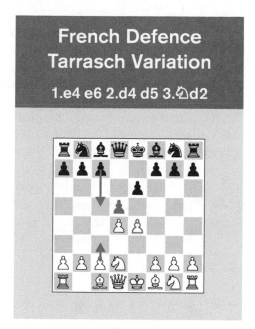

French Defence Tarrasch Variation

1.e4 e6 2.d4 d5 3.♘d2

To defend the e4-pawn with 3.♘d2 seems less natural than to do so with 3.♘c3. However, the former has the virtue of rendering ...♝b4 ineffective. Tarrasch began to play it towards the end of the 19th century, as a means of avoiding the **Winawer Variation** 3.♘c3 ♝b4, which was beginning to be seen as a valid alternative to the **Classical French** 3.♘c3 ♘f6.

Another plus of 3.♘d2 is that in the face of the thematic and omnipresent ...c7-c5 pawn advance in the French, White is ready to support the centre with c3. On the downside we have the knight standing in the way of the bishop on c1, but more concretely the lack of pressure on the centre (i.e. d5) compared to ♘c3 allows for the immediate ...c7-c5 advance. Even if it does not solve all of Black's problems, this is one of the most popular moves.

The fact that White has no immediate threats means that Black has an ample choice of continuations. Remember that with 3...dxe4 you transpose to the Rubinstein Variation, which we will discuss later. In ascending order of popularity the variations at Black's disposal are:

A)   3.   ...   ♝f8-e7

This was occasionally played by Oleg Romanishin during the 1970s and remained a rarity until there was a boom in its popularity at the end of the 20th century, in part thanks to its adoption by big names such as Morozevich and Lputian. The idea, besides getting off the beaten path, is to wait and see what White does, with the chance of making ...c5 more effective than on the third move; for example, after *4.♝d3 c5! 5.exd5?* (5.dxc5 is forced and a good move) *5...♛xd5!*

Black gets an improved version of the analogous variation after 3...c5, which we will look at further on.

**   4.   ♘g1-f3**

is the most solid and the most frequent.

**   4.   ...   ♘g8-f6**

Now White's best option seems to be

**   5.   e4-e5**

5.♝d3 c5! is good for Black. And after

5.	...	**♘f6-d7**
6.	**♝f1-d3**	**c7-c5**
7.	**c2-c3**	**♘b8-c6**

you magically transpose to the 7.♘gf3 gambit line of the variation with 3...♘f6!.

B)   **3.   ...   a7-a6**

As above, Black wants to play an improved version of 3...c5. After 4.e5!?, the move 4...♗d7 – with the idea of ...♗b5 – is interesting.

Therefore, if White does not wish to re-enter the 3...c5 variation with 4.♘gf3 c5!, the most incisive move would appear to be

4.   ♗f1-d3

This is connected with the idea of opening up play after

4.   ...   c7-c5
5.   d4xc5!   ♗f8xc5
6.   ♘g1-f3

White has a freer game; however, Black's position is playable.

C)   **3.   ...   ♘b8-c6**

The controversial **Guimard Variation**. Developing while attacking a pawn cannot be that bad. However, voluntarily blocking his c-pawn is not natural to a French player and, ignoring its objective value, most people continue to see it as an ugly move.

4.   ♘g1-f3!

4.c3 e5!? is not necessarily advantageous for Black, but it makes life more complicated for White.

4.   ...   ♘g8-f6
5.   e4-e5   ♘f6-d7

We have reached a strange position in which the c6-knight blocks the natural advance of the c-pawn. However, Black is ready to attack the head of the white pawn chain with ...f7-f6. In addition, the d2-knight does not have any particularly inviting squares to go to; so much so, that it usually goes to b3 or f1. Besides 6.♗b5!? – in the style of the **Ruy Lopez** – White has two good alternatives:

C1)   **6.   ♘d2-b3**

To set the c1-bishop free.

6.   ...   a7-a5

Not so much with the intention of ...a5-a4, but rather with the idea of ...b6 and ...♗a6.

7.	a2-a4	b7-b6
8.	♗f1-b5	♘c6-a7
9.	♗b5-d3	

White has the freer game.

C2)

6.	♗f1-e2	f7-f6
7.	e5xf6	♕d8xf6
8.	♘d2-f1!	♗f8-d6
9.	♘f1-e3	0-0
10.	0-0	

Here, White's position is slightly preferable.

D)   **3. ...**   **c7-c5**

The most thematic response, even if it is less popular than 3...♘f6. Black takes advantage of the timidly placed knight on d2 to fight back in the centre. White generally responds with

4. e4xd5

even if the flexible 4.♘gf3, with unforced transpositional possibilities, is becoming popular. Now Black must make the big strategic decision: should he take back with the queen or with the pawn?

D1)   **4. ...**   **♕d8xd5**

An increasingly large number of players are choosing this move, which leads to sharp positions that are reminiscent of some **Sicilian** lines. Even if it is not necessarily the best move, the capture by the queen is definitely a nuisance for White, who would normally prefer to proceed more quietly. Generally he reacts with

5. ♘g1-f3!

The sacrifice is only temporary:

5.	...	c5xd4
6.	♗f1-c4	♕d5-d6!

The best square for the queen.

7.	0-0	♘g8-f6
8.	♘d2-b3	♘b8-c6
9.	♘b3xd4	♘c6xd4
10.	♘f3xd4	a7-a6
11.	♖f1-e1	♕d6-c7

Attacking the bishop on c4 and preparing ...♗d6.

12.	♗c4-b3	♗f8-d6

More solid is 12...♗d7.

13.	♘d4-f5!?	♗d6xh2+
14.	♔g1-h1	0-0

15. ♘f5xg7!

This position still has not been fully evaluated, notwithstanding the many games that have been played with it. The following is a representative line that will give you an idea of the possible complications that can ensue:

15. ...   ♖f8-d8!

Capturing with 15...♚xg7 appears to give White the advantage after 16.♛d4!.

16. ♛d1-f3   ♚g8xg7
17. ♗c1-h6+!   ♚g7-g6!
18. c2-c3!

Threatening with a devastating check on c2.

18. ...   ♘f6-h5!

To play ...f5.

19. ♗h6-c1!

Threatening 20.♛g4+. Now, probably Black's safest option is to return the piece with

19. ...   ♗h2-f4!
20. g2-g4   ♘h5-g3+!
21. f2xg3   ♗f4xc1
22. ♖a1xc1   b7-b6

with equality.

D2)   4. ...   e6xd5

The most solid. Without fear Black accepts the isolated pawn on d5, putting his faith in his greater piece activity.

Tarrasch proposed the same strategic concept in his eponymous defence to the **Queen's Gambit** (1.d4 d5 2.c4 e6 3.♘c3 c5!?). This move is very popular with strong players; however, it has few adherents at lower levels, where there is an instinctive mistrust of the isolated queen's pawn: that is, if it is black! The point being that when the isolated queen's pawn is white, players seem to be much more aware of its dynamic potential. Just think of the Sicilian with 2.c2-c3, which is popular at all levels, where the isolated d4-pawn is seen more as a means of favourably opening the game (by the d4-d5 advance) than a static weakness.

5.   ♘g1-f3

5.♗b5+!? ♗d7 6.♛e2+ ♗e7 7.dxc5 is interesting.

5. ...   ♘b8-c6

Black prefers to develop the g8-knight to e7. 5...c4 seems premature, while 5...♘f6 6.♗b5+ ♗d7 7.♗xd7+ ♘bxd7 8.0-0 ♗e7 9.dxc5 ♘xc5 10.♘b3 ♘ce4 11.♘fd4! – with the idea of f3 or ♛f3 – would appear to be slightly advantageous for White, even if after 11...♛d7!, Black's position is perfectly playable.

6.   ♗f1-b5

It is better to postpone taking on c5 so that the black bishop moves twice.

6.	...	♗f8-d6
7.	d4xc5	♗d6xc5
8.	0-0	♘g8-e7
9.	♘d2-b3	♗c5-d6

9...♗b6 is also playable. White can then respond with the effective 10.♖e1 followed by 11.♗e3, neutralizing the activity of the annoying black bishop.

10. ♖f1-e1

10.♘bd4!? is interesting.

10.	...	0-0
11.	♗c1-g5	♗c8-g4

We have arrived at a typical position in this line, for which the percentage of draws is unusually high: around 60%!

E) 3. ... ♘g8-f6

is the most popular, the most ambitious, and the move which best represents the spirit of the French Defence.

4. e4-e5 ♘f6-d7

A typical 'French' centre has been created, and we are presented yet again with the eternal question: is this a strong or a weak centre? There is a basis for a white kingside initiative, but Black's counterplay with ...c7-c5 and ...f7-f6 can be very dangerous. At this point White must make an important strategic decision: either support the centre with f2-f4 or give preference to piece development with ♗d3.

5.c3!? is a waiting move, but you will transpose to one of the two systems immediately below, depending on White's 6th move.

5.♘gf3!? is also playable – it transposes to the gambit that we will deal with in Variation E21.

E1) 5. f2-f4

In a certain sense this is the most logical move: White enlarges his centre and to avoid suffocation Black must react energetically before his opponent finishes development. To that end, apart from putting pressure on d4, it is often necessary to take radical measures, such as the pawn advances ...f6 and ...g5!

5.	...	c7-c5
6.	c2-c3	♘b8-c6
7.	♘d2-f3	

Allowing the king's knight to develop to e2 (or h3).

7. ...	**♛d8-b6**
8. g2-g3	

Keeping d4 defended: the light-squared bishop seeks a future on h3, and in doing so leaves the g2-square vacant for the king! 8.♘e2 is possible, leading to the Steinitz Variation. However, the most popular alternative nowadays is 8.a3!? which, like 6.a3 in the Advance Variation, prevents irritating checks from b4.

8. ...	**c5xd4**
9. c3xd4	**♝f8-b4+**
10. ♚e1-f2	

And we see the first consequences of White's late development (*after 10.♝d2? Black can calmly take on d4*). Now after 10...f7-f6 or 10....g7-g5, the position is extremely tense with chances for both sides. It is true that White's centre will collapse, but with Black's pawn advances on the kingside it is not clear which of the two exposed kings is more vulnerable.

E2)   5.   ♝f1-d3

White places his pieces more modestly on their natural squares and seeks to limit Black's counterplay, with the idea

of profiting from his positional advantages in the long term. In particular the e5-square, if occupied by a trusty knight, could cause Black many problems in the middlegame as well as in the endgame.

5. ...	**c7-c5**
6. c2-c3	**♞b8-c6**

Now White has two options:

E21)   7.   ♞g1-f3

The increasingly popular choice, which introduces a poisonous pawn sacrifice:

7. ...	**♛d8-b6**

After 7...♝e7 8.0-0, a recent hot idea is the move **8...g5!?** (*with the point of 9.♖e1? g4, winning the knight!*). However, this still needs to be accurately assessed. Curiously, this position can also be reached via the variation 3...♝e7 (!)

8. 0-0	

The placement of the white pieces makes it difficult to defend the d4-pawn, so White leaves it to its fate.

8. ...	**c5xd4**
9. c3xd4	**♞c6xd4**
10. ♞f3xd4	**♛b6xd4**
11. ♞d2-f3	**♛d4-b6**
12. ♛d1-a4!	

With the idea of going to g4. Black will be wise to prevent this with

12. ...	**♛b6-b4!**
13. ♛a4-c2	**♛b4-c5!**

If White does not want a draw by repetition, he can try to win with

14. ♛c2-e2

With compensation that practical play has demonstrated to be more than adequate. Not that White's position is winning, but in practice these positions are difficult for Black to play; unless he happens to be a computer.

E22)   7. ♘g1-e2

Continuing the policy of solidity, keeping the f3-square vacant for the other knight.

7. ...	**c5xd4**

After 7...f6?!, without the exchange on d4, the move 8.♘f4! is very strong.

8. c3xd4	**f7-f6!**

At times it is better to attack the head of the pawn chain: in this variation the b6-square is not always the best place for the black queen. 8...♘b6 – with the idea of ...a5-a4, ...♗d7 and queenside play – has fallen slightly into disuse. It teeters on the edge of being playable.

9. e5xf6

The aggressive 9.♘f4, which attacks e6 and threatens ♛h5+, is now met by 9...♘xd4 10.♛h5+ ♚e7 11.exf6+ ♘xf6 12.♘g6+ hxg6 13.♛xh8 ♚f7 and practical play has demonstrated that Black receives adequate compensation for the exchange.

9. ...	**♘d7xf6**

This is more natural than 9...♛xf6, even though the latter move has its supporters.

10. 0-0

Or first 10.♘f3.

10. ...	**♗f8-d6**
11. ♘d2-f3	

We have arrived at one of the **key positions of the Tarrasch Variation**. Thousands of games have not been sufficient to make clear what Black's best plan is.

E221)   11. ...   ♛d8-b6

Putting pressure on d4 and b2.

12. b2-b3

The pawn sacrifice 12.♗f4 is playable, but White aims for a positional advantage.

12. ...	**0-0**
13. ♗c1-f4	**♗d6xf4**
14. ♘e2xf4	**♘f6-e4**
15. ♘f4-e2!	**♗c8-d7**
16. ♘e2-g3	**♘e4xg3**
17. h2xg3	

As often happens in these variations, it is not clear which weakness is greater: White's d4-pawn or Black's e5-square.

E222)   11. ...   ♛d8-c7

Preventing the thematic ♗f4.

12. ♗c1-g5

With the idea of going to g3! The move 12.g3 is also interesting – always with the idea in mind of exchanging the dark-squared bishops after 12...0-0 13.♗f4. Now Black maintains equality with the aggressive 13...♘g4!?.

12. ...　　　0-0

13. ♗g5-h4!

Black was threatening the annoying 13...♘g4, which would now simply be met by ♗g3. At this point

13. ...　　　♘f6-h5

seems to be the most logical step. The latest find here is

14. ♕d1-c2!

since 14.♖c1 g6!, with the idea of applying pressure to d4 with the ♕ on g7, has proved to be good for Black (*now 14...g6? does not work because of 15.♗xg6*).

14. ...　　　h7-h6

15. ♗d3-g6

Now Black sacrifices the exchange:

15. ...　　　♖f8xf3

16. g2xf3　　♗d6xh2+

17. ♔g1-h1　　♘h5-f4

18. ♘e2-g3!

And we have a position which is difficult to weigh up, notwithstanding the many games played from this position.

E223) 11. ...　　　0-0

Simply continuing his development. White almost always proceeds with the strategically appealing

12. ♗c1-f4

which, however, allows Black a certain amount of counterplay:

12. ...　　　♗d6xf4

13. ♘e2xf4　　♘f6-e4!

Among the various moves which are playable at this point (14.g3, 14.♘e2 and 14.♘h5), the most popular at the moment is the unnatural-looking

14. ♕d1-c1

Defending the f4-knight and preparing a transfer to the excellent e3-square. A delightful though unforced line that often occurs is

14. ...　　　♘e4-g5!

15. ♘f3xg5　　♕d8xg5

16. ♗d3xh7+!?　♔g8xh7

17. ♘f4xe6

which exploits the undefended black queen and the intermediate check on f8 to obtain a rook and 2 pawns for a knight and a bishop. If Black either exchanges queens or defends the rook with the queen, the resulting positions seem to be easier for White to play, even if they are not objectively superior from his point of view.

Tal,Mikhail
Portisch,Lajos

Montreal 1979 (15)

1.e4 e6 2.d4 d5 3.♘d2 c5 4.exd5 exd5 5.♗b5+ ♗d7 6.♕e2+ ♗e7 7.dxc5 ♘f6 8.♘b3 0-0 9.♘f3 ♖e8 10.♗e3 a6 11.♗d3 ♗a4 12.♘fd4 ♘bd7 13.0-0-0 ♘xc5 14.♘f5 ♗f8 15.♘xc5 ♗xc5 16.♕f3 ♗xe3+ 17.♘xe3 ♖c8 18.♗f5 ♖c5 19.♘d4 ♗c6 20.b4 ♖b5 21.a4 ♖b6 22.a5 ♖b5 23.♕f4 b6 24.♗d3 bxa5 25.♗xb5 axb5 26.♖hd1 axb4 27.♔b2 ♕c8 28.♖xb4 ♘e4 29.♖d3 ♘c5 30.♖a3 ♘a4+ 31.♔c1 ♗d7 32.♕d6 ♗c6 33.♖d3 h6 34.♖f4 ♕e6 35.♕xe6 fxe6 36.♘g4 e5 37.♖f5 ♘c5 38.♖c3 ♗d7 39.♖xe5　　　1-0

Pillsbury,Harry
Maroczy,Geza

Paris 1900 (6)

1.e4 e6 2.d4 d5 3.♘d2 ♘f6 4.e5 ♘fd7 5.f4 c5 6.c3 ♘c6 7.♘gf3 ♗e7 8.♗d3 ♕b6 9.dxc5 ♘xc5 10.♘b3 ♘xb3 11.axb3 ♗d7 12.b4 ♖c8 13.♕e2 a6 14.♗e3 ♕c7 15.♕f2 ♘b8 16.♗b6 ♕c6 17.0-0 0-0 18.♖a5 f5 19.♔h1 ♖ce8 20.♗c5 ♕c7 21.♗xe7 ♖xe7 22.g4 ♘c6 23.♖aa1 fxg4 24.♕h4 g6 25.♕xg4 ♖g7 26.h4 ♘e7 27.♘d4 ♘f5 28.♗xf5 gxf5 29.♕h5 ♕d8 30.♖g1 ♖f7 31.♕h6 ♕e7 32.♘f3 ♔h8 33.♔h2 ♖f8 34.h5 ♖g4 35.♘g5 ♖xf4 36.♘f7+ ♕xf7 37.♕xf4 ♕xh5+ 38.♔g3 ♕e2 39.♔h4 ♖c8 40.♖ae1 ♕xb2 41.♔h3 ♖xc3+ 42.♖g3 ♖c2 43.♖h1 ♖c8 44.♕h6 ♕xe5 45.♕xh7+ ♔xh7 46.♔g2X　　　1-0

Iordachescu,Viorel
Volkov,Sergey

Moscow 2007 (4)

1.e4 e6 2.d4 d5 3.♘d2 ♘f6 4.e5 ♘fd7 5.♗d3 c5 6.c3 ♘c6 7.♘gf3 ♗e7 8.0-0 g5 9.dxc5 ♘dxe5 10.♘xe5 ♘xe5 11.♘b3 ♕c7 12.f4 ♗xc5+ 13.♘xc5 ♕xc5+ 14.♖f2 ♘xd3 15.♕xd3 g4 16.b3 ♗d7 17.♗e3 ♕b5 18.♕d4 ♖g8 19.f5 exf5 20.♕e5+ ♗e6 21.♖xf5 0-0-0 22.♖f2 a6 23.♗f4 ♕c6 24.♖d1 b5 25.c4 ♔b7 26.cxb5 ♕xb5 27.a4 ♕d7 28.♖d4 ♕e7 29.♕e1 ♔a8 30.♕e2 ♕a7 31.♗e3 ♗c8 32.♕d2 ♖ge8 33.♖f1 ♕b6 34.♗f2 ♖e4 35.b4 f5 36.b5 h5 37.♖d1 ♕e6 38.♖xe4 fxe4 39.♕d4 ♕e7 40.♖c1 ♖e8 41.♗e3 ♕d7 42.♖c6 h4 43.♕b6 ♕b7 44.♕c5 ♖b8 45.♖c7　　　1-0

Tarrasch,Siegbert
Kürschner,Max

Nuremberg m 1891

1.e4 e6 2.d4 d5 3.♘d2 ♘f6 4.e5 ♘fd7 5.♗d3 c5 6.c3 ♘c6 7.♘e2 cxd4 8.cxd4 ♗b4 9.0-0 ♘f8 10.f4 f5 11.exf6 gxf6 12.♘f3 ♕b6 13.♔h1 ♗d7 14.a3 ♗e7 15.f5 0-0-0 16.♘f4 ♔b8 17.♖e1 ♗c8 18.fxe6 ♖d6 19.♗f5 ♘d8 20.b4 ♘dxe6 21.♕b3 ♕d8 22.♖a2 ♘g5 23.♗xc8 ♔xc8 24.♖ae2 ♘e4 25.♘xd5 ♖xd5 26.♖xe4 ♘g6 27.♖xe7 ♘xe7 28.♖xe7 ♕xe7 29.♕xd5 ♔b8 30.h3 ♕c7 31.♗e3 ♖e8 32.♗g1 ♔a8 33.♕c5 ♕d7 34.d5 b6 35.♕c6+ ♕xc6 36.dxc6 ♖e6 37.b5 a6 38.a4 ♖e4 39.♗d4 f5 40.a5 axb5 41.axb6 ♖e6 42.b7+ ♔b8 43.♗e5+　　　1-0

French Defence
Rubinstein Variation

1.e4 e6 2.d4 d5 3.♘c3/d2
dxe4 4.♘c3/d2xe4

When White defends the e4-pawn with ♘c3 or ♘d2 on his third move, Black has an interesting joint variation (in the sense that it can arise from both 3.♘d2 and 3.♘c3): the controversial **Rubinstein Variation** 3...dxe4. After 4.♘xe4, the position is reminiscent of the **Caro-Kann** with the difference that there is a black pawn on e6 instead of on c6. The fact that the light-squared bishop can no longer develop to f5 is an obvious disadvantage, yet it is also true that the freeing ...c7-c5 advance takes place in one move and the c8-bishop can always develop later to b7 or to c6 via d7. Obviously, White has a freer game and a nice space advantage, and this was reason enough for Tarrasch to condemn the variation. However, practice has shown us that Black's position is solid and that a patient player can obtain reasonable positions, with the added advantage that there is not much theory to study.

After many years in a slump, the Rubinstein Variation has become relatively popular on the professional circuit as a means of obtaining draws against players of the same level. However, it is rare at lower levels, where defensive technique is not as refined.

4. ...   ♘b8-d7

The direct 4...♘f6 can be followed by 5.♘xf6+!, either leaving the black queen exposed on f6 or spoiling Black's pawn structure in the event of 5...gxf6. The move 4...♗d7 pops up every now and then (compared to ...b6 and ...♗b7 this does not weaken the b5- and c6-squares) and after 5.♘f3 ♗c6 6.♗d3 Black has a solid, but perhaps excessively passive position. Let us return to 4...♘d7.

5. ♘g1-f3   ♘g8-f6
6. ♘e4xf6+

Simplifying the position, but White does not lose a tempo retreating the knight.

6. ...   ♘d7xf6
7. ♗f1-d3   c7-c5

The most natural reaction. White will obtain active piece play in an open position:

8. d4xc5!   ♗f8xc5
9. ♕d1-e2

Thus, White reserves the possibility of a solid approach with 0-0, ♗g5 and ♖ad1, or a more aggressive one with ♗d2/g5 and 0-0-0. In both cases, opening theory claims a small advantage for White, but in practical play the ensuing positions provide each player with possibilities.

Steinitz,Wilhelm
Bird,Henry
London m2 1866 (9)

1.e4 e6 2.d4 d5 3.♘c3 dxe4 4.♘xe4 ♘c6 5.♘f3 ♘f6 6.♘xf6+ ♕xf6 7.♗g5 ♕f5 8.♗d3 ♕g4 9.h3 ♕xg2 10.♖h2 ♕xh2 11.♘xh2 ♘xd4 12.♗b5+ **1-0**

Volokitin,Andrey
Nakamura,Hikaru
Lausanne 2005 (3)

1.e4 e6 2.d4 d5 3.♘c3 dxe4 4.♘xe4 ♗d7 5.♘f3 ♗c6 6.♗d3 ♘d7 7.0-0 ♘gf6 8.♘g3 ♗e7 9.♖e1 ♗xf3 10.♕xf3 c6 11.c3 0-0 12.♗f4 ♖e8 13.♖ad1 ♕b6 14.♗c1 c5 15.dxc5 ♘xc5 16.♗c2 ♖ad8 17.♖xd8 ♗xd8 18.♘h5 ♘xh5 19.♗xh7+ ♔xh7 20.♕xf7 ♖f8 21.♕xf8 ♘d3 22.♕f3 ♘hf4 23.♗xf4 ♘xe1 24.♕e4+ ♔h8 25.b3 ♕a6 26.♕xe1 ♕xa2 27.♕d1 ♗b6 28.♗g3 ♕b2 29.c4 ♕c3 30.♔h1 e5 31.h3 ♗d4 32.♔h2 ♔g8 33.♕b1 a6 34.♗h4 ♕d2 35.♕g6 ♕f4+ 36.♗g3 ♕f7 37.♕g5 ♕e6 38.♕d8+ ♔h7 39.♕h4+ ♔g8 40.♕e4 b5 41.f4 bxc4 42.fxe5 ♗c5

43.bxc4 a5 44.♕a8+ ♔h7 45.♕xa5 ♕xc4 46.e6 ♔g6 47.♕c7 ♕d4 48.h4 ♕g1+ 49.♔h3 ♕h1+ 50.♔h2 ♕c1 51.♕e5 ♕a3+ 52.♗g3 ♔h7 53.h5 ♗e7 54.♕f5+ ♔h8 55.♕g6 ♗f8 56.♔h2 ♕c5 57.h6 gxh6 58.♗h4 ♕d6+ 59.♔h3 ♗g7 60.♕e4 ♔g8 61.♕f5 ♕a3+ 62.♗g3 ♕e7 63.♗h4 ♕a3+ 64.♕f3 ♕c1 65.e7 ♕c8+ 66.♔h2 ♕e6 67.♕h5 ♕e5+ 68.♕xe5 ♗xe5+ 69.♗g3 ♗xg3+ 70.♔xg3 ♔f7 71.♔g4 ♔xe7 72.♔h5 ♔f6 73.♔xh6 ♔f5 74.♔h5 ♔f6 75.g4 ♔g7 76.♔g5 ♔h7 77.♔f6 ♔h6 78.g5+ ♔h7 79.♔f7 ♔h8 80.♔g6 **1-0**

Tarrasch,Siegbert
Rubinstein,Akiba
San Sebastian 1911 (6)

1.e4 e6 2.d4 d5 3.♘c3 dxe4 4.♘xe4 ♘d7 5.♘f3 ♘gf6 6.♗d3 ♗e7 7.0-0 0-0 8.♘xf6+ ♘xf6 9.♘e5 c5 10.dxc5 ♕c7 11.♕e2 ♗xc5 12.♗g5 ♘d7 13.♘xd7 ♗xd7 14.♖ad1 ♗c6 15.♕h5 g6 16.♕h4 ♖fe8 17.♖fe1 ♗e7 18.♗xe7 ♕xe7 19.♕xe7 ♖xe7 20.♗e4 ♖c8 21.c3 e5 22.♖d6 ♗xe4 23.♖xe4 f5 24.♖a4 b6 25.g4 e4 26.gxf5 gxf5 27.♔f1 ♔f7 28.♖ad4 ♖e6 29.♖d7+ ♖e7 30.♖4d5 ♖xd7 31.♖xd7+ ♔g6 32.♖xa7 ♖d8 33.♖a6 ♖d2 34.♖xb6+ ♔g5 35.♔e1 ♖c2 36.♖b5 ♔g4 37.h3+ ♔xh3 38.♖xf5 ♖xb2 39.♖f4 ♖xa2 40.♖xe4 h5 41.c4 ♔g2 42.♖f4 ♖c2 43.♖h4 ♔f3 44.♔d1 ♖xf2 45.c5 ♔e3 46.♖xh5 ♔d4 **½-½**

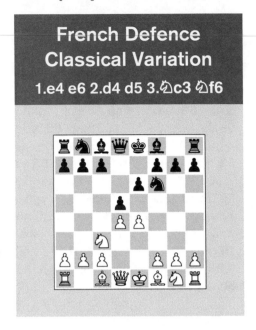

French Defence
Classical Variation

1.e4 e6 2.d4 d5 3.♘c3 ♘f6

White's third most played move remains, even if by only a small margin, 3.♘c3.

White is not worried about the knight getting pinned or about blocking his c-pawn. His greater central control produces sharper positions, and therefore this variation is usually preferred by aggressive players. This is not an academic consideration, as is demonstrated by the fact that **3...c5?** is an excellent move in the **Tarrasch Variation**, but here it is a grave mistake. *4.exd5 exd5 and then 5.dxc5!* follows, with a clear advantage for White.

Back to 3.♘c3. The classical 3...♘f6 is more solid than 3...♗b4, the Winawer Variation. At the end of the 20th century it experienced a revival, probably because it is a way to avoid the excessive amount of accumulated theory pertaining to the Winawer. White can now defend e4 by advancing the pawn or by pinning the ♘f6.

A)   4. e4-e5

The so-called **Steinitz Variation**. White gains space on the kingside, but Black's typical reaction of ...c7-c5 is now more effective because of the knight on c3.

4.   ...   ♘f6-d7

Now White usually supports the e5-pawn with

5. f2-f4

and leaves the d4-square, when it is cleared by dxc5 or ...cxd4, for his pieces. The very old move 5.♘ce2 has recently become fashionable, thanks to the efforts of Shirov and Anand. After 5...c5, the centre can be supported with 6.c3. The ensuing positions resemble, and at times transpose to, the Tarrasch Variation with 3...♘f6. After 6...♘c6 7.f4

7...♕b6 (or 7...b5!?) 8.♘f3 f6!?, you have a double-edged position with chances for both sides.

5.	...	c7-c5
6.	♘g1-f3	♞b8-c6
7.	♗c1-e3!	

Reaching the variation's key position. Black now has three options.

A1)   **7.**   **...**   **a7-a6**

Preparation for queenside counterplay with 8...b5. White maintains a good positional advantage thanks to his control of the d4-square with a timely dxc5.

A2)   **7.**   **...**   **♕d8-b6**

Counterattacking b2, even if there is

| 8. | ♞c3-a4! | ♕b6-a5+ |
| 9. | c2-c3 | c5xd4 |

9...c4!? is playable, but 10.b4! gives White a slight edge.

10.	b2-b4!	♞c6xb4
11.	c3xb4	♗f8xb4+
12.	♗e3-d2	♗b4xd2+
13.	♞f3xd2	

Practice has shown that the white knight is stronger than Black's three pawns.

A3)   **7.**   **...**   **c5xd4**

For the abovementioned reasons, Black usually opts for this solid line.

| 8. | ♞f3xd4 | ♗f8-c5 |
| 9. | ♕d1-d2 | |

Black can now exchange twice on d4 and continue with 11...♕b6; but the resulting endgame, though manageable, is not exactly exhilarating. Black can also maintain the tension:

9.	...	0-0
10.	0-0-0	a7-a6
11.	h2-h4	♞c6xd4

In order to play ...b7-b5.

12.	♗e3xd4	b7-b5
13.	♖h1-h3	b5-b4
14.	♞c3-a4	♗c5xd4
15.	♕d2xd4	a6-a5

White's apparent central control is something of an illusion: in practice, opposite-side castling and Black's counterplay on the c-file will mean that there are good chances for both players. This is confirmed by the statistics, which show Black doing very well. However, it must be noted that, curiously, the black players had a higher average Elo rating than the white players.

This is also true of the 3...c5 line in the French Tarrasch. It is evident that this is one of those lines which is greatly appreciated by highly-rated players, but much less so by mere mortals.

B)   4. ♗c1-g5

The **old main line** is positionally justified by the fact that the exchange of the bad dark-squared bishop for the opponent's good dark-squared bishop is theoretically recommended for White. However, it is also true that every piece exchange will assist the ambitions of the player with the more cramped position; in this case, Black.

After 4.♗g5, Black has three variations at his disposal. All three are very different in terms of their competitive and strategic characteristics. If Black wants to win, then the McCutcheon Variation is certainly the right choice. In terms of fighting spirit and strategic characteristics, it is correctly considered to be the connecting link between the **Classical French** and the **Winawer**.

B1)   4. ...   ♗f8-b4

Here we have the controversial **McCutcheon Variation**. There are those who have said that after 4...♗b4,

both players are worse off! Indeed, after the main line sequence

5.	e4-e5	h7-h6
6.	♗g5-d2!	♗b4xc3
7.	b2xc3!	♘f6-e4
8.	♕d1-g4	g7-g6

– 8...♔f8!? is probably better than its reputation –

9.	♗f1-d3	♘e4xd2
10.	♔e1xd2	c7-c5

both kings would prefer to be somewhere quieter. There are evident weaknesses on Black's kingside, and the pawn advance h4-h5, often combined with the manoeuvre ♖h3-g3, can be very dangerous for Black. However, the king on d2 gives Black chances of quick counterplay with ...cxd4 and ...♕a5+, for example:

11.	♘g1-f3	♘b8-c6
12.	h2-h4	c5xd4
13.	c3xd4	♕d8-a5+
14.	♔d2-e3	b7-b6
15.	♕g4-f4	♗c8-a6
16.	♕f4-f6	♖h8-g8

and it is not clear which of the two kings is more exposed to danger.

B2)   4. ...   d5xe4

The **Burn Variation**, which has evident similarities to the **Rubinstein**. However, with the Burn, the presence of the bishop on g5 offers Black the favourable possibility of exchanging pieces, which is always most welcome in cramped positions.

5.   ♘c3xe4   ♗f8-e7
6.   ♗g5xf6!

The best response, which does not lose time defending e4, and does not excessively simplify matters, as is the case with 6.♘xf6+.

After 6...♗xf6 and 7.♘f3, we have a typical position in which White has a small central domination (d4-pawn against e6-pawn). White either seeks to quietly exploit his minute advantage, or he castles queenside and tries a pawn assault on the black king.

More combative is the alternative move

6.   ...   g7xf6!?

Along the lines of the **Bronstein-Larsen Variation** of the **Caro-Kann**, with the difference that Black has the bishop pair. The books claim that White has a small advantage, but in reality you reach those typical, strategically complex positions where the stronger player will win.

B3)   4.   ...   ♗f8-e7

The **Classical Variation** of the **Classical French**! The most strategic and solid of the alternatives has lost a lot of its past popularity. This is more a question of fashion than objective consideration.

5.   e4-e5

is by far the most popular response. The **Anderssen Variation** 5.♗xf6 is considered to be a bit of a museum piece, but like many variations that have fallen into disuse, it may only need a bit of spit and polish, and it will prove to be playable.

5.   ...   ♘f6-d7

Tartakower's move 5...♘e4 has not stood the test of time.

At this point White is at a crossroads; and as is so often the case, the choice is between aggression and solidity.

B31)   6.   h2-h4!?
The historic **Chatard-Alekhine Attack**, which remains a dangerous weapon, even though Black has nothing to fear with correct play. It is difficult to say which is the best continuation for Black. Taking twice on g5 after 8.♕d3 (or 8.♘h3) gives White obvious compensation, but whether it is sufficient to provide him with an advantage is still uncertain.

Black has several playable moves (6...a6, 6...0-0, 6...h6), but the most combative is

6. ...   c7-c5!

A fearless move, as Black knows that his king will have to go to e7:

7. ♗g5xe7!   ♔e8xe7!

Perhaps 7...♕xe7 is playable, but it obliges Black to make a risky sacrifice after 8.♘b5! 0-0! 9.♘c7 cxd4 10.♘xa8.

8. f2-f4

Unlike in the **Classical Variation**, Black has already advanced his pawn to c5, and the queen is ready to move across to the queenside. On the other hand, the king's position on e7 is a bit of a worry.

8. ...   ♕d8-b6
9. ♘c3-a4   ♕b6-a5+
10. c2-c3   b7-b6!

Preparing the thematic ...♗a6, with a satisfactory position.

B32) 6. ♗g5xe7   ♕d8xe7
7. f2-f4   0-0

The immediate 7...c5? is an error because of 8.♘b5!, after which the knight threatens to go to c7, and also to give an annoying check on d6.

8. ♘g1-f3   c7-c5

We have a position that has been reached in hundreds of games. Black will obviously play on the queenside; at times Black — when White does not exchange on c5 and castles queenside — plays ...c5-c4. For his part, White can castle queenside, launching a kingside attack using his pawns and the bishop on d3. Otherwise, when Black plays ...f7-f6, White will play exf6 and then place his two rooks on the d- and e-files, with the aim of controlling the centre: in particular the e5-square. If Black does not respond dynamically to this, he will have to play the classic endgame where a centrally-placed white knight dominates Black's bad bishop. The game generally continues with

9. ♕d1-d2

9.♗d3, threatening the classic sacrifice on h7 followed by ♘g5+ and ♕h5, can be comfortably met by 9...f6!.

9. ...   ♘b8-c6
10. d4xc5!

Here Black can continue with the ambitious 10...♕xc5, which prevents White's kingside castling and prepares ...♘b6 after 11.0-0-0, followed by ...♗d7 and ...♘c6-a5-c4, with a strong initiative against White's king. The problem is that Black must always be careful. After 11.♗d3, the ♗xh7+ sacrifice, followed by ♘g5+ and ♕d3, though not necessarily winning, gives White a dangerous attack. This position is a tough one to evaluate. Anything could happen.

If instead Black has more positional inclinations he can play

| 10. ... | f7-f6!? |
| 11. e5xf6 | ♕e7xf6! |

It is best to keep control of e5.

| 12. g2-g3 | ♘d7xc5 |
| 13. 0-0-0 | ♖f8-d8 |

Not 13...♗d7? 14.♘xd5! exd5 15.♕xd5+.

14. ♕d2-f2!

The most recent idea.

14. ...	b7-b6
15. ♗f1-g2	♗c8-d7
16. ♖h1-e1	

with a small plus for White.

Kamsky,Gata
Socko,Bartosz

Turin ol 2006 (4)

1.e4 e6 2.d4 d5 3.♘c3 ♘f6 4.e5 ♘fd7 5.f4 c5 6.♘f3 ♘c6 7.♗e3 cxd4 8.♘xd4 ♗c5 9.♕d2 0-0 10.g3 ♘xd4 11.♗xd4 a6 12.♗xc5 ♘xc5 13.♕d4 ♕c7 14.♗d3 b5 15.a3 ♗d7 16.0-0 ♘a4 17.♘e2 ♖fc8 18.g4 a5 19.f5 ♕c5 20.b4 ♕xd4+ 21.♘xd4 ♘c3

22.♘b3 axb4 23.axb4 ♘a4 24.♔f2 exf5 25.gxf5 ♖e8 26.♖fe1 ♘b2 27.♖xa8 ♖xa8 28.e6 fxe6 29.♘c5 ♗e8 30.fxe6 ♔f8 31.♔e3 ♘xd3 32.cxd3 ♖a2 33.♔d4 ♔e7 34.h3 ♖h2 35.♖e3 ♗g6 36.♔xd5 ♗f5 37.♖f3 g6 38.d4 ♖e2 39.♔c6 ♖xe6+ 40.♘xe6 ♗e4+ 41.d5 ♗xf3 42.♘g5 ♗g2 43.♘xh7 ♗e4 44.h4 ♗g2 45.♘g5 ♔f6 46.♔c5 ♔e7 47.♘e6 ♔f6 48.♘d4 ♔e5 49.d6 ♗h3 50.♘xb5 **1-0**

Teichmann,Richard
John,Walter

Ostend-B 1907 (13)

1.e4 e6 2.d4 d5 3.♘c3 ♘f6 4.♗g5 ♗b4 5.e5 h6 6.♗e3 ♘e4 7.♕g4 ♔f8 8.♗d3 ♘xc3 9.a3 ♗a5 10.♗d2 c5 11.bxc3 cxd4 12.cxd4 ♗xd2+ 13.♔xd2 ♕g5+ 14.♕xg5 hxg5 15.♖f1 ♘c6 16.♘e2 ♔e7 17.f4 gxf4 18.♖xf4 ♗d7 19.♖hf1 ♖af8 20.h3 f5 21.exf6+ gxf6 22.♖4f2 ♖h6 23.c3 ♔d6 24.♘f4 f5 25.♖e1 ♘a5 26.♖fe2 ♖c8 27.♖b1 b6 28.♖e3 ♖g8 29.♔e1 ♖c8 30.♔d2 ♗a4 31.♗f1 ♘b3+ 32.♔e1 ♘a5 33.♖b2 ♗d7 34.g3 ♖e8 35.h4 ♘c6 36.♖d2 ♘e7 37.♗e2 ♘g8 38.♘d3 ♖e7 39.♘e5 ♘f6 40.♗d3 ♗e8 41.♖f2 ♖c7 42.♔d2 ♗h5 43.♖f1 ♗e8 44.♘f3 ♗h5 45.♘g5 ♘e4+ 46.♗xe4 dxe4 47.♔c2 ♖h8 48.♔b2 ♗g4 49.♖f4 ♗h5 50.♖f2 ♗g4 51.♖f1 ♖g8 52.♖f2 ♔d5 53.♖h2 b5 54.♖f2 a5 55.♖f4 b4 56.axb4 axb4 57.cxb4 ♖c4 58.♖a3 ♖xb4+ 59.♔c3 ♖b5 60.♔d2 ♖gb8 61.♖f1 ♖b2+ 62.♔e3 ♖8b3+ 63.♖xb3 ♖xb3+ 64.♔f2 e3+ 65.♔g2 ♖d3 66.♖e1 ♖d2+ 67.♔f1

♖d3 68.♔g2 e2 69.♘h3 ♔xd4
70.♘f4 ♖d2 71.♔f2 e5 72.♘g2 ♖d3
73.♖a1 ♖f3+ 74.♔g1 ♖xg3 75.♔f2
♖f3+ 76.♔g1 f4   0-1

Nataf,Igor-Alexandre
Riazantsev,Alexander
Portugal tt 2006 (1)

1.e4 e6 2.d4 d5 3.♘c3 ♘f6 4.♗g5
♗e7 5.e5 ♘fd7 6.h4 c5 7.♗xe7
♔xe7 8.♕g4 ♘c6 9.dxc5 ♘dxe5
10.♕xg7 ♖g8 11.♕xh7 ♗d7
12.0-0-0 ♕a5 13.♕h6 d4 14.♘ge2
dxc3 15.♘xc3 ♖ad8 16.♘e4 ♘g4
17.♕d2 ♕xa2 18.♕d6+ ♔e8
19.♗d3 ♗c8 20.♕c7 ♕a1+ 21.♔d2
♕a5+ 22.♕xa5 ♘xa5 23.♖a1 ♘c4+
24.♔e2 f5 25.♗xc4 fxe4 26.♖xa7
♖f8 27.f3 exf3+ 28.gxf3 ♘e5
29.♗b5+ ♗d7 30.♖xb7 ♗xb5+
31.♖xb5 ♘xf3 32.c3 ♘e5 33.h5 ♖g8
34.h6 ♖g2+ 35.♔e3 ♖dd2 36.c6
♘c4+ 37.♔f3 ♖df2+ 38.♔e4 ♖g4+
39.♔d3 ♖d2X   0-1

Stefansson,Hannes
Kortchnoi,Viktor
Gothenburg Ech-tt 2005 (3)

1.e4 e6 2.d4 d5 3.♘c3 ♘f6 4.♗g5
♗e7 5.e5 ♘fd7 6.♗xe7 ♕xe7 7.f4
♘b6 8.♘f3 ♗d7 9.♕d2 a6 10.h4
♘c6 11.h5 h6 12.♘d1 ♘a7 13.♘e3
♗b5 14.0-0-0 c5 15.f5 ♗xf1
16.♖dxf1 ♘c6 17.c3 0-0-0 18.♘h4
cxd4 19.cxd4 ♘c4 20.♘xc4 dxc4
21.fxe6 ♕xe6 22.♘f3 ♖d7 23.♖h4
♖hd8 24.♖d1 ♔b8 25.♕c3 ♘e7
26.♘e1 ♘d5 27.♕h3 ♕xh3 28.♖xh3
♘f4 29.♖e3 ♖xd4 30.♖xd4 ♖xd4
31.♘f3 ♘xg2 32.♖e2 ♖g4 33.♔d2
♘f4 34.♖e4 ♖g2+ 35.♔c3 ♘xh5
36.♘d4 ♘g3 37.♖f4 ♘e2+ 38.♘xe2
♖xe2 39.♖xf7 g5 40.♖h7 ♖xe5
41.♖xh6 g4 42.♔xc4 ♖g5 43.♖h2
g3 44.♖g2 ♔c7 45.♔d4 ♔b6
46.♔e3 ♔c5 47.♔f3 ♔b4 48.♔e2
♔c4 49.♔e3 ♖g7 50.♖c2+ ♔d5
51.♖d2+ ♔e5 52.♖g2 ♔f5 53.♔f3
a5 54.b3 b5   0-1

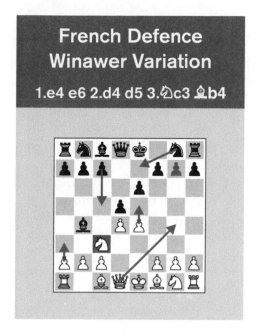

French Defence Winawer Variation

1.e4 e6 2.d4 d5 3.♘c3 ♝b4

At a deep level this is very logical: Black indirectly attacks the e4-pawn without allowing White to gain a tempo with the pawn advance e4-e5, and reserves e7 for his king's knight. The obvious drawback is that the bishop on b4 very often ends up being exchanged for the knight on c3, with a consequent weakening of the dark squares, which in some variations can result in the black king's safety being put in jeopardy. However, Black enjoys long-term advantages thanks to the doubled white pawn on c3 and the excellent play offered on the queenside — at least in the **Classical Winawer**. Like all the openings, it has virtues which compensate for its defects. Nonetheless, the **Winawer** manages to polarize opinions in a particularly pronounced fashion. This becomes clear when you consider the fact that former World Champion Mikhail Botvinnik used it for years as his main weapon against 1.e4, while another World Champion, Bobby Fischer,

notwithstanding the poor results he had against the Winawer (or perhaps for that very reason!), considered it to be positionally unsound!

4.e5 is the move most often chosen by White. However, before looking at that, we will have a brief look at the minor alternatives. While none of these put the soundness of the Winawer in doubt, they can be most dangerous if Black is not sufficiently prepared.

A)   **4. a2-a3**
The most direct.
    4. ...   **♝b4xc3+**
    5. b2xc3   **d5xe4**
White concedes the e4-pawn with the idea of exploiting the enemy's weakened kingside with
    6. ♕d1-g4
The gambit 6.f3?! is interesting but probably not completely sound.
    6. ...   **♘g8-f6!**
    7. ♕g4xg7   **♖h8-g8**
    8. ♕g7-h6   **♘b8-d7**
    9. ♘g1-e2   **c7-c5**

Black reaches a balanced position in which the weakness of the dark squares is compensated for by better development. In practical play, the results are slightly in Black's favour, which is a simple enough explanation for this line's lack of popularity with white players.

B)   4. ♕d1-g4

Another very direct line: g7 is undefended and White attacks it.

    4. ...   ♘g8-f6!

Black must always react energetically to justify the positional deficiencies of the Winawer.

    5. ♕g4xg7   ♖h8-g8
    6. ♕g7-h6

Again, Black must respond dynamically:

    6. ...   c7-c5!

After 6...dxe4?! 7.♘e2!, White is better.

    7. e4-e5   c5xd4
    8. a2-a3   ♗b4-f8!

    9. ♕h6xf6   ♕d8xf6
    10. e5xf6   d4xc3

with a small advantage for Black.

C)   4. ♗c1-d2

The **Keres Gambit**. White prevents the creation of a doubled pawn on c3 but allows the e4-pawn to be taken.

    4. ...   d5xe4
    5. ♕d1-g4!

Alekhine played 5.♘xe4?, but after 5...♕xd4 White does not have sufficient compensation.

    5. ...   ♘g8-f6

Or 5...♕xd4 6.0-0-0 h5! 7.♕e2!? ♗d7 8.♘xe4, with an unclear game.

    6. ♕g4xg7   ♖h8-g8
    7. ♕g7-h6   ♕d8xd4!
    8. 0-0-0   ♗b4-f8!

An excellent idea of Bronstein's, which he played in his 1950 match against Isaac Boleslavsky.

    9. ♕h6-h4   ♖g8-g4
    10. ♕h4-h3   ♕d4xf2!
    11. ♗f1-e2   ♖g4-h4!

Deliberately rising to the bait.

    12. ♕h3xh4   ♕f2xh4
    13. g2-g3

This would appear to win back the queen with interest, but in reality there is:

    13. ...   e4-e3
    14. g3xh4   e3xd2+
    15. ♔c1xd2   ♗c8-d7

and if one of the players is better off, it is Black. He may have lost the exchange, but the two united passed e- and f-pawns are supported by his two bishops, and they will soon start to advance. White's position is not easy to play.

D)   4. e4xd5   e6xd5
    5. ♗f1-d3

This move has been relatively popular since the 1990s as a reasonably safe way of avoiding the strategic complexities of the Winawer, ending up with a sort of improved version of the Exchange Variation. After the exchange on c3, if Black develops his knight to e7 to avoid the pin with ♗g5, plans centred around ♕h5 have proved to be troublesome. When this line was first used, players had difficulty dealing with it. However, after a while, the remedy was found:

5. ...   c7-c6!

This allows the b4-bishop to return to d6 after 6.a3; or, after the natural 6.♘e2, Black can continue with 6...♘e7 without having to fear ♕h5.

E)   4. ♘g1-e2

One of the most solid alternatives to 4.e5, which is very popular at low levels of play, where there is a tendency to avoid the doubled c-pawn.

4. ...   d5xe4

Both 4...♘f6 and 4...♘c6 are also playable.

5. a2-a3

The idea is that if Black wants to keep the e4-pawn he will have to do without his dark-squared bishop.

5. ...   ♗b4xc3+

5...♗e7 6.♘xe4 ♘f6 is also perfectly playable, giving Black an improved version of the Rubinstein Variation.

6. ♘e2xc3

Now the avaricious 6...f5?! is perhaps not as bad as people say: however, it does give White a promising position after 7.f3! exf3 8.♕xf3.

Therefore the best thing is to counterattack on the d4-square:

6. ...   ♘b8-c6!
7. d4-d5!?

A logical attempt to open up the game for the two bishops. 7.♗b5 ♘e7 8.♘xe4 a6 leads to equality.

7. ...   e6xd5
8. ♕d1xd5   ♘g8-e7

and neither player has the advantage.

We will now return to the **main move**:

4. e4-e5

White's closing of the centre would indicate a reaction on the flank and indeed, **4...c5** is the most popular move here. Leaving aside 4...♘e7, which usually leads back to the main line, there are valid alternatives that are often based on the attempt to exchange the bad c8-bishop for White's good one with ...b7-b6. These alternatives are positionally justified, although it is important to underline that Black remains dangerously behind in development, and that White has a big space advantage. You are therefore dealing with lines that are suitable for solid and patient players who like to manoeuvre behind their own lines. There also exists another incredible alternative, which we will look at first:

A)   4. ...   ♗b4-f8!?

Compared to the normal Advance Variation, White already has his knight on c3 and it's his turn to move! However, Black will try to prove that the knight is badly placed on c3, where it blocks the c2-pawn. In addition, on f8 the bishop defends g7 from the ♕g4 incursion and Black prepares ...b6 and ...♗a6. If White believes these considerations to be valid, he could continue with the even more paradoxical **5.♘b1!?** returning to the 3.e5 variation... But usually White is sceptical and continues with the natural 5.♘f3. Black's tournament results, though not exceptional, are acceptable.

Please note that you can often reach this position via the Steinitz Variation(!!) with the move sequence 3...♘f6 4.e5 ♘g8.

B)   4. ...   ♕d8-d7

This move is more 'normal', even if it appears unnatural: it serves to defend g7 from aside. Black will play ...f7-f5 if White moves his queen to g4.

This side-defence of g7 is better achieved from d7 than from e7, because it leaves the e7-square vacant for the knight, whereas the c8-bishop develops to a6. Usually, White proceeds with

5. a2-a3   ♗b4xc3+

The move 5...♗f8!? is also playable here, for the reasons explained before... but why play the Winawer if you are not prepared to concede the bishop?

6. b2xc3   b7-b6

The obvious strategic objective is to exchange the bad bishop.

7. ♕d1-g4

The most energetic.

7. ...   f7-f5
8. ♕g4-g3   ♗c8-a6
9. ♗f1xa6   ♘b8xa6
10. ♘g1-e2

Heading for f4.

10. ...   ♘a6-b8!

With the intention of going to c4 via c6-a5.

11. ♘e2-f4   ♔e8-f7!?

Preparing ...♘e7; *the move 11...♘c6 is too risky because of 12.♘xe6! ♕xe6 13.♕xg7 and White would appear to have the advantage.* White in effect has a certain initiative after

    12. ♕g3-f3   ♘g8-e7
    13. ♕f3-h5+!   ♔f7-g8
    14. ♖h1-g1

with the idea of advancing the pawn to g4. However, Black's position is very solid and not easy to break down.

C)   4. ...   b7-b6

Prophylactically defending g7 turns out to be unnecessary.

    5. ♕d1-g4   ♗b4-f8

This could be the reply to 5.a3, too, although 5...♗xc3+ 6.bxc3 ♘e7 is more in the spirit of the Winawer.

    6. ♗c1-g5   ♕d8-d7
    7. f2-f4   ♗c8-a6

White has a tiny edge.

As we have pointed out above, the most popular move is

    4. ...   c7-c5

which puts White's centre in crisis. Here the most common continuation is 5.a3, which aims to solidify the centre. However, two important alternatives for White are worth noting..

A)   5. ♗c1-d2

    5. ...   ♘g8-e7!

White's idea was ♘b5 with the unpleasant threat of a check on d6. Black therefore hurries to castle. *For this reason the natural-looking 5...cxd4?! is of doubtful merit: if the black king has to move to f8, White's attack can become very dangerous.*

    6. ♘c3-b5

6.a3 and 6.dxc5!? are playable, even though not problematic for Black.

    6. ...   ♗b4xd2+
    7. ♕d1xd2   0-0
    8. c2-c3

White has preserved the integrity of his centre, but at the price of a slight lag in development and his b5-knight is away from the action. Black will be able to reach equality by developing normally.

B)   5. ♕d1-g4

Not as dangerous here as it is on the 7th move, when — after the exchange on c3

– the centre is less fluid. However, the move should not be treated lightly.

5. ...   ♘g8-e7

Naturally, Black will not lose time defending g7. He seeks counterplay speculating on White's unstable centre.

6. ♘g1-f3!

A positional choice. *6.♕xg7?! is premature because of 6...♖g8 7.♕h6! cxd4 8.a3 ♗xc3+ (with the queen on h7, the move 8...♕a5 would be extremely powerful, as after 9.axb4 ♕xa1 the bishop on c1 would now be unprotected) 9.bxc3 ♕c7 and Black has an improved version of the main line 7.♕g4.* Back to 6.♘f3. Now the simplest reply is

6. ...   c5xd4
7. ♘f3xd4   ♘e7-g6!

which counterattacks the e5-pawn: defending it with a piece is not easy and f2-f4 leaves the white queenside in trouble after ...♘c6 and ...♕a5.

Let's return to the **main line**.

5. a2-a3

At this point the normal continuation is 5...♗xc3+, which we will call the **Classical Winawer**. We will take a look at this after we have examined two alternatives for Black.

The first is 5...cxd4, which is rather rare: the second option 5...♗a5 is becoming ever more popular.

A)   5. ...   c5xd4

Starting a tactical sequence typical of the Nimzo-Indian, where after a2-a3 Black takes on d4 so he can retreat the bishop to e7.

But here White has another possibility:

6. a3xb4!

Damaging his own pawn structure: however, White obtains play on the dark squares that is more promising than in the normal Winawer.

6. ...   d4xc3
7. ♘g1-f3!

7.bxc3?! ♕c7 gives Black the advantage.

7. ...   ♘g8-e7
8. ♗f1-d3

White often loses a pawn; on the other hand, he has the freer game and the two bishops.

B)   5. ...   ♗b4-a5

The **Armenian Variation**, which has been very fashionable since the late 1990s and is now threatening the historical domination of the **Classical Winawer**. Yet, strangely it had not been dignified with a name until a short time ago, on account of its successful adoption by the Armenian grandmasters Smbat Lputian and Rafael Vaganian.

The concept is very logical: instead of stabilizing the centre with an exchange on c3, Black keeps the tension, forcing White to take extreme measures: we are referring to **Alekhine's energetic move**

6. b2-b4!

In the past this response was considered so strong that players were discouraged from playing 5...&a5. However, as is often the case, many of opening theory's old conclusions have been proved to be only partially true or even outright wrong. Still, although 6.b4 remains the most popular move, the search for alternative continuations that give an opening advantage is becoming more frequent; moves such as 6.&d2!? or even 6.dxc5!?.

The idea of 6.b4 is that after the obvious, but probably dubious 6...cxb4 7.&b5!, White obtains a clear advantage, at least according to the opening theory of the past. However, after 7...&c6! 8.axb4 &xb4+ 9.c3 &e7 10.&a3

you reach a distinctly improved version of the **Sicilian Wing Gambit**. This is certainly not easy for Black to meet. However, is this enough to justify speaking of an objective advantage for White? Whatever the answer to that may be, the best move is

6. ...   c5xd4!

White, as is so often the case in the opening, can choose between an aggressive and a solid continuation.

B1)   7. ♕d1-g4

The immediate 7.bxa5 dxc3 8.♕g4 ♘e7 is simply a transposition.

7. ...   ♘g8-e7
8. b4xa5

8.♕xg7 also transposes.

8. ...   d4xc3
9. ♕g4xg7   ♖h8-g8
10. ♕g7xh7   ♘b8-c6

Let's look at the interesting position that has arisen, which is very reminiscent of the analogous position in the **Classical Winawer**.

Material is equal (the a5-pawn will disappear soon), but strategically both positions have evident virtues and defects. White is behind in development and must defend e5; in compensation he has control of the dark squares, and in the endgame the h-pawn may be a winning trump card. For his part, Black quickly prepares ...0-0-0 with ...♕c7/a5 and ...♗d7, if necessary sacrificing the f7-pawn, and he will activate his pieces – in particular his rooks – on the kingside, and the e7-knight, moving it to f5, or to d5 after ...d5-d4.

Returning to concrete variations, White usually defends e5 with the ambitious

11. f2-f4

This move does not contribute to White's development, which is already lagging, and the bishop on c1 becomes bad. However, it reinforces the centre and prepares the insidious ♘f3-g5. The move 11.♘f3 is also playable, and after 11...♕c7! (preventing ♘g5) 12.♗f4 or 12.♗b5, the resulting positions are double-edged and give both players possibilities. A good example is the famous drawn game between Fischer and Tal in 1960.

Let's return to the position after 11.f4.

11. ...	♕d8xa5
12. ♘g1-f3	♗c8-d7
13. ♘f3-g5!?	

Or, more solidly, 13.♖b1 0-0-0 14.♕d3.

| 13. ... | ♖g8xg5!? |
| 14. f4xg5 | 0-0-0 |

with compensation for the exchange and a position that is difficult to evaluate.

B2)   7. ♘c3-b5

The most solid alternative.

| 7. ... | ♗a5-c7 |
| 8. f2-f4 | |

8.♘f3 provides less reliable control of the centre, in view of 8...♘c6 9.♗f4 ♘ge7 with the idea of ...♘g6.

| 8. ... | ♗c8-d7! |

The latest idea. Its intention is to exchange the bad bishop if White's knight doesn't take on c7.

9. ♘g1-f3

If 9.♘xc7+ ♕xc7 10.♘f3 ♘e7 11.♗d3 a6, with the idea of ...♗b5, Black maintains equality.

| 9. ... | ♗d7xb5 |
| 10. ♗f1xb5+ | ♘b8-d7! |

Here the knight has better prospects than on c6, as it is able to transfer to c4 via b6.

11. 0-0	♘g8-e7
12. ♘f3xd4	0-0
13. ♗b5-d3	g7-g6!

White has a good space advantage and the two bishops, but Black is solid on the kingside, and can reasonably hope to exploit the weaknesses on White's queenside created by the pawn advance b2-b4. If the pawn were on b2, White would probably be better. However, the position as it stands is dynamically balanced.

The Classical Winawer

5. ...	♗b4xc3+
6. b2xc3	

Here we have the key position of the Classical Winawer.

For the moment White's centre is sufficiently solid, and the usual pressure applied by Black to d4, which is typical of many French variations, is less effective here, given that White has a second c-pawn with which to support the centre. Black's trump cards are the weaknesses of the white a-pawn, the c2-pawn and the c4-square, which can be effectively occupied by a knight. In addition, Black can exert strong pressure along the c-file. The position has all the characteristics of a slow manoeuvring struggle.

Naturally, White has his own trumps to play: he will seek to exploit the weakness on g7, moving the queen to g4; or develop his pieces more solidly and naturally, hoping to put his dark-squared bishop to good use when the game inevitably opens. Black can castle either kingside or queenside, and attack the head of the white pawn chain by ...f7-f6. In the lines with kingside castling, he can advance the pawn to c4 to prevent the opening of attacking lines for White; White sometimes opens up the game with the 'sacrilegious' dxc5. It is no wonder that the Classical Winawer is considered to be such a strategically complex opening.

Now, 6...♘e7 is the natural move, demonstrating that Black is not afraid of the attack on g7 with ♕g4. However, if you wish to avoid the complications that this involves, there are two alternatives:

A) 6. ... ♕d8-a5

Another case of re-evaluation.

7. ♗c1-d2 ♕a5-a4!

Not so much to attack d4 as to prevent a3-a4.

8. ♕d1-g4!

8.♕b1 does not produce anything special, as there is 8...c4; while after 8.♘f3 b6!, Black frees himself of the bad bishop with ...♗a6, with equality.

8. ...   g7-g6!?

An example of the beautiful complexity of chess: every position has its own individual nature. This move has always been considered to be inferior to the thematic 8...♘e7, which concedes the g7-pawn in exchange for an initiative. But here 8...g6 is actually the best move. The difference is the attack on the c2-pawn, which is not easy to defend. This is so crucial that the best move seems to be the paradoxical

9. ♕g4-d1!

A pendulum manoeuvre that also occurs in other variations of the Winawer.

9. ...   b7-b6!

Safer than the premature 9...cxd4?! which, by opening lines, highlights the weakness of the dark-square complex.

10. h2-h4   h7-h5
11. ♘g1-f3   ♗c8-a6

and the position is balanced.

B)   6. ...   ♕d8-c7

As in the 4...♕d7 variation, Black takes measures against ♕g4, defending g7 from aside, with the difference that c7 is a more natural square.

7. ♕d1-g4

White plays this all the same. However, here it would be interesting to transpose to the positional main line with 7.♘f3, considering that in this variation the black queen is more actively placed on a5.

7. ...   f7-f5

With 7...♘e7 you transpose to the Poisoned Pawn Variation, which we will look at later. However, 6...♕c7 is generally played in order to avoid this line.

An alternative option is 7...f6, keeping more tension in the pawn structure.

8. ♕g4-g3   c5xd4

If 8...♘e7?! is played immediately, then 9.♕xg7 ♖g8 10.♕xh7 cxd4 11.♔d1! is strong.

9. c3xd4   ♘g8-e7
10. ♗c1-d2

Now 10.♕xg7?? would simply lose a rook.

10. ...   0-0
11. ♗f1-d3   b7-b6
12. ♘g1-e2

With its eye firmly on f4!

12. ...   ♗c8-a6
13. ♘e2-f4   ♕c7-d7
14. h2-h4

White has an unpleasant kingside initiative, but if Black likes to play the French, this should not worry him too much.

Now back to the **main line**.

| **6. ...** | **♘g8-e7** |

We finally examine the move which is the most popular and the most combative. The diagram shows White's principal options. He has various plans to choose from.

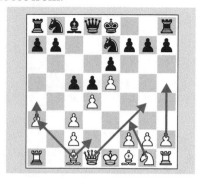

The most direct is to move the queen to g4, but the slower-paced plans 7.h4-h5 and 7.♘f3 – with or without a3-a4 – are also played.

The Poisoned Pawn Variation

| **7. ♕d1-g4** |

The most aggressive reply. Now Black usually sacrifices the g7-pawn with 7...♕c7 or 7...cxd4, which usually transposes. Alternatively, he can defend it with the solid 7...♔f8 or the provocative-looking 7...0-0.

A) | **7. ...** | **♔e8-f8** |

A solid alternative. The king is safer here than after kingside castling. However, the development problems of the h8-rook could become a factor.

| **8. h2-h4** |

This move, with the idea of ♖h3-g3, seems the best, even if the strange 8.♗d2!? (to discourage ...♕a5) is interesting.

| **8. ...** | **♕d8-a5** |
| **9. ♗c1-d2** | **♕a5-a4** |

Thematic.

10. ♖h1-h3!	**♘b8-c6**
11. h4-h5	**h7-h6**
12. ♕g4-f4	**♗c8-d7!**
13. ♖h3-f3	**♗d7-e8**

In true French fashion, White has a dangerous kingside initiative and Black has promising queenside play. Opening books claim a certain advantage for White, but in over-the-board play anything could happen.

B) | **7. ...** | **0-0** |

Black castles without fear of White's queen; the counterplay obtained by a well-timed ...f5 is sufficient to maintain a dynamic balance. Until a few years ago this so-called Warsaw Variation was viewed as a reasonable way to get off the beaten track and avoid a lot of theory. This is no longer the case; its recent popularity has made it topical, with the inevitable explosion of related theory.

| **8. ♗f1-d3!** |

This is by now considered to be the best: delaying ♘f3 gives White the possibility to retreat his queen to d1 in some variations, when Black is forced to weaken his position with ...g6 because of ♕h5.

8. ... f7-f5

The safest. 8...♘bc6 is playable, but you need to have a good knowledge of the variations that follow. 9.♕h5! is a little crude but effective: 9...♘g6! *(9...h6? has proved to be good for White: 10.♗xh6! gxh6 11.♕xh6)* 10.♘f3 ♕c7 11.h4!? cxd4! 12.♔d1! and White has a dangerous initiative, even if not necessarily a winning one.

9. e5xf6 ♖f8xf6
10. ♗c1-g5

10.♕h5 h6!? 11.g4 ♘bc6! 12.g5 g6! 13.♕xh6 ♖f7 14.♗xg6 ♖g7 15.♗d3 e5 with good counterplay for Black.

10. ... ♖f6-f7

10...♘d7 is interesting but the compensation for the exchange after 11.♕h4! appears doubtful.

11. ♕g4-h5 g7-g6
12. ♕h5-d1!

Again this recurring theme: the queen returns to its home square.

12. ... ♘b8-c6
13. ♘g1-f3 ♕d8-f8!
14. 0-0

In theory, White has a small advantage thanks to his control of the dark squares, but in practice Black's kingside initiative means that both players have chances.

C) 7. ... ♕d8-c7

This remains the most popular move in the Classical Winawer.

8. ♕g4xg7

8.♗d3 is interesting. After 8...cxd4 (8...c4!? is playable and perhaps safer) 9.♘e2 dxc3 10.♕xg7 ♖g8 11.♕xh7 ♘bc6 (11...♕xe5!?) 12.♗f4 ♗d7 13.0-0 0-0-0, we have another **Poisoned Pawn** type situation that is hard to assess.

8. ... ♖h8-g8
9. ♕g7xh7 c5xd4

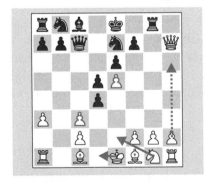

It should be remembered that Black's 7th and 9th moves can be played in reverse order.

This key position is analogous to the more famous one from the **Sicilian Najdorf**, and is therefore called the **Poisoned Pawn Variation of the**

Winawer. How much poison the pawn actually contains is the question that lies before us. The dual threat against e5 and c3 allows Black to recover the pawn (10.cxd4?? would lose the a1-rook after 10...♕c3+), after which the strategic considerations are the same as those already discussed in the **Armenian Variation** with ♕g4.

White now has two possibilities to deal with Black's threats:

C1)   10. ♔e1-d1

A rare line, but a very dangerous one where Black needs to know his stuff. White protects himself against the queen fork on c3 and the queen check on e5 in an unnatural way. In compensation, the knight can later develop to f3, where it is definitely more active than on e2.

10. ...	**♘b8-c6**
11. ♘g1-f3	**d4xc3**

Safer than the other capture 11...♘xe5 12.♗f4 ♕xc3 13.♘xe5! ♕xa1+ 14.♗c1 d3! 15.♕xf7+ ♔d8 16.♕f6! dxc2+, with a position that is difficult to weigh up.

12. ♘f3-g5	**♘c6xe5**
13. ♗c1-f4	

13.f4 f6! appears to be good for Black.

13. ...	**♕c7-b6!**
14. ♗f4xe5	**♖g8xg5**
15. ♕h7-h4!	**♖g5-g8**
16. ♕h4-d4	**♕b6xd4+**
17. ♗e5xd4	

Who is better off? Black has a good mass of pawns in the centre, but it may not be a good idea to advance them, as they could become a target for White's two bishops.

If this position is not Black's cup of tea, he might prefer the complications that ensue after 11...♘xe5!?.

C2)   10. ♘g1-e2

Defending c3 and, indirectly, e5.

10. ...	**♘b8-c6!**

If 10...♕xe5? 11.cxd4, and White simply has an extra pawn.

11. f2-f4	

11.cxd4? ♘xd4! – again the theme of the queen check on c3.

11. ...	**♗c8-d7**
12. ♕h7-d3	

Forcing Black to clarify the position in the centre and freeing the path for the h-pawn which is ready to march all the way to h8!

12. ...	**d4xc3**

This position has been reached hundreds of times and it is still not clear which of White's many alternatives is the best.

He can take on c3 with the queen or the knight, or he can move the c1-bishop to e3 or the rook to b1. Another alternative is to advance the h-pawn. White tries to organize his forces, which at the moment are not harmoniously placed. He hopes to make the most of the extra pawn that he will have, the two bishops, and the passed h-pawn.

For his part, Black will castle queenside and seek to activate his pieces by placing one knight on f5 and the other on c4 by way of a5. Sometimes he will play ...f7-f6 to undermine White's centre and activate the d7-bishop, moving it to g6 via e8, and he often pushes ...d5-d4, to break open the white king's position. It is not possible here to examine all of the variations exhaustively. We will therefore present only one of the many possible lines, which is, however, indicative of the strategic and tactical complexity of the system.

13. ♘e2xc3!?   a7-a6
To stop ♘b5.
14. ♖a1-b1
Always a useful move, and in this case it is particularly venomous.

14. ...   ♘c6-a5!
After the mechanical 14...0-0-0?, there follows 15.♕xa6!.
15. h2-h4   ♘e7-f5
Threatening 16...♖g3.
16. ♖h1-h3   0-0-0
17. h4-h5   ♘a5-c4

with a position that is truly difficult to assess.

In these situations, opening experts usually hedge their bets and make do with 'good possibilities for both players'.

Classical Winawer – Positional Lines

Now we will have a look at the positional lines in the **Classical Winawer**, where White does not seek to capture the g7-pawn, but instead is happy to emerge from the opening phase with his pieces harmoniously placed and, at the most, with some expansion on the kingside without decentralizing his queen.

The first of the three variations that we will examine is the least common:

A)   7. h2-h4

7.	...	♘b8-c6
8.	h4-h5	♕d8-a5
9.	♗c1-d2	♗c8-d7!?

Black is correct in continuing to develop without worrying about the weakening of the dark-square complex.

Alternatively, 9...h6 10.♕g4 ♘f5 11.♗d3 ♘ce7 12.dxc5! gives White a freer game.

9...cxd4 10.cxd4 ♕a4 12.♘f3!? ♘xd4 is playable, even if by playing 13.♗d3 White achieves excellent compensation for the pawn.

10. h5-h6

At this point White must follow through with his idea, as after the banal developing move 10.♘f3 the move 10...h6! would be good, since ♕g4 is no longer playable.

| 10. | ... | g7xh6! |
| 11. | ♘g1-f3 | 0-0-0 |

Black's lead in development compensates for his structural weaknesses.

B)   7. ♘g1-f3

In view of the possible transpositions to line B, which we have just looked at, or to D, the final line, we will now deal with the variations in which White does not play either h2-h4 or a3-a4.

B1)   7. ...   ♗c8-d7!?

With the idea of ...♗a4. Here the following unaesthetic move is interesting:

| 8. | d4xc5!? | ♗d7-a4 |
| 9. | ♖a1-b1 | |

The active placement of White's pieces compensates for his bad pawn structure.

B2)   **7. ...**   ♛**d8-a5**

is playable:

     8.   ♝**c1-d2**   ♞**b8-c6**

     9.   ♝**f1-e2**

For 9.a4, see Variation D below.

     9. ...   ♝**c8-d7**

    10. 0-0   **c5-c4!**

Not 10...♛a4? on account of 11.♛b1!, after which both 12.♛xb7 and 12.♝b5 are threatened.

    11. ♞**f3-g5!?**

    11. ...   **h7-h6**

    12. ♞**g5-h3**

The manoeuvre ♞f3-g5-h3, to get to f4 and, if necessary, h5, is common in these variations.

    12. ...   ♞**e7-g6!**

Now the position is approximately balanced.

B3)   **7. ...**   **b7-b6**

The idea of exchanging the bad bishop with ...♝a6 is particularly good here.

     8.   ♝**f1-b5+**   ♝**c8-d7**

     9.   ♝**b5-d3!**

With this manoeuvre White has prevented ...♝a6.

     9. ...   **c5-c4**

    10. ♝**d3-f1**

In order to move the bishop to g2 or to h3 later on.

    10. ...   ♝**d7-a4!**

Black obstructs the pawn on a3: for this reason the variation with ...b6, which is excellent here, is not as good after 7.a4, when the a4-square becomes inaccessible for Black. For this reason, many experts consider that 7.a4 is in fact the most accurate of White's solid alternatives.

    11. h2-h4   **h7-h6**

    12. h4-h5   ♚**e8-d7!**

Black has brought his king to safety; and after

    13. g2-g3

he obtains a satisfactory position with

    13. ...   ♛**d8-g8!**

The idea is to put the c2-pawn under pressure with ...♛h7.

C)   **7. a3-a4**

This move is not played so much to open the a3-f8 diagonal for the dark-squared bishop, which rarely happens, but more to prevent Black from occupying the a4-square with the bishop or the queen. It also assists a possible ♗b5, which is often a useful move.

7.	...	♘b8-c6
8.	♘g1-f3	♛d8-a5
9.	♗c1-d2	

White prefers to keep the queens on the board: the old 9.♛d2 is rarely played today, and does not cause problems for Black: 9...♗d7 10.♗a3 cxd4 11.cxd4 ♛xd2+ 12.♔xd2 ♘f5.

| 9. | ... | ♗c8-d7 |

This is a tabiya position.

10. ♗f1-b5

This move is in the spirit of the **Ruy Lopez** and it has become more popular than the more natural 10.♗e2 or 10.♗d3. White seeks to discourage

...f7-f6 and in some variations adds a drop of poison to the threat of c3-c4. The idea is that if Black plays 10...a6, White can take on c6 or, better still, retreat to e2, after which the weakness on b6 should become apparent. This is a subtlety, as something can only be considered a weakness if it can be exploited.

10.	...	a7-a6
11.	♗b5-e2	f7-f6!?
12.	c3-c4	♛a5-c7
13.	c4xd5	♘e7xd5
14.	c2-c4	♘d5-e7
15.	e5xf6	g7xf6
16.	d4-d5!?	

In this position, anything can happen. The weakness on b6, which is absent in the analogous variation with 10.♗e2, does not appear to be significant. If Black does not like the very open character of this line, he can choose to close the position with 10...c4!?, or protect himself against the c3-c4 advance with 10...♛c7. Alternatively, he can safely continue with 10...f6.

All of these alternatives lead to acceptable games. This confirms that in most openings the number of playable moves is much greater than you might think. Some variations are much more popular than others simply because we tend to copy the moves played by champions.

Ragozin,Viacheslav
Botvinnik,Mikhail

Moscow 1936

1.e4 e6 2.d4 d5 3.♘c3 ♗b4 4.a3
♗xc3+ 5.bxc3 dxe4 6.♕g4 ♘f6
7.♕xg7 ♖g8 8.♕h6 c5 9.♘e2 ♘c6
10.♗b2 ♗d7 11.♖d1 ♖g6 12.♕e3
♕a5 13.dxc5 0-0-0 14.♘g3 ♘g4
15.♕xe4 ♕xc5 16.♖d2 ♕b6 17.♗c1
f5 18.♕c4 ♕b1 19.♘e2 ♕b6 20.♘f4
♖gg8 21.♗d3 ♔b8 22.♕b3 ♕c7
23.♖e2 e5 24.♘e6 ♗xe6 25.♕xe6
e4 26.♗b5 ♘ce5 27.c4 ♘xh2
28.♖xh2   0-1

Steinitz,Wilhelm
Winawer,Szymon

Paris 1867

1.e4 e6 2.d4 d5 3.♘c3 ♗b4 4.exd5
exd5 5.♗d3 ♗e6 6.♘f3 h6 7.0-0
♗xc3 8.bxc3 ♘d7 9.♖b1 ♘b6
10.♘e5 ♘e7 11.f4 ♗f5 12.♗xf5 ♘xf5
13.♗a3 ♘d6 14.f5 ♘e4 15.f6 g6
16.♕g4 ♕c8 17.♕xg6 ♕e6 18.♕g7
0-0-0 19.♘xf7 ♘xc3 20.♘xd8 ♖xd8
21.f7 ♘d7 22.♖be1 ♘e2+ 23.♔h1
c5 24.♗xc5 ♕e4 25.f8♕ ♘xf8
26.♖xf8 ♘g3+ 27.♕xg3 ♖xf8
28.♗xf8   1-0

Capablanca,Jose Raul
Alekhine,Alexander

Buenos Aires Wch m 1927 (1)

1.e4 e6 2.d4 d5 3.♘c3 ♗b4 4.exd5
exd5 5.♗d3 ♘c6 6.♘e2 ♘ge7 7.0-0
♗f5 8.♗xf5 ♘xf5 9.♕d3 ♕d7
10.♘d1 0-0 11.♘e3 ♘xe3 12.♗xe3
♖fe8 13.♘f4 ♗d6 14.♖fe1 ♘b4
15.♕b3 ♕f5 16.♖ac1 ♘xc2 17.♖xc2
♕xf4 18.g3 ♕f5 19.♖ce2 b6
20.♕b5 h5 21.h4 ♖e4 22.♗d2 ♖xd4
23.♗c3 ♖d3 24.♗e5 ♖d8 25.♗xd6

♖xd6 26.♖e5 ♕f3 27.♖xh5 ♕xh5
28.♖e8+ ♔h7 29.♕xd3+ ♕g6
30.♕d1 ♖e6 31.♖a8 ♖e5 32.♖xa7
c5 33.♖d7 ♕e6 34.♕d3+ g6
35.♖d8 d4 36.a4 ♖e1+ 37.♔g2
♕c6+ 38.f3 ♖e3 39.♕d1 ♕e6 40.g4
♖e2+ 41.♔h3 ♕e3 42.♕h1 ♕f4
43.h5 ♖f2   0-1

Alekhine,Alexander
Nimzowitsch,Aaron

Bled 1931 (6)

1.e4 e6 2.d4 d5 3.♘c3 ♗b4 4.♘e2
dxe4 5.a3 ♗xc3+ 6.♘xc3 f5?! 7.f3!
[7.♗c4 ♘f6 8.♗g5 0-0 9.♕d2 ♘c6
10.0-0-0 ♔h8 11.f3↑ exf3 12.gxf3±
Maroczy-Seitz, Györ 1924; 7.♗f4!? ♘f6
8.f3 (8.♕d2 0-0 9.0-0-0 ♘h5 10.♗c4
♘c6 11.f3! (11.♘e2? ♗e7 12.f3 ♘xf4
13.♘xf4 ♘d5∓ Pilnik-Stahlberg, Mar
del Plata 1943) 11...exf3 (11...♘xf4?
12.♕xf4 ♕xd4 13.♘b5 c5 14.c3±)
12.gxf3 ♘xf4 13.♕xf4 ♕d6 14.♕e3
♔h8 15.f4±) 8...0-0 (8...exf3 9.♕xf3
♕xd4? 10.♘b5+− Alekhine) 9.fxe4
♘xe4 10.♘xe4 fxe4 11.♕d2 ♘d7
12.♗e2 c5 Thomas-Nimzowitsch,
Marienbad 1925] 7...exf3 8.♕xf3
♕xd4 [8...♕h4+ 9.g3 ♕xd4 10.♗f4!
(10.♘b5!? (Alekhine) 10...♕d8
(10...♕c5 11.♗e3 ♕e7 12.♗g5!)
11.♗f4 ♘a6 12.♖d1 ♕e7 13.♘d6+!
cxd6 14.♗xd6 ♕f7 15.♖xa6±) 10...c6
11.♕h5+ g6 12.♕e2 ♕g7 13.0-0-0±
(Larsen) 13...♘f6 14.♕d2 ♔f7 15.♗h6
♕g8 16.♗c4 ♕e8 17.g4!±; 8...♘f6
9.♗f4 (9.♗g5) 9...0-0 10.0-0-0 c6
11.h3 ♘d5 12.♘xd5 ♕xd5 13.♕c3!±
Matokhin-Birnov, USSR 1949] 9.♕g3!
[9.♗e3!? ♕g4 10.♕f2 ♘f6 11.h3 ♕g6
12.0-0-0 0-0 13.♗c4 ♘c6 14.g4
Chalabi-Mashian, Munich ol 1958;

9.♘b5!? ♛h4+ 10.g3 ♛e7 11.♛c3! ♘a6 (11...c6 12.♗f4) **12.♗f4 ♘f6 13.♗g2 0-0 14.0-0-0 ♘e8 15.♖he1** Tilevic-Rabinovich, Sverdlovsk 1957] **9...♘f6!? 10.♛xg7 ♛e5+?** [≥ 10...♖g8!] **11.♗e2 ♖g8 12.♛h6 ♖g6 13.♛h4± ♗d7?!** [13...♖xg2? **14.♗f4+−** Alekhine; 13...♖g4!? 14.♛f2 ♘c6 15.0-0 ♖g7 Kmoch] **14.♗g5! ♗c6?** [14...♘c6] **15.0-0-0+− ♗xg2 16.♖he1 ♗e4 17.♗h5 ♘xh5 18.♖d8+ ♔f7 19.♛xh5** [19...♔g7 20.♘xe4 fxe4 21.♗h6++−] **1-0**

Steiner,Lajos
Nimzowitsch,Aaron

Berlin 1928 (10)

1.e4 e6 2.d4 d5 3.♘c3 ♗b4 4.e5 c5 5.♗d2 ♘e7 6.a3 ♗xc3 7.bxc3 c4 8.h4 h5 9.♗e2 ♘f5 10.g3 g6 11.♗g5 ♛a5 12.♛d2 ♘c6 13.♗f6 ♖g8 14.♘h3 ♔d7 15.♘g5 ♖h6 16.f3 ♔c7 17.g4 ♖e8 18.♗g7 ♘g8 19.gxh5 gxh5 20.f4 ♘ce7 21.♗xh5 ♘f5 22.♗xf7 ♘xg7 23.♗xe8 ♘xe8 24.♘f7 ♘gf6 25.exf6 ♘xf6 26.♘g5 ♘h5 27.♛e3 ♗d7 28.♛e5+ ♔b6 29.♛d6+ ♗c6 30.♔d2 a6 31.♘xe6 ♔a7 32.♖ag1 ♖e8 33.♖g6 ♖c8 34.♖hg1 ♛b5 35.♛b4 ♖h8 36.♛xb5 axb5 37.f5 ♖h7 38.f6 ♗e8 39.♘g5 ♖c7 40.♖h6 **1-0**

Lasker,Emanuel
Nimzowitsch,Aaron

Zurich 1934 (10)

1.e4 e6 2.d4 d5 3.♘c3 ♗b4 4.e5 c5 5.♗d2 ♘e7 6.♘b5 ♗xd2+ 7.♛xd2 0-0 8.c3 ♘f5 9.g4?! [9.♗d3!] **9...♘h4!∓** (Keres) **10.g5 cxd4 11.cxd4 ♘c6 12.0-0-0 ♛a5!∓**

13.♔b1 [13.♛xa5!?] **13...♛xd2 14.♖xd2 f6!∓ 15.gxf6** [15.f4? fxe5] **15...gxf6 16.♗h3** [seeking salvation in a tactical skirmish] **16...fxe5 17.♘c7 ♖b8 18.♘xe6 ♖f6 19.♘c7 ♗xh3 20.♘xh3 ♘f3 21.♖dd1 exd4 22.♘xd5 ♖f5 23.♘df4 ♖bf8 24.♘d3 ♘ce5 25.♘xe5 ♖xe5 26.♘g1!? ♘g5! 27.h4 ♘e6 28.♖h2 ♖e4?! 29.f3! ♖e3 30.♖e2! ♖f4 31.♖xe3 dxe3 32.♖d3 ♖xh4 33.♖xe3 ♘d4 34.♖e4 ♖xe4** [34...♘xf3? 35.♖e8+ ♔f7 36.♘xf3 ♖h1+ 37.♖e1!+−] **35.fxe4 ♔f7 36.♔c1 ♔f6 37.♔d2 ♔e5! 38.♔e3 h5 39.a3** [39.♘h3!?] **39...a5 40.♘h3 ♘c2+** [40...♘e6] **41.♔d3** [41.♔d2 ♘d4 42.♔e3 ♘e6] **41...♘e1+ 42.♔e2 ♘g2 43.♔f3 ♘h4+ 44.♔e3 ♘g6 45.♘g5 ♔f6 46.♘h7+ ♔g7 47.♘g5 ♔f6 48.♘h7+ ♔e7! 49.♘g5** [49.♔d4 ♘f8! 50.♘g5 ♘e6+!−+] **49...♘e5 50.♔d4 ♔d6 51.♘h3 a4 52.♘f4 h4 53.♘h3 b6! 54.♘f4 b5 55.♘h3 ♘c6+ 56.♔e3 ♔c5 57.♔d3 b4! 58.axb4+ ♔xb4 59.♔c2 ♘d4+ 60.♔b1 ♘e6! 61.♔a2** [61.♔c2 ♔c4 62.♘f2 ♘g5!−+ Reinfeld] **61...♔c4 62.♔a3 ♔d4! 63.♔xa4 ♔xe4 64.b4 ♔f3 65.b5 ♔g2!** [it is mate in 19 moves according to the six-piece tablebases] **0-1**

Fischer,Robert
Tal,Mikhail

Leipzig ol 1960 (5)

1.e4 e6 2.d4 d5 3.♘c3 ♗b4 4.e5 c5 5.a3 ♗a5 6.b4 cxd4 7.♛g4 ♘e7 8.bxa5 dxc3 9.♛xg7 ♖g8 10.♛xh7 ♘bc6 11.♘f3 ♛c7 12.♗b5 ♗d7 13.0-0 0-0-0 14.♗g5 ♘xe5 15.♘xe5 ♗xb5 16.♘xf7 ♗xf1 17.♘xd8 ♖xg5

18.♘xe6 ♖xg2+ 19.♔h1 ♕e5
20.♖xf1 ♕xe6 21.♔xg2 ♕g4+ ½-½

Naiditsch,Arkady
Yusupov,Artur
Germany Bundesliga 2006/07 (9)

1.e4 e6 2.d4 d5 3.♘c3 ♗b4 4.e5
♘e7 5.a3 ♗xc3+ 6.bxc3 c5 7.♕g4
0-0 8.♗d3 ♘bc6 9.♕h5 ♘g6 10.♘f3
♕c7 11.♗e3 ♘ce7 12.h4 ♗d7
13.♕g4 f5 14.♕h3 h6 15.h5 ♘h8
16.g4 c4 17.♗e2 fxg4 18.♕xg4 ♘f5
19.♔d2 b5 20.♘h4 ♘xe3 21.fxe3
♘f7 22.♘f3 ♘d8 23.♖hg1 ♗e8
24.♘h4 a5 25.♗f3 ♖b8 26.e4 dxe4
27.♗xe4 b4 28.axb4 axb4 29.♖af1
♖xf1 30.♖xf1 b3 31.cxb3 cxb3
32.♗d3 ♖c8 33.c4 ♕b7 34.♔e3 b2
35.♘g6 ♗f7 36.♕e4 ♖b8 37.d5
♕a7+ 38.♔e2 b1♕ 39.♖xb1 ♕a2+
40.♔f1 1-0

Nijboer,Friso
Timman,Jan
Hilversum ch-NED 2006 (5)

1.e4 e6 2.d4 d5 3.♘c3 ♗b4 4.e5 c5
5.a3 ♗xc3+ 6.bxc3 ♘e7 7.♕g4 ♕c7
8.♕xg7 ♖g8 9.♕xh7 cxd4 10.♘e2
♘bc6 11.f4 ♗d7 12.♕d3 dxc3
13.♘xc3 a6 14.♖b1 ♖c8 15.h4 ♘f5
16.♖h3 ♘cd4 17.h5 ♕c5 18.♖xb7
♘b5 19.♘e4 1-0

Sokolov,Andrey
Yusupov,Artur
Riga m 1986 (3)

1.e4 e6 2.d4 d5 3.♘c3 ♗b4 4.e5 c5
5.a3 ♗xc3+ 6.bxc3 ♘e7 7.♘f3 b6
8.a4 ♗a6 9.♗xa6 ♘xa6 10.0-0 ♘b8
11.dxc5 bxc5 12.c4 0-0 13.cxd5
♘xd5 14.♕d3 h6 15.c4 ♘e7 16.♕e4
♘d7 17.♖b1 ♕a5 18.♖d1 ♖ad8

19.♕c2 ♘xe5 20.♘xe5 ♕c3 21.♕e2
♕xe5 22.♗e3 ♘f5 23.♕f3 ♖xd1+
24.♖xd1 ♘d4 25.♗xd4 cxd4
26.♕d3 ♖d8 27.g3 ♕c5 28.f4 ♕b4
29.♖a1 a5 30.h4 h5 31.♖b1 ♕xa4
32.♖b5 g6 33.♔g2 ♕a2+ 34.♔f3 a4
35.♖b6 ♔g7 36.♖b1 ♔g8 37.♖b6
♕a1 38.♔e2 a3 39.♖a6 ♕b2+
40.♕d2 d3+ 0-1

Pogrebissky,Iosif
Botvinnik,Mikhail
Leningrad ch-URS 1939 (13)

1.e4 e6 2.d4 d5 3.♘c3 ♗b4 4.e5 c5
5.a3 ♗xc3+ 6.bxc3 ♘e7 7.♘f3
♘bc6 8.♗d3 ♕a5 9.♕d2 c4 10.♗e2
♕a4 11.0-0 [11.h4; 11.♘g5] 11...♗d7
12.♘g5 h6 13.♘h3 0-0-0 14.f4 f6
15.♘f2 h5 16.♘d1 ♘f5 17.♘b2 ♕a5
18.a4 g5!∓ [Fine] 19.♘d1 g4 20.exf6
♖df8 21.♗a3 ♖xf6 22.♗b4 ♘xb4
23.cxb4 ♕b6 24.c3 ♕c7 25.♗b2
♖hf8 26.♗d1 ♘e7 27.g3 ♖h8
28.♗c2 h4 29.♔g2 ♘f5 30.♗xf5
♖xf5 31.♕e2 ♖fh5 32.♖h1 e5
33.dxe5 ♗f5 34.♖ag1 hxg3 35.♔f1
♖xh2 36.♖xh2 ♖xh2 0-1

Rabinovich,Ilya
Botvinnik,Mikhail
Leningrad ch-URS 1939 (4)

1.e4 e6 2.d4 d5 3.♘c3 ♗b4 4.e5 c5
5.a3 ♗xc3+ 6.bxc3 ♘e7 7.♘f3 ♗d7
8.a4 ♕a5 9.♕d2 ♘bc6 10.♗d3 c4
11.♗e2 f6 12.♗a3 0-0-0 13.0-0 ♘f5
14.g4? [14.♖fb1!? h5 15.h4; 14.♖fe1]
14...♘fe7 15.♖fb1 ♕a6? 16.a5±
♖df8 17.♘e1 fxe5 18.♘d3!± cxd3
19.♗xd3 ♕xa5 20.♗xe7 ♕c7
21.♗xf8 ♖xf8 22.♗b5 ♖f4 23.h3 a6
24.♗xc6 ♗xc6 25.♖e1 e4 26.♖e3
♗b5 27.♖g3 g5 28.♔g2 ♕f7

29.♕e3 ♕f6 30.♖e1 ♗e8 31.♕e2
♔b8 32.♖b1 ♗b5 33.♕e3 ♗e8
34.♕e2 ♔c7 35.♖h1 ♗g6 36.♖e1
♗e8 37.♖h1 h5 38.♔g1 ♗b5
39.♕e1 h4 40.♖e3 ♗c4 41.♖h2 b6
42.♕a1 ♕f8 43.♖g2 a5 44.♕a4
♕e7 45.♕a1 ♔b7 46.♕a4 ♖f8
47.♖e1 ♕d6 48.♕a1 ♔a6 49.♖e3 b5
50.♕b2 ♖f3 51.♔h1 ♖f6 52.♔g1
♔b6 53.♖h2 ♖f7 54.♖g2 ♖f3
55.♔h1 ♖f8 56.♔g1 ♖f6 57.♖h2
♔c6 58.♖g2 ♖f3 59.♔h1 ♗f1
60.♖xf3 exf3 61.♖h2 a4 62.♔g1 a3
63.♕c1 ♗c4 64.♕xg5 a2 65.♕c1 e5
66.dxe5 ♕xe5 67.♕a1 ♕e2   0-1

Smyslov,Vasily
Botvinnik,Mikhail

Moscow ch-URS 1944 (8)

1.e4 e6 2.d4 d5 3.♘c3 ♗b4 4.e5 c5
5.a3 ♗xc3+ 6.bxc3 ♘e7 7.a4 ♘bc6
8.♘f3 ♕a5 9.♗d2 c4 10.♘g5 [10.h4
(Steiner); 10.g3!] 10...h6 11.♘h3 ♘g6
12.♕f3?! [12.f4 ♗d7 13.g1 (Fine);
12.♗e2 ♗d7 13.♗h5±] 12...♗d7
13.♘f4 ♘xf4 14.♕xf4 ♘e7! 15.h4
♗xa4!∓ 16.h5 [16.♗e2 ♕b5 17.♗d1]
16...♕b5!∓ 17.♔d1 [17.♖c1]
17...♖c8!∓ 18.♗c1 [18.♗e2 ♖c6 19.g4?
♗xc2+ 20.♔xc2 ♕b3+ 21.♔c1
♖b6-+] 18...♖c6 19.♗e2 [19.g4!?]
19...♖a6 20.♔d2 0-0 [a questionable
move. White now develops a strong initiative on the kingside; ≥ 20...♕d7 21.g4
♗b5] 21.g4! [21.♗a3? ♗xc2! 22.♗xe7
♕b2! Botvinnik] 21...f6! 22.exf6 ♖xf6
23.♕c7 [23.♕e3] 23...♖f7 24.♕d8+

♔h7 25.f4! ♕a5!? 26.♕b8 [26.♕xa5
♖xa5 27.♗a3] 26...♘c6 27.♕e8 ♖e7
28.♕g6+?! [28.♕f8!? ♕d8 29.♕xd8
♘xd8 30.g5⇄ Botvinnik] 28...♔g8
29.♗a3 [29.g5!? ♕xd4!? 30.gxh6 e5]
29...e5?! [29...♕c7! 30.♖hf1 ♗b4!
(30...♘e5? 31.fxe5 ♗e8 32.♖f8+ ♔xf8
33.♕h7) 31.♗xb4 ♗e8!∓] 30.fxe5?
[30.dxe5 Botvinnik; 30.♗xe7 ♘xe7]
30...♘xd4! [30...♘xe5 31.♕xa6 ♕xa6
32.♗xe7± Fine] 31.♗b4 [31.♕xa6 bxa6
32.♗xe7 ♘xe2-+] 31...♕d8 32.♕xa6
bxa6 33.cxd4 ♖b7! 34.♖xa4 ♕g5+
35.♔d1 a5 [35...c3! mates in 6 moves]
36.♗f3 ♖xb4 37.♗xd5+ ♔f8 38.♖f1+
♔e8 39.♗c6+ ♔e7 40.♖xb4 ♕xg4+
                                    0-1

Fischer,Robert
Larsen,Bent

Denver m 1971 (1)

1.e4 e6 2.d4 d5 3.♘c3 ♗b4 4.e5
♘e7 5.a3 ♗xc3+ 6.bxc3 c5 7.a4
♘bc6 8.♘f3 ♗d7 9.♗d3 ♕c7 10.0-0
c4 11.♗e2 f6 12.♖e1 ♘g6 13.♗a3
fxe5 14.dxe5 ♘cxe5 15.♘xe5 ♘xe5
16.♕d4 ♘g6 17.♗h5 ♔f7 18.f4
♖he8 19.f5 exf5 20.♕xd5+ ♔f6
21.♗f3 ♘e5 22.♕d4 ♔g6 23.♖xe5
♕xe5 24.♕xd7 ♖ad8 25.♕xb7
♕e3+ 26.♔f1 ♖d2 27.♕c6+ ♖e6
28.♗c5 ♖f2+ 29.♔g1 ♖xg2+
30.♔xg2 ♕d2+ 31.♔h1 ♖xc6
32.♗xc6 ♕xc3 33.♖g1+ ♔f6
34.♗xa7 g5 35.♗b6 ♕xc2 36.a5
♕b2 37.♗d8+ ♔e6 38.a6 ♕a3
39.♗b7 ♕c5 40.♖b1 c3 41.♗b6 1-0

Sicilian Defence

1.e2-e4 c7-c5

In the **Sicilian Defence**, Black advances his pawn to c5 so as to make it as difficult as possible for White to achieve the ideal pawn centre, which consists of pawns on e4 and d4. Until the end of the 1920s, Black almost always preferred to directly occupy the centre with the classical move 1...e5. However, the Sicilian Defence has a big advantage over this move: usually White responds to ...c5 by advancing his pawn to d4 and then recaptures with the knight (the **Open Sicilian**). This gives Black the advantage of a central pawn majority; an e-pawn and d-pawn against the single white e-pawn. This structure has strategic characteristics that are more complex than those of the Open Games, and Black can end up with a variety of very different pawn formations. White, for his part, can castle kingside or queenside. He can play strategically, or he can violently attack the black king by making use of his space advantage and better piece development, and the increased mobility granted by these factors.

White directs his forces to the kingside, and Black seeks an initiative on the queenside, exploiting the semi-open c-file. There are, of course, the inevitable exceptions: a striking example is the **Sveshnikov Variation**, in which Black develops a strong kingside initiative against the white king! This complexity is well suited to the taste of modern players, who like to be able to determine the strategy of their own game, and not have it determined too much by the strategic intentions of their opponent, even if this relative autonomy entails greater risks. The Sicilian was virtually never played in the 19th century: it enjoyed a boom in the second half of the 20th century, and it is as vital and popular as ever at the beginning of the new millennium. Kasparov, whom many consider to be the strongest player of all time, played it almost exclusively, and his contributions, especially in the **Najdorf Variation**, have led to the creation of a very large body of theory. However, we are still far from plumbing the depths of this defence.

Minor Variations

2.♘f3 and 3.d4 leads to the Open Sicilian. However, there are quite a few players who, for one reason or another, prefer one of the following minor variations. These variations may not be quite as sharp as the main lines, but they should not be underestimated by Black. In particular, the **Sicilian with 2.c3** — otherwise known as the **Alapin Variation** — has become so popular lately that it is only because of convention that it is still classified as a minor system.

Wing Gambit

1.	**e2-e4**	**c7-c5**
2.	**b2-b4**	

The **Wing Gambit** has never been popular with elite players, and for the few who do use it at this level it is only brought out as a surprise weapon. White plays 2.b4 with the intention of giving up a pawn, in order to construct a strong pawn centre with 3.d4; or he will activate his pieces with 3.a3. Against correct play, White does not seem to gain sufficient compensation for the pawn. However, in practice it is not easy for Black to defend his position.

Morra Gambit

Here is another gambit for adventure lovers, even if it is more positional by nature than most of the other gambits:

1.	**e2-e4**	**c7-c5**
2.	**d2-d4**	**c5xd4**
3.	**c2-c3**	**d4xc3**
4.	**♘b1xc3**	

White gives up a pawn for development, and above all to make the c- and d-files available for occupation by his rooks. Black, denied his usual active play on the queenside, has to operate in a cramped and passive position for many moves.

White usually develops his pieces very aggressively (usually: ♘f3, ♘c3, ♗f4, ♗c4, ♕e2, ♖fd1, ♖ac1) and Black must defend with precision. Black usually establishes a **Scheveningen** set-up (e6, d6, a6, ♘f6, ♘c6, ♗e7, ♗d7, ♕c7 or ♕b8) and normally delays kingside castling. A modern treatment of the **Morra Gambit** by Black involves advancing the pawn to e5: a drastic measure to prevent e4-e5 (which in many continuations causes Black serious problems).

More rarely Black fianchettoes on the kingside in the style of the **Dragon Variation**. The **Siberian Variation** has become a very fashionable choice recently:

4.	**...**	**♘b8-c6**
5.	**♘g1-f3**	**e7-e6**
6.	**♗f1-c4**	**♕d8-c7**
7.	**♕d1-e2**	**♘g8-f6**
8.	**0-0**	**♘f6-g4**

with the venomous idea of responding to *9.h3??* with *9...♞d4* and Black wins the queen.

9.	♞c3-b5	♛c7-b8	
10.	h2-h3	h7-h5!	
11.	g2-g3	a7-a6!	
12.	♞b5-c3	♝f8-c5	
13.	♝c1-f4	♞g4-e5	

White does not have sufficient compensation for the pawn. The Morra Gambit is very popular at amateur level, but is viewed with suspicion by grandmasters. In view of this reservation, it is surprising how often these elite players decline the gambit and prefer to continue with 3...♞f6, transposing to positions from the **Alapin Variation**. Other ways of declining the Morra are 3...d5 or 3...d3.

In conclusion, Black's extra pawn should count in the long term: at least in theory. However, as it happens, in the ensuing endgames the extra pawn is not always enough to guarantee a win.

2.f4 Variation

1.	e2-e4	c7-c5
2.	f2-f4	

This attack achieved a certain popularity in the 1970s thanks to the efforts of Bent Larsen and Tony Miles. Black can seek to break up White's aligned pawns in the centre with ...e6 and ...d5. Or he can immediately play 2...d5 to produce a kind of improved **Scandinavian**:

2.	...	d7-d5
3.	e4xd5	♛d8xd5

3...♞f6!? is an interesting gambit

4.	♞b1-c3	♛d5-d8

Black's c5-pawn is without doubt more useful than White's f4-pawn.

For this reason White usually postpones f4 until the third move, first preventing 2...d5 with 2.♞c3.

Mariotti,Sergio
Kuzmin,Gennady
Leningrad 1977 (15)

1.e4 c5 2.b4 cxb4 3.d4 d5 4.e5 ♞c6 5.a3 ♛b6 6.♞e2 ♝f5 7.axb4 ♞xb4 8.♞a3 ♖c8 9.♞f4 ♝xc2 10.♛g4 e6 11.♝b5+ ♞c6 12.♞xd5 ♛d8 13.♞xc2 ♛xd5 14.♖b1 h5 15.♛h3 ♛e4+ 16.♔d1 ♛g4+ 17.♛xg4 hxg4 18.♝a4 ♖c7 19.♝xc6+ ♖xc6 20.♖xb7 ♞e7 21.♖xa7 ♖c8 22.♖a4 ♞d5 23.♝d2 ♖b8 24.♔e2 ♝e7 25.g3 0-0 26.♞e3 ♖b2 27.♞xd5 exd5 28.♖d1 ♖c8 29.♔f1 ♖cc2 30.♝e1 ♝g5 31.♖a5 ♔h7 32.♖xd5 ♔g6 33.♖d6+ ♔f5 34.♖d7 ♔g6 35.d5 ♝e3 36.♖d6+ ♔h7 37.fxe3 ♖xh2 38.♖d2 ♖bxd2 39.♝xd2 ♖xd2 40.e4 ♖d3 41.♔f2 ♖f3+ 42.♔g2 ♖d3 43.e6 fxe6 44.♖xe6 ♔g8 45.d6 ♔f7 46.♖e7+ ♔f6 47.e5+ ♔f5 48.♔f2 ♔e4 49.d7 1-0

Messa,Roberto
Keogh,Eamon
Berlin tt 1980

1.e4 c5 2.d4 cxd4 3.c3 dxc3 4.♞xc3 d6 5.♝c4 ♞c6 6.♞f3 e6 7.0-0 ♝e7

8.♕e2 a6 9.♖d1 ♕c7 10.♗f4 ♘f6
11.♖ac1 0-0 12.♗b3 ♖d8 13.♘d5
exd5 14.exd5 ♕d7 15.dxc6 bxc6
16.♘e5 ♕b7 17.♘xf7 d5 18.♘xd8
♗xd8 19.♗a4 ♗g4 20.♗xc6 ♕xc6
21.♕xg4 ♕e8 22.♕f3 ♗b6 23.♗e3
♗xe3 24.♕xe3 ♕d7 25.h3 ♖e8
26.♕b6 ♖e6 27.♕c7 ♕xc7 28.♖xc7
1-0

Fischer,Robert
Kortchnoi,Viktor
Buenos Aires 1960 (14)

1.e4 c5 2.♘f3 a6 3.d4 cxd4 4.c3
dxc3 5.♘xc3 ♘c6 6.♗c4 d6 7.0-0
♘f6 8.♗g5 e6 9.♕e2 ♗e7 10.♖fd1
♕c7 11.♖ac1 0-0 12.♗b3 h6 13.♗f4
e5 14.♗e3 ♕d8 15.♘d5 ♘xd5
16.♗xd5 ♗d7 17.♘d2 ♘b4 18.♗b3
♗g5 19.♗xg5 ♕xg5 20.♘f3 ♗g4
21.♖c7 ♕d8 22.♖xb7 ♖b8 23.♖xb8
♕xb8 24.h3 ♗xf3 25.♕xf3 ♘c6
26.♕d3 ♘d4 27.♗c4 a5 28.b3 ♕b4
29.f4 ♔h7   ½-½

Fischer,Robert
Naranja,Renato
Meralco 1967

1.e4 c5 2.♘c3 ♘c6 3.♘ge2 e5
4.♘d5 ♘f6 5.♘ec3 ♗e7 6.♗c4 0-0
7.d3 h6 8.f4 d6 9.f5 b6 10.h4 ♗b7
11.a3 ♖c8 12.♘xf6+ ♗xf6 13.♕h5
♘e7 14.♗g5 d5 15.♗xf6 dxc4
16.♕g4 g6 17.dxc4 ♕d6 18.♗xe7
♕xe7 19.fxg6 fxg6 20.♕xg6+ ♕g7
21.♕xg7+ ♔xg7 22.♖d1 ♖cd8
23.♖xd8 ♖xd8 24.♘d5 b5 25.cxb5

♗xd5 26.exd5 c4 27.a4 ♖xd5
28.♔e2 ♖d4 29.♖d1 ♖e4+ 30.♔f3
♖f4+ 31.♔e3 c3 32.b3   1-0

Antoms,Guntars
McShane,Luke
Leon Ech-tt 2001 (1)

1.e4 c5 2.♘c3 ♘c6 3.f4 g6 4.♘f3
♗g7 5.♗c4 e6 6.f5 ♘ge7 7.fxe6
dxe6 8.0-0 ♘d4 9.d3 ♘ec6! 10.♗g5
♘xf3+ 11.♕xf3 ♗d4+ 12.♗e3
♗xe3+ 13.♕xe3 ♕d4 14.♕xd4
cxd4 15.♘b5 ♔e7 16.♖ae1 ♗d7
17.♘c7?! ♖ac8 18.♘d5+ ♔d6
19.♘f6 ♘e5! 20.c3 dxc3 21.bxc3
♗a4!?↑ 22.♖b3? ♗xb3 23.axb3
♘xd3 24.♖d1 ♖xc3–+ 25.♖f3 ♔e7
26.♘g4 ♖d8 27.♘f2? ♘xf2 28.♖xd8
♖xf3   0-1

Kovalev,Andrey
Kovalevskaya,Ekaterina
Moscow 2002 (1)

1.e4 c5 2.♘c3 ♘c6 3.f4 g6 4.♘f3
♗g7 5.♗c4 e6 6.0-0 ♘ge7 7.e5 d5
8.exd6 ♕xd6 9.♘e4 ♕c7 10.d3 0-0
11.♕e1 ♘f5 12.g4 ♘fd4 13.♘fg5 h6
14.c3 b5 15.cxd4 bxc4 16.f5 exf5
17.♗f4 ♕d8 18.gxf5 ♗xf5 19.d5
♘d4 20.dxc4 hxg5 21.♘xg5 f6
22.♘e6 ♗xe6 23.dxe6 ♖e8 24.♕e4
f5 25.♕g2 ♖xe6 26.♖ae1 ♕e8
27.♖xe6 ♘xe6 28.♖e1 ♖d8 29.b4
♕f7 30.♗e3 cxb4 31.c5 ♗d4
32.♗xd4 ♖xd4 33.♕a8+ ♔g7 34.c6
♘g5 35.♖c1 ♕d5 36.♕xa7+ ♔h6
                                  0-1

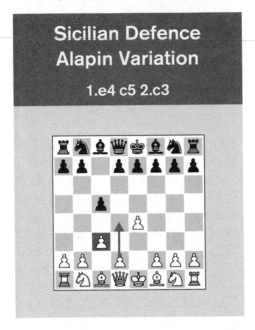

Sicilian Defence Alapin Variation

1.e4 c5 2.c3

This variation deserves special attention because of its noteworthy current popularity.

In a certain sense, 2.c3 is the most logical way to proceed; White seeks to create the ideal pawn centre, i.e. pawns on the d4- and e4-squares. White wants to play 3.d4: if then 3...cxd4, he recaptures with the c3-pawn.

The move 2.c3 also has its disadvantages: it is not a developing move, as is the normal 2.♘f3; but the main problem is that it denies the b1-knight the possibility to develop to its natural destination, the c3-square. This is not an esoteric point, as it allows Black effective counterplay against the undefended e4-pawn, with the opportunity to reach improved versions of the **Alekhine** (2...♘f6), the **Scandinavian** (2...d5), or the **French** (2...e6 and 3...d5).

However, Black can also ignore his adversary's 'threat' to conquer the centre if he wants to, and continue with ...d6, ...♘f6, ...g6, ...♗g7 and ...0-0. But this allows White to maintain a slight advantage.

Here is a more detailed look at these five approaches that Black can use against the Alapin Variation.

A)   2.   ...   d7-d5
Aiming to exploit the fact that White, having already occupied the c3-square, will not be able to attack the black queen on d5. This variation often leads to positions with an isolated d4-pawn, with the usual strategic considerations for both colours that this entails. Here Black can very actively play ...♗g4, with or without ...♘f6; or otherwise, continue more modestly with **...e7-e6**, leaving the c8-bishop on its home square.

3.   e4xd5   ♕d8xd5
4.   d2-d4

Black can now choose between two equally valid moves:

A1)   4.   ...   ♘b8-c6
**   5.   ♘g1-f3   ♗c8-g4**
Putting maximum pressure on d4.
**   6.   ♗f1-e2   c5xd4**

7. c3xd4   e7-e6

and Black has fair prospects.

A2)   4. ...   ♞g8-f6
5. ♞g1-f3

and Black has a variety of replies: 5...♞c6, 5...♝g4 and the prudent 5...e6.

The resulting positions are typical isolated queen's pawn structures: White has an initiative which can become unpleasant for Black in the middlegame, and he has good piece activity, which can often threaten the black king. On the other hand, if Black patiently plays through to the endgame, the weakness of the isolated d4-pawn could prove to be in his favour.

B)   2. ...   ♞g8-f6

The second method is certainly more active, and for this reason also riskier. It consists of a direct counterattack against c4.

Here Black, in a way similar to the **Alekhine Defence**, seeks to encourage White to advance his pawn to e5, believing that he will then be able to effectively counterattack the centre with ...d7–d6. On the other hand, the c2–c4 pawn advance, which is so common in many Alekhine variations, now takes one extra tempo.

3. e4-e5   ♞f6-d5
4. d2-d4   c5xd4

Now White can recapture on d4 with the pawn or the queen. In the latter case, after 5.♕xd4 e6 6.♞f3 ♞c6 7.♕e4 (best), Black should be able to obtain balanced play with either the logical 7...d6 or the courageous 7...f5.

Alternatively, he can postpone the capture with the flexible

5. ♞g1-f3

not immediately revealing his intentions. Black can respond to 5.♞f3 in three ways: 5...d6, which is interesting but largely untried; 5...e6, which appears to be passive, but is very solid; and

5. ...   ♞b8-c6

which is the most common, and to which White has two alternative responses:

B1)   6. c3xd4   d7-d6
7. ♝f1-c4

The most incisive; 7.♞c3 is also interesting.

7. ...   ♞d5-b6
8. ♝c4-b5

Stronger than 8.♗b3, which does not cause Black any problems.

8. ... d6xe5!

The only move that allows Black to reach a balanced game.

B2) 6. ♗f1-c4

White's modern continuation, which is sharper and more complicated.

6. ... ♘d5-b6
7. ♗c4-b3 d7-d6
8. e5xd6 ♕d8xd6
9. 0-0

The c3-pawn, and possibly the b2-pawn, is in effect sacrificed to exploit the lead in development and White's highly dynamic piece placement. However, Black should be able to equalize if he knows his theory and defends carefully.

C) 2. ... e7-e6

This third line is perhaps the most solid of all.

3. d2-d4 d7-d5

The idea behind this line is to deploy the pawns along the lines of the French Defence. If White now plays e4-e5 we have effectively transposed to the Advance Variation of the French.

4. e4xd5 e6xd5

A typical position arising from the 3...c5 line of the **Tarrasch Variation of the French**, but in this case White already has his pawn on c3, which makes it easier for Black to equalize. However, the position is a little dry and gives Black few opportunities to win.

D) 2. ... d7-d6

Black's fourth approach is to ignore his adversary's 'threat' to conquer the centre. However, this allows White much freer play. For example,

3. d2-d4 ♘g8-f6
4. ♗f1-d3! c5xd4
5. c3xd4 g7-g6
6. ♘b1-c3

and after 6...♗g7, if White plays the correct move 7.h3! before he develops his king's knight,

Black will not easily reach a satisfactory position. It is important to prevent the

f3-knight from being pinned, as that would weaken the defence of d4. For this reason Black can attempt

>**6.** ... ♞b8-c6
>**7.** ♞g1-f3

7.♞e2!?, to meet 7...♝g4 with 8.f3.

>**7.** ... ♝c8-g4

But now 8.d5! is strong, forcing Black to concede the bishop pair with 8...♝xf3 9.♛xf3 ♞e5 10.♝b5+, as 8...♞e5 is followed by 9.♞xe5!.

E)
>**2.** ... e7-e5
>**3.** ♞g1-f3 ♞b8-c6
>**4.** ♝f1-c4

White has an unpleasant initiative.

Sveshnikov,Evgeny
Satyapragyan,Swayangsu
Dubai 2004 (2)

1.e4 c5 2.c3 d5 3.exd5 ♛xd5 4.d4 g6 5.♞f3 ♝g7 6.dxc5 ♛xc5 7.♛b3 ♞f6 8.♝e3 ♛a5 9.♝c4 0-0 10.0-0 ♞c6 11.♞g5 e6 12.♝d2 ♛c7 13.♝e2 ♞d5 14.♝c5 ♜d8 15.♜fd1 ♞a5 16.♛a3 b6 17.♝b4 ♞c6 18.♞de4 h6 19.♞f3 ♞cxb4 20.cxb4 ♛c2 21.♞c3 ♝xc3 22.bxc3 ♛xe2 23.♛c1 ♝b7 24.♛xh6 ♞f6 25.♜e1 ♛xf2+ 0-1

Lasker,Emanuel
Bernstein,Ossip
New York 1940

1.e4 c5 2.c3 d5 3.exd5 ♛xd5 4.d4 e6 5.♞f3 ♞c6 6.♝e2 cxd4 7.cxd4 ♝b4+ 8.♞c3 ♞f6 9.0-0 ♛d6 10.a3 ♝a5 11.♛a4 0-0 12.♝g5 a6 13.♝xf6 gxf6 14.♜ad1 b5 15.♛b3 ♝c7 16.♞e4 ♛e7 17.♛c3 ♝b7 18.d5 ♝e5 19.♞xe5 ♞xe5 20.f4 ♜ac8 21.d6 ♛d8 22.♞xf6+ ♛xf6 23.♛xe5 ♛xe5 24.fxe5 ♜c5 25.d7

♜d8 26.♞h5 ♜xe5 27.♝xf7+ ♚g7 28.♜d3 ♜g5 29.g3 ♜d5 30.♜xd5 ♝xd5 31.♝e8 a5 32.♜f7+ ♚g8 33.♚f2 ♝c6 34.♜e7 e5 35.♝f7+ ♚f8 36.♜e8+ ♜xe8 37.♝xe8 1-0

Jonkman,Harmen
Adly,Ahmed
Wijk aan Zee C 2006 (10)

1.e4 c5 2.c3 d5 3.exd5 ♛xd5 4.d4 ♞c6 5.♞f3 cxd4 6.cxd4 e5 7.♞c3 ♝b4 8.♝d2 ♝xc3 9.♝xc3 e4 10.♞e5 ♞xe5 11.dxe5 ♞e7 12.♝e2 ♝d7 13.0-0 ♝c6 14.♛c1 ♝e6 15.♜d1 ♞g6 16.♜d6 ♛e7 17.♝b4 0-0 18.♜xg6 ♛xb4 19.♜xg7+ ♚xg7 20.♛g5+ ♚h8 21.♛f6+ ♚g8 22.♛g5+ ♚h8 23.♛f6+ ♚g8 24.♛g5+ ♚h8 25.♛f6+ ½-½

Tiviakov,Sergey
Sakaev,Konstantin
Khanty Mansiysk 2005 (3)

1.e4 c5 2.c3 ♞f6 3.e5 ♞d5 4.♝c4 ♞b6 5.♝b3 c4 6.♝c2 ♞c6 7.♞f3 ♛c7 8.♛e2 g5 9.h3 ♝g7 10.0-0 ♞xe5 11.♞xg5 d5 12.a4 ♝d7 13.a5 ♞c8 14.♞f3 ♞g6 15.d4 cxd3 16.♝xd3 e5 17.a6 ♞ce7 18.axb7 ♛xb7 19.♝a6 ♛c7 20.♞a3 0-0 21.♞b5 ♛c6 22.♝e3 ♞f5 23.♜fd1 ♞xe3 24.fxe3 ♛b6 25.♚h1 e4 26.♞h2 ♞e7 27.♞d4 ♜ab8 28.♜d2 ♚h8 29.♛f2 f5 30.g3 ♞g6 31.♞e2 ♝e6 32.♞d4 ♝d7 33.b4 ♞e5 34.♜da2 ♞c6 35.♞e2 ♝e6 36.♜a3 ♝g8 37.♞f1 ♞e5 38.♞f4 ♛h6 39.♝e2 ♞g6 40.♞h5 ♝e5 41.b5 ♜bc8 42.♜xa7 ♜xc3 43.♜1a2 ♜b3 44.h4 ♜b1 45.♜2a6 d4 46.exd4 ♝d5 47.♛g2 f4 48.gxf4 ♝xf4 49.♜d7 ♝c4 50.♞xf4 ♝xe2 51.♜xg6 ♛xh4+ 52.♛h3 ♛xh3+ 53.♞xh3 hxg6 0-1

Tiviakov,Sergey
Carlsen,Magnus

Wijk aan Zee 2007 (1)

1.e4 c5 2.c3 ♘f6 3.e5 ♘d5 4.♘f3
♘c6 5.♗c4 ♘b6 6.♗b3 d5 7.exd6
♕xd6 8.♘a3 a6 9.0-0 ♗f5 10.d4
cxd4 11.♘xd4 ♘xd4 12.cxd4 e6
13.♕f3 ♕d7 14.d5 ♘xd5 15.♖d1
♗xa3 16.bxa3 0-0 17.h4 ♖ac8
18.♗xd5 exd5 19.♖xd5 ♕e6 20.♖xf5
♕e1+ 21.♔h2 ♖xc1 22.♖xc1 ♕xc1
23.♕xb7 ♕xa3 24.♕d5   ½-½

Mamedyarov,Shakhriyar
Shanava,Konstantin

Chalkidiki jr 2003 (7)

1.e4 c5 2.c3 ♘f6 3.e5 ♘d5 4.d4
cxd4 5.♕xd4 e6 6.♘f3 ♘c6 7.♕e4
d6 8.♗b5 ♗d7 9.c4 ♘c7 10.exd6
♗xd6 11.0-0 ♘b4 12.♗xd7+ ♕xd7
13.♘c3 ♕c6 14.a3 ♘ba6 15.♕e2
0-0 16.b4 ♕e8 17.♘e4 ♗e7 18.♗f4
♕c8 19.♗d6 ♗xd6 20.♘xd6 ♕b8
21.♕e4 b6 22.♖ad1 ♘e8 23.♘xe8
♕xe8 24.♘g5 f5 25.♕xe6+ ♕xe6
26.♘xe6 ♖f7 27.♖fe1 h6 28.♖d6
♖e7 29.♔f1 ♖ae8 30.♖e3 f4 31.♖e2
♖c8 32.f3 ♔f7 33.c5   1-0

Godena,Michele
Kozul,Zdenko

Nova Gorica 2000 (3)

1.e4 c5 2.♘f3 e6 3.c3 ♘f6 4.e5 ♘d5
5.d4 cxd4 6.cxd4 d6 7.♗c4 ♘c6 8.0-0
♗e7 9.♕e2 0-0 10.♖d1 a6 11.♘c3
♘xc3 12.bxc3 dxe5 13.dxe5 ♕a5
14.♕e4 g6 15.♗h6 ♖d8 16.♖xd8+
♕xd8 17.♕f4 ♕c7 18.♖d1 ♗d7 19.♘g5
♗e8 20.♖d6 ♖d8 21.♘e4 f5 22.♗xe6+
♔h8 23.♗g5 ♖a8 24.♗f6+ ♗xf6
25.♘xf6 ♗f7 26.♕h6 ♗xe6 27.♖xe6
♖g8 28.♘xg8 ♕g7 29.♖d6   1-0

Sanz Alonso,Francisco Javier
Miles,Anthony

Amsterdam zt 1978 (15)

1.e4 c5 2.c3 ♘f6 3.e5 ♘d5 4.d4
cxd4 5.cxd4 b6 6.♘f3 e6 7.a3 ♗e7
8.♗d3 ♗b7 9.0-0 ♘a6 10.♖e1 ♘ac7
11.♘bd2 0-0 12.♘e4 f5 13.exf6 gxf6
14.♕d2 ♖f7 15.♕h6 ♖g7 16.♕h3 f5
17.♗h6 fxe4 18.♖xe4 ♘f6 19.♖h4
♗f8 20.♗xg7 ♗xg7 21.♖e1 ♗xf3
22.gxf3 ♕e7 23.♔h1 ♔f7 24.f4 ♖g8
25.f5 ♕d6 26.fxe6+ dxe6 27.♕f3
♔e7 28.♗c4 ♘cd5 29.♖e5 ♕c6
30.♗f1 ♗h8 31.♖h3 h5 32.♖g3 ♖f8
33.♗h3 ♘g4   0-1

Vlassov,Nikolay
Ponomariov,Ruslan

Moscow 2002 (1)

1.e4 c5 2.c3 e6 3.d4 d5 4.exd5
exd5 5.♘f3 ♘c6 6.♗e3 cxd4
7.♘xd4 ♗d6 8.♗e2 ♘f6 9.0-0 0-0
10.♘d2 ♖e8 11.♖e1 a6 12.♘f1 ♘e5
13.♗g5 h6 14.♗h4 ♘g6 15.♗g3
♗c5 16.♗f3 ♖xe1 17.♕xe1 ♕b6
18.♘b3 ♗f5 19.♘xc5 ♕xc5 20.♕d2
♘e4 21.♗xe4 dxe4 22.♖e1 ♕c6
23.♕d4 ♖e8 24.c4 ♘f8 25.♘e3
♗g6 26.♘d5 ♘e6 27.♕c3 f6 28.♖d1
♘c5 29.♘b4 ♕c8 30.♖d6 e3 31.f3
e2 32.h3 ♘a4 33.♕d2 e1♕+
34.♗xe1 ♖xe1+ 35.♔h2 ♖e8
36.♘d5 ♕f5 37.♖d7 ♕e5+ 38.f4
♕xb2 39.♘e7+ ♔h7 40.♕d5 ♘c3
41.♕xb7 ♕xb7 42.♖xb7 ♗e4
43.♖a7 ♖b8 44.f5 ♖b2 45.♔g3
♖xa2 46.♔f4 ♗xg2 47.♔e3 ♘e4
48.♘d5 h5 49.♘f4 ♘d6 50.♘xh5
♘xf5+ 51.♔d3 ♖a3+ 52.♔d2 ♔h6
53.♘f4 ♗e4 54.c5 g5 55.♘e6 ♖d3+
56.♔e1 ♘d4 57.♖xa6 ♔g6 58.h4
♘xe6 59.♖xe6   0-1

Sicilian Defence Minor Systems after

1.e2-e4 c7-c5 2.♘c3 ♘c6

Chameleon System

After

    2. ♘b1-c3   ♘b8-c6

(or 2...e6 or 2...d6), White sometimes proceeds with

    3. ♘g1-e2

This way, White keeps the option of d2-d4 on the next move, transposing to one of the Open Sicilian variations. Alternatively, he can prepare a fianchetto with g2-g3, transposing to a kind of Closed Sicilian. The name of the variation is inspired by its chameleon-like capacity to suddenly transform from a closed variation into an Open Sicilian.

This can be a headache for Black, who might end up having to play Open Sicilian variations which are not part of his repertoire: for example, after 2...♘c6 3.♘ge2 and 4.d4, a player who intended to play the Najdorf will now find it impossible to do so. The move 3...e5 is a radical way to avoid being tricked into playing unknown or lit-

tle-liked variations, obviously if 2...♘c6, or 2...d6, has already been played. But you pay a price: the ugly weakness of the d5-square.

The Grand Prix Attack

After

    2. ♘b1-c3   ♘b8-c6

the move

    3. f2-f4

is a dangerous continuation. Usually Black opens the diagonal for the king's bishop with

    3. ...   g7-g6

and after playing ...e7-e6, the king's knight goes to e7. White, for his part, continues with ♘f3, ♗c4 (or the positional ♗b5). At this point it is not uncommon for White to **sacrifice a pawn on f5** in exchange for a dangerous initiative against the king in the following typical variation:

    4. ♘g1-f3   ♗f8-g7
    5. ♗f1-c4   e7-e6
    6. f4-f5!?

However, it must be said that if Black knows the ensuing complications he can emerge out of them in good shape:

    6. ...   ♘g8-e7!

7.	f5xe6	f7xe6
8.	d2-d3	d7-d5!
9.	♗c4-b3	b7-b5!

It is curious that the idea of the f4-f5 sacrifice isn't from the Sicilian but from the **English Opening**. You reach the same type of position with the English Opening — with reversed colours. We suggest you have a look at the famous 1969 Saidy-Fischer game, in which Fischer played the positional sacrifice ...f4.

The **Grand Prix Attack** is an effective weapon to use against fans of the **Najdorf** or **Dragon Variations**, as both groups generally play 2...d6 after 2.♘c3, thus denying themselves the opportunity to play ...d7-d5 in one move, as you would normally do in the main line.

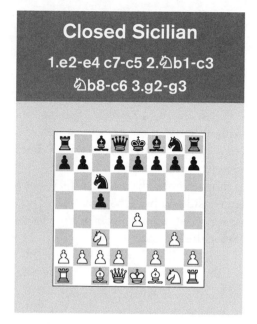

Closed Sicilian

1.e2-e4 c7-c5 2.♘b1-c3 ♞b8-c6 3.g2-g3

In the past decades, the **Closed Sicilian** was popular with players like Vasily Smyslov and Boris Spassky. Today, too, it has its admirers at all levels — from beginners to grandmasters.

By playing 2.♘c3 before opening the diagonal for the fianchetto, White anticipates ...d7-d5, which liberates Black's game. The most common response is 2...♘c6, after which White plays 3.g3, with the idea of developing the f1-bishop to g2.

Another good plan for Black is 2...e6 (or 3...e6) to prepare ...d7-d5: this is good for players who do not mind playing with hanging or isolated pawns, in positions where good piece play compensates for static weaknesses.

The bishop on g2 exerts further influence on d5, reinforcing central control, and only later will White shift his focus to the kingside. Beginners should note that to attack effectively on the flanks, the centre should be closed, or

otherwise you must have good control over it.

The Closed Sicilian is characterized by White's intention to not open the position with ♘f3 and d2-d4, but instead to play a manoeuvring game marked by the development of the bishop to g2 and expansion on the kingside. The price to be paid for this is a certain weakening of the queenside. In the main line Black usually continues with 3...g6, to place the dark-squared bishop on g7, from where it can support counterplay on the queenside (...♖b8, ...♗b7-b5-b4).

This system utilizes ideas from the **English Opening** (with reversed colours): 1.c4 e5 2.♘c3 ♘c6 3.g3 g6. However, in the Sicilian, White's extra tempo changes things slightly.

3.	...	g7-g6
4.	♗f1-g2	♗f8-g7
5.	d2-d3	

we have the **typical Closed Sicilian position**.

5.	...	d7-d6

As we will see, the most common plan begins with 6.f4. However, recently the move 6.♗e3 has become increasingly popular, especially with players at low to medium levels.

The manoeuvre ♗e3-♕d2-♗h6, with the idea of ♗xg7, h4-h5-hxg6 and ♕h6, is very dangerous if Black responds mechanically. However, White needs to be careful as well. There is a trap that he can fall into: After 6...e6 7.♕d2 ♘ge7 8.♗h6 0-0 9.h4 ♗xh6 10.♕xh6 f6!, *if White now continues with the thematic 11.h5??, Black wins the queen with 11...g5 followed by ...♔h8 and ...♘g8.* On the other hand, if White plays the correct move 11.♕d2, he has a small plus.

A good plan for Black seems to be to leave the knight on g8 and to begin immediate queenside counterplay with 6...♖b8, and after 7.♘ge2 (threatening d4) 7...♘d4 8.0-0 e6 9.♕d2 b5 or 9...♘e7, Black has sufficient counterplay. However, as we have already said,

6. f2-f4

is the most common move, planning a pawn storm on the kingside. Black

seeks counterplay by expanding on the queenside with ...b5-b4.

Black fundamentally has four approaches:

- develop the king's knight to the natural f6-square. However, placing the knight here has the defect that it is a little exposed to the advance of White's pawns;

- prepare immediate counterplay on the queenside with ...♖b8 and ...b7-b5-b4, postponing the decision of how to develop the kingside.

- play the direct ...e7-e5 along the lines of the Botvinnik Variation of the English Opening, with reversed colours;

- play ...e7-e6 and develop the king's knight to e7.

The last two options are the most frequently played:

A)   6. ...   e7-e5

An ambitious continuation, which at first glance seems illogical, as it blocks the extended control of the dark-squared diagonal and helps White to open the f-file. However, Black takes possession of the e5-square. Play is more fluid, and it is suitable for players who prefer positions that are more open than those that are produced by 6...e6.

7. ♘g1-h3

This move is often chosen because of the following traps that can easily ensnare an unsuspecting Black player. White aims for the f4-f5 advance, and therefore it is best if the knight does not interfere with the scope of the rook on the f-file after kingside castling.

After natural moves like 7...♘ge7 8.0-0, Black may play, as so often happens, the natural-looking *8...0-0?. Now White plays the sacrifice 9.f5! obtaining a very good position.*

If instead Black plays the more prudent 8...♘d4!, again White can either offer a sacrifice with 9.f5!? or play the quieter 9.♗e3.

Probably the safest thing for Black to do is to exchange immediately on f4, on the 7th move.

	7. ...	e5xf4

White cannot recapture with the pawn, because of 8...♗xh3 and 9...♕h4+, gaining a piece. After White recaptures with the knight or the bishop, he will control the d5-square and have pressure on the f-file. However, Black will be left with some trumps: the very active g7-bishop and the d4- and e5-squares for the knights.

B)   6. ...   e7-e6

The most common continuation. Black fights against the f4-f5 push more effectively this way, and in the event that White prepares for this advance with g3-g4, Black has the option of taking a radical step to prevent it: ...f5; the g8-knight develops to e7, where it is less exposed to White's pawn storm and exerts influence on the key f5-square.

The following gambit line has been popular recently:

7.	♘g1-f3	♘g8-e7
8.	0-0	0-0
9.	♗c1-e3	♘c6-d4

To prevent 10.d4.

10. e4-e5!?

White opens up the position for his two bishops, frees the e4-square for the c3-knight, forces a weakening of the d6- and c5-squares, and if Black captures on e5 he can exploit the f-file for his attack. Black can defend himself, but his task is not easy.

This gambit is not White's only option. Interesting alternatives are: 10.♖b1 (used by the young Anatoly Karpov), 10.♕d2, or the new idea 10.♗f2, in order to be able to recapture on d4 with the knight without being forked.

In conclusion, the Closed Sicilian, while certainly not the antidote to the Sicilian, has a big plus: it is not necessary to memorize hundreds of variations. It is sufficient just to develop a feel for the typical positions which, because they are strategically complex, tend to favour the stronger player rather than the one who is better prepared.

Adams,Michael
Kramnik,Vladimir

Las Vegas FIDE-Wch 1999 (5)

1.e4 c5 2.♘c3 ♘c6 3.g3 g6 4.♗g2 ♗g7 5.d3 d6 6.♗e3 e5 7.♕d2 ♘ge7 8.f4 ♘d4 9.♘f3 0-0 10.0-0-0 exf4 11.♗xf4 ♘xf3+ 12.♖xf3 ♕b6 13.♖b1 ♗e6 14.♗h6 ♖ae8 15.♗xg7 ♔xg7 16.♔h1 f6 17.a3 d5 18.b4 cxb4 19.♖xb4 ♕c7 20.♘b5 ♕d7 21.♘d4 ♗g8 22.♖e3 ♘c6 23.♘xc6 ♕xc6 24.h4 b6 25.♔h2 ♕c5 26.d4 ♕d6 27.exd5 ♗xd5 28.♗xd5 ♕xd5 29.c4 ♕f7 30.d5 ♖xe3 31.♕xe3 ♖e8 32.♕d3 ♕e7 33.♖b2 ♕e1 34.♕d2 ♕xd2+ 35.♖xd2 ♔f7 36.a4 ♖e4 37.a5 ♖xc4 38.axb6 axb6 39.♖b2 ♖d4 40.♖xb6 ♖xd5 41.♖b7+ ♔g8 42.♔g2 h5 43.♔f3 ♖e5 44.♖a7 ♔f8 45.♖b7 ♖e7 46.♖b6 ♔f7 47.♖a6 ♖d7 48.♖b6 ♔e7 49.♖a6 ♖d6 50.♖a5 ♔e6 51.♖a3 ♔e5 52.♖e3+ ♔f5 53.♖a3 ♖d5 54.♖e3 g5 55.hxg5 fxg5 56.♖a3 g4+ 57.♔e3 ♖e5+ 58.♔f2 ♖c5 59.♖a4 ♖c2+ 60.♔g1 ♖e2 61.♔f1 ♖d2 62.♔g1 ♔e5 63.♖a5+ ♖d5 64.♖a4 ♖d1+ 65.♔f2 ♖d2+ 66.♔g1 ♔f5 67.♖f4+ ♔e5 68.♖a4 ♖d4 69.♖a5+ ♔e4 70.♖xh5 ♔f3 71.♖a5 ♖d1+ 72.♔h2 ♖d2+ 73.♔g1 ♖g2+ 74.♔h1 ♖e2 75.♔g1 ♔xg3 76.♖a3+ ♔f4 77.♖b3 g3 78.♖b8   ½-½

Short,Nigel
Kramnik,Vladimir

Wijk aan Zee 2005 (12)

1.e4 c5 2.♘c3 ♘c6 3.g3 g6 4.♗g2 ♗g7 5.d3 d6 6.♗e3 ♖b8 7.♕d2 b5 8.f4 b4 9.♘d1 ♕b6 10.♘f3 ♘h6 11.a3 a5 12.axb4 axb4 13.h3 f5

14.0-0 0-0 15.♗f2 e6 16.♘e3 ♘f7 17.♘c4 ♕c7 18.♖fe1 ♖d8 19.exf5 exf5 20.c3 bxc3 21.bxc3 d5 22.♘ce5 ♘fxe5 23.fxe5 ♘xe5 24.♘xe5 ♗xe5 25.♕g5 ♗b7 26.♖a7 ♖d7 27.c4 ♕d6 28.cxd5 ♗f6 29.♕f4 ♕xf4 30.gxf4 ♖bd8 31.♖e6 ♗xd5 32.♖xd7 ♗xe6 33.♖xd8+ ♗xd8 34.♗xc5   ½-½

Bachin,Vitaly
Motylev,Alexander

Sochi tt 2005 (5)

1.e4 c5 2.♘c3 ♘c6 3.g3 g6 4.♗g2 ♗g7 5.d3 d6 6.f4 e5 7.♘f3 ♘ge7 8.♗e3 ♘d4 9.h3 b5 10.0-0 b4 11.♘d5 ♘xd5 12.exd5 ♘xf3+ 13.♕xf3 0-0 14.♖ab1 f5 15.a4 exf4 16.♗xf4 g5 17.♗d2 ♗d7 18.b3 ♕f6 19.♖be1 ♖ae8 20.♕d1 ♕g6 21.♗f3 g4 22.♗h1 ♖xe1 23.♕xe1 ♖e8 24.♕d1 h5 25.♗f4 ♗c3 26.♔h2 ♕f6 27.h4 ♗c8 28.♗g2 ♕h7 29.♗d2 ♕e5 30.♗f4 ♕f6 31.♗d2 ♕e5 32.♗f4 ♕e7 33.♕c1 a5 34.♗d2 ♗xd2 35.♕xd2 ♕e3 36.♕d1 ♕g6 37.♕a1 ♕d2 38.♖d1 ♕e3 39.♖f1 ♖e5 40.c3 ♕xd3 41.cxb4 axb4 42.♕c1 ♕e3 43.♕c4 ♕d2 44.♕b5 ♖e2 45.♖g1 f4 46.♕b8 f3 47.♕xd6+ ♗e6 48.♔h1 ♕xd5 49.♕f8 ♖xg2 50.♖xg2 fxg2+ 51.♔h2 ♕d4 52.♕e8+ ♗f7 53.♕c6+ ♔g7 54.♕xg2 ♗xb3 55.a5 ♗d5 56.♕e2 ♕e4 57.♕f1 ♕f3   0-1

Spassky,Boris
Hort,Vlastimil

Bugojno 1978 (3)

1.e4 c5 2.♘c3 ♘c6 3.g3 g6 4.♗g2 ♗g7 5.d3 d6 6.f4 e5 7.♘h3 ♘ge7

8.0-0 ♘d4 9.f5 gxf5 10.♕h5 h6
11.♖f2 ♗e6 12.♗e3 ♕d7 13.♖af1
0-0-0 14.♘d5 fxe4 15.♘xe7+ ♕xe7
16.♗xd4 cxd4 17.♖xf7 ♕e8
18.♗xe4 ♖f8 19.♗f5 ♕xf7 20.♕xf7
♖xf7 21.♗xe6+ ♖fd7 22.♖f7 ♔c7
23.♗xd7 ♖xd7 24.♖xd7+ ♔xd7
25.♔g2 ♔e6 26.♔f3 d5 27.♔g4 ♔f6
28.♔h5 ♗f8 29.♘g1 b5 30.♘e2 a5
31.g4 a4 32.h4 b4 33.b3 a3 34.♘g3
e4 35.g5+ hxg5 36.hxg5+ ♔e6
37.♔g4 ♗g7 38.♘h5 ♗f8 39.g6 e3
40.♔f3 ♔f5 41.g7   1-0

Short,Nigel
Ye Jiangchuan
Shenyang 2000 (3)

1.e4 c5 2.♘c3 ♘c6 3.g3 g6 4.♗g2
♗g7 5.d3 d6 6.♘h3 e5 7.f4 ♘ge7
8.0-0 h6 9.♗e3 exf4 10.♘xf4 0-0
11.♕d2 ♔h7 12.♖ae1 ♖b8 13.♘cd5
♘xd5 14.exd5 ♘e7 15.♗f2 ♘f5
16.♗e4 b5 17.g4 ♕g5 18.♔h1 ♗e5
19.gxf5 ♗xf4 20.♗e3 ♗xe3
21.♕xe3 gxf5 22.♗g2 ♖g8 23.♗h3
♕xe3 24.♖xe3 ♖g5 25.♖e7 ♔g6
26.♖xa7 b4 27.♖c7 ♔f6 28.d4 cxd4
29.♖d1 ♗a6 30.♗g2 ♗e2 31.♖d2
♖e8 32.h4 ♖g4 33.♖c6 f4
34.♖xd6+ ♔g7 35.♖xd4 h5 36.♖b6
f3 37.♖xg4+ hxg4 38.♖xb4 f5
39.d6 ♖d8 40.♖d4 ♔f6 41.c3 ♔e5
42.h5 f4 43.d7 fxg2+ 44.♔xg2
♗f3+ 45.♔g1 g3 46.h6 ♗e4 47.♖a4
                                    0-1

Spassky,Boris
Geller,Efim
Sukhumi m 1968 (4)

1.e4 c5 2.♘c3 d6 3.g3 ♘c6 4.♗g2 g6
5.d3 ♗g7 6.f4 ♘f6 7.♘f3 0-0 8.0-0
♖b8 9.h3 b5 10.a3 a5 11.♗e3 b4
12.axb4 axb4 13.♘e2 ♗b7 14.♕d2
♖a8 15.♖ab1 ♕a5 16.b3 ♖fc8 17.f5
♕b6 18.g4 ♖a2 19.♘c1 ♖a5 20.♕f2
♕c7 21.♘e2 ♖a2 22.♖bc1 ♕d8
23.♘f4 ♕e8 24.♘g5 ♘d4 25.fxg6
hxg6 26.♘d5 ♘xb3 27.e5 ♘xc1
28.♗xc1 ♗xd5 29.♗xd5 ♘xd5
30.♕h4 ♘f6 31.exf6 exf6 32.♕h7+
♔f8 33.♘e4 ♕e5 34.♗f4 ♕d4+
35.♔h1 ♖c6 36.♗h6 ♗xh6 37.♕h8+
♔e7 38.♘xf6 ♗f4 39.g5 ♔e6
40.♕e8+ ♔f5 41.♕xf7 ♖c7 42.♕xc7
♔xg5 43.♕e7 ♕e3 44.♘e4+ ♔h5
45.♕h7+ ♗h6 46.♕d7 ♗f4 47.♘f6+
♔g5 48.♘d5   1-0

Spassky,Boris
Geller,Efim
Sukhumi m 1968 (6)

1.e4 c5 2.♘c3 d6 3.g3 ♘c6 4.♗g2
g6 5.d3 ♗g7 6.f4 ♘f6 7.♘f3 0-0
8.0-0 ♖b8 9.h3 b5 10.a3 a5 11.♗e3
b4 12.axb4 axb4 13.♘e2 ♗b7 14.b3
♖a8 15.♖c1 ♖a2 16.g4 ♕a8 17.♕e1
♕a6 18.♕f2 ♘a7 19.f5 ♘b5 20.fxg6
hxg6 21.♘g5 ♘a3 22.♕h4 ♖c8
23.♖xf6 exf6 24.♕h7+ ♔f8 25.♘xf7
♖xc2 26.♗h6 ♖xc1+ 27.♘xc1 ♔xf7
28.♕xg7+ ♔e8 29.g5 f5 30.♕xg6+
♔d7 31.♕f7+ ♔c6 32.exf5+   1-0

Sicilian Defence
Minor Systems with 2.♘f3

1.e2-e4 c7-c5 2.♘g1-f3

In response to 2.♘f3, there are three moves that are significantly more popular than any others. In ascending order of popularity they are:
- 2...d6
- 2...♘c6
- 2...e6

We will examine them in reverse order. However, first we will look at the rarely played 2...g6, 2...a6, and 2...♘f6.

These lines do not have good reputations. It is doubtlessly true that White can obtain a certain advantage, but, as is so often the case with minor variations, this is not always sufficient to bring victory against correct play. In addition, it is not rare that their surprise value shifts the balance in Black's favour.

Hyper-Accelerated Dragon

2. ...   g7-g6

This line has been given its name by some experts to distinguish it from the standard **Dragon** and the **Accelerated Dragon**. Some play this move with the aim of transposing to an Accelerated Dragon, while avoiding the troublesome **Maróczy Bind** (white pawns on e4 and c4).

3. d2-d4   c5xd4

Now, the recapture by the f3-knight indeed transposes to the Accelerated Dragon. However, after

4. ♕d1xd4   ♘g8-f6

Bronstein had the interesting idea of

5. ♗f1-b5!?

The idea is to play e4-e5 without having to deal with ♘c6.

To avoid this variation, some players try 3...♗g7!?, and *if White plays 4.c4, hoping to transpose into the Maróczy Bind, Black can deviate with the interesting and little-explored 4...♕a5+ or 4...♕b6*. Naturally, White has other options, such as **4.dxc5!**.

White can also try another means to take the game away from typical Dragon positions: 3.c3, with the aim of creating an **Alapin** position in which Black has already played ...g7-g6.

O'Kelly Variation

2. ...   a7-a6

In many Sicilian variations, Black advances his pawn to a6 to prevent ♗b5 or ♘b5 at various stages of the game, and also with the intention to continue with ...b5 and possibly ...b4 and ...♗b7. If this is so, why not immediately play ...a7-a6? Among other things, this continuation offers the advantage that if White continues with the thematic 3.d4, Black achieves easy equality with 3...cxd4 4.♘xd4 e5!. After all, unlike in variations such as the **Sveshnikov** or the **De La Bourdonnais**, the knight is denied the b5-square, and after 5.♘f5 we have 5...d5!, and Black is better.

White's best strategic option is to forget about d2-d4 and instead directly play into one of the minor variations of the Sicilian in which the ...a7-a6 advance proves to be of little use, for example with 3.c3 or 3.c4. However, in a closed position the loss of one tempo with the a-pawn may not be such a bad thing, and you avoid many highly theoretical lines.

Nimzowitsch Variation

> **2. ...**   **♘g8-f6**

This move produces another interesting system, which many call the **Nimzowitsch Variation**.

Black plays a type of **Alekhine Defence** in which White has his knight already on f3 and Black has already advanced his pawn to c5.

It is not clear which of the two players benefits the most from this.

However, in the main line, White seems to maintain a certain advantage with correct play:

> **3. e4-e5!**   **♘f6-d5**
> **4. ♘b1-c3!**   **e7-e6**

4...♘xc3 5.dxc3 is advantageous for White.

> **5. ♘c3xd5**   **e6xd5**
> **6. d2-d4**   **♘b8-c6**
> **7. d4xc5**   **♗f8xc5**
> **8. ♕d1xd5**

and White has a small plus. It should be noted, though, that it is not easy for White to remember the details of all the complications that can arise, seeing how infrequently you come across this

235

defence in tournaments. Therefore, the Nimzowitsch Variation can be a very dangerous weapon because of its surprise value.

Adams,Michael
Tkachiev,Vladislav
France tt 1999/00 (8)

1.e4 c5 2.♘f3 g6 3.d4 ♗g7 4.d5 d6 5.♗b5+ ♗d7 6.a4 ♘f6 7.♘c3 0-0 8.0-0 ♘a6 9.♖e1 ♗xb5 10.♘xb5 ♖e8 11.h3 h6 12.♖a3 ♘b4 13.♖ae3 e6 14.c3 ♘a6 15.♘xd6 ♕xd6 16.e5 ♕xd5 17.♖d3 ♕a2 18.exf6 ♗xf6 19.♗xh6 c4 20.♖d2 ♕b3 21.♕xb3 cxb3 22.♗e3 b6 23.♖d7 ♘b8 24.♖c7 ♖d8 25.♘d2 ♘a6 26.♖c4 ♘c5 27.♖e2 ♘b7 28.♘xb3 ♖d1+ 29.♔h2 ♖ad8 30.♗d4 ♗xd4 31.♘xd4 ♘c5 32.a5 ♖c1 33.♘c6 ♖d7 34.axb6 axb6 35.♖b4 ♔g7 36.♘e5 ♖b7 37.♘c4 b5 38.♘d6 ♖d7 39.♖d2 ♔f8 40.♖xb5 ♘a4   1-0

Euwe,Max
Rubinstein,Akiba
The Hague 1921 (5)

1.e4 c5 2.♘f3 ♘f6 3.e5 ♘d5 4.d4 cxd4 5.♕xd4 e6 6.c4 ♘c6 7.♕d1 ♘de7 8.♗d2 ♘g6 9.♕e2 ♕c7

10.♗c3 b6 11.h4 d6 12.exd6 ♗xd6 13.♘bd2 ♘f4 14.♕e3 ♗c5 15.♕e4 f5 16.♕c2 0-0 17.g3 ♘g6 18.h5 ♘ge5 19.♘xe5 ♘xe5 20.b4 ♗xf2+ 21.♔xf2 ♘g4+ 22.♔e2 ♕xg3 23.♗d4 ♗b7 24.♖h3 ♕d6 25.♕c3 e5 26.♗g1 f4 27.c5 ♕h6 28.♔e1 e4 29.♖h4 ♕g5 30.♕h3 ♘e3 31.♗xe3 fxe3 32.♗c4+ ♔h8 33.♘f1 ♕f6   0-1

Short,Nigel
Ostermeyer,Peter
Solingen 1986 (2)

1.e4 c5 2.♘f3 ♘f6 3.e5 ♘d5 4.♘c3! ♘xc3 5.dxc3 ♘c6 6.♗f4 h6 7.♗c4 e6 8.♕e2 b6 9.0-0-0 ♗b7 10.h4 ♕c7 11.♖d2 0-0-0 12.♖hd1 ♗e7 13.♔b1 ♘a5 14.♗a6 ♗xa6 15.♕xa6+ ♕b7 16.♕e2 ♕c6 17.c4 ♘b7 18.h5 ♘a5 19.b3 ♕b7 20.g4 g5 21.♗g3 ♘c6 22.c3 ♖hf8 23.♖d3 f5 24.exf6 ♖xf6 25.♖e3 ♖df8 26.♘d2 e5 27.♘e4 ♖e6 28.♖ed3 ♘b8 29.♖d6 ♕c7 30.♖6d5 d6 31.b4 ♘c6 32.bxc5 bxc5 33.♔a1 ♔b7 34.♘xc5+ dxc5 35.♖d7 ♗d6 36.♖xc7+ ♔xc7 37.♕e4 ♖ff6 38.f3 ♖e7 39.♗f2 ♘b8 40.♕a8 ♘c6 41.♖b1 ♔d7 42.♕b7+ ♗c7 43.♗xc5   1-0

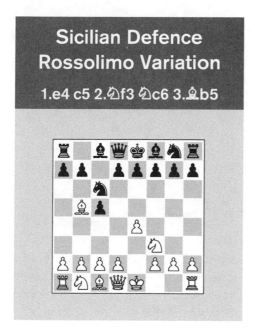

Sicilian Defence Rossolimo Variation

1.e4 c5 2.♘f3 ♘c6 3.♗b5

The **Rossolimo Variation** is the most important of the minor variations available to White in response to 2...♘c6. It is named in honour of the Ukrainian-born player who successfully employed it from the 1940s. Its recent popularity would seem to be tied to white players' growing respect for the **Sveshnikov Variation**. An ever increasing number of them will not 'risk' 3.d4 and would rather steer the game into complex strategic positions, which give the better player good chances of victory.

White's position is very flexible: he can push a pawn to c3 and d4; he can exchange the bishop for the c6-knight, or otherwise bring it back to f1 after ♖e1; he can try to establish strategic positions, or choose a violent gambit continuation. In short, it is ideal for players who prefer to 'play' instead of 'remember'.

To better understand the positions that ensue, you should keep in mind the 'sister' variations in the **English Opening** where Black plays ♗b4: 1.c4 e5 2.♘c3 ♘f6 3.♘f3 ♘c6 4.g3 ♗b4

which are closely related.
Otherwise there is 4.e3 ♗b4!?.

Leading to the same positions with an extra tempo – or one less – depending on which way you look at it.

After 3.♗b5, Black has three replies, (ignoring 3...d6, which you usually arrive at with the move sequence 2...d6 3.♗b5+ when Black opts for 3...♘c6): 3...♘f6, 3...e6 and 3...g6.

A)	3. ...	♘g8-f6
	4. e4-e5	♘f6-d5
	5. 0-0	

Thus, White can establish an insidious set-up, notwithstanding its apparently modest appearance. The e5-pawn is an irritating intruder, which White sets about to overprotect with 6.♖e1, in accordance with the teachings of Nimzowitsch. This gives White a certain initiative, and Black must play with great precision to get through the following part of the game unscathed.

B)   3. ...   e7-e6

A move that is often played. The idea is to avoid doubled pawns on c6 by playing 4...♞ge7 (if White does not immediately play 4.♗xc6). At this point, the natural 4.0-0 follows (4.♘c3 is also possible). However, the immediate 4.♗xc6!?, before Black takes the measure to prevent the doubling of his pawns, is interesting and increasingly popular.

B1)   4. 0-0   ♞g8-e7
**   5. ♘b1-c3   a7-a6**
**   6. ♗b5xc6   ♞e7xc6**
**   7. d2-d4   c5xd4**
**   8. ♘f3xd4**

we have reached a strange **Open Sicilian** position which is very reminiscent of the **Taimanov Variation**, in which the absence of White's light-squared

bishop is compensated for by a big lead in development.

But Black's position is solid, and in the long term the bishop pair could be to his advantage. Strangely, however, White's statistical performance is above average!

Instead of playing 5.♘c3, it would seem to be more logical to play 5.♖e1, to preserve the bishop, which can now retreat to f1 after 5...a6.

Alternatively, there is 5.c3, to enable the bishop to retreat to c2, with the secondary ambition of occupying the centre with the d- and e-pawns. The resulting game is double-edged.

B2)   4. ♗b5xc6

Now Black's best move is

**   4. ...   b7xc6!**

If White prematurely seeks to exploit the weak dark squares with 5.e5, this will be in vain because of 5...f6!.

Therefore, a better plan for White would include 5.0-0 and ♖e1; or 5.d3, ♘bd2-c4 and, if possible, e5; or otherwise the opening of the long diagonal for his bishop with b2-b3. Black responds with the classic manoeuvre ...♘e7-g6, and it is not rare to play ...f7-f6 to prevent White from playing e4-e5, leaving the d7-pawn with the more ambitious task of occupying the centre by advancing ...d5.

However, Black's most common choice remains

C)   3. ...   g7-g6

C1)   4. ♗b5xc6!?

This unprovoked capture is interesting.

4. ...   b7xc6

The less active 4...dxc6 is also played a lot, after which White can initiate dangerous aggressive plans with ♘c3, d3, ♗e3, ♕d2, and 0-0-0.

5.   0-0   ♗f8-g7
6.   ♖f1-e1

At this point the eccentric-looking **6...♘h6!** is the most popular move, and it is also probably the strongest. The knight does not develop to f6, as this would invite e4-e5. It does not go to e7 either, because the advance ...e7-e6 needed to make this possible would weaken the d6- and f6-squares.

After 6...♘h6 Black proceeds with ...f7-f6, always with the idea of preventing e4-e5, the knight on h6 repositions to f7, the d-pawn advances to d6 and his companion will possibly go to e5; and then Black should have reasonable prospects.

C2)   4. 0-0

This remains the most common continuation.

4. ...   ♗f8-g7
5.   ♖f1-e1

The immediate 5.c3 is commonly played, with the idea of conquering the centre with d2-d4.

5. ...   ♘g8-f6

239

Black is now less afraid of e4-e5, as the ♞f6 can go to c7 by way of d5, attacking the bishop on b5. Now that White has castled kingside, after ♗xc6, Black recaptures with the d-pawn and places the c7-knight on e6, aiming for the outpost d4, with a solid position. Therefore White usually chooses

6. c2-c3 0-0
7. d2-d4 d7-d5!

Black plays this without first exchanging on d4, to avoid clearing the c3-square for the knight on b1.

8. e4-e5 ♞f6-e4

And Black has a satisfactory position.

Rossolimo,Nicolas
Kottnauer,Cenek
Bad Gastein 1948 (10)

1.e4 c5 2.♞f3 ♞c6 3.♗b5 e6 4.0-0 ♞f6 5.♖e1 d5 6.exd5 ♞xd5 7.♞e5 ♕c7 8.♕f3 ♗d6 9.♞xc6 bxc6?? [9...0-0!] 10.♕xd5 **1-0**

Bologan,Viktor
Radjabov,Teimour
Turin ol 2006 (5)

1.e4 c5 2.♞f3 ♞c6 3.♗b5 e6 4.♗xc6 bxc6 5.d3 ♞e7 6.♕e2 ♕c7 7.♞g5 ♞g6 8.f4 c4 9.0-0 cxd3 10.cxd3 ♗c5+ 11.♔h1 f6 12.♞h3 0-0 13.♞c3

d5 14.♞a4 ♗d6 15.♗e3 ♗a6 16.♗c5 ♖fe8 17.exd5 cxd5 18.♕e3 ♗b5 19.♗xd6 ♕xd6 20.♞c3 ♗a6 21.♕d4 ♞e7 22.♞f2 ♞f5 23.♕a4 ♖eb8 24.♕a3 ♕xa3 25.bxa3 ♖b2 26.♔g1 ♖c8 27.♖fc1 ♞d4 28.♞cd1 ♖xc1 29.♖xc1 ♖xa2 30.♞c3 ♖xa3 31.♔f1 ♞b3 **0-1**

Naiditsch,Arkady
Nataf,Igor-Alexandre
Germany Bundesliga 2006/07 (7)

1.e4 c5 2.♞f3 ♞c6 3.♗b5 e6 4.♗xc6 bxc6 5.b3 d5 6.♞c3 ♗a6 7.d3 ♞f6 8.♗b2 ♕a5 9.♕d2 c4 10.dxc4 dxc4 11.e5 ♞d7 12.♞e4 ♕xd2+ 13.♞fxd2 ♖b8 14.0-0-0 c5 15.♖he1 ♞b6 16.f4 cxb3 17.♞xb3 ♞a4 18.♗a3 ♗b7 19.♞d6+ ♗xd6 20.exd6 ♔d7 21.♗xc5 ♗xg2 22.♗a3 ♖hc8 23.♖d4 ♗c6 24.f5 ♗b5 25.♖f4 exf5 26.♖e7+ ♔d8 27.♖xf7 ♗d7 28.♖xg7 ♞c3 29.♖g8+ ♗e8 30.♖xf5 ♞xa2+ 31.♔b2 ♞c3 32.♖e5 ♞a4+ 33.♔c1 ♔d7 34.♞d4 ♖d8 **1-0**

Fischer,Robert
Spassky,Boris
Belgrade/Sveti Stefan m 1992 (11)

1.e4 c5 2.♞f3 ♞c6 3.♗b5 g6 4.♗xc6 bxc6 5.0-0 ♗g7 6.♖e1 e5 7.b4!? cxb4 8.a3 c5 9.axb4 cxb4 10.d4 exd4 11.♗b2 d6 12.♞xd4! ♕d7?! [12...♞f6!?] 13.♞d2 ♗b7 14.♞c4 ♞h6 [14...♞f6 15.♞xd6+ ♕xd6 16.e5 ♕d5 17.exf6+ ♔d8 18.♞b3!+−; 14...♞e7!?] 15.♞f5! ♗xb2 [15...♞xf5 16.exf5+ ♔f8 17.f6+−] 16.♞cxd6+ ♔f8 [16...♔d8 17.♞xh6! ♗xa1 18.♕xa1+−] 17.♞xh6 f6 [17...♗xa1 18.♕xa1+−] 18.♞df7! ♕xd1 19.♖axd1 ♔e7 20.♞xh8 ♖xh8

21.♘f5+! gxf5 [21...♔e6 22.♖d6+ ♔e5 23.♖d7 ♗c6 24.♖e7+ ♔f4 25.♘e3+−] **22.exf5+ ♗e5 23.f4 ♖c8 24.fxe5 ♖xc2 25.e6 ♗c6 26.♖c1! ♖xc1 27.♖xc1 ♔d6 28.♖d1+ ♔e5 29.e7 a5 30.♖c1!** [30.e8♕+? ♗xe8 31.♖e1+ ♔d4 32.♖xe8 b3 33.♖b8 ♔c3 34.♖c8+=] **30...♗d7 31.♖c5+ ♔d4 32.♖xa5 b3 33.♖a7 ♗e8 34.♖b7 ♔c3 35.♔f2 b2 36.♔e3 ♗f7 37.g4!** [Zugzwang; 37.♖b8?] **37...♗c2 38.♔d4 b1♕ 39.♖xb1 ♗xb1 40.♔c5 ♔c2 41.♔d6** **1-0**

Shirov,Alexey
Kramnik,Vladimir
Novgorod 1994 (7)

1.e4 c5 2.♘f3 ♘c6 3.♗b5 g6 4.♗xc6 dxc6 5.h3 e5 6.d3 f6!?N 7.c3!? ♘h6 8.0-0 ♘f7 9.♗e3 g5! 10.♘e1 ♗e6 11.♘d2 h5 12.a3 a5 13.♕e2 b6 14.♘c2 ♖a7! 15.d4? [15.♖fd1!] **15...cxd4 16.cxd4 ♖d7 17.dxe5 ♘xe5∓ 18.♖fd1** [18.f4? ♗c5] **18...♗e7 19.♘f1 ♗c4 20.♖xd7 ♕xd7 21.♕d2 ♗d3!?** [21...c5∓] **22.♕c3□ ♗xe4 23.♘g3 ♗d5! 24.♗xb6 h4 25.♘e2 g4 26.♘f4 ♗e4?T 27.♖e1! ♕f5 28.♘e6! ♖g8 29.♘cd4 ♘f3+! 30.♔f1??** [30.♕xf3 gxf3 31.♘xf5 ♗xf5 32.♘d4!=] **30...♗d3+ 31.♖e2 ♗xe2+ 32.♔xe2 ♕e4+ 33.♕e3 ♘xd4+ 34.♘xd4 ♕xe3+ 35.♔xe3 gxh3 36.gxh3 ♖g5!? 37.♘xc6 ♗c5+ 38.♗xc5 ♖xc5 39.♘d4 a4 40.♔d3 ♖c1!** **0-1**

Adams,Michael
Chandler,Murray
Southend rapid 2001 (2)

1.e4 c5 2.♘f3 ♘c6 3.♗b5 g6 4.♗xc6 dxc6 5.d3 ♗g7 6.h3 ♘f6 7.♘c3 ♘d7

8.♗e3 e5 9.♕d2 ♕e7 10.♗h6 0-0 11.♗h2 ♖d8 12.♘g4 ♘f8 13.♗xg7 ♔xg7 14.♕h6+ ♔g8 15.0-0-0 c4 16.dxc4 ♗xg4 17.hxg4 ♕c5 18.f3 ♕xc4 19.♖xd8 ♖xd8 20.♕g5 ♖e8 21.♕e3 ♕d4 22.♕xd4 exd4 23.♘e2 ♘e6 24.♔d2 ♖d8 25.b3 b5 26.♖a1 c5 27.a4 a6 28.axb5 axb5 29.♖a5 ♖b8 30.♔d3 ♗g7 31.f4 ♖b7 32.f5 ♘d8 33.♖a6 ♖c7 34.g5 gxf5 35.exf5 ♗c6 36.♖b6 ♘b4+ 37.♔d2 ♘d5 38.♖xb5 ♘e3 39.♘g3 ♔f8 40.f6 ♔e8 41.♘e4 ♔d7 42.♔d3 c4+ 43.bxc4 ♖xc4 44.♖b7+ ♖c7 45.♘c5+ ♔c6 46.♖xc7+ ♔xc7 47.♘e6+ ♔d6 48.♘xd4 ♘xg2 49.♔e4 ♘e1 50.c3 ♔d7 51.♘f3 ♘c2 52.c4 ♘b4 53.♔f5 ♘c2 54.♘e5+ ♔e8 55.♔e4 ♘b4 56.c5 ♘a6 57.c6 ♘c7 58.♘c4 ♘e6 59.♘d6+ ♔f8 60.♔d5 ♔g8 61.♘e4 ♘c7+ 62.♔d6 ♘b5+ 63.♔d7 h5 64.gxh6 ♔h7 65.♘d6 **1-0**

Ivanchuk,Vasily
Filippov,Valery
Chalkidiki tt 2002 (7)

1.e4 c5 2.♘f3 ♘c6 3.♗b5 g6 4.♗xc6 dxc6 5.d3 ♗g7 6.h3 ♘f6 7.♘c3 ♘d7 8.♗e3 e5 9.♕d2 ♕e7 10.♗h6!? ♗xh6 11.♕xh6 f6 12.♘h4!? ♕f8 13.♕d2 ♕e7 14.0-0-0± f5 15.g3 f4 16.♘g2 fxg3 17.fxg3 ♘f8 18.h4 h5 19.♖df1 ♘e6 20.♖f2 ♘d4 21.♕g5! ♕xg5+□ 22.hxg5 ♖f8□ 23.♖hf1 ♖xf2 24.♖xf2± ♗e6 25.♘a4 b6 26.c3 ♘b5 27.♘h4 0-0-0!? 28.c4 ♖xd3 29.cxb5 cxb5 30.♘c3 b4 31.♖f6! ♗c4 32.♘d5+− ♗xa2 33.♘f3! ♖d4□ 34.♘f6! ♖c4+ 35.♔d2 ♗b1 36.♔e3 a5 37.♘xg6 a4 38.♖f1 a3 39.♖xb1 a2 40.♖a1 b3 41.♘xe5 **1-0**

Akopian,Vladimir
Kuzubov,Yury

Gibraltar 2007 (9)

1.e4 c5 2.♘f3 ♘c6 3.♗b5 g6 4.♗xc6 dxc6 5.d3 ♗g7 6.h3 b6 7.♘c3 ♘h6 8.♗e3 f6 9.♕d2 ♘f7 10.0-0-0 e5 11.♘h2 ♗e6 12.f4 exf4 13.♗xf4 ♕d7 14.♘f3 0-0-0 15.d4 cxd4 16.♘xd4 ♔b7 17.♕e2 ♕e7 18.♘xc6 ♔xc6 19.♘d5 ♕e8 20.♕a6 ♗f8 21.♕xa7 ♗c5 22.b4 ♕d7 23.♕a6
1-0

Rossolimo,Nicolas
Romanenko,N.

Bad Gastein 1948

1.e4 c5 2.♘f3 ♘c6 3.♗b5 g6 4.0-0 ♗g7 5.♖e1 ♘f6 6.♘c3 ♘d4 7.e5 ♘g8 8.d3 ♘xb5 9.♘xb5 a6?! 10.♘d6+! exd6 11.♗g5! ♕a5 [11...♕b6 12.exd6+ ♔f8 13.♖e8+! ♔xe8 14.♕e2+ ♔f8 15.♗e7+ ♔e8 16.♖e1! and mate soon follows] 12.exd6+ ♔f8 13.♖e8+! ♔xe8 14.♕e2+ ♔f8 15.♗e7+ ♔e8 [15...♘xe7 16.♕xe7+ ♔g8 17.♘g5 and mate on f7] 16.♗d8+! ♔xd8 [16...♔f8 17.♗xa5+−] 17.♘g5! 17.♘g5 ♘h6 18.♕e7X
1-0

Morozevich,Alexander
McShane,Luke

England tt 2000/01 (9)

1.e4 c5 2.♘f3 ♘c6 3.♗b5 g6 4.0-0 ♗g7 5.c3 ♘f6 6.d4 cxd4 7.cxd4 ♘xe4 8.d5 ♘d6 9.♘a3 a6 10.♕a4 ♘a7 11.♗d3 0-0 12.♖e1 b5 13.♕h4 ♗b7 14.♗h6 f6 15.♗xg7 ♔xg7 16.♖ad1 ♘ac8 17.♘c2 ♘f7 18.♘e3 ♘cd6 19.♘d4 ♖e8 20.♕h3 ♖c8 21.♗b1 ♖c7 22.f4 ♕b8 23.♖f1 ♕a7 24.♔h1 e6 25.f5 e5 26.fxg6 hxg6 27.♕f3 f5 28.♘exf5+ gxf5 29.♘xf5+ ♘xf5 30.♕xf5 d6 31.♕g6+ ♔f8 32.♕xd6+ ♖ee7 33.♖xf7+ ♔xf7 34.♖f1+ ♔g8 35.♕g6+
1-0

Sandipan,Chanda
Himanshu,Sharma

New Delhi 2006 (9)

1.e4 c5 2.♘f3 ♘c6 3.♗b5 g6 4.0-0 ♗g7 5.h3 ♘f6 6.e5 ♘d5 7.♖e1 ♕c7 8.♘c3 ♘xc3 9.dxc3 ♘xe5 10.♘xe5 ♗xe5 11.♕d5 ♗d6 12.♗h6 a6 13.♗a4 ♖b8 14.♖xe7+ ♗xe7 15.♖e1 ♔d8 16.♖xe7 ♔xe7 17.♕e4+ ♔f6 18.g4 g5 19.♕f5+ ♔e7 20.♗xg5+ ♔f8 21.♗h6+
1-0

Sicilian Defence Variations with ...♛b6

One of the minor variations for Black which is currently reasonably popular, has the idea of developing his queen to b6 in the first few moves, in other words: before completing the development of the other pieces.

It is true that on b6 the queen is not as well placed as it could be, especially if it blocks the path of the b-pawn when it is still on b7. However, it can always reposition to c7, which is the square it most usually develops to in the Sicilian.

The advantage of the annoying move ...♛b6 is that it applies pressure on the d4-knight, usually forcing it to go to b3, where it is less active and dangerous than on d4.

And if White brings the knight back to d4 after the queen on b6 repositions to c7? He would find himself playing a Sicilian with loss of a tempo! The manoeuvre ...♛d8-b6-c7 by Black requires two tempi, while White's ♘f3-d4-b3-d4 requires three!

1.	e2-e4	c7-c5
2.	♘g1-f3	♘b8-c6
3.	d2-d4	c5xd4
4.	♘f3xd4	♛d8-b6

This is the most common line. Black directly attacks the knight on d4. The move ...♛b6 also makes sense in other variations.

Those interested in the move ...♛b6 in various Sicilian lines should note the following:
- 1.e4 c5 2.♘f3 ♘c6 3.d4 cxd4 4.♘xd4 ♘f6 5.♘c3 ♛b6;
- the **Anti-Sozin Variation** 6...♛b6;
- the **Poisoned Pawn Variation of the Najdorf**;
- the **Kengis Variation** 1.e4 c5 2.♘f3 e6 3.d4 cxd4 4.♘xd4 ♛b6.

Shabalov, Alexander
Yermolinsky, Alex
Saint Paul 2000 (6)

1.e4 c5 2.♘f3 ♘c6 3.d4 cxd4 4.♘xd4 ♛b6 5.♘b5 a6 6.♗e3 ♛d8 7.♘d4 ♘f6 8.♘c3 e5 9.♘f5 d5 10.exd5 ♘b4 11.♘g3 ♘fxd5 12.♘xd5 ♛xd5 13.♛xd5 ♘xd5 14.♗d2 ♘b4 15.♔d1 ♗e6 16.a3 ♘c6 17.♗d3 g6 18.♖e1 f5 19.♗c3 0-0-0 20.f3 ♗h6 21.♔e2 ♖hf8 22.♔f2 e4 23.♗f1 ♘d4 24.♗xd4 ♖xd4 25.fxe4 ♗d2 26.♖ed1 fxe4+ 27.♔g1 ♗g4 28.♖db1 ♗e3+ 29.♔h1 ♗f2 30.c3 ♖dd8 31.♘xe4 ♗f5 32.♗d3 ♖xd3 33.♘xf2 ♖d2 34.♖f1 ♖xb2 35.♔g1 ♖d8 36.g4 ♗d7 37.♖ab1 ♖xb1 38.♖xb1 ♗c6 39.♖d1 ♖e8 40.h4 ♖e2 41.♖d4 ♖a2 42.♖f4 ♖xa3 43.♖f7 h5 44.g5 ♖xc3 45.♖f6 a5 46.♖xg6 a4 47.♖d6 a3 48.♖d2 ♖g3+ 49.♔h2 ♖g2+ 50.♔h3 b5 **0-1**

Kuzmin, Alexey
Sveshnikov, Evgeny
Moscow ch-city 1987

1.e4 c5 2.♘f3 ♘c6 3.d4 cxd4
4.♘xd4 e5 5.♘b5 d6 6.c4 ♗e7
7.♘1c3 a6 8.♘a3 h6 9.♗e2 ♗e6
10.0-0 ♗g5 11.♘c2 ♘ge7 12.b3
♗xc1 13.♖xc1 ♘g6 14.♗g4 0-0
15.♘e3 ♘d4 16.♘e2 ♕f6 17.♘xd4
exd4 18.♘f5 ♘e5 19.♗e2 ♗xf5
20.exf5 b5 21.f4 ♘d7 22.cxb5 axb5

23.♗xb5 ♘c5 24.a4 d3 25.♔h1 ♕d4
26.♖c4 ♕d5 27.♖c3 ♖fe8 28.♖xc5
dxc5 29.♕xd3 ♕xd3 30.♗xd3 ♔f8
31.♔g1 ♔e7 32.♗b5 ♖ed8 33.♖e1+
♔f6 34.♖e5 ♖d4 35.♖xc5 ♖xf4
36.♗c4 ♖d8 37.h3 ♖d1+ 38.♔h2
♖d2 39.♖c7 ♖xf5 40.♖xf7+ ♔g6
41.♖xf5 ♔xf5 42.a5 ♔e5 43.a6 ♔d4
44.♗b5 ♔c5 45.♗c4 g5 46.♔g3
♔b6 47.♗f1 ♖d4 48.♗c4 ♖f4 49.♗e2
♔a7 50.♔h2 ♖e4 51.♗d3   ½-½

246

Sicilian Defence Sveshnikov/ Lasker-Pelikan Variation

1.e4 c5 2.♘f3 ♘c6 3.d4 cxd4 4.♘xd4 ♘f6 5.♘c3 e5

The move **5...e5** characterizes the **Sveshnikov Variation**, which was already being dabbled with occasionally by Bird and World Champion Emanuel Lasker as early as the end of the 1800s and the beginning of the 1900s. However, it was only towards the end of the 1970s that it became genuinely popular. At the beginning of this new century its reputation is better than ever: practically all the best players — Kramnik, Shirov, Topalov, Lautier, Ivanchuk, Leko (and towards the end of his career, Kasparov) — use the Sveshnikov relatively frequently! Not bad for a variation that was originally considered to be unsound. This does not mean that assessments based on positional considerations are no longer valid; it is just that today more importance is given to the dynamic features of a position. In the case in question, it is

true that the d5-square is weakened, but Black's good piece activity makes it difficult, if not impossible, for White to exploit this weakness. This system remains one of the best if Black is playing for a win, even if that entails taking greater risks. In addition, with the proliferation of open tournaments, it is common to encounter players of all levels. As a result, a dangerous opening, though perhaps not completely sound, can be a very useful addition to your repertoire. We will now have a closer look at specific variations. After 5...e5, the best response is certainly

> **6. ♘d4-b5**

To try and exploit the hole on d6. Black continues with

> **6. ... d7-d6**

because, unlike in the **De La Bourdonnais Variation**, the f6-square is not available to the queen anymore. Therefore 6...a6? would be a bad error.

> **7. ♗c1-g5**

is the most popular move at this point. However, we will first take a brief look at two alternatives:

A) White can prevent Black's planned moves ...a6 and ...b5 by immediately playing 7.a4

and then relocating the b5-knight via a3-c4.

B) Alternatively, White can completely change the distinctive features of the position with 7.♘d5, which forces the exchange 7...♘xd5. After 8.exd5

we have a typical position with a queenside pawn majority for White. He will try to prepare the c2-c4-c5 advance and Black will seek counterplay on the kingside, gaining leverage with the e5- and f5-pawns. Many black players consider this continuation to be so unpleasant that they prefer to play the move 5...e6 instead of the thematic 5...e5. In this way, after 6.♘db5 (considered to be the best) 6...d6 7.♗f4 e5 8.♗g5, you transpose into the **main line of the Sveshnikov** with 7.♗g5, with both players having made an extra move. However, there is a price to be paid: after 5...e6, Black must be ready for the disagreeable possibility that White will continue with 6.♘xc6 bxc6 7.e5.

Kasparov, playing with the white pieces, has scored some brilliant victories using this variation.
We will now go back to **7.♗g5**.

As we said before, this is the most popular continuation. The pin on the f6-knight accentuates the weakness of the d5-square.
This can be considered the initial position of the Sveshnikov system.

7. ...   a7-a6

White now usually retreats the knight immediately with

8. ♘b5-a3

as it was discovered that the 'classical' 8.♗xf6 gxf6 9.♘a3 gives Black good play after 9...f5!.
In the past players now continued with 8...♗e6. However, from the 1970s onwards players started to employ the move

8. ...   b7-b5!

This followed a more modern interpretation of the position by the Russian grandmasters Evgeny Sveshnikov and Gennady Timoschenko. It is often called the Cheliabinsk Variation, to differentiate it from the older 8...♗e6 variation.
Now we are at a major crossroads: White can play the 'positional' 9.♘d5, or the aggressive 9.♗xf6.

A) 9. ♘c3-d5 ♗f8-e7

Black also has 9...♕a5+ 10.♗d2 ♕d8, inviting a draw by repetition after 11.♗g5.

10. ♗g5xf6 ♗e7xf6
11. c2-c3

To make way for the a3-knight. After 11...0-0 12.♘c2, Black obtains dynamically balanced positions with either 12...♗g5, to exchange the bad bishop, or 12...♖b8, anticipating the thematic a2-a4 by applying indirect pressure to the b2-pawn.

B) 9. ♗g5xf6

The most common choice.

9. ... g7xf6

9...♕xf6 is an error because of 10.♘d5 ♕d8 11.♗xb5!.

Black has grave weaknesses in his pawn structure, especially on the kingside.

However, this is fully compensated for by several advantages: a strong central pawn formation, the bishop pair, and counterattacking possibilities on the g-file.

10. ♘c3-d5

Now we have another important crossroads, but this time for Black: the modern 10...♗g7 or the classical 10...f5.

B1) 10. ... ♗f8-g7

The Novosibirsk Variation is the modern choice. By delaying ...f5, Black seeks to immediately remove the d5-knight with ...♘e7.

White can choose between 11.c3 (Black will be wise to meet this with the immediate ...f6-f5, with good play) and

11. ♗f1-d3 ♘c6-e7

The most logical, but 11...♗e6 is also playable.

12. ♘d5xe7 ♕d8xe7

Play has become complicated. Black has the possibility of the pawn break ...f5, to take possession of the centre with ...d6-d5 later. The resulting positions have inspired varying evaluations.

B2) 10. ... f6-f5

This can be defined as the principal move of the entire defence.

This very complex position has been studied at great depth – chiefly the following two lines:

White tries to control the light squares, in particular f5, with ♘ce3 and ♗d3. The game should be fairly balanced.

B21)   11. ♗f1-d3
11.♗xb5!? should not give White much for the piece after 11...axb5 12.♘xb5 ♖a4!.

11. ...	♗c8-e6

12. ♕d1-h5
A more prudent line is 12.0-0 ♗xd5! 13.exd5 ♘e7 14.c3!, with balanced play.

12. ...	♖h8-g8!
13. g2-g3	♖g8-g4!

with chances for both sides.

B22)   11. c2-c3   ♗f8-g7
Considered to be the best.

12. e4xf5	♗c8xf5
13. ♘a3-c2	♗f5-e6

Anand, Viswanathan
Ponomariov, Ruslan
Wijk aan Zee 2003 (7)

1.e4 c5 2.♘f3 ♘c6 3.d4 cxd4 4.♘xd4 e5 5.♘b5 d6 6.♘1c3 a6 7.♘a3 ♘f6 8.♘c4 b5 9.♘e3 b4?! 10.♘cd5! ♘xe4 11.a3 bxa3 12.♖xa3 g6 13.c3! ♗d7? 14.♘c4± ♖b8 15.♗e3 f5 16.♗b6 ♖xb6 17.♘cxb6 ♗h6 18.♗d3! 0-0 19.♗xe4 fxe4 20.0-0 ♗e6 21.♖xa6 ♕h4 22.♕e2 ♘d8 23.♖a8+– ♔g7 24.g3! ♗g4 25.gxh4 ♗xe2 26.♖fa1 g5 27.♘d7! ♖f5 28.♖xd8 gxh4 29.♖g8+! ♔f7 30.♖a7 ♖f3 31.♘7f6+ ♔e6 32.♖e7+ ♔f5 33.♘g4 ♗d2 34.♘ge3+   1-0

Karpov, Anatoly
Sveshnikov, Evgeny
Moscow ch-URS 1973 (3)

1.e4 c5 2.♘f3 e6 3.d4 cxd4 4.♘xd4 ♘c6 5.♘b5 ♘f6 6.♘1c3 d6 7.♗f4 e5 8.♗g5 a6 9.♘a3 b5 10.♘d5 ♗e7 11.♗xf6 ♗xf6 12.c3 0-0 13.♘c2 ♗g5 14.a4 bxa4 15.♖xa4 a5 16.♗c4 ♖b8 17.b3 ♗e6 18.♕a1 g6 19.0-0 ♕d7 20.♖d1 f5 21.exf5 gxf5 22.b4 axb4 23.cxb4 ♔h8 24.b5 ♗xd5 25.♖xd5

♘e7 26.♕xe5+ dxe5 27.♖xd7 ♘c8 28.♖c7 ♗d8 29.♖c6 ♘b6 30.♖b4 ♘xc4 31.♖cxc4 ♗b6 32.♔f1 ♖fd8 33.♔e2 ♗a5 34.♖b3 ♖d2+ 35.♔e3 f4+ 36.♔e4 ♖xf2 37.♔xe5 ♖xg2 38.♘d4 ♖xh2 39.♖c6 ♗b6 40.♘e6 f3 41.♖xf3 ♖h5+ 42.♔f6 ♖xb5 43.♖d6 ♖b2 44.♔e7 ♗a5   ½-½

Anand,Viswanathan
Kasparov,Garry

Linares 2005 (6)

1.e4 c5 2.♘f3 ♘c6 3.d4 cxd4 4.♘xd4 ♘f6 5.♘c3 e5 6.♘db5 d6 7.♗g5 a6 8.♘a3 b5 9.♘d5 ♗e7 10.♗xf6 ♗xf6 11.c3 0-0 12.♘c2 ♗g5 13.a4 bxa4 14.♖xa4 a5 15.♗c4 ♖b8 16.♖a2 ♔h8 17.♘ce3 g6 18.0-0 f5 19.♕a4!? ♗d7 20.♘b5 ♖xb5?! 21.♕xb5 ♘b4 22.♕xa5 ♘xa2 23.♕xa2 fxe4 24.b4 ♗e6 25.c4 ♕c8 26.♕b3 ♔g7 27.♖b1 ♗f7 28.♖d1 h5 29.♕c2 ♕a8 30.h3?! [30.b5 ♗h4 31.g3±] 30...♗h4! 31.♖f1 ♕f8 32.b5 ♗c8 33.♘c3 ♗b7 34.♘ed5 ♕c8 35.♕e2 ♗xd5 36.♘xd5 ♕c5 37.b6? ♕d4 38.♕c2 ♔h7 39.♔h2 ♖xf2 40.♖xf2 ♗xf2 41.♕c1 e3 42.b7 ♕a7 43.♕b1 e2 44.♘e7 ♗g3+   ½-½

Anand,Viswanathan
Van Wely,Loek

Wijk aan Zee 2006 (9)

1.e4 c5 2.♘f3 ♘c6 3.d4 cxd4 4.♘xd4 ♘f6 5.♘c3 e5 6.♘db5 d6 7.♗g5 a6 8.♘a3 b5 9.♘d5 ♗e7 10.♗xf6 ♗xf6 11.c3 ♗g5 12.♘c2 ♖b8 13.a4 bxa4 14.♘cb4 ♗d7 15.♗xa6 ♘xb4 16.cxb4 0-0 17.0-0 ♗c6 18.♖xa4 ♗xa4 19.♕xa4 ♕e8N 20.♕xe8 ♖fxe8 21.b5 f5 22.b6! fxe4 23.h4?! ♗d2? 24.b7 ♔f7 25.♖d1

♗h6 26.♘b4 ♔e7 27.♘d5+ ♔f7 28.g4 ♗f4 29.♖e1 g5 30.♖e2! ♖ed8 31.♘b4! d5 32.♘c6 ♖g8 33.♘xb8 ♖xb8 34.h5! ♔e7 35.♔f1 d4 36.♖c2 e3 37.fxe3 dxe3 38.♖c7+ ♔f6 39.♖xh7 e4 40.♗c4 ♖d8 41.♖f7+ ♔e5 42.♖d7   1-0

Ivanovic,Bozidar
Sveshnikov,Evgeny

Krk tt 1976

1.e4 c5 2.♘f3 ♘c6 3.d4 cxd4 4.♘xd4 ♘f6 5.♘c3 e5 6.♘db5 d6 7.♗g5 a6 8.♗xf6 gxf6 9.♘a3 b5 10.♘d5 f5 11.♗d3 ♗e6 12.c4 ♕a5+ 13.♔f1 ♗xd5 14.exd5 ♘d4 15.cxb5 axb5 16.♘c2 ♘xc2 17.♕xc2 e4 18.♕c6+ ♔e7 19.♗xb5 ♖a7 20.♕e8+ ♔f6 21.g4 ♖e7 22.♕b8 ♔e5 23.f4+ ♔xf4 24.♔e2 ♔e5 25.♖hf1 fxg4 26.b4 ♗g7 27.bxa5 ♖xb8 28.♖ab1 f5 29.a6 f4 30.♗c6 f3+ 31.♔f2 ♖xb1 32.♖xb1 ♔f4 33.♖b4 ♗c3 34.♖c4 ♗a5 35.♔f1 ♗b6 36.♗b7 h5 37.♖c6 e3 38.♖c4+ ♔g5   0-1

Shirov,Alexey
Grischuk,Alexander

Wijk aan Zee 2003 (8)

1.e4 c5 2.♘f3 ♘c6 3.d4 cxd4 4.♘xd4 ♘f6 5.♘c3 e5 6.♘db5 d6 7.♗g5 a6 8.♘a3 b5 9.♗xf6 gxf6 10.♘d5 f5 11.♗d3 ♗e6 12.0-0 ♗xd5 13.exd5 ♘e7 14.c3 ♗g7 15.♕h5 e4 16.♗c2 ♕c8 17.♖ae1 0-0 18.♗b3 a5! 19.♕g5 ♕b7! 20.f3 h6 21.♕f4?!N a4 22.♗c2 b4 23.cxb4 ♕xb4 24.fxe4 ♘g6! 25.♕xf5 ♗xb2 26.e5! ♗xe5 27.♘b1 ♖ae8?! 28.♗e4? ♗f4!–+ 29.g3 ♖e5 30.♕g4 ♖xe4 31.♖xe4 ♕xe4 32.gxf4 ♖b8   0-1

Spassky,Boris
Sveshnikov,Evgeny

Moscow ch-URS 1973 (12)

1.e4 c5 2.♘f3 ♘c6 3.d4 cxd4
4.♘xd4 ♘f6 5.♘c3 e6 6.♘db5 d6
7.♗f4 e5 8.♗g5 a6 9.♘a3 b5
10.♗xf6 gxf6 11.♘d5 f5 12.♗d3
♗e6 13.0-0 ♗g7 14.♕h5 h6 15.c3
0-0 16.♘c2 fxe4 17.♗xe4 f5 18.♘f4
♗d7 19.♗d5+ ♔h7 20.♕g6+ ♔h8
21.♘h5 ♕e7 22.♘b4 ♘xb4
23.♗xa8 ♖g8 24.cxb4   1-0

Tseshkovsky,Vitaly
Sveshnikov,Evgeny

Sochi 1974 (8)

1.e4 c5 2.♘f3 ♘c6 3.♘c3 ♘f6 4.d4
cxd4 5.♘xd4 e5 6.♘db5 d6 7.♗g5
a6 8.♘a3 b5 9.♗xf6 gxf6 10.♘d5 f5
11.♗d3 ♗e6 12.♕h5 ♗g7 13.c3 0-0
14.g4 fxg4 15.♘c2 f5 16.♘de3 f4
17.♘xg4 ♔h8 18.♖g1 ♖b8 19.a3 a5
20.♔f1 ♕d7 21.♘e1 ♕f7 22.♕h4
♕e7 23.♕h5 ♗f7 24.♕h3 ♗c4
25.♖d1 ♘d8 26.♘f3 ♗f6 27.♗xc4
bxc4 28.♘xf6 ♖xf6 29.♘h4 ♕e6
30.♕g2 ♕f7 31.♘f5 ♕f8 32.♕g4
♘f7 33.♕e2 ♘h6 34.♘xh6 f3
35.♕xc4 ♕xh6 36.♕c7 ♖xb2
37.♕c8+ ♖f8 38.♕g4 ♖xf2+
39.♔xf2 ♕xh2+ 40.♖g2 fxg2+
41.♔e3 ♖g8   0-1

Anand,Viswanathan
Leko,Peter

Dortmund 2003 (1)

1.e4 c5 2.♘f3 ♘c6 3.d4 cxd4
4.♘xd4 ♘f6 5.♘c3 e5 6.♘db5 d6
7.♗g5 a6 8.♘a3 b5 9.♗xf6 gxf6
10.♘d5 f5 11.c3 ♗g7 12.exf5 ♗xf5
13.♘c2 0-0 14.♘ce3 ♗e6 15.♗d3 f5
16.0-0 ♖a7 17.♕h5 ♖af7 18.♖ad1

♘e7 19.♘xe7+ ♕xe7 20.♗c2 e4
21.♘d5 ♗xd5 22.♖xd5 ♔h8 23.f4 b4
24.cxb4 ♗xb2 25.♗b3 ♗a3 26.♕d1
♕a7+ 27.♕d4+ ♕xd4+ 28.♖xd4
♖e7 29.♔f2 a5 30.♖xd6 ♗xb4
31.♖d5 ♔g7 32.♔e2 ♖f6 33.♖c1 ♖g6
34.g3 ♖h6 35.h4 ♖g6 36.♖xf5 ♖xg3
37.♖g5+ ♖xg5 38.hxg5 h6
39.gxh6+ ♔xh6 40.♖c6+ ♔h7
41.♔e3 ♖g7 42.♗e6 ♖g3+ 43.♔xe4
♖c3 44.♗c4 ♖h3 45.♖a6 ♖h6
46.♗e6 ♖h4 47.♖a7+ ♔g6 48.♗f7+
♔f6 49.♗b3 ♗d6 50.♖f7+ ♔g6
51.♖f5 ♖h1 52.♖d5 ♖e1+ 53.♔f3
♗b4 54.♗c4 ♔f6 55.♖b5 ♖d1
56.♖b6+ ♖d6 57.♖b7 ♖d4   ½-½

Anand,Viswanathan
Leko,Peter

Wijk aan Zee 2005 (2)

1.e4 c5 2.♘f3 ♘c6 3.d4 cxd4
4.♘xd4 ♘f6 5.♘c3 e5 6.♘db5 d6
7.♗g5 a6 8.♘a3 b5 9.♗xf6 gxf6
10.♘d5 f5 11.c3 ♗g7 12.exf5 ♗xf5
13.♘c2 0-0 14.♘ce3 ♗e6 15.♗d3 f5
16.0-0 ♖a7 17.a4 ♘e7 18.♘xe7+
♖xe7 19.axb5 axb5 20.♗xb5 d5
21.♖a6 f4 22.♘c2!? ♗c8N 23.♖a8
♕d6 24.♘b4 ♗b7 25.♖a7?! d4
26.♗a6? ♗xg2!-+ 27.♗c4+ ♔h8
28.♖a6 ♕c5 29.♔xg2 f3+ 30.♔h1
♕xc4 31.♖c6 ♕b5 32.♖d6 e4
33.♖xd4 ♗xd4 34.♕xd4+ ♕e5
35.♕xe5+ ♖xe5 36.♘c2 ♖b8
37.♘e3 ♖c5 38.h3 ♖xb2 39.c4 ♖g5
40.♔h2 ♔g8 41.h4 ♖g6 42.♔h3 ♔f7
43.♘f5 ♖c2 44.♘e3 ♖d2 45.c5 ♔e6
46.c6 ♖g8 47.c7 ♖c8 48.♔g3 ♖xc7
49.♔f4 ♖d4 50.♖a1 ♖f7+ 51.♔g3
♖d8 52.♖a6+ ♔e5 53.♘g4+ ♔d5
54.♘f6+ ♖xf6 55.♖xf6 ♔e5 56.♖h6
♖g8+ 57.♔h3 e3   0-1

Sicilian Defence Accelerated Dragon

1.e4 c5 2.♘f3 ♘c6 3.d4 cxd4 4.♘xd4 g6

The **Accelerated Dragon** is one of the oldest of the Sicilian variations. It made its distant debut in 1851 in London.

The venerable age of the Accelerated Dragon should not come as a surprise if you stop to think about how the ideas behind the Sicilian have developed. If the aim of 1...c5 is to take control of the d4-square, then as a consequence 2...♘c6 appears to be the most logical continuation, as is the opening up of the diagonal so as to control d4 further with the fianchettoed bishop on g7. This logic was irresistible to the early pioneers of opening theory; it is therefore understandable that the first examples of the modern Dragon type positions with 2...d6 did not appear until the 20th century.

In the preceding years Black tried to deal directly with the famous **Maróczy Bind**, which takes its name from grandmaster Géza Maróczy (1870-1951), who was one of the strongest Hungarian players of all time. This formation, which was first played at the beginning of the 20th century, is renowned for its great solidity and reliability. Frustrated by the difficulties presented by the Maróczy formation, players started to experiment with 2...d6.

Profiting from the fact that the knight is still on b1, White seizes firm control of the centre with **5.c4** (this is the key move of the Maróczy Bind) and greatly reduces Black's chances for counterplay.

In the beginning, this did not appear to be so worrying for Black, in that it was widespread usage to first play 4...♘f6, and only after 5.♘c3 to continue with 5...g6. In this way White no longer has the c2-c4 pawn advance at his disposal. However, it did not take long to discover that after the sequence 6.♘xc6 bxc6 7.e5!

7...♘g8 (a sad necessity, as the pawn sacrifice 7...♘d5 8.♘xd5 cxd5 9.♕xd5 ♖b8 fails to 10.e6! fxe6? 11.♕e5! hitting two rooks), White is better, notwithstanding the fact that the pawn on e5 is so far advanced that it could become subject to a counterattack.

Then someone thought of substituting 2...♘c6 with 2...d6 so that the pawn advance to e5 would no longer be possible. And this is how the 'normal' Dragon came to make its debut in 1924: 1.e4 c5 2.♘f3 d6 3.d4 cxd4 4.♘xd4 ♘f6 5.♘c3 g6. The name 'accelerated' was added later and indicates the opening of the fianchetto diagonal on the 4th move instead of on the 5th as occurs with the 'standard' Dragon.

This means that the standard Dragon has the virtue of preventing the Maróczy Bind, but as we will see in the section that deals with the Maróczy, all that glitters is not gold. The problem is that there is less central influence exerted on the centre with 2...d6 compared to 2...♘c6, and this means that White can more freely choose continuations that would be dubious against the Accelerated variation. A good example of this is the popular 9.0-0-0 in the **Yugoslav Attack** in the standard **Dragon**. As always, the final choice boils down to questions of taste and style of play. The Accelerated Dragon could be an excellent choice, if a player does not mind the positional struggle that ensues after the imposition of the Maróczy Bind.

Maróczy Bind

We will look at

5. c2-c4

in some depth, both because it is popular, and because it is also objectively the best move. You must remember that it is not uncommon to reach the Maróczy pawn formation by means of the Symmetrical English: 1.c4 c5 2.♘f3 g6 3.d4 cxd4 4.♘xd4 ♘c6 5.e4.

At this point Black generally responds with

5. ...   ♗f8-g7

The following subtle sequence is also popular: 5...♘f6 6.♘c3 d6!?. Only after 7.♗e2 or 7.f3 (*after 7.♗e3 Black has the unpleasant intrusion of 7...♘g4*), Black proceeds with 7...♘xd4, before White plays ♗e3, with the object of forcing White to take on d4 with the queen. This modern approach is called the **Gurgenidze Variation**, and it is characterized by an early exchange on d4, which reduces White's options. After 8.♕xd4 ♗g7

Black moves his queen to a5; the c8-bishop to e6; the f8-rook (after castling) to c8; and then the a-pawn to a6, preparing ...b5, exerting a lot of pressure on the queenside. White, for his part, can seek aggressive counterplay on the kingside with f4-f5. He can also develop his queen's bishop to e3 (or to g5), retreat the queen to d2 and then play a timely ♘d5 (without castling, so the king can recapture on d2). If this is followed by an exchange of queens, an endgame or, better still, a queenless middlegame ensues that is often favourable for White.

After the likely exchange on d5, White can choose e4xd5, which means he will then exert a certain amount of pressure on the e7-pawn by means of the semi-open e-file. Alternatively, he can play c4xd5, hoping to control or exploit the open c-file. When this file is open, it is common for the major pieces to be exchanged there. The ensuing endgame is very often in White's favour, because of his space advantage and the possibility to exploit the weak c6-square, against which Black will be induced or forced to play ...b7-b6 or ...b7-b5.

Now we will return to 5...♗g7. After the obvious moves

> **6. ♗c1-e3 ♘g8-f6**
> **7. ♘b1-c3**

Black must make his first big choice: 7...♘g4, or 7...0-0 (with or without ...d6).

A) 7. ... ♘f6-g4

The **Simagin Variation**.

This continuation fell into slight disrepute from the beginning of the 1970s, but now it is again considered to be playable.

> **8. ♕d1xg4 ♘c6xd4**

Now the best move is, curiously,

> **9. ♕g4-d1!**

to safeguard the queen against the latent threat posed by the bishop on c8, to defend c2, and also to attack the knight on d4. Now Black can continue with the aggressive but dubious 9...e5, or with the more reliable

> **9. ... ♘d4-e6**

The knight is well placed on e6: there, it controls c5, d4 and f4, and in the variations with ...♕a5 it also sometimes supports the pawn push ...g6-g5 [!]. This can be seen in the following line, which at first sight appears to contravene the most fundamental strategic principles:

> **10. ♖a1-c1 ♕d8-a5**

> **11. ♕d1-d2 b7-b6**
> **12. ♗f1-e2 ♗c8-b7**
> **13. f2-f3 g6-g5!?**
> **14. 0-0 h7-h5!?**
> **15. ♖f1-d1**

White has a slight space advantage, but Black's position is flexible and playable.

B)   **7. ...**   **0-0**
       8. ♗f1-e2

with two likely continuations: 8...d6 or 8...b6.

B1)   **8. ...**   **d7-d6**
       9. 0-0   **♗c8-d7**

and you reach one of the key positions of the defence.

Strangely, you can also arrive at this position by means of the **King's Indian Defence**: 1.d4 ♘f6 2.c4 g6 3.♘c3 ♗g7 4.e4 d6 5.♘f3 0-0 6.♗e2 c5 (instead of the more common 6...e5) 7.0-0 cxd4 8.♘xd4 ♘c6 9.♗e3 ♗d7.
In this position Black's typical plan is to exchange on d4, move the bishop to c6 in order to force White to play f3; then transfer the f6-knight to c5 via d7; advance the pawn to a5; and close the game by placing pawns on the dark squares. Black's defensive strategy would make it advisable to exchange the dark-squared bishops, to limit White's offensive possibilities, and leave him with the 'bad' e2-bishop. For his part, White will patiently prepare slow play on the queenside with ♖ab1, ♖fc1, ♙a3 and ♙b4. That is, when it is tactically feasible to do so. However, it should not be presumed that opening up the position will always favour White!

B2)   **8. ...**   **b7-b6**

An alternative to 8...d6 that has its fans, in part because of a couple of traps that White can fall for! After
       9. 0-0   **♗c8-b7**
if White plays the solid
       10. f2-f3

he obtains the customary space advantage with slightly the better chances. However, if he tries to be clever, speculating on an exchange on g7 with a following check on d4, his plan will backfire: 10.♕d2?! ♘xd4 11.♗xd4 e5! 12.♗xe5 ♘xe4 (now yes) and Black has the advantage. Or 10.♖c1? ♘xd4 11.♗xd4 ♗h6! winning at least a pawn or the exchange.

Standard Accelerated Dragon

Back to the initial position of the Accelerated Dragon.
If White does not like the idea of the positional struggle inherent to the **Maróczy Bind**, he can deviate with the more direct
       5. ♘b1-c3   **♗f8-g7**
       6. ♗c1-e3   **♘g8-f6**

Now White must show the utmost care. Black has not yet played ...d6 and here he can play ...d7-d5, which in various Dragon variations frees the defender's game, in one tempo. In addition, some of the lines with ...♛b6 are particularly effective in this defence.

White can choose between the pseudo-active 7.♘xc6, the solid 7.♗e2 and the aggressive 7.♗c4.

A) **7. ♘d4xc6   b7xc6**
8. e4-e5

8. ...   ♘f6-g8

The pawn sacrifice 8...♘d5!? is playable and Black's compensation should be sufficient.

With the text, Black should be able to equalize after either 9.f4 ♘h6 or 9.♗d4 f6.

B) **7. ♗f1-e2   0-0**
8. ♘d4-b3!

To prevent ...d7-d5. Now Black usually replies 8...d6, transposing to the classical lines of the standard Dragon.

It is worth remembering that if in this position, White tries to steer the game in the direction of the **Yugoslav Attack of the Dragon Variation** with *7.f3?! 0-0 8.♛d2?!, Black can obtain good play with 8...d5!* (here requiring only one tempo).

C) **7. ♗f1-c4**

This can be considered the most aggressive move.

White tries to get back into the **main lines of the Dragon Variation** by castling queenside and initiating a pawn storm on the kingside; alternatively, he

257

can continue more solidly with h2-h3 and 0-0.

Black can allow this if he wishes, but he also has the possibility to enter quieter variations; or, if he likes, more aggressive ones.

C1)   7.   ...   ♛d8-a5

The 'quiet' variation which, thanks to the combined threat of 8...♞xe4 and 8..♛b4, forces White to castle kingside. This greatly reduces the dynamic rhythm of the game. Black now has a position which is not particularly active, but playable.

The most popular line in this variation is:

8.	0-0	0-0
9.	♝c4-b3	d7-d6
10.	h2-h3	♝c8-d7
11.	f2-f4	♞c6xd4
12.	♝e3xd4	♝d7-c6
13.	♛d1-d3	

and White has an edge.

If Black intends to be more bellicose, he can continue with the normal

C2)   7.   ...   0-0

to which White may respond by establishing the classic set-up of the Yugoslav Attack: f3, ♛d2 and 0-0-0.

8.   ♝c4-b3

White has to play this way in order to defend b2! *8.f3?! allows 8...♛b6!*

9.♝b3 ♞xe4!, and Black is better. Please take note of a typical error often made at this point, even by many strong players: *8...♞a5?* (It is natural to want to rid yourself of the strong bishop on b3) *and now 9.e5 ♞e8 allows for the brilliant 10.♝xf7+! ♚xf7 11.♞e6!!*

and White wins material, as happened in a famous game between Fischer and Reshevsky, New York 1958.

Back to **8.♝b3.** The hyper-aggressive variation that we referred to is 8...a5, threatening ...a4 followed by ...♞xe4. White can react solidly with 9.a4 or defend e4 with 9.f3. Now Black can play 9...d5!?.

After correct play, as with 10.♗xd5! ♘xd5 11.exd5 ♘b4 12.♘de2 ♗f5 13.♖c1, White should have a small advantage, albeit of a type that requires great skill to exploit.

The latest development is that White simply allows Black to carry out his plans, playing 9.0-0!, as after 9...a4 10.♘xa4 ♘xe4, Black is seriously hampered by the weakness of the b6-square. The standard variation is

8. ...   d7-d6

and we have returned to an 'almost normal' Dragon position. 'Almost' in the sense that after

9. f2-f3   ♗c8-d7
10. ♕d1-d2

White has already moved the bishop to b3, whereas in the Dragon, in the strict sense of the term, you usually prefer to first play h2-h4 or castle queenside. The

bishop on b3 gives Black an additional possibility: the **Parma Variation**:

10. ...   ♘c6xd4
11. ♗e3xd4   b7-b5!?

For a long time this was considered to be one of the best anti-Yugoslav Attack variations. However, nowadays we are not so sure: after

12. h2-h4   a7-a5
13. a2-a4   b5xa4
14. ♘c3xa4

Black still has difficulties to overcome.

Bacrot, Etienne
Tiviakov, Sergey
Wijk aan Zee 2006 (2)
1.e4 c5 2.♘f3 ♘c6 3.d4 cxd4 4.♘xd4 g6 5.c4 ♘f6 6.♘c3 d6 7.♘c2 ♗g7 8.♗e2 ♘d7 9.♗d2 ♘c5 10.0-0 0-0 11.b4 ♘e6 12.♖c1 ♘ed4 13.♘xd4 ♘xd4 14.♗e3 ♘xe2+ 15.♕xe2 ♗e6 16.♘d5 ♕d7 17.♖fd1 b6 18.b5 f5 19.exf5 ♖xf5 20.♘b4 ♗f7 21.♘c6 ♖e8 22.♕d3 ♖c8 23.♕e4 ♖c7 24.a4 h5 25.h3 ♕e6 26.♕xe6 ♗xe6 27.♖e1 ♗c8 28.a5 bxa5 29.♗xa7 ♔f7 30.♗b6 ♖xc6 31.bxc6 a4 32.♖ed1 a3 33.♗d4 ♗xd4 34.♖xd4 ♗e6 35.♖d5 ♔e8 36.♖xf5 gxf5 37.♖a1 ♔d8 38.♖xa3 ♔c7 39.♖e3 ♗xc4 40.♖xe7+ ♔xc6 41.f3   1-0

Ivanchuk,Vasily
Anand,Viswanathan

Buenos Aires 1994 (3)

1.e4 c5 2.Nf3 Nc6 3.d4 cxd4 4.Nxd4 g6 5.c4 Nf6 6.Nc3 d6 7.Be2 Nxd4 8.Qxd4 Bg7 9.Be3 0-0 10.Qd2 Be6 11.0-0 Qa5 12.Rab1! Rfc8 13.b3 Nd7 14.Rfc1 Qd8 15.Nd5 Nc5 16.Bf3 a5 17.h4 Bxd5 18.exd5 Qd7 19.Qe2! Re8 20.h5 Qf5?! 21.Rd1 Be5 22.g4 Qc8 23.Kg2 Bg7 24.Rh1 Nd7 25.hxg6 hxg6 26.Rh4→ a4 27.Rbh1 axb3 28.axb3 Ra1 29.R1h3! Qa8 30.Rh7 Qa2 31.Rxg7+!! Kxg7 32.Bd4+ f6 33.Qe3 Nf8 34.Be4!! Kf7 35.Rh8!
1-0

Kasparov,Garry
Kasimdzhanov,Rustam

Batumi tt rapid 2001 (11)

1.e4 c5 2.Nf3 Nc6 3.d4 cxd4 4.Nxd4 g6 5.c4 Nf6 6.Nc3 d6 7.f3 Nxd4 8.Qxd4 Bg7 9.Be3 0-0 10.Qd2 Be6 11.Rc1 Qa5 12.Bd3 Rfc8 13.b3 a6 14.Ne2 Qxd2+ 15.Kxd2 Nd7 16.Nf4 Nc5 17.Be2 a5 18.h4!± Na6 19.Rb1 Nb4 20.a3 Nc6 21.Nxe6 fxe6 22.f4 Kf7 23.h5 Nd4 24.Bd3 e5 25.f5 g5! 26.h6! Bf6 27.g4 Nf3+ 28.Ke2 Nd4+ 29.Kf2 e6? 30.Rh5?± Rc7! 31.a4 Rg8 32.Rhh1 Re8 33.Rhd1 Ra8 34.Bd2 Rc6 35.Bc3 Rb6 36.Bxd4!? exd4 37.e5 Bxe5?± 38.fxe6+ Ke7 39.Ke2! Rf8 40.Rf1 Bf4 41.Bf5 Rh8 42.Kd3 Be5 43.Be4 Bf4 44.Bf5 Be5 45.Kc2! Bf4 46.Rbd1 Be3 47.Be4 Kxe6 48.Bd5+ Kd7 49.Rf7+ Kc8+— 50.Rg7 Bf4 51.Rxd4 Be5 52.Rd3 Rf8 53.Rxh7 Rf2+ 54.Rd2 Rxd2+ 55.Kxd2 Rxb3 56.Re7 Rh3 57.h7 b6 58.Be4 Kd8 59.Rb7 Bd4 60.Bf5 Ke8 61.Rd7 Be5 62.Rb7 Bd4 63.Bg6+ Kd8 64.Bh5 Ra3 65.Rxb6 Kc7 66.Rb5 Rxa4 67.Rxg5 Rb4 68.Kd3 Bb2 69.Rxa5 Kd7 70.Ra8
1-0

Short,Nigel
Larsen,Bent

Brussels 1987 (11)

1.e4 c5 2.Nf3 Nc6 3.d4 cxd4 4.Nxd4 g6 5.c4 Bg7 6.Be3 Nf6 7.Nc3 Ng4 8.Qxg4 Nxd4 9.Qd1 Ne6 10.Rc1 Qa5 11.Be2 b6 12.0-0 Bb7 13.f3 g5 14.a3 Qe5 15.Qd2 h5 16.Rfd1 d6 17.b4 h4 18.Nd5 Kf8 19.Bf1 Bc6 20.Qd3 Nf4 21.Nxf4? gxf4 22.Bd4 Qxd4+ 23.Qxd4 Bxd4+ 24.Rxd4 Rh5 25.c5!? dxc5 26.bxc5 b5 27.e5 h3! 28.Re1 hxg2 29.Bxg2 Rc8 30.Rxf4 Rd5 31.e6 f6∓ 32.h4 Rxc5 33.Bh3 Bc6 34.Kf2 Rhd5 35.Re3 f5 36.h5 Kg7 37.h6+ Kxh6 38.Rh4+ Kg7 39.f4 Rc2+?? 40.Ke1 Rc1+ 41.Ke2 Be8 42.Rg3+ Bg6 43.Rh5?? Rc2+ 44.Ke1 Rc3 45.Rxc3 Bxh5 46.Rc7 Kf6 47.Rxa7 Rd4 48.Bxf5!? Kxf5 49.Rxe7 Rd5 50.a4 bxa4 51.Ra7 Rd4 52.Ra5+ Kg4 53.e7 Be8 54.f5 Kg5 55.Ra8 Re4+ 56.Kd2 Rxe7 57.Kc3 Kxf5 58.Kb2 Ke4 59.Rd8 Bd7 60.Rb8 Kd4 61.Rb7 Re2+ 62.Ka3 Re3+ 63.Kb2 a3+ 64.Ka1 Be6 65.Rb1 Kc3 66.Rc1+ Kb4 67.Rb1+ Bb3 68.Rc1 Re2 69.Rg1 Rd2 70.Rg4+ Bc4 71.Rg1 Bd3 72.Rc1 Bc2 73.Ka2 Be4+ 74.Ka1 Bd3Z
0-1

Leko,Peter
Piket,Jeroen
Tilburg 1997 (7)

1.e4 c5 2.♘f3 ♘c6 3.d4 cxd4
4.♘xd4 g6 5.c4 ♗g7 6.♗e3 ♘f6
7.♘c3 ♘g4 8.♕xg4 ♘xd4 9.♕d1
♘e6 10.♖c1 ♕a5 11.a3 b6 12.♗d3
g5 13.0-0 ♗b7 14.♖c2 ♗xc3 15.♖xc3
♕e5 16.♖e1 h5 17.♗d2 ♖h6 18.h4?!
♖g6 19.hxg5 ♘xg5 20.♕xh5 ♕g7
21.♔f1 ♘e6 22.g3 0-0-0 23.♗e3?
♖h8 24.♕f3 ♖h2 25.c5 ♖f6
26.cxb6+ ♔d8 27.♗f4 ♘d4! 28.♕e3
♕g4 29.♕xd4 ♕f3?? 30.♕xd7+! 1-0

Adams,Michael
Gonzalez,Bernal Manuel
Istanbul ol 2000 (2)

1.e4 c5 2.♘f3 ♘c6 3.d4 cxd4
4.♘xd4 g6 5.c4 ♗g7 6.♗e3 ♘f6
7.♘c3 0-0 8.♗e2 d6 9.0-0 ♗d7
10.♖e1 ♘xd4 11.♗xd4 ♗c6 12.♗d3
a5 13.♕d2 ♘d7 14.♗xg7 ♔xg7
15.♖e3! h6 16.♗e2!?± a4 17.h4!
♕a5 18.h5 g5 19.♖f1 ♕e5 20.♘d5
a3 21.bxa3?⇄ e6 22.g3 ♔h8
23.♔h2 g4! 24.♘b4 ♘f6 25.♘xc6
bxc6 26.♕d1 ♘xe4 27.♔g1 f5
28.♗d3 d5 29.cxd5 exd5?∓
30.♗xe4 fxe4 31.♕xg4 ♖a7 32.♖c1
♕b2 33.♖f1 ♖g7 34.♕d1 ♕e5
35.♕c2 ♖f6 36.a4 ♖e7 37.♖fe1
♕d6?⇄ 38.♕b2! ♔h7 39.a5! c5?±
40.♖b3! d4?+− 41.♖b6 ♕e5
42.♖xe4! ♕xe4 43.♖xf6 ♕e1+
44.♔h2 ♕e2 45.♕b3?± ♕xh5+
46.♔g2 ♖e1 47.♕f7+ ♕xf7
48.♖xf7+ ♔g6 49.♖d7 ♔f5≌
50.♖d5+ ♔e4 51.♖xc5 ♖e2?+−
52.a4 ♖a2 53.a6 ♖xa4 54.f3+! ♔e3

55.♖e5+ ♔d2 56.♖e6 h5 57.f4 ♖a5
58.♔f3 d3 59.♖d6 ♔c2 60.♔e3 ♖a3
61.♖d5 ♖xa6 62.♖c5+ ♔d1 63.♔xd3
1-0

Svidler,Peter
Carlsen,Magnus
Morelia/Linares 2007 (7)

1.e4 c5 2.♘f3 ♘c6 3.♘c3 g6 4.d4
cxd4 5.♘xd4 ♗g7 6.♗e3 ♘f6 7.♗c4
0-0 8.♗b3 e6 9.0-0 d5 10.exd5
♘xd5 11.♘xd5 exd5 12.c3 ♘a5
13.♕d3 ♘xb3 14.axb3 a6 15.♕d2
♖e8 16.♖fe1 ♗d7 17.♘c2 ♗c6
18.♗d4 f6 19.♖xe8+ ♕xe8 20.h3
♕f7 21.♘b4 ♗f8 22.♘xc6 bxc6
23.b4 ♗d6 24.b5 cxb5 25.♗xf6 a5
26.♗d4 ♕f4 27.♕xf4   ½-½

Shirov,Alexey
Ivanchuk,Vasily
Wijk aan Zee 1999 (13)

1.e4 c5 2.♘f3 ♘c6 3.♘c3 g6 4.d4
cxd4 5.♘xd4 ♗g7 6.♗e3 ♘f6 7.♗c4
0-0 8.♗b3 d6 9.f3 ♗d7 10.♕d2
♘xd4 11.♗xd4 b5 12.h4 a5 13.a4
bxa4 14.♘xa4 ♗e6 15.♘b6 ♖a6
16.♘d5 ♗xd5 17.exd5 ♕c7 18.♖a4
♖b8 19.h5 ♘xh5 20.♗xg7 ♔xg7
21.g4 ♘f6 22.♕h6+ ♔g8 23.♖f4
♕c5 24.♖xf6 exf6 25.♔d1 ♖xb3
26.cxb3 ♕xd5+ 27.♔c2 ♖c6+
28.♔b1 ♕d3+ 29.♔a2 g5 30.♕xf6
♕g6 31.♕e7 ♔g7 32.♖d1 h6
33.♕d7 ♖a6 34.♕c8 ♖b6 35.♕c7
♖a6 36.♕c8 ♖a7 37.♕c6 d5
38.♕c3+ f6 39.♖xd5 a4 40.bxa4
♕f7 41.♕b3 ♖xa4+ 42.♕xa4
♕xd5+ 43.♕b3 ♕a5+ 44.♕a3
♕d5+ 45.♕b3   ½-½

Sicilian Defence Minor Systems after 2...e6

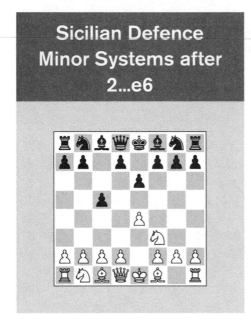

After 2...e6, White can decide not to advance the pawn to d4, to avoid some of the better-known theory.

With 3.d3 or 3.♕e2, you generally transpose into variations of the King's Indian Attack, which is arrived at with the following moves: ♘f3, g3, ♗g2, 0-0, d3, ♘bd2 and e4. The precise order of the moves is usually not so important. It is so named because White is playing a King's Indian Defence with colours reversed.

White can also open the diagonal for his queen's bishop with 3.b3 or seek to transpose to the Alapin with 3.c3 or, with the non-committal moves 3.♘c3 or 3.c4, to an Open Sicilian on the next move.

Psakhis,Lev
Strikovic,Aleksa
Erevan ol 1996 (3)
1.e4 c5 2.♘f3 e6 3.d3 ♘c6 4.g3 d5 5.♕e2 ♘f6 6.♗g2 ♗e7 7.0-0 0-0 8.e5

♘e8 9.c4 ♘c7 10.♘c3 ♖b8 11.♖d1 b5 12.b3 f5!? 13.cxd5 exd5 14.d4 ♗a6 15.♕e3 ♘e6 16.♘e2 b4 17.dxc5 ♗xc5 18.♕d2 ♕b6 19.♘f4 ♘xf4 20.gxf4 ♖bd8 21.♗b2 d4 22.♘g5 ♖fe8 [22...♘e7!] 23.♖ac1 ♘e7 24.♖xc5 ♕xc5 25.♘e6 ♕b6 26.♘xd8 ♖xd8 27.♗xd4 ♕g6 28.♕xb4 ♘c6 29.♕c3 ♗b7 30.♔h1!+− h5T 31.♖d2 h4 32.h3 ♖c8 33.♕b2 ♕f7 34.♖c2 ♕d7 35.♗e3 ♘b4 36.♖xc8+ ♕xc8 37.♕d4 ♗xg2+ 38.♔xg2 ♕b7+ 39.♔h2 a5 40.e6 ♘d5 41.♕e5 ♘e7 42.♕xa5   1-0

Zhang Zhong
Kobalia,Mikhail
Ubeda 2001 (8)
1.e4 c5 2.♘f3 e6 3.d3 ♘c6 4.g3 ♘ge7 5.♗g2 g6 6.0-0 ♗g7 7.c3 0-0 8.d4 cxd4 9.cxd4 d5 10.e5 ♘f5 11.♘c3 f6 12.g4 ♘fe7 13.exf6 ♖xf6 14.♗e3 ♖f8 15.♕d2 ♗d7 16.h3 ♘c8 17.♖fe1 ♘d6 18.b3 ♕a5 19.♖ac1 ♖ac8 20.♕d3 ♘b4 21.♕b1 ♘c6 22.♕d3 ♘b4 23.♕d2 ♘c6 24.♗f4 ♘f7 25.♕e3 ♘b4 26.h4 ♘xa2 27.♘xa2 ♕xa2 28.h5 ♕a3 29.hxg6 hxg6 30.♕d3 ♕e7 31.♖xc8 ♗xc8 32.g5 ♘d6 33.♗xd6 ♕xd6 34.♕xg6 ♕f4 35.♖e3 ♕f5 36.♕xf5 ♖xf5 37.♗h3 ♖f8 38.♔g2 ♖e8 39.♖c3 ♗d7 40.♖c7 ♗c6 41.♗g4 ♔f8 42.♔g3 a5 43.♗h5 ♖a8 44.♗f7 a4 45.bxa4 ♖xa4 46.♗xe6 ♗e8 47.♖xb7 ♖a3 48.♖b4 ♗h5 49.♗xd5 ♗xf3 50.♗xf3 ♖d3 51.d5 ♗e5+ 52.♔g2 ♖d2 53.♔f1 ♗d4 54.♗e2 ♗c5 55.♖b5 ♗d4 56.♖b3 ♔e7 57.♖f3 ♔d6 58.♖f5 ♗c5 59.g6 ♗d4 60.♖f7 ♖a2 61.♗g4 ♔xd5 62.♖d7+ ♔c5 63.♖xd4 ♔xd4 64.g7   1-0

Sicilian Defence Pin Variation

1.e4 c5 2.♘f3 e6 3.d4 cxd4 4.♘xd4 ♘f6 5.♘c3 ♗b4

This is a direct, but not completely sound attempt to immediately attack the e4-pawn. Played by Owen and Bird as far back as the second half of the 19th century, this variation has always been viewed with a certain suspicion. It had a brief revival in the 1970s, when it was played with a new idea: an exchange sacrifice. However, it was soon discovered that White gains a concrete advantage with correct play, and the variation returned to obscurity. However, it can be a valid surprise weapon: indeed, if White is unaware of the correct antidote, he can easily lose his way in the ensuing complications.

6. e4-e5!

The only move that can give Black a headache. It is a strange fact that the effectiveness of this move was not appreciated until the 1930s: for decades be-fore this, players had responded auto-matically with 6.♗d3.

6. ...   ♘f6-d5

The alternatives are inferior. However, the kingside weakness (g7) is more significant than the doubled pawn on c3 and there are two ways White can gain a good advantage.

A)   7. ♗c1-d2

The solid approach.

7. ...	♘d5xc3
8. b2xc3	♗b4-e7
9. ♕d1-g4	0-0
10. ♗d2-h6	g7-g6
11. h2-h4!	

White refuses to take the bait and he con-tinues to attack with excellent chances.

B)   7. ♕d1-g4

The aggressive approach.

7. ... **0-0!?**

and here is the exchange sacrifice we mentioned before

8. &c1-h6 **g7-g6**

9. ♕g4-g3!

The new idea is not to immediately accept the exchange sacrifice, in order to better exploit the weakness in Black's kingside position.

Taubenhaus,Jean
Schlechter,Carl

Ostend 1905 (8)

1.e4 c5 2.♘f3 e6 3.d4 cxd4 4.♘xd4 ♘f6 5.♘c3 &b4 6.&d3 ♘c6 [6...e5 7.♘e2 ♘c6 8.&d2 d6 9.0-0 &e6 10.a3 &a5 11.♖e1 h6 12.f4 &b6+ 13.♔h1 ♘g4 14.♖f1 ♘xh2↑ Grünwald-Meister, Berlin 2006] **7.&e3 d5 8.♘xc6 bxc6 9.e5 ♘d7 10.♕g4 &f8 11.f4 ♖b8 12.♘d1 g6 13.h4 h5 14.♕e2 ♘c5 15.c3 ♘xd3+ 16.♕xd3 c5 17.♕e2 &e7 18.♘f2 ♕a5 19.♕c2 &a6 20.a4 ♔f8 21.g3 ♕b6 22.b4 d4 23.bxc5 &xc5 24.&c1 ♔g7 25.♘e4 ♕c6 0-1**

Wagman,Stuart
Barle,Janez

Biel 1981

1.e4 c5 2.♘f3 e6 3.d4 cxd4 4.♘xd4 ♘f6 5.♘c3 &b4 6.e5 ♘d5 [6...♕c7? 7.exf6 &xc3+ 8.bxc3 ♕xc3+ 9.♕d2 ♕xa1 10.c3 ♕b1 11.fxg7 ♕e4+ 12.&e2 ♖g8 13.♘b5 ♕xg2 14.♖f1 ♘a6 15.♘d6+ ♔d8 16.♕d4 b6 17.♕f6+ ♔c7 18.♘b5+ 1-0 Pavlovic-Petrovic, Belgrade 2006] **7.&d2 ♘xc3 8.bxc3 &a5 9.♕g4 0-0 10.&d3 d6 11.♘f3 g6 12.h4 dxe5 13.h5 f5 14.&xf5 exf5 15.♕c4+ ♖f7 16.hxg6 hxg6 17.♘g5 ♕c7 18.♕h4 ♔f8 19.♘xf7 ♔xf7 20.♕h7+ ♔e6**

21.♕xg6+ ♔d5 22.♖h6 ♘c6 23.♕g8+ ♔c5 24.♖b1 b5 25.&e3+ ♔d4 26.&xd4+ exd4 27.♕f8+ ♔c4 28.♕g8+ ♔c5 29.♖xb5+ ♔xb5 30.♕d5+ ♕c5 31.a4+ 1-0

Del Rio Angelis,Salvador Gabriel
Sulskis,Sarunas

Port Erin 2003 (5)

1.e4 c5 2.♘f3 e6 3.d4 cxd4 4.♘xd4 ♘f6 5.♘c3 &b4 6.e5 ♘d5 7.&d2 ♘xc3 8.bxc3 &a5 9.&d3 d6 10.f4 dxe5 11.fxe5 ♕c7 12.0-0 &xc3 13.&xc3 ♕xc3 14.♘b5 ♕c5+ 15.♔h1 0-0 16.♘d6 ♕xe5 17.♘xf7 ♖xf7 18.&xh7+ ♔xh7 19.♖xf7 ♔g8 20.♖e7 &d7 21.♖b1 ♘c6 22.♕g4 ♘d7 23.♖xe6 ♕c3 24.♖e7 ♘f8 25.♖d1 ♖e8 26.♖xe8 &xe8 27.♕f3 ♕xf3 28.gxf3 ♘e6 29.♔g2 ♔f7 30.♔f2 ♔f6 31.♔e3 g5 32.♖b1 &c6 33.♖b4 ♘f4 34.♖c4 ♔e5 35.♔f2 &d5 36.♖a4 a6 37.a3 &c6 38.♖a5+ ♔f6 39.♖c5 ♘h3+ 40.♔e3 ♔e6 41.♖c4 ♘f4 42.♖d4 a5 43.♖d8 a4 44.♖g8 ♔f6 45.♖f8+ ♔g7 46.♖c8 ♘g2+ 47.♔f2 ♘h4 48.♔g3 &xf3 49.c3 &c6 50.♖a8 ♘g6 0-1

Lalic,Bogdan
Sulava,Nenad

Pula 1997 (9)

1.e4 c5 2.♘f3 e6 3.d4 cxd4 4.♘xd4 ♘f6 5.♘c3 &b4 6.e5 ♘d5 7.&d2 ♘xc3 8.bxc3 &e7 9.♕g4 0-0 10.&h6 g6 11.h4 d6 [11...♕a5 12.♕g3 d6 13.♘b5 ♘d7 14.h5 ♘xe5 15.f4 &d7 16.fxe5 &xb5 17.&xb5 ♕xb5 18.&xf8 Czarnota-Sulskis, Warsaw Ech 2005 (1-0, 68)] **12.h5 ♕a5 13.♘b5 a6 14.hxg6 fxg6 15.&xf8 &xf8 16.♖xh7 1-0**

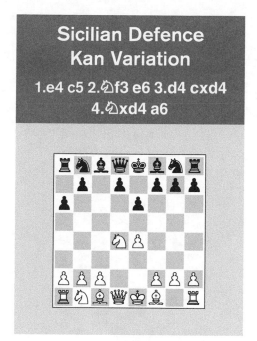

Sicilian Defence
Kan Variation

1.e4 c5 2.♘f3 e6 3.d4 cxd4
4.♘xd4 a6

The move sequence 1.e4 c5 2.♘f3 e6 3.d4 cxd4 4.♘xd4 a6 leads to one of the oldest positions in the Sicilian Defence. It was used in several of Adolf Anderssen's games in the middle part of the 19th century, and by Louis Paulsen towards the end of the same century. However, it only started to become popular from the beginning of the 1950s onwards, due to good results achieved by the Soviet player Ilya Kan. It is statistically one of the best lines for Black in the Sicilian. Though this is in part a comment on its objective worth, it also reflects the fact that the **Kan** is greatly appreciated by strong players, who find its flexibility attractive.

There is sometimes a little confusion about the nomenclature of the 'sister' **Taimanov** and **Paulsen variations**, in part because of possible transpositions. Both Kan and Mark Taimanov were more recent players than Paulsen, and so it was natural that until the 1960s opening theory would include their contributions within the Paulsen Variation. However, as theory developed each variation acquired its own name, even if this is not consistently observed by opening manuals.

After 1.e4 c5 2.♘f3 e6 3.d4 cxd4 4.♘xd4, we will use the following names:

> 4...a6 – **Kan Variation**;
> 4...♘c6 – **Paulsen-Taimanov**;
> 4...♘c6 5.♘c3 a6 6.♗e2 ♘ge7 – **Taimanov** (in the strict sense);
> 4...♘c6 5.♘c3 a6 6.♗e2 ♛c7 – **Paulsen** (in the strict sense).

From what we have said so far, you will now realize how subtle the distinctions are. For example, when playing the Kan, Black only needs to play ...♘c6 and he will suddenly find himself in the Paulsen-Taimanov variation.

It is interesting to know that in the past the Paulsen Variation used to be reached almost exclusively via the Kan (4...a6). Nowadays, black players more commonly prefer to reach the Paulsen through 4...♘c6. This trend is also because modern players, who are well-versed in the intricacies of the Kan, like to develop the b8-knight to c6. Otherwise, its placement there is delayed.

To make matters even more confusing, it should be remembered that when Black plays ...d6 (either after 4...a6 or after 4...♘c6 5.♘c3) and develops the bishop to e7, he transposes to the **Scheveningen Variation**. This is something that happens often, as in this way Black avoids the dangers associated with the **Keres Attack** (see page 308).

We will consider 5.♗d3 to be the main line of the Kan. Before we look at it, we will examine the alternatives:

A)   5. c2-c4

Adopting the **Maróczy Bind** pawn formation, as in the **Kalashnikov**, the **Anti-Taimanov** and the **Accelerated Dragon**.

Now the advance ...d7-d5 by Black will prove to be difficult.

At first, this was considered to be a sort of positional refutation of the Kan. However, today it is not viewed with fear: Black can respond directly with 5...♘f6 and then 6.♘c3 ♗b4, which produces tactically complex play. This is particularly the case in the variation 7.♗d3 ♘c6 8.♘xc6 dxc6 9.e5 ♕a5 10.exf6 ♗xc3+, where White's initiative used to be seen as very promising. However, in reality Black has more than sufficient resources. Also good is the solid 6...♕c7, which controls e5 and creates a typical **Hedgehog Defence** formation (this variation acquired its name because the e6-d6-b6-a6 pawn formation reminded players of the thorny spines of a hedgehog). This variation is willingly used by modern players who are unconcerned by White's space advantage.

B)   5. ♘b1-c3

This tends to lead to positions found in the **Paulsen-Taimanov Variation** where every now and then Black plays 5...♘c6. However, if Black wants to remain in the orbit of the **Kan**, he can play the completely re-evaluated

    5. ...   b7-b5

In old opening books this was considered doubtful because of

    6. ♗f1-d3!

However, in fact after 6...♕b6 — a recent move that is very fashionable — or 6...d6, Black's results have been acceptable.

Still, the classical 5...♕c7 is also playable.

C)   5. ♗f1-d3

The principal move of the **Kan Variation**.

This is not such a natural-looking move; generally we are advised to place the bishops on open diagonals. However, in this case there are many advantages that come with this move. Substantially, it is a question of timing: by defending the e4-pawn with the bishop, White postpones the development of the knight to c3, to reserve the option of c2-c4 for a more opportune moment than the 5th move.

Nonetheless, this flexible developing move allows White, if he wants, to still develop the knight to c3, transposing to common variations of the Scheveningen in which the d3-bishop can become a threat after the pawn advances f2-f4 and e4-e5. Moreover, in some variations the white queen – unobstructed by a bishop on e2 – can relocate directly to the kingside.

After 5.♗d3, Black has an ample choice of moves besides 5...d6, which is one of many ways to transpose to the **Scheveningen Variation**. Some of the available moves are: 5...b5, 5...b6, 5...♘e7 or even 5...d5, which until not long ago was considered to be premature. However, the most popular are the following:

C1)   **5. ...**   **♗f8-c5**

To try to exploit the presence of the undefended d4-knight by attacking it immediately, and after 6.♘b3, retreating the bishop to a7 or e7.

C2)   **5. ...**   **♕d8-b6**

This is all the rage with Sicilian players at the moment. The resulting positions are still largely unexplored.

C3)   **5. ...**   **♘b8-c6**

is the classical continuation. Now it is seen more rarely, but this is only a question of fashion.

C4)   **5. ...**   **g7-g6**

Here a student could protest, 'But doesn't everybody say that with an e6-d7 pawn structure you shouldn't advance the pawn to g6, as it creates ugly weaknesses on d6 and f6?' This is true, but as always, general principles must be considered in the context of each particular case. Here, the weakness in question is not easy to exploit, since the d3-bishop obstructs the d-file. In addition, the move ...♗g7 will gain a tempo by attacking the undefended knight on d4.

C5)   **5. ...**   **♘g8-f6**

The most popular move at the moment, taking advantage of White's inability to advance the pawn to e5 because of 6...♕a5+ followed by 7...♕xe5.

After 6.0-0 (threatening 7.e5), you continue with 6...♕c7 or 6...d6 to establish a classic **Hedgehog formation** in the event that White plays c2-c4.

Ehlvest,Jaan
Kasparov,Garry

Linares 1991 (10)

1.e4 c5 2.♘f3 e6 3.d4 cxd4 4.♘xd4 a6 5.c4 ♘f6 6.♘c3 ♕c7 7.♗d3 ♗e7 8.f4 d6 9.♕e2 ♘c6 10.♘f3 ♘d7 11.a3 ♗f6 12.♗e3 ♗xc3+ 13.bxc3 e5 14.f5 ♘cb8 15.0-0 ♘c5 16.♗c2 ♘bd7 17.♖fd1 ♘f6 18.♘d2 ♗d7 19.♗g5 ♗c6 20.♕f3 0-0-0 21.♖e1 h6 22.♗h4 ♖dg8 23.♔h1 ♘fd7 24.♘f1 g5 25.♗f2 h5 26.♕d1 h4 27.♕b1 ♘f6 28.♗xc5 dxc5 29.♘e3 ♕a5 30.♕b2 h3 31.g3 ♘xe4 32.♗xe4 ♗xe4+ 33.♔g1 ♖d8 34.♘g4 ♗xf5 35.♘xe5 ♕c7 36.♕f2 ♗e6 37.♖ab1 ♖d6 38.♖b2 ♖hd8 39.♖be2 f6 40.♘g6 ♗xc4   0-1

Spassky,Boris
Fischer,Robert

Reykjavik Wch m 1972 (21)

1.e4 c5 2.♘f3 e6 3.d4 cxd4 4.♘xd4 a6 5.♘c3 ♘c6 6.♗e3 ♘f6 7.♗d3 d5 8.exd5 exd5 9.0-0 ♗d6 10.♘xc6 bxc6 11.♗d4 0-0 12.♕f3 ♗e6 13.♖fe1 c5 14.♗xf6 ♕xf6 15.♕xf6 gxf6 16.♖ad1 ♖fd8 17.♗e2 ♖ab8 18.b3 c4 19.♘xd5 ♗xd5 20.♖xd5 ♗xh2+ 21.♔xh2 ♖xd5 22.♗xc4 ♖d2 23.♗xa6 ♖xc2 24.♖e2 ♖xe2 25.♗xe2 ♖d8 26.a4 ♖d2 27.♗c4

♖a2 28.♔g3 ♔f8 29.♔f3 ♔e7 30.g4 f5 31.gxf5 f6 32.♗g8 h6 33.♔g3 ♔d6 34.♔f3 ♖a1 35.♔g2 ♔e5 36.♗e6 ♔f4 37.♗d7 ♖b1 38.♗e6 ♖b2 39.♗c4 ♖a2 40.♗e6 h5 41.♗d7
          0-1

De la Paz,Frank
Milov,Vadim

Morelia 2007 (3)

1.e4 c5 2.♘f3 e6 3.d4 cxd4 4.♘xd4 a6 5.♗d3 ♘e7 6.0-0 ♘bc6 7.♗e3 ♘xd4 8.♗xd4 ♘c6 9.♗c3 b5 10.a3 e5 11.♘d2 d6 12.b4 ♗e7 13.a4 ♖b8 14.axb5 axb5 15.♘b3 0-0 16.♘a5 ♕c7 17.♗d2 ♗e6 18.c3 d5 19.♕e2 ♖fd8 20.♗xb5 ♘xa5 21.♖xa5 dxe4 22.c4 ♖xb5 23.cxb5 ♕c2 24.♖c1 ♕b2 25.♕e1 ♖xd2 26.♖a8+ ♗f8 27.♖b1 ♕d4 28.b6 ♗d5 29.♖aa1 ♖d3 30.b5 h6 31.h3 e3 32.fxe3 ♖xe3   0-1

Sulskis,Sarunas
Hansen, Sune Berg

Calvia ol 2004 (12)

1.e4 c5 2.♘f3 e6 3.d4 cxd4 4.♘xd4 a6 5.♗d3 ♗c5 6.c3 d6 7.0-0 ♘f6 8.♕e2 e5 9.♘f3 ♗e6 10.h3 h6 11.♖d1 ♕c7 12.♘bd2 0-0 13.♘f1 ♘c6 14.♘g3 d5 15.♗xh6 dxe4 16.♕d2 exd3 17.♗xg7 ♘h7 18.♘h5 f6 19.♕h6 e4 20.♗xf8 ♖xf8 21.♕g6+ ♔h8 22.♕xe4 ♗f7 23.♕h4 ♘e5 24.♘xe5 fxe5 25.♖xd3 ♗xh5 26.♕xh5 ♗xf2+ 27.♔h1 e4 28.♖d5 ♕f7 29.♕e5+ ♘f6 30.♖ad1 e3 31.♖d8 ♖xd8 32.♖xd8+ ♔g7 33.g4 ♕g6 34.♔g2 ♕e4+ 35.♕xe4 ♘xe4 36.♖e8 e2 37.♖xe4 e1♕ 38.♖xe1 ♗xe1 39.♔f3 ♔f6 40.♔e4

♔e6 41.a4 a5 42.♔d4 ♗h4 43.♔c5 ♗d8 44.b4 axb4 45.cxb4 ♔d7 46.a5 ♗e7+ 47.♔c4 ♗d8 48.♔d5 ♔c7 49.b5 ♗h4 50.♔e6 ♗e1 51.a6 bxa6 52.bxa6 ♔b6 53.g5   **1-0**

Anand,Viswanathan
Svidler,Peter
Cap d'Agde rapid 2003 (2)

1.e4 c5 2.♘f3 e6 3.d4 cxd4 4.♘xd4 a6 5.♗d3 ♗c5 6.♘b3 ♗a7 7.0-0 ♘c6 8.♘c3 ♘f6 9.♕e2 d6 10.♗e3 b5 11.♗xa7 ♖xa7 12.♕e3 0-0 13.♖fd1 ♖d7 14.h3 ♗b7 15.a4 b4 16.♘e2 ♕c7 17.a5 ♖c8 18.♘ed4 ♘e5 19.♕e2 ♘c4 20.♖dc1 e5 21.♘f5 d5 22.exd5 ♗xd5 23.♘d2 ♘xd2 24.♕xd2 ♘e4 25.♕xb4 ♘c5 26.♗f1 ♗e6 27.♘e3 ♖d4 28.♕b6 ♕xb6 29.axb6 ♖b4 30.♗xa6 ♘xa6 31.♖xa6 ♖xb2 32.c4 h5 33.c5 ♖b5 34.c6   **1-0**

Nakamura,Hikaru
Epishin,Vladimir
Gibraltar 2007 (7)

1.e4 c5 2.♘f3 e6 3.d4 cxd4 4.♘xd4 a6 5.♗d3 ♗c5 6.♘b3 ♗e7 7.♗e3 d5 8.exd5 ♕xd5 9.♘c3 ♕xg2 10.♗e4 ♕h3 11.♕d4 ♘f6 12.0-0-0 ♘bd7 13.♖hg1 g6 14.♖g3 ♕h5 15.♗g5 h6 16.♗f3 ♕xh2 17.♗e3 e5 18.♕a4 e4 19.♘xe4 ♘xe4 20.♗xe4 ♕h4 21.♘c5 b5 22.♕d4 ♘f6 23.♕d5 ♘xc5 24.♗xc5   **1-0**

Taubenhaus,Jean
Tarrasch,Siegbert
Ostend 1905 (18)

1.e4 c5 2.♘f3 e6 3.d4 cxd4 4.♘xd4 a6 5.♗d3 ♘c6 6.c3 ♘f6 7.♗e3 d5 8.♘d2 ♗e7 9.0-0 0-0 10.f4 dxe4

11.♘xe4 ♘d5 12.♘xc6 ♘xe3 13.♘f6+ ♗xf6 14.♗xh7+ ♔xh7 15.♕h5+ ♔g8 16.♘xd8 ♘xf1 17.♘xf7 ♖xf7 18.♖xf1 ♗d7 19.♖f3 ♖af8 20.♖h3 g5 21.♖g3 ♗d8 22.♖xg5+ ♗xg5 23.♕xg5+ ♖g7 24.♕e5 ♖g6 25.♕e4 ♖gf6 26.g3 ♗c6 27.♕d3 ♖8f7 28.♕d8+ ♔h7 29.♕d3+ ♔g7 30.♕e3 ♖d7 31.c4 ♖d1+ 32.♔f2 ♖h1 33.♕e5 ♖xh2+ 34.♔e3 ♖g2 35.♕g5+ ♔f7 36.♕h5+ ♖g6 37.♕h7+ ♖g7 38.♕h5+ ♔g8 39.♕e5 ♖2xg3+ 40.♔d4 ♖3g6 41.b4 ♖f7 42.b5 axb5 43.cxb5 ♗d5 44.a4 ♖g4 45.♔e3 ♖fxf4 46.♕b8+ ♖f8 47.♕d6 ♖f3+   **0-1**

Byrne,Robert
Andersson,Ulf
Amsterdam IBM 1979 (12)

1.e4 c5 2.♘f3 e6 3.d4 cxd4 4.♘xd4 a6 5.♗d3 g6 6.b3 d6 7.0-0 ♗g7 8.♗b2 ♘f6 9.c4 0-0 10.♘c3 ♘bd7 11.♖e1 ♖e8 12.♗f1 b6 13.♕d2 ♗b7 14.♖ad1 ♕c7 15.f3 ♖ad8 16.♕f2 ♘e5 17.♖c1 d5 18.exd5 [18.cxd5 ♘fg4 19.♕g3 ♘d3!! 20.♕xc7 ♗xd4+ 21.♔h1 ♘df2+ 22.♔g1 ♘h3+ 23.♔h1 ♘gf2X] 18...♘fg4 19.♕g3 ♘xf3+ 20.gxf3 [20.♘xf3 ♕c5+] 20...♗xd4+ 21.♔h1 ♕xg3 22.hxg3 ♘e3–+ 23.♗d3 exd5 24.cxd5 ♘xd5 25.♖xe8+ ♖xe8 26.♗e4 ♗xc3 27.♗xc3 ♘xc3 28.♗xb7 ♘xa2 29.♖c6 a5 30.♖xb6 ♖b8 31.♔g2 ♔f8 32.♖b5 ♘b4 33.♔f2 ♔e7 34.♔e3 ♔d6 35.♔d4 ♔c7 36.♖xb4 axb4 37.♗d5 ♔d6 38.♗xf7 ♖f8 39.♗d5 ♖f5 40.♗e4 ♖g5 41.g4 h5   **0-1**

Sicilian Defence
Paulsen-Taimanov

1.e4 c5 2.♞f3 e6 3.d4 cxd4

4.♞xd4 ♞c6

It should be stressed that you can reach the same position with the move order 1.e4 c5 2.♞f3 ♞c6 3.d4 cxd4 4.♞xd4 e6.

Every opening has its good and bad points. Compared to the Kan, the positive feature here is that since d4 is controlled by the ♞c6, the most unpleasant move 5.♝d3 becomes impossible. Moreover, the move 5.c4 loses a lot of its effectiveness here, as after 5...♞f6 6.♞c3 ♝b4, White's centre is already under pressure.

Another reason why the **Paulsen-Taimanov Variation** is so popular is that Black always has the option of ...d7-d6 in the main lines. In this way he can transpose to the **Scheveningen Variation**, having avoided the dangerous **Keres** and **English Attacks**, which can be so formidable against the standard Scheveningen.

On the minus side, Black can no longer flexibly develop the b8-knight to d7, as is the case in many Sicilian variations. Black does not control the b5-square, because he has not played ...a6. So the first continuation that will be examined is 5.♞b5, which some refer to as the **Anti-Taimanov Variation**. This is not as popular as it once was (for example, it was one of Fischer's favourites). However, it remains one of White's main lines; the second being 5.♞c3.

A)   5.   ♞d4-b5   d7-d6

Now there are two continuations for White: 6.c4 and 6.♝f4.

A1)   6.   c2-c4

Bringing about the classic **Maróczy Bind pawn formation** (pawns on e4 and c4)

and Black responds by taking up the **Hedgehog Defence pawn formation**.

It is true that White loses time with the manoeuvre ♘d4-b5-c3 (or a3) in comparison to sister systems that are brought about by the **English Opening**, the **Sicilian Kan Variation**, or the **Queen's Indian Defence**. However, it is not uncommon for Black to move the knight from c6 to d7 by way of b8! As you will have noted, the slow manoeuvring style of play which is typical of these variations, is the appropriate way to handle all Hedgehog-like formations, even if they are produced by different openings. It is only when White attacks b6 with ♗e3 and ♕b3 that the variations have their own specific features.

The importance of White's space advantage was overestimated in the past. In practice, Black's position has proved to be difficult to attack; either with gradual manoeuvres, where White maintains his space advantage; or with aggressive attempts in which White tries to attack Black's king with his f- and g-pawns. In response to the latter approach, Black's usual counter-measure is an opportune pawn advance ...d6-d5. If White plays g2-g4, the manoeuvre ...h6, ...♘h7 and ...♘g5 is also effective.

When White plays the more solid f2-f3 and takes counter-measures against Black's ...d5 pawn break with ♔h1 and ♗f1, Black has the interesting sequence ...♗e7-d8-c7; or, alternatively, ...♔h8, ...♖g8 and then ...g5-g4 to undermine the white pawn chain.

A2)   6. ♗c1-f4

This is a more direct approach.

6.   ...   e6-e5
7. ♗f4-e3

We have reached a position which is very reminiscent of the **Lasker-Pelikan Variation**, which can also be reached by means of the **Kalashnikov** (but with one move less for both players!).

But White's most frequent choice remains the natural developing move:

B)   5. ♘b1-c3

By 5...d6 Black can now transpose to standard lines of the **Scheveningen** in which he has not yet developed his king's knight. Not moving the knight could be advisable, as you can avoid several dangerous continuations by White.

At this point it makes virtually no difference in which order Black plays ...a6 and ...♕c7. However, the most common first move is

271

| 5. | ... | **a7-a6** |

It is worth noting some popular alternative lines for White (regardless of in which order ...a6 and ...♕c7 are played): 6.♗e2, which remains the most frequently played, as well as the more recent 6.♗e3.

B1)   6. ♘d4xc6

This is only usual in response to 5...a6.

| 6. | ... | **b7xc6** |
| 7. | **♗f1-d3** | |

The position produced is different from what you usually find in the Sicilian Defence. Black's centre is reinforced and there is no longer a knight on d4, which is so unpleasant for Black in the Sicilian. However, in compensation White can develop his pieces in an natural and active fashion. Moreover, the move ...a6 proves to be pointless and the bishop on c8 is not a pretty sight. In short, virtues and defects compensate for each other, but the relative novelty of the line is appealing to those players who are attracted to territory which is still theoretically unexplored.

B2)   6. g2-g3

Another variation that is employed quite a lot by white players.

It prepares for a kingside fianchetto (as mentioned, in response to either 5...a6 or to 5...♕c7). In the other Sicilian variations this indicates White's desire for a quiet game that avoids the critical lines. However, here the fianchetto contains a drop of poison: the e4-pawn, which is often under pressure in the Paulsen, is now well protected, the g2-bishop bears down on the queenside, and at times tactical motifs centred on ♖e1 and the sacrificial move ♘d5 are possible. The game becomes fundamentally positional in nature, but current theoretical assessments give White a small but unpleasant initiative. Indeed, so much so, that probably the best option for Black is to play d7-d6 on the 7th move (after protecting the c6-square well with 6...♕c7 – if this has been played on the 5th move, now 6...a6 is required to avoid the irritating move ♘db5), transposing to a Scheveningen variation that should not cause Black great problems.

B3)   6. ♗c1-e3   ♕d8-c7

| 7. | **♕d1-d2** | **♘g8-f6** |
| 8. | **f2-f3** | |

This variation, running along the lines of the **English Attack**, has recently become more popular.

White plans for the usual kingside expansion. Given that Black can still play ...♗b4 and seek counterplay in the centre with ...d7-d5, it has always been thought that the second player has easy counterplay. However, things are not so simple and White's initiative remains dangerous.

B4)   6. ♗f1-e2

This classical move remains the **main line**.

Instead of 6...♕c7, Black can continue with the **Taimanov Variation** in the strict sense of the term, by playing 6...♘ge7, with the aim of exchanging on d4 and bringing out the white queen, in order to gain a tempo with ...♘c6. Therefore White avoids the exchange with 7.♘b3, which has come to be seen as the main line. 7...b5 8.♗e3 ♘g6 9.0-0 ♗e7 10.a4 b4 11.a5! (threatening 12.♗b6) 11...♖b8 12.♘a4

with a slight edge for White.

6.   ...   ♕d8-c7

The classical move, controlling e5 and preparing ...♘f6.

7.   0-0   ♘g8-f6

8.   ♗c1-e3

Now we are in the **key position of the Paulsen**, in which Black can put White's centre under pressure with 8...b5 or the more commonly played

8.   ...   ♗f8-b4

From a statistical point of view, 8...♗b4 is one of Black's most trustworthy options. This should come as no surprise, since if White proceeds mechanically he can easily find himself in difficulty. Therefore White's best move – unless of course you already know what it is – is not very easy to find:

9.   ♘c3-a4!

A curious move: it decentralizes the knight and leaves the e4-pawn unde-

273

fended. Now 9...♘xe4?! is weak because of 10.♘xc6 followed by 11.♘b6 and 12.♕d4.

9.   ...   ♗b4-e7

By pulling back the bishop, the threat of ...♘xe4 becomes more powerful. Also playable is the old 9...0-0 10.♘xc6 bxc6 11.♘b6 ♖b8 12.♘xc8 ♖fxc8 13.♗xa6, and after 13...♖d8 or 13...♖f8, Black regains the pawn because of the weaknesses on e4, b2 and h2, with an unclear game.

10. ♘d4xc6   b7xc6
11. ♘a4-b6   ♖a8-b8
12. ♘b6xc8   ♕c7xc8

Unlike the analogous variation with 9...0-0, the bishop is not on b4. Now that b2 is under attack, Black can allow e4-e5.

13. e4-e5   ♘f6-d5
14. ♗e3-c1   ♗e7-c5
15. c2-c4   ♘d5-e7
16. b2-b3   ♕c8-c7
17. ♗c1-b2

Black's position is cramped but playable. It should be remembered that Black can always transpose to the **Scheveningen** with **8...♗e7** or **8...d6**.

Karpov,Anatoly
Kasparov,Garry

Moscow Wch m 1984 (3)

1.e4 c5 2.♘f3 e6 3.d4 cxd4 4.♘xd4 ♘c6 5.♘b5 d6 6.c4 ♘f6 7.♘1c3 a6 8.♘a3 ♗e7 9.♗e2 0-0 10.0-0 b6 11.♗e3 ♗b7 12.♕b3 ♘a5 13.♕xb6 ♘xe4 14.♘xe4 ♗xe4 15.♕xd8 ♗xd8 16.♖ad1 d5 17.f3 ♗f5 18.cxd5 exd5 19.♖xd5 ♗e6 20.♖d6 ♗xa2 21.♖xa6 ♖b8 22.♗c5 ♖e8 23.♗b5 ♖e6 24.b4 ♘b7 25.♗f2 ♗e7 26.♘c2 ♗d5 27.♖d1 ♗b3 28.♖d7 ♖d8 29.♖xe6 ♖xd7 30.♖e1 ♖c7 31.♗b6   1-0

Almasi,Zoltan
Ivanchuk,Vasily

Polanica Zdroj 2000 (8)

1.e4 c5 2.♘f3 ♘c6 3.d4 cxd4 4.♘xd4 e6 5.♘b5 d6 6.♗f4 e5 7.♗e3 ♘f6 [7...f5? 8.♘1c3! f4 9.♘d5! fxe3 10.♘bc7+ ♔f7 11.♕f3+ ♘f6 12.♗c4 ♘d4! 13.♘xf6+ d5 14.♗xd5+ ♔g6? 15.♕h5+ ♔xf6 16.fxe3 ♘xc2+ 17.♔e2 1-0 Morphy-Anderssen, Paris 1858 — this modern line was already played 150 years ago!] 8.♗g5 a6 9.♘5c3 ♗e7 10.♘d2?! [10.♗xf6!?] 10...♗g4 11.♗e2 ♗xe2 12.♘xe2 d5= 13.♗xf6 ♗xf6 14.0-0 0-0 15.c4 dxe4 16.♘xe4 ♗e7 17.c5?! ♕c7 18.♕b3 ♖ad8 19.♖fd1 g6 20.♕c4 ♘a5 21.♕b4 ♔g7 22.♘2c3?! ♘c6 23.♕c4 f5 24.♘d6 ♗xd6 25.cxd6 ♖xd6 26.♖xd6 ♕xd6 27.♖d1 ♘d4 28.f4 b5 29.♕d3 ♖d8 30.♔h1 b4 31.♘e2 ♘b5! 32.♕xd6 ♖xd6 33.♖xd6 ♘xd6 34.fxe5 ♘c4 35.b3 ♘xe5 36.♘f4 a5 37.h4 ♔f6 38.♔g1 ♘g4 39.♘d3 ♔e6−+ 40.♘c5+ ♔d6! 41.♘b7+ ♔c7   0-1

Macieja,Bartlomiej
Rublevsky,Sergey

Rethymnon tt 2003 (7)

1.e4 c5 2.♘f3 e6 3.d4 cxd4 4.♘xd4 ♘c6 5.♘b5 d6 6.♗f4 e5 7.♗e3 a6 8.♘5c3 ♘f6 9.♗c4 ♗e6 10.♘d5 ♘xe4 11.♗b6 ♕g5 12.♘c7+ ♔d7 13.♗xe6+ fxe6 14.♘xa8 ♕xg2 15.♖f1 ♗e7 16.♘d2 ♖xa8 17.c3 ♘xd2 18.♕xd2 ♕xh2 19.0-0-0 ♕f4 20.♗e3 ♕f5 21.♖g1 g6 22.f4 e4 23.♖g3 ♖f8 24.♖g5 ♕f7 25.♖g3 d5 26.♔b1 ♔c8 27.♖h1 ♗d6 28.♖h6 ♕c7 29.♖gh3 ♖f7 30.♖h1 ♗f8 31.♖6h2 ♔b8 32.♕g2 ♗d6 33.♕g4 ♕d7 34.♖h6 ♗f8 35.♖6h3 ♘a5

36.b3 ♘c6 37.♕g1 ♗d6 38.♖h6 ♗f8
39.♖6h3 ♔a8 40.♕g2 ♗d6 41.♖h6
e5 42.fxe5 ♘xe5 43.♖d1 ♘d3
44.♗d4 ♗f4 45.♖h3 ♕f5 46.♖f1 ♕e6
47.♕h1 h5 48.♕g2 ♕f5 49.♖hh1 e3
50.♕e2 ♕e4 51.♔a1 ♘b4 52.♔b2
♘c6 53.♗b6 ♖f8 54.♖h3 ♖e8
55.♖d1 ♖e6 56.♗c5 ♔b8 57.♖d3
♘e5 58.♖dxe3 ♗xe3 59.♖xe3 ♕f5
60.♗d4 ♘d3+ 61.♕xd3 ♕xd3
62.♖xd3 g5 63.♖e3 ♖g6 64.♖e8+
♔c7 65.♖h8 h4 66.♖h5 ♔d6 67.♗e3
g4 68.♖xh4 g3 69.♖h6   1-0

Fischer,Robert
Tal,Mikhail
Bled 1961 (2)

1.e4 c5 2.♘f3 ♘c6 3.d4 cxd4
4.♘xd4 e6 5.♘c3 ♕c7 6.g3 ♘f6?!
7.♘db5! ♕b8 8.♗f4 ♘e5 9.♗e2 ♗c5
10.♗xe5 ♕xe5 11.f4 ♕b8 12.e5 a6
13.exf6 axb5 14.fxg7 ♖g8 15.♘e4
♗e7 16.♕d4 ♖a4 17.♘f6+ ♗xf6
18.♕xf6 ♕c7 19.0-0-0 ♖xa2 20.♔b1
♖a6 21.♗xb5 ♖b6 22.♗d3 e5
23.fxe5 ♖xf6 24.exf6 ♕c5 25.♗xh7
♕g5 26.♗xg8 ♕xf6 27.♖hf1 ♕xg7
28.♗xf7+ ♔d8 29.♗e6 ♕h6
30.♗xd7 ♗xd7 31.♖f7 ♕xh2
32.♖dxd7+ ♔e8 33.♖de7+ ♔d8
34.♖d7+ ♔c8 35.♖c7+ ♔d8
36.♖fd7+ ♔e8 37.♖d1 b5 38.♖b7
♕h5 39.g4 ♕h3 40.g5 ♕f3
41.♖e1+ ♔f8 42.♖xb5 ♔g7 43.♖b6
♕g3 44.♖d1 ♕c7 45.♖dd6 ♕c8
46.b3 ♔f7 47.♖a6   1-0

Landa,Konstantin
Zunker,Reinhard
Bad Wiessee 2005 (2)

1.e4 c5 2.♘f3 e6 3.♘c3 ♘c6 4.d4
cxd4 5.♘xd4 ♕c7 6.♗e2 a6 7.0-0

♘f6 8.♗e3 b5 9.♘xc6 dxc6 10.f4 b4
11.e5 ♘d5 12.♘xd5 cxd5 13.♕d4
♕a5 14.a3 bxa3 15.c3 ♗d7 16.b4
♕a4 17.♗d1 ♕c6 18.♖xa3 ♕c4
19.♕xc4 dxc4 20.♗f3   1-0

Nisipeanu,Liviu-Dieter
De la Riva Aguado,Oscar
Spain tt 2006 (2)

1.e4 c5 2.♘f3 ♘c6 3.d4 cxd4
4.♘xd4 e6 5.♘c3 ♕c7 6.♗e3 a6
7.♗e2 ♘f6 8.0-0 ♗b4 9.♘a4 0-0
10.♘xc6 bxc6 11.♘b6 ♖b8 12.♘xc8
♖fxc8 13.♗xa6 ♖f8 14.♗d3 ♗d6
15.g3 ♗e5 16.a4 ♗xb2 17.♖a2 d5
18.exd5 ♘xd5 19.♗d2 ♗f6 20.a5
♖fd8 21.a6 ♘c3 22.♗xc3 ♗xc3
23.♕f3 ♗d4 24.♗e4 ♖d6 25.♖d1
♗a7 26.♖xd6 ♕xd6 27.♖a1 ♕c5
28.♖d1 ♕b6 29.♖d7 f5 30.♗d3 ♖d8
31.♖b7 ♕c5 32.♔g2 h6 33.♕e2
♔h8 34.f4 ♖d6 35.♕e5   1-0

Efimenko,Zahar
Miladinovic,Igor
Zlatibor tt 2006 (6)

1.e4 c5 2.♘f3 ♘c6 3.d4 cxd4
4.♘xd4 ♕c7 5.♘c3 e6 6.♗e2 a6
7.0-0 ♘f6 8.♗e3 ♗b4 9.♘a4 ♗e7
10.♘xc6 bxc6 11.♘b6 ♖b8 12.♘xc8
♕xc8 13.♗d4 ♕c7 14.e5 ♘d5 15.b3
a5 16.g3 c5 17.♗b2 a4 18.♗c4 ♘b6
19.♗b5 c4 20.♗d4 axb3 21.cxb3
cxb3 22.♕xb3 0-0 23.a4 ♘d5 24.a5
♗c5 25.♖ac1 ♗xd4 26.♖xc7 ♘xc7
27.♕d3 ♗xb5 28.♖b1 ♘c3 29.♖xb8
♖xb8 30.a6 ♘b5 31.♔g2 g6 32.f4
♔f8 33.g4 ♔e8 34.♕h3 ♘c3 35.a7
♖b2+ 36.♔f1 ♖b1+ 37.♔g2 ♖g1+
38.♔f3 ♗xa7 39.♕xh7 ♖f1+
40.♔g2 ♖f2+ 41.♔h1 ♘c5 42.♕h8+
♗f8 43.♕h3 ♘d5 44.♕b3 ♗b4   0-1

Sicilian Defence
Four Knights Variation

1.e4 c5 2.♘f3 ♘c6 (2...e6) 3.d4 cxd4 4.♘xd4 ♘f6 5.♘c3 e6 (5...♘c6)

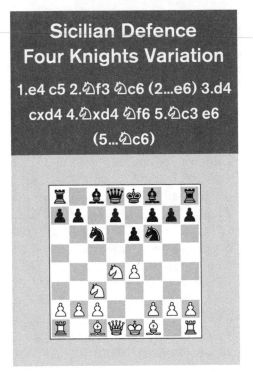

This variation has the ECO code B45, which classifies it as a sub-variation of the **Paulsen-Taimanov** (4...e6 5.♘c3 ♘f6). In reality, most of the time the position is reached by playing 2...♘c6 and 4...♘f6.

At the moment the following line is popular: 6.♘xc6 bxc6 7.e5 ♘d5

8.♘e4, which gains space and fixes the weakness on d6, but the price to be paid for this is a reinforced black centre. The following common sequence is indicative of the variation's complexity: 8...♕c7 9.f4 ♕b6! 10.c4 ♗b4+ 11.♔e2! f5 12.♘f2 ♗a6 13.♔f3! ♘e7 14.♗e3 ♗c5 15.♗xc5 ♕xc5 16.♕d6

with an unbalanced position where both players have chances.
However,

6. ♘d4-b5

remains the most logical and it is also the most popular: the weakness on d6 is put under further pressure. The usual reply is

6. ...   ♗f8-b4

This is the move which defines the Sicilian Four Knights. Naturally, with 6...d6 7.♗f4 e5 8.♗g5 you transpose to the **Lasker-Pelikan Variation**, with an extra move played by both sides.

Given that the thematic 7.♘d6+, as well as 7.♗f4, gives Black good counterplay, the most frequent move by far has become the solid

7. a2-a3

White contents himself with the small advantage of the two bishops. The game becomes a slow positional struggle after

7. ... ♗b4xc3+
8. ♘b5xc3 d7-d5

Black opens the position after conceding the two bishops to White, in order to free his game

9. e4xd5 e6xd5

It is true that Black has a weak pawn on d5 and is without his dark-squared bishop. However, after the usual sequence

10. ♗f1-d3 0-0
11. 0-0 d5-d4
12. ♘c3-e2

we have a position which is different to the classic isolated d-pawn positions. Here the pawn has advanced to d4. Black has gained a good space advantage and control of the d5-square. White maintains a minimal plus, but it is difficult to gain anything concrete, as is apparent from the unusually high draw rate.

Therefore, on the whole, this variation is good for a black player who is happy to draw.

If Black wants to fight for the full point, then the percentage of victories for Black (10%) is certainly not encouraging. This is particularly clear when it is compared to the overall win rate of 29% for the Sicilian, higher than for any other of Black's defences, and testimony to the Sicilian's combative nature.

Adams,Michael
Radjabov,Teimour

Enghien les Bains 2003 (6)

1.e4 c5 2.♘f3 e6 3.d4 cxd4 4.♘xd4 ♘f6 5.♘c3 ♘c6 6.♘xc6 bxc6 7.e5 ♘d5 8.♘e4 ♕c7 9.f4 ♖b8?! 10.♗d3 ♕b6 11.♕e2 ♗e7N 12.c4?! ♗b4+? [12...f5!] 13.♔f1 f5 14.exf6 ♘xf6□ 15.♘xf6+! gxf6 16.♗e3± ♕a5?! 17.♔f2 ♗e7 18.c5! d5 19.cxd6 ♗xd6 20.♖hd1± ♔e7 21.♔g1 ♗c5 22.♗xc5+ ♕xc5+ 23.♔h1 ♕b4?! 24.♕e3 ♕a5 25.b3 ♗d7 26.♗c4 ♖bd8 27.♖e1+- ♕b6 28.♕g3 ♖dg8 29.♕h3 1-0

Anderssen,Adolf
Paulsen,Louis

Leipzig m 1876 (1)

1.e4 c5 2.♘f3 e6 3.♘c3 ♘c6 4.d4 cxd4 5.♘xd4 ♘f6 6.♘db5 ♗b4 7.♘d6+ ♔e7 8.♗f4 e5 9.♘f5+ ♔f8 10.♗g5 d5 11.exd5 ♕xd5 12.♘e3 ♕a5 13.♘c4 ♗xc3+ 14.bxc3 ♕xc3+ 15.♗d2 ♕d4 16.c3 ♕e4+ 17.♗e3 ♘d5 18.f3 ♕h4+ 19.♗f2 ♕d8 20.♕b3 ♘f4 21.♖d1 ♕e7 22.g3 ♘e6 23.♗g2 g6 24.0-0 ♔g7 25.♖fe1 ♕c7 26.♖d5 f6 27.♘d6

♘g5 28.♘xc8 ♖hxc8 29.♖b5 b6 30.f4 ♘f7 31.fxe5 fxe5 32.♖f1 ♘d6 33.♗xc6 ♕xc6 34.♖xe5 ♘f5 35.g4 ♕f3 36.♖e7+ ♔h8 37.gxf5 ♕g4+ 38.♗g3 ♖c4 39.fxg6 ♖d8 40.♕xc4

1-0

Shirov,Alexey
Grischuk,Alexander

Linares 2001 (5)

1.e4 c5 2.♘f3 ♘c6 3.d4 cxd4 4.♘xd4 ♘f6 5.♘c3 e6 6.♘db5 ♗b4 7.a3 ♗xc3+ 8.♘xc3 d5 9.♗d3!? d4 10.♘e2 e5 11.0-0 0-0 12.h3 ♖e8 13.♘g3 ♗e6!?N 14.f4 exf4 15.♗xf4 ♘d7 16.♕h5 g6?! 17.♕h6→ ♕f6?! 18.♗g5 ♕g7 19.♕h4 ♘ce5 20.♗h6 ♕h8 21.♘f5! ♗xf5 22.exf5 ♘xd3 23.cxd3 ♕e5 24.♖f4 ♘c5 25.♖af1 ♘xd3 26.fxg6! fxg6 27.♖f7! ♘c5 28.♖g7+ ♔h8 29.♖ff7+− ♘e6 30.♖xg6 d3 31.♖g4 ♖g8 32.♖xh7+

1-0

Kasparov,Garry
Grischuk,Alexander

Cannes rapid 2001 (2)

1.e4 c5 2.♘f3 ♘c6 3.d4 cxd4 4.♘xd4 ♘f6 5.♘c3 e6 6.♘db5 ♗b4 7.a3 ♗xc3+ 8.♘xc3 d5 9.exd5 exd5 10.♗d3 0-0 11.0-0 d4! 12.♘e2!? ♗g4!? 13.♗g5 ♕d6 14.♖e1!? ♖fe8 15.♕d2 ♗xe2! 16.♗f4!?N ♕d7

17.♖xe2 ♖xe2 18.♕xe2 ♖e8 19.♕f1 ♕e6 20.h3 [±/=] 20...h6 21.♖d1 ♘d5 22.♗g3 ♘f6 23.♗f4 ♘d5 24.♗d2 ♘e3! 25.fxe3 dxe3 26.♕e2 exd2 27.♕xe6 ♖xe6 28.♖xd2 ♔f8 29.♗c4 [↔d] 29...♖e7 30.♔f2 [±/=] 30...♖c7 31.♗e2 ♔e7 32.c3 ♘e5 33.♖d4 ♖c6 34.a4 ♖b6!? 35.b4△ ♖c6 36.♖e4 f6 37.c4 b6 38.♔e3 ♖d6?! 39.c5! bxc5 40.bxc5 ♖d5 41.♖b4□ ♖xc5 42.♖b7+ ♔d6 43.♖xa7 ♖c3+ 44.♔f2 g5 45.♖a6+ ♖c6 46.♔e3 ♖xa6 47.♗xa6 f5 48.♗c8? ♘c4+! 49.♔f3 ♘b6 50.♗xf5 ♘xa4= 51.♔g4 ♔e5 52.♗c2 ♘c5 53.♔h5 ♔f6 54.♗xh6 ♘e6 55.g3 ♘d4 56.♗d3 ♘f3 57.♗e2 ♘e5 58.♔h5 ♘g6   ½-½

Almasi,Zoltan
Wippermann,Till

Germany Bundesliga 2005/06 (12)

1.e4 c5 2.♘f3 ♘c6 3.d4 cxd4 4.♘xd4 ♘f6 5.♘c3 e6 6.♘db5 ♗b4 7.a3 ♗xc3+ 8.♘xc3 d5 9.exd5 exd5 10.♗d3 0-0 11.0-0 d4 12.♘e2 ♕d5 13.♘f4 ♕d6 14.♘h5 ♘xh5 15.♕xh5 h6 16.♕h4 ♗d7 17.♗f4 ♕d5 18.♖ad1 f5 19.c4 ♕f7 20.♕g3 ♕f6 21.b4 ♔h8 22.h4 ♖fe8 23.♖fe1 ♗e6 24.b5 ♘a5 25.♗e5 ♕f7 26.♗xd4 ♗xc4 27.♗xf5 ♖xe1+ 28.♖xe1 ♘b3 29.♗b2 ♖f8 30.♗g6 ♕d5 31.♗xg7+   1-0

Sicilian Defence Moscow Variation

1.e4 c5 2.♘f3 d6 3.♗b5+

Setting up the **Maróczy Bind pawn formation** (pawns on c4 and e4) either immediately or after 5.0-0, is even more justifiable here than usual, as there is no light-squared bishop that can become bad. However, Black can get perfectly playable positions by fianchettoing along the lines of an **Accelerated Dragon**, or advancing the pawn to e6 and establishing a **Hedgehog Defence**. For example, Black has no problems after

5.	...	♘b8-c6
6.	0-0	g7-g6
7.	d2-d4	c5xd4
8.	♘f3xd4	♗f8-g7
9.	♗c1-e3	♘g8-f6
10.	f2-f3	0-0
11.	♘b1-c3	♕d7-d8!?

which leaves the d7-square available for the knight.

The most popular minor variation in response to 2...d6 is 3.♗b5+. White aims for quiet positions, which are comparatively unexplored. However, it is important to have a positional understanding of the various pawn structures that can occur.

White's percentage of wins is not extraordinary, and the high number of draws is an indication of the line's solidity.

The following three are all plausible continuations: 3...♗d7, 3...♘c6 and 3...♘d7.

A)   3.   ...   ♗c8-d7
The solid line.
    4.   ♗b5xd7+
Again Black has to choose between the aggressive 4...♘xd7 and the solid
    4.   ...   ♕d8xd7
which is the most popular.
    5.   c2-c4

B)   3.   ...   ♘b8-c6

This non-committal move often arises from the **Rossolimo Variation** (2...♘c6 3.♗b5 d6).

4. 0-0   ♗c8-d7

White can continue with

5. ♖f1-e1

which defends the e4-pawn and prepares for a possible retreat of the bishop to f1.

Alternatively, you can continue with 5.c3, and then d2-d4, in some tactical lines sacrificing the e4-pawn for a strong initiative in the centre. For example, 5...♘f6 6.♖e1 a6 7.♗xc6 ♗xc6 8.d4!? ♗xe4 9.♗g5, with optimum compensation for the pawn.

If instead White immediately plays 4.d4, after 4...cxd4 5.♕xd4 you transpose to the **Hungarian Variation** 1.e4 c5 2.♘f3 d6 3.d4 cxd4 4.♕xd4 ♘c6 5.♗b5.

C)   3. ...   ♘b8-d7

This ambitious move is the riskiest of the three. Black puts his faith in the bishop pair and the substantially solid nature of the position, but the price he pays is a cramped game that entails an abundance of tactical dangers. The variation is therefore playable, but Black should have a good knowledge of the lines involved.

4. d2-d4

White immediately opens the game so as to make the most of the shortcomings in Black's cramped position.

4. ...   ♘g8-f6

5. ♘b1-c3

Now Black has basically two approaches:

C1)   5. ...   c5xd4

6. ♕d1xd4

Now Black regularly advances the e-pawn chasing the queen away.

6. ...   e7-e5

It is true that this leaves Black with a weak backward d6-pawn. However, in an age when the **Sveshnikov** and **Kalashnikov Variations** are hugely popular, this can no longer scare anyone; even if White keeps an unpleasant initiative with correct play.

C2)   5. ...   a7-a6

The ambitious approach, which aims to gain the advantage of the bishop pair: however, Black is behind in development after

6. ♗b5xd7+   ♘f6xd7

The resulting position is fraught with danger for Black. Ideas such as ♘d5 are in the air, and Black must defend himself with accuracy if he wants to come out of this alive. For example,

7.	0-0	e7-e6
8.	♗c1-g5	♛d8-c7
9.	d4xc5!?	♞d7xc5
10.	♖f1-e1	

White is exerting unpleasant pressure on the centre.

Timman,Jan
Ivanchuk,Vasily
Amsterdam 1994 (6)

1.e4 c5 2.♞f3 d6 3.♗b5+ ♗d7 4.♕e2 ♞f6 5.♗xd7+ ♕xd7 6.e5 dxe5 7.♞xe5 ♕e6 8.♞a3 ♞fd7 9.♞ac4 ♞xe5 10.♞xe5 f6 11.♞c4 ♕xe2+ 12.♔xe2 ♞c6 13.c3 e5 14.a4 ♗e7 15.d3 0-0-0 16.♗e3 b6 17.f3 ♖d7 18.g4 ♖hd8 19.♖hd1 ♗f8 20.h4 ♞e7 21.a5 ♔b7? 22.axb6 axb6 23.♖a3 ♞d5 24.♖da1 ♗e7 25.h5 g6?! 26.♖a7+ ♔c6 27.♖xd7 ♖xd7 28.hxg6 hxg6 29.g5! b5 30.gxf6 ♗xf6 31.♞a5+ ♔b6 32.♞b3 ♞xe3 33.♔xe3 c4?! 34.♖a6+! ♔xa6 35.♞c5+ ♔a5 36.♞xd7 ♗g5+ 37.♔e4 ♗c1 38.dxc4 ♗xb2 39.c5! ♗xc3 40.c6 ♔a6 41.♔d5 ♗a5 42.♞c5+ ♔a7 43.♔d6 ♔b8 44.♔d7 g5 45.♞d3! b4 46.♞xb4 e4 47.fxe4

g4 48.♞a6+! ♔a7 49.c7 ♗xc7 50.♞xc7 g3 51.♞b5+ ♔b6 52.♞d4
1-0

Ivanchuk,Vasily
Miton,Kamil
Havana Capablanca mem 2006 (5)

1.e4 c5 2.♞f3 d6 3.♗b5+ ♗d7 4.♗xd7+ ♞xd7 5.0-0 ♞gf6 6.♕e2 e6 7.b3 ♗e7 8.♗b2 0-0 9.c4 a6 10.d4 cxd4 11.♞xd4 ♕a5 12.♞c3 ♖fe8 13.♖ad1 ♖ac8 14.f4 b5 15.e5 b4 16.exf6 bxc3 17.♗xc3 ♕xc3 18.fxe7 ♞f6 19.g4 d5 20.g5 ♞e4 21.f5 ♖xe7 22.f6 ♖d7 23.cxd5 ♖xd5 24.♕xe4 ♖cd8 25.♖f3 ♕c5 26.♖fd3 e5 27.fxg7 ♖xd4 28.♕e3 ♕d5 29.♖xd4 exd4 30.♕f4 d3 31.♖d2 ♕c5+ 32.♖f2 ♕d5 33.♖d2 ♖e8 34.♔f2 ♖e4 35.♕f6 ♖e5 36.♖xd3 ♖f5+
0-1

Rublevsky,Sergey
Harikrishna,Pentala
Foros 2006 (7)

1.e4 c5 2.♞f3 d6 3.♗b5+ ♞d7 4.0-0 ♞f6 5.♖e1 e5 6.c3 ♗e7 7.d4 0-0 8.h3 a6 9.♗f1 b5 10.d5 ♞e8 11.a4 ♖b8 12.b3 ♞c7 13.♞a3 ♞h8 14.♞c2 g6 15.♗h6 ♖g8 16.♞e3 ♗f8 17.♗xf8 ♕xf8 18.axb5 axb5 19.♖a7 ♗b7 20.♕a1 ♖a8 21.♖xb7 ♖xa1 22.♖xa1 c4 23.♖xc7 cxb3 24.♖xd7 ♕c8 25.♖xf7 ♖g7 26.♖xg7 ♔xg7 27.c4 bxc4 28.♞xc4
1-0

Lilienthal,Andor
Kotov,Alexander
Moscow ch-URS 1940 (12)

1.e4 c5 2.♞f3 d6 3.♗b5+ ♞d7 4.d4 cxd4 5.♕xd4 ♞f6 6.♗g5 ♕a5+ 7.♞c3 a6 8.b4 ♕d8 9.♗xf6 gxf6

10.♗xd7+ ♗xd7 11.♘d5 b5 12.♘h4
♖c8 13.♘f5 ♗xf5 14.exf5 ♗g7
15.0-0 0-0 16.♖ae1 ♖e8 17.♖e2 ♘c6
18.♖fe1 e5 19.fxe6 fxe6 20.♖xe6
♖xe6 21.♖xe6 ♖xc2 22.♕e3 ♘f8
23.h4 h5 24.♖e7 ♕c8 25.♖a7   1-0

Dvoretsky,Mark
Pohla,Harry
Viliandi 1972

1.e4 c5 2.♘f3 d6 3.♗b5+ ♘d7 4.d4
cxd4 5.♕xd4 ♘f6 6.♗g5 e6 7.♘c3
♗e7 8.0-0-0 0-0 9.♖he1 [9.h4!?]
9...♕a5 10.♗xd7 ♗xd7 11.♗xf6 gxf6
[11...♗xf6 12.e5 ♗e7 13.exd6 ♗f6
14.♘e5±] 12.e5 fxe5 13.♘xe5 ♖fd8
[13...♗c6 14.♖d3?? (14.♘xc6 bxc6
15.♖d3+−) 14...dxe5 15.♖xe5 ♕b4!−+
Dvoretsky-Scholseth, St John 1988]
14.♘xd7 [14.♕g4+!! ♔f8 15.♘xf7!
(15.♘xd7+ ♖xd7 16.♖d5 ♕b6!
(16...exd5? 17.♕xd7 ♖e8 18.♔b1 d4
19.♕b5!+−) 17.♖xe6!? fxe6 18.♕xe6
♕c6! 19.♖f5+ ♔g7 20.♖f7+ ♔h8
21.f4!?±) 15...♔xf7 16.♖d5!! exd5
(16...♕a6 17.♖f5+!) 17.♕h5+ ♔f8
18.♕h6+ Tal; 14.♘d5!? dxe5!
(14...♗g5+ 15.♔b1 dxe5 16.♕xe5 ♗d2

17.♘f6+ ♔g7 18.♘h5+ ♔f8 19.♕g7+!
♔e7 20.♕f6+ ♔f8 21.♖e5 ♕b4
22.a3+−) 15.♘xe7+ ♔f8 16.♕d6
♗b5!∞] 14...♖xd7 15.♘e4 [15.♖d3
♕g5+ 16.♔b1 ♕f6; 15.♖e3 ♗g5 16.f4
e5 17.♖xe5 ♕xe5 18.♕xe5 dxe5
19.♖xd7 ♗xf4+∞] 15...h6?!
[15...♗xa2!; 15...e5?! 16.♘f6+ ♗xf6
17.♕g4+ ♔h8 18.♕xd7 ♕xa2 19.c3±]
16.♖e3 ♔h7 17.♖f3! ♖f8 18.♔b1 b6
[18...f5? 19.♘c5+−] 19.♕e3 ♗g5?
[19...♕h5!] 20.♕d3 f5 21.♘xg5+
hxg5 22.♖h3+ ♔g7 [22...♔g6
23.♕e2!] 23.♕e3 f4 24.♕xe6 ♕f5
25.♕h6+ ♔f7 26.♖xd6   1-0

Spanton,Timothy
Marusenko,Petr
Hastings 2005/06 (4)

1.e4 c5 2.♘f3 d6 3.♗b5+ ♘d7 4.d4
♘f6 5.♘c3 cxd4 6.♕xd4 h6 7.♗e3
e5 8.♕d3 ♗e7 9.♗c4 0-0 10.♘h4 d5
11.exd5 e4 12.♘xe4 ♘xe4 13.♘g6
♘d6 14.♘xf8 ♘e5?? [in a good position Black overlooks almost the same
mate that Kramnik would suffer one
year later against Deep Fritz] 15.♕h7+
1-0

Sicilian Defence Minor Variations

1.e2-e4 c7-c5 2.♘g1-f3 d7-d6

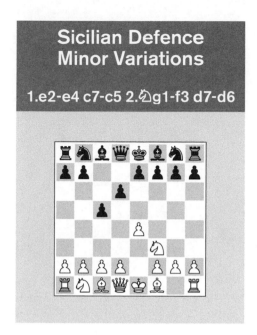

After 2...d6 White can play other quiet lines and avoid a lot of theory. Curiously, the beginner's move

3. ♗f1-c4

has become popular: with the pawn already on d6 the freeing pawn advance to d5 is not usually played, as this would require another tempo and White continues solidly with d3, c3, ♗b3, ♘bd2 etc., along the lines of the **Closed Variation of the Ruy Lopez**.

Another frequently used line is

3. c2-c3

which, compared to 2.c3 in the **Alapin**, has its own specific features. After

3. ...   ♘g8-f6!

the e4-e5 pawn advance is no longer possible and so the game develops into a slow struggle characterized by a lot of manoeuvring. White can start with 4.♗e2 as 4...♘xe4 is impossible on account of 5.♕a4+.

Now a look at some other minor systems: after the normal

3. d2-d4

Black sometimes continues with

3. ...   ♘g8-f6

By postponing the exchange on d4 by one move, Black seeks to take a bit of the sting out of minor continuations such as 4.♕xd4 or 5.f3, since after 4.♘c3 White no longer has the possibility to play c2-c4. However, White can deviate with 4.dxc5!, with good prospects of obtaining an edge.

3. d2-d4   c5xd4

Here, there is another very popular minor variation:

4. ♕d1xd4

The **Hungarian Variation**. If Black attacks the queen with

4. ...   ♘b8-c6
5. ♗f1-b5

and after the exchange on c6, White will usually continue with ♗g5 and 0-0-0, with a lot of pressure on the centre and good piece play. For example, after

5. ...	♗c8-d7
6. ♗b5xc6	♗d7xc6
7. ♘b1-c3	♘g8-f6
8. ♗c1-g5	e7-e6
9. 0-0-0	♗f8-e7
10. ♖h1-e1	0-0
11. ♔c1-b1	

or 11.♕d2, White's free play compensates for his opponent's bishop pair.
If, on the other hand, Black does not attack the queen immediately (playing, for example, 4...a6), White can continue with 5.c4, setting up the classic **Maróczy Bind formation**. Or he can develop normally with ♘c3, ♗e3, etc.

Every now and then (after 1.e4 c5 2.♘f3 d6 3.d4 cxd4) the following minor line will pop up in a tournament game:

4. ♘f3xd4   ♘g8-f6
5. f2-f3

White protects e4 with the f-pawn to delay the development of the queen's knight, and in so doing, he is able to play c2-c4. However, Black can respond effectively in the centre with

5. ...   e7-e5!

obtaining good play.

After the standard

5. ♘b1-c3

Black is the one who can get off the beaten path with

5. ...   e7-e5

This move is not often played because it does not have a good reputation. However, for now at least, there is no apparent refutation.

6. &f1-b5+! &c8-d7
7. &b5xd7+ ♕d8xd7

If White now continues with the thematic 8.♘f5, the situation is not clear after 8...♘xe4. White will probably have to content himself with a slight advantage after 8.♘f3.

The same idea can be achieved by playing ...e7-e5 one move earlier, instead of ...♘f6, with probable transpositions.

Another minor line is one that enjoyed a certain popularity in the 1990s: after 1.e4 c5 2.♘f3 d6 3.d4 cxd4 4.♘xd4 ♘f6 5.♘c3:

5. ... &c8-d7

This was frequently played by grandmaster Viktor Kupreichik. Even though 5...&d7 is not played often, it does have its objective validity. On d7 the bishop supports the knight on c6 and it is ready to go to c6 after the exchange of the enemy's knight in the centre, which is a move that always makes Black's position less cramped. This variation enjoys particularly good results, perhaps because of its surprise effect. An excellent idea for White is to use an **English Attack** set-up (f3, g4, h4, &e3, 0-0-0), in which the d7-bishop is less useful than in other Sicilian variations.

5. ... ♘b8-d7

is another rare variation which has a surprisingly high win rate. It was used a few times by Bent Larsen. However, it should come as no surprise that it does well, given that ...♘bd7 is a natural developing move in the Sicilian, and therefore should be perfectly playable.

Godena, Michele
Rowson, Jonathan
Verona 2006 (4)
1.e4 c5 2.♘f3 d6 3.&c4 ♘f6 4.d3 ♘c6 5.♘bd2 g6 6.0-0 &g7 7.c3 0-0 8.&b3 b5 9.♖e1 a5 10.a4 b4 11.♘f1 &a6 12.&g5 ♘d7 13.&d5 ♖c8 14.&xc6 ♖xc6 15.♕d2 bxc3 16.bxc3 ♘e5 17.♘xe5 dxe5 18.c4 ♖d6 19.♕c2 f6 20.&e3 ♖xd3 21.&xc5 ♖d7 22.♘e3 ♕c7 23.&a3 ♖fd8 24.♘d5 ♕a7 25.c5 e6 26.c6 ♖f7 27.c7 ♖c8 28.&c5 ♕b7 29.♖ab1 exd5 30.♖xb7 &xb7 31.&b6 d4 32.&xa5 ♖e8 33.♖b1 &c8 34.♖b8 ♔h8 35.♕c4 ♖ff8 36.&b4 ♖g8 37.a5 &f8 38.&xf8 ♖exf8 39.a6 1-0

Salov, Valery
Ljubojevic, Ljubomir
Buenos Aires 1994 (6)
1.e4 c5 2.♘f3 d6 3.d4 cxd4 4.♘xd4 ♘f6 5.f3 e5 6.&b5+ &d7 7.&xd7+

♕xd7 8.♘f5 d5 9.♗g5 dxe4 10.♗xf6 ♕xd1+ 11.♔xd1 gxf6 12.fxe4 ♘c6 13.c3 ♖g8 14.g3 ♖d8+ 15.♘d2 ♘e7 16.♔c2 ♔d7 17.♖ad1 ♔c6 18.♘f3 ♖xd1 19.♘xe7+ ♗xe7 20.♖xd1 ♖d8 21.♖xd8 ♗xd8 22.♘h4 ♗e7 23.♘f5 ♗f8 24.b4 ♔d7 25.♔b3 ♔c6 26.♔c4 a6 27.a4 b6 28.g4 b5+ 29.♔b3 ♔d7 30.♘e3 ♗h6 31.♘d5 ♗g5 32.c4 ♔c6 33.♘c3 bxc4+ 34.♔xc4 ♗h4 35.♘d5 ♗g5 36.h3 ♗h4 37.♘e7+ ♔d7 38.♘f5 ♗e1 39.b5 axb5+ 40.♔xb5 ♗d2 41.♔b6 ♗e1 42.a5 ♗f2+ 43.♔b7 ♔e6 44.♔c6 **1-0**

Bosch,Jeroen
Dvoiris,Semen

Leeuwarden 1997 (4)

1.e4 c5 2.♘f3 d6 3.d4 cxd4 4.♘xd4 ♘f6 5.f3 e5 6.♗b5+ ♘bd7 7.♘f5 a6 8.♗xd7+ ♕xd7 9.♗g5 d5 10.♗xf6 gxf6 11.♘c3 ♗b4 12.0-0 ♗xc3 13.bxc3 dxe4 14.fxe4 ♕xd1 15.♖axd1 ♗e6 16.a4 b5 17.axb5 axb5 18.♘e3 ♔e7 19.♘d5+ ♗xd5 20.♖xd5 ♖ab8 21.♖fd1 ♖hc8 22.♖d7+ ♔e8 23.♖a7 ♖a8 24.♖xa8 ♖xa8 25.♔f2 ♖c8 26.♖d3 ♖c4 27.♖e3 ♔e7 28.♔e2 h5 29.♔d3 f5 30.exf5 ♔f6 31.♖e1 ♔xf5 32.♖b1 ♖g4 33.g3 h4 34.♖f1+ ♔e6 35.♖g1 hxg3 36.hxg3 f5 37.♖b1 ♖xg3+ 38.♔d2 ♖g2+ 39.♔d3 e4+ 40.♔d4 ♖d2+ 41.♔e3 ♖xc2 42.♖b3 b4 **0-1**

Ganguly,Surya Shekhar
Zugic,Igor

Calvia ol 2004 (11)

1.e4 c5 2.♘f3 d6 3.d4 cxd4 4.♘xd4 ♘f6 5.♘c3 ♗d7 6.♗g5 e6 7.♘db5 ♗c6 8.♗xf6 gxf6 9.♕h5 a6 10.♘d4

♗d7 11.0-0-0 ♘c6 12.♘xc6 bxc6 13.h4! ♕b6 14.♖h3 c5?! [14...♖b8 15.♘a4 ♕c7] 15.♖f3 ♗e7 [15...♗g7 16.e5!] **16.e5! dxe5?** [16...♖b8! 17.exf6 (17.exd6 ♕xb2+ 18.♔d2 ♗xd6 with counterplay) 17...♗f8 the solid centre and the bishop pair offer good compensation for the pawn] 17.♖xd7! ♔xd7 18.♕xf7 ♖a7 19.♘c4 ♔d8 20.♗xe6 c4 21.♗xc4 ♖d7 22.♘d5 ♕a5 23.b4! ♕a4 24.♘b6 ♕xb4 25.♘xd7 ♔xd7 26.♖b3 **1-0**

Kosintseva,Nadezhda
Sedlak,Nikola

Moscow 2007 (7)

1.e4 c5 2.♘f3 d6 3.d4 cxd4 4.♘xd4 ♘f6 5.♘c3 ♗d7 6.♗g5 e6 7.♘db5 ♗c6 8.♗xf6 gxf6 9.♕h5 a6 10.♘d4 ♗d7 11.0-0-0 b5 12.f4 ♘c6 13.♔b1 ♕b6 14.♘xc6 ♗xc6 15.f5 ♗e7 16.♕h6 ♕c5 17.♗d3 e5 18.g4 b4 19.♘e2 d5 20.♘g3 0-0-0 21.exd5 ♗xd5 22.♗e4 ♗c4 23.b3 ♗b5 24.g5 ♖xd1+ 25.♖xd1 ♖d8 26.♖xd8+ ♗xd8 27.gxf6 ♗b6 28.a4 bxa3 29.♕d2 ♕g1+ 30.♔a2 ♗d4 31.c3 ♗e3 32.♕d5 ♕c1 33.♕b7+ ♔d8 34.♕e7+ ♔c8 35.♕f8+ ♔c7 36.♕e7+ ♗d7 37.♕xa3 ♕xc3 38.b4 ♕c4+ 39.♕b3 ♗b5 40.♕xc4+ ♗xc4+ 41.♔b2 ♗d4+ 42.♔a3 ♗g1 43.h3 ♗f2 44.♘h5 ♗h4 45.♗f3 ♔d6 46.♘g7 ♗xf6 47.♘e8+ ♔e7 48.♘c7 ♔d7 49.♘d5 ♗d8 50.♘e3 ♗d3 51.♔b3 e4 52.♗h5 ♗b6 53.♘d5 ♗d4 54.♘f4 ♗f1 55.♗xf7 ♗e5 56.♗e6+ ♔d6 57.♘d5 ♗xh3 58.♘e3 ♗d4 59.♘c4+ ♔e7 60.♗c8 ♗f1 61.♗xa6 e3 62.♘e5 ♗xa6 63.♘c6+ ♔f6 64.♘xd4 h5 65.♘c2 h4 66.b5 h3 **0-1**

Classical Sicilian Minor Variations

1.e2-e4 c7-c5 2.♘g1-f3 d7-d6 (2...♘c6) 3.d2-d4 c5xd4 4.♘f3xd4 ♘g8-f6 5.♘b1-c3 ♘b8-c6 (5...d6)

We have reached the position which is best known as the **Classical Sicilian**. White has some interesting alternatives to the popular 6.♗g5 (see following section).

A)   6. f2-f4

With this move White seeks to steer the game towards a **Scheveningen**-type position. However, Black should have no problems in reaching a balanced position after 6...e5!.

B)   6. ♗c1-e3

A normal developing move which, after the predictable 6...e6, gives White the option of establishing an **English Attack set-up** with f2-f3, 0-0-0, g2-g4 etc. That is even more dangerous here, as the black knight, which is already on c6, makes Black's position a little rigid (against the English Attack the knight is better placed on d7). However, Black can try to upset White's plans with 6...e5 or with the ambitious 6...♘g4, and he should not have too much difficulty in reaching a balanced game.

C)   6. f2-f3

This is also played with the idea of setting up the **English Attack**. Therefore, Black should respond energetically with 6...e5.

D)   6. ♗f1-e2

After this classical continuation Black has various options: the **Classical Dragon** with 6...g6, the **Scheveningen** with 6...e6, or the **Boleslavsky Variation** with

6. ...   e7-e5

Black has excellent performance statistics in this variation. However, this is largely because of White's frequent choice of the weak 7.♘b3?! instead of the correct 7.♘f3!. In the analogous **Najdorf** position (6.♗e2 e5), 7.♘b3 is the most popular, so it is natural to ask why it is dubious here. The answer is simple: here, after 7...♗e7 8.0-0 0-0 9.♗e3, Black only needs one tempo to play 9...a5, and after 10.a4 ♘b4 he has excellent counterplay.

The move discussed in this section, ...e5, has played an important role in the historical development of the Sicilian. This is because it featured in the first example where weakening the d5-square in order to gain space in the centre was considered to be legitimate. It can thus be seen as the ideological forefather of many variations in which Black advances the pawn to e5 in the Sicilian.

7. ♘d4-f3!   h7-h6!

It is necessary to prevent ♗g5, which would lessen Black's control of d5.

8. 0-0	**♗f8-e7**
9. ♖f1-e1	**0-0**
10. h2-h3	**♗c8-e6**
11. ♗e2-f1	

White takes measures against the freeing move ...d6-d5 by attacking e5. In response Black repositions the c6-knight to d7 with

11. ...   ♘c6-b8!

- in the style of the **Breyer Variation of the Ruy Lopez** – with balanced play.

For 6.♗c4, we refer you to the Section on the **Sozin-Velimirovic Variation**.

Sicilian Defence Richter-Rauzer

1.e4 c5 2.♘f3 d6 3.d4 cxd4 4.♘xd4 ♘f6 5.♘c3 ♘c6 6.♗g5

In old opening reference books, the move 6.♗g5 against the Classical Sicilian was called the **Anti-Dragon System.** And indeed the initial idea was to prevent 6...g6, as after 7.♗xf6, Black is left with bad doubled pawns. It was only after the Classical Sicilian had been developed that the move 6.♗g5 was used for its objective merits.

After the usual reply of 6...e6 the German master Kurt Richter first thought of the continuation 7.♘xc6 bxc6 8.e5, which today is considered to be objectively dubious. However, it did have the merit of kindling interest in 6.♗g5. Later the Russian opening expert Vsevolod Rauzer (1908-1941) conceived the plan which is still considered to be the best today: combining 6.♗g5 with the developing moves

♕d2 and 0-0-0. This applies pressure on the d6-pawn and in addition White retains the latent positional threat to take on f6 when Black cannot recapture with a piece. It is true that Black quite often allows this to happen, putting his faith in his bishop pair and the solid nature of his position after ...gxf6. In this case Black castles queenside or keeps his king in the centre, in view of his weakened kingside structure.

After 6.♗g5, Black usually plays 6...e6. Otherwise, he can choose from some minor variations that accept the creation of doubled pawns.

6...♗d7 is a move that is worth noting.

An unprepared white player can be taken by surprise when confronted with this. The move is connected with some venomous tactical lines with ...♕a5, ...♖c8 and a possible exchange sacrifice on c3.

Let's go back to the usual

6. ... e7-e6

which avoids the creation of a doubled pawn on f6.

7. ♕d1-d2

Now there are two principal continuations:

A)   **7. ...**   ♗f8-e7

This is the most solid option.

     8. 0-0-0   **0-0**

The most frequently played move is

     9. f2-f4

which produces a complicated position. A popular continuation is:

9. ...	♞c6xd4
10. ♕d2xd4	♕d8-a5
11. ♗f1-c4	♗c8-d7
12. e4-e5	d6xe5
13. f4xe5	♗d7-c6
14. ♗g5-d2	♞f6-d7
15. ♞c3-d5	♕a5-d8
16. ♞d5xe7+	♕d8xe7

The weakness of the e5-pawn is compensated for by White's two bishops and space advantage.

Back to White's 9th move. It is worth noting that since the 1980s many play-ers have switched their allegiance to the alternative move

     9. ♞d4-b3

which immediately highlights the weakness on d6.

B)   **7. ...**   **a7-a6**

Black immediately prevents 8.♞db5, which will be dangerous after the dou-bling of White's major pieces on the d-file.

     8. 0-0-0

B1)   **8. ...**   **h7-h6**

This immediate challenge is designed to definitively eliminate White's ever-present threat to take on f6. It has its drawbacks: after 9.♗f4, there is great pressure on d6. But above all, White has a nice position after he establishes an **English Attack-like set-up** (f3, g4, h4):

   9. ♗g5-e3

This is very dangerous, as 8...h6 has created a target that White can utilize to open up lines of attack on the kingside.

B2)   8. ...   ♗c8-d7

To avoid being exposed to a pawn storm, Black sometimes delays castling and (after 7...a6 8.0-0-0) plays this move instead of 8...h6, thus reserving the possibility of castling queenside in some cases.

   9. f2-f4

Now there are various strategic options: Black can break up White's aligned central pawns with 9...h6 10.♗h4 g5.

After 11.fxg5, the move 11...♘g4 follows.

Alternatively, Black can expand on the queenside with 9...b5.

Another option is to continue with the normal developing move

   9. ...   ♗f8-e7

In this last case, White usually proceeds with

   10. ♘d4-f3

Putting pressure on the d6-pawn.

   10. ...   b7-b5

   11. ♗g5xf6

11.e5!? is also interesting, After the text Black can sacrifice the d6-pawn with 11...♗xf6, which was a popular continuation in the 1960s; however, it is not completely sound. Alternatively, he can continue with the solid

   11. ...   g7xf6

producing a pawn structure which is common in these variations. White seeks to put the e6-pawn under pressure with the advance f4-f5, g2-g3, ♗f1-h3 and the manoeuvre ♘c3-e2-f4, in order to force Black to play ...e6-e5 with a resulting weakness on d5. Black has the two bishops, usually he castles queenside and grabs space on that flank.

In conclusion, the **Richter–Rauzer** is a variation that does not involve forced tactical lines, which are common in the **Dragon**, the **Najdorf** and the **Sozin**. It is strategically subtle and complex, and it is thus well suited to players who expect to win by virtue of their better general understanding of the game.

Tal,Mikhail
Kortchnoi,Viktor
Montpellier ct 1985 (8)

1.e4 c5 2.♘f3 d6 3.d4 cxd4 4.♘xd4 ♘f6 5.♘c3 ♘c6 6.♗g5 e6 7.♕d2 ♗e7 8.0-0-0 0-0 9.♘b3 a5 10.a4 d5 11.♗b5 dxe4 12.♕xd8 ♗xd8 13.♖he1 ♘a7 14.♗c4 h6 15.♗xf6 gxf6 16.♘xe4 f5 17.♘d6 ♗c7 18.g3 b6 19.♘xf5 exf5 20.♗d5 ♗e6 21.♗xa8 ♖xa8 22.♘d4 ♗d5 23.♖e7 ♖c8 24.♘b5   1-0

Morozevich,Alexander
Avrukh,Boris
Turin ol 2006 (13)

1.e4 c5 2.♘f3 ♘c6 3.d4 cxd4 4.♘xd4 ♘f6 5.♘c3 d6 6.♗g5 e6 7.♕d2 a6 8.♘xc6 bxc6 9.0-0-0 d5 10.e5 h6 11.♗h4 g5 12.♗g3 ♘d7 13.h4 g4 14.♕e2 ♖g8 15.♕d3 ♖b8 16.♕h7 ♖g7 17.♕h8 ♕a5 18.♖d3 d4 19.♖xd4 ♖xb2 20.♔d2 ♘b6 21.♗d3 ♘d5 22.♖c4 ♗b7 23.♖e1 ♖b4 24.♖ee4 c5 25.a3 ♖xc4 26.♖xc4 ♘b6 27.♖f4 ♘d5 28.♖c4 ♘b6 29.♖f4 c4 30.♖xc4 ♘xc4+ 31.♗xc4 ♗e4 32.♕xh6 ♖h7 33.♕e3 ♗h6 34.♗f4 ♗xf4 35.♕xf4 ♗g6 36.g3 ♖h5 37.♕xg4 ♖xe5 38.♕d4 ♖c5 39.f4 ♔e7 40.g4 ♖c6 41.♗d3 ♗xd3 42.cxd3 ♖c7 43.g5 ♕xa3 44.♕f6+ ♔e8 45.♕h8+ ♔d7 46.♘e2 ♕b4+ 47.♔e3 ♖c2 48.♕h5 ♕d2+ 49.♔d4 ♔e7 50.♕f3 ♕xe2 51.♕b7+ ♔f8   0-1

Yakovenko,Dmitry
Hou Yifan
Moscow 2007 (3)

1.e4 c5 2.♘f3 d6 3.d4 cxd4 4.♘xd4 ♘f6 5.♘c3 ♘c6 6.♗g5 e6 7.♕d2 a6 8.0-0-0 ♘xd4 9.♕xd4 ♗e7 10.f4 b5 11.♗e2 ♗b7 12.♗f3 ♖c8 13.♗xf6 gxf6 14.♔b1 ♖c5 15.♖he1 ♕c7 16.f5 0-0 17.♖e3 ♔h8 18.♕d2 ♖g8 19.♘e2 ♗f8 20.♖d3 ♖e5 21.♘g3 ♗e7 22.♕h6 ♕d8 23.♖xd6 ♗xd6 24.♖xd6 ♕f8 25.♕xf6+ ♕g7 26.♕xg7+ ♔xg7 27.♔c1 ♖c8 28.♖d7 ♗c6 29.♖a7 ♖a8 30.♖c7 ♗e8 31.♘h5+ ♔f8 32.f6 b4 33.♘f4 ♖a5 34.♔b1 ♖b8 35.♘d3 e5 36.g4 h6 37.h4 ♖ab5 38.g5 hxg5 39.hxg5

R8b7 40.Rc4 a5 41.b3 R7b6 42.a4
bxa3 43.Ka2 Rb8 44.Kxa3 Bd7
45.Rc7 Be8 46.Bg4 R8b7 47.Rc4
Rb8 48.Bf5 Rd8 49.Rc7 Rdb8
50.Re7 R8b7 51.Rxb7 Rxb7
52.Nxe5 Rb8 53.c4 Rd8 54.c5 Rd1
55.c6 Rc1 56.Kb2   1-0

Short,Nigel
Ljubojevic,Ljubomir
Amsterdam 1988 (4)

1.e4 c5 2.Nf3 d6 3.d4 cxd4 4.Nxd4
Nf6 5.Nc3 Nc6 6.Bg5 e6 7.Qd2 a6
8.0-0-0 h6 9.Be3 Bd7 10.f4 b5
11.Bd3 Be7 12.Kb1 b4 13.Nce2
0-0 14.h3 Qc7 15.g4 Qb7 16.Ng3
Nxd4 17.Bxd4 Bc6 18.Rhe1 Rfe8
19.g5 hxg5 20.fxg5 Nd7 21.Bxg7
Kxg7 22.Nh5+ Kg6 23.e5+ Kxh5
24.Qf4 Bxg5 25.Qxf7+ Kh4
26.Qh7+ Kg3 27.Qh5 Kh2
28.Qxg5 Rg8 29.Rd2+ Bg2
30.Qf4+ Rg3 31.Be4 Qxe4
32.Qxe4   1-0

Anand,Viswanathan
Shirov,Alexey
Paris rapid 1992 (2)

1.e4 c5 2.Nf3 d6 3.d4 cxd4 4.Nxd4
Nf6 5.Nc3 Nc6 6.Bg5 e6 7.Qd2 a6
8.0-0-0 h6 9.Be3 Qc7 10.f3 Rb8
11.g4 Ne5 12.h4 b5 13.Qg2 b4
14.Nb1 Nc4 15.Bxc4 Qxc4 16.g5
Nd7 17.b3 Qc7 18.g6 Nc5 19.gxf7+
Qxf7 20.Nd2 e5 21.Nc6 Rb6
22.Na5 Rb5 23.Ndc4 Be6 24.Kb1?
Qc7! 25.f4 Rxa5 26.Nxa5 Qxa5
27.fxe5 dxe5 28.Qg6+ Ke7 29.Rd2
Qc7? 30.Rf1?! Nd7 31.Rdf2 Qd6
32.Kc1 a5 33.h5 Kd8 34.Rd2 Qc6

Adams,Michael
Kozul,Zdenko
Belgrade tt 1999 (2)

1.e4 c5 2.Nf3 d6 3.d4 cxd4 4.Nxd4
Nf6 5.Nc3 Nc6 6.Bg5 e6 7.Qd2 a6
8.0-0-0 Bd7 9.f4 b5 10.Bxf6 gxf6
11.Kb1 Qb6 12.Nxc6 Bxc6 13.Qe1
Be7 14.Bd3 a5?! 15.f5N b4?!
16.Ne2 e5 17.Ng3± Qc5 18.Qe2
Rc8 19.b3! 0-0 20.Bc4 Kh8
21.Rhe1 Rg8 22.Qh5! Be8 23.Qh6
Qb6 24.Nh5 Qd8 25.Rd2+− Rg5
26.Red1 Bc6 27.Nxf6 Rg7 28.Nh5
Rg4 29.Nf6 Rg7 30.g4 Qb6 31.h3
Rd8 32.Nh5 Rgg8 33.Bxf7 Bg5
34.Qe6 Rgf8 35.Rxd6 Rxd6
36.Qxe5+ Rf6 37.Nxf6   1-0

Zelcic,Robert
Kozul,Zdenko
Pozega 2000 (7)

1.e4 c5 2.Nf3 Nc6 3.d4 cxd4
4.Nxd4 Nf6 5.Nc3 d6 6.Bg5 e6
7.Qd2 a6 8.0-0-0 Bd7 9.f4 b5
10.Bxf6 gxf6 11.Kb1 Qb6 12.Nxc6
Bxc6 13.Qe1 Ra7 14.f5 Qc5
15.Bd3 Rc7 16.Qh4 Be7 17.Ne2 e5
18.Qh6 a5 19.Qg7 Rf8 20.Qxh7 a4
21.Qh6 a3 22.b3 Rg8 23.Qc1 Rxg2
24.Rdg1 Rxe2 25.Bxe2 Bxe4
26.Bd3 Bxh1 27.Rg8+ Bf8
28.Qxh1 d5 29.Qf1 Ke7 30.Qe1
Qd4 31.Qc1 b4 32.Rh8 Rc3 33.Rh7
e4 34.Qf4 Rxc2   0-1

35.Kb1 a4 36.Bxh6! Rxh6
37.Rxf8+ Kc7 38.Qg5 Nxf8
39.Qxg7+ Bd7 40.Qxf8 Rxh5
41.Qxb4 Rh6? 42.Rd5 Qb6
43.Qc3+ Kb7?? 44.Rxd7+   1-0

Spassky,Boris
Zhukhovitsky,Samuel

Leningrad 1957 (4)

1.e4 c5 2.♘f3 ♘c6 3.d4 cxd4
4.♘xd4 ♘f6 5.♘c3 d6 6.♗g5 e6
7.♕d2 a6 8.0-0-0 ♗d7 9.f4 ♗e7
10.♘f3 h6 11.♗xf6 gxf6 12.f5 ♕c7
13.♔b1 0-0-0 14.♗c4 ♔b8 15.♗b3
♖c8 16.♘e2 exf5 17.exf5 ♗xf5
18.♘c3 ♗f8 19.♘d4 ♘xd4 20.♕xd4
♖g8 21.♕xf6 ♗g6 22.♕f2 ♗g7
23.♘a4 ♖ge8 24.♖hf1 ♖e4 25.♘b6
♖ce8 26.♘d5 ♕c5 27.♘f4 ♗d4
28.♕h4 ♗e5 29.g3 a5 30.a4 ♖b4
31.♘xg6 ♖xh4 32.♘xh4 f6 33.♘f5
h5 34.♖d5 ♕c7 35.♖b5 b6 36.♘e3
♗d4 37.♘d5 ♕d8 38.♖f4 ♗c5
39.♖xf6 ♖e2 40.♖f7 ♖f2 41.♖h7
♖xh2 42.♘xb6 ♗xb6 43.♗d5 ♔c8
44.♖b7 ♕e8 45.♖5xb6 ♕e1+
46.♔a2 ♖xc2 47.♖a6 ♖c7 48.♖b8+
♔d7 49.♖f8 ♕b4 50.♖f7+ ♔d8
51.♖f4 ♕d2 52.♖f8+   1-0

Fischer,Robert
Spassky,Boris

Reykjavik Wch m 1972 (18)

1.e4 c5 2.♘f3 d6 3.♘c3 ♘c6 4.d4
cxd4 5.♘xd4 ♘f6 6.♗g5 e6 7.♕d2
a6 8.0-0-0 ♗d7 9.f4 ♗e7 10.♘f3 b5
11.♗xf6 gxf6 12.♗d3 ♕a5 13.♔b1
b4 14.♘e2 ♕c5 15.f5 a5 16.♘f4 a4
17.♖c1 ♖b8 18.c3 b3 19.a3 ♘e5
20.♖hf1 ♘c4 21.♗xc4 ♕xc4
22.♖ce1 ♔d8 23.♔a1 ♖b5 24.♘d4

♖a5 25.♘d3 ♔c7 26.♘b4 h5 27.g3
♖e5 28.♘d3 ♖b8 29.♕e2 ♖a5
30.fxe6 fxe6 31.♖f2 e5 32.♘f5 ♗xf5
33.♖xf5 d5 34.exd5 ♕xd5 35.♘b4
♕d7 36.♖xh5 ♗xb4 37.cxb4 ♖d5
38.♖c1+ ♔b7 39.♕e4 ♖c8 40.♖b1
♔b6 41.♖h7 ♖d4 42.♕g6 ♕c6
43.♖f7 ♖d6 44.♕h6 ♕f3 45.♕h7
♕c6 46.♕h6 ♕f3 47.♕h7 ♕c6 ½-½

Fischer,Robert
Spassky,Boris

Reykjavik Wch m 1972 (20)

1.e4 c5 2.♘f3 ♘c6 3.d4 cxd4
4.♘xd4 ♘f6 5.♘c3 d6 6.♗g5 e6
7.♕d2 a6 8.0-0-0 ♗d7 9.f4 ♗e7
10.♗e2 0-0 11.♘f3 h6 12.♗h4 ♘xe4
13.♗xe7 ♘xd2 14.♗xd8 ♘xf3
15.♘xf3 ♖fxd8 16.♖xd6 ♔f8
17.♖hd1 ♔e7 18.♘a4 ♗e8 19.♖xd8
♖xd8 20.♘c5 ♖b8 21.♖d3 a5
22.♖b3 b5 23.a3 a4 24.♖c3 ♖d8
25.♘d3 f6 26.♖c5 ♖b8 27.♖c3 g5
28.g3 ♔d6 29.♘c5 g4 30.♘e4+
♔e7 31.♘e1 ♖d8 32.♘d3 ♖d4
33.♘ef2 h5 34.♖c5 ♖d5 35.♖c3
♘d4 36.♖c7+ ♖d7 37.♖xd7+ ♗xd7
38.♘e1 e5 39.fxe5 fxe5 40.♔d2 ♗f5
41.♘d1 ♔d6 42.♘e3 ♗e6 43.♔d3
♗f7 44.♔c3 ♔c6 45.♔d3 ♔c5
46.♔e4 ♔d6 47.♔d3 ♗g6+ 48.♔c3
♔c5 49.♘d3+ ♔d6 50.♘e1 ♔c6
51.♔d2 ♔c5 52.♘d3+ ♔d6 53.♘e1
♘e6 54.♔c3 ♘d4   ½-½

Sicilian Defence Dragon Variation

1.e4 c5 2.♘f3 d6 3.d4 cxd4 4.♘xd4 ♘f6 5.♘c3 g6

The name **Dragon** came about at the beginning of the 20th century and it was the happy brainchild of the Ukrainian master Fedor Duz-Khotimirsky. He was crazy about astronomy, and he noted that there was an analogy between the form of the pawn structure d6-e7-f7-g6-h7 and the dragon-shaped Draco Constellation; as a result, the fire-breathing beast of Greek mythology finds itself in chess opening theory.

As mentioned before, the modern version of the Dragon with the move order 2...d6 and 5...g6 did not make its debut until 1924, when it was employed in a Réti-Tartakower game played in New York. It was created as a means of preventing the **Maróczy Bind** (5.c4), which White can use against the **Accelerated Dragon** (2...♘c6 and 4...g6).

In the past it was also common to use a type of **Deferred Dragon** via the Classical Sicilian: 1.e4 c5 2.♘f3 d6 3.d4 cxd4 4.♘xd4 ♘f6 5.♘c3 ♘c6 with the idea of advancing the pawn to g6 on the 6th move.

However, **Rauzer's move** 6.♗g5! (see the previous section) with the idea of creating doubled pawns on the f-file in the event of 6...g6,

meant that this move sequence was not very attractive for black players wishing to fianchetto on the kingside.

Before we look at the modern variations, we will examine the development of the f1-bishop to e2 with the intention of castling kingside as soon as possible. Part of the purpose of looking at this move first is to put things in a historical context.

In the early years of this opening, White almost always played 6.♗e2.

Classical Variation

6. ♗f1-e2   ♗f8-g7

and now:

A)   7. ♗c1-e3   ♘b8-c6
8. 0-0   0-0
9. ♘d4-b3!

Preventing the central thrust 9...d5.

9.	...	♝c8-e6
10.	f2-f4	

The **key position of the Classical Dragon**. Black's resources seem to be adequate after 10...♞a5, 10...♛c8 or, better still, 10...♜c8.

In recent years, positionally-minded players have been using 7.♝e3 less often, and instead it has become popular to employ the solid plan:

B)	7.	0-0	♞b8-c6
	8.	♞d4-b3	0-0
	9.	♜f1-e1	

White intends to play 10.♝f1, with the idea of ♞d5 and ♝g5. The resulting pressure is not enough to give him an objective advantage, but it can still be annoying for Black.

The following positional line became reasonably popular in the 1980s, mainly because of its adoption by Karpov: 9.♝g5.

However, this line is not seen very frequently these days.

Fianchetto Variation

	6.	g2-g3

This fianchetto development of the king's bishop, which avoids lines that are too sharp or overly theoretical, has always enjoyed a certain popularity with players who wish to enter a more strategically-orientated game.

However, with correct play, Black will not have any problems in achieving a satisfactory position with chances for both sides, for example:

6. ...   ♘b8-c6!?

with the idea to exchange on d4. Against this White's best continuation is probably

7.   ♘d4-e2!?

after which a phase of slow positional manoeuvring follows. The ensuing positions offer equal chances for both players.

Levenfish Variation

6.   f2-f4

The **Levenfish** is another variation which has always had its admirers. This is perhaps because *after the spontaneous 6...♗g7, the move 7.e5! gives White a dangerous initiative.*

If Black does not have a good knowledge of the narrow path that leads to a likely draw, there is a good chance he will be beaten.

The safest option for Black is to prevent the pawn advance e4-e5 with

6.   ...   ♘b8-c6

with a balanced position.

The real theoretical revolution regarding the Dragon started in 1936 with the advent of:

The Yugoslav Attack

6.   ♗c1-e3

This set-up was championed by the same person who co-developed the **Richter-Rauzer Variation**! For this reason the ensuing line involving queenside castling is often also called the **Rauzer Variation**, and it first appeared in the game Rauzer-Chekhover played in the Young Masters Championship of 1936.

With 6.♗e3 followed by 7.f3 (or vice versa as Rauzer used to prefer), White ambitiously plans for ♕d2, 0-0-0, ♗c4, g2-g4, h2-h4-h5, ♗h6, ♗xg7, h5xg6, ♕h6+, ♘d5 and checkmate!

Naturally, White is not the only player moving his pieces, and on the queenside Black is often the first to be able to threaten the safety of the opponent's king. The ensuing sharp lines can become some of the most complex in opening theory.

6.   ...   ♗f8-g7

7.   f2-f3   0-0

Or also the immediate 7...♘c6.

8.   ♕d1-d2   ♘b8-c6

We have arrived at the first big theoretical crossroads.

Black is ready to play the freeing advance 9...d5. White can try to stop this with either 9.♗c4 or 9.g4, or otherwise ignore it with 9.0-0-0.

A) 9. g2-g4

This prevents 9...d5, which would be met by 10.g5, after which 11.♘xd5 simply wins the d-pawn. However, compared to 9.0-0-0, White's position becomes more rigid. Usually the g2-g4 advance as part of a general attack on the kingside is played only when necessary.

The most common continuation is:

9. ...	♗c8-e6
10. 0-0-0	

After 10.♘xe6 fxe6, the weakness on f3 becomes apparent.

10. ...	♘c6xd4
11. ♗e3xd4	♕d8-a5

12. a2-a3	♖a8-b8
13. h2-h4	♖f8-c8

Now White usually simplifies with 14.♘d5, followed by the exchange of queens. He contents himself with a microscopic advantage, without risking a direct assault on Black's castled king.

B) 9. 0-0-0

Ignoring Black's 'threat' and putting his faith in his lead in development and the pressure on the d-file. Black can decide against 9...d5, and instead play 9...♘xd4.

B1) 9. ... ♘c6xd4

10. ♗e3xd4	♗c8-e6

But after

11. ♔c1-b1!	

White has a slight advantage.

Here is an advantage compared to the line with 9.g4. 11.♔b1! prevents the move 11...♕a5, which would be met by 12.♘d5. Black must prepare ...♕a5 by first using two tempi with ...♕c7 and ...♖fc8. He leaves the f8-square to the king to thwart the intermediate check ♘d5xe7+ after ♘d5 ♕d2, which would otherwise be disastrous.

B2)   **9. ...**   **d6-d5**

This is Black's thematic reaction in the Yugoslav Attack. The resulting position is sharper than after 9...♘xd4. Strictly speaking, the d-pawn push is a pawn sacrifice:

10. e4xd5   **♘f6xd5**
11. ♘d4xc6   **b7xc6**

White rarely ventures to accept it; even if after 12.♘xd5 cxd5 13.♕xd5

it is not clear if Black has sufficient compensation after 13...♕c7.

White's generally preferred continuation is

12. ♗e3-d4   **e7-e5**
13. ♗d4-c5

Now Black offers an exchange sacrifice with

13. ...   **♗c8-e6**

banking on his control of the dark-square complex. However, White rarely accepts this Greek gift and continues

14. ♘c3-e4

with a complex position.

C)   **9. ♗f1-c4**

This 'standard' move prevents ...d5 and places the bishop aggressively on the diagonal that points straight at the black king.

However, as always in the opening, a move that brings advantages also has weaknesses: the bishop, be it on c4 or b3 – its usual retreat square – is exposed to an advance by Black's a- and b-pawns; and then after the thematic manoeuvre ...♘e5-c4, it is exchanged for the black knight. Therefore, it is worth asking yourself whether it is worth moving the bishop to b3 only to have it exchanged off. However, Black too must spend time – three moves – to move the knight from b8 to c4. In these variations, opposite-side castling is normal and an extra tempo can be decisive. After 9.♗c4, Black continues to develop:

9. ...   ♗c8-d7
10. 0-0-0

And now Black has several plans at his disposal. It is worth remembering that White can advance the h-pawn before he castles, but this usually leads to a transposition to the main line.

C1)   10. ...   ♕d8-a5

Historically the first approach to development was to place the black queen on a5, then ...♖fc8 and ...♘e5-c4, followed by ...♖xc4. In some variations that were created later, Black plays ...b7-b5 in order to recapture on c4 with the pawn, and frontally attack

White's castled kingside position along the b-file. For White's part, his plan is generally: h4-h5, a possible g2-g4, ♔b1 – which denies Black several tactical possibilities – ♗h6, etc.

Nowadays, only a few enthusiasts play this line.

11. ♗c4-b3   ♖f8-c8

12. ♔c1-b1   ♘c6-e5
13. h2-h4   ♘e5-c4
14. ♗b3xc4   ♖c8xc4
15. ♘d4-b3

Black's best choice is probably to move the queen back to d8, which really makes you doubt the validity of the whole variation.

C2)   10. ...   ♖a8-c8

Currently much more common.

11. ♗c4-b3   ♘c6-e5
12. h2-h4

We are now at another crossroads.

C21)   **12. ...**   **♘e5-c4**
        13. ♗b3xc4   **♖c8xc4**
        14. h4-h5

White sacrifices a pawn for a kingside initiative. After 14...♘xh5 15.g4 ♘f6, White has many playable moves, ranging from the aggressive 16.e5 or 16.♗h6 to more solid moves such as 16.♘de2, 16.♘b3 or 16.♔b1. Against all these options, Black appears to have adequate resources with which he can keep the game dynamically balanced.

C22) **12. ...**   **h7-h5**

The **Soltis Variation**, which has been very popular recently.

In the early days of the Dragon it seemed contradictory to play a move that allowed White to open files on the kingside by the g2-g4 advance. However, practical play has shown that the two moves that White needs to make in preparation for g2-g4 allow Black to find adequate counterplay.

The plan to remove the g7-bishop with 13.♗h6 does not seem to give White an advantage either after 13...♘c4, or 13...♗xh6 14.♕xh6 ♖xc3!

A thematic exchange sacrifice which is practically forced.

Therefore the most popular move has become the preparatory

      13. ♗e3-g5

White removes the bishop from e3 and, reserving the possibility to exchange on f6, he renders the imminent pawn advance g2-g4 more incisive.

It took a long time before black players found an adequate response in this position. The solution was the strange move

      13. ...   **♖c8-c5!**

First played by Genna Sosonko in 1976.

On the 5th rank this rook has both a defensive and an attacking role. It supports the advance ...b7-b5 and in many variations prepares an exchange sacrifice taking the g5-bishop, or the knight after ♘d5. Without this resource the Soltis Variation would not have passed the test of time.

Réti,Richard
Tartakower,Savielly

New York 1924 (11)

1.♘f3 g6 2.e4 c5 3.d4 cxd4 4.♘xd4 ♘f6 5.♘c3 d6 6.♗e2 ♗g7 7.0-0 ♘c6 8.♗e3 0-0 9.♘b3 ♗e6 10.f4 ♕c8 11.h3 ♘e8 12.♕d2 f5 13.exf5 gxf5 14.♖ae1 ♔h8 15.♘d4 ♗g8 16.g4 ♘xd4 17.♗xd4 e5 18.♗e3 fxg4 19.♗xg4 ♗e6 20.f5 ♗xf5 21.♖xf5 ♖xf5 22.♕d3 e4 23.♘xe4 h5 24.♘g3 hxg4 25.♘xf5 ♕e6 26.♖e2 ♗e5 27.♗d4 ♘f6 28.hxg4 ♖g8 29.♗xe5 dxe5 30.♖h2+ ♘h7 31.♘e3 ♖g7 32.♕d8+ ♖g8 33.♕d3 ♖g7 34.♕e4 ♔g8 35.♖d2 ♘f6 36.♖d8+ ♔f7 37.♕xb7+ ♔g6 38.♕f3 ♔g5 39.♖d2 e4 40.♕g3 ♖d7 41.♖xd7 ♘xd7 42.♕f2 ♘c5 43.♕f5+ ♕xf5 44.gxf5 ♘a4 45.b3 ♘c3 46.a4 a5 47.♔f2 ♘a2 48.♔e2 ♔f6 49.♔d2 ♘b4 50.♔c3 ♗e5 51.f6 ♔xf6 52.♔d4 ♔e6 53.♔xe4 ♔d6 54.♔d4 ♘c6+ 55.♔c4 ♘a7 56.c3 ♔c6 57.♔d4 ♘b6 58.♘c4+ ♔a6 59.♔d5 ♘c8 60.♔e6   1-0

Karpov,Anatoly
Sosonko,Genna

Bad Lauterberg 1977 (1)

1.e4 c5 2.♘f3 d6 3.d4 cxd4 4.♘xd4 ♘f6 5.♘c3 g6 6.♗e2 ♗g7 7.0-0 ♘c6 8.♘b3 0-0 9.♗g5 ♗e6 10.♔h1 a5 11.a4 ♘d7 12.f4 ♘b6 13.f5 ♗c4 14.♗xc4 ♘xc4 15.♕e2 ♘b6 16.♕b5 ♘d4 17.♘xd4 ♗xd4 18.♖ad1 ♗g7 19.♗e3 ♘d7 20.♘d5 ♖e8 21.c3 ♗e5 22.♗b6 ♘xb6 23.♘xb6 ♖a6 24.♘c4 ♕b8 25.♘xa5 ♖c8 26.♘c4 ♗xh2 27.♘b6 ♖xb6 28.♕xb6 ♗e5 29.a5 ♖c6 30.♕e3 ♕c7 31.♖d5 ♖a6 32.♕d3 ♔g7 33.♖b5 g5 34.♕d5 ♖a7

35.g4 ♕c8 36.♔g2 ♕d7 37.c4 ♕e8 38.b3 ♕d8 39.♕d2 f6 40.♖h1 ♗f4 41.♕c3 ♕h8 42.♕h3 h5 43.♕xh5 ♕xh5 44.♖xh5 ♗d2 45.b4   1-0

Inarkiev,Ernesto
Khalifman,Alexander

Khanty Mansiysk 2005 (1)

1.e4 c5 2.♘f3 d6 3.d4 cxd4 4.♘xd4 ♘f6 5.♘c3 g6 6.♗e3 ♗g7 7.f3 a6 8.♕d2 b5 9.0-0-0 ♗b7 10.♗h6 ♗xh6 11.♕xh6 ♘bd7 12.♔b1 ♖c8 13.♕d2 b4 14.♘ce2 ♕b6 15.h4 h5 16.♘c1 d5 17.exd5 ♘xd5 18.♖e1 e5 19.♘db3 a5 20.♘d3 0-0 21.♕f2 ♕c7 22.g4 a4 23.♘bc1 a3 24.gxh5 axb2 25.♘b3 e4 26.fxe4 ♘c3+ 27.♔xb2 ♘xe4 28.♕h2 ♕c3+ 29.♔b1 ♗d5 30.♖d1 ♕f6 31.♗h3 ♗xb3 32.axb3 ♖a8 33.♘b2 ♘c3+ 34.♔c1 ♖a1+ 35.♔d2 ♘xd1 36.♖xd1 ♕xb2 37.♖xa1 ♕d4+   0-1

Rauzer,Vsevolod
Chekhover,Vitaly

Leningrad 1936 (8)

1.e4 c5 2.♘f3 d6 3.d4 cxd4 4.♘xd4 ♘f6 5.♘c3 g6 6.f3 ♗g7 7.♗e3 0-0 8.♕d2 ♘c6 9.0-0-0 ♘xd4 10.♗xd4 ♗e6 11.♔b1 ♖c8 12.h4 ♘h5 13.♗xg7 ♔xg7 14.♘d5 ♗xd5 15.exd5 ♘g3 16.♖h2 e5 17.dxe6 fxe6 18.h5 ♘xh5 19.♕xd6 ♕xd6 20.♖xd6 ♖fd8 21.♖xd8 ♖xd8 22.♔c1 ♘g3 23.♗d3 ♖d4 24.♖h3 ♘h5 25.g3 b6 26.♔d2 ♖d5 27.♔e3 ♖g5 28.♔f2 ♖a5 29.a3 ♘f6 30.♖h4 ♖c5 31.♖d4 ♖d5 32.♖c4 ♖c5 33.♖xc5 bxc5 34.b4 cxb4 35.axb4 ♘d5 36.b5 ♘c3 37.♔e3 e5 38.♗c4 h5 39.♔d3 ♘a4 40.♗d5 g5 41.♗c6 h4 42.gxh4 gxh4 43.f4   ½-½

Lahno,Katerina
Jobava,Baadur

Dubai 2004 (2)

1.e4 c5 2.♘f3 d6 3.d4 ♘f6 4.♘c3
cxd4 5.♘xd4 g6 6.♗e3 ♗g7 7.f3
♘c6 8.♕d2 0-0 9.0-0-0 d5 10.♔b1
♘xd4 11.e5 ♘f5 12.exf6 exf6
13.♗c5 d4 14.♗xf8 ♕xf8 15.♘e2N
♘e3 16.♖c1 ♘c4! 17.♕xd4 b5 18.c3
♗f5+ 19.♔a1 ♖d8 20.♕f2 ♖d2
21.♕xa7 ♘xb2 22.♘d4 ♘a4!
23.♘xb5? ♘xc3!! 24.♗c4 ♘xb5
25.♕e3 ♗d3!   0-1

Timman,Jan
Miles,Anthony

Bad Lauterberg 1977 (2)

1.e4 c5 2.♘f3 d6 3.d4 cxd4 4.♘xd4
♘f6 5.♘c3 g6 6.♗e3 ♗g7 7.f3 0-0
8.♕d2 ♘c6 9.0-0-0 d5 10.exd5
♘xd5 11.♘xc6 bxc6 12.♗d4 e5
13.♗c5 ♗e6 14.♘e4 ♖e8 15.h4 ♖b8
16.g4 f5 17.gxf5 gxf5 18.♘d6 ♖f8
19.♘c4 ♔h8 20.♖g1 ♗f6 21.♕h6
♖f7 22.♗h3 ♖d7 23.♗d6 ♘f4
24.♖d2 ♖b5 25.♗f1 ♖d5 26.♖xd5
♘xd5 27.♗xe5 ♖f7 28.♕g5 ♕f8
29.♗xf6+ ♖xf6 30.♘e5 ♘e7 31.♗c4
♗xc4 32.♘d7   1-0

Shirov,Alexey
Tiviakov,Sergey

Dos Hermanas 2003 (5)

1.e4 c5 2.♘f3 d6 3.d4 cxd4 4.♘xd4
♘f6 5.♘c3 g6 6.♗e3 ♗g7 7.f3 ♘c6
8.♕d2 0-0 9.♗c4 ♘d7 10.0-0-0 ♘b6
11.♗b3 ♘a5 12.♕d3 ♗d7 13.♔b1
♖c8 14.g4 ♘ac4 15.h4 ♘e5 16.♕e2
a5 17.h5 a4 18.hxg6 axb3 19.gxh7+
♔h8 20.cxb3 e6 21.f4 ♘c6 22.♘db5

d5 23.♕f2 ♘a8 24.♗c5 ♘e7 25.f5
f6 26.exd5 e5 27.♘d6 ♖c7 28.♘de4
♖c8 29.d6 ♘c6 30.♘d5 ♖f7 31.g5
♘d4 32.♗xd4 exd4 33.gxf6 ♗xf6
34.♘exf6 ♖xf6 35.♕xd4 ♗xf5+
36.♔a1   1-0

Karpov,Anatoly
Gik,Evgeny

Moscow 1968

1.e4 c5 2.♘f3 d6 3.d4 cxd4 4.♘xd4
♘f6 5.♘c3 g6 6.♗e3 ♗g7 7.f3 0-0
8.♗c4 ♘c6 9.♕d2 ♕a5 10.0-0-0
♗d7 11.h4 ♘e5 12.♗b3 ♖fc8 13.h5
♘xh5 14.♗h6 ♗xh6 15.♕xh6 ♖xc3
16.bxc3 ♕xc3 17.♘e2 ♕c5 18.g4
♘f6 19.g5 ♘h5 20.♖xh5 gxh5
21.♖h1 ♕e3+ 22.♔b1 ♕xf3
23.♖xh5 e6 24.g6 ♘xg6 25.♕xh7+
♔f8 26.♖f5 ♕xb3+ 27.axb3 exf5
28.♘f4 ♖d8 29.♕h6+ ♔e8 30.♘xg6
fxg6 31.♕xg6+ ♔e7 32.♕g5+ ♔e8
33.exf5 ♖c8 34.♕g8+ ♔e7
35.♕g7+ ♔d8 36.f6   1-0

Hracek,Zbynek
Cebalo,Miso

Medulin tt 2002 (3)

1.e4 c5 2.♘f3 d6 3.d4 ♘f6 4.♘c3
cxd4 5.♘xd4 g6 6.♗e3 ♗g7 7.f3 0-0
8.♕d2 ♘c6 9.♗c4 ♗d7 10.0-0-0
♕a5 11.♗b3 ♖fc8 12.h4 ♘e5 13.h5
♖xc3 14.bxc3 ♘xh5 15.♗h6 ♗xh6
16.♕xh6 ♘f6 17.♔b2 ♖c8 18.♕e3
♕c5 19.♖h4 a5 20.♖dh1 e6 21.a4
b5 22.axb5 a4 23.♗a2 ♗xb5
24.♖xh7 ♘xh7 25.♕h6 ♕xc3+
26.♔b1 ♗c4 27.♕xh7+ ♔f8
28.♗xc4 ♖xc4 29.♕h4 ♔e8 30.♕f6
♔d7 31.♖h8 ♖c8 32.♖xc8 ♔xc8
33.♘e2 ♕b4+   0-1

Nunn,John
Ward,Christopher

England tt 1997/98 (5)

1.e4 c5 2.♘f3 d6 3.d4 cxd4 4.♘xd4 ♘f6 5.♘c3 g6 6.♗e3 ♗g7 7.f3 ♘c6 8.♕d2 0-0 9.♗c4 ♗d7 10.0-0-0 ♕a5 11.h4 ♘e5 12.♗b3 ♖fc8 13.g4 b5 14.h5 ♘c4 15.♗xc4 bxc4 16.♗h6 ♗h8 17.♘f5 ♖e8 18.♕g5 ♕b6 19.hxg6 fxg6 20.♗g7 ♗xg7 21.♘xg7 ♖eb8 22.♘h5 ♘xh5 23.gxh5 ♗e8 24.b3 cxb3 25.axb3 ♕c5 26.♘d5 ♖b7 27.♘xe7+ ♖xe7 28.♕xe7 ♖c8 29.♖h2 gxh5 30.♖g2+ ♗g6 31.♖xd6 ♕e3+ 32.♖gd2 ♖f8 33.♖d8 ♖xd8 34.♕xd8+ ♔g7 35.♕d4+ ♕xd4 36.♖xd4 h4 37.♔d2 h3 38.♔e3 ♔h6 39.♔f4   1-0

Grischuk,Alexander
Bu Xiangzhi

Calvia ol 2004 (14)

1.e4 c5 2.♘f3 ♘c6 3.♘c3 g6 4.d4 cxd4 5.♘xd4 ♗g7 6.♗e3 ♘f6 7.♗c4 0-0 8.♗b3 d6 9.f3 ♗d7 10.h4 h5 11.♕d2 ♘a5 12.♗h6 ♘xb3 13.♘xb3 a5 14.♘d4 ♗xh6 15.♕xh6 ♕b6 16.0-0-0 ♖fc8 17.g4 ♖xc3 18.bxc3 ♕c5 19.♖d3 ♕e5 20.gxh5 ♘xh5 21.♖g1 ♘f4 22.♖e3 ♖c8 23.♖g5 ♕f6 24.♖xa5 e5 25.♘b3 d5 26.exd5 ♗f5 27.d6 ♕xd6 28.♖axe5 ♕a3+ 29.♔d2 ♕d6+ 30.♘d4 ♘e6 31.♔e1 ♖xc3 32.♘xe6 ♖xe3+ 33.♕xe3 ♗xe6 34.a3 ♕c7 35.h5 ♕xc2 36.hxg6 ♕b1+ 37.♔f2 ♕c2+ 38.♔g3   1-0

Smirnov,Igor
Fedorov,Alexey

Moscow 2007 (3)

1.e4 c5 2.♘f3 d6 3.d4 cxd4 4.♘xd4 ♘f6 5.♘c3 g6 6.♗e3 ♗g7 7.f3 ♘c6

8.♕d2 ♗d7 9.♗c4 0-0 10.0-0-0 ♘e5 11.♗b3 ♖c8 12.♔b1 ♖e8 13.g4 b5 14.g5 b4 15.♘ce2 ♘h5 16.f4 ♘c4 17.♗xc4 ♖xc4 18.b3 ♖c7 19.f5 ♕a8 20.♕d3 a5 21.♖hf1 a4 22.♖f2 axb3 23.cxb3 ♗c8 24.fxg6 fxg6 25.♘b5 ♗a6 26.♕d5+ ♕xd5 27.♖xd5 ♗b7 28.♘a7 ♖d7 29.♘c6 ♗b7 30.♘xb4 e6 31.♖b5 ♗xe4+ 32.♔c1 d5 33.♗c5 d4 34.♖a5 e5 35.a4 ♗f5 36.♖a7 ♖c8   0-1

Karpov,Anatoly
Kortchnoi,Viktor

Moscow m 1974 (2)

1.e4 c5 2.♘f3 d6 3.d4 cxd4 4.♘xd4 ♘f6 5.♘c3 g6 6.♗e3 ♗g7 7.f3 ♘c6 8.♕d2 0-0 9.♗c4 ♗d7 10.h4 ♖c8 11.♗b3 ♘e5 12.0-0-0 ♘c4 13.♗xc4 ♖xc4 14.h5 ♘xh5 15.g4 ♘f6 16.♘de2 ♕a5 17.♗h6 ♗xh6 18.♕xh6 ♖fc8 19.♖d3 ♖4c5 20.g5 ♖xg5 21.♖d5 ♖xd5 22.♘xd5 ♖e8 23.♘ef4 ♗c6 24.e5 ♗xd5 25.exf6 exf6 26.♕xh7+ ♔f8 27.♕h8+   1-0

Ljubojevic,Ljubomir
Miles,Anthony

Brussels 1986 (9)

1.e4 c5 2.♘f3 d6 3.d4 cxd4 4.♘xd4 ♘f6 5.♘c3 g6 6.♗e3 ♗g7 7.f3 0-0 8.♕d2 ♘c6 9.♗c4 ♗d7 10.h4 ♖c8 11.♗b3 h5 12.0-0-0 ♘e5 13.g4 hxg4 14.h5 ♘xh5 15.♗h6 e6 16.♖dg1 ♕f6 17.♗xg7 ♕xg7 18.fxg4 ♘f6 19.g5 ♘h5 20.♘ce2 ♘c4 21.♕b4 a5 22.♕xb7 ♘e5 23.c3 ♘d3+ 24.♔b1 ♘c5 25.♕b6 ♕e5 26.♗c2 ♖b8 27.♕xa5 ♖xb2+ 28.♔xb2 ♘d3+   0-1

Anand,Viswanathan
Kasparov,Garry

New York Wch m 1995 (11)

1.e4 c5 2.♘f3 d6 3.d4 cxd4 4.♘xd4 ♘f6 5.♘c3 g6 6.♗e3 ♗g7 7.f3 0-0 8.♕d2 ♘c6 9.♗c4 ♗d7 10.0-0-0 ♘e5 11.♗b3 ♖c8 12.h4 h5 13.♔b1 ♘c4 14.♗xc4 ♖xc4 15.♘de2 b5 16.♗h6 ♕a5 17.♗xg7 ♔xg7 18.♘f4 ♖fc8 19.♘cd5 ♕xd2 20.♖xd2 ♘xd5 21.♘xd5 ♔f8 22.♖e1 ♖b8 23.b3 ♖c5 24.♘f4 ♖bc8 25.♔b2 a5 26.a3 ♔g7 27.♘d5 ♗e6 28.b4 axb4 29.axb4 ♖c4 30.♘b6 ♖xb4+ 31.♔a3 ♖xc2 **0-1**

Zuidema,Coen
Sosonko,Genna

Netherlands tt 1975/76 (9)

1.e4 c5 2.♘f3 d6 3.d4 cxd4 4.♘xd4 ♘f6 5.♘c3 g6 6.♗e3 ♗g7 7.f3 ♘c6 8.♕d2 0-0 9.♗c4 ♗d7 10.0-0-0 ♘e5 11.♗b3 ♖c8 12.h4 h5 13.♗g5 ♖c5 14.♖he1 b5 15.f4 ♘c4 16.♗xc4

bxc4 17.e5 ♕b6 18.♗xf6 ♖b8 19.b3 exf6 20.e6 fxe6 21.♘xe6 ♗xe6 22.♘a4 cxb3 23.♘xb6 bxa2 24.♔b2 ♖xb6+ 25.♔a3 ♖a6+ 26.♔b4 ♖c4+ 27.♔b5 ♖b6+ 28.♔a5 f5 29.♖e3 ♖b1 30.♖a3 ♗c3+ **0-1**

Almasi,Zoltan
Golubev,Mikhail

Germany Bundesliga 2003/04 (2)

1.e4 c5 2.♘f3 d6 3.d4 cxd4 4.♘xd4 ♘f6 5.♘c3 g6 6.♗e3 ♗g7 7.f3 ♘c6 8.♕d2 0-0 9.♗c4 ♗d7 10.h4 ♘e5 11.♗b3 ♖c8 12.0-0-0 h5 13.♗g5 ♖c5 14.♔b1 ♖e8 15.♗h6 ♗h8 16.g4 ♕a5 17.g5 ♘h7 18.f4 ♘c4 19.♕d3 ♘a3+ 20.♔c1 e6 21.♘ce2 d5 22.exd5 exd5 23.f5 ♘xc2 24.♗xc2 ♗xf5 25.♘xf5 ♕xa2 26.♘fd4 ♕a1+ 27.♔d2 ♕a5+ 28.♘c3 ♖c4 29.♘b3 ♕b4 30.♔c1 ♖xc3 31.bxc3 ♗xc3 32.♖df1 d4 33.♖h3 a5 34.♖hf3 ♕a3+ 35.♔d1 ♕e7 36.♘d2 ♕d7 37.♖xf7 ♕g4+ 38.♕f3 ♗xd2 39.♕xg4 **1-0**

Sicilian Defence Scheveningen Variation

1.e4 c5 2.♘f3 d6 3.d4 cxd4
4.♘xd4 ♘f6 5.♘c3 e6

This variation, characterized by black pawns on e6 and d6, which control many squares on the 5th rank, can also be reached by playing Black's 2nd and 5th moves in reverse order; in particular, if Black dislikes the possible simplification with 3.♗b5+.

It is currently very popular, especially with top level players. It had its official debut in 1923, when Euwe used it against Maróczy in the Dutch town of Scheveningen, which is how it got its name. As with other variations of the Open Sicilian (when White advances his pawn to d4), Black is left with an extra centre pawn.

The e6- and d6-pawns perform a defensive role and Black's counterplay is focused on the queenside along the c-file and the use of the a- and b-pawns, which are generally played to a6 and b5, but sometimes the a-pawn goes directly

to a5. For his part, White has a good space advantage and this allows him to implement a number of strategies, marked by their varying degrees of aggressiveness. However, most of the time White concentrates on kingside play and he usually limits himself to preventive measures on the queenside (such as a2-a4, to stop ...b7-b5).

All this means that the **Scheveningen** produces positions which are strategically highly complex. They are also more flexible than, for example, the comparatively rigid **Dragon Variation**, even if in some variations of the Scheveningen – such as the **Velimirovic Attack** – there are also long sequences of forced moves that leave little space for personal interpretation. Another example of the Scheveningen's greater flexibility is evident when you compare it with its sister variation, the **Najdorf**, to which there are many transpositions. The fact that ...a7-a6 has not yet been played allows for more options in some lines. For example, it is not uncommon to develop the bishop to c6 via d7, after the exchange of knights on d4.

Black also has an advantage compared to the Najdorf in the lines where White develops his king's bishop to c4, as Black can immediately put White's centre under pressure; for example, with the manoeuvre ♘b8-a6-c5, from where the knight can defend e6 and possibly be exchanged for the bishop on b3.

Another example is

6. ♗c1-g5

which for years has been the main line against the **Najdorf**. But here it is not as effective, since after

| 6. | ... | | ♗f8-e7 |

and 7...h6, Black has some tactics based on the motif ...♘xe4.

However, it is true that with the pawn already played to e6, the freeing advance to e5, which is so frequent in the Najdorf, requires an extra tempo.

The variations that we will look at are: 6.g3, 6.♗e3, 6.g4, 6.f4 and 6.♗e2. For the lines in which the king's bishop is developed to c4, we refer you to the following section.

Fianchetto Variation

| 6. | g2-g3 |

This is a positional variation, as are all the lines against the Sicilian that feature a fianchetto. Its aim is to make the ...d7-d5 advance more difficult. How-

ever, unlike other white fianchetto variations, play can easily become very aggressive here. Once White stabilizes the centre, he can attack on the kingside by advancing the g-pawn again in a kind of **Keres Attack Deferred**.

The following line is a typical example:

6.	...	a7-a6
7.	♗f1-g2	♕d8-c7
8.	0-0	♘b8-c6
9.	a2-a4!?	♗f8-e7
10.	♗c1-e3	0-0
11.	♕d1-e2	♖a8-b8
12.	f2-f4	♘c6-a5
13.	♖a1-d1	♘a5-c4
14.	♗e3-c1	

with a complicated game and chances for both sides.

English Attack

| 6. | ♗c1-e3 |

This line is very fashionable nowadays. We really should call it the **Scheveningen English Attack**. Developed in the 1980s, it is above all the work of a group of English grandmasters – most famously John Nunn, Nigel Short and Murray Chandler.

White imitates the **Yugoslav Attack** against the **Dragon** with ♗e3, f3, ♕d2,

0-0-0, g4 and h4, in order to start a direct attack against Black's king.

Black cannot remain passive in the face of this initiative, so he usually responds energetically in the centre with ...a7-a6, ...b7-b5, ...♗b7, ...♘d7-c5 and the thematic ...d6-d5.

The resulting positions are very complex, so you will need steady nerves and a good memory. With time the following has established itself as the main line (look at the games at the end of this section):

6.	♗c1-e3	a7-a6
7.	♕d1-d2	b7-b5
8.	f2-f3	♘b8-d7
9.	g2-g4	h7-h6
10.	0-0-0	♗c8-b7
11.	h2-h4	b5-b4!
12.	♘c3-a4	♕d8-a5
13.	b2-b3	♘d7-c5
14.	a2-a3!	♘c5xa4
15.	a3xb4	♕a5-c7
16.	b3xa4	d6-d5
17.	e4-e5	♘f6-d7
18.	f3-f4	♘d7-b6

and Black's compensation for the pawn is difficult to evaluate.

Please note that this variation is classified under the Scheveningen because of convention. In reality, most of the time you will reach it via the Najdorf when White plays 6.♗e3 (or 6.f3) and Black prefers to play 6....e6 – which is often the case – instead of the thematic 6...e5, or the modern 6...♘g4.

The Keres Attack

6. g2-g4

The much-feared Keres Attack is the principal bugbear for Scheveningen devotees. White immediately expands on the kingside with decidedly unfriendly intentions.

It had its victorious debut in 1943 when it was used by the Estonian champion Paul Keres in a game against Efim Bogoljubow. This was the first of many victories that this attack has notched up, and it has become so feared that many prefer to first play 5...a6 (Najdorf), so that the g4-square is still controlled by two pieces, and only after White replies 6.♗e2, 6.♗e3, or 6.f4, transpose with 6....e6 to the Scheveningen. However, obviously, the Najdorf leaves you with problems to deal with too. Number one is 6.♗g5, as we have already mentioned.

Back to 6.g4. Now the moves 6...♘c6 and 6...a6 are playable; but after 7.g5, White has achieved the space advantage he was seeking. For this reason

6. ...   h7-h6

is the most popular move for Black. It has its advantages and disadvantages. White's initiative is slowed down, in the sense that if he wants to play h2-h4 and g4-g5 he must first defend the rook on h1, and when the pawn advance takes place, the h8-rook can play a more active role. In addition, the extra tempo that is gained allows Black to make the thematic pawn advance ...d6-d5.

However, by playing 6...h6 Black has weakened his kingside and castling there is out of the question; yet castling queenside also has its risks.

White's most common continuation is

7. h2-h4   ♘b8-c6
8. ♖h1-g1

Now Black usually responds with

8. ...   h6-h5!?

To break up White's pawn front and create an outpost on g4.

Also here we should underline that there is another possible transposition from the **Najdorf**. If after

6. ...   a7-a6

White plays

7. ♗c1-e3

– instead of 7.g5 –

the position has transposed to the **Perenyi Attack**. This has the ECO code B81, but it is usually reached via the Najdorf (after 5...a6 6.♗e3 e6 7.g4!?), and rarely by means of the Scheveningen (after 6.♗e3 a6 7.g4). The variation is very dangerous (for both players!). A good example is:

7. ...   e6-e5!?
8. ♘d4-f5   g7-g6

Now White is virtually forced to sacrifice a piece with

9. g4-g5   g6xf5
10. e4xf5

and Black, instead of retreating the knight from f6 must respond energetically with

10. ...   d6-d5!
11. g5xf6

11.♕f3 d4 12.0-0-0 is another frequent guest of the tournament arena.

11. ...	**d5-d4**
12. ♗f1-c4	

The theoretical implications of recent play from this position have yet to be fully explored.

Scheveningen with 6.f4

White has another very interesting line to play against the Scheveningen:

6.	**f2-f4**

This variation is characterized by White playing fairly aggressively without burning all his bridges. This is particularly the case when White proceeds (if Black allows) with ♕f3 and 0-0-0, and then attacks on the kingside with his pawns. If Black plays ...a7-a6 you transpose to variations more usually reached by way of the **Najdorf**, but classified under the Scheveningen Variation. However, Black can also forgo ...a7-a6 and play other promising lines with ...♘xd4 and ...♗d7-c6, or push the pawn to e5 at the right moment. This costs a tempo, but it does break up White's pawn front.

Notwithstanding all this,

6. ...	**a7-a6**

remains the most played move in response to 6.f4. Usually there follows

7. ♕d1-f3	**♕d8-b6**

with sharp play and possibilities for both sides. For example: 8.♘b3 ♕c7 9.g4 b5 10.♗d3 ♗b7 11.g5 ♘fd7.

Classical Variation

6.	♗f1-e2

This remains a popular choice.

White usually proceeds with ♗e3, f4, 0-0, and a possible a4, ♔h1, and then it is not rare for him to put the bishop on d3, the queen on g3, and after ♖ad1 or ♖ae1, to get ready for the pawn advance e4-e5. He can also calmly plan a possible g2-g4-g5 push. White's pieces are flexibly placed, and he must be careful to prevent Black's counterplay, which can become very menacing in case White rushes ahead without sufficient thought. For his part, Black can continue in classical fashion by exchanging on d4, in order to put White's centre under pressure with ...♛c7, ...a7-a6, ...b7-b5, ...♝b7 and ...b5-b4.

If White puts his pawn on a4, to limit Black's activity on the queenside, Black can adopt a type of **Hedgehog formation** which is very adaptable and difficult to dent.

Therefore, as in the 6.f4 line, it has recently become more popular to forgo the 'Najdorf' pawn advance ...a7-a6, and instead immediately seek counterplay in the centre with ...♞xd4 (obviously after ...♞c6) followed by ...♝d7-c6. Alternatively, Black can push his pawn to e5, which simplifies, and gives Black a playable position, even if there are fewer prospects of winning.

Another modern set-up, which in the past was underestimated, is for Black to develop his knight to d7 instead of c6. It is certainly more passively placed here and has less influence on the centre. However, if Black manages to successfully complete his development, he can then relocate it actively on c5, or on the c4-square via b6.

Of the many plans and strategies available, we will look at the main line, by which we mean the line that is most frequently played in tournaments:

6.	...	a7-a6
7.	0-0	♝f8-e7
8.	f2-f4	0-0
9.	♔g1-h1	♛d8-c7
10.	a2-a4	

White can also refrain from this and instead opt for the old plan, which is more direct and entails more risk: 10.♛e1 ♞c6 11.♝e3 ♞xd4 12.♝xd4 b5 13.a3 ♝b7 14.♛g3, with sharp play.

10.	...	♞b8-c6
11.	♝c1-e3	

For the reasons explained above, this position is more often reached via the **Najdorf**.

Here is an example of the type of play that can follow:

11.	...	♜f8-e8
12.	♝e2-f3	♜a8-b8
13.	g2-g4	♞c6xd4
14.	♝e3xd4	e6-e5
15.	f4xe5	d6xe5
16.	♝d4-a7	♜b8-a8
17.	g4-g5	♜e8-d8
18.	♛d1-e2	♞f6-e8
19.	♝a7-e3	♝c8-e6

with a complicated position.

Movsesian,Sergey
Sakaev,Konstantin
Panormo Ech blitz 2002 (10)

1.e4 c5 2.♞f3 d6 3.♞c3 a6 4.d4 cxd4 5.♞xd4 ♞f6 6.g3 e6 7.♝g2 ♛c7 8.0-0 ♞c6 9.♜e1 ♝e7 10.♞xc6 bxc6 11.e5 dxe5 12.♜xe5 0-0 13.♝f4 ♛b7 14.♞a4 ♜d8 15.♛f3 ♞d5 16.♝d2 ♝f6 17.♜e4 e5 18.♜ae1 ♞e7 19.♝a5 ♜d5 20.♝c3 ♝f5 21.♜b4 ♛c7 22.♞b6 ♜ad8 23.♞xd5 cxd5 24.g4 ♝e6 25.g5 ♝xg5 26.♝xe5 ♛xc2 27.♛g3 ♝h6

28.♖b7 ♘f5 29.♕c3 ♕a4 30.♕c7
♖f8 31.♗d6 ♘xd6 32.♕xd6 ♗f4
33.♕e7 ♕c6 34.h3 ♗d6 35.♖xe6
1-0

Anand,Viswanathan
Topalov,Veselin

Sofia 2005 (1)

1.e4 c5 2.♘f3 d6 3.d4 cxd4 4.♘xd4
♘f6 5.♘c3 a6 6.♗e3 e6 7.f3 b5
8.g4 h6 9.♕d2 b4 10.♘a4 ♘bd7
11.0-0-0 ♘e5 12.b3 ♗d7 13.♘b2
d5 14.♗f4 ♘xf3 15.♘xf3 ♘xe4
16.♕d4 f6 17.♗d3 ♗c5 18.♗xe4
♗xd4 19.♗g6+ ♔f8 20.♖xd4 a5
21.♖e1 ♗e8 22.♘h4 e5 23.♖d2 a4
24.bxa4 ♔g8 25.♗g3 d4 26.♖d3
h5 27.♗xe8 ♕xe8 28.g5 ♖c8 29.g6
♖h6 30.♖xd4 ♖xg6 31.♘xg6 ♕xg6
32.♖d2 ♖c3 33.♖ed1 ♔h7 34.♔b1
♕f5 35.♗e1 ♖a3 36.♖d6 ♖h3 37.a5
♖xh2 38.♖c1 ♕e4 39.a6 ♕a8
40.♗xb4 h4 41.♗c5 h3 42.♘d3
♖d2 43.♖b6 h2 44.♘f2 ♕d5
45.♗e3 ♖e2 46.♖b3 f5 47.a7 ♖xe3
48.♖xe3 ♕b7+ 49.♖b3 ♕xa7
50.♘h1 f4 51.c4 e4 52.c5 e3 53.c6
e2 54.c7 ♕xc7 55.♖xc7 e1♕+
56.♖c1 ♕e4+ 57.♔a1 ♕d4+
58.♔b1 ♕e4+ 59.♔a1 ♕d4+
60.♔b1 ♕e4+ ½-½

Kasparov,Garry
Topalov,Veselin

Wijk aan Zee 2001 (7)

1.e4 c5 2.♘f3 d6 3.d4 cxd4 4.♘xd4
♘f6 5.♘c3 a6 6.♗e3 e6 7.f3 b5 8.g4
h6 9.♕d2 ♘bd7 10.0-0-0 ♗b7 11.h4
b4 12.♘a4 ♕a5 13.b3 ♘c5 14.a3
♘xa4 15.axb4 ♕c7 16.bxa4 d5
17.e5 ♘d7 18.f4 ♘b6 19.♖h3 ♘c4
20.♕c3 ♖c8 21.♗d2 ♗e7 22.♗e1

♖b8 23.f5 ♗c8 24.♗xc4 dxc4
25.♕f3 ♗d7 26.fxe6 fxe6 27.g5
hxg5 28.hxg5 ♖xh3 29.♕xh3 ♕xe5
30.♕h5+ ♔f8 31.♘f3 ♕e3+
32.♔b2 ♗e8 33.♕h8+ ♔f7 34.♗c3
1-0

Fedorov,Alexey
Vera,Reynaldo

Linares 2002 (6)

1.e4 c5 2.♘f3 d6 3.d4 cxd4 4.♘xd4
♘f6 5.♘c3 a6 6.f3 e6 7.♗e3 b5 8.g4
h6 9.♕d2 ♘bd7 10.0-0-0 ♗b7 11.h4
b4 12.♘a4 ♕a5 13.b3 ♘c5 14.a3
♘xa4 15.axb4 ♕c7 16.bxa4 d5
17.e5 ♘d7 18.f4 ♘b6 19.♖h3 ♘xa4
20.♗f2 ♖c8 21.♗e1 ♖b8 22.f5 ♗c8
23.♖b3 ♖b6 24.fxe6 fxe6 25.g5
♗d7 26.♕d3 hxg5 27.♕g6+ ♔d8
28.♕xg5+ ♔c8 29.♖dd3 ♔b7
30.♖f3 g6 31.♔b1 ♖h5 32.♕xg6
♕xe5 33.♗f2 ♖h8 34.♖f7 ♖d6
35.♖a3 ♔a8 36.♖xd7 ♖xd7 37.♖xa4
♗d6 38.♖xa6+ ♔b7 39.♘xe6 ♖c8
40.♖a7+ 1-0

Keres,Paul
Bogoljubow,Efim

Salzburg 1943 (1)

1.e4 c5 2.♘e2 e6 3.d4 cxd4 4.♘xd4
♘f6 5.♘c3 d6 6.g4 ♘c6 7.g5 ♘xd4
8.♕xd4 ♘d7 9.♗e3 a6 10.♗e2 ♕c7
11.f4 b6 12.f5 ♘e5 13.fxe6 fxe6
14.a4 ♗e7 15.h4 ♕c5 16.♕d2 ♕c7
17.♖f1 ♗b7 18.♗d4 ♖f8 19.0-0-0
♖xf1 20.♖xf1 ♗d8 21.♕f4 ♘g6
22.♕g4 ♕e7 23.♕h5 e5 24.♗e3
♗c7 25.♕xh7 ♘f4 26.♗xf4 exf4
27.♗h5+ ♔d7 28.♗g4+ ♔c6 29.♕f5
b5 30.♕d5+ ♔b6 31.♕d4+ ♔c6
32.♘d5 1-0

Karpov,Anatoly
Dorfman,Iosif

Moscow ch-URS 1976 (8)

1.e4 c5 2.♘f3 d6 3.d4 cxd4 4.♘xd4 ♘f6 5.♘c3 e6 6.g4 ♗e7 7.g5 ♘fd7 8.h4 ♘c6 9.♗e3 a6 10.♕e2 ♕c7 11.0-0-0 b5 12.♘xc6 ♕xc6 13.♗d4 b4 14.♘d5 exd5 15.♗xg7 ♖g8 16.exd5 ♕c7 17.♗f6 ♘e5 18.♗xe5 dxe5 19.f4 ♗f5 20.♗h3 ♗xh3 21.♖xh3 ♖c8 22.fxe5 ♕c4 23.♖dd3 ♕f4+ 24.♔b1 ♖c4 25.d6 ♖e4 26.♖he3 ♖xe3 27.♖xe3 ♕xh4 28.♕f3 ♕xg5 29.♖e1 ♕g2 30.♕f5 ♖g6 31.♖f1 ♕d5 32.dxe7 ♔xe7 33.♕f4 a5 34.♕h4+ ♔e8 35.♕xh7 ♕f3 36.♕h8+ ♔e7 37.♕h4+ ♔e8 38.♕c4 ♕b7 39.b3 ♖e6 40.♖g1 ♖xe5 41.♖g8+ ♔e7 42.♕h4+ ♔d7 43.♕f6 ♖e7 44.♕f5+ ♔d6 45.♕xa5 ♖e5 46.♕d8+ ♔e6 47.♔b2 f6 48.♖f8 ♕g7 49.♕c8+ ♔d5 50.♕c4+ **1-0**

Karpov,Anatoly
Sax,Gyula

Linares 1983 (3)

1.e4 c5 2.♘f3 e6 3.d4 cxd4 4.♘xd4 ♘f6 5.♘c3 d6 6.g4 h6 7.♖g1 ♗e7 8.♗e3 ♘c6 9.♕e2 ♗d7 10.h4 ♘xd4 11.♗xd4 e5 12.♗e3 ♗c6 13.♕d3 ♕a5 14.0-0-0 ♘xe4 15.♘xe4 d5 16.♕b3 dxe4 17.♗c4 ♖f8 18.♖d5 ♗xd5 19.♗xd5 ♖d8 20.♗c4 ♗b4 21.c3 b5 22.♗e2 ♗d6 23.♕d5 ♔e7 24.♗c5 ♗xc5 25.♕xe5+ ♔d7 26.♕xc5 ♕c7 27.♕f5+ ♔e7 28.♕xe4+ ♔d7 29.♕f5+ ♔e7 30.♖e1 ♖d6 31.♗c4+ ♔d8 32.♗xb5 a6 33.♗a4 g6 34.♕f3 ♔c8 35.♖e7 ♖d1+ 36.♔xd1 ♕xe7 37.♕a8+ ♔c7 38.♕a7+ ♔d6 39.♕b6+ **1-0**

Nevednichy,Vladislav
Sax,Gyula

Hungary tt 2001/02 (5)

1.e4 c5 2.♘f3 e6 3.d4 cxd4 4.♘xd4 ♘f6 5.♘c3 d6 6.g4 h6 7.♗g2 ♘c6 8.h3 ♗d7 9.f4 ♘xd4 10.♕xd4 ♗c6 11.♗e3 ♗e7 12.0-0-0 ♘d7 13.♕d2 ♕c7 14.h4 b5 15.g5 ♘b6 16.b3 0-0-0 17.♕d3 b4 18.♘b5 ♕b7 19.♘d4 ♗d7 20.♕d2 d5 21.exd5 ♘xd5 22.♘f5 ♗c6 23.♘xe7+ ♕xe7 24.♗d4 ♘c3 25.♖de1 ♘b5 26.♗xc6 ♘xd4 27.♕g2 ♕c7 28.♗a8 ♖d7 29.gxh6 gxh6 30.♖e5 f6 31.♖e4 ♔b8 32.♖d1 ♖hd8 33.♖d3 a5 34.♖e1 ♘e2+ 35.♔b1 ♘xf4 36.♖xd7 ♘xg2 37.♖xc7 ♘xe1 38.♖e7 **0-1**

Timman,Jan
Smeets,Jan

Hilversum ch-NED 2006 (6)

1.e4 c5 2.♘f3 d6 3.d4 ♘f6 4.♘c3 cxd4 5.♘xd4 a6 6.♗e3 e6 7.g4 e5 8.♘f5 g6 9.g5 gxf5 10.exf5 d5 11.♕f3 d4 12.0-0-0 ♘bd7 13.♗c4 ♕c7 14.♗xd4 exd4 15.♖he1+ ♘e5 16.gxf6 ♗d6 17.♖xd4 ♗d7 18.♗xf7+ ♔d8 19.♕d5 ♘xf7 20.♕xf7 ♔c8 21.♘d5 ♕a5 22.b4 **1-0**

Naiditsch,Arkady
Belov,Vladimir

Moscow 2007 (2)

1.e4 c5 2.♘f3 d6 3.d4 cxd4 4.♘xd4 ♘f6 5.♘c3 a6 6.♗e3 e6 7.g4 e5 8.♘f5 g6 9.g5 gxf5 10.exf5 d5 11.gxf6 d4 12.♗c4 ♕c7 13.♕d3 dxe3 14.f4 ♗b4 15.0-0-0 ♗xc3 16.bxc3 ♘c6 17.♖hg1 ♖f8 18.♕xe3 ♗xf5 19.♕c5 ♖d8 20.♗d5 ♖xd5 21.♖xd5 ♗e6 22.♖d6 exf4 23.♖g7

313

♗d7 24.♖d1 ♗e6 25.♖e1 ♕c8
26.♕d6 ♗d7 27.♕xf4 ♕d8 28.♖eg1
♕b8 29.♕h6 ♕d6 30.♖1g2 ♕a3+
31.♔d1 ♕xc3 32.♖7g3 ♕a1+
33.♔d2 ♕d4+ 34.♔c1 ♕a1+
35.♔d2 ♕d4+ 36.♔c1 ♕c5 37.♖d2
♕e5 38.c3 ♕c5 39.♕f4 ♕e5
40.♕f2 ♕a5 41.♕f4 ♕e5   ½-½

Polgar,Judit
Kasparov,Garry
Geneva rapid 1996 (3)

1.e4 c5 2.♘f3 d6 3.d4 cxd4 4.♘xd4
♘f6 5.♘c3 a6 6.f4 e6 7.♕f3 ♕b6
8.♘b3 ♕c7 9.g4 b5 10.g5 ♘fd7
11.♗e3 ♘b6 12.0-0-0 ♘8d7 13.♕h3
b4 14.♘e2 ♘c4 15.♔b1 ♗b7
16.♘ed4 ♘xe3 17.♕xe3 g6 18.♗h3
♕b6 19.♖hf1 0-0-0 20.c3 ♔b8
21.cxb4 ♕xb4 22.♖c1 ♘c5 23.♖fd1
♗e7 24.e5 ♘xb3 25.axb3 ♖c8
26.♗f1 ♕b6 27.b4 ♖hd8 28.b5 axb5
29.♗xb5 dxe5 30.♕xe5+ ♗d6
31.♕e3 ♖xc1+ 32.♖xc1 ♗c7
33.♘c6+ ♗xc6 34.♕xb6+ ♗xb6
35.♖xc6 ♗e3 36.♖c4 ♖d5 37.♖e4
♗d2 38.♗e8 ♖f5 39.♖d4 ♗xf4
40.♖d8+ ♔c7 41.♖d7+ ♔c8 42.♖xf7
♔d8 43.♖xf5 exf5 44.♗f7 ♔e7
45.♗g8 ♔f8 46.♗d5 ♗xh2 47.♔c2
♗f4 48.♔d3 ♗xg5 49.b4 ♗d8
50.♔e3 ♔g7 51.♔f4 ♔f6 52.b5 h5
53.♔g3 g5 54.♔f3 g4+ 55.♔g2 h4
56.♔f2 ♗b6+ 57.♔g2 h3+ 58.♔g3
♔g5 59.♔h2 ♗c7+ 60.♔g1 g3   0-1

Pantaleoni,Claudio
Zoldan,Matteo
Bratto 1997 (2)

1.♘f3 d6 2.e4 c5 3.d4 cxd4 4.♘xd4
♘f6 5.♘c3 e6 6.f4 a6 7.♕f3 ♕b6
8.♘b3 ♕c7 9.♗d3 b5 10.g4 ♗b7

11.g5 ♘fd7 12.♗d2 ♘c5 13.0-0 ♘c6
14.♖ae1 g6 15.♘d5 exd5 16.exd5+
♘e7 17.♗a5 ♕c8 18.f5 ♘xb3
19.fxg6 ♕c5+ 20.♖f2 ♗xd5
21.gxf7+ ♔d7 22.♕g4+ ♔c6
23.cxb3 ♘g6 24.♗b4 ♘e5 25.♖xe5
♕xf2+ 26.♔xf2 dxe5 27.♗e4 ♗c5+
28.♗xc5 ♔xc5 29.b4+ ♔d4
30.♕d1+ ♔xe4 31.♕f3+ ♔d4
32.♕e3+ ♔c4 33.♕c3X   1-0

So,Wesley
Belov,Vladimir
Manila 2006 (9)

1.e4 c5 2.♘f3 d6 3.d4 cxd4 4.♘xd4
♘f6 5.♘c3 a6 6.f4 e6 7.♕f3 ♕b6
8.♘b3 ♕c7 9.♗d3 b5 10.g4 ♗b7
11.g5 ♘fd7 12.♕h3 g6 13.♖f1 ♗g7
14.f5 exf5 15.exf5 0-0 16.♗e3 ♖e8
17.0-0-0 ♘e5 18.♗e4 ♗xe4
19.♘xe4 ♘bd7 20.♘xd6 ♘c4
21.♘xc4 bxc4 22.fxg6 hxg6
23.♖xd7 ♖xe3 24.♖fxf7 ♗xb2+
25.♔b1 ♖xh3 26.♖xc7 ♗e5
27.♖ce7 cxb3 28.axb3 ♖xh2 29.♖f1
♗g7 30.♖e6 ♔h7 31.♖c6 a5
32.♔a2 ♖e8 33.♖f7 ♖e1 34.b4 a4
35.♖xg7+ ♔xg7 36.b5 ♖ee2
37.♔b1 ♖e5   0-1

Svidler,Peter
Lautier,Joel
Calvia ol 2004 (10)

1.e4 c5 2.♘f3 e6 3.d4 cxd4 4.♘xd4
♘c6 5.♘c3 a6 6.♗e2 d6 7.♗e3 ♘f6
8.f4 ♗e7 9.♕d2!? 0-0 10.0-0-0 ♘d7
11.♗f3 ♖b8 12.♘ce2 ♕a5 13.♘xc6!
♕xd2+ 14.♖xd2 bxc6 15.♖hd1 ♘b6
16.♗xb6! ♖xb6 17.♖xd6!± ♗xd6
18.♖xd6 e5 19.fxe5 ♖e8 20.♘d4
♔f8 21.e6 ♗xe6 22.e5 ♗c4 23.b3
♗f1 24.♘xc6 g5 25.a4 g4 26.♗d5

♖xe5 27.♖d8+ ♖e8 28.♖d7 ♖e1+
29.♔b2 ♖d1 30.♖xf7+ ♔e8
31.♖e7+ ♔f8 32.♖e5 ♖d2 33.♔c1!
♖f2 34.♖g5 ♔e8 35.♖xg4 ♔d7
36.♘e5+ ♔d6 37.♘c4+ ♗xc4
38.♗xc4 ♔c5 39.♗d3 h6 40.a5
♖bf6 41.♔b2 ♖2f4 42.♖g7 ♖f7
43.♖g3 ♔b4 44.♗xa6 ♔xa5 45.♗d3
♖f2 46.♖h3 ♖7f6 47.♖h5+ ♔b6
48.g4 ♖d6 49.♔a3 ♖g2 50.h3 ♖g3
51.♔b4 ♖d4+ 52.♔c3 ♖d6 53.♔c4
♖f3 54.b4+− ♖f4+ 55.♔b3 ♖f3
56.♔a4 ♖g3 57.♗e4 ♖c3 58.♗d3
♔b7 59.h4 ♖c8 60.g5 hxg5 61.hxg5
♖d4 62.g6 ♖g4 63.♗f5   1-0

Ljubojevic,Ljubomir
Andersson,Ulf

Wijk aan Zee 1976 (3)

1.e4 c5 2.♘f3 e6 3.d4 cxd4 4.♘xd4
♘c6 5.♘c3 ♕c7 6.♗e2 a6 7.0-0 ♘f6
8.♗e3 ♗e7 9.f4 d6 10.♕e1 0-0
11.♕g3 ♗d7 12.e5 dxe5 13.fxe5
♘xe5 14.♗f4 ♗d6 15.♖ad1 ♕b8
16.♖d3 ♘e8 17.♘e4 ♗c7 18.♖c3
♘c6 19.♗xc7 ♘xd4 20.♗d3 ♕a7
21.♘c5 ♗b5 22.♗e5 ♘c6 23.♗xh7+
♔xh7 24.♖f4 f6 25.♖h4+ ♔g8
26.♕h3 ♘d8 27.♗d4 b6 28.♘xe6
♘xe6 29.♕xe6+ ♕f7 30.♕e4 g5
31.♖h6 ♖a7 32.♖ch3 ♕g7 33.♖g6
♖ff7 34.c4   1-0

Fernandes,Antonio
Arlandi,Ennio

Leon Ech-tt 2001 (5)

1.e4 c5 2.♘f3 e6 3.d4 cxd4 4.♘xd4
♘f6 5.♘c3 d6 6.♗e3 a6 7.♗e2 ♕c7
8.f4 ♗e7 9.0-0 0-0 10.♔h1 ♘c6
11.♕e1 ♘xd4 12.♗xd4 b5 13.a3
♗b7 14.♕g3 ♗c6 15.♖ad1 ♕b7

16.♗f3 ♖ac8 17.♖fe1 b4? 18.axb4
♕xb4 19.♘d5! ♗xd5 20.♗c3 ♕a4
21.exd5 ♕xc2 22.dxe6 ♖c7 23.♗e4
♕a4? 24.♗xf6 ♗xf6 25.exf7+ ♔h8
26.♕h3   1-0

Anand,Viswanathan
Kasparov,Garry

New York Wch m 1995 (9)

1.e4 c5 2.♘f3 d6 3.d4 cxd4 4.♘xd4
♘f6 5.♘c3 a6 6.♗e2 e6 7.0-0 ♗e7
8.a4 ♘c6 9.♗e3 0-0 10.f4 ♕c7
11.♔h1 ♖e8 12.♗f3 ♗d7 13.♘b3
♘a5 14.♘xa5 ♕xa5 15.♕d3 ♖ad8
16.♖fd1 ♗c6 17.b4 ♕c7 18.b5 ♗d7
19.♖ab1 axb5 20.♘xb5 ♗xb5
21.♕xb5 ♖a8 22.c4 e5 23.♗b6 ♕c8
24.fxe5 dxe5 25.a5 ♗f8 26.h3 ♕e6
27.♖d5 ♘xd5? 28.exd5 ♕g6 29.c5
e4 30.♗e2 ♖e5 31.♕d7 ♖g5 32.♖g1
e3 33.d6 ♖g3 34.♕xb7 ♕e6
35.♔h2   1-0

Adams,Michael
Topalov,Veselin

Wijk aan Zee 2006 (2)

1.e4 c5 2.♘f3 d6 3.d4 cxd4 4.♘xd4
♘f6 5.♘c3 a6 6.♗e2 e6 7.0-0 ♗e7
8.a4 ♘c6 9.♗e3 0-0 10.f4 ♕c7
11.♔h1 ♖e8 12.♗f3 ♗f8 13.♕d2
♘a5 14.b3 ♖b8 15.♖ad1 ♘c6
16.♗f2 ♘d7 17.♗g3 ♘xd4 18.♕xd4
b5 19.axb5 axb5 20.b4 g6 21.e5 d5
22.f5 gxf5 23.♘xd5 ♕c4 24.♕d2 h6
25.h3 exd5 26.♗xd5 ♕xb4 27.c3
♕c5 28.♖xf5 ♖e6 29.♖xf7 ♘b6
30.♖df1 ♘xd5 31.♖xf8+ ♕xf8
32.♖xf8+ ♔xf8 33.♕xd5 ♔e8
34.♗h4 ♗d7 35.♗f6 b4 36.♕e4
♗c8 37.cxb4 ♖b7 38.♕g6+ ♔d7
39.♕xh6 ♔c7 40.♕f4 ♔b8 41.h4
♖c7 42.h5   1-0

Sicilian Defence
Sozin-Velimirovic Attack

1.e4 c5 2.♘f3 d6 3.d4 cxd4
4.♘xd4 ♘f6 5.♘c3 ♘c6/a6
6.♗c4

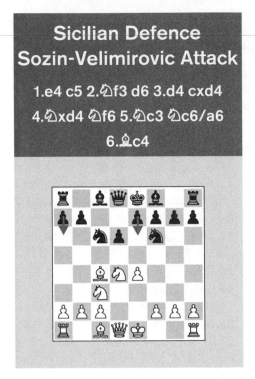

In this section we will discuss the variations in which White plays ♗c4 on the 6th move against the **Scheveningen**, the **Najdorf**, or the **Classical Sicilian**. It is evident that there are many strategic similarities and transpositions, and thus it seemed logical to look at them together rather than in the respective sections for each variation. The development of the bishop to c4 gives a clear strategic quality to each variation.

The Russian master Veniamin Sozin (1896-1956), whose name has become attached to this system, was not the first to play 6.♗c4. You can see examples of it being played occasionally in some 19th century games. However, Sozin was the first to show what White's best plan is in some games that were played in the 1930s. This plan is to combine ♗c4 with the advance f2-f4 and a pos-

sible further advance to f5, in order to rapidly apply pressure on e6, and thus add some sense to the development of the bishop to the a2-g8 diagonal, where it would otherwise be less influential.

It is not without reason that the game plan of the highly popular **English Attack**, i.e. the pawn advances f2-f3, g2-g4 and h2-h4, does not include the development of the bishop to c4, and indeed in the Sozin this pawn configuration proves to be largely ineffective. The only exception, in this sense, is the main line of the **Dragon**, in which this set-up does include ♗c4. However, in this case the bishop mainly has the prophylactic role of preventing ...d6-d5.

Another great advocate of the deployment of the f1-bishop to c4 during the 1960s was the future 11th World Champion, Bobby Fischer, who came up with many new ideas for White — and for Black! In recognition of his many contributions, some experts attach his name to Sozin's when denoting the whole system. However, we will call it by its usual name.

Fischer Attack

7.♗b3 is called the **Fischer Attack** only if it is played in the **Najdorf**; that is, after

| 5. | ... | a7-a6 |
| 6. | ♗f1-c4 | e7-e6 |

or via the **Scheveningen** (5...e6 6.♗c4) when Black plays 6...a6.

7.   ♗c4-b3!?

With this precautionary retreat by the c4-bishop to b3, White is making a move that will be necessary sooner or later (even if 7.0-0 and 7.a3 are both playable).

Black usually seeks immediate counterplay on the queenside with the manoeuvre ...♘bd7-c5, or with ...b7-b5.

The move 7...♘bd7 is fashionable at the moment, but was considered to be theoretically bad in the past. It was played more than once by Kasparov in his 1993 World Championship match against Short.

After 8.f4 ♘c5

practice has shown that Black's position is perfectly playable.

7. ...   b7-b5

White continues more often than not with

8. 0-0

The direct 8.f4 followed by f4-f5 is playable, but does not give more than equality.

8. ...   ♗f8-e7!

The old main line was 9.f4 0-0 10.e5 dxe5 11.fxe5 ♘fd7, which is now slightly out of use, since Black has more than adequate resources.

9. ♕d1-f3!

This has now become all the rage. Played by Fischer in 1960, its real popularity began when Kasparov adopted it in the 1990s.

Here we have a rare case where play, when restricted exclusively to pieces, proves to be dangerous.

Black's problem is that the threat of 10.e5 cannot be prevented with the natural-looking 9...♗b7 because of 10.♗xe6! fxe6 11.♘xe6, with a strong attack. Therefore play proceeds with

9. ...   ♕d8-c7
10. ♕f3-g3   0-0
11. ♗c1-h6!   ♘f6-e8

Now White has an unpleasant kingside initiative. However, with correct play, Black should be able to maintain the balance.

Now we will look at how we can get to this position via the **Classical Sicilian**:

1. e2-e4   c7-c5
2. ♘g1-f3   d7-d6
3. d2-d4   c5xd4

4.	♘f3xd4	♘g8-f6
5.	♘b1-c3	♘b8-c6
6.	♗f1-c4	e7-e6

We will now examine the positions where White does not develop his queen to f3, but instead to e2, with both kingside and queenside castling. The most common continuation is

7.	♗c1-e3	a7-a6

8. ♗c4-b3

The more flexible 8.0-0 (for 8.♕e2 see the **Velimirovic Attack** further on) 8...♗e7 9.♗b3 0-0 10.f4 ♘xd4 11.♗xd4 b5 12.e5 dxe5 13.fxe5 ♘d7 14.♘e4 ♗b7 15.♘d6 ♗xd6 16.exd6 ♕g5

leads to a complex position that is difficult to assess.

8.	...	♗f8-e7
9.	f2-f4	

With the move 9.♕e2 you transpose to a Velimirovic Attack in which White has retreated his bishop a little prematurely to b3. This allows ...♘a5, but with the difference that White cannot retreat the bishop to d3, as you can in the standard Velimirovic line.

9.	...	0-0
10.	♕d1-f3	

We can call this position the **Classical Sozin**, as it was played this way in the 1930s. White searches for a balance between aggressiveness and solidity, and he prepares an initiative on the kingside without burning all his bridges behind him.

Velimirovic Attack

Here is another famous variation where White's light-squared bishop is developed to c4. You should note that White can only enter this variation if Black plays the **Classical Sicilian** (1.e4 c5 2.♘f3 d6 3.d4 cxd4 4.♘xd4 ♘f6 5.♘c3 ♘c6).

6.	♗f1-c4	e7-e6
7.	♗c1-e3	♗f8-e7

7...a6 8.♕e2 ♕c7 9.0-0-0 ♗e7 is a transposition of moves.

8.	♕d1-e2	

White's idea is to prepare queenside castling while keeping control of g4, to be able to push the g-pawn without the need to play f2-f3. It became popular in 1965, following some brilliant victories by its creator, the Yugoslav GM Dragoljub Velimirovic. It was sometimes played by Fischer; he used this variation in a famous game with Larsen in 1970, which he lost. This aggressive line has never achieved the popularity of the **Richter-Rauzer**: probably because most players prefer not to play such a one-dimensional line, and instead would rather play something strategically more complex.

Black generally continues with

8.	...	a7-a6
9.	0-0-0	♛d8-c7
10.	♗c4-b3	

This is a prophylactic move, which is necessary to be able to play g2-g4.

Now Black must choose. He can leave the king in the middle and play on the queenside with 10...♞a5, exchanging it for the bishop on b3, but this leaves White with the strong knight on d4. Instead, Black can immediately play 10...0-0. In the latter case, White's plan is the brutal manoeuvre g2-g4, ♖h1-g1-g3-h3 and, then g4-g5, ♛e2-h5-h7 checkmate! However, Black will not just sit there twiddling his thumbs, and in practice it is difficult to pull this off.

A)   11. g2-g4

This is best met by

11. ...   ♞c6xd4

when White must recapture with the rook, since *12.♗xd4 e5 13.♗e3 ♗xg4 14.f3 ♗e6 gives no compensation for the sacrificed pawn.*

12. ♖d1xd4

This prevents 12...e5 thanks to 13.♖c4 (gaining a tempo by attacking the queen) followed by g4-g5 and ♞c3-d5. Therefore, Black continues with

12.	...	b7-b5
13.	g4-g5	♞f6-d7
14.	♖h1-g1	♞d7-c5

and White can try and add some sense to the rook's placement on d4 by clearing the way to h4 with 15.e5!?. Black would be wise to not accept the proffered pawn immediately; instead he should respond with 15...d5 16.♖h4 ♛xe5, with a position that is not easy to evaluate.

B)   11. ♖h1-g1

11. ...   ♘f6-d7
11...b5 12.g4 b4 13.♘xc6 ♛xc6 14.♘d5 is another highly sacrificial line.

12. g2-g4   ♘d7-c5
Now the normal continuation would be 13.g5.

However, at this point White can play a courageous two-piece sacrifice:

13. ♘d4-f5!?   b7-b5
14. ♗b3-d5!?

For examples of these lines, see the games at the end of this section.

As you have doubtlessly noted, when you play these variations, you are living on a razor's edge. Exhilarating perhaps, but not to the taste of every black player, who has alternatives such as ...♘c6-a5xb3, or postponing kingside castling and first mobilizing his queenside pawns.

To finish we have prepared a table (see next page) which presents the various systems in which White can play ♗c4.

A) Classical Sicilian

1.	e2-e4	c7-c5
2.	♘g1-f3	d7-d6
3.	d2-d4	c5xd4
4.	♘f3xd4	♘g8-f6
5.	♘b1-c3	♘b8-c6
6.	♗f1-c4	

Please note: after the normal 6...e6, the game will head for either the **Velimirovic Attack** or the **Classical Sozin**. But Black can avoid this and enter less theoretical lines like 6...♗d7 or the more popular 6...♕b6. Then, after 7.♘db5, or 7.♘b3, you reach positions which are similar to the **Classical Scheveningen**: 7...a6 8.♗e3 ♕c7 9.♗e2. *Do not forget about the common error 6...g6? 7.♘xc6 bxc6 8.e5!.*

B) Scheveningen

1.	e2-e4	c7-c5
2.	♘g1-f3	d7-d6
3.	d2-d4	c5xd4
4.	♘f3xd4	♘g8-f6
5.	♘b1-c3	e7-e6
6.	♗f1-c4	

♗c4 is less frequently played against the **Scheveningen** than against the **Najdorf** or the **Classical Sicilian** because of the popularity of the **Keres Attack**.
Here, Black can avoid the usual set-up by not playing ...♘c6, for example:

6.	...	♗f8-e7
7.	♗c4-b3	

Now Black could defer the 'Najdorf' ...a6 and directly play his knight to c5 via a6, preparing to exchange it for the light-squared bishop when he chooses to. 6...♘c6 would transpose to subsection 1).

C) Najdorf

1.	e2-e4	c7-c5
2.	♘g1-f3	d7-d6
3.	d2-d4	c5xd4
4.	♘f3xd4	♘g8-f6
5.	♘b1-c3	a7-a6
6.	♗f1-c4	e7-e6

Now, after

7.	♗c4-b3!?	

we have the **Fischer Attack**. 7.0-0 is also playable. The alternative 7.♗e3 is ambitious but double-edged; after 7...b5 8.♗b3 b4!?, it isn't clear if White will get sufficient compensation for the e4-pawn.

Short,Nigel
Kasparov,Garry
London Wch m 1993 (8)

1.e4 c5 2.♘f3 d6 3.d4 cxd4 4.♘xd4 ♘f6 5.♘c3 a6 6.♗c4 e6 7.♗b3 ♘bd7 8.f4 ♘c5 9.e5 dxe5 10.fxe5 ♘fd7 11.♗f4 b5 12.♕g4 h5 13.♕g3 h4 14.♕g4 g5?! 15.0-0-0 ♕e7 16.♘c6! ♘xb3+ 17.axb3 ♕c5 18.♘e4! ♕xc6 19.♗xg5 ♗b7 20.♖d6!! ♗xd6 21.♘xd6+ ♔f8 22.♖f1 ♘xe5 23.♕xe6 ♕d5 24.♖xf7+!! ♘xf7 25.♗e7+ ♔g7□ 26.♕f6+ ♔h7 27.♘xf7 ♕h5□ 28.♘g5+ ♔g8 29.♕e6+ ♔g7 30.♕f6+ ♔g8 31.♕e6+ ♔g7 32.♗f6+ ♔h6 33.♘f7+ ♔h7 34.♘g5+ ♔h6 35.♗xh8+ [35.♘f7+±] 35...♕g6 36.♘f7+ ♔h7 37.♕e7 ♕xg2? [37...♔g8!!] 38.♗e5? [38.♗d4!+−] 38...♕f1+ = 39.♔d2 ♕f2+ 40.♔d3 ♕f3+ 41.♔d2 ♕f2+ [another example (in addition to Fischer-Geller) of the tremendous complexity of the Sicilian: even the best players in the world can make serious mistakes in these complicated variations] ½-½

Nisipeanu,Liviu-Dieter
Grischuk,Alexander
Foros 2006 (8)

1.e4 c5 2.♘f3 d6 3.d4 cxd4 4.♘xd4 ♘f6 5.♘c3 a6 6.♗c4 e6 7.♗b3 ♘bd7 8.♗g5 h6 9.♗xf6 ♕xf6 10.0-0 g5 11.f4 ♗g7 12.e5 dxe5 13.f5 e4 14.♘ce2 exf5 15.♖xf5 ♕b6 16.♖xf7 ♗f6 17.♕d2 ♘e5 18.♖xf6 ♕xf6 19.♖f1 ♕b6 20.♘c3 ♘c6 21.♗f7+ ♔d8 22.♕f2 ♕xd4 23.♖d1 ♕xd1+ 24.♘xd1 ♔e7 25.♘e3 ♗e6 26.♗xe6 ♔xe6 27.♕f5+ ♔e7 28.♕xe4+ ♔d6 29.♕d3+ ♔e6 30.♕g6+ ♔d7 31.♘c4 ♖ad8 32.♕d6+ ♔e8 33.♕e6+ ♔f8 34.♕f6+ ♔g8 35.♕g6+ ♔f8 36.h3 ♖g8 37.♕f6+ ♔e8 38.♘d6+ 1-0

Fischer,Robert
Rubinetti,Jorge
Palma de Mallorca 1970 (17)

1.e4 c5 2.♘f3 d6 3.d4 cxd4 4.♘xd4 ♘f6 5.♘c3 e6 6.♗c4 a6 7.♗b3 b5 8.0-0 ♗b7 9.♖e1 ♘bd7 10.♗g5 h6 11.♗h4 ♘c5 12.♗d5 exd5 13.exd5+ ♔d7 14.b4 ♘a4 15.♘xa4 bxa4 16.c4 ♔c8 17.♕xa4 ♕d7 18.♕b3 g5 19.♗g3 ♘h5 20.c5 dxc5 21.bxc5 ♕xd5 22.♖e8+ ♔d7 23.♕a4+ ♗c6 24.♘xc6 1-0

Morozevich,Alexander
Kasparov,Garry
Astana 2001 (3)

1.e4 c5 2.♘f3 d6 3.d4 cxd4 4.♘xd4 ♘f6 5.♘c3 a6 6.♗c4 e6 7.♗b3 b5 8.0-0 ♗e7 9.♕f3 ♕c7 10.♕g3 0-0 11.♗h6 ♘e8 12.♖ad1 ♗d7 13.f4 ♘c6 14.f5 ♘xd4 15.♖xd4 ♗f6 16.♖d3 ♗e5 17.♕g4 b4 18.f6 g6 19.♘e2 a5 20.♗xf8 ♔xf8 21.♕h4 a4 22.♕xh7 ♕a7+ 23.♔h1 ♘xf6 24.♕h6+ ♔e7 25.♗c4 ♕c5 26.b3 axb3 27.♗xb3 ♗b5 28.♘f4 ♗xf4 29.♕xf4 ♕e5 30.h3 g5 31.♕f2 g4 32.♕b6 ♘d7 33.♕f2 ♘f6 34.♕b6 ♖h8 35.♖xd6 ♕xd6 36.♕xd6+ ♔xd6 37.♖xf6 ♖h7 38.♔h2 ♔e5 39.♖f2 gxh3 40.gxh3 ♗c6 41.♗c4 ♗xe4 42.♖e2 f5 43.♗d3 ♔f4 44.♗xe4 fxe4 45.♖f2+ ♔e3 46.♖f8 e5 47.♖e8 ♖c7 48.♖xe5 ♔f4

49.♖b5 ♖xc2+ 50.♔g1 e3 51.♖xb4+ ♔f3 52.♖b1 ♖g2+ 53.♔h1 e2 54.a4 ♔f2 55.a5 ♖g5 56.♔h2 ♖xa5 57.h4 ♖a3 **0-1**

Megaranto,Susanto
Dominguez,Lenier
Turin ol 2006 (7)

1.e4 c5 2.♘f3 d6 3.d4 cxd4 4.♘xd4 ♘f6 5.♘c3 a6 6.♗c4 e6 7.♗b3 b5 8.0-0 ♗e7 9.♕f3 ♕c7 10.♕g3 0-0 11.♗h6 ♘e8 12.♖ad1 ♗d7 13.a3 ♘c6 14.♘xc6 ♗xc6 15.♖fe1 ♕b7 16.f3 a5 17.♘e2 a4 18.♗a2 b4 19.axb4 ♕xb4 20.♗c1 ♘f6 21.♘d4 ♗d7 22.♕f2 ♖fc8 23.g4 ♗b5 24.c3 ♕a5 25.e5 dxe5 26.♖xe5 ♖c5 27.♖ee1 ♗c4 28.♗b1 ♕c7 29.f4 g6 30.h3 ♗d5 31.♗d3 ♖b8 32.f5 gxf5 33.gxf5 ♔h8 34.fxe6 ♖g8+ 35.♔f1 ♘h5 36.exf7 ♘g3+ 37.♔g1 ♘e2+ 38.♔f1 ♘g3+ 39.♔g1 ♘e2+ 40.♔f1 ♘g3+ 41.♔g1 **½-½**

Fischer,Robert
Spassky,Boris
Reykjavik Wch m 1972 (4)

1.e4 c5 2.♘f3 d6 3.d4 cxd4 4.♘xd4 ♘f6 5.♘c3 ♘c6 6.♗c4 e6 7.♗b3 ♗e7 8.♗e3 0-0 9.0-0 a6 10.f4 ♘xd4 11.♗xd4 b5 12.a3 [12.e5 (this is the main line) 12...dxe5 13.fxe5 ♘d7 14.♘e4 ♗b7 15.♘d6 ♗xd6 16.exd6 ♕g5 17.♖f2; 17.♕e2] 12...♗b7 13.♕d3 a5 14.e5 dxe5 15.fxe5 ♘d7 16.♘xb5 ♘c5 17.♗xc5 ♗xc5+ 18.♔h1 ♕g5 19.♕e2 ♖ad8 20.♖ad1 ♖xd1 21.♖xd1 h5 [21...♗e3! 22.♘d6 ♗c6 23.♘c4 ♗f4 24.♔g1 a4 25.♗a2 h5∓] 22.♘d6? [22.♘d4!] 22...♗a8 23.♗c4 h4 24.h3 ♗e3 25.♕g4 ♕xe5 26.♕xh4 [26.♘xf7 ♔xf7

27.♗xe6+ ♔f6!] 26...g5! [26...♕xb2!?] 27.♕g4 ♗c5! 28.♘b5 ♔g7 29.♘d4 ♖h8?! [29...♖d8] 30.♘f3 ♗xf3 31.♕xf3 ♗d6? [31...♖h4!∓] 32.♕c3 ♕xc3 33.bxc3= ♗e5 34.♖d7 ♔f6 35.♔g1 ♗xc3 36.♗e2 ♗e5 37.♔f1 ♖c8 38.♗h5 ♖c7 39.♖xc7 ♗xc7 40.a4 ♔e7 41.♔e2 f5 42.♔d3 ♗e5 43.c4 ♔d6 44.♗f7 ♗g3 45.c5+ **½-½**

Friedel,Joshua
Zavadsky,Peter
Las Vegas 2006 (2)

1.e4 c5 2.♘f3 d6 3.d4 cxd4 4.♘xd4 ♘f6 5.♘c3 ♘c6 6.♗c4 e6 7.0-0 ♗e7 8.♗e3 0-0 9.♗b3 a6 10.f4 ♕c7 11.♕e2 b5 12.f5 ♘xd4 13.♗xd4 b4 14.fxe6 bxc3 15.exf7+ ♖xf7 16.♗xf7+ ♔xf7 17.♕h5+ ♔g8 18.♗xf6 ♕a7+ 19.♔h1 gxf6 20.♕d5+ ♔f8 21.bxc3 ♕b7 22.♕h5 ♕xe4 23.♕h6+ ♔f7 24.♖ae1 ♕g6 25.♕e3 ♗f8 26.♕e8+ ♔g8 27.♕c6 ♖b8 28.♕c7 ♖a8 29.♖f3 ♔h8 30.♖g3 ♕h5 31.♕c4 **1-0**

Fischer,Robert
Geller,Efim
Skopje 1967 (2)

1.e4 c5 2.♘f3 d6 3.d4 cxd4 4.♘xd4 ♘f6 5.♘c3 ♘c6 6.♗c4 e6 7.♗e3 ♗e7 8.♗b3 0-0 9.♕e2 ♕a5 10.0-0-0 ♘xd4 11.♗xd4 ♗d7 12.♔b1 ♗c6? [≥ 12...♖fc8] 13.f4 ♖ad8 14.♖hf1 b5 15.f5!! b4 16.fxe6! bxc3 17.exf7+ [17.♖xf6!] 17...♔h8 18.♖f5! ♕b4 19.♕f1! ♘xe4 20.a3? [20.♕f4!!+—] 20...♕b7 21.♕f4 ♗a4!! 22.♕g4 ♗f6! 23.♖xf6 ♗xb3! [Fischer resigned, having seen 24.♖f4 ♗a2+—+] **0-1**

Velimirovic,Dragoljub
Sofrevski,Jovan

Titograd ch-YUG 1965 (7)

1.e4 c5 2.♘f3 ♘c6 3.d4 cxd4 4.♘xd4 e6 5.♘c3 d6 6.♗e3 ♘f6 7.♗c4 ♗e7 8.♕e2 a6 9.0-0-0 ♕c7 10.♗b3 ♘a5 11.g4 b5 12.g5 ♘xb3+ 13.axb3 ♘d7 14.♘f5 exf5 15.♘d5 ♕d8 16.exf5 0-0 17.f6 gxf6 18.♗d4 ♘e5 19.gxf6 ♗xf6 20.♖hg1+ ♗g7 21.♗xe5 dxe5 22.♕xe5 f6 23.♘e7+ ♔f7 24.♕h5+   1-0

Fedorov,Alexey
Lutsko,Igor

Minsk ch-BLR 2005 (1)

1.e4 c5 2.♘f3 ♘c6 3.d4 cxd4 4.♘xd4 ♘f6 5.♘c3 d6 6.♗c4 e6 7.♗e3 a6 8.♕e2 ♕c7 9.0-0-0 ♗e7 10.♗b3 0-0 11.♖hg1 b5 12.g4 b4 13.♘xc6 ♕xc6 14.♘d5 exd5 15.g5 ♘xe4 16.♗xd5 ♕a4 17.♗d4 ♗f5 18.♗xe4 ♗xe4 19.♕xe4 ♖fe8 20.♔b1 ♗f8 21.♕d3 ♕c6 22.h4 ♕e4 23.h5 ♖ac8 24.♗e3 ♖e6 25.♕xe4 ♖xe4 26.♖d5 ♖ec4 27.♖c1 ♗e7 28.b3 ♖e4 29.♖cd1 ♖c6 30.♖5d4 ♖xd4 31.♖xd4 a5 32.♖d5 ♗d8 33.♖b5 ♔f8 34.♗d4 ♖c8 35.♔b2 g6 36.hxg6 hxg6 37.c3 bxc3+ 38.♗xc3 ♔e8 39.♗xa5 ♗xa5 40.♖xa5 ♔d7 41.a4 ♖h8 42.♖a7+ ♔e6 43.♖c7 ♖h2 44.♖c2 ♖g2 45.a5 ♖xg5 46.b4 ♖b5 47.♔b3 d5 48.a6 ♖b8 49.♔a4 d4 50.b5 ♔d5 51.a7 ♖a8 52.b6 d3 53.♖d2 ♔c6 54.♔a5   1-0

Movsziszian,Karen
Spraggett,Kevin

Tarragona 2006 (4)

1.e4 c5 2.♘f3 d6 3.d4 ♘f6 4.♘c3 cxd4 5.♘xd4 ♘c6 6.♗c4 e6 7.♗e3

♗e7 8.♗b3 a6 9.♕e2 0-0 10.0-0-0 ♕c7 11.♖hg1 b5 12.g4 b4 13.♘xc6 ♕xc6 14.♘d5 exd5 15.g5 ♘xe4 16.♗xd5 ♕a4 17.♗d4 ♗f5 18.♗xe4 ♗xe4 19.♕xe4 ♕xa2 20.♕xe7 ♖ae8 21.♕c7 ♖e4 22.♗e3 ♖c4 23.♕xd6 b3 24.♔d2 ♖xc2+ 25.♔e1 ♕xb2 26.♕d3 a5 27.♖g4 ♖c3 28.♕d2 ♖c2 29.♕d3 ♖c3 30.♕e4 ♕a3 31.♖h4 g6 32.♗d4 ♖c1 33.♖xh7 ♕b4+ 34.♔e2 ♖c2+ 35.♔f3 ♕xd4 36.♖xd4 ♔xh7   1-0

Sokolov,Andrey
Salov,Valery

Nikolaev 1983

1.e4 c5 2.♘f3 ♘c6 3.d4 cxd4 4.♘xd4 ♘f6 5.♘c3 d6 6.♗c4 e6 7.♗e3 a6 8.♕e2 ♕c7 9.0-0-0 ♗e7 10.♗b3 0-0 11.♖hg1 ♘d7 12.g4 ♘c5 13.♘f5 b5 14.♗d5 ♗b7 15.g5 exf5 16.g6 hxg6 17.♖xg6 ♘e5 18.♖xg7+ ♔xg7 19.♖g1+ ♘g6 20.exf5 ♖h8 21.♗d4+ ♗f6 22.fxg6 fxg6 23.♕g4 ♖h6 24.♗xf6+ ♔h7 25.♖e1 ♗d5 26.♘xd5 ♕c8 27.♖e7+ ♔g8 28.♖g7+ ♔f8 29.♖g8+ ♔xg8 30.♘e7+   1-0

Fedorov,Alexey
Lanka,Zigurds

Pula Ech-tt 1997 (8)

1.e4 c5 2.♘f3 ♘c6 3.d4 cxd4 4.♘xd4 ♘f6 5.♘c3 d6 6.♗c4 e6 7.♗e3 ♗e7 8.♕e2 a6 9.0-0-0 ♕c7 10.♗b3 0-0 11.♖hg1 ♘d7 12.g4 ♘c5 13.♘f5 b5 14.♗d5 ♗b7 15.g5 ♖fc8 16.♖g3 ♘e5 17.♖h3 ♘g6 18.♕h5 ♘f8 19.♘xg7 ♗xd5 20.♕h6 e5 21.♘h5 ♘ce6 22.exd5 b4 23.dxe6 ♘xe6 24.♘f6+ ♗xf6 25.gxf6   1-0

Sicilian Defence
Najdorf Variation

**1.e4 c5 2.♘f3 d6 3.d4 cxd4
4.♘xd4 ♘f6 5.♘c3 a6**

The advance ...a7-a6 on the 5th move is the move that defines the **Najdorf Variation**. It has become the most popular of all Sicilian variations. This is hardly a surprise, as it was the mythical champion Bobby Fischer's favourite choice during the 1960s and 1970s. In addition, from the 1980s on, Garry Kasparov used it almost exclusively. Champion players have always dictated chess opening fashion. We may not be able to play like these guys, but we can at least play their openings!

Played by Esteban Canal as far back as 1929 (!), 5...a6 was also used by the Czechoslovakian Karel Opocensky in the 1930s. It became popular in the 1940s and acquired its name in honour of the Polish-Argentinian player Miguel Najdorf (1910-1997), one of the strongest non-Soviet players after the Second World War.

We are dealing with a very flexible concept: Black plays the move ...a6, which is always useful in the Sicilian; he maintains the option to advance the pawn to e6 (transposing to the **Scheveningen**) or to e5, depending on the circumstances and the personal taste of the player. This is Kasparov's approach, and he generally opted for ...**e6** when White chose positional continuations such as 6.♗e2. Fischer, on the other hand, preferred to remain in the spirit of Najdorf with the thematic pawn advance to e5.

You should note that the move 5...a6 is played to make ...e7-e5 possible without receiving check on b5: if 5...e5 is played immediately, it gives the white knight advantageous access to the f5-square, as explained in the section on minor variations after 2...d6.

A reader may well ask why a move like ...e5 is so important in the Najdorf, given the hole it creates on d5?

The answer lies in the fact that the Najdorf is at heart an ambitious line that aims to put the e4-pawn under pressure! In the Open Sicilian, with the white d-pawn gone, and the f-pawn on f4, the 'poor' e-pawn is subject to attack by the adversary's pieces. *When the hypermodernists provocatively claimed that 1.e4 was an error, they may have been partially correct!* Black blocks the path of the e4-pawn with ...e5, preventing that extra step forward that is so dangerous in the standard variations; he then exchanges on f4 and begins to attack it with ...b5 to develop the bishop to b7, with ...♘d7-c5 and sometimes with ...♖e8.

In some exemplary games by Fischer and other Najdorf experts this plan is carried out brilliantly.

Naturally, the ...e5 push does not always work in Black's favour. It does not take much to find yourself in strategically lost positions, as some of the young Karpov's adversaries discovered the hard way. That said, it is understandable that **6.♗g5** was the first and most popular anti-Najdorf continuation, since with the f6-knight already pinned, the move 6...e5 creates a weakness on d5 which is more easily exploitable by White than in the other variations.

We will now have a look at White's alternatives on the 6th move.

A)   6. ♖h1-g1

Recently this strange move has appeared, which is played with the idea of a g2-g4 advance.

B)   6. a2-a4

This could be a good idea for those who do not want to get bogged down in too much theory. It prevents ...b7-b5, therefore it cannot be bad.

C)   6. g2-g3

The **Fianchetto Variation** is relatively popular with players who like quiet positions. After 6...e5, the knight can retreat to e2 or to b3, in both cases with a slow positional struggle. Naturally, ...e7-e6 leads to positions dealt with in the section on the **Scheveningen Variation**.

D)   6. h2-h3

This is the move that Bobby Fischer played a few times when he had to fight against the Najdorf himself. White's idea includes a g2-g4 pawn advance and, if Black plays ...e7-e5, to retreat the knight to e2 and then reposition it on g3.

However, with 6...e6! Black can transpose to the **Scheveningen**, in which h2-h3 is of doubtful use.

E)   6. ♗f1-d3

Of the minor variations, this best justifies the idea of the Najdorf's 6...e5: after 7.♘de2

Black obtains a comfortable position with ...♘bd7 and ...b5.

Please note the valid opportunity to exploit the fact that the d4-knight is undefended with 6...♘c6 and also 6...g6.

We shall now turn to the 'serious' options, at least from a statistical frequency viewpoint.

F)   6. ♗f1-c4

We have already discussed this move in the section on the **Sozin-Velimirovic Attack**.

G)   6. f2-f4

An interesting move. It is sufficiently aggressive and there are not too many variations that you have to remember.

In Najdorf style there is

6. ...   e7-e5

Black can also opt for 6...e6, which transposes to the **Scheveningen**, or he can choose the flexible 6...♕c7 or 6...♘bd7.

7. ♘d4-f3   ♘b8-d7
8. a2-a4

Preventing ...b7-b5.

8. ...   ♗f8-e7
9. ♗f1-d3

The ambitious 9.♗c4 is also playable here.

9. ...   0-0
10. 0-0

We have reached a strategically complex position that is rich in possibilities for both players.

Black can gain a pawn with 10...exf4 with the idea – after 11.♗xf4 – to take on b2 with the queen (after ...♕b6 check). Otherwise, in the event of the prophylactic 11.♔h1, he can try to defend the extra pawn on f4 with 11...♘h5.

Naturally, such greediness has its risks. Black can instead play the more solid

10. ...   ♘d7-c5
11. ♔g1-h1   e5xf4
12. ♗c1xf4

327

White has some prospects of an initiative on the kingside, but Black's piece activity gives him sufficient counterplay.

You should also note another possibility on the 8th move for Black:

8. ...   ♕d8-c7

This queen move prevents the white bishop from establishing itself on c4. The objective is a kingside fianchetto, but after 9.♗d3 g6 10.0-0 ♗g7 11.♕e1 0-0 12.♕h4 b6 13.♔h1 ♗b7 14.fxe5 dxe5 15.♗h6

White has a dangerous kingside initiative.

Beliavsky,Alexander
Tal,Mikhail
Moscow ch-URS 1973 (11)
1.e4 c5 2.♘f3 d6 3.d4 cxd4 4.♘xd4
♘f6 5.♘c3 a6 6.a4 ♘c6 7.♗e2 e5
8.♘b3 ♗e7 9.0-0 0-0 10.f4 ♘b4
11.♔h1 ♗e6 12.f5 ♗d7 13.♗g5 ♗c6

14.♗xf6 ♗xf6 15.♗c4 ♖c8 16.♕e2
♕c7 17.♖fd1 ♖fd8 18.♘d2 ♘xc2
19.♖ac1 ♘d4 20.♕g4 ♕e7 21.♘f3
b5 22.axb5 axb5 23.♘d5 ♗xd5
24.♗xd5 ♘c2 25.h4 ♘e3 26.♕h5
♖xc1 27.♖xc1 ♘xd5 28.exd5 e4
29.♖e1 ♖e8 30.♕g4 ♗xb2 31.♖e3
h6 32.♘d2 ♕a7 33.♖xe4 ♕a1+
34.♔h2 ♖xe4 35.♘xe4 ♗e5+ 36.g3
♕a2+ 37.♔h3 ♕xd5 38.♕f3 ♔f8
39.♕e3 ♗d4 40.♕f4 ♕e5 41.♕f3
d5 42.♘d2 b4 43.♘b3 ♗e3   0-1

Alexeev,Evgeny
Arizmendi Martinez,Julen
Biel 2006 (4)
1.e4 c5 2.♘f3 d6 3.d4 ♘f6 4.♘c3
cxd4 5.♘xd4 a6 6.g3 e5 7.♘b3 ♘bd7
8.a4 b6 9.♗g2 ♗b7 10.0-0 ♗e7
11.♖e1 ♖c8 12.♘d2 ♖c5 13.♘f1 ♕a8
14.♗g5 h6 15.♗xf6 ♘xf6 16.♘e3 g6
17.♕d3 0-0 18.f4 exf4 19.gxf4 ♖h5
20.♖f1 d5 21.♘exd5 ♘xd5 22.exd5
♗f6 23.♖ad1 ♗g7 24.f5 ♗e5 25.h3
♖g5 26.♘e4 ♖xf5 27.♖xf5 gxf5
28.♘g3 f4 29.♘f5 ♕d8 30.♘xh6+
♔g7 31.♘f5+ ♔h8 32.♕e2 ♕f6
33.♕h5+ ♔g8 34.♘h6+   1-0

Dominguez,Lenier
De Firmian,Nick
Istanbul ol 2000 (13)
1.e4 c5 2.♘f3 d6 3.d4 cxd4 4.♘xd4
♘f6 5.♘c3 a6 6.f4 e5 7.♘f3 ♘bd7
8.a4 ♗e7 9.♗d3 0-0 10.0-0 exf4
11.♔h1 ♘c5 12.♗xf4 ♗g4 13.♕d2
♖c8 14.♖ae1 ♖e8 15.♘d4 ♕d7
16.a5 ♗h5 17.♘f5 ♗g6 18.♗g5 ♗d8
19.♗xf6 ♗xf6 20.♘d5 ♗d8 21.b4
♘xd3 22.cxd3 ♖e5 23.♘fe3 ♖c6
24.♘c4 ♖e8 25.♕f4 h6 26.♕g3
♗xe4 27.♘cb6 ♖xb6 28.♘xb6 ♗xb6

29.♖xe4 ♖xe4 30.dxe4 ♗d4 31.♕d3 ♗e5 32.♖c1 g6 33.♕h3 ♕e7 34.♕xh6 ♗g7 35.♖c8+ ♗f8 36.♕f4 d5 37.♖c7 ♕e6 38.e5 ♗d6 39.♖xb7 ♗xe5 40.♕f1 d4 41.b5 ♕d5 42.bxa6 d3 43.♖b1 ♔g7 44.♕f3 ♕d4 45.♖f1 f5 46.♕b7+ ♔h6 47.a7 d2 48.a8♕ d1♕ 49.♕f8+ ♔g5 50.♕be7+ ♔g4 51.h3+   1-0

Ivanchuk, Vasily
Kasparov, Garry
Amsterdam 1994 (4)

1.e4 c5 2.♘f3 d6 3.d4 cxd4 4.♘xd4 ♘f6 5.♘c3 a6 6.f4 ♕c7 7.♕f3 g6 8.♗e3 ♗g7 9.h3 e5 10.fxe5 dxe5 11.♗h6 ♗xh6 12.♕xf6 0-0 13.♘d5 ♕a5+ 14.b4 ♕d8 15.♘e7+ ♕xe7 16.♕xe7 exd4 17.♗c4 ♘c6 18.♕c5 ♗e3 19.♖f1 ♘d8 20.♖f3 ♗e6 21.♖xe3 dxe3 22.♗xe6 ♘xe6 23.♕xe3 a5 24.b5 ♖ac8 25.0-0-0 ♖c5 26.♖d5 b6 27.♕g3 ♖c7 28.♕d6 ♖fc8 29.♖d2 ♖b7 30.g4 ♘c5 31.♕f6 h6 32.e5 ♖e8 33.h4 ♔h7 34.h5 g5 35.♖d6 ♖e6 36.♕d8 ♔g7 37.a3 a4 38.♔b2 ♖be7 39.♖xb6   1-0

Sicilian Defence
Najdorf 6.♗e2

1.e4 c5 2.♘f3 d6 3.d4 cxd4
4.♘xd4 ♘f6 5.♘c3 a6 6.♗e2

This **Classical Variation** is becoming more and more popular. White simply wants to develop naturally before starting to play actively. The ensuing lines are of a positional nature, but this does not necessarily mean that they are easier to handle: as in its sister variation in the Scheveningen, tactical play usually starts after the opening phase.

Yet again, Black has basically two choices:

A) To play e6, transposing to the **Scheveningen** (see the Scheveningen section for a detailed examination);

B) To continue with the thematic 6...e5. We have already elaborated on the advantages and disadvantages of this pawn advance.

6.	...	e7-e5
7.	♘d4-b3	♗f8-e7
8.	0-0	0-0

White can continue with the aggressive

9. ♗c1-e3

the subtle

9. ♔g1-h1

or the solid

9. a2-a4

Each of these produces complicated positions that contain plenty of possibilities for both players. Generally, White seeks to exploit the weakness of the d5-square, and is careful to limit Black's counterplay. He then aims to create a kingside initiative with the pawn advance f2-f4.

Sometimes, an alternative strategy is to occupy the d5-square with the knight, to recapture with the e4-pawn and then to make the most of his queenside pawn majority with the pawn advances b2-b4 and c2-c4-c5.

Karpov, Anatoly
Polugaevsky, Lev

Moscow m 1974 (6)

1.e4 c5 2.♘f3 d6 3.d4 cxd4 4.♘xd4 ♘f6 5.♘c3 a6 6.♗e2 e5 7.♘b3 ♗e7 8.0-0 ♗e6 9.f4 ♕c7 10.a4 ♘bd7 11.♔h1 0-0 12.♗e3 exf4 13.♖xf4 ♘e5 14.a5 ♘fd7 15.♖f1 ♗f6 16.♘d5 ♗xd5 17.♕xd5 ♕xc2 18.♘d4 ♕xb2 19.♖ab1 ♕c3 20.♘f5 ♕c2 21.♖be1

♘c5 22.♘xd6 ♘cd3 23.♗xd3 ♘xd3 24.♖d1 ♘b4 25.♕xb7 ♖ab8 26.♕a7 ♕c6 27.♗f4 ♖a8 28.♕f2 ♖ad8 29.♕g3 ♕c3 30.♖f3 ♕c2 31.♖df1 ♗d4 32.♗h6 ♘c6 33.♘f5 ♕b2 34.♗c1 ♕b5 35.♘h6+ ♔h8 36.♘xf7+ ♖xf7 37.♖xf7 ♗f6 38.♕f2 ♔g8 39.♖xf6 gxf6 40.♕xf6   1-0

Short,Nigel
Gelfand,Boris

Amsterdam 1996 (2)

1.e4 c5 2.♘f3 d6 3.d4 cxd4 4.♘xd4 ♘f6 5.♘c3 a6 6.♗e2 e5 7.♘b3 ♗e7 8.0-0 ♗e6 9.f4 ♕c7 10.♔h1 0-0 11.f5 ♗c4 12.g4 h6 13.g5 hxg5 14.♗xg5 ♘bd7 15.♖g1 ♖fc8 16.♗xc4 ♕xc4 17.♕f3 ♘f8 18.a3 b5 19.♘d2 ♕c6 20.♕h3 ♔e8 21.♕h8+ ♗f8 22.♗xf6 ♘xf6 23.♖xg7 a5 24.♖g3 b4 25.♕xf6 bxc3 26.bxc3 ♕b7 27.♖b1 ♕e7 28.♕h8 ♖ab8 29.♖bg1 ♔d7 30.c4 ♖b2 31.♖c3 ♕d8 32.♕h7 ♔e8 33.♖g8 ♕f6 34.♔g2 ♔d7 35.♘f1 ♗e7 36.♖g7 ♖f8 37.♘e3 ♕h4 38.♕xh4 ♗xh4 39.c5 dxc5 40.♖xc5 a4 41.♔f3 ♗e7 42.♖d5+ ♔c7 43.♖xe5 ♗xa3 44.♖a5   1-0

Efimenko,Zahar
Onischuk,Vladimir

Poltava ch-UKR 2006 (1)

1.e4 c5 2.♘f3 d6 3.d4 cxd4 4.♘xd4 ♘f6 5.♘c3 a6 6.♗e2 e5 7.♘b3 ♗e7 8.0-0 0-0 9.♖e1 ♗e6 10.♗f3 ♘bd7 11.a4 ♕c7 12.a5 ♖fc8 13.♗e3 b5 14.axb6 ♘xb6 15.♘a5 ♖ab8 16.♘d5 ♘bxd5 17.exd5 ♗d7 18.♘c6 ♗xc6 19.dxc6 e4 20.♗e2 ♕xc6 21.♗xa6 ♖c7 22.c4 d5 23.♗b5 ♕e6 24.♗f4 ♗d6 25.cxd5 ♕e7 26.♗xd6 ♕xd6 27.♗c6 g6 28.b3 ♖d8 29.h3

♕e5 30.♕e2 ♖e7 31.♖a4 ♔g7 32.♖c4 h5 33.b4 g5 34.b5 g4 35.♕e3 h4 36.b6 ♔h7 37.b7   1-0

Svidler,Peter
Polgar,Judit

Dos Hermanas 1999 (9)

1.e4 c5 2.♘f3 d6 3.d4 cxd4 4.♘xd4 ♘f6 5.♘c3 a6 6.♗e2 e5 7.♘b3 ♗e7 8.0-0 0-0 9.♗e3 ♗e6 10.♘d5 ♘bd7 11.♕d3 ♗xd5 12.exd5 ♘c5 13.♕d2 ♘fe4 14.♕b4 a5 15.♕b5 ♕c7 16.♖fd1 b6 17.♕c4 f5 18.♗d3 ♕d8 19.♘xc5 ♘xc5 20.a3 ♖c8 21.♕b5 e4 22.♗f1 ♗f6 23.♖ab1 ♗e5 24.b4 axb4 25.♖xb4 ♘d7 26.♖c4 ♖xc4 27.♕xc4 ♕e8 28.♖e1 ♘f6 29.h3 ♘d7 30.♕c7 f4 31.♗c1 e3 32.♗b5 exf2+ 33.♔xf2 f3   0-1

Short,Nigel
Polgar,Judit

Budapest 2003 (8)

1.e4 c5 2.♘f3 d6 3.d4 cxd4 4.♘xd4 ♘f6 5.♘c3 a6 6.♗e2 e5 7.♘b3 ♗e7 8.0-0 0-0 9.♔h1 ♘c6 10.♗e3 ♗e6 11.♕d2 d5 12.exd5 ♘xd5 13.♘xd5 ♗xd5 14.♖fd1 ♗xb3 15.axb3 ♕xd2 16.♖xd2 ♖ad8 17.♖ad1 ♖xd2 18.♖xd2 ♖d8 19.♗d3 g6 20.c3 a5 21.f3 h6 22.g3 ♗g5 23.f4 exf4 24.gxf4 ♗f6 25.♔g2 g5 26.♗c4 ♖e8 27.♖e2 gxf4 28.♗xf4 ♖xe2+ 29.♗xe2 ♔g7 30.♗g4 ♗g5 31.♗c7 ♗d8 32.♗g3 ♔g6 33.♗c8 b6 34.♔f3 f5 35.♗d7 ♘e7 36.♗h4 ♔f7 37.♗f2 ♗c7 38.h4 h5 39.♔e2 f4 40.♔f3 ♘g6 41.♗f5 ♘e5+ 42.♔e4 ♘g4 43.♗d4 ♘e3 44.♗h3 ♘g4 45.♔f5 ♘e3+ 46.♔g5 ♘c2 47.♗f2 ♘e3 48.♔xh5 ♔f6 49.♗g4 ♗d6 50.♗e1 ♗f8 51.b4 axb4 52.cxb4

♘d5 53.b5 ♗b4 54.♗xb4 ♘xb4
55.♗e2 ♔f5 56.♔h6 ♔f6 57.♔h5
♔f5 58.b3 ♘d5 59.♗d3+ ♔e5
60.♔g4 ♘f6+ 61.♔f3 ♘g8 62.h5
♘h6 63.♗g6 ♘g8 64.♗c2 ♘h6
65.♗d3 ♘g8 66.♔g4 ♘f6+ 67.♔g5
f3 68.h6 f2 69.♔g6 ♘d5 70.♗c4
♔e4 71.♔f7 ♘e3 72.♗e2 ♘f5 73.h7
♔e3 74.♗f1 ♘g3 75.♗g2   1-0

Wirig,Anthony
Moradiabadi,Elshan
Nancy 2007 (8)
1.e4 c5 2.♘f3 d6 3.d4 cxd4 4.♘xd4
♘f6 5.♘c3 a6 6.♗e2 e5 7.♘b3 ♗e7

8.0-0 0-0 9.♔h1 b6 10.f4 ♗b7
11.♗f3 ♘bd7 12.♘d5 ♖c8 13.c3 a5
14.a4 ♗a6 15.♖e1 ♘xd5 16.exd5 f5
17.♗e2 ♗xe2 18.♕xe2 ♗f6 19.♗e3
♘c5 20.♕b5 exf4 21.♗xf4 ♘e4
22.♖f1 ♕e8 23.♕d3 g5 24.♗e3
♕h5 25.♗d4 ♖ce8 26.♔g1 g4
27.♘d2 ♗xd4+ 28.♕xd4 g3 29.h3
♕e2 30.♖ae1 ♕xd2 31.♖xe4
♕xd4+ 32.♖xd4 ♖e2 33.♖f3 f4
34.♖dxf4 ♖e1+ 35.♖f1 ♖xf4
36.♖xe1 ♖xa4 37.♔f1 ♖f4+ 38.♔g1
♖f2 39.♖e3 ♖xb2 40.♖xg3+ ♔f7
41.♖f3+ ♔g6 42.c4 a4 43.♔f1 ♖c2
44.♖e3 ♔f5   0-1

Sicilian Defence Najdorf 6.♗e3

1.e4 c5 2.♘f3 d6 3.d4 cxd4
4.♘xd4 ♘f6 5.♘c3 a6 6.♗e3

This move was barely dealt with, if at all, in the old opening tomes. It underwent a sudden boom in the 1990s, and is now one of the most commonly played moves.

As it was introduced by Murray Chandler, Nigel Short and John Nunn in the 1980s, it was to become known as the **English Attack**.

White prepares for ♕d2 and 0-0-0 followed by f2-f3 (more rarely by f2-f4) and g2-g4, with an initiative on the kingside.

Black has fundamentally three continuations at his disposal: 6...e6, 6...e5 and 6...♘g4.

A)   6. ...   e7-e6

is the most popular, but leads into the realms of the **Scheveningen Variation** (see that section).

B)   6. ...   e7-e5

A response in pure Najdorf style. Now White can retreat the knight to a solid position on f3, with the plan to castle kingside and limit Black's queenside counterplay with a2-a4-a5, or White may choose the more aggressive and more frequently played

7. ♘d4-b3

which leaves the passage open for the f-pawn, and he can prepare to castle queenside, which is followed by opposite-side pawn storms. The main line is

7.	...	♗c8-e6
8.	♕d1-d2	♘b8-d7
9.	f2-f3	♗f8-e7
10.	g2-g4	h7-h6
11.	0-0-0	b7-b5
12.	h2-h4	♘d7-b6

with a complicated position and chances for both sides.

C)   6. ...   ♘f6-g4

This move, which was not even mentioned in the old opening manuals, was perhaps the most frequent of all in the 1990s! Yet another clear indication that opening theory is far from exhausted and new contributions keep cropping up. Often a move is not part of opening theory simply because it has not been played yet – or at least, not often enough!

7.	♗e3-g5	h7-h6
8.	♗g5-h4	g7-g5
9.	♗h4-g3	♗f8-g7
10.	♗f1-e2	h6-h5

Now we have a position that is difficult to evaluate.

It is easy to see why people have such differing views about this line: Black has lost a tempo to move the knight to a fairly unstable position on g4. On the other hand, White has moved his bishop four times to put it on g3, whereas his adversary's bishop has already taken control of the long dark-squared diagonal. Naturally, the price Black pays for his piece activity is the strategically doubtful advance of his g- and h-pawns, which denies the black king a quiet refuge on the kingside. However, this assessment is academic and should not be seen as immutable: it

is not rare in practice that Black, having taken control of the centre, will use his g- and h-pawns to apply pressure on White's castled king's position! The most common continuation is

11.	♗e2xg4	♗c8xg4
12.	f2-f3	♗g4-d7
13.	♗g3-f2	♘b8-c6
14.	0-0	e7-e6

Black has an active position and the bishop pair, while White has a better pawn structure.

Given the effectiveness of 6...♘g4, players are increasingly resorting to

> **6. f2-f3!?**

to prevent the knight move, and then they enter the 6.♗e3 variation.

Black can try to take advantage of the negative aspects of this idea with

> **6. ...   ♕d8-b6!?**

Kryvoruchko,Yury
Kovchan,Alexander
Alushta tt 2006 (1)

1.e4 c5 2.♘f3 d6 3.d4 cxd4 4.♘xd4 ♘f6 5.♘c3 a6 6.♗e3 e5 7.♘de2 ♗e6 8.f4 ♘g4 9.♗g1 g6 10.h3 ♘f6 11.g4 exf4 12.♘xf4 ♘c6 13.♕d2 ♘e5 14.0-0-0 ♘f3 15.♕e3 ♘xg1 16.e5 ♗h6 17.♖xd6 ♘d7 18.♘e4 ♗xf4 19.♕xf4 ♕a5 20.♖xe6+ 1-0

Anand,Viswanathan
Kasparov,Garry

Linares 2002 (10)

1.e4 c5 2.♘f3 d6 3.d4 cxd4 4.♘xd4 ♘f6 5.♘c3 a6 6.♗e3 e5 7.♘b3 ♗e6 8.f3 ♘bd7 9.g4 b5 10.g5 b4 11.♘e2 ♘h5 12.♕d2 a5 13.♘g3 ♘xg3 14.hxg3 a4 15.♘c1 ♕a5 16.♘d3 d5 17.exd5 ♕xd5 18.♗g2 ♕b5 19.♗h3 ♗xh3 20.♖xh3 ♗e7 21.♖h4 f5 22.0-0-0 b3 23.a3 ♖c8 24.c3 ♘f8 25.♖h2 ♘g6 26.♘b4 ♖d8 27.♘d5 ♔f7 28.♕d3 ♕xd3 29.♖xd3 f4 30.gxf4 exf4 31.♘xf4 ♘xf4 32.♖xd8 ♖xd8 33.♗xf4 ♖d3 34.♖h3 ♔g6 35.♗d2 ♗d8 36.♖g3 ♗e7 37.♖h3 ♗d8 38.♖g3 ♔f5 39.♔d1 ♗c7 ½-½

Adams,Michael
Hansen,Sune Berg

Calvia ol 2004 (3)

1.e4 c5 2.♘f3 d6 3.d4 cxd4 4.♘xd4 ♘f6 5.♘c3 a6 6.♗e3 e5 7.♘b3 ♗e6 8.f3 ♘bd7 9.♕d2 b5 10.0-0-0 ♖c8 11.♔b1 ♗e7 12.g4 ♘b6 13.g5 ♘h5 14.♕f2 ♘c4 15.♗xc4 ♖xc4 16.♖hg1 ♕b8 17.♘d5 ♗d8 18.♘d2 ♖c8 19.♘f1 ♗xd5 20.♖xd5 0-0 21.♘g3 ♘xg3 22.hxg3 f6 23.gxf6 ♗xf6 24.♕d2 ♖c6 25.♖d1 ♗e7 26.f4 ♖fc8 27.fxe5 dxe5 28.♖d7 ♗f8 29.♕d5+ ♔h8 30.♗a7 ♕a8 31.♕xe5 ♖xc2 32.♗d4 ♖c1+ 33.♖xc1 ♖xc1+ 34.♔xc1 ♕c6+ 1-0

Quezada,Yuniesky
Karjakin,Sergey

Calvia ol 2004 (11)

1.e4 c5 2.♘f3 d6 3.d4 cxd4 4.♘xd4 ♘f6 5.♘c3 a6 6.♗e3 e5 7.♘b3 ♗e6 8.f3 ♘bd7 9.♕d2 b5 10.0-0-0 ♘b6 11.♕f2 ♘c4 12.♗xc4 bxc4 13.♘c5

♗e7 14.♘5a4 ♖b8 15.♘b6 0-0 16.♔b1 ♖b7 17.♘cd5 ♘xd5 18.♘xd5 ♖b5 19.♗b6 ♕d7 20.a4 ♖xd5 21.exd5 ♗f5 22.g4 ♗g6 23.f4 exf4 24.♖he1 ♗f6 25.g5 ♗xg5 26.♗d4 ♕xa4 27.♖g1 ♗f6 28.♗xf6 gxf6 29.♕d2 ♖b8 30.♕c3 ♖b5 31.♖d2 f3 32.h4 ♖a5 33.♕a3 ♕xa3 34.bxa3 ♗f8 35.♖d4 ♖xa3 36.♖xc4 ♖e3 37.♖f1 ♗e4 38.♔c1 f5 39.♖f2 ♔e7 40.♖a4 ♗xd5 41.♔d2 ♖e5 42.♖xa6 ♗e4 43.c4 ♖c5 44.♖a4 ♔f6 45.♔e3 ♔e5 46.♖d2 h5 47.♔f2 ♖c8 48.♔e3 ♖c6 49.♖a5+ ♔e6 50.♖a4 ♖c8 51.♖a6 ♖xc4 52.♖axd6+ ♔e5 53.♖a6 ♖c3+ 54.♔f2 ♖c1 55.♖h6 ♖h1 56.♔g3 f4+ 57.♔f2 ♖h2+ 58.♔e1 ♖xh4 59.♖h8 ♔f5 60.♖g8 ♔f6 61.♔f2 ♖g4 62.♖e8 ♔f5 63.♖f8 f6 64.♖h8 ♖g5 65.♖h6 ♖g2+ 66.♔e1 ♖xd2 67.♔xd2 ♔g4 68.♖h8 ♔g3 69.♖g8+ ♔f2 70.♖h8 h4 71.♖xh4 ♔g3 0-1

Karjakin,Sergey
Anand,Viswanathan

Wijk aan Zee 2006 (1)

1.e4 c5 2.♘f3 d6 3.d4 cxd4 4.♘xd4 ♘f6 5.♘c3 a6 6.♗e3 e5 7.♘b3 ♗e6 8.f3 ♗e7 9.♕d2 0-0 10.0-0-0 ♘bd7 11.g4 b5 12.g5 b4 13.♘e2 ♘e8 14.f4 a5 15.f5 a4 16.♘bd4 exd4 17.♘xd4 b3 18.♔b1 bxc2+ 19.♘xc2 ♗b3 20.axb3 axb3 21.♘a3 ♘e5 22.h4 ♖a5 23.♕c3?! ♕a8 24.♗g2 ♘c7!! 25.♕xc7 ♖c8 26.♕xe7 ♘c4! 27.g6 hxg6 28.fxg6 ♘xa3+ 29.bxa3 ♖xa3 30.gxf7+ ♔h7 31.f8♘+ ♖xf8 32.♕xf8 ♖a1+ 33.♔b2 ♖a2+ 34.♔c3 ♕a5+ 35.♔d3 ♕b5+ 36.♔d4 ♖a4+ 37.♔c3 ♕c4+ 0-1

Ivanchuk, Vasily
Topalov, Veselin
Morelia/Linares 2007 (2)

1.e4 c5 2.♘f3 d6 3.d4 cxd4 4.♘xd4 ♘f6 5.♘c3 a6 6.♗e3 e5 7.♘f3 ♗e7 8.♗c4 0-0 9.0-0 ♗e6 10.♗xe6 fxe6 11.♘a4 ♘g4 12.♕d3 ♘xe3 13.♕xe3 b5 14.♘b6 ♖a7 15.♘d5 ♖b7 16.♕d2 ♘c6 17.♖ad1 ♖d7 18.♕c3 ♘b8 19.♘xe7+ ♕xe7 20.♖d3 h6 21.♖fd1 ♖fd8 22.h4 ♔h7 23.♖1d2 ♕f8 24.♕b3 ♕e8 25.a4 ♕g6 26.axb5 axb5 27.♖e3 ♘a6 28.♕xb5 ♘c5 29.♕c4 ♖a7 30.♖e1 ♕e8 31.b4 ♘a4 32.♕b3 ♘b6 33.♖ed1 ♖ad7 34.♕d3 ♖c8 35.c3 ♖a7 36.♕e3 ♖a6 37.♕e2 ♘c4 38.♖a2 ♖ac6 39.♖a7 ♖6c7 40.♖da1± ♕f7?? 41.♕xc4! 1-0

Ivanchuk, Vasily
Shirov, Alexey
Wijk aan Zee 2001 (11)

1.e4 c5 2.♘f3 d6 3.d4 cxd4 4.♘xd4 ♘f6 5.♘c3 a6 6.♗e3 ♘g4 7.♗g5 h6 8.♗h4 g5 9.♗g3 ♗g7 10.h3 ♘f6 11.♗c4 ♕b6 12.0-0 ♘xe4 13.♘xe4 ♕xd4 14.♘xd6+ exd6 15.♕e2+ ♗e6 16.♗xe6 0-0 17.♖ad1 ♕f6

18.♗d5 ♘c6 19.c3 ♖ad8 20.♖fe1 ♕g6 21.a4 ♔h7 22.♗xc6 bxc6 23.♕xa6 d5 24.a5 f5 25.♗e5 ♖a8 26.♕b6 ♖f7 27.b4 f4 28.f3 h5 29.♕f2 ♗h6 30.♗d4 g4 31.hxg4 hxg4 32.fxg4 f3 33.gxf3 ♖af8 34.♔g2 ♖xf3 35.♕xf3 ♖xf3 36.♔xf3 ♕c2 37.a6 ♕h2 38.♗e5 ♕a2 39.♖a1 ♕c2 40.a7 ♕d3+ 41.♔f2 1-0

Kasimdzhanov, Rustam
Anand, Viswanathan
San Luis Wch-FIDE 2005 (4)

1.e4 c5 2.♘f3 d6 3.d4 cxd4 4.♘xd4 ♘f6 5.♘c3 a6 6.♗e3 ♘g4 7.♗g5 h6 8.♗h4 g5 9.♗g3 ♗g7 10.h3 ♘e5 11.♘f5 ♗xf5 12.exf5 ♘bc6 13.♘d5 e6 14.fxe6 fxe6 15.♘e3 0-0 16.♗e2 ♕e7 17.0-0 ♖ad8 18.♗h5 ♔h8 19.♖e1 d5 20.a4 ♘c4 21.♘xc4 dxc4 22.♕g4 ♕b4 23.♕xe6 ♖d2 24.♖ad1 ♘d4 25.♕e4 ♘f5 26.♗e5 ♖xf2 27.♗f3 ♖d2 28.♗xg7+ ♔xg7 29.♕e5+ ♕f6 30.a5 ♘h4 31.♕c7+ ♖f7 32.♕e5+ ♖f6 33.♗h5 ♘g6 34.♗xg6 ♖xd1 35.♖xd1 ♔xg6 36.♕e4+ ♔g7 37.♖d7+ ♔g8 38.♕h7+ 1-0

Sicilian Defence
Najdorf 6.♗g5

**1.e4 c5 2.♘f3 d6 3.d4 cxd4
4.♘xd4 ♘f6 5.♘c3 a6 6.♗g5**

The last of the alternatives is the old main line 6.♗g5. Though it is not so commonly played now, its appeal remains unaltered.

The move was very popular from the 1950s until the 1980s – or, more precisely, the line that continues with 7.f4 was by far the most common variation. With the advent of a burgeoning amount of theory, creative players started to look for alternatives in unexplored areas, as they had become tired of the fact that memory was becoming as important a factor as understanding. For this reason, the move 6.♗g5 was to become a rarity in the 1990s, at least at the higher levels. However, lower-level players have always continued to show a marked preference for this historically important and fascinating variation. Their choice is probably inspired by the hope of a quick checkmate or of encountering an unprepared adversary. In the first years of the new millennium there has been a return of interest at the higher levels. This is perhaps because the quantity of theory for the so-called minor variations has now also reached disturbing proportions. After

6. ... e7-e6

White almost always continues with

7. f2-f4

with the idea of e4-e5. 7.♕f3, which was popular in the early days of the variation, is now very rare. After 7.f4 there is a major crossroads: Black has a healthy choice from six major continuations which are all perfectly playable, plus two minor lines (7...♗d7 and 7...h6). All of these have a lot of related theory and they are strategically very divergent as well; small wonder that 6.♗g5 is a daunting prospect for the lazy player!

A) 7. ... ♘b8-c6

The most recent of the alternatives is now part of established theory. A move that applies pressure to the centre would appear to be logical, since the moves ♗g5 and f2-f4 have isolated the bishop on the kingside, with a resulting weakness of the dark squares in the centre and on the queenside. The question is if the pawn advance e4-e5, which

Black does not appear to be worried about, is good or bad for White.

White has two continuations, both of which produce unclear positions:

A1)

8.	e4-e5	h7-h6
9.	♗g5-h4	g7-g5

Or 9...♘xd4!?.

10.	f4xg5	♘f6-d5
11.	♘c3xd5	e6xd5
12.	e5xd6	♗f8xd6
13.	♕d1-e2+	

with complicated play.

A2)

8.	♘d4xc6	b7xc6
9.	e4-e5	h7-h6
10.	♗g5-h4	g7-g5
11.	f4xg5	♘f6-d5
12.	♘c3-e4	

Or 12.♘xd5.

12. ...		♕d8-b6

and the black king's precarious position seems to be compensated for by the weaknesses on White's queenside.

B)   **7. ...**   **♘b8-d7**

Another way to prevent e4-e5, and also enabling the ...b7-b5 push. When Black develops the bishop to e7, you transpose to the main line with 7...♗e7, but here Black's idea is to immediately activate his pieces on the queenside.

8.	♕d1-f3	♕d8-c7
9.	0-0-0	b7-b5

Now White has three continuations:

B1)

10.	♗f1xb5	a6xb5
11.	♘d4xb5	♕c7-b8
12.	e4-e5	♖a8-a5!
13.	e5xf6	g7xf6
14.	♗g5-h6!	♗f8xh6
15.	♘b5xd6+	♔e8-e7

With two pawns for the piece and the black king out in the open, White would appear to have abundant compensation: in reality practice has taught us that it is a struggle for White to maintain equality.

B2)   10. e4-e5

Aiming to sacrifice two pieces!

10. ...	**♗c8-b7**
11. ♕f3-h3	**d6xe5**
12. ♘d4xe6	**f7xe6**
13. ♕h3xe6+	**♗f8-e7**
14. ♗f1xb5	

Alternatives like 14.♘xb5 and 14.♗xf6 often tend to end in a draw as well.

14. ...	**a6xb5**
15. ♘c3xb5	**♕c7-c6**
16. ♘b5-d6+	**♔e8-d8**
17. f4xe5	**♔d8-c7!**

with a chaotic position whose extreme consequences have yet to be fully examined. However, the unwritten law of chess harmony teaches us that it is rare that such violent methods can refute variations with a solid positional foundation. A draw is the most likely result.

B3)   10. ♗f1-d3

White contents himself with increasing the pressure, and as such this is the most dangerous line.

10. ...	**♗c8-b7**
11. ♖h1-e1	

Now Black can transpose with 11...♗e7 to the main line Najdorf (7...♗e7), or otherwise maintain a position of a more individual nature with 11...0-0-0, or with

11. ...	**♕c7-b6**

After this last move, the sacrifice

12. ♘c3-d5!?

is not forced, but it is interesting. If Black is wise, he will not accept the piece (*after 12...exd5, 13.♘c6!! is very strong*), instead he should sacrifice his queen: 12...♕xd4! 13.♗xf6 gxf6 14.♗xb5 ♕c5 15.b4! ♕xb5 16.♘c7+ ♔e7 17.♘xb5 axb5, with unclear play.

C)   7.   ...   ♕d8-c7

A logical move: before playing ...b7-b5, Black protects himself against the e4-e5 push without worrying about doubled pawns on the f-file.

8.   ♕d1-f3   b7-b5

White doesn't seem to gain an advantage with either the solid 9.♗xf6 gxf6 or the aggressive 9.0-0-0 b4 10.e5 ♗b7 11.♘cb5!? axb5 12.♗xb5+ ♘bd7! 13.♕h3 b3!.

It is surprising that this variation is not played more often.

Polugaevsky Variation

D)   7.   ...   b7-b5

This famous variation is named after its creator, the Russian grandmaster Lev Polugaevsky (1934-1995). He devot-

edly played the variation from 1959 until the 1990s, and it has never been refuted. Like the **Dragon Variation** it always rises from the ashes. Despite all this, it has never been as popular as the other variations. This is perhaps because of the excessive risks involved if you have not memorized a truly large number of lines.

After the thematic

8.   e4-e5   d6xe5
9.   f4xe5

Black does not lose a piece on account of

9.   ...   ♕d8-c7

and now we have reached a major crossroads: White can defend e5 to maintain his space advantage, but he will be left with a weak e5-pawn. He can also take on f6 conceding a central

pawn and his dark-squared bishop, and put his faith in the lead in development that he gains.

D1)   **10. ♕d1-e2   ♘f6-d7**
        11. 0-0-0   ♗c8-b7

11...♘c6 is also interesting.

        12. ♕e2-g4

Now Black can play either the cautious 12...♕b6 to parry the threat of 13.♘xe6, or the bold 12...♕xe5. White can meet the latter with the optimistic 13.♗xb5; however, it is better to choose 13.♗e2, with the idea of ♗f3, which keeps Black under long-term pressure. Years of practical play have shown that White is unable to overcome the surprising resilience of Black's positions in both these lines.

D2)   **10. e5xf6   ♕c7-e5+**
        11. ♗f1-e2   ♕e5xg5

After 12.0-0 or the refined 12.♕d3, nobody has yet found a way to squeeze any advantage out of White's lead in development, even if it is evident that Black is walking on a tightrope.

Poisoned Pawn Variation

E)   **7. ...   ♕d8-b6**

This is the famous **Poisoned Pawn Variation**. Since its inception, it has always been the subject of controversy. Its colourful name would suggest a scant regard for the validity of the variation, but the experience gained from years of practical play is that the b2-pawn often proves to be a tasty morsel for Black, and not a small pellet of poisonous bait! The Poisoned Pawn Variation first appeared in tournament play in the 1950s and it was at first underestimated, in part due to the brilliant victories with the white pieces obtained by Keres and Tal. However, there is nothing as persuasive as victory, and Fischer's successes in the 1960s with the black pieces quickly changed the opinion of opening scholars and players alike. This is made evident by the fact that 7...♕b6 was Kasparov's favourite move. However, rarely anyone felt brave enough to take him on with this line. In a certain sense, 7...♕b6 is perhaps Black's most logical move: with the dark-squared bishop no longer controlling b2 and e3, White's queenside is put under immediate pressure.

        8. ♕d1-d2

The timid 8.♘b3 is playable, but brings no advantage.

        8. ...   ♕b6xb2

White has two continuations:

E1)   9. ♘d4-b3

The most solid. It seems unnatural to take the ♘d4 away from the centre, but the threat of a2-a3 and ♖a2 forces Black to act.

9.   ...   ♕b2-a3

9...♘c6 is also playable as after 10.a3 ♘a5 11.♖a2, 11...♘xb3 saves the queen.

10. ♗g5xf6   g7xf6
11. ♗f1-e2   h7-h5
12. 0-0

and White's compensation is difficult to evaluate.

E2)   9. ♖a1-b1

The most natural, and it is considered to be the strongest, even if statistically the results are in Black's favour!

9.   ...   ♕b2-a3

The following attempts fail to give White an advantage: 10.e5, 10.♗xf6 and 10.♗e2.
The same goes for

10. f4-f5   ♘b8-c6
11. f5xe6   f7xe6
12. ♘d4xc6   b7xc6

Here the positions become tactically highly complex after either the solid 13.♗e2, or

13. e4-e5!?   d6xe5

13...♘d5 is another line.

14. ♗g5xf6   g7xf6
15. ♘c3-e4

Some continuations have been deeply studied until the endgame stage: with correct play Black maintains at least equality. However, it obvious that we are dealing with very risky lines that do not offer many opportunities for personal interpretation.

F)   **7. ...**   **♗f8-e7**

The so-called **Main Line**. Black delays counterplay on the queenside and develops naturally on the kingside. White continues with

     8. ♕d1-f3

to prepare queenside castling.

An attentive student might ask why the queen is moved to f3 and not to d2, as is the case in the Richter-Rauzer. This is because on f3 the queen is more usefully placed than on d2: it is easier to transfer it to g3 or to h3 and the advance e4-e5 will gain force when Black plays ...b7-b5. Above all, the move 8.♕d2 would lead to a tactical problem here after 8...h6! and if 9.♗h4 ♘xe4!.

Back to 8.♕f3. At this point we are at an important crossroads: 8...h6 or 8...♕c7.

F1)   **8. ...**   **h7-h6**

The **Gothenburg Variation**, whose ambitious idea is

     9. ♗g5-h4   **g7-g5!?**

To break up the white pawn formation on the kingside. This variation made its simultaneous (!) debut in the 1955 Interzonal tournament in Gothenburg. Remarkably, three Argentinean players, Pilnik, Panno and Najdorf, played it at the same time against three Soviet champions: Spassky, Geller and Keres, respectively. The result: three victories for White!

The implied verdict has not changed with time: against correct play Black has an uphill battle maintaining equality after

     10. f4xg5   **♘f6-d7**
     11. ♘d4xe6!

11.♕h5 also makes a lot of sense.

     11. ...   **f7xe6**
     12. ♕f3-h5+   **♚e8-f8**
     13. ♗f1-b5!!

The move played by Geller in the previously mentioned stem game, and the one that is still considered to be the best.

Fischer came up with the best defence three years later: 13...♖h7! (Gligoric-Fischer, Portoroz 1958). After 14.0-0+ ♚g8 15.g6 ♖g7 16.♖f7 ♗xh4

343

17.♕xh6, according to the most recent analysis the white attack remains strong and promising.

The idea of playing ...h6 and, on the retreat of the bishop to h4, to continue with ...g5 to give the white f4-pawn a kick, and place the d7-knight on the e5 outpost is a characteristic strategic manoeuvre. We have already seen this manoeuvre in the **Richter-Rauzer**, and we will see it again in Variation F21 with 10.♗d3 – see below.

F2)   8. ...   ♕d8-c7

The most frequent response. It prevents 9.♗c4, or rather this is the explanation given in the chess opening bibles.

9. 0-0-0   ♘b8-d7

We find ourselves confronted with another big dilemma for White: 10.♗d3 or 10.g4?

F21)   10. ♗f1-d3

Moving the last undeveloped piece to a natural square and inaugurating a strategy of central play.

10. ...   b7-b5

Consistent, but there exists a playable alternative that is safer: 10...h6 (an example of the irony of chess – this safe idea stems from the highly risky Gothenburg Variation) 11.♗h4 g5!?

and the interesting idea of making a positional pawn sacrifice becomes apparent: 12.fxg5 ♘e5 13.♕e2 ♘fg4.

Back to 10...b5.

Play continues with 11.♖he1 ♗b7. Now White can continue with **Velimirovic's sacrifice** 12.♘d5!?, which is interesting but probably unsound (please go to the appendix to look at the brilliant victory by Velimirovic when he first uncorked his sacrifice). However, White is not forced to play this sacrifice and he can play the quieter 12.♕g3

and then after 12...b4!? (12...0-0-0 had its trial by fire in the first Spassky-Fischer match, in Reykjavik 1972), the sacrifice on d5 becomes even more dangerous. However, it should not worry Black too much; provided that he is well prepared!

F22) 10. g2-g4

A standard attacking move in the Sicilian.

In this situation, there are two problems: the bishop on g5 obstructs g4-g5 and Black can still castle queenside, thwarting, at least partly, White's pawn storm.

Therefore White is required to take energetic measures before Black can quietly complete his development.

10. ...　　　　**b7-b5**
11. ♗g5xf6

To speed up the initiative.

11. ...　　　　**♘d7xf6**

Fischer's move 11...gxf6!? is hardly ever played now, but it is not as bad as it might seem.

12. g4-g5　　　　**♘f6-d7**
13. f4-f5!

13.a3 seems slow for the reasons explained above.

13. ...　　　　**♗e7xg5+**

To accept the pawn seems best; after 13...♘c5 14.f6 gxf6 15.gxf6 ♗f8 16.♖g1! ♗d7 17.♖g7!!, practical play has demonstrated that White has a highly dangerous initiative.

14. ♔c1-b1　　　　**♘d7-e5**
15. ♕f3-h5

Attacking e6 and g5.

15. ...　　　　**♕c7-e7**

Or 15...♕d8.

16. ♘d4xe6　　　　**♗c8xe6**
17. f5xe6　　　　**g7-g6**
18. e6xf7+

White gets back the pawn with a position which is difficult to evaluate: Black's king is a little exposed, the d6-pawn is weak, and the d5-square is in White's hands... yet this is not enough to yield a decisive advantage! The powerful knight on e5 and his control of the dark-square complex gives Black sufficient counterplay.

Timman,Jan
Gelfand,Boris
Wijk aan Zee 2002 (8)

1.e4 c5 2.♘f3 d6 3.d4 cxd4 4.♘xd4 ♘f6 5.♘c3 a6 6.♗g5 e6 7.f4 ♘bd7 8.♕f3 ♕c7 9.0-0-0 b5 10.♗xb5 axb5 11.♘dxb5 ♕b8 12.e5 ♖a5 13.exf6 gxf6 14.♗h6 ♗xh6 15.♘xd6+ ♔e7 16.♔b1 ♖d8 17.♖he1 ♘b6 18.♘cb5 ♖xb5 19.♘xb5 ♖xd1+?! [19...♘c4] 20.♖xd1 ♗xf4 21.g3 ♗e5 22.♕a3+ ♔e8 23.♘d6+ ♗xd6 24.♕xd6 ♕xd6 25.♖xd6 ♘d5 26.c4 ♔e7

345

27.♖c6 ♗b7 28.cxd5! ♗xc6 29.dxc6
♔d6 30.g4!   1-0

Chiburdanidze,Maia
Dvoiris,Semen

Tallinn 1980

1.e4 c5 2.♘f3 d6 3.d4 cxd4 4.♘xd4
♘f6 5.♘c3 a6 6.♗g5 e6 7.f4 ♘bd7
8.♕f3 ♕c7 9.0-0-0 b5 10.♗d3 ♗b7
11.♖he1 ♕b6 12.♘d5!? exd5?
[12...♕xd4!] 13.♘c6!! ♗xc6
14.exd5+ ♗e7 15.dxc6 ♘c5
16.♗xf6 gxf6 17.♗f5 ♕c7 18.b4
♘e6 19.♕h5 ♘g7 20.♗d7+ ♔f8
21.♕h6 d5 22.♖xe7 ♔xe7 23.♖e1+
♔f8 24.♕xf6 ♔g8 25.♖e7 ♖f8
26.♗e6 ♕xe7 27.♕xe7 fxe6 28.c7
h5 29.♕xf8+ ♔xf8 30.c8♕+ ♔f7
31.♕xh8   1-0

Spassky,Boris
Rashkovsky,Nukhim

Moscow ch-URS 1973 (8)

1.e4 c5 2.♘f3 d6 3.d4 cxd4 4.♘xd4
♘f6 5.♘c3 a6 6.♗g5 e6 7.f4 ♕c7
8.♗d3 [8.♕f3] 8...♘bd7 9.♕e2 b5?!
[9...♗e7] 10.0-0-0 ♗b7 [10...b4
11.♘d5! exd5 12.exd5+ ♗e7 13.♖he1
♘b8 14.♗xf6 gxf6 15.♗f5! ♖a7
16.♗xc8 ♖xc8 17.g4 ♘d8 18.♘f5 ♖e8
19.♖d3 ♕d7 20.♖e3±] 11.♖he1 ♗e7
[11...0-0-0!?] 12.e5! dxe5 13.fxe5
♘d5 14.♗xe7?! [14.♘xe6! fxe6
(14...♗xg5+ 15.♘xg5 ♘xc3 16.bxc3
♕xc3 17.♕g4 ♕a3+ 18.♔d2 ♕a5+
19.♔e2 Keres) 15.♕h5+ ♔d8
16.♘xd5 ♗xd5 17.♗xe7+ ♔xe7
18.♕g5+ ♔e8 19.♕xg7] 14...♘xc3
15.♕g4 ♘xd1 [15...♔xe7?
16.♘xe6!+−] 16.♘xe6 ♕c6?
[16...fxe6! 17.♗d6 ♕b6 18.♕xe6+!
(18.♕g5?! ♘f6!) 18...♔d8 19.♗f5

♗c6 20.♖xd1 ♖e8 21.♕f7 ♕e3+
22.♔b1 ♕e2 23.♔c1 ♕e3+=]
17.♘xg7+ ♔xe7 18.♕g5+ f6
[18...♔f8 19.♘f5] 19.exf6+ ♔d8
20.f7+ ♔c7 21.♕f4+   1-0

Tal,Mikhail
Polugaevsky,Lev

Alma-Ata m 1980 (2)

1.e4 c5 2.♘f3 d6 3.d4 cxd4 4.♘xd4
♘f6 5.♘c3 a6 6.♗g5 e6 7.f4 b5 8.e5
dxe5 9.fxe5 ♕c7 10.♗xb5+ axb5
11.exf6 ♕e5+ 12.♕e2 ♕xg5
13.♘dxb5 ♖a5 14.fxg7 ♗xg7
15.♘e4 ♕e5 16.♘bd6+ ♔e7 17.0-0
f5 18.♖ad1 ♖d5 19.♕c4 ♖xd1
20.♖xd1 fxe4 21.♘xc8+ ♔f7
22.♘d6+ ♔g6 23.♘xe4 ♘a6 24.♘f2
♘c5 25.b4 ♘a4 26.♘g4 ♕f5
27.♘e3 ♕b2 28.♕h4 ♕e5 29.♕g4+
♔h6 30.♖e1 ♗f6 31.b5 ♖f8 32.b6
♗g5 33.♕g3 ♕xg3 34.hxg3 ♔g7
35.♘g4 ♘c4 36.♖xe6 ♖b8 37.♖c6
♘xb6 38.♖c7+ ♔g8 39.c4 ♘a4
40.♔f2 ♖b2+ 41.♔f3 ♖xa2 42.♔e4
♖e2+ 43.♔f5 ♗e7 44.♘f6+ ♗xf6
45.♔xf6 ♘b6 46.g4 ♖xg2 47.♔g5
♖d2 48.c5 ♘d7 49.c6 ♖d5+ 50.♔h6
♖d6+ 51.♔g5 ♘e5 52.♖c8+ ♔g7
53.♖c7+ ♘f7+ 54.♔f5 h6 55.♔e4
♔f6 56.♖c8 ♖d1 57.♖f8 ♖d6 58.♖c8
♘g5+ 59.♔e3 ♔e7 60.♔f4 ♘f7
61.♔g3 ♖d3+ 62.♔g2 ♖c3 63.♖c7+
♔f6 64.♖c8 ♘e5 65.c7 ♘f7 66.♖g8
♖xc7 67.♔g3 ♖c1 68.♖a8 ♘e5
69.♖f8+ ♔g7 70.♖f5 ♖c3+   0-1

Beliavsky,Alexander
Polugaevsky,Lev

Moscow Spartakiad 1979

1.e4 c5 2.♘f3 d6 3.d4 cxd4
4.♘xd4 ♘f6 5.♘c3 a6 6.♗g5 e6

7.f4 b5 8.e5 dxe5 9.fxe5 ♛c7
10.exf6 ♛e5+ 11.♗e2 ♛xg5
12.0-0 ♛e5 13.♘f3 ♗c5+ 14.♔h1
♛xf6 15.♘e4 ♛e7 16.♘fg5 0-0
17.♘xf7 ♖xf7 18.♖xf7 ♔xf7
19.♗h5+ ♔g8 20.♘xc5 ♘d7
21.♘xe6 ♗b7 22.♗f3 ♗xf3
23.♛xf3 ♖e8 24.♘d4 ♛e1+
25.♛f1 ♛b4 26.♘b3 ♘f6 27.c3
♛h4 28.♘d4 ♘g4 29.♘f3 ♛f2
30.h3 ♛xf1+ 31.♖xf1 ♘f6 32.♔g1
♖e2 33.♖f2 ♖e3 34.♖d2 ♘e4
35.♖d8+ ♔f7 36.♔f1 ♘c5 37.♖d5
♘a4 38.♖d2 h6 39.♘d4 ♖e4
40.♘e2 ♖e7 41.♔e1 h5 42.♔d1 h4
43.b3 ♘c5 44.♖d4 ♔f6 45.♖xe4
♘xe4 46.♔c2 ♔e5 47.♔d3 ♘f2+
48.♔e3 ♘d1+ 49.♔d2 ♘f2 50.♘d4
♔f4 51.♘e6+ ♔g3 52.♔e3 ♘d1+
53.♔d4 ♔xg2 54.c4 bxc4 55.bxc4
♔xh3 56.c5 ♘b2 57.c6 ♘a4
58.♘f4+ ♔g3 59.♘d5 h3 60.c7 h2
61.c8♛ h1♛ 62.♛c7+ ♔h4
63.♛d8+ ♔g3 64.♛g5+ ♔h2
65.♛h5+ ♔g1 66.♛d1+ ♔h2
67.♛xa4 ♛a1+ 68.♔c5 (78) 1-0

12...♘xe4 13.♘xe4 ♗xh4 14.f5!
exf5 15.♗b5+ axb5 [15...♔e7
16.♛f4 g5 17.♛e3! ♗e6 (17...fxe4
18.♛xe4+ ♗e6 19.♘c4±; 17...axb5
18.♘xd6+! ♔xd6 (18...♗e6
19.♘xf5++–) 19.♖ad1+ ♔c7
20.♛e5+ ♔b6 21.♛d4+ (21.♛xh8
♘c6 22.g3 ♗e6∞) 21...♔c7
22.♛e5+=) 18.♗c4∞] 16.♘xd6+
♔f8 17.♘xc8 ♘c6 18.♘d6 ♖d8
19.♘xb5 ♛e7 20.♛f4 g6 21.a4 ♗g5
22.♛c4 ♗e3+ 23.♔h1 f4 24.g3 g5
[24...♘e5!] 25.♖ae1 ♛b4
26.♛xb4+ ♘xb4 27.♖e2 ♔g7
[27...♘c6∓] 28.♘a5 b6 [28...♖d7!?]
29.♘c4 ♘d5 30.♘cd6 ♗c5
[30...♔g6!?] 31.♘b7 ♖c8
[31...♘e3!–+ Tal] 32.c4 ♘e3 33.♖f3
♗xc4 34.gxf4 g4 35.♖d3 h5 36.h3
♘a5 37.♘7d6 ♗xd6 38.♘xd6 ♖c1+
39.♔g2 ♘c4 40.♘e8+ ♔g6 41.h4!
f6 42.♖e6 ♖c2+ 43.♔g1 ♔f5
44.♘g7+ ♔xf4 45.♖d4+ ♔g3
46.♘f5+ ♔f3 47.♖ee4 ♖c1+
48.♔h2 ♖c2+ 49.♔g1 ½-½

Spassky,Boris
Fischer,Robert
Reykjavik Wch m 1972 (7)

1.e4 c5 2.♘f3 d6 3.d4 cxd4 4.♘xd4
♘f6 5.♘c3 a6 6.♗g5 e6 7.f4 ♛b6
8.♛d2 ♛xb2 9.♘b3 ♛a3 [9...♘c6
10.♗xf6 (10.a3 ♘a5!) 10...gxf6
11.♘a4 ♛a3 12.♘b6 ♖b8 13.♘c4
♛a4 White has good compensation for
the pawn; 9...♘bd7 is possible in view
of 10.a3?! ♘c5] 10.♗d3 ♗e7 11.0-0
h6 12.♗h4 [12.♗xf6 ♗xf6 13.e5
(with chances for both sides) 13...dxe5
(13...♗e7 14.♖fe1!) 14.♘e4]

Spassky,Boris
Fischer,Robert
Reykjavik Wch m 1972 (11)

1.e4 c5 2.♘f3 d6 3.d4 cxd4 4.♘xd4
♘f6 5.♘c3 a6 6.♗g5 e6 7.f4 ♛b6
8.♛d2 ♛xb2 9.♘b3 ♛a3 10.♗xf6
gxf6 11.♗e2 h5 12.0-0 ♘c6 13.♔h1
♗d7 14.♘b1 ♛b4 15.♛e3 d5?
[15...♘e7!] 16.exd5 ♘e7 17.c4 ♘f5
18.♛d3! h4? [18...♖c8] 19.♗g4 ♘d6
20.♘1d2 f5? 21.a3 ♛b6 22.c5 ♛b5
23.♛c3 fxg4 24.a4+– h3 25.axb5
hxg2+ 26.♔xg2 ♖h3 27.♛f6 ♘f5
28.c6 ♗c8 29.dxe6 fxe6 30.♖fe1
♗e7 31.♖xe6 1-0

Qi Jingxuan
Karpov,Anatoly
Hannover 1983 (13)

1.e4 c5 2.♘f3 d6 3.d4 cxd4 4.♘xd4 ♘f6 5.♘c3 a6 6.♗g5 e6 7.f4 ♕b6 8.♕d2 ♕xb2 9.♘b3 ♕a3 10.♗xf6 gxf6 11.♗e2 h5 12.0-0 ♘c6 13.♔h1 ♗d7 14.♘b1 ♕b4 15.♕e3 ♘e7! 16.c4 f5 17.a3 ♕a4 18.♘c3 ♕c6 19.♘d4 ♕c5 20.exf5 ♗g7 21.fxe6 fxe6 22.♖ad1 ♗xd4 23.♕xd4 ♕xd4 24.♖xd4 ♘f5 25.♖d2 ♖c8 26.♖f3 ♔e7 27.♔g1 h4 28.♗d3 ♖c5 29.♗xf5 ♖xf5 30.♖fd3 ♖xf4 31.♖xd6 ♗c6 32.c5 ♖hf8 33.h3 ♖f1+ 34.♔h2 ♖c1 35.♖6d3 ♖ff1 36.♘d1 e5 37.♘f2 ♖g1 38.♘d1 ♖e1 39.♖d6 e4 40.♖2d4 a5 41.♘f2 e3 42.♖xh4 exf2 43.♖h7+ ♔e8 44.♖h8+ ♔f7   0-1

Short,Nigel
Kasparov,Garry
London Wch m 1993 (4)

1.e4 c5 2.♘f3 d6 3.d4 cxd4 4.♘xd4 ♘f6 5.♘c3 a6 6.♗g5 e6 7.f4 ♕b6 8.♕d2 ♕xb2 9.♘b3 ♕a3 10.♗xf6 gxf6 11.♗e2 ♘c6 12.0-0 ♗d7 13.♔h1 h5 14.♘d1 ♖c8 15.♘e3 ♕b4 16.c3 ♕xe4 17.♗d3 ♕a4 18.♘c4 ♖c7 19.♘b6 ♕a3 20.♖ae1 ♘e7 21.♘c4 ♖xc4 22.♗xc4 h4 23.♗d3 f5 24.♗e2 ♗g7 25.c4 h3 26.g3 d5 27.♗f3 dxc4 28.♖e3 c3 29.♖xc3 ♗xc3 30.♕xc3 0-0 31.♖g1 ♖c8 32.♕f6 ♗c6 33.♗xc6 ♖xc6 34.g4 ♘g6 35.gxf5 exf5 36.♕xf5 ♕xa2 37.♕xh3 ♕c2 38.f5 ♖c3 39.♕g4 ♖xb3 40.fxg6 ♕c6+   0-1

Luther,Thomas
Kasimdzhanov,Rustam
Essen 2002 (3)

1.e4 c5 2.♘f3 d6 3.d4 cxd4 4.♘xd4 ♘f6 5.♘c3 a6 6.♗g5 e6 7.f4 ♕b6 8.♕d2 ♕xb2 9.♘b3 ♕a3 10.♗xf6 gxf6 11.♗e2 h5 12.0-0 ♘d7 13.♔h1 h4 14.h3 b6 15.♖ad1 ♗b7 16.f5 ♖c8 17.fxe6 fxe6 18.♕d4 ♗e7 19.♗g4 ♘c5 20.♖f3 ♘xb3 21.cxb3 ♕c5 22.♗xe6 ♕xd4 23.♖xd4 ♖c5 24.♘d5 b5 25.♖d1 ♖h5 26.♘xf6+ ♗xf6 27.♖xf6 ♖he5 28.♗f5 d5 29.♗g6+ ♔d8 30.exd5 ♖cxd5 31.♖xd5+ ♗xd5 32.♖f2 ♔e7 33.♔h2 ♔d6 34.♗d3 ♖e1 35.♗e2 ♔c5 36.♗f3 ♗e6 37.♖e2 ♖xe2 38.♗xe2 ♗b4 39.a4 ♗xb3 40.♗xb5 axb5 41.axb5 ♔xb5   ½-½

Keres,Paul
Fuderer,Andrija
Gothenburg izt 1955 (16)

1.e4 c5 2.♘f3 d6 3.d4 cxd4 4.♘xd4 ♘f6 5.♘c3 a6 6.♗g5 e6 7.f4 ♕b6 8.♕d2 ♕xb2 9.♖b1 ♕a3 10.e5 ♘fd7 11.f5 ♘xe5 12.fxe6 fxe6 13.♗e2 ♘bc6 14.♘xc6 bxc6 15.♘e4 d5 16.0-0 ♕a4 17.♗h5+ ♔d7 18.♖xf8   1-0

Bilek,Istvan
Fischer,Robert
Stockholm izt 1962 (5)

1.e4 c5 2.♘f3 d6 3.d4 cxd4 4.♘xd4 ♘f6 5.♘c3 a6 6.♗g5 e6 7.f4 ♕b6 8.♕d2 ♕xb2 9.♖b1 ♕a3 10.e5 dxe5 11.fxe5 ♘fd7 12.♗c4 ♗e7 13.♗xe6 0-0 14.0-0 ♗xg5 15.♕xg5 h6 16.♕h4 ♕xc3 17.♖xf7 ♖xf7 18.♕d8+ ♘f8 19.♗xf7+ ♔xf7 20.♖f1+ ♔g6 21.♖xf8 ♗d7 22.♘f3

♕e3+ 23.♔h1 ♕c1+ 24.♘g1 ♕xc2 25.♖g8 ♕f2 26.♖f8 ♕xa2 27.♖f3 ♔h7   0-1

Tal,Mikhail
Tolush,Alexander
Leningrad ch-URS 1956 (17)

1.e4 c5 2.♘f3 d6 3.d4 cxd4 4.♘xd4 ♘f6 5.♘c3 a6 6.♗g5 e6 7.f4 ♕b6 8.♕d2 ♕xb2 9.♖b1 ♕a3 10.e5 dxe5 11.fxe5 ♘fd7 12.♘e4 ♕xa2 [12...h6!] 13.♖b3 ♕a1+ 14.♔f2 ♕a4 15.♗b5 [15.♘xe6!+−] 15...axb5 16.♘xb5 f6 17.exf6 gxf6? [17...♕xe4!] 18.♖e1 ♖a6 19.♗xf6 ♘xf6 20.♘xf6+ ♔f7 21.♖f3 ♕h4+ 22.♔f1 e5 23.♕d5+ ♗e6 24.♘d7+ ♔g6 25.♘xe5+ ♔g7 26.♖g3+ ♕xg3 27.♕xb7+ ♘d7 28.hxg3 ♖b6 29.♕c7 ♗c5 30.♘xd7 ♗c4+ 31.♖e2   1-0

Radjabov,Teimour
Anand,Viswanathan
Rishon-le-Zion Wch blitz 2006 (5)

1.e4 c5 2.♘f3 d6 3.d4 cxd4 4.♘xd4 ♘f6 5.♘c3 a6 6.♗g5 e6 7.f4 ♕b6 8.♕d2 ♕xb2 9.♖b1 ♕a3 10.e5 dxe5 11.fxe5 ♘fd7 12.♘e4 h6! 13.♗h4 [13.♗b5!?!] 13...♕a4? 14.♗e2 ♘c6? 15.♘xe6!+− g5 16.♘f6+   1-0

Radjabov,Teimour
Karjakin,Sergey
Cap d'Agde rapid 2006 (3)

1.e4 c5 2.♘f3 d6 3.d4 cxd4 4.♘xd4 ♘f6 5.♘c3 a6 6.♗g5 e6 7.f4 ♕b6 8.♕d2 ♕xb2 9.♖b1 ♕a3 10.e5 dxe5 11.fxe5 ♘fd7 12.♘e4 h6 13.♗h4 ♕xa2! 14.♖d1 [a recent and quite successful attempt at rehabilitation] 14...♕b2?! 15.♕e3 ♗c5 16.♗e2

♘c6 17.c3 [17.♘xe6!!] 17...♕a3 18.0-0 0-0 19.♘f6+ ♘xf6 20.♗xf6! ♘xd4 21.♖xd4 ♗xd4 22.♕xd4 gxf6 23.exf6 ♕a5 24.h4 ♔h7 25.♗d3+ ♕f5 26.♖e1 ♖g8 27.♔h2 a5 28.g4 ♕xd3 29.♕xd3+ ♔h8 30.♖e5 ♖xg4 31.♖h5 ♖g6 32.♕d8+ ♔h7 33.♕e7   1-0

Motylev,Alexander
Anand,Viswanathan
Wijk aan Zee 2007 (2)

1.e4 c5 2.♘f3 d6 3.d4 cxd4 4.♘xd4 ♘f6 5.♘c3 a6 6.♗g5 e6 7.f4 ♕b6 8.♕d2 ♕xb2 9.♖b1 ♕a3 10.e5 h6 11.♗h4 dxe5 12.fxe5 ♘fd7 13.♘e4 ♕xa2 14.♖d1 ♕d5! [Kasparov's suggestion] 15.♕e3 ♕xe5 16.♗e2 ♗c5! 17.♗g3 ♗xd4 18.♖xd4 ♕a5+ 19.♖d2 0-0 20.♗d6 ♖d8 21.♕g3 ♕f5 22.♗e5 ♕g6 23.♕h4 ♘c6 24.0-0 [24.♗h5] 24...f5 25.♗h5 ♕h7 26.♗b2 fxe4 27.♖f7 ♖f8 28.♕f2? [28.♖xg7 ♕xg7 29.♗xg7 ♔xg7 30.♕g3+ ♔h8 31.♕g6=] 28...♖xf7 29.♕xf7+ ♔h8 30.♖f2 e5 31.♕d5 ♘f6   0-1

Anand,Viswanathan
Van Wely,Loek
Wijk aan Zee 2007 (9)

1.e4 c5 2.♘f3 d6 3.d4 cxd4 4.♘xd4 ♘f6 5.♘c3 a6 6.♗g5 e6 7.f4 ♕b6 8.♕d2 ♕xb2 9.♖b1 ♕a3 10.e5 h6 11.♗h4 dxe5 12.fxe5 ♘fd7 13.♘e4 ♕xa2 14.♖d1 ♕d5 15.♕e3 ♕xe5 16.♗e2 ♗c5 17.♗g3 ♗xd4 18.♖xd4 ♕a5+ 19.♖d2 0-0 20.♗d6 ♘c6 [Black deviates from the previous game] 21.♗xf8 ♘xf8 22.0-0∞ ♗d7 23.♘d6 ♘e5 24.♘xb7 ♕c7 25.♘d6 f6 26.c4 ♗c6 27.♖a1 ♘fd7 28.♕d4 a5

29.♘b5 ♕b6? [29...♕b7!] 30.♕xb6 ♘xb6 31.♖d6 ♘bd7 32.♘d4 ♗e4 33.♘xe6 a4 34.♘c7 ♖a5 35.♖a6 ♖xa6 36.♘xa6 ♗c6 37.c5 ♗b7 38.♖c1 ♘c6 39.♘c7 ♘d4 40.♗c4+ ♔f8 41.♖d1   1-0

Fischer,Robert
Geller,Efim
Monte Carlo 1967 (11)

1.e4 c5 2.♘f3 d6 3.d4 cxd4 4.♘xd4 ♘f6 5.♘c3 a6 6.♗g5 e6 7.f4 ♕b6 8.♕d2 ♕xb2 9.♖b1 ♕a3 10.f5 ♘c6 11.fxe6 fxe6 12.♘xc6 bxc6 13.e5 ♘d5 14.♘xd5 cxd5 15.♗e2 dxe5 16.0-0 ♗c5+ 17.♔h1 ♖f8 18.c4 ♖xf1+ 19.♖xf1 ♗b7 20.♗g4 dxc4 21.♗xe6 ♕d3 22.♕e1 ♗e4 23.♗g4 ♖b8 24.♗d1 ♔d7 25.♖f7+ ♔e6 0-1

Beliavsky,Alexander
Timman,Jan
Tilburg 1981 (11)

1.e4 c5 2.♘f3 d6 3.d4 cxd4 4.♘xd4 ♘f6 5.♘c3 a6 6.♗g5 e6 7.f4 ♕b6 8.♕d2 ♕xb2 9.♖b1 ♕a3 10.f5 ♘c6 11.fxe6 fxe6 12.♘xc6 bxc6 13.e5 dxe5 14.♗xf6 gxf6 15.♘e4 ♗e7 16.♗e2 h5 17.♖b3 ♕a4 18.♘xf6+ ♗xf6 19.c4 ♖a7 20.0-0 ♖d7 21.♕e3 ♕xa2 22.♖xf6 ♕a1+ 23.♗f1 ♖g7 24.♖b8 ♔e7 25.♖f2 ♕d4 26.♕f3 e4 27.♕f4 ♖g4 28.♕c7+ ♕d7 29.♖xc8 ♕xc7 30.♖xc7+ ♔d6 31.♖a7 e3 32.♖e2 ♖e4 33.♖xa6 ♔c5 34.♖a3   1-0

Porreca,Giorgio
Bertok,Mario
Zagreb 1955 (3)

1.e4 c5 2.♘f3 d6 3.d4 cxd4 4.♘xd4 ♘f6 5.♘c3 a6 6.♗g5 e6

7.f4 ♗e7 8.♕f3 ♘c6 9.0-0-0 ♘xd4 10.♖xd4 ♕c7 11.♗h4 b5 12.g4 ♗b7 13.♗g2 ♖c8 14.♕e2 ♘xe4 15.♘xe4 ♗xe4 16.♗xe4 ♗xh4 17.g5 h6 18.♖hd1 ♖d8 19.a4 hxg5 20.axb5 gxf4 21.bxa6 ♕b6 22.♖a4 ♖d7 23.♔b1 ♔e7 24.♖d3 ♕g1+ 25.♔a2 ♗f2 26.♖d1 ♕xh2 27.♖h1 ♗g1 28.♖xh2 ♖xh2 29.♕g4 ♗e3 30.♕xg7 d5 31.♗xd5 exd5 32.♕e5+ ♔f8 33.♕b8+ ♔g7 34.♖xf4 ♗xf4 35.♕xf4 ♖g2 36.♕d4+ ♔g6 37.a7 ♖xa7+ 38.♕xa7 ♖xc2 39.♕d4 f5 40.♕xd5 ♔g5 41.♔b1 ♖f2 42.b4 ♔g4 43.b5 f4 44.b6 f3 45.♕d4+ ♔g3 46.b7 ♔g2 47.b8♕   1-0

Geller,Efim
Panno,Oscar
Gothenburg izt 1955 (14)

1.e4 c5 2.♘f3 d6 3.d4 cxd4 4.♘xd4 ♘f6 5.♘c3 a6 6.♗g5 e6 7.f4 ♗e7 8.♕f3 h6 9.♗h4 g5 10.fxg5 ♘fd7 11.♘xe6 fxe6 12.♕h5+ ♔f8 13.♗b5 ♘e5 14.♗g3 ♗xg5 15.0-0 ♔e7 16.♗xe5 ♕b6+ 17.♔h1 dxe5 18.♕f7+ ♔d6 19.♖ad1+ ♕d4 20.♖xd4+ exd4 21.e5+ ♔c5 22.♕c7+ ♘c6 23.♗xc6   1-0

Gligoric,Svetozar
Fischer,Robert
Portoroz izt 1958 (21)

1.e4 c5 2.♘f3 d6 3.d4 cxd4 4.♘xd4 ♘f6 5.♘c3 a6 6.♗g5 e6 7.f4 ♗e7 8.♕f3 h6 9.♗h4 g5 10.fxg5 ♘fd7 11.♘xe6 fxe6 12.♕h5+ ♔f8 13.♗b5 ♖h7! 14.♕g6 ♖f7 15.♕xh6+ ♔g8 16.♕g6+ ♖g7 17.♕xe6+ ♔h8

18.♗xd7 ♘xd7 19.0-0-0 ♘e5
20.♕d5 ♗g4 21.♖df1 ♗xg5+
22.♗xg5 ♕xg5+ 23.♔b1 ♕e7
24.♕d2 ♗e6 25.g3 ♖d8 26.♖f4
♕g5 27.♕f2 ♔g8 28.♖d1 ♖f7 29.b3
♕e7 30.♕d4 ♘g6 31.♖xf7 ♕xf7
32.♕e3 ½-½

Luther,Thomas
Ott,Frank
Höckendorf ch-GER 2004 (5)

1.e4 c5 2.♘f3 d6 3.d4 cxd4 4.♘xd4
♘f6 5.♘c3 a6 6.♗g5 e6 7.f4 h6
8.♗h4 ♗e7 9.♕f3 ♕c7 10.0-0-0
♘bd7 11.♗d3 g5 12.fxg5 ♘e5
13.♕e2 ♘fg4 14.♘f3 ♘xf3 15.♕xf3
hxg5 16.♗g3 ♘e5 17.♗xe5 dxe5
18.♖df1 ♖h7 19.h4 b5 20.♔b1 ♖g7
21.hxg5 b4 22.g6 bxc3 23.gxf7+
♔d7 24.f8♕ ♗xf8 25.♕xf8 ♔c6
26.♗c4 ♕e7 27.♗xe6 ♖b8 28.♗d5+
♔c7 29.♕xe7+ ♖xe7 30.b3 ♗b7
31.♗xb7 ♔xb7 32.♖h3 ♖g8 33.♖xc3
♖xg2 34.♖f5 ♖e2 35.♖c4 ♖e6
36.♔b2 ♖b6 37.a3 a5 38.a4 ♖h2
39.♖f8 ♗b7 40.♖d8 ♖h4 41.♖d5
♔b6 42.♖b5+ ♔a6 43.♖c8 1-0

Velimirovic,Dragoljub
Ljubojevic,Ljubomir
Umag ch-YUG 1972 (6)

1.e4 c5 2.♘f3 d6 3.d4 cxd4 4.♘xd4
♘f6 5.♘c3 a6 6.♗g5 e6 7.f4 ♗e7
8.♕f3 ♕c7 9.0-0-0 ♘bd7 10.♗d3 b5
11.♖he1 ♗b7 12.♘d5 ♘xd5 13.exd5
♗xg5 14.♖xe6+ fxe6 15.♘xe6 ♕a5
16.♕h5+ g6 17.♕xg5 ♖g8 18.♖d2
♘f8 19.♘xf8 ♕d8 20.♘xh7 ♕xg5
21.fxg5 ♔f7 22.♘f6 ♖h8 23.g3 ♗c8
24.h4 ♗f5 25.♗xf5 gxf5 26.h5 ♖a7
27.♖f2 1-0

Spassky,Boris
Fischer,Robert
Reykjavik Wch m 1972 (15)

1.e4 c5 2.♘f3 d6 3.d4 cxd4 4.♘xd4
♘f6 5.♘c3 a6 6.♗g5 e6 7.f4 ♗e7
8.♕f3 ♕c7 9.0-0-0 ♘bd7 10.♗d3 b5
11.♖he1 ♗b7 12.♕g3 0-0-0 13.♗xf6
♘xf6 14.♕xg7 ♖df8 15.♕g3 b4
16.♘a4 ♖hg8 17.♕f2 ♘d7 18.♔b1
♔b8 19.c3 ♘c5 20.♗c2 bxc3 21.♘xc3
♗f6 22.g3 h5 23.e5 dxe5 24.fxe5
♗h8 25.♘f3 ♖d8 26.♖xd8+ ♖xd8
27.♘g5 ♗xe5 28.♕xf7 ♖d7 29.♕xh5
♗xc3 30.bxc3 ♕b6+ 31.♔c1 ♕a5
32.♕h8+ ♔a7 33.a4 ♘d3+ 34.♗xd3
♖xd3 35.♔c2 ♖d5 36.♖e4 ♖d8
37.♕g7 ♕f5 38.♔b3 ♕d5+ 39.♔a3
♕d2 40.♖b4 ♕c1+ 41.♖b2 ♕a1+
42.♖a2 ♕c1+ 43.♖b2 ♕a1+ ½-½

Kholmov,Ratmir
Bronstein,David
Kiev ch-URS 1964 (17)

1.e4 c5 2.♘f3 ♘f6 3.♘c3 d6 4.d4
cxd4 5.♘xd4 a6 6.♗g5 e6 7.f4 ♗e7
8.♕f3 ♕c7 9.0-0-0 ♘bd7 10.g4 b5
11.♗xf6 gxf6 12.f5 ♘e5 13.♕h3 0-0
14.g5 b4 15.gxf6 ♗xf6 16.♖g1+
♔h8 17.♕h6 ♕e7 18.♘c6!! ♘xc6
19.e5! ♗g5+ 20.♖xg5 f6 21.exd6
♕f7 22.♖g3 bxc3 23.♗c4 cxb2+
24.♔b1 ♘d8 25.♖dg1 ♖a7 26.d7
♖xd7 27.fxe6 ♘xe6 28.♗xe6 ♖d1+
29.♖xd1 ♗xe6 30.♔xb2 ♖b8+
31.♔a1 ♗xa2 32.♖gd3 ♕e7
33.♔xa2 ♕e6+ 34.♖b3 1-0

Vuckovic,Bojan
Nakamura,Hikaru
Bermuda 2002 (5)

1.e4 c5 2.♘f3 d6 3.d4 cxd4 4.♘xd4
♘f6 5.♘c3 a6 6.♗g5 e6 7.f4 ♗e7

8.♕f3 ♕c7 9.0-0-0 ♘bd7 10.g4 b5
11.♗xf6 ♘xf6 12.g5 ♘d7 13.f5 ♗xg5+
14.♔b1 ♘e5 15.♕h5 ♕e7 16.♘xe6
♗xe6 17.fxe6 g6 18.exf7+ ♔xf7
19.♕h3 ♔g7 20.♘d5 ♕d8 21.♕c3 ♖a7
22.♕a3 ♕b8 23.h4 ♗h6 24.h5 a5
25.♗e2 b4 26.♕g3 ♖f7 27.hxg6 hxg6
28.♗h5 ♕f8 29.♖hg1 ♗f4 30.♘xf4
♖xf4 31.♗xg6 ♖g4 32.♕xe5+ dxe5

33.♖xg4 ♖h2 34.♗f5+ ♔h6 35.♖g6+
♔h5 36.♖c6 ♕d8 37.♖c1 ♕h4 38.♖c7
♔g5 39.a4 ♖h1 40.♖xh1 ♕xh1+
41.♔a2 ♔f4 42.♖c4 ♕d1 43.♗e6 ♔e3
44.♗d5 ♔d2 45.♖c8 ♔c1 46.♗b3 ♕e2
47.♖c4 ♔d2 48.♖c5 ♕xe4 49.♖xa5
♔c1 50.♖d5 ♕e2 51.a5 e4 52.♖d6 e3
53.a6 ♕g2 54.♖e6 ♕g7 55.c3 ♕g2
0-1

Index of Players

The numbers refer to pages.
If the page number is **bold** the player was Black.

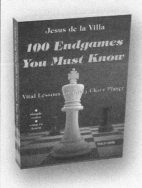